D1345756

❈ TAMMY WYNETTE ❈

TAMMY WYNETTE

Tragic Country Queen

Jimmy McDonough

SIMON &
SCHUSTER

London · New York · Sydney · Toronto

A CBS COMPANY

First published in Great Britain by Simon & Schuster UK Ltd, 2010
A CBS COMPANY

1 3 5 7 9 10 8 6 4 2

Simon & Schuster UK Ltd
1st Floor
222 Gray's Inn Road
London WC1X 8HB

www.simonandschuster.co.uk

Simon & Schuster Australia
Sydney

A CIP catalogue record for this book is available
from the British Library.

Frontispiece: Al Clayton/ Southern Historical Collection, Wilson Library,
University of North Carolina at Chapel Hill

Text design by Carla Bolte

ISBN: 978-1-84737-062-4

Printed in the UK by CPI Mackays, Chatham ME5 8TD

For my mother

Janet Wicht McDonough

an artist

Reality can never fulfill fantasy's expectations. Why? Because fantasy is always perfect.

—*Dark Dreams,* Hazelwood and Michaud

Sometimes it's hard to be a woman.

—"Stand by Your Man," Sherrill and Wynette

Contents

❋ TAMMY WYNETTE ❋

Dear Tammy,

I figure I should drop you a line now and then, say hello, tell you how it's going. Don't worry, I won't spill all the beans—I can't. There's just too much about you that will never be resolved. I don't think anybody knows the whole story—not even your last husband, Mr. Tammy Wynette himself, George Richey.

Allow me to bore you with a story concerning your favorite recording. You know, the one that brought together the three men in your life. Billy Sherrill, the person who discovered you, produced it. He helped you pen the lyrics, as did George Richey, and this particular number was inspired by the collapse of your marriage to Jones, the great love of your life.

A few years back a dame I was crazy about was about to walk out the door and I was losing my mind. In the midnight hours I once again turned to you, digging out the dusty old vinyl to spin your masterpiece, "'Til I Can Make It on My Own."

And each time I played the song it hurt worse than the time before. I hated it, and I hated you. I wanted to take that record and smash the damn thing. Instead I just played it again.

For we both know what that record's about, and it isn't making it on your own.

You never, ever wanted to be alone. Tammy had to have a man, your friends all tell me. Tammy just had to have a man.

Virginia's in the House

I believe you have to live the songs.

—Tammy Wynette

October 1968. The Country Music Association Awards. After a peppy introduction by Roy Rogers and Dale Evans, Tammy Wynette wafts to the mic like she's in a trance. Skinny as a matchstick, wearing a fancy, futuristic housecoat dress, Tammy looks like her ratted-out beehive and big lapels might consume her at any second. "Just a country girl's idea of glamour," explains Dolly Parton. "Tammy didn't have any more fashion sense than I did, really. I always say me and Tammy, we got our clothes from Fifth and Park—that was, the fifth trailer in the park."

Wynette's a striking woman, with an elegant neck, beautiful lips, and a stunning profile, but one with an extreme, elongated face set beneath feline, close-set eyes. Unimaginative types who don't savor esoteric looks might be dim-witted enough to consider her a tad homely. Hell, head-on Wynette looks like a Siamese cat in a wig hat. Not that Tammy was particularly vain. As she told Alanna Nash, "my neck's too long, my nose has a hump in it, my boobs are too saggy and the kids call me 'weenie butt' 'cause I have no rear end."

"Tammy never had the movie star looks of her lesser rivals, but she had a tough beauty, a no-messin' allure," wrote the KLF's Bill Drummond, who would collaborate with Wynette near the end of her life on a wacky and improbable dance hit, "Justified and Ancient." Only twenty-six, Tammy already seems a bit shopworn. The mountain of makeup can't completely hide the worry, the fear, the dark circles lurking below tired eyes. She stands so stiff you'd think the hanger was still in the damn dress.

And then this tiny, troubled wisp of a human being opens her mouth,

3

and out comes an atom-bomb voice. The band's playing too fast, which only accentuates her odd phrasing. "Our little boy turned four years old . . ."

The particular song she's singing tonight is a cockamamie number called "D-I-V-O-R-C-E," and its content is a bit much—a mother spelling out "the hurtin' words" so Junior can't understand that Mommy's split with Daddy "becomes final today." But Wynette invests the song with such feeling that anybody with half a heart would have to acknowledge the sheer conviction on display, the utter reality of her pain. For when Tammy sings, as her longtime producer Billy Sherrill once said, there is "a tear in every word."

When she gets to the chorus, Wynette belts out the words with the force of an air-raid siren, yet barely bats an eyelash. There's zero body language— the drama's all in the voice. She doesn't act out the song or punch her fist in the air; in fact, she barely moves an inch. Tammy the statue. Until a Tin-seltown choreographer teaches her some questionable dance steps in the mid-eighties, Wynette will remain frozen onstage. The antistyle of Tammy's wax-figure performances absolutely mystified Dolly Parton. "I could not believe that *all* of that voice and *all* that sound was comin' out of a person standin' totally still. I'd think, 'How is she doin' that?' It seems like you'd have to lean into your body or bow down into it or *somethin'* to get all of that out. I've never seen anything like it to this day. I was in awe of her. I thought she had one of the greatest voices of all time."

Wynette finishes her devastating performance and meekly walks off the stage. She wins Female Vocalist of the Year tonight, as she would the following year—and the one after that. For all her talent, she is not only a genuinely humble person, but, unfortunately, one with little self-confidence. "She never knew she was Tammy Wynette," said more than one friend.

September 30, 1982. The White House. Performing at a barbecue for President Ronald Reagan, Tammy serenades the commander in chief with her signature song, "Stand by Your Man." The day before, she'd sung it in Alabama for that steely firebrand of the South, George Wallace. A few years previous she'd done it for Jimmy Carter. Indifferent to politics, Tammy likes 'em all. "She didn't know anything about what was goin' on in the world," said her friend Joan Dew. "She wasn't interested. It wasn't that she was stupid, she just didn't care." For Reagan, Wynette is wearing a "red antebellum gown with a hoopskirt which was just gorgeous," said her hairdresser Jan

Smith, who had not only flown in with the coveted dress, but had to "buy it a ticket and sit it next to me."

There they were, the president, the country singer, and her hairdresser, "walking across the White House lawn," Smith recalled. "All of a sudden Tammy pokes me, I look down and she sticks her foot out and wiggles it! She was barefoot under that dress."

Barefoot on the White House lawn. Classic Tammy. As is what transpires during her performance. She parks herself down in the president's lap and sings "Stand by Your Man" right in Ronnie's face. The act isn't unusual for Wynette—during live shows, she'd often go out in the audience, zero in on some hapless husband, and melt him down in a similar fashion. But this is the president. "I didn't know it wasn't proper protocol," claimed Miss Tammy. "*He* certainly didn't say anything." As far as Wynette's performance went, "I had goose bumps," the Gipper confessed to the *New York Times*. Months later, on June 20, 1983, Tammy sings for the president at a catfish dinner in Jackson, Mississippi. "He *kissed* Tammy!" said Jan Smith. A photo of the smooch wound up in the *Globe*. "Ronald Reagan definitely had a thing for Tammy. After it was over, Tammy said to me, 'Oh, my God, Jan, that was so embarrassing! He swabbed my tonsils!' Well, Nancy Reagan got real out of joint about it."

When Tammy belts out "Stand by Your Man," "the more than 2,000 Republicans responded as if it were a theme song," noted the *Times*. Which is funny, because so have an untold number of drag queens, gay men, and lesbians. A song with a sublimely fuzzy center, "Stand by Your Man" is open to interpretation, enabling all kinds to claim it either as an anthem or as patriarchal propaganda. Whatever your politics, if you really listen, it can be a hard number to resist. Just about everybody at some point in his or her life has fallen victim to a selfless, perhaps unhealthy, passion for another, and Wynette delivers the lyric as a matter of life and death.

Tammy would live to sing "Stand by Your Man" to five presidents and countless lesser luminaries. Not bad for a country girl from Itawamba County, Mississippi. "She went from a little nowhere place to talkin' with the president," said cousin Jane Williams. "She did not have anything. She did it herself."

Summer, 1996. Lincoln City, Oregon. Tammy is performing at the grand opening of the Chinook Winds Casino. She has been in ever-declining health due to wrenching intestinal problems that cause her continual and excruciating pain. She also has a serious and decades-long addiction to painkillers, the powerful synthetic opiate Dilaudid among them. Sometimes a plane would be dispatched to pick up her narcotics; others, the drugs would be FedExed in. Just when Tammy got her hands on the package was a matter of concern for band and crew. If Wynette took too big a taste, she'd be zonked out, and the show would be an uphill battle. The band even had a saying to clue one another in that Tammy was seriously under the influence: "Virginia's in the house." Virginia Pugh was Tammy's real name, and when Virginia's name was invoked, it indicated an overmedicated Wynette. As backup singer Karyn Sloas explained, "We'd always say, 'Is Virginia doin' the show, or is Tammy?' And if Virginia was doin' the show, I would be prepared to sing a little bit more. Virginia clearly did the show in Lincoln City."

Yes, Virginia was in the house with a vengeance that night. Yvonne Abdon and Karyn Sloas, her backup singers, were used to covering for Wynette when she was in vocal distress. "She had hand signals that she would give us if she was not able to hit the last note," said Sloas. A fist behind her back meant she wasn't going to hit that high F at the climax of "Stand by Your Man"; an open palm indicated, "Get this song over with as quick as possible."

But a far weirder drama is unfolding onstage tonight. "We noticed Tammy was singing a lot slower," said Tammy's guitar player (and Karyn's husband) David Sloas. "She was doin' a pretty bad show, noddin' off between songs," said Yvonne Abdon, who sometimes had to sidle up to Wynette midsong and nudge her out of a nod. Tammy had a ritual she'd perform every night when back on the bus after the show. "She'd start getting sleepy and start playin' with her rings," said Yvonne. One by one they'd come off and she'd totter back to her bed.

Which is what Tammy begins to do this night in Lincoln City. The only problem is that Wynette is still onstage, in front of an audience and in the middle of "Stand by Your Man" when she plops down on her stool and starts preparing for bed. "It was pitiful," said Abdon. "Karyn and I just looked at each other."

When Tammy fails to deliver a line near the end of the song, Karyn Sloas, said David, "jumped in and started singin'." As Wynette stands there in a daze, fumbling with her baubles, the curtain is abruptly brought down. "They helped Tammy to her dressing room, and she doubled over in phenomenal pain," said Sloas. "The next day was canceled. The Chinook Winds people were very upset. This was their opening weekend." Sloas, who continued working the road post-Wynette, said casino vets were still muttering about the debacle over a decade later.

It was a scenario that reoccurred with depressing frequency in her final years. For Tammy was trapped. Trapped in an addiction she couldn't conquer, trapped by illness that brought on endless pain, and, many insist, trapped in a marriage to manager/husband George Richey that made everything worse.

"She seemed kind of desperate to me," said the bluntly honest Charley Abdon, her drummer since 1985. "I think she knew Richey used her a bit. I mean, we *all* used her a little bit. I was there to make a livin'. I wish Tammy would've quit. She really should've. It's a sad story."

Few recording artists achieve the kind of success Tammy Wynette did. In total, she had more than twenty number one hits, several of which she'd cowritten. Tammy was the first country artist to go platinum, and her total sales now loom somewhere past the thirty-million mark. If there is one person who her musicians and producers compare her to, it is Elvis. Guitarist Chip Young, who recorded with both, felt they were "very similar. Tammy just had that charisma." Her tale is equally mythical. "She went from bein' a beautician to the queen of country music," said Emmylou Harris.

"I have big imagination, and big hopes. I do everything big," said Wynette. With five husbands (one lasting only forty-four days), four kids, thirty-plus operations, Tammy also was harassed, endured financial disaster, and even escaped a strange, unsolved kidnapping attempt many suspected she'd had a hand in herself. One newspaper ran an article consisting solely of headlines from her various mishaps and maladies. To top it all off, husband number three was George Jones, Wynette's idol. During their stormy seven-year marriage, they'd record what many critics consider the greatest country duets of all time. "Every woman wants her very own personal hero," said writer Holly Gleason. "That he also happened to be a legendary vocal pyrotechnist, too, spoke volumes to the perfection of the fairy tales she believed in."

Tammy loved country music with near-Pentecostal fervor and was known to chew out friends and family members that belittled her art form. "It's honest music," said Wynette. "It tells a story. It has a beginning, middle, and an end . . . it's what people live. It's what a lot of rock artists don't write about. They sugarcoat things." Tammy sings of cheating husbands, suffering wives, kids' lives wrecked by divorce. The down and dirty stuff that grinds us all down on a daily basis. If you're a woman, she could be singing your life. If you are a man, she might be compelling for darker reasons. Wynette sings of love in a rather disturbing fashion. Her music ain't for sissies.

Wynette is such an extreme character that she instantly polarizes. Academics quarrel over the content of "D-I-V-O-R-C-E." "In this song," writes Cenate Pruitt, "the male exists only to torment the narrator, with no real explanation offered as to why the divorce is taking place at all, as it seems the narrator is entirely content to remain in the marriage, despite whatever issues it may have." Not exactly, counters Kenneth E. Morris: "The singer's perspective was that of a divorced mother in moral and sentimental alliance with her children against an egotistical and uncaring ex-husband."

"Poor Tammy, she confused people—with her sultry album covers and husky, yearning voice, singing all those songs about family values and keeping your man satisfied, right in the middle of women's lib," said Lisa Miller, an acclaimed Australian singer-songwriter. "But when I listened to Tammy I didn't hear a downtrodden woman. I heard a vulnerable one with enormous inner strength. She seemed to draw from a deeper well. She had this incredible ache in her voice and the ability to deliver her lines with utter conviction, to hit notes with such bull's-eye precision, and to move from in-your-ear intimacy to soaring notes that threaten to cut your head off! This was so thrilling."

The voice, the voice. What can one say? It bewitches you. Tammy just has that "out in the country sound," to steal a line David "Honeyboy" Edwards used to describe fellow bluesman Elmore James. "A conversational mezzo-soprano with just enough grain to sound vulnerable" is the accurate if bloodless description Jon Pareles gave it in the *New York Times*. As her producer Billy Sherrill pointed out, when you got down to it, Tammy really didn't have the greatest range, but, boy, could she go from loud to soft and back again. Not to mention the fact that Wynette does weird and wondrous things to words simply by singing them. "She could just milk a vowel," said Emmylou Harris. "She could give so much melody to just, like, *one syllable*. But it never sounded contrived."

It's easy to pick on Tammy, dismiss her as an unsavory cartoon. But it's more interesting to really listen to her, because she is a far more complicated and intriguing figure than the garish, glossy surface might suggest. Stephen

Holden, another *Times* critic, noted that Wynette's "blend of dependency and determination" had "less to do with camp than with her skill at building emotionally truthful songs around everyday catchphrases and socking them out in a voice that embodies the pain and resilience of long-suffering working-class women." Sherrill put it a simpler way: "She speaks for the woman who's been kicked in the ass all her life."

There is a noble quality to the lady. When I think of Tammy's music, something Julia Blackburn once wrote about Billie Holiday often comes to mind. "Even the saddest songs were full of courage. It was as if just the fact of singing was in itself a triumph and a way of dealing with despair." But Wynette has never gotten the accolades of a Holiday, even though she is just as great a singer. Billie's blend of dependency and determination is somehow more palatable. Patsy, Loretta, Dolly long ago crossed over to the kind of harmless-icon status acceptable enough for even the fatally bland audience of public radio to embrace, approve, and buy at a coffee shop kiosk. Tammy remains a harder sell. "Not many people I know 'get' Tammy Wynette," noted Lisa Miller. Wynette still disturbs, still gets under the skin.

Those who love Tammy, however, do so fiercely. "She had fans—scary fans," said former Sony executive Mike Martinovich, who would undoubtedly admit to being something of a scary Tammy fan himself. Michelle Broussard Honick ran Wynette's fan club in the late seventies and early eighties and experienced the darker side of such an enterprise. "There were some fans who would call her Our Lady. It was almost a religious thing for them."

Wynette has influenced a legion of singers. Her admirers run the gamut from Barbra Streisand to Melissa Etheridge, not to mention that lovable, chainsaw-wielding punk rock terrorist Wendy O. Williams, who dared to record a screechy and unlistenable "Stand by Your Man" duet with Motorhead's Lemmy Kilmister. Producer/arranger Jack Nitzsche—famous for his work with the Rolling Stones, Phil Spector, and countless others—was so in awe of Wynette he literally got down and kissed her feet when he first met her. Although only two *King of the Hill* episodes were completed before Wynette died, director Mike Judge felt Tammy lent authenticity to his animated TV comedy about working-class Texas life by providing the voice of Tilly Hill, Hank's mom. "She's the real deal. It was like getting Marlon Brando."

As far as female country singers go, forget it. Tanya Tucker, Martina McBride, Rosanne Cash, Shelby Lynne, Wynonna, Lorrie Morgan—it would be harder to find somebody who *doesn't* namecheck Wynette. Modern-day country diva Faith Hill confessed, "It's hard for me to listen to her records without crying."

Far away in Australia, Lisa Miller recalled the galvanizing moment she first heard Tammy Wynette sing. "The record shop guy dropped the needle on 'Send Me No Roses.' I felt shivers immediately, the kind you can only get when you hear something really pure, organic, and rare. Her voice evoked classic images of truck-stop jukeboxes and neon signs. Her sound epitomized this romantic country and western world to me." Tammy upped the ante for Lisa. With her own music, Miller vowed "to make records that sounded like they were produced by Billy Sherrill, but above all trying to sound as much like myself as Tammy sounded like herself."

"I listened to her so much," said Emmylou Harris. "She was so distinctive . . . it seemed so effortless. She was the real article . . . she really influenced the way I sing." Harris first met Wynette after standing in line to get her autograph at the Stardust Club in Waldorf, Maryland. When she told Tammy she was aiming at a singing career, Wynette encouraged her, talking to her for over half an hour. "She made me feel like she had known me," said Emmylou. "It was not an act, it was real."

Over and over I heard about Wynette's kindness. The first time artist June Zent, who did many a painting for Tammy, met Wynette at her Florida vacation home, she mentioned her favorite Tammy song was "You and Me." Wynette picked up a guitar and "we sang it together," said Zent. "I had just met her, and she literally gave me a concert there on the bed! Tammy immediately put me at ease." Robert Duvall isn't all that fond of giving interviews, but he was happy to recount how Wynette waived a ten-thousand-dollar fee so he could use a George and Tammy duet as the title song for his 1977 rodeo documentary, *We're Not the Jet Set*. "Tammy was so gracious," said Duvall.

"She was the kind of woman who could be deathly ill, and still want to cook you biscuits," said writer Holly Gleason, who wasn't alone when she noted how, when Tammy greeted you, there was "always some question about a small detail of your life, a record you were loving, a place she'd had dinner, or how much fun she'd had with the grandbaby by the pool. So many stars lose touch with those small things. Tammy built a life on it."

Phoebe Gloeckner quotes Wynette's 1967 hit "Your Good Girl's Gonna Go Bad" near the end of her classic graphic novel *Diary of a Teenage Girl*. She met Tammy briefly out on the road at Marriott's Great America in Santa Clara, California. "She was the queen that evening. I had been waiting the whole night to meet Tammy Wynette. Finally, we knocked on the door of her bus. She opened the door and hesitated to let us in—but she did, with reserved kindness. She was all alone and seemed to be trying to recover from her performance.

"Tammy didn't really quite smile, although I couldn't say she wasn't friendly. She stood with regal posture, didn't say much, and her face was not at all expressive—she had a beautiful, very pale face, like a statue. I remember that Tammy seemed to hold herself back, like a queen—graciously, and with some humility and sense of duty, mixing with the rabble, hiding her own pain in deference to the needs of the crowd. She signed a little piece of paper for me. . . . She seemed lonely."

Three decades later Gloeckner could still recall the details of Wynette's full-length black halter-neck dress. Tammy had that kind of effect on people. Tough guys—grizzled veterans of the music business—wept while remembering her.

"Tammy was a paradox," says country music historian Robert K. Oermann. "She was weak and strong. It's interesting to contrast her life with, say, Loretta Lynn's. Loretta often sang about being rebellious against men and yet stayed married to the same guy her whole life. Tammy embodied the pliant female, and yet was incredibly independent."

Tammy and Loretta were buddies. "To be that close to someone in the business and not be jealous of 'em is a great feeling," said Wynette, who was known to suffer jealousy a time or two in her life. Loretta first met Tammy when she was out on the road with then-husband Don Chapel and his daughter Donna. "She was workin' her little butt off, fixin' hair for everybody. I thought to myself, 'Y'know, I'm glad I'm not a beautician or I'd be right in the same boat.'"

Lynn immediately recognized Wynette as a great singer, admired her style. "Yeah, I'd say Tammy had a presence. Tammy looked different than all the other singers. She had her own look, could fix her hair any way. She was wearin' falls—she did that without anybody knowin'. You didn't forget Tammy. Whatever the fashion was, Tammy was it."

One night in the mid-seventies Wynette surprised Lynn by showing up out on the road uninvited. "Do you know, she checked out of the hospital and come to see me in Atlanta, Georgia? Here Tammy comes. She just showed up, she didn't call. She was in her hospital gown and she had a fur coat over her like she was in mink, y'know. I said, 'You're in the hospital!' Tammy says, 'I *was.*' She spent the night, got on a plane early the next morning, and flew back to her hospital. I couldn't believe it."

Then there was the awards show in Los Angeles when Tammy hid out in Loretta's dressing room. She was secretly dating Burt Reynolds at the time and didn't want to run into his other paramour. "She says, 'Now, you make sure I don't run into Dinah Shore.' I said, 'How come, Tammy?' She says, 'Well, I've been goin' with Burt.' I said, 'Oh, my God! A good friend you are to Dinah!' It was really funny. We didn't have no trouble that night, but Tammy left her hat. I've got it in the museum."

On one occasion the ladies spent some time together in Hawaii. The house had no air-conditioning, and they sprawled on couches "like two trained seals," said Wynette. "We were awful," remembered Lynn. "Tammy'd get off the couch, I'd say, 'Tammy, make me a bologna sandwich.' Then she'd say, 'Loretty, would you make me a bologna sandwich?' We were waitin' on each other like that. We spent days there just doin' nothin'. It was good." They started to write a song together, "We Ain't Done Too Bad for a Couple of Good Ol' Girls," but never finished it. "It was very hard for me and Tammy to get away from everybody else," said Loretta.

"We knew each other like a book. I could tell when she wasn't feelin' good. Her eyes. That would be a dead giveaway. I could always look at her and tell what she was goin' through. And she'd have to come out with it. But when her and I got together we didn't want to talk about the hard times. Tammy wasn't in for a lot of sadness—she wanted to hear good stuff. When we got together we lived it up. Yes, we did."

I think it's safe to say that Wynette's death was something Lynn has never really recovered from. "That was somethin' that really hit me hard. I don't know if I'll ever get as close to another girl singer. I've tried not to. Let me tell you, I really loved Tammy."

A few little details to give some flavor to this most fascinating creature: Tammy loved to shop. "Before the show the first thing Tammy wanted to do was hit the mall," said her friend and biographer Joan Dew. "She could scout out and go through a mall like a vacuum cleaner. It was unbelievable." And she loved a bargain. "She was notorious for getting a five-thousand-dollar Bob Mackie dress and then buying some Kmart shoes to go with it," noted daughter Georgette.

Along with a pair of garish clip-on earrings (Wynette never got her ears pierced)—the bigger, the better. Everybody remembers the gigantic red plastic peace sign earrings. "No matter what kind of dress I'd do," said her slightly exasperated costume designer Jef Billings, "she'd go out and find big earrings."

Wynette was a hellacious Southern cook. Her friends still grow weak at the memory of her peanut butter and banana pudding, chocolate pie, and especially her ham and dumplings. "It was the best thing you ever put in your mouth," sighed hairdresser and friend Nan Crafton. "She'd call up and say, 'Makin' ham 'n' dumplings,' and we'd *all* go." But what did Wynette like to ingest best out on the road? "Junk food," said Crafton. "The worst fair food. Mexican food. She liked all that fried lard and chicken." (Wynette confessed to one interviewer, "A hot dog is still my favorite food.")

Tammy hated TV spots for feminine hygiene. "If a commercial about tampons came on, she'd get up, turn it off and start rantin' and ravin'," said her friend Kelli Haggard-Patterson. "Tammy was so pissed off, she wanted to go to Congress—'They need to have these commercials taken *off!*'"

Tammy loved sleeping on her bus—even when she got off the road, she'd stay on the bus a night before moving into the house. And God forbid you should shut that bus down while she was catching forty winks. "One time in Washington, D.C., we parked in an underground garage and they made us turn the bus off," said Nan. "I'll never forget it. Tammy had a blue peignoir nightgown on and she came flyin' through that cabin like she was floatin'—'WHO TURNED THE BUS OFF?! I don't care *what* they say!' Number one rule, you never turned the bus off."

Wynette required white noise in the form of a blaring TV when she slept. "She had to have it on full bore," recalled hairdresser Barbara Hutchison, who'd try to turn it down a hair and get some sleep of her own. "She'd have sleepin' pills underneath her and everything else and still wake up—'What's the TV doin' off? I can't hear it! Turn it back up a little bit.'" Wynette kept up her beautician's license twenty years after hitting the big time just in case "the music thing doesn't work out."

Wynette could be self-centered. More than one friend pointed to the section in her autobiography dealing with her aunt Carolyn's disfiguring car crash. Wynette adored Carolyn, who was like a big sister to her. On the way to the hospital with her mother, stepfather, and grandparents, little Tammy caught sight of a purple dress in a store window. Wynette desperately wanted the dress. Her grandfather, whom she called "Daddy," told her they couldn't stop, they had to get to the hospital. Tammy voiced her love for the outfit once more, and Daddy had them turn the car around so he could get it for her, hospital or no hospital. Wynette would have a similar effect on many of the men that entered her life.

Tammy was always taking in stray dogs—or stray people. On holidays, she'd go to the local shelter and invite some of the less fortunate back to her house and feed them. "Wynette was always for the underdog," said her childhood pal Linda Cayson. "You didn't pick on a little kid or mistreat a dog when she was around."

Wynette's favorite perfume was Private Collection by Estée Lauder. Martha Dettwiller once went to visit Wynette in a Vegas hotel and, suddenly realizing she didn't have her room number, went around sniffing the suites. Sure enough, she detected the scent of Wynette. "Private Collection," Dettwiller recalled, was floating around the air "like a haze." Once Tammy saw you, added Martha, "She had a way of sayin' your name so that you knew you were special. You knew that your name was safe in her mouth. That's a gift that very few people have."

Although Wynette didn't advertise it, she was a spiritual person. "When it come to God, Tammy knew who he was," said Loretta Lynn. Wynette, who never failed to include gospel numbers in her show, said, "When I die I'm going to either one of two places, and I'm going to do my best to get to the good one. I don't expect any jewels in my crown, but I do hope I'll have a crown."

There have been two books written about Tammy Wynette, 1979's *Stand by Your Man*, an autobiography as told by Tammy to Joan Dew, and the posthumous *Tammy Wynette: A Daughter Recalls Her Mother's Tragic Life and Death* (2000), by her daughter Jackie Daly and Tom Carter. The latter is basically a grim indictment of Wynette's last husband, George Richey; the former ends with Tammy's marriage to Richey in 1978.

A classic country autobiography, down to the sultry, sad Norman Seeff cover photo, *Stand by Your Man* cemented Wynette's version of the first half of her life. Not that she'd ever know it. "To tell you the honest-to-God truth, I don't think Tammy ever read the book," admitted Dew, who teamed up with Wynette's hairdresser Nanette Crafton to playfully quiz her on the contents. "We decided we'd ask her some pertinent questions about the book. She didn't know the answers. It was funny. Tammy didn't care."

The press loved Wynette, and they believed her—so much so that her version of the events of her life pretty much went unchallenged, at least until 1978, the year of her alleged kidnapping. Rosemary Bowen-Jones, producer of an excellent 1986 BBC documentary on Wynette, *Stand by Your Dream*, recognized the inescapable shortcomings encountered when such a project is created in collusion with its subject. "When you're someone like that, you've kind of rehearsed your life," said Bowen-Jones of Tammy. "It's a story that's been told. She's written the songs, she'd done so many interviews." It left Rosemary wondering, "Is it true, is it made up, how much is real?"

Another quandary was Wynette's propensity for telling tall tales. "She would exaggerate a story," said Charlene Montgomery, who was around Tammy frequently during the Jones years. "It would start out small. We'd leave Nashville, I'd hear Tammy tell a story about somethin' that happened. Well, we'd run into somebody like Jan Howard, I'd hear Tammy tell the story again and she'd add about four lines. Then we'd run into another group of people, she'd add another three or four lines. It would just get bigger 'n' bigger 'n' bigger. By the time we got through with the tour, the story was just completely out of control. Huge!"

Wynette got so inspired listening to your life, she'd swipe a detail or two for her own. One day on the road Montgomery told her about the last whipping she got from her father. "Whipped me with a belt buckle," Charlene told Tammy, who was shocked. As was Charlene when the tale wound up as an autobiographical anecdote in Wynette's book, where she says her mother hit her with the buckle end of a belt "hard enough to draw blood." There were times when Wynette felt she had to improve on reality. As Patsy Sledd, backup singer during the original George and Tammy tours, recalled, "I'd tell Tammy a story, she'd go, 'George, you got to hear this!' She didn't *ever* tell it straight. She'd never tell the truth! She'd turn it around to make it the way she wanted it to come out." Second husband Don Chapel recalled Tammy utilizing details gleaned from the tabloid tales of others to forge her own mythology. After Wynette read how Zsa Zsa Gabor was stripped of her diamonds in an elevator burglary, she exclaimed to Don, "What a good way to get publicity!" Later Chapel read an identical story, only this time the victim was Tammy.

Another challenge to documenting Wynette: as open and honest as she appeared to be in her music, as a person Tammy was "very guarded," said backup singer Karyn Sloas. "She would relax, tell you too much, then the next day totally shut down—'I've let you in, you saw too much, this never happened.'"

"I write about things I can't talk about," said Tammy, and there were plenty of subjects that fit that description. She was not one to confide or reveal. Cathye Leshay, governess to Wynette's children, was closer to Wynette than most. Even she felt the wall. At one point Cathye was cleaning Tammy's house in Jupiter, Florida, when she found a note in the bedroom. It was addressed to Leshay. In it Tammy thanks Cathye for taking care of her children. "This is somethin' I'll have the rest of my life. A little piece of notepaper. And she didn't sign it or nothin'," said Leshay, choking up. "Tammy didn't give it to me. She just made sure that I found it. This would not have been anything that she would've ever come and said to me." Echoing something I'd heard from many others, Leshay concluded, "Tammy didn't get real personal with people. I don't know what the deal was."

This is a book about the singers that live the songs, and therein lies a certain darkness.

"Sad songs are what move people," Lorrie Morgan told me. "We want to know other people are in pain, because that's what we relate to. Unfortunately we're all in pain.

"Years ago I sang a song about a divorce—I was nineteen years old, not even married yet. I looked at the producer and I said, 'I'm sorry, but I don't feel it, I haven't lived it. I can't sing this song, I can't relate to it.' 'You don't have to relate to it to sing it.' I said bullshit, you have to relate to somethin'. You have to. You *have* to be brokenhearted.

"Y'know what my brother told me a long time ago? I was goin' through a really bad time. I mean, it was like I was chasin' disaster, chasin' it. He said, 'Lorrie, just because you sing country songs doesn't mean you have to live 'em.' And I thought, 'You're wrong. You have to live what you sing. You have to *live* it.'"

"My life's not a fairy tale," insisted Wynette. "I'm not Snow White." Once you immerse yourself in Tammy's world, it's a hard notion to shake. Her later years in particular were agonizing to document. I kept returning to the records. The more I unearthed, the more haunting her music became.

Writer Alanna Nash, who interviewed Wynette, felt the intense intimacy of Tammy's voice, "how it just gets into your bloodstream and takes over. This is a woman who lived with a tremendous amount of pain, physically and emotionally. The fact she was able to channel it really speaks to her artistry."

Tammy Wynette never found what she was looking for. A white knight, a Prince Charming, that heart of gold. "I Still Believe in Fairy Tales." "Take Me to Your World." "That's the Way It Could Have Been." "You and Me." "Stand by Your Man." Listen to the songs on her fifty-plus albums one after the other and it becomes strangely oppressive, this singular pursuit of l-o-v-e. Tammy never relents.

She wanted life to whisk her off her high-heeled feet, to be as passionate as the feverish cover of some romance novel. Instead Tammy Wynette wound up dying in public an inch at a time, her emaciated, addicted, tormented face plastered across the cover of every grocery store tabloid. "Unfortunately the drama of her life overshadows her position as a performer," said Alanna Nash. "Her death is so painful to me I can hardly stand to think about it. It's almost like speaking about some kind of horrible murder. It couldn't get any more tabloid, really."

So who was Tammy Wynette? Did the sadness in the songs determine the sadness in her life, or vice versa? Was she simply a being cursed with a taste for self-destruction to rival that of any rock star? Was Tammy betrayed by those who claimed to love her? Did she jump, or was she pushed? I'm not certain there's a clear-cut answer to any of it.

One thing I do know. She was a great artist, and it is time to document her life with the intensity and honesty Tammy deserves. I want you to feel this woman's presence as deeply as I feel her songs. I want you to stand by Tammy Wynette.

Nettiebelle

The Southern air. It's filled with rambling ghosts and disturbed spirits.

—Bob Dylan

Oh, I wish Daddy could be here right now. You can never lose your talent,
he used to say. You can lose everything else, but you can't lose your talent.

—Baby Jane Hudson (Bette Davis), *Whatever Happened to Baby Jane?*

Eyes on the horizon and lost in a dream, that was Wynette. It was hot
in the fields, the sun determined to fry everything in sight, and while
she might've been standing there looking forlorn in her cotton-picking outfit of long britches, hat, and gloves, just fidgeting in the Mississippi dirt,
playing on the screen in her Technicolor mind was a hot country band
fronted by George Jones himself, with none other than Wynette Pugh facing him on the mic. Bright lights, loud honky-tonk music—why, even the
clouds of cigarette smoke she conjured up sent a shiver down her spine. Yes,
life would be like a big Hollywood movie: glamorous and perfect . . .

Wynette just loved how that man phrased a ballad. So did her mother,
Mildred. "She bought every single record George ever did," said Wynette
years later. The burr-headed, beady-eyed singer from Texas they called "the
Possum" was one of the few things mother and daughter agreed upon. Mildred had many a Jones record, including his latest duet with Melba Montgomery, "We Must've Been Out of Our Minds." Wynette knew every word
of the lyric, every lick of George's vocal, and she also knew, given half a
chance, she could sing better than that ol' Melba Montgomery.

"Girl, go back to work!" Mildred's hollering snapped Wynette right back to
the cotton patch. She looked down at the dusty, half-empty sack in her tired,
nervous hands and felt like a deflated balloon. Reality was always a rough landing for Wynette. But nobody was going to stop her dream. Nobody. Not even
Mother.

"I'm proud to be country," said Wynette. "I'm not hillbilly, I'm a country
girl." "Hillbilly" was a word she despised, because it meant "you don't know

anything." As for working in the fields, "I hated pickin' cotton worse than anything in the world," she'd declare in interview after interview. Wynette saw the farm as a one-way ticket to nowheresville. She was determined to escape. Said her lifelong pal Linda Cayson, "One of the things we always talked about was, we were never goin' to marry a farmer." While Wynette would grow up to be a formidable Southern cook, she had a dislike for a central ingredient early on. "It was chicken 'n' dumplings, fried chicken, chicken everything. . . . I thought at the time it was the worst life ever."

It was contradictions like these that made Wynette so compelling. Decades later, when she was Nashville royalty living in a million-dollar mansion behind formidable gates bearing her initials and a doorbell that chimed "Stand by Your Man," Tammy kept a handful of the last cotton she'd picked from her grandfather Chester Russell's farm. It was displayed in a fifteen-hundred-dollar Lalique crystal bowl. Wynette never forgot where she came from, even if she liked the reminder in a very expensive dish.

Tammy Wynette is often lumped in with Dolly Parton and Loretta Lynn as some sort of classic country "girl singer" triumvirate (itself unfairly reductive of these three very distinct characters; how often do you hear "George and Johnny and Merle"?) with similar dirt-poor beginnings. Contrary to the legend, Wynette did not crawl out of abject poverty, and it's an important distinction, as every bio of her invariably begins by making such a claim.

The very scholarly Paula Fox, writing about the popular autobiographies of all three in her highfalutin' dissertation "Recycled 'Trash': Gender and Authenticity in Country Music Autobiography" notes, "Country authenticity presumes humble origins, anti-intellectualism and literary naivete." No doubt, but Lynn and Parton came into the world a bit more "'umble" than their pal Tammy. Loretta's family couldn't afford shoes or meat and had to walk ten miles to the hospital when Loretta was sick. "I don't want to go back to it," she wrote. "I remember being hungry too much." Dolly says in her book that she grew up "poor—very poor. In fact, my daddy couldn't afford to pay Dr. Thomas for delivering me, so he gave him a sack of cornmeal."

Wynette's beginnings were decidedly less grim. "If we had a dime or a quarter pocket change we was doin' real good," said childhood friend Agnes Wilson. "Maybe Wynette would have a dollar and change in her pocket. She had money at school that the other kids didn't have. Well, Wynette was rich

as far as we were concerned. Chester would give her anything she wanted."
At Christmas her grandfather Chester Russell handed her an envelope with
fifty dollars in it, an unheard-of amount in Wynette's neck of the woods.

Utter the words "picking cotton," though, and a cliché appears. Nowhere
in her 1979 autobiography does Wynette actually claim poverty, although
she does suggest as much in the intro to her 1990 cookbook, as well as in
remarks like, "I don't know if anybody can appreciate satin without having
worn a sackcloth dress." This isn't to suggest Wynette was fibbing; maybe
she gave up explaining or perhaps she just acquiesced to the myth. She'd
certainly know total destitution once she married and left home, but not in
childhood. Chester might've been extremely thrifty, but he was far from
destitute. An early article on Tammy's background even had Mildred complaining, "They make it sound like she was real hard up. While we didn't
have a lot of money, Wynette never wanted for anything, either."

Ask Wynette's friends just how much cotton she actually picked and
you'll get some pointed replies. Said former sister-in-law Nancy Byrd, "By
no standards did she have to stay out of school like some of the kids did to
help gather the crops. Wynette didn't exert herself too much out there." Her
friend Holly Ford agreed: "If Wynette picked cotton, it wasn't like hard
labor, that they were starvin' to death. She probably picked cotton so she
could put on shorts and get a suntan." John Wilson, who worked alongside
Wynette in the fields and later dated her, disagreed: "Some of the people
talk about her not workin' . . . A lotta days I picked cotton with her, pulled
corn, made molasses. She was one of the hands. Mr. Russell paid her just
like he paid us." Wynette got two dollars for every pound. "Wynette *did*
have to pick cotton," explained cousin Jane Williams. "Not because she was
poor, just because Chester demanded it."

Thomas Chester "Mr. Ches" Russell owned six hundred acres in Itawamba
County, Mississippi, ran his own gin mill, and was on the board of the local
college, grade school, and bank. "In each community you have some folks
that have the power to get things done," said relative Gerald Jetton. "They
don't want the notoriety, they don't want to be out in front, but they know
what's happenin' and what's *gonna* happen. Chester was pretty
ambitious."

Not that you'd know it by looking at Mr. Ches, for he looked like any
other dusty sharecropper driving an old Ford. "He always dressed in overalls," said Wynette. "We never knew we had a dime." The way some relatives

talk, Chester might've held on to every ten-cent piece he ever made, which definitely added up. "I know he had money in more than one bank at the end," said Jane Williams.

Mention Russell's name to a local and you'll see a smiling face. "Chester, he was a *wooon*derful man," said Agnes Wilson. "He had a truck, and if people in the community got sick with no way to get 'em to the doctor, he'd get up at two o'clock in the morning. My daddy thought I was dead with a spasm, and Ches carried me to a doctor in the middle of the night." Itawamba County was "the poorest place in the thirties and forties," said Agnes. "There was no bathrooms, no runnin' water . . . Ches Russell had a house that was painted and warm, and probably more modern than anybody else's." Chester doted on his granddaughter, whom he called Nettiebelle.

"Life was so 'Billie Joe'–ish," Wynette once said of her childhood, referring to Bobbie Gentry's melancholy 1967 hit of small-town gossip and suicide. Work in Itawamba County was hard to come by. Wynette didn't have electricity until the second grade and didn't have a phone until she left home. Chester would read her bedtime stories by kerosene lamp.

"Everything we had to eat was prepared from scratch—using fresh, natural ingredients we either picked or slaughtered that same day," said Wynette, dismayed by the latter. "My grandfather had a brother who was a marksman. All I had to hear was, 'Send Claude after his rifle.' I hid in a closet until it was all over." Wynette started in the kitchen at age nine, when her mother gave her the choice to either work in the field or prepare food for the farmhands. She became a formidable cook. "She loved nothing more than to have a houseful of people and cook for 'em—the more the merrier," said daughter Jackie. "I don't think she knew how to cook small amounts. Mom loved sittin' around the table with everybody. She would always say grace. Always."

Red Bay, population 3,374, is a sleepy little northwest Alabama town butted up against the Mississippi border, a peaceful oasis that seems blissfully unaware of modern madness. Incorporated in 1907, Red Bay has one motel, one AM radio station, and one restaurant, not counting the usual fast-food chains. The median income for an individual here is $27,596. There are twenty-one churches in the ten-mile-square town. The ones I passed, curiously enough, all sported little sayings on their welcome signs that seemed preoccupied with keeping the womenfolk in line.

Main Street's popular Bay Theater, where Wynette received her first smooch from A. G. Stepp* in the balcony (separate seating for blacks and whites) is long gone. "We'd go to the movie, then we'd go to the drugstore," said cousin Jane Williams. "Kids played outside, they didn't sit in front of a TV." People here are friendly. Everybody knows everybody, not to mention everything about everybody, and you get the feeling that while life has improved economically, the invasion of television, chain stores, and the Internet is helping render the landscape as bland as the rest of America. The old values are in full force here: God, family, and work.

In Wynette's day church was the center of all social life. "We lived in church," she said. "Saturday night for the youth meetin's, Sunday night for the preachin', and Wednesday night for prayer meetin'." "There was no place else to go," said Agnes Wilson. "Entertainment was just a word you didn't know." "We liked to go to church, because friends were there—and *boys*," said Linda Cayson. "If you dated, that's mostly where you went." As Mississippi and Alabama were dry states at the time, there were no nightclubs or honky-tonks. "It was the only place we had to go to sing," said Wynette.

She proudly stated, "My father's people were Church of God Pentecostal, and my mother's people were Baptist. I myself am true Southern Mission-ary Baptist." She attended Providence Baptist Church and volunteered to play piano for the congregation at the tender age of nine (her forthrightness then even embarrassed her mother). Wynette found Providence a bit stuffy compared to the much funkier Oak Grove Church of God, where believers spoke in tongues as they shook with the spirit and gospel songs were revved up by the rawest of electric guitars. One can imagine little Wynette's eyes growing wide as the backwoods fire-and-brimstone testifying rocked the walls. "They really got cookin' over there," she recalled. "Rockin' gospel, more like black gospel music."

From grandmother Margaret "Mama" Pugh, Wynette learned the mys-teries of Sacred Harp or shape-note singing, where the congregation's en-semble results in a harmonically complex hypnotic drone. "Fa-so-la singin'" is what Wynette called it: "where they teach you to sing all the notes and never the words." Mama Pugh played the organ and "lived and breathed music," according to Wynette.

There are those who harrumph that Wynette didn't spend much time in a house of worship once she became a star, but according to her uncle Gerald

---

*Stepp is now a minister. I didn't have the heart to inquire about that kiss.

Jetton, if they doubted her faith, they didn't know the real Wynette. "She didn't advertise it. You could just sense that Wynette was spiritual and thought deeply about religion—in the way that she treated people, in her honesty about things, and in her wanting to do good for other folks.... You can tell if a person lives the Christian values or whether they just pay lip service to them. Wynette lived those values."

And the Baptist creed that "a wife is to submit herself to the servant leadership of her husband" was not one Wynette quarreled with, at least on the surface. "I was taught the old, true South," she said. "Daddy made all the decisions. A man's word was law. That's what bothers me so much when people make fun of 'Stand by Your Man.' That's all I knew."

Tammy Wynette burst into the world as Virginia Wynette Pugh* the afternoon of May 5, 1942, at the Mississippi home of Chester Russell. "There wasn't any town," said her mother Mildred. "It was all farm. There weren't but eight hundred people in all of Itawamba County." It was an austere six-room white frame house with a porch in back and front, plus a storm cellar, a necessary addition for the part of the country they called "Tornado Alley." Russell had built the home himself fourteen years before, using lumber taken from his six-hundred-acre farm. Chester's land joined the Alabama border, and Wynette often referred to the small nearby town of Red Bay as her hometown. "My top half comes from Mississippi and my bottom half from Alabama," she wisecracked to the press.†

Mildred Faye Russell was twenty when she gave birth to her only daughter, and her husband, William Hollis Pugh, was five years older. A country woman of imposing size and stature with olive skin and luminous blue eyes, she was incapable of putting on airs. Mildred was a people person, one that could talk you to death. She picked cotton on her father's farm and taught school. "Mildred went on in later years and extended her education

---

*She didn't acquire her show business moniker until 1966, so for the most part I'll refer to her as Wynette until then.

†When it comes to musicians, Alabama's got most states beat. To name but a few: Hank Williams, Nat King Cole, W. C. Handy, Dinah Washington, the Louvin Brothers, Wilson Pickett, Arthur Alexander, Clarence Carter, Percy Sledge, the Delmore Brothers, Jake Hess, and Jim Nabors. When I asked Hurschel Wiginton, leader of the Nashville Edition, the vocal group that sang backgrounds on many a Tammy Wynette record, why so many musicians came from Alabama, he said, "I think all of us were pretty hungry. We tried harder."

where she could teach. That was very unusual for anybody 'round here and took great determination," said Agnes Wilson. Unfortunately for Wynette, she substitute-taught at her daughter's own school.

Mildred was highly thought of in the community, but was also known to be bossy, domineering. "She was a Russell, and she had her own ways about everything," said relative Dan Hall. "Anything she wanted, wrong or right, she got it." Her daughter would be much the same way. "I was spoiled," confessed Wynette.

Although everybody called the new baby Wynette (sometimes "Nette" for short), Mildred had named her Virginia in tribute to a nurse that had cared for her husband in a Memphis hospital. Just five months before Wynette's birth, Hollis had been told he had an inoperable brain tumor. "He was dying, and knew he was dying," said Wynette. A lanky, dark-haired, handsome fellow, intense and unsmiling, he looks, in the few portraits I've seen, as if he could've stepped out of a Walker Evans photo. Hollis had dreamt of a career as a professional musician, and had even recorded two little demonstration records that hung on Wynette's walls for many a year, but they were too beat up to extract a single note from. She'd never know what her father's music sounded like.

Hollis and his brother Carl patterned themselves after the Delmore Brothers, a hot Alabama duo popular at the Grand Ole Opry in the thirties that hit big on King Records some years later with such numbers as 1949's "Blues Stay Away from Me" and the suberb "Trouble Ain't Nothin' but the Blues." The Pugh brothers "sounded just like 'em," said Agnes Wilson. "They could sing as good as the Delmore Brothers could." Cousin Dan Hall knew Hollis well. "I run with him. Good guy. Hollis played guitar, regular outlaw music. Every weekend we'd get together, three of us. Hollis's brother had a four-string Spanish guitar. And he could play it, too."

By the Christmas after Wynette's birth, Hollis had lost his sight, and, according to her book, he turned ornery in the weeks before his death on February 13, 1943. Hollis's last happy moments were spent at the piano, little Wynette in his lap, as he guided her tiny hands to pick out the keys. "Mother said that he called her one day sitting at the piano with me on his knees and said, 'Give her music lessons. I want her to play this thing when I'm gone,'" she explained.

"My father inspired me and gave me the hope, but I don't remember him," said Wynette, and in ferreting through hours and hours of interviews with her, you notice one subject inevitably chokes her up: the father she never knew. Many of Wynette's closest female friends throughout her life expressed a similar opinion when it came to the lasting effect Hollis's early death had: in her many relationships and marriages with older men, Wynette was searching for the father figure she never had.

Despite a grandfather and a stepfather (Foy Lee) that both did their best to raise her, the loss of Hollis hovered over her, a sad shadow never to fully disappear. Lillian Turner, who played on Wynette's high school basketball team, remembered Wynette breaking everybody's heart in the girl's locker room by singing "Daddy's Girl." Another friend, Martha Chumbley, recalled an odd sorrow enveloping Wynette one day: "Her mother had come back from somewhere and bought her a new dress and all this stuff, and Wynette said, 'I have always gotten everything I ever wanted, but I didn't get what I needed.'"

Music kept her father's spirit alive, and it didn't take long for Wynette to start fulfilling her father's dying wishes. "I loved an audience from the time I could walk," she said, and one of the first songs she learned on the piano was taught to her by Chester. It was a little ditty that his wife, Flora, considered wildly inappropriate. Said Wynette, "Every time we had company he'd say, 'Nettiebelle, go sing "Sally, Let Your Bangs Hang Down,"'* and my grandmother would nearly die! She'd say, 'Chester, she's singing that dirty song again!' and it would thrill granddaddy to death."

After Hollis died, Mildred moved to Memphis for a while to work in a wartime airplane factory, and Wynette remained on the farm with Chester and Flora. The couple slept in separate rooms, and Wynette would share her grandfather's bed until she hit puberty, at which point he made her sleep in her own bed, a move that truly dismayed Wynette. She disliked sleeping by herself, and later in life often had one or another daughter for company under the covers. "I hate being alone," she'd tell an interviewer.

Wynette called her grandparents Mama and Daddy, while Mildred, noted Linda Cayson with a little chuckle, was assigned a more reserved title: "Mother." The Russells were strict, particularly Flora. "Mama and Daddy bossed us all, including my mother," said Wynette. "If I did something

---

*Lyric: "Sally caught me peepin' and she thought it was a sin."

naughty my mother wouldn't punish me. She would say to her mother, 'Mama, Wynette needs a whipping.' And I'd usually get it."

Chester doled out a whipping every now and again as well. Wynette was capable of hard work—Linda can recall a day when she picked over two hundred pounds of cotton—but she was equally adept at weaseling out. One day when Wynette was ten Chester told her if she picked fifty pounds she could quit at noon and go to the Tupelo fair she desperately wanted to attend. Wynette headed over to the field early when the cotton was still wet, knowing that would help her cheat on the weight. And although Chester had warned her repeatedly not to pad her sack with rocks as they could spark a fire in the mill, Wynette was an impulsive creature. "I wanted to quit . . . so I filled my sack full of rocks. And I went to the wagon and I emptied it myself so nobody would know."

Lazing around back on the porch before leaving for town, Wynette caught sight of the black smoke drifting up from the mill and knew her goose was cooked. "I saw Daddy get on the tractor and start towards the house, so I started runnin'." Hundreds of pounds of cotton had been lost, and Chester was fit to be tied. "Nettiebelle, the faster you run, the harder I'll whip when I catch you," he growled at Wynette, who'd tripped and fell trying to get away. "I cut my knee and I thought, 'Maybe that'll help.'" It didn't. Chester took after her with a cotton stalk. "He wore me out. He whipped me awful!" But Wynette still went to the fair.

When Wynette turned four, her mother married Foy Lee. Foy worked the farm for Chester and stayed married to Mildred—or Millerd, as he called her—for the rest of her life. When Wynette hit the big time, they'd watch her children, who knew them affectionately as Mee-Maw and Pee-Paw. Easygoing, unexcitable, and just as country as he could be, Foy let his wife take the driver's seat. "I think Mildred pretty much told him what to do," said Linda Cayson. The couple rarely fought, unless Foy hit the sauce.

After Wynette had become a star, her hairdresser Jan Smith once took Foy to the racetrack. Without Mildred around to boss him, he enjoyed a nip or two. "Well, Pee-Paw just got drunker and drunker," recalled Jan. "He said to me, 'You can't tell Millerd this! If Millerd knew this she'd quit me, she'd quit me for sure.'" Jan promised not to tell, and Foy let her in on a little secret: "Y'know, if you just keep a little bottle of vanilla flavorin' in your pocket and drink a little, people will think you've been eatin' cake instead of drinkin'."

By the time they made it to the box, no amount of vanilla extract could hide the fact that Foy was drunk as a skunk. Jan dragged him back to the car to sleep it off. "Pee-Paw was over six feet tall and had the longest arms you've ever seen. I took his shoes because I thought, 'He won't go anywhere without his shoes.'" But when they got back to the car, Foy had vanished.

"I went up to a policeman standin' at the main gate. I said, 'You seen a real tall man around here? With a jacket with cuffs up to his elbows and no shoes?'

"'Lost his five hundred dollars?' said the cop. 'He's at the jail.'"

Jan ran over to the police station, told them they had Tammy Wynette's stepfather locked up, and a deal was struck.

"You can have Pee-Paw, but we all want a signed album," said the cops. ("It was more like thirty!" insisted Jan.)

Pee-Paw had a dry sense of humor—so dry, in fact, he often didn't know how funny he was. Charley Abdon, Wynette's longtime drummer, recalled standing next to Foy at a Malden, Missouri, show when he drawled out a line that made Abdon's jaw drop. "Ol' Pee-Paw looked over, saw some girl out in the audience, and said, 'By God, I'd break her down like a shotgun.' I thought, what a thing for an old geezer to say!"

For all his antics, Foy could calm Mildred down when she got riled up over Wynette, whom he adored. And Wynette felt the same about Foy. "She loved him to death," said Linda. "Foy was real good to her." Agnes Wilson recounted one of the first things Wynette did after she became a star. "When she got the first big check, Wynette said, 'Foy, you go down to the dealership and you pick out a car you want and I'll pay for it.' That's how much she thought of him. It burned Mildred, 'cause she thought it should've been for her."*

Wynette was a rambunctious little jitterbug, well known for her agile acrobatic stunts and her basketball maneuvers on Hopewell's red-dirt court. A left-handed player, Wynette felt self-conscious because she was the only one wearing blue jeans. Chester wouldn't let her wear the shorts the rest of the girls wore. "I can see up the legs of them britches," he said. "I ain't havin' that." Chester finally relented after Flora sewed elastic bands into the hem to close any offending gaps. Named Miss Offense in her high school year-

---

*Not that Mildred was any happier when her daughter surprised her with a new Lincoln. "Mee-Maw went out there, looked at it, and said, 'I don't want that thing, it looks like a Ford in the back.' Tammy said, 'Well, when did your ass get so fine you couldn't ride a Ford?' Mildred wanted a Cadillac, and she took to her bed."

book, Wynette made the all-state team both in 1958 and the following year, but "her heart wasn't in it," said Nancy Byrd. Her real love was music. "We'd ride the bus to basketball games, and Wynette would lead the group in singin' songs," said teammate Betty Chasteen. "She had a beautiful loud voice and she just raised the roof on that bus." Added classmate Bobby Canup, "Wynette could hit that high E! Most people could not go that high."

Wynette might've been an only child, but Mildred's sister Carolyn was just five years old when Wynette was born, and the two girls were close as any sisters. "Carolyn was the one who had the sense," said Linda. "Kind of calmed Wynette down." Wynette idolized her and, at age five, would tag along with Carolyn to Hopewell School (later called "Bounds-X"), the three-room grade school just five hundred yards from their home. Wynette was already a ham. "I remember Carolyn coming in one day from school and she said, 'Mama, I can't stand this any longer, she's driving me crazy. Every time she gets a chance she stands on the benches and sings and sings!'"

It was at Hopewell that Wynette, now in the sixth grade, stood up and told the class what she wanted to do with her life: "I want to be a singer, or an actress." The kids all laughed, prompting teacher Leman Burch to whack his desk with a ruler and tell them, "You can be anything you want in life if you want it bad enough." Wynette would never forget those words.* Burch described Wynette as "a leader. When I wanted all the girls to do something, all I had to do was win Wynette. . . . She would always take charge of a project."

At Hopewell, Wynette found a soul mate in Linda Cayson (then Loden). "We just bonded instantly," said Linda. "I just loved her from day one." The two girls lived near each other and, since they had no phone, often made plans to leave their homes at the same time. "We'd meet on the road 'bout halfway and either come back to my house or her house," said Cayson, who noted the road to Wynette's house was actually paved. There was many a sleepover, and the two girls were inseparable. "When you saw one you saw the other," said friend Bobby Canup.

"We spent an awful lot of time together growin' up," said Linda. "We've been up and down all these hills 'n' hollers around here, oh, yes, Lord. When

---

*According to Linda Cayson, Wynette was a talented actress. "In the eighth grade, we did a class play at Hopewell—'Henpecked Henry.' She played the lead in it, Henry's wife. Wynette was really good."

Wynette was a kid, she was just happy as could be, and just funny." The pair got into all sorts of mischief (invariably instigated by Wynette), like tying rocks and a can to the tail of one of Chester's little old dogs, Jack, and watching it scamper off in a panic. "I'm tellin' you, I remember Mr. Russell bearin' on us about doin' Jack that way," said Cayson, laughing. Linda's father ran a general store and one old customer liked to serenade the two girls with "Curly-Headed Baby." Unfortunately he had a harelip. "Wynette, she'd get the biggest kick out of getting him to sing, because he couldn't talk plainly, it was just mumblin'. Wynette would get so tickled."

Linda was quiet and not as popular as Wynette, but if somebody dared pick on her, they were in for it. When a schoolyard bully tried to beat Linda up, little Wynette got in the would-be assailant's face and, unable to bring herself to cuss the girl out, told her she was "nothin' but an old Russian," which in those days meant "Communist," certainly no compliment. Or the time in the eleventh grade when everybody was trying out for the school play. "Wynette got her part but I didn't get mine, they gave it to another girl—so she refused to be in the play," said Cayson. "She would defend me to the end. We were fierce for each other."

At age six Wynette and Linda discovered they both shared a passion for music. "Mr. Ches had a piano," recalled Cayson. "Wynette was always on it. Often we played it together—I played one end, she'd be on the other. We just started singin', and both realized we could harmonize. She sang the real high parts and I sang the low parts, two-part harmony as close as any sisters. I think Wynette was born with it in her. Even as a child I knew her voice was going to be special. She was rehearsin' for the world."

"Oh, she was a good girl," Mildred said of her daughter in an early press clipping. "But we just couldn't tear her away from that radio." Mildred remembered finding Wynette standing by the heater one day, weeping. "I asked her what was wrong, and Wynette said some country singer had died." The family radio was one of the only conduits to that big world outside. Wynette and Carolyn would tune to the Grand Ole Opry on the weekends, and Linda remembers how she and Wynette heard such artists as Ernest Tubb, Hank Snow, and Roy Acuff on WERH, a tiny station out of nearby Hamilton, Alabama. "We listened to the country radio all the time," said Cayson, who recalled weeping with Wynette over the 1953 Jean Shepard–Ferlin Husky duet, "A Dear John Letter." "Lord, we just thought that was the *saddest* song." Patsy Cline and Skeeter Davis were two Wynette favorites. And she had an ear for such early R & B as the Coasters, the Platters, and Ray Charles.

"Mother's record collection influenced me a lot," said Wynette. At night in her room, she'd play one Hank Williams song over and over, his mournful and stark 1949 guitar-and-vocal demo recording of unrequited love entitled "No One Will Ever Know." "I'll cry myself to sleep and wake up smiling," sang Hank, his lyrics tailor-made for the stoic-but-only-on-the-surface character Wynette would become. The vinyl copy of *The Immortal Hank Williams* dwarfed her tiny Mickey Mouse record player. As Wynette told Dolly Carlisle, "I'd lie on my stomach sleeping, and I'd take my finger and scratch the needle back to the beginning and I'd play it over and over." After Hank moaned "I'll cry myself to sleep and wake up smiling" for the tenth time, Wynette would finally drift off to dreamland.*

White Southern gospel music was another major influence. Listen to *Inspiration*, her stunning 1969 gospel album, or the spine-tingling rendition of "Precious Memories" she recorded with the Masters V in 1987. "Those old songs mean the world to me," said Wynette. "I feel strange when I don't do a gospel song in a show. If not for Him, I wouldn't have a voice."

The white male gospel quartets of the 1950s could whip female audience members into the sort of frenzy one would soon associate with Elvis. They were a far cry from "the forced, prissy smiles, poodle dog hairstyles, and ghastly leisure suits that later came to dominate the genre," said David Vest, who would later play piano for Wynette during her early days in Birmingham.

Vest saw the Blackwood Brothers at age ten in 1953 and vividly remembers how women "swooned and screamed" when tenor Bill Shaw stepped up to the mic to do "Over the Moon." Vest also witnessed flamboyant, mustachioed pianist (and ordained Baptist minister) Hovie Lister electrifying

---

*In 1991, Wynette brought the house down on a Hank Williams, Jr.–hosted TV show by belting out a seemingly off-the-cuff verse of "No One Will Ever Know" that left Hank Jr. and his other guests shaking their heads in wonder. "Your dad was my hero," she told Hank Jr. "Always will be." One laments that Tammy was never afforded the opportunity (like so many of her male counterparts, including George Jones) to record a Hank tribute album.

crowds with his group the Statesmen. "Lister would throw off his suit coat, let his hair fall suddenly in his face, kick back the bench, looking like the devil incarnate seizing control of a gospel quartet. Then he would race over to the microphone and take over the lead vocal, shouting with abandon, in Pentecostal camp meeting style. . . . He could really peddle the snake oil, too. When I first heard Jerry Lee Lewis, at least half a decade after my first exposure to Hovie Lister, I knew exactly where he was coming from." The Statesmen's debonair high tenor Denver Crumpler was a big favorite of Wynette's.

The Statesmen and the Blackwood Brothers toured together for "All-Night Sings," multiple-act extravaganzas put together by quartet singer and promoter Wally Fowler. "Smooth silk vs. Harris tweed" is how Vest described this particular battle of the bands. "The Statesmen were much more 'manly' sounding in their close harmony. The Blackwoods were three high harmonies, anchored by an impossibly low bass singer. They sang black repertoire without trying to sound 'black.' James Blackwood is to white gospel music what Maybelle Carter is to country. He took the music of Wynette's childhood and went national with it."

Mildred and Foy would put money aside to attend the All-Night Sings, which Linda Cayson recalled attending with Wynette. "We were sittin' there both just amazed. Wynette said, 'Lin, I've got chill bumps,' and I said, 'I do, too.'" During a short first stay in Memphis, Wynette, just like the young Elvis, headed over to radio station WMPS to stare through the glass as the Blackwoods did their radio show. Later in life Wynette would perform with James Blackwood, and he'd sing at her mother's funeral. "James Blackwood has been a hero of mine for my entire life," Wynette wrote in 1997. "I find myself still in awe."

It should be noted that it was in Memphis that a twelve-year-old Wynette had her one brief but significant encounter with Elvis.* Mildred had a job working at University Park Cleaners on North McLean Boulevard for Carney and Auzella Moore. Carney's brother Scotty was a guitarist, and his group rehearsed up in the hat-blocking department above the shop. The singer in the band was Elvis Presley. Wynette would listen to them rehearse, or watch

---

*In her autobiography and in countless interviews, Wynette repeatedly stated she was ten at the time, but Presley didn't start playing with Scotty Moore until 1954, the year Moore dates meeting Wynette in his own book. During one TV interview she dated the encounter to 1957.

Scotty trade licks with an old black guy who worked there. "She was fascinated by guitars," recalled Moore.

Wynette remembered standing at the foot of the stairs with Auzella looking up at Elvis and his crew. "They just looked like teenagers with greasy hair," she told Holly George-Warren. "And Auzella said, 'My, my, my, look at the stars.' Elvis turned around and said, 'One of these days I'll wrap you up in hundred-dollar bills.' I will never forget that. She just laughed."

That Christmas, when Auzella went to Presley's three-bedroom house to deliver some gifts, Wynette tagged along. Newly signed to RCA Records, Elvis wasn't there, but she got an eyeful of the newfound Presley opulence. "The carpet came up to my ankles," said Wynette, who rushed home to tell Mildred all about it. "I said, 'Oh, mother, you've never seen anything like this, the carpet was white and the walls were white and the tree set right in the middle . . . it was just gorgeous.'" One detail made a big impression on little Wynette: Elvis was making a living with his music. "I thought, gosh, how neat."

At eight years of age, both Wynette and Linda took piano lessons from Phelam Ganus, a strict disciplinarian who wrote out his music and expected you to go home and learn it. Not interested in homework, Wynette would make him play the piece until she could play it by ear. Ganus soon caught on and refused. As Wynette told it, "The music teacher told mother and me, 'You're wasting my time and your time, Mrs. Lee. She's not listening to what I tell her. She plays what she hears.'" When Wynette visited Ganus not long before he died in the mid-seventies, the old man took one look at the tall blonde superstar and said, "I knew someday you'd make something of yourself, but I don't like the color of your hair. It used to be brown." Then Ganus drifted off to sleep.

Cousin Jane recalled Wynette playing the piano at their house until the wooden bench she sat on turned white from her perspiration. "When it came to music, she could hear somethin' on the radio and she'd play it—this wasn't somethin' that was taught her, it was just *in* her."

Flute, piano, organ, and accordion—Wynette could play them all. At age twelve she learned chords on the guitar from her father's brother Harrod, who, having lost an arm working for the railroad, used his one hand to position her fingers on the frets. "Wynette was always performin'," said friend Holly Ford. "Piano, accordion, you name it, she could play it all. You never had to ask her twice." At school recess Wynette would beeline to the auditorium for the old keyboard there. "She'd get on that piano and she'd start singin,' and it would make chills over you," said Agnes Wilson.

Wynette sang in a bunch of little vocal groups that included local kids like Nancy Byrd, Gayra Falls, Kenneth and Morris Miller, Tommy Brewer, Geraldine Tharp, and Agnes Wilson. "I would sing the beat, Wynette would sing the high part, and my sister would sing the alto," said Wilson. The one constant was Linda, although Agnes never sang with her and Wynette together. "I didn't have a way to get different places. Their mothers had automobiles."

Around age ten or eleven, Wynette and Linda started singing together in public, and people still remember their performances. "Wynette was a very talented young lady," said Jamie Cole, who sang with Wynette and Linda at the Oak Grove Church of God. "When she would sing a song, even in church, Wynette would put all of her heart into it, see? She wanted to show her emotions." For the most part, Wynette and Linda sang gospel songs, but they also did "In the Pines" and "a lot of Everly Brothers—we could harmonize good on those," as Linda recalled. "We had one song everywhere we went we'd have to sing, 'Swing Low, Sweet Chariot.' We fixed us an arrangement that wasn't really like the original."

Mildred "was probably the first one that realized we were pretty good," said Linda. "First church we ever sang at was a place called Mount Gilead. Just a little bitty one-room church. Mildred carried us over there."

In 1987 the BBC went to Alabama and reunited Wynette with her old singing partners Agnes and Linda. Wilson visited with Wynette on the bus and recalled how nervous she was before the filming at her mother's old house of worship, the tiny Providence Baptist Church. Agnes was "the one who prayed for us all through school if we was losin' in ball games. I was known as the prayer warrior. Wynette said, 'Well, Agnes, it's been a *loooong* time, and if you ever prayed, you better be a-prayin' for us that we can get through this.'"

In the BBC film Wynette sits at the church piano with Linda and Agnes on either side, and as you listen to this trio gathered under a lazy ceiling fan trading lilting harmonies on "I'll Fly Away" to the twenty or so people in the pews, you hunger to go back in time and see what the world was like for the young singer.

Little churches led to bigger ones. "I remember one time us goin' to

Tupelo because we had been invited to sing at this big church," said Linda. "It had carpet on the floors and padded seats! We never had been in a church like that before." Wynette loved to rattle her perpetually nervous little pal. "She knew if she ever got me tickled I could not hush. I'd be sittin' there shakin',' and that just tickled her to death."

Although they never won, Mildred drove Wynette and Linda to talent contests all over the area. "Mildred was all for things like that," said Cayson. "She wanted Wynette to be somebody. I think that her preference would've been for Wynette to keep singin' gospel. Mildred always wanted Wynette to make it big, but she wanted her to do it *Mildred's* way."

On one trip to Tupelo, they performed on live TV. "We were on the mornin' show, Freddie and Kay Bane. All the lights were real hot." A fly landed right on Linda's chest during their song, but the duo somehow made it through their performance intact. "It was scary for me, but it wasn't for Wynette. She always had nerves of steel . . . yeah, she'd try *anything.*"

Brother Verde Collier, Linda's Methodist minister, featured the two song-birds on his weekly Saturday morning radio show on WERH in Hamilton, Alabama. "My mother would let me drive her car, which was a '51 Ford," Wynette told Holly George-Warren. "The next weekend Lin's Daddy would let her have the car, and she'd drive. And we'd sing two songs every Satur-day and, my, we thought we were something."

That led to a spot singing on WERH with local legend Carmol Taylor, who had a band called Carmol Taylor and His Country Pals. After giving many hopefuls their first taste of showbiz, Taylor would go on to cowrite numerous songs with Wynette's producer, Billy Sherrill. (According to en-gineer Lou Bradley, Carmol was one of the few people who could get into the elusive producer's office on a regular basis. "He was a big ol' rawboned country boy from north Alabama. Carmol kept 'em honest. He was their country leavening agent.")

Saturday nights Wynette and Linda would join Carmol and his band over at Hamilton's skating rink, the Skatetorium. It was a big deal at the time. "The area around here didn't have one," said Agnes Wilson. "It was a modern-day thing!" As Wynette put it, "We'd sing a while and stop, and everybody would skate. Then we'd sing some more."

Wynette and Linda had sung in church, on the radio, and at the Skate-torium, but it was only the beginning, at least as far as Wynette was con-cerned. As Cayson recalled, "She'd say, 'We're gonna make it big one of these days, and we're gonna call ourselves Gwen'—Wynette loved the name Gwen—'and Lin.'" Linda would nod in agreement, humoring her friend, but Wynette was dead serious. "She really believed it. Wynette had big dreams even back then."

"From the time Wynette entered Tremont High School, it was like a great wind came through," said classmate Holly Ford. "Nothing was ever the same. She was born to be a star."

Wynette claimed in her autobiography and in various interviews that she was never that popular and was even picked on at times. She felt she was heavy and her thin brown hair "mousy." This says more about Wynette's tremendous sensitivity than how she was seen by others, because when I shared these opinions with her old friends they just laughed.

"She was just really popular," maintained Linda Cayson. "Boys always liked her. 'Cause she was very pretty." And famous for her tan. "When we'd come back to school, brown was not the word for it," said friend Martha Chumbley. "Everybody wanted to be brown just like Wynette." And to attend her birthday party. "The roads would just be full of cars and kids," said Chumbley. Wynette was even voted Miss Tremont High in 1960. "She shouldn't have been," insisted classmate Bobby Canup. "I mean, somebody who was failing could be Miss Tremont High? That's not correct, y'see." But that was Wynette. "Get Wynette to talkin', she could charm a snake," said Holly Ford.

Wynette was a rebel. Adventurous, fun-loving. And fearless. Linda Cayson has fond memories of an impromptu photo shoot one day when they played hooky. "Her granddaddy had a big ol' lake, so we skipped school. Carried a lunch and a camera and went over to that ol' lake. And I don't know how many different outfits we had taken over there. She posed in a bathin' suit! Oh, she was just like a movie star." Holly Ford recalled a sleepover when Wynette decided to take a late-night dip in Chester's lake. "Wynette just stripped off her clothes, jumped in that pond— Honey, you couldn't have paid me a million dollars to get in there with those snakes. Didn't faze her. I just think she walked through life like she owned it. Wynette felt no fear. She just floated through whatever with the greatest of ease."

And when it came to her own life, particularly her exceedingly complex love life, Wynette was quite the storyteller. "She could spin a tale," said

Ford. "Wynette just wrapped you up. You felt like you had a front-row seat. She had such detail, she could paint a picture with words. Anything she told, if it was no more than, 'I went to the beauty shop today, had my hair done, and stopped by and got a Coke'—y'know, just somethin' very trivial—she could just make you want to hear it again. Wynette could've talked to a blind person, and they'd have thought they had their sight back."*

Wynette even hypnotized a teacher or two. Miss Jamerson taught typing, bookkeeping, shorthand—"the things that women had to take back then," as Ford put it. Wynette would launch into some dramatic tale about her love life, and all class work would grind to a halt. "The bell would ring, and we hadn't done a thing! I mean, Wynette could even keep the teacher from sayin', 'Okay, that's enough.' Miss Jamerson enjoyed just listenin' to her, too, and we would get tickled at just *how much* she enjoyed it."

One gets the idea that citizens of Red Bay still find the adventures of the young Wynette Pugh a little shocking, although once you get them to spill a few of the beans, the stories are fairly innocuous. Just asking one of her classmates to confirm that she was considered a rebel, he whispered, "She was . . . but don't say that I said it." No doubt if Wynette had been a boy, nobody would've thought twice, but this was the 1950s in a small Southern town. She was well aware of the double standard and wrote in her autobiography how angry it made her "to hear a girl called names for doing the same thing a boy will brag about."

Which isn't to say that Wynette's constant craving for male attention wasn't a little unnerving. "She *always* had guys that were in love with her," said former sister-in-law Nancy Byrd. "I'm tellin' ya! Even the young boys— if you asked them, they'd tell you that they had dates with Wynette! Little guys that were not popular and considered themselves lucky if they got one girl to date 'em!"

Martha Chumbley agreed. "She dated some that didn't date very much. It wasn't just that she was for the wild ones and the ones that dated all the girls—she dated quiet ones, too. She dated a lot of different boys."

"She was into datin' and boys long before we were," said Holly Ford. "Guys just *loved* bein' around her. Wynette always had these many, many boy-

*Decades later, on Wynette's bus, listening to her tales of romance with Burt Reynolds, Holly felt like she was back in high school. "You almost fell in love with Burt yourself just hearin' her tell about him. Wynette was just in love with love."

friends, so you felt she was more like a married woman. And we thought she was just a little more advanced than we were. She lived a much more exciting life by *far*."

Who was Wynette seeing now? And just what was she doing with them? It was the talk of Tremont High. "Everybody would speculate but nobody would know for sure," said one pal. Back when we were growin' up and you did something, you didn't want nobody to know it. Wynette didn't care!"

Naturally, this led to the telling of tales of questionable veracity. One friend whispered of a secret after-party at Wynette's house that had gained her the nickname Wine-ette. "*Wine*-ette. Not *win*-ette. I said, 'Why?' 'Because she kept that bottle of wine under her mattress!' Whether she did or not, I don't know. The kids would say, '*Wyyyyyyy*-nette' and everybody would know what you meant." Then there was the day a slightly risqué letter detailing her amorous adventures she'd sent a friend ended up on the Tremont High bulletin board.

"Everybody was readin' it," confessed Bobby Canup. "Wynette jerked it down before I got to read the first sentence or two. They said it was full of mushy stuff. Wynette turned bloodred and she said, 'That so-and-so, I'll kill her for that!'" Her escapades resulted in such gossip that some parents looked down on Wynette. "My mother would not have wanted me to have gone with her," said one classmate.

Bobby Canup, who dated Wynette's pal Linda Cayson, took it upon himself to find out what was so special about Wynette. One day he spotted her outside the school auditorium where the kids hung out. "I decided I was gonna get me one o' them kisses. She came back in that auditorium door and she said, 'Hey, Bobby,' and I said, 'Hey,' and I grabbed her and I laid one on her. She done looked startled—she said, 'You oughtta get Linda, not me!' She was the first girl I ever kissed. Behind the stage when I wasn't supposed to!"

But apparently Virginia Pugh was more talk than action. At least according to her autobiography, in which she states she remained a virgin until her wedding night. This anomaly didn't stop Wynette from playing the role of high school vamp to the hilt. "She knew about sex before I ever knew it existed," said one classmate who preferred not to be identified. "Wynette introduced a lot of those ideas to us. It was just so much fun bein' around somebody who could at least *talk* about it. Now I can look back and think maybe she didn't do all the things that she implied. . . . She was so much more mature-minded, and she just had a sexuality about her."

Wynette kept her classmates in suspense not only over her current romance, but where it might take her the following weekend—and everybody was enlisted in the plot, said Holly Ford. "She was goin' to elope, it was this one and it was that one, and the intrigue of passin' notes and helpin' her, getting her all set to run away. . . . We'd get so involved that we'd just work ourselves up into a fever!" By the following Monday, Wynette would return to school, unmarried and already on to a new romance. "It wasn't like we were upset—'Gosh, you put us through all of that?!' She'd turn around and do it the next week! There's no tellin' how many times we went through all the drama of getting her ready to elope—and then she'd just come back to school!"

Wynette loved the attention, and she could be brazen. Nancy Byrd and her brother Euple accompanied Wynette on a trip to Fulton to buy some shoes for graduation. "Well, she was just all over Euple, just in love with him." When they returned home, Nancy ran an errand with Wynette plus another guy she'd dated. "And she was all over *him* and in love." Nancy laughed in disbelief. "She'd keep two or three on a string and keep 'em all happy. It always amazed me. They all thought that they were THE one. I thought it was an extremely good talent myself. And I don't think Wynette had to compromise herself, if you know what I mean."

One person who wasn't the least bit entertained by Wynette's shenanigans was Mildred. "It didn't sit well with her," said Linda Cayson. "Nothin' sat well with her. That was the trouble. I think she wanted to pick everything Wynette did. She wanted to pick her boyfriends. If there was one she didn't approve of, it was hard for Wynette to have anything to do with them." Added Nancy Byrd, "She wanted Wynette to be the model Southern lady. Mildred didn't like her dating older men."

Mildred could be a formidable opponent. She was big and short-tempered, and meant business when provoked. "When we was little, I thought a lot of Mee-Maw, and I was half scared of her," said Linda Cayson. Granddaughter Jackie Daly remembers visiting Mildred and Foy as a child. "They wanted us to play—she locked us out of the house and said, 'You can't come in until it's time to eat.' It was getting dark, and we were wantin' in. They had this field behind their house, just woods. Mee-Maw told us the wolves were gonna get us. I'll never forget it. Scared me to death."*

Friction between mother and daughter began early. "Wynette had an 'I'm all grown up and I know what I'm gonna be' attitude from about ten or twelve," said Agnes Wilson. Wynette would get mad at her grandfather, sulk, then carry her cot on her back to Foy and Mildred's house—until, that is, Wynette would get into it with her mother and go tromping back to Chester's. "She could throw some fits," said Wilson.

"Mildred was strict," said Linda Cayson. "She just disapproved of a lot of things. She wanted Wynette to be perfect. And kids can't be perfect." Although nobody dared share this opinion with either Mildred and Wynette, the consensus was that they were just too much alike, each as stubborn as a mule and determined to get her own way. "I think it was a love/hate relationship, because Mee-Maw was very demanding," said daughter Jackie. "Mom was rebellious, and was that way, really, until she died."

Wynette lived briefly with Mildred and Foy in Memphis, then suddenly returned home to the farm, later claiming it was because of a postcard her grandparents had sent telling her the gym teacher was giving her outfit away to another girl. According to her aunt Hazel Hall, there was a more compelling reason for her swift return to Itawamba County—she was out of control. "Wynette bawled and squalled over going, then she run off down there. Mildred watched her like a hawk. The babysitter didn't work out, Wynette wouldn't listen to her. Mildred had to bring her back to Uncle Chester. She said, 'Somebody's gonna kill her.'"

Wynette smoked, which drove her mother crazy. Cigarettes made her pal Linda ill, but she'd still keep Wynette company when she'd slip off to Mildred and Foy's outhouse for a clandestine puff. During the summer Linda and Wynette would go off to Birmingham together to visit relatives, and on one particular trip Wynette smoked all week long. The return home was a disaster. "We rode a Trailways bus and we got off at Red Bay," Cayson recalled. "And her mama was there to pick us up. Wynette had a little ol' low-cut dress and she had a pack of cigarettes tucked down in her bra." Linda laughed at the memory. "When Wynette stepped off, she had to kinda bend over and—*ha!*—

---

*Late in life Mildred was leaving the hospital one day only to be accosted by a purse-snatcher. "She took that pocketbook and swung at him," said her friend Helen Hutchison. "He didn't get it. Honey, she had a gun in her pocketbook!"

Mildred just reached up and got that pack of cigarettes stuck down in her bosom. Oh, Lord, that was a bad, long trip home. Rave and rant. Rave and rant. I'm tellin' ya, boy, Mildred could put a hurtin' on you."

Wynette had an aunt in Red Bay, Hazel Hall, whom she considered her "second mother" and often turned to for help. "Mildred gave her a lotta hard whippin's," said Hazel. "I was sorry for her. I never did whip her. She wanted to slip things by her mother, hide everything, and done a pretty good job of it. I think Mildred knew, but she couldn't stop it."

"Wynette would come see us so she could do what she wanted to do," said cousin Jane Hall. "She'd spend the night, but she might not get in until later. Wynette would just sneak off and do things. My bedroom was upstairs so she could just come in the front door and zip up the stairs."

Wynette's antics weren't always so funny to her friends, like the night Holly Ford had a bunch of girls over for a sleepover in their senior year. "We were eatin' potato chips, drinkin' Coke, we were all just havin' a good time," said Ford. Suddenly they realized Wynette had vanished. Somehow they figured out she had snuck off to meet a much older guy she was crazy about, D. C. Byrd. "I almost had a heart attack," said Ford. "I thought my mother was probably gonna beat me to death, if Wynette's mother didn't. Thinkin', 'What if they have a car wreck, what if she gets caught?' I was so worried. And angry that Wynette took away this happy time and put us, especially me, through this much stress." Around midnight Wynette magically reappeared. "Do you think any of us girls said anything? We enjoyed hearin' all about it! Every little detail. You could forgive Wynette for anything."

One of Wynette and Mildred's first big showdowns was over a boy named Billy Cole. He was nineteen; Wynette was fifteen and in the sixth grade. They met at Oak Grove Church of God. "Billy Cole and his brother Jamie were sons of the preacher man," said Holly. "Popular, well-liked, good boys. They were in church every time the doors opened." Wynette and Linda sang with the brothers and then started dating them. "More or less our goin' together consisted of bein' together at singin's 'n' stuff," said Linda. "That was Wynette's first big love. She thought Billy was somethin'. He was really good lookin'. I liked his brother James. Mildred wanted her to double-date, so I brought up the rear."

At some point Wynette had a fight with Billy, sending her into a tizzy. "They had a spat, and Wynette took blush or rouge and made her eyes red so it would look like she was cryin'," said friend Betty Chasteen. "Wynette was always just real dramatic," added Linda. "Real dramatic."

Wynette decided that she and Billy were going to become husband and wife. Young newlyweds were not uncommon in Wynette's neck of the woods, but she knew Mildred would have a fit, so it was kept very hush-hush. "That 'get married' bit was Wynette's idea instead of his," said Linda. "She was the one that ordered the rings . . . Wynette was determined, I'll put it thataway." Wynette mail-ordered the eight-dollar rings and had them sent to the school instead of home, but Mildred uncovered the plot before Wynette even had a chance to show Billy his golden ring.

"You know why she didn't marry him?" asked Bobby Canup. "Ches and his wife was gonna go somewhere and leave Wynette, and she was gonna run off and get married. So I told mother, 'Well, Wynette's gonna get married this weekend.' 'She is?' 'Yeah, she's gonna run off with Billy Cole.' So you wouldn't believe what happened. All of a sudden Ches Russell drove up and delivered a truckload of concrete blocks. My mother went out there and said, 'Well, I hear Wynette's getting married this weekend.' He went, 'WHAT?' 'The kids are sayin' she's gonna run off with Billy Cole this weekend, you was goin' somewhere.' 'Well, I'm goin' somewhere, but *she's* goin' with me.' So I'm the one that knocked her out of marryin' Billy Cole. I didn't mean to!"

An angry Mildred showed up at Tremont High. As Nancy Byrd remembered, "They had a confrontation, and I can remember Wynette was tryin' to take a whole box of St. Joseph's aspirin because she had cried 'til she had a headache. We were afraid she was overdosin'! She scared all us girls to death. Wynette felt things very deeply."

There would be no more dates with Billy Cole. Mildred "stopped all of that," said Linda. "Wynette was so mad, she couldn't see straight. She wasn't cryin'—just mad as all get-out. Rantin' and ravin'!"

Just because Mildred had won the last round didn't mean the fight was over. "I'm a Taurus," Wynette said. "Telling me I can't is like waving a red flag in front of a bull." Wynette was determined to get out from under her family's rule one way or another. That her friend Linda had gotten married in their junior year only upped the ante.

"When I first got married she came to my little apartment. Wynette thought that would be the most wonderful thing, to be married. So I think right then she set her mind that she was gonna get married, too. Wynette always said the only reason in the world that she married was because I married. I hate that. Because I made a mistake—and Wynette did, too."

But those ugly realities were off in some pesky future. Wynette was too busy dreaming to think rationally. "I'd lay awake at night and think, 'Oh, boy, I'll be in my own house and have my own curtains, my own dishes, I won't have to do anything anybody tells me.'"

Just seventeen years old, Wynette was at a crossroads. "I dreamed of being a singer, but I also wanted to be a housewife and mother like my girlfriends." For the time being, the path taken was the one that was expected of her. "One side of me needs singing and the life on the road," Wynette said in a 1981 interview. "But I was raised to believe in marriage as a woman's greatest fulfillment and I guess deep down that's what I still believe."

Wynette went off and married Euple Byrd, five years her senior. And she did it a month before graduation, which meant she wouldn't finish school. That would really stick it to her mother. Not only that, but Euple was known to drink the occasional beer. That practically warranted the death penalty in ol' Mildred's eyes.

Did Wynette love Euple? Nobody who knew her then thought so. "I *will* love him," she told herself.

Once men and relationships entered Wynette's life, a chaos ensued. Giddy romances, mad infatuations, backstreet affairs . . . yet when the drama died down and the dust cleared, Wynette was often left holding nothing.

There was something that she wanted so desperately. A perfect marriage? A white-picket-fence life? A happy ending? Whatever it was would forever elude her. Somehow she knew this. You can see it in those sad, hurting eyes. You can hear it in that voice.

"It was like there was always a void in her life," said Linda Cayson. "Like she was searchin' for somethin' that she couldn't find. Somethin' missin'."

Euple

In almost every marriage there is a selfish and an unselfish partner. A
pattern is set up and soon becomes inflexible, of one person always
making the demands and one person always giving way.

—Iris Murdoch, *A Severed Head*

I say what I want to say. I go where I want to go. Nobody tells me no.

—Tammy Wynette

"Everybody liked Euple," says friend Bobby Canup. "He was an easy-
goin', real nice person." Linda Cayson agrees. "Euple was a good guy.
I liked him. He was just as nice and friendly and funny as he could be."
Agnes Wilson adds a caveat: "Euple was a sweet, friendly boy . . . he just
didn't have money." "That wasn't the Euple Byrd that we know, the one
Wynette wrote about," insists friend Judy Allen. "Like he was worthless and
all that." His sister Diane Bruff chimes in: "Euple Byrd was a fine man, and
anybody would tell you that he would give you the shirt off his
back . . . Wynette was the wild one."

The Byrd family feels they have been somewhat demonized in both
Wynette's autobiography and the subsequent 1981 TV movie. According to
Wynette, Euple is the first husband that stood in the way. He had his wife
arrested for being an unfit mother, wanted her committed, and laughed at
her dream. In the movie, the Byrd family appears to be little more than a
bunch of toothless hillbillies. The wounds still haven't healed. The Byrds
"weren't prosperous," said one friend. "But they were good people. They did
not deserve to be made to look like these mountain people idiots. They
portrayed 'em cruelly."

The story of Wynette and Euple is a tangled mess. Unfortunately Euple
is dead, as is Wynette's mother, Mildred, and to my knowledge neither was
ever interviewed about this turbulent time in Wynette's life and the central
role each of them played in it. The accepted account is Wynette's autobiography, by its very nature a one-sided telling of the tale. The remaining living
witnesses paint a somewhat more complex picture.

———

"Wynette dated every one of the Byrd boys—even my husband," said Weir Byrd's wife, Nancy. (Wynette's pursuit of the Byrds is somewhat legendary—Judy Allen recalled that at the time, "One of the Byrd sisters made the comment, 'Mama, Daddy may not be safe.'") Although Wynette dated Weir and Don as well as Euple, the Byrd boy she really had in the sights of her love gun was the oldest of the brothers, D.C.

"D.C. was a nice-lookin' man," said Judy. "Slicked-back, real wavy black hair. Tall, dark, and handsome, you'd say." D.C. was a "ladies' man," said Nancy Byrd. "The type you'd see in the movies." He had a little Clark Gable mustache, and an impressive set of wheels. "'54 Mercury convertible," Bobby Canup recalled. "In the service he'd made a continental kit and extended the fenders eighteen inches so that thing was long, had that continental kit on the back. He didn't think about gravel roads around here, y'see—that thing would drag 'bout every time he hit the road. The girls went wild."

Wynette barely devotes a sentence to the relationship in her book, but her old Red Bay friends and relatives know better. "Lord, Wynette was crazy about D.C.," said his sister, Diane Bruff. "He and his first wife, they separated over Wynette." D.C. had dropped out of school to join the air force. When he returned and his marriage broke up, "Wynette was determined she was gonna marry him," said Martha Chumbley. But in between dates with Wynette, D.C. was still seeing his former wife. "Wynette would tell us at school about D.C. callin' her—and all the time us knowin' he was slippin' and goin' with the girl that he married!" Then D.C. remarried his wife. "It just like to broke Wynette's heart," said Nancy Byrd.

Suddenly Euple entered the picture. He was a handsome redheaded fellow, crazy about Wynette. Not that the torch she carried for his brother had been snuffed out. "Wynette was always getting these melodramatic letters from him, even when she was dating Euple," said one relative. "I hate to tell this, but she was accused of goin' back up in the woods and meetin' up with D.C. even after they were married."

Her classmates at Tremont had patiently followed all of Wynette's romances, but this saga left them a bit befuddled. "That was the one area that we just couldn't understand—we thought D.C. was so *old*," said Holly Ford. "Then Euple bein' able to overlook the fact that his own *brother* and Wynette had this little episode . . ." Linda Cayson liked Don Byrd and doubled-dated with Wynette and Euple. "I don't think she was all that crazy about him," she said. "She just wanted to get away from Mildred."

Further complicating matters, Wynette was also dating her substitute math teacher, John Wilson. A half dozen years Wynette's senior, John had somehow managed to win her mother's approval. But he soon enlisted for military duty. "Mildred wanted us to get married before I went over," Wilson recalled. This plan backfired, as it only succeeded in pushing Wynette deeper into the arms of Euple.

There is no doubt Wynette cast a spell over men. Interview those who have been involved with this dame, and their eyes glaze over as they stare into the distance. Wynette didn't like the spell to be broken, either, even after she was through with them. Later Martha Chumbley would date one of her old boyfriends a few times after Wynette had married. Wynette heard about it, and when she saw Martha in church, she said ominously, "Don't you do anything I wouldn't do." There was something odd about the way Wynette made the comment. "It was like she was jealous, even though she was married."

Wynette spent her last year of school either fighting Mildred or not speaking to her. Her mother meddled in her dates. She and Foy would show up two cars away at the drive-in movie. They'd trail Wynette to basketball games, then demand that they leave simultaneously so Wynette and her date could follow them home. Mildred bird-dogged her daughter's every move, embarrassing and angering her. She longed to have a mother like Linda's, who'd sit up with them and joke about boys. Mildred was relentless, and Wynette refused to toe the line.

One day in church Euple whispered a marriage proposal in her ear. Shortly thereafter Wynette got home thirty minutes late after a date with him, and a ferocious argument with her mother ensued. It was the last straw for Wynette. The next day at school she called Euple and consented to his proposal. (Nancy Byrd recalled a specific reason for the union. "Wynette really actually thought she was pregnant when she married Euple. She was sittin' on the front porch at my husband's mother's and she cried. Wynette said she didn't have any choice, she had to get married, she was pregnant. I remember her tellin' me that she had miscarried . . . I never even did believe Wynette was pregnant, to tell you the truth.")

Wynette being not quite of legal age, Mildred refused to sign the papers and demanded she vacate the house. Foy agreed to sign for her, allowing Euple and Wynette to head for nearby Fulton, where they tied the knot. The preacher's wife was the only witness. It was the spring of 1959. Wynette was seventeen, Euple twenty-six. "Everybody was totally surprised she married Euple," said Betty Chasteen. "She was in love with D.C."

For their honeymoon, the couple had nowhere to go but his family's house. I can see 'em drivin' up in Mom and Daddy's yard just as plain as day," said Euple's sister Diane. "Wynette had a little feather hat and a cream-colored suit. They were in a black car, maybe Euple borrowed it from D.C." It was not the most romantic of wedding nights. "Wynette got a bad ear infection," said Wanda Byrd. "Euple had to take her to the doctor that night and get her ear lanced."

According to Wynette, things got no better once the couple returned to Euple's old house for their first romp in the conjugal bed. The way she tells it, the event sounds more like a dreary stag film than romance novel. The dusty wood floors were cold, the worn-out bedsprings noisy. "No soft music, no candlelight, no champagne, and no satin sheets," she wrote. There were many more disappointments to come.

Mother and daughter didn't speak to each other for some time after the wedding. "Wynette and Euple came and stayed a week with my husband right after they got married, because she didn't want Mildred to know where they were," said Agnes Wilson. And what was Mildred's state of mind at the time? "Highly upset," Agnes admitted.

The couple's first home was a shabby three-room apartment in Tupelo, where Euple had gotten construction work. Wynette worked at the Genesco shoe factory. Euple was soon laid off, and, according to Nancy Byrd, Wynette didn't last long at Genesco. "There was a little girl workin' down there from a family of, like, sixteen kids. She was not of age, and Wynette turned her in at the personnel office, and the child got fired. Some of 'em were sort of getting after Wynette because of what she had done, and Wynette just up and quit."

They went back to Tremont, where Euple lost another job. "They just moved everywhere, wouldn't stay in one place," said Martha Chumbley. "Wynette sold their furniture I don't know how many times. They'd move, she'd sell her furniture, then she'd get some more furniture." Wynette said they moved because Euple couldn't or wouldn't keep a job; others are skeptical. "It's strange—after Wynette left him, Euple never moved anymore," said Martha Chumbley. "He stayed in Birmingham."

Wynette and her relatives have maintained that Euple just wasn't very interested in work. "Nice guy, but he didn't have a whole lot of ambition," said Gerald Jetton. "Euple was not what you'd call a go-getter," said Jane Williams. "He just liked doing what he wanted to do, and didn't feel like he was responsible for a family." Added Jane's father (and Wynette's uncle) Dan Hall with an air of finality, "Euple was a good dog trader."

In Euple's defense, there wasn't much work to go around in Itawamba County. "There wasn't any labor for men in this area," said Agnes Wilson. "You could not get a job unless you wanted to cotton-farm or saw-mill. Or bootleg whiskey. When the factories came in, they were for women only. Now there might be four or five men that would be mechanics or upkeep, but as far as a general hirin' of men, it didn't happen. My husband didn't have any jobs, either. I worked in a sewin' factory for years. My husband would help me garden and help me can, do stuff to make a livin' at home."

"Euple was painted as a person that wouldn't hold jobs," said Nancy Byrd. "The reason why he changed so many jobs was he was followin' her! Wynette would up and leave. Take off and go to Memphis to sing up there." Euple would poke fun at his wife's interest in "hillbilly music." "He didn't want me to sing at all," she insisted. Wynette was the sensitive kind, anyway. It wouldn't have taken much to derail her confidence.

Overwhelmed by her marriage, Wynette said she set aside any desire for music. Not exactly, says Euple's family. Recalled Nancy Byrd, "She'd go sing in these roadhouses, and he'd go with her. I remember one time in Alabama someplace where Wynette was supposedly singin', we thought it was gonna be a big concert. Got there and Wynette was the only one singin' at this old school."

The only criticism they remember is that Euple wanted her to wait until the kids were older. "He didn't hold her back," recalled sister Martha Byrd. "Whatever Wynette wanted, he tried to please her. Euple was just that type of person."

After spending the first six months of their marriage wandering, the Byrds had nowhere to go except back to her family. Wynette was pregnant and wanted to reconcile with Mildred. Chester allowed Wynette and Euple to move into an old pioneer log house that he owned just north of the house she was born in. Built by settler George Bounds in 1844, it was in terrible condition. "I had no electricity, no running water, no plumbing, and no stove," recalled Wynette. "I cooked in a big black pot inside my fireplace." There was a price to be paid for returning home. "They didn't help 'em at all," said Linda Cayson. "Euple wasn't Mildred's choice. It was kinda like, 'Well, you made your bed, now you have to lie in it.'"

Wynette had been the center of attention in school. Boys followed her everywhere, girls wanted to be her confidante. She had gotten a taste of local fame by singing with Linda on radio and TV. If she needed something, Chester took care of it. Now she was pregnant, living in an old shack with someone she didn't really love, an outcast in her own family. "She wasn't real happy," said Linda. "Wynette didn't have nothin' when she was married to Euple, and I think she resented that."

Some locals used to the rougher ways of life back then scoff at Wynette's complaints, but Linda Cayson saw firsthand. One day she visited, and Wynette made lunch—a little hamburger made out of sausage. "That's all that was in that house, and that's the truth." Cayson helped her insulate the drafty cabin by tacking up cardboard boxes from her father's store. "That house was so cold."

Soon there were children in the cabin. Daughter Gwendolyn Lee was born on April 15, 1961; Jacquelyn Faye (named in honor of Jackie Kennedy, but spelled the Wynette way) came on August 21, 1962. In order to slip off to the spring a hundred yards away for potable water, Wynette would park the heavy iron leg of the bed on Gwen's dress so she couldn't wander off. She boiled diapers clean in her big black pot and bathed her tots in a big wooden tub. The couple couldn't even afford a radio. "My life was dull, drab, and exhausting," said Wynette.

It seemed to some that the former Miss Tremont had been exiled to Mildred Lee's Home for Wayward Daughters. Holly Ford ran into her when she was pregnant. "She looked really bad. You know how women get those liver spots on their face? I felt sorry for her. That wasn't a good time in Wynette's life. She knew she had to get out and get some kind of training. Wynette wasn't one that could just sit at home to be barefoot and pregnant her whole life."

After a job for Euple in Red Bay enabled them to move into an actual house with indoor plumbing, Wynette, borrowing the twenty-five-dollar monthly tuition from Mildred, started attending Mrs. McGuire's School of Beauty in 1963. It was also around then that she started dyeing her hair blonde, beginning the transformation that would result in Tammy Wynette.

Her schooling was interrupted by a brief move to Memphis that rekindled her interest in music. Wynette said work for Euple brought them there; at least one person in Memphis said that she'd already left her husband and was living alone. Mary Forbess was the proprietor of Mary's Place. "Had a bar, piano against the wall, maybe five tables," she said. One day Wynette had ventured into her downstairs bar, the first she'd ever entered. "Wynette was walkin' down Front Street, she heard music comin' out of the doorway, Carl McVoy playin' the piano," said Forbess. McVoy was Mary's boyfriend at the time, and when he wasn't doing construction work he'd come in and tickle the ivories.

An older cousin of Jerry Lee Lewis, McVoy played boogie-woogie stylings that had actually been an early influence on Jerry Lee, and Carl himself put out a few rockabilly singles in the late fifties and early sixties on Hi, Philips, and Tri Records. (A bluesy version of Slim Harpo's "Rainin' in My Heart" was McVoy's most popular number.) "Carl could play just like Jerry Lee," said Mary. "But he wanted to drink and party more than he wanted to play music."

Forbess offered Wynette a waitressing job. Wynette's version was that she had to ask Euple first; Mary claimed "she had left her husband and rented a place where I lived." Whatever the particulars, Wynette worked the three p.m. to midnight shift and started performing, if only for a handful of drunks. "We found out Wynette could sing and we just loved it," said Forbess. "She'd just sing when she wanted to. Wynette played that ol' ragged piano I had. She had an accordion and she'd play that. Wynette was country." Wynette regaling a few drunken patrons in a tiny Memphis saloon with a little ditty on the accordion must've been a sight to behold.

To McVoy's ears, too, Wynette was "strictly country," and he was the first person to point her in the direction of Nashville. Music City might've been a mere 185 miles from Red Bay, but as far as Wynette was concerned it could've been on the moon. She'd never entertained the idea. McVoy's suggestion would rattle around Wynette's brain a while. She soon vanished from Mary's bar. "Wynette didn't stay in Memphis real long, don't know if it was six months," said Forbess. "She went back home, I don't know why."

Wynette was in such a hurry she left with two kids' bicycles that belonged to Mary.*

Wynette returned to Tremont with Euple in tow and finished beauty school while he worked in construction. According to Wynette, the couple continually fought over sex. He wanted it; she was uninterested and felt guilty. "I found it very disappointing . . . it wasn't anything like movies and novels led you to believe," wrote Wynette. "I felt cheated."† Wynette had a prolonged and serious kidney infection, which only complicated the matter. Finally Wynette demanded that Euple leave. Every few days he'd return, resulting in more arguments.

The couple then wound up in Tupelo. Wynette waited tables and worked as a chiropractor's receptionist. In the middle of 1964 Wynette was pregnant again. She begged her family physician, Dr. Robert Pegram, not to tell Euple. Wynette was contemplating a divorce. She went home and tried to tell her husband it was over.

The only version we have of the following events is Wynette's. None of her friends seems to have been in touch with her. Maybe it was just too painful a situation for Wynette to acknowledge to anyone. One night she and Euple had a fight that turned into a screaming match, resulting in what must've have been a nervous breakdown for Wynette. Unable to speak, her kidney infection now almost life threatening, she was hospitalized for depression and received twelve shock treatments. "They were horrible, but they helped me," she said. On her release from the hospital, Wynette was determined to file for divorce.

This did not sit well with Mildred. "There was no such thing as divorce in my family . . . they thought I was the worst thing in the world for doing that," said Wynette. "They tried to *make* me work it out." Throughout her life, Wynette considered divorce her greatest sin. The fact she'd been married five times pained and embarrassed her. Despite Wynette's strength in extracting herself from relationships that were clearly no good for her, inside she felt she brought great shame to her family.

---

*It would take Carl McVoy a while to catch on that Tammy Wynette and Wynette Byrd were one and the same. As Mary recalled, laughing, "Carl called one day years later and said, 'We need Wynette to come to Memphis and play at the Western Lounge, we're lookin' for somebody to play country music.' I said, 'Carl, she was just on *Hee Haw.'*"

†Noted longtime friend and hairdresser Jan Smith, "I'm not sure Tammy ever had a climax . . . because if she'd had a climax, she'd want another one, wouldn't she?"

Her first marital failure was particularly torturous. Whatever Mildred might've thought about Euple in the beginning, he was now part of the family, and, much to Wynette's displeasure, she now sided with him. Diane Bruff recalled Mildred got physical with her pregnant daughter one day in the driveway of her apartment. "She knocked Wynette down because of the way she was doin' in her driveway. Mildred herself said, 'I knocked the h-e-double-l out of her.'"

Euple and Wynette continued to fight, make up, then fight some more. One night she came home to find all her possessions gone. Euple had cleaned the place out.* As she sat on the floor of her empty apartment crying, there was a knock on the door, and there stood an officer of the law. Wynette thought he must be there to investigate the hijacking of her belongings, but the cop announced he was arresting her for being an unfit mother and her kids would be taken away. Euple was using Wynette's breakdown and subsequent hospital stay against her.

Wynette claimed her family physician showed up at the police station to attest to her sanity, and the matter was dropped. Another crisis occurred a few weeks later when she went to pick up her kids at day care. Euple and Mildred had already retrieved Gwen and Jackie, and Wynette said they were conspiring to have her committed. She spotted her kids playing in Mildred's yard and hustled them into the car. Euple came out of the house to see Wynette driving off, igniting a high-speed chase that ended at the Tupelo courthouse, where Wynette put a bond in place to keep her husband away.

At least one relative disputes this version of events. "*Wynette* took the children and left Euple. The way I understood it, she was with this guy at this motel. Mildred went with Euple—they went in and they took the kids away from her, took them over to Mildred's. Wynette claimed in her book she didn't know where her children were—she knew *exactly* where those girls were, because they were with her own mother."

Apparently Wynette's infatuations were a problem throughout her marriage. Said Diane Bruff, "When they were livin' in Tupelo, Wynette was singin' in a nightclub over there, and she brought a sailor home with her!

*Nancy Byrd said that Euple told her the same story but with Wynette being the one who had left and taken everything. It happened later, when the couple lived in Birmingham. "They were in a rented furnished apartment," she recalled. "Euple came in one day from work and all that was left was a quilt and pillow."

How would you like to have your wife bring a man home?" Knowing her, Wynette probably just wanted some attention, not sex, but that desire alone was too much for the time and place she was living in. "One night she asked my ex-husband and my brother Don to take her to a *movie*. Euple, he was workin'," said Diane. "That was the way she was. Wynette was an outgoin' person—but she took it too far, see."

Even Hazel Hall, a woman who loved Wynette like a daughter and who seemed loath to speak critically of her, said, "Wynette wasn't good to Euple. She run around on him. I was ashamed of some of the things she did. I said, 'Well, you oughtn'a done him that way.' Wynette said, 'I didn't care.' And she didn't!"

Wynette mentions none of this in her book, except to say that Euple insisted the baby she was carrying wasn't his, a claim she said was disproved by a blood test. Whatever the particulars, it seems obvious that Wynette was trapped in a relationship she shouldn't have been in—and that Euple had the misfortune to be in love with a very complicated woman.

"Euple did the best he could. He wasn't a mean person," said Agnes Wilson. "Wynette had her own ideas. She clashed with Euple just like she clashed with her mother. He had a hard time. There was no controllin' Wynette."

What was Wynette to do? She could've just given in, learned to behave herself, and been a good little wife and daughter. "Mildred wanted Wynette to stay around home and go to beauty school," said John Wilson. "She didn't much want that. Wynette wanted to be in the music world."

Wynette made up her mind to leave town. There was nowhere left to go in Red Bay, nothing left to do. Her marriage was in shambles. She was alienated from her family. Wynette must've felt the whole world was looking down on her. She had two kids to feed and another on the way. Brave move? It was insane. Wynette didn't have a dime to her name.

Wynette decided she'd head to Birmingham to stay with her father's relatives. She didn't tell Euple, and she didn't tell her mother. She just up and left.

"I remember the day she told me she was leavin'," said Linda Cayson, clearly disturbed by the memory. "She says, 'I'm gonna leave, I'm gonna get outta here.' I worried about Wynette, I really didn't want her to strike out like that. I was afraid. I said, 'Wynette, you can't, you don't have any money.'

She said, 'Well, I'll make it some way.'" Linda wouldn't see her again until after she'd made it in Nashville.

Dan Hall recalled a desperate-looking Wynette stopping by the house on her way out of town. "She had an ol' wore-out '55 Ford car. She told my wife, 'I ain't got no gas and I got no money to go to Birmingham.' Hazel carried that car over to the service station, filled it up with gas, and gave her a five-dollar bill."

Wynette said her good-byes, hopped in the car, and headed off down the highway. It must've been a lonely trip. She was going against her mother, her husband, even what she'd heard preached in church. This was not the sort of thing a twenty-two-year-old pregnant married woman with two kids was supposed to do.

Said one friend, "When she went to Birmingham, nobody wanted her to go. Even her own kinfolks disowned her."

It's *Country Boy Eddie* Time

Q: Are they two separate people, Wynette Pugh and Tammy Wynette?

A: Yeah, they're two separate people. Wynette Pugh was a scared little farm girl that made a lot of mistakes. And then there's Tammy Wynette, who got most of her education on the road—and [who has to] be what the Tammy Wynette name implies when I go out on stage.

—Tammy Wynette

I'm a goddamn image, not a person.

—Joan Crawford

"She was standing in the doorway like an apparition," said a wistful David Vest. It was the first time he laid eyes upon Wynette Byrd, and she was auditioning for *Country Boy Eddie*, an early-morning Birmingham TV show. Vest was the piano player in the band, and from where he sat, he could see she was one glamorous-looking creature. "Like Kim Novak or Jean Seberg. Plain black dress, no makeup, hair tied back, very simple . . . there was a statuesque quality to her. Noble, regal."

On the surface, the "Pittsburgh of the South" was a strange choice for Wynette. "There was really no country music scene at all," said Vest. "The big scene was gospel." At the time Birmingham had been making the national news for rather unsavory reasons. A year before Wynette arrived, the city had been home to a Baptist church bombing that left four black children dead. In full reign as governor of Alabama, pugnacious upstart George Wallace was working his unique brand of Machiavellian magic, his white-power platform resulting in racial unrest throughout the state.

Wynette arrived in Birmingham in the fall of 1964. Her grandparents William and Margaret Pugh lived in a tiny two-bedroom house with one of her father's sisters, her husband, and their child. Somehow they made room for Wynette, who immediately began looking for work, only to find her Mississippi beautician's license was worthless in the state of Alabama. She headed back to school, enrolling in Dolly Pardon's American Beauty College, wearing big smocks to hide the fact she was pregnant. (It was against state rules to attend the school "with child.") By this point Wynette was grindingly poor. "I thought, 'Well, if getting into country music was a ridiculous idea before, it's really out of the question now.' But the dream wouldn't die."

Aiding that dream were the Pughs. They were a musical bunch that encouraged Wynette's interest in singing, particularly her uncle Harvey True-love, who had been in her father's band, and his wife, Athalene. During family pickin' parties Harvey played guitar, Wynette tickled the ivories, and all three sang together. Harvey, who had a job as head engineer at WBRC, made the first real step in Wynette's career possible. The station broadcast an early-morning show for the farming crowd hosted by the one and only Gordon "Country Boy Eddie" Burns.

Born in Warrior, Alabama, in 1931, Country Boy Eddie is a colorful character in Birmingham TV history. "I wanted to have me a country-western show," he said. "I went and talked to Channel 6 about it, didn't do any good. Went to 13, and they put me on." A born hustler, Eddie had a mighty talent for selling commercial time on his show, which originally broadcast late at night. "The first week I billed three thousand dollars—that was a lot of money. They thought I couldn't sell that time."

Channel 6 lured Eddie back, giving him the early-morning slot he wanted, five a.m. As David Vest noted, previous to Eddie's arrival the station had been showing a test pattern at that hour. "They thought Eddie was a fool, but being a rural fella himself, he knew all these farm people got up early, and if they had something to watch, they'd turn it on."

"That was 1957," says Eddie. "Stayed on thirty-eight years, two hours a day, Monday through Friday, five to seven a.m. We kind of ad-libbed the show for two hours." Locals savor the memory of the craziness that constituted the *Country Boy Eddie* show. "Eddie could get fifty-six minutes of commercials into an hour program," said Mark Colvin. "You have never seen anything like it in your life. He'd have a singer come out, they'd get a little two-bar intro, *doo doot doot*, 'My Love . . . ,' and Eddie'd cut 'em right off. 'That's fine! Let's have a big hand for her—and talk to *you* about some of those fine people down at Ellis Feed and Seed.' And these wannabes would get up at three in the morning, fix their hair, and go down to the studio *hoping* Eddie would let them sing, and when he did, he wouldn't let 'em finish a song. He had too many commercials to run!"

"Eddie was a go-getter," recalled former Birmingham DJ Fred Lehner. "Eddie didn't worry a lot about detail, he just charged straight ahead. He would've made the world's greatest used-car salesman. I loved the guy, but, man, I wouldn't let him carry my wallet around. Eddie used to imitate a mule on television. He'd hold his bottom lip out and sound like a damn mule—*hee haw, hee haw.*" In addition, Eddie played the fiddle "quite badly," said Vest, who fondly recalled Eddie as "all bullshit, all the time . . . a confabulator who used to claim to have degrees in psychology and to have been a psych-ops expert in the Korean War." No doubt such moxie aided Eddie in attracting such names as the Stanley Brothers and the Osborne Brothers to make appearances. "If you came through Alabama and you were tryin' to sell a record, you came on the show," said Vest.

Eddie had quite the collection of oddballs for a band. There was Whitey Puckett, an albino clarinet player who was legally blind and usually schnockered. Puckett, who drove a '58 Edsel with a red-tipped cane decoratively attached to the front grille, carried a bucket of vodka that he drank from with a dipper as he drove down the street. "People jumped up on the sidewalk and into alleys to get out of his way," noted Vest, who played piano in the band for the princely sum of thirty-five bucks a week. Bass player Butterbean Flippo drew on his own freckles with the aid of a Magic Marker.

Johnny Gore, who played electric guitar and briefly toured with Wynette after she signed with Epic, was described by Vest as "a ladies' man who played hot guitar but tended to solo all the way through every song." There was a steel player whose name is forgotten, plus three acoustic guitarists, among them Mason "Tex" Dixon, who'd recorded some great country singles on various no-name labels (and a man Vest "expected to die of apoplexy every time Eddie didn't let him sing a number"), not to mention Johnny Cash soundalike Bill Compton, whose fabulous local hit "Iron Man" was an ode to the fifty-six-foot-tall cast-iron statue of Vulcan the band passed on the drive to work. Actress and author Fannie Flagg was also a regular after Wynette left, contributing a zany weather-girl routine. Eddie even cut a self-penned theme song, "Hanging in There on a Rusty Fishhook."

Augmenting this ragtag musical assembly was Mule Man, some poor would-be actor who donned a cape while scaling the walls of the studio ("I think Eddie might've given him gas money," said Vest) and Mickey the Fire-Eater, an Italian fellow from the Birmingham projects who "had a badly crippled leg but was always challenging someone to a fight."

Into this beautiful mess tumbled a nervous Wynette Byrd. Her uncle Jack had talked Eddie into letting his niece audition.* "I said, 'Well, bring her on up here, Harvey,'" recalled Eddie. "I said, 'Let me hear you sing one.' I thought she was terrific. I said, 'You can be on any time you want to.'" Wynette was ecstatic. As she often said later, the thirty-five-dollar salary was icing on the cake, as she would've performed for free. Wynette made her debut on *Country Boy Eddie* singing Patsy Cline's "Sweet Dreams," although due to her bulging belly, she was only unveiled to the world from the waist up.

Wynette crawled out of bed at four a.m. to appear on the show, then ran over to Pardon's beauty school (and later the Midfield Beauty Salon) to put in an eight-hour shift. Relatives in the Byrd clan watched the kids. She was adept at hairstyling and found working in a salon entertaining. "It was a center for gossip," admitted Wynette, who'd later confess to having seen the movie *Shampoo* four times. Wynette might've been working around the clock, but inside she was lost in a dream. "I knew the words to every song on the radio. People used to look at me like I was crazy when I'd be in the supermarket, just singin' away; not paying attention to where I was or what I was pickin' up."

David Vest, who's written about Wynette on numerous occasions (and gone on to record and tour as a blues pianist), occupies a significant place in her story: he's the first musician who recorded her and recognized her originality, and was privy to a rare glimpse into her inner being at the time. Vest, who was from Huntsville, Alabama, was a year younger than Wynette and hung around the folk/rock crowd. He and Wynette were the youngest members of Eddie's band. "I always called Wynette my 'runnin' pardner.' 'How's my little runnin' pardner?' She was just a straight shooter. Wynette didn't have a whole lotta time for goofin' off."

Eddie has made claims that Wynette got piles of fan mail once she started appearing on the show, but Vest scoffed at that. He maintained that Wynette was just one more band member competing for Eddie's airtime. "She was never a special part of the show. If Wynette ever sang two songs in one hour, it was a rare thing." She faced the usual challenges of being the only

*In other versions of the story, Wynette said she got the gig after complaining to Eddie that he had no female vocalists.

woman in the outfit. "At one point everybody in that band but me claimed to have slept with her," said Vest. "I knew none of it was true."

Eddie hauled the band out for many a personal appearance, none more disastrous than a country music extravaganza at Birmingham's Albert Boutwell Municipal Auditorium put on by a dubious promoter named Larry Sunbrock. Acts included Red Foley, Sonny James, the Wilburn Brothers, and Hank Williams, Jr., as well as, Vest noted, "a special appearance by the reigning Miss World." Wynette did a number and sang backup during the rest of the show, which was interrupted by a seeming tragedy. "A stretcher appeared, and the promoter, Sunbrock, was on it," wrote Vest. "Someone whispered that he had suffered a heart attack."

Red Foley wanted to stop the show, but the gallant Sunbrock waved him off from his stretcher, telling him, "The show must go on." It was all a con. "Sunbrock was whisked away by an ambulance. Later someone came backstage and announced that the gate receipts were missing. It was rumored that a satchel of money had been carried out on the stretcher, under the sheet." Nobody got a dime.

"I believe that it's the soulfulness that you are born with," said Ray Charles in a 1994 interview. "You can teach a person to sing, you can actually do that . . . but you cannot teach them to sing with *feelin'*. They either have it in them—or they don't." Cliché? I suppose. But in Wynette's case it appears to be true. According to David Vest, the soul she possessed "was there at the beginning. Wynette always sang the same way. She was right on that note every time, like an arrow and a target."

What material was Wynette doing in the beginning? Classic country: Kitty's "It Wasn't God Who Made Honky Tonk Angels," Loretta's "Don't Come Home A-Drinkin' (With Lovin' on Your Mind)," Norma Jean's "Let's Go All the Way," and Jeannie Seely's "Don't Touch Me." "The minute you heard her, she had you by the heart," Vest writes. Wynette "sang nothing she didn't believe in. She knew exactly where the center of the great tradition lay. She lived in it."

Physically, Wynette did nothing as she sang. "I had never seen her do anything to 'sell' a song," writes Vest, and this characteristic, which would be such a mesmerizing aspect of her persona, appears to have arisen out of fear rather than design. "She was very stiff. Nervous about bein' in public. Bein' exposed." Sometimes she'd get so deep into a song, she'd stop and start over, "singing in a harder tone. . . . It was this combination of great confidence and great nervousness. To see both of those things be so strong in somebody was kind of unusual. She'd just stand there and sing. You'd see her go down inside the song and bring it out. Wynette felt the song so deeply. The less she did, the more she entertained you."

At some point Wynette asked Vest if he'd assist in recording some demos in preparation for her inevitable pilgrimage to Music City. His friend Homer Milam had a little studio, and, figuring Wynette should have something original to pitch, Vest offered to conjure up some material. "I'd never written a song in my life," he said. Into the studio they went, Vest accompanying Wynette on piano before a solitary mic and a reel-to-reel tape recorder. The intrepid duo had only a vague idea of how to proceed. "Nobody does a country demo with a piano—but we were," David noted. Wynette called off the takes and Vest acted as his own engineer, running over to stop the tape between songs.

Whatever it was that constituted the tragic magic that the world would soon know as Tammy Wynette, you can already hear it on this nine-minute-plus collection of short songs—especially on the one he'd written for her, a sad, stark number entitled "Sing Me a Lonesome Song." She vocalizes the lyrics softly, plainly, but with great conviction. Barely into her twenties, Wynette already knew plenty about lonesome songs and how to convey them, and this recording is the first glimmer of her greatness. (Unfortunately, none of Vest's demos have seen release, outside of a snippet of "Sing Me a Lonesome Song" used in a 2005 BBC documentary.)

Wynette had a surprise for Vest. At the end of recording the songs he'd brought, she asked how much tape was left. Enough for another number, Vest told her. "She said, 'Well, I got one I was foolin' with—can we try it?'" With that, Wynette unveiled a song called "Matrimony." "I had no idea she had ever written anything, or that she could play a note on any instrument," said Vest. They worked up an arrangement and cut it in a couple of takes. A song about "a lost and lonely wife" that has "failed the test" and who "can show you all the ways to slip around," it has to be read as an autobiographical look at the wreckage of her marriage to Euple. "If you're headed for that thing called matrimony, I hope you have much better luck than me," she sings. During the first take Wynette was so overcome she had to begin again. "The line that she choked on was, 'You can't tell me how it feels to be a lost and lonely wife,'" recalled Vest. It's a bleak little song; as Vest has written, Wynette "made marriage sound like Devil's Island or Botany Bay."

"That's the kind of thing she was writin'—tough stuff about marriage," he said. "So later, when they shoved Wynette out there and had her sing 'Stand by Your Man,' it was kind of odd to me, compared to the kind of stuff that she had been writing." (Such feelings are still to be found in Wynette's Nashville recordings—they just lurk in the delivery rather than the words. She could make the happiest lyrics about the male/female union sound tortured, "Stand by Your Man" included.)

That sadness so core to Wynette's sound is front and center in these demos. "It was almost a regal bearing that Wynette had," said Vest. "There was something majestic about it that made it far deeper than any ordinary little sadness." To say it was because she'd grown up without a father or to blame it on a broken heart strikes Vest as simplistic.

"I don't think you can point to one or two things that had happened in her life . . . it was like some itch you can't scratch, hunger you can't fill. Tennyson talks about 'Idle tears, I know not what they mean, from the depths from some divine despair' . . . I just think that lookin' for some one cause or explanation is probably futile."

Wynette was in tune with something much deeper, something universal. She knew the sort of despair that comes on a rainy night when you're staring through a filthy windshield at an overlit convenience store and you don't have a dollar to your name. There was a stain of sadness on her voice, and thankfully for the rest of us, it would never, ever come clean.

After gigs Wynette and David would reconvene at a café next to Big-Hearted Eddie's, a used-car lot that was one of *Country Boy*'s sponsors. Each table had a jukebox, and they'd sit there and turn the playlist pages inside the glass dome—*clack, clack, clack*—and listen to the music of the day, including such Wynette favorites as Charlie Louvin, Roy Orbison, and Jean Shepard. "To watch her listen to great music was an intense experience," said Vest. "She was so impatient with bad stuff—'Who played *that* crap?' Wynette knew her country.

"There'd be a new song by George Jones and Melba Montgomery. She'd go, 'Listen to this, right up to the bridge—see how they do that? Puts chills all over me.' And George Jones? Wynette thought she belonged in his league. 'Matter of fact, I could sing that better than Melba Montgomery.'

It was like a center fielder sayin', 'I could get to that ball.' Just pointin' out a fact.

"Wynette believed in her voice. I think she knew from the start that she belonged among the best country singers. Wynette wanted her place at the table, and she was on a mission to get what belonged to her. She didn't say it arrogantly or presumptuously, but Wynette had this just quiet confidence that if there was any justice and she was heard she'd have an audience."

Wynette and Vest even attempted to make a go of it as a "happy hour" piano bar duo. During one 1966 gig in some Homewood, Alabama, lounge, Vest coaxed Wynette into doing the Beatles' latest—"Yellow Submarine." "She about hit me over the head for doin' that to her," said Vest ruefully. "Imagine Tammy Wynette singin', 'We all live in a yellow submarine.'"

After this particular job they stopped at a drive-in restaurant out on the Bessemer Super Highway. A carhop delivered their vanilla milk shakes. Vest had noticed that the boozy clientele back at the bar had unnerved his little runnin' pardner. "They were sittin' all around the piano blowin' smoke in her face, laughin', red-faced drunks. She leaned over and said, 'Do they have to be so close? I can't stand 'em bein' so close to me.' She was very tense that night, so when we stopped and had our milk shake I said, 'What was that all about?'"

Vest's question unlocked a rare confession from Wynette. She had terrible anxiety that went beyond any stage fright. "The fear went back a long way, that every waking moment was spent fighting it back. . . . She had thoughts of asking doctors to try to remove it surgically. She looked at me to see if I thought she was crazy. . . . She told me she could not remember a night when she didn't lie down afraid to go to sleep, afraid of what might happen, what she might dream, what she might remember. Afraid to let go and rest because the pain and the fear might overwhelm her."

Vest saw tears welling in her eyes. "I just let her talk," he said. "Later she seemed a little nervous about bein' so revealin' and talkin' so much." Wynette asked him not to tell anybody what she'd shared with him. "I never did, until after she was dead. I never said it to a soul."

Vest, who hadn't been romantically involved with Wynette, saw her one last time before she left Birmingham. They had been looking for work at a joint called the Pussycat-A-Go-Go Club and said good-bye in the parking lot. "We didn't talk that night," Vest recalled. "She stood looking in my eyes.

Then, without warning, she kissed me. Before I could react, she was walking away."

Tina Denise Byrd arrived in the world March 27, 1965. Three months premature, she weighed only two pounds, three ounces and was just eleven inches long. Wynette had to borrow money from her uncle for the hospital bill, which would spiral upward to a few thousand dollars as Tina was diagnosed with spinal meningitis just four months into her life. She'd be kept in isolation for seventeen days, a distraught Wynette by her side, in the same dress and tennis shoes she wore to the beauty salon, the outfit augmented by an operating cap and face mask.

Wynette managed to slip her hands through holes in the incubator to massage Tina's little back—that is, when the infant wasn't convulsing. Meanwhile, Wynette dropped from 112 to 90 pounds, racked with guilt over the situation and her life in general. Inside she wondered, "Was God punishing me because I wanted a divorce from a man I should never have married in the first place?"

Wynette's marriage to Euple was in the final stages of decay. He'd followed her to Birmingham, but according to Wynette he stayed just one night, a trick pulled only so that she would have to refile her divorce petition. David Vest never saw the inside of Wynette's apartment, nor did he meet her soon-to-be ex-husband. As he remembered it, "Euple was tryin' to get the kids back from her, so she was hidin' from him. He wouldn't leave her alone. Sendin' messages, havin' people call her. She sounded like a woman concerned about being stalked."

Wanda Byrd, Euple's sister, recalled her brother being torn up over the situation. "She wouldn't let him see the kids, and he would cry. I would tell him, 'Euple, don't worry about it. When those girls get old enough, they will come back to you.'" At least one friend recalled Wynette's having an affair with a nameless married man who'd visit with her years later out on the road.

Once Tina was born, Euple returned again, and, both agreeing to give it one more chance, the Byrd family moved into a twenty-three-dollar-a-month apartment in Elyton Village, a Birmingham project. Wynette claimed that after a few months he went to work one day and never returned.

There would be a final unexpected encounter with her ex-husband, and it grew into one of those Tammy tales she told time and again post-stardom.

It came on the very day Wynette left Birmingham for Nashville. Euple took a gander at the old car packed full of kids, coloring books, and assorted crap and drawled, "So you're going to Nashville to be a hillbilly singer, huh?" He just had to use that word Wynette hated so—"hillbilly."

Wynette told him she was going to try. Euple chuckled and said, "Dream on, baby. Dream on."

Ten years later Wynette would be headlining a Birmingham auditorium. She came out after the show to sit on the edge of the stage and autograph memorabilia. Who should be waiting in line with a glossy photo of Tammy Wynette he wanted signed by the artist herself? None other than Euple Byrd.

And sign it she did: "Dream on, baby. Love, Tammy."

Euple wouldn't see her again for years. As Wynette rose to superstardom, he faded into the Birmingham night. When she published her autobiography in 1979, the Byrd family was crushed. "It really hurt my parents," said Diane Bruff. Her father, who was very fond of Wynette, wept. "I told him, 'Dad, don't worry about it. People that know Wynette know what it is.'" Euple didn't discuss it. "He'd kinda shrug it off and go ahead," said Martha Byrd. "Euple was the type—he didn't like to say bad things about other people. It hurt him, I'm sure."

Sometime in the eighties Euple got back in touch with his daughters. "I asked him why he didn't have any contact with us before," said Jackie. "He wanted to wait until we were old enough to make the decision. During hard times that Tina and I had, he'd Western Union money." When Euple would visit, he'd bring toys for the girls, even for Georgette, Wynette's child with George Jones.

"He didn't want me to feel left out, especially bein' the youngest and littlest," said Georgette. "Euple was very good to me. When I had my twins, Euple was one of the first people after my family to come to my house and see my children."

Eventually Euple's relationship with his daughters led to a mending of the fences with Wynette. Her pal Linda Cayson came up from Alabama to visit and found an unexpected guest. "I was never so shocked. Euple was there at the house! Wynette laughed—she said it got to where they had him at Christmastime." During one visit Wynette asked him if he'd sit for a family portrait. "Now, Euple told me this out of his own mouth," one relative recalled. "Well, she called a photographer over there, to snap all the children, him, and Wynette. And she had her hand on his leg—just like they were still married!" Euple died in a car crash in November 1996. Wynette drove into town on her tour bus to attend the service. "I just remember when she walked in the funeral home everything got really quiet," said one of those present. "It was almost like Jesus Christ had walked in."

"Instead of getting back behind the family, she sat on the front row, and we had to sit further back," said Diane Bruff. "And I thought, 'Well, my Lord, the way you talked about Euple and done him . . . ,' but I didn't say anything." During the visitation, Wynette had been her usual dramatic self. "They told us not to touch Euple," said Diane. "And Wynette walked up to that casket, ruffled up his hair, and got down over him like he was still her husband."

Whatever faults Euple had, in the end, according to one relative, he provided for their daughters a little better than his superstar ex-wife would. "The ironic thing about it was Euple had life insurance policies for all three of those girls—not large ones, but as it turned out, the girls got more money from their daddy than they got from their own mother."

It was hard for some of the Byrds to reconcile with Wynette. "I loved Wynette," said Diane. "I didn't after she talked about my family like she did. Loretta Lynn told how hard she had it, and she told the truth. She wasn't constantly throwin' off on a man. I had to do a lot of prayin' about it because I hated her." Nancy Byrd tried to remain charitable. "I don't think she really even thought about it hurtin' anybody . . . Wynette just lived in this unrealistic dream world. She was lost in her dream."

Just about everybody who knew Euple says the same thing: Wynette was the love of his life. At least one of his daughters is in agreement. "After he died Gwen and I went through his stuff," said Jackie. "He had clippings, articles about Mom in boxes."

"He never got over Wynette," said Diane. "'Til the day he died, Euple never quit lovin' her. He never quit lovin' Wynette."

Back to that Birmingham housing project in 1965. Wynette continued to grind out a living working at *Country Boy Eddie* and the beauty salon. Some nights she sang at local hot spots Lois's Horseshoe Lounge and the Pink Elephant. Tina was somehow managing slowly to recover.

Wynette had also been hanging around WYAM, a 500-watt Bessemer, Alabama, country station a few miles from Midfield Beauty Salon. It was there she met DJ Fred Lehner. "The first time she opened her mouth to sing, I said, 'Good Lord, listen to this,'" said Lehner, who recorded a dozen or so demos in the tiny station. (Wynette didn't reveal much; neither Lehner nor David Vest knew about the other's recording her.) This time Tammy accompanied herself on an old piano that had suffered through a couple of floods. "She was extremely fast on pickin' up the feeling of the song, what it should sound like," recalled Lehner. "When it came to music, she wasn't intimidated by anything."

Only one of the dozen or so songs that Lehner recorded has seen the light of day, an inconsequential ditty entitled "You Can Steal Me" that was later chosen to open her career-spanning boxed set, *Tears of Fire.* When the collection came out in 1992, Wynette maintained that she had no idea the piece existed. "Somebody had taped me without me knowin' it," she insisted to Ralph Emery. (Wynette also asserted that she had cowritten the song, which is credited solely to Lehner.) It seems like a ridiculous claim, as Lehner took her to the studio several times to cut material, all of which he'd written, save a cover of "Release Me" and a gender-switched version of the George Jones 1962 hit "She Thinks I Still Care."

Lehner used Wynette's demos to get his material cut by established artists. His recording of Wynette and local singer Sid Linard duetting on "The Way Things Were Goin'" led to a cover by Johnny Paycheck and Mickey Evans, while "You Can Steal Me" reached number 33 on the country charts in 1967 by Bonnie Guitar. "Bonnie came by the radio station, and I gave her a copy of the song that Tammy had demoed for me. A few days later I got a call from a guy by the name of George Richey. He said, 'I love your song, I'm gonna cut it. Who's the demo singer?'" Richey, then Bonnie Guitar's producer, would eventually marry and manage Wynette.

Lehner remembered the squalor that Wynette lived in at the time. "There was almost nothin' there—a sofa, two little girls runnin' around dirty in diapers. It was a low-rent housing project in a poor section of Birmingham." Wynette's kidney problems persisted, and Lehner had to drive her to the hospital one night. "She was sickly, but it didn't slow her down. She was a hardworkin' girl and she knew what she wanted."

Wynette accompanied Fred and his wife, Jane, on a two-day trip to the National Disc Jockey Convention in Nashville in October 1965. The country music mecca overwhelmed her, but not enough to prevent Wynette from making her first live appearance in Music City, USA. Directly in front of the Ryman Auditorium, then home to the Grand Ole Opry, local station WENO had parked a flatbed truck complete with a band, alongside a sign that invited any would-be's in the crowd to step up and try a number. Bold little Wynette climbed aboard and belted out "Your Cheatin' Heart." "It was windy, and she was complainin' 'bout her hair," recalled Jane Lehner. "Typical woman stuff." Three years on from this inauspicious debut, Wynette would be a member of the Opry, standing at the microphone alongside then man of her dreams, George Jones.

The Lehners shuttled Wynette over to the area around Sixteenth and Seventeenth Avenues known as Music Row. Clustered there were the Nashville record companies, producers, and publishers, and Wynette dutifully made the rounds. "Jane and I would sit in the car while she'd go up and knock on a door," said Fred. "I never saw any sign of frustration. Wynette had kind of a quiet confidence . . . she knew somethin' was gonna happen."

She returned to Birmingham with her engine revved. One way or another Wynette had to return to Nashville. Help came from new convert Charles Colvin, one of the unsung heroes in Wynette's life. Colvin owned a little recording studio and had cowritten songs with local soul legend Tony Borders. He believed in Wynette and financed further trips to Nashville, where he tried to introduce her to people in the business. It was Motel 6 all the way, because she had no money, and neither did he. "I remember him saying they had to share the same room," said Colvin's son, Mark. "He was a married man, so he had to be real careful about stayin' in his spot and her in her spot."

Wynette was determined to beat the odds. "She was single-minded," said Lisa Wallace, future wife of George Wallace, just another aspiring singer hanging around the set of the *Country Boy Eddie* show at the time. "She'd say, 'I been to Nashville over the weekend, I don't know whether to sign with United Artists or Decca or this one or that one.' We would all just sneer and kinda laugh, because we thought she was makin' it up. Boy, next thing I know, she's not kidding."

Naysayers only fueled Wynette's ambition. As she'd boast many times

in her life, "Don't tell me I can't do something, 'cause I'll show you I can."
Joni Thornton, another aspiring Birmingham singer, used to sneak into the
Pink Pussycat as a teen to listen to Wynette sing. Thornton knew her only
from a distance, but the one night she spent sharing a table as Wynette
talked of pursuing her dream is indelible in her mind. "I'll remember it
forever. She just hit her fist on the table, put her arm in the air, and said
that she was goin' to Nashville—and gonna do whatever she had to do to
make it."

Around this time Wynette managed to snag a gig singing backup at a
Porter Wagoner appearance. Apparently she impressed Porter, because he
invited her out on the road for a fifty-dollar-a-night, ten-date tour of Alabama
and Georgia. She didn't rate a spot on the tour bus, so she followed behind
in an old VW bug with her aunt Earleen. She took to life on the road immediately. Whatever doubts Wynette had about a music career, she insisted
"there was no turning back after that." Surely this was the break that she
was waiting for. Porter would have to recognize her talent, get her a record
deal, and make her a star. It didn't happen. "He never said a word," said
Wynette, who returned to the beauty salon job in despair. But she main-
tainted that the "depression turned to anger," only intensifying her resolve
to conquer Nashville, come hell or high water. "I'm the only one Porter
helped by not helping," she said wryly.*

And so in January 1968, Wynette packed up her '59 Chevy and hit the
road once more. "You wouldn't believe that car," she recalled. "I had a tricycle

---

*Just when these dates with Wagoner took place is another mystery. Wynette says she
stepped in right after Norma Jean left his show, but according to Steve Eng's meticulously
researched biography of Wagoner, Norma Jean left in 1967. Wynette had already
embarked on a recording career by then. Second husband Don Chapel insists that she
exaggerated the event, and that she told him she'd only sung for him on one date. (Before
he passed away, Wagoner declined to be interviewed for this book.) Dolly Parton, of
course, wound up as Norma Jean's replacement, and Chapel says that, despite Tammy's
later friendship with Parton, at the time she was "in total dread fear of Dolly," as they
both entered the *Billboard* charts in December 1967, and she felt Dolly might "upstage"
her success.

Parton has a story she loves to tell, one she repeated at Tammy's memorial service.
Wynette once asked her, "What if Porter claims we all slept with him?" "Don't worry,
Tammy," Dolly told her. "Half of the people will think he's lying and the other half will
just think we had bad taste."

According to author Randall Reise, Wagoner wrote an unpublished memoir in which
he boasted of a "brief, loveless affair" with Wynette during her early Nashville days.
When asked about the subject, Tammy said, "Let's put it this way: if Porter was Adam
and I was Eve, there would have been no Cain and Abel."

tied on top of it, everything hangin' off the back, two little kids in the backseat . . . everything I owned was in that car."

She had no job awaiting her in Nashville, and no backup plan other than her beautician's license. The eggs were all in one basket. She hardly knew a soul in Nashville, and unlike in Birmingham, she had no relatives there to lean on. Wynette was still estranged from her family in Red Bay, but Mildred was never very far from her mind. "I had to prove to my mother I could do it."

Wynette headed off down the highway for another home in a new town. "The most frightening time in my life would have to be when I went to Nashville with the three kids and had no job, no money, no husband. I don't think it could've been any worse at that point . . . I was really desperate."

There wasn't another husband—yet. But she already had another suitor awaiting in Nashville. His name was Don Chapel, and he worked at the Anchor Motel. You could say he was in show business—more important, country music show business. And he even knew George Jones.

Dear Tammy,

I took a break from the grimness of your early years by losing myself in old issues of your Tammy Wynette Fan Club Newsletter *(later known as* First Lady News*). These particular copies were from the seventies, just a few folded-over sheets with black-and-white photos, handmade with love. There was a lot of information to be gleaned, particularly from the questions sent in by fans. One admirer inquired if you like makeup. "Only when I'm onstage, and even then I'm very conservative" was the response. Now, did you really expect anybody to believe that whopper?*

Your number one soap opera at the time was Days of Our Lives. *You were crazy over that Ray Stevens ballad "Misty." Favorite actress: Bette Davis. Favorite movies:* Whatever Happened to Baby Jane? *and* Hush . . . Hush, Sweet Charlotte. *Favorite British singer: Tom Jones. You loved to fish, particularly for grouper and crappie. In 1978 you arrived before a cheering crowd at an Omaha rodeo in the back of a Cadillac convertible wearing a white pantsuit and a brown vest.*

Most curiously, you list your favorite all-time performer as that baggy-pantsed comic Red Skelton, whose act you attended in Las Vegas in 1965. Yes, Wynette Pugh aka Tammy Wynette went to Vegas and saw Clem Kadiddlehopper back in '65. I can't get this stupid little fact out of my head. I've literally spent a few hours ruminating on it.

How the hell did you end up in Vegas? You didn't have a dime to your name in 1965. You couldn't even pay the rent! Was it a hairdresser's convention? I figure there must've been a man involved. Did you gamble, drink, sin? Were you constantly looking over your shoulder to see if Euple was on your trail?

Biographers are tortured by such arcane matters, Tammy. They think by sifting through such obscure details they'll unearth the one true answer that will solve the riddle of their subject. But that never happens. Biographers can't break into people's heads. Believe me, I've tried just about everything, short of a hammer and chisel. You can never step inside somebody's soul. Especially yours.

Your early years were so grimy and vague. Something happened to you, Tammy. I mean something beyond divorce and shock treatments and poverty. You just shut down, clicked off. You didn't tell people your feelings, hardly ever. As far as I know you didn't confide in or confess to anybody. As cliché as it sounds, you only ever revealed yourself in the music. Thank God you found your way to Music City.

Girl Singer

I decided I was going to make it as a singer . . . or kill myself trying.

—Tammy Wynette

Located at West End and Twentieth, the Anchor Motel was a cut-rate overnight stop favored by thrifty travelers and starving musicians. NASHVILLE'S ONLY UPTOWN MOTEL—TILE BATHS WITH GLASS SHOWER DOORS—WALL TO WALL CARPETING—FREE TV IN EACH ROOM, read the postcards. Don Chapel was working the front desk when a call came in that would alter the course of his life. Some chick wanting a room. She claimed to be a songwriter, one with a very important appointment to see Porter Wagoner. "Turned out to be a lie," said Chapel. "He wasn't even in town."

A Shriners convention had descended on Music City, and Don was swamped. By the time Wynette Byrd arrived in her borrowed and beat-up VW bug, the only room left was the bridal suite. She took it. Later that night Chapel got a call at the front desk.

"This is Virginia. You know there's no TV in the bridal suite?"

"Yes, ma'am, I know that," Chapel replied wearily.

"Can I come down there in the lobby and watch TV?" Don, thinking nothing of it, said of course. "She was smarter than I thought . . . in a cunning way," he mutters now.

Wynette drifted into the lobby and started to gab. Chapel let her know he was a singer and songwriter, too. One who'd recently signed with Musicor Records, the current home of George Jones. And Jones himself had cut a couple of Don's songs. The fact that Don had a connection to Wynette's longtime hero must've lit a marquee's worth of lightbulbs in that pretty little head. Chapel soon noticed that Wynette carried around a couple of dog-eared loose-leaf notebooks in which she'd transcribed the lyrics to all of

George's songs. "Handwritten, every song he ever recorded," he noted woefully. "I shoulda seen it right then, dammit."

Chapel got off work at eleven and escorted Wynette on a night out on the town. They wound up at Possum Holler, a nightclub belonging to Jones. Wynette got up and sang Loretta's "Don't Come Home A-Drinkin'" to a tepid response. They made their way back to the Anchor Motel in the wee, wee hours. Don walked Wynette to her room. "I turned to leave and she said, 'Well, I don't know about you, but I'm goin' to *bed*.'" Chapel, who had been divorced about six months earlier, couldn't refuse an invitation to the bridal suite. "I scoop her up, carry her across the threshold like we're married. Big joke." Once inside, Don spied a detail that made his heart ache. "Now this is the God's truth—she had her panties hanging on a clothesline in the bathroom. And they're full o' holes. You know how *cheap* panties are?"

They made with the loving, and Chapel refutes any claims that Wynette was an apathetic participant. "She was insatiable . . . we spent a week in that motel . . . we had food brought in." After the first night Don smuggled her into his own room at the motel, which was against employee rules. The manager came knocking: "You got a woman in that room?" "You want the truth?" responded Don, who was fired on the spot. Chapel informed his boss the lady in question was soon to be a Nashville superstar, then boasted he'd be back in a year to buy the joint.

Wynette had to head to Birmingham to return the car she'd borrowed and pick up her kids. Don drove her to her apartment and remained in the vehicle as she ventured in. Little did he know Euple lurked inside. "I'm sittin' in the driveway. I could've been killed! She told me she was divorced!" Not two weeks into the relationship and it was already a rough ride for Don.

Don Chapel is yet another curious male figure in the life of Tammy Wynette. The way Wynette told the story, he was primarily famous for two things: being the husband George Jones brazenly stole Tammy from as well as being the man who distributed nude pictures of his wife once she started becoming famous (a charge he emphatically denies). But Chapel is far more than an amusing footnote. The fact is that Don helped Wynette at a time when she had nowhere else to turn.

I liked Don. Big hair, a big attitude, even a big Web site. Yes, after all these years Don's still in the game and he's just the sort of character Nashville could use more of today. Chapel is not always the easiest man to read.

At times he hints at dark plots, hit men, and murders, the full story of which he says will only be revealed in his own book, one he's titling "Don Chapel: Fatally Wounded by George Jones and Tammy Wynette." He can be a little cantankerous, a bit paranoid, and remains hurt and angry over his media portrayal. And for good reason, for his part of the Tammy saga has been continually told without him. Chapel feels he and his family were obliterated by the sort of mythmaking stories that haphazardly roll off, as he put it, "the tongues of stars that have become so famous whatever they say is perceived as the truth." Wynette and George Jones have voiced their versions repeatedly in documentaries, interviews, and their own autobiographies. "Nobody interviewed me," he said. "Nobody said, 'Don, how was this? Tell it how it was.'"

One of six children, Don Chapel* aka Leon Amburgey grew up dirt-poor in Letcher County, Kentucky. His main musical influence, like that of so many others in this book, was gospel. Music was a big deal to the Amburgey clan—Don's dad pawned his carpentry tools to buy his daughter a banjo. Starting in 1936, three of his siblings toured the Southeast as the Sunshine Sisters, one of the first all-female string bands. Two of the three embarked on solo careers. Jean Chapel, a rockabilly sensation billed as "the female Elvis," became a respected songwriter whose songs were cut by, among others, Eddy Arnold, Patsy Cline, Kitty Wells, and George Jones. Another sister, Martha Carson, earned the title "First Lady of Gospel," and her 1951 hit "Satisfied" was a million-seller.

Don signed to Musicor Records shortly before Wynette Byrd arrived. Two singles sung and written by Chapel and produced by "Pappy" Daily, longtime associate of George Jones, were released in 1966, and Jones would record three of Chapel's songs in 1967. Wynette's fast climb up the charts quickly eclipsed Don's success, but when they met, he had the leg up, being the one with a recording contract and songwriting credits. In her book Wynette makes it sound as if she came to Nashville a handful of times, moved there, then landed a record deal, but there is a six-month period in 1966 she doesn't account for, when Don tried to help her and took her out on the road.

After being tossed out of the Anchor Motel, Wynette got an apartment

---

*Chapel declines to state his age.

in East Nashville, no easy feat in itself. It's hard to believe, but the powers that be in the city of Nashville were embarrassed by its reputation as the country music capital of the world. "The ruling class preferred to call Nashville 'The Athens of the South' because of the number of its colleges and universities," wrote Brenda Lee in her autobiography. "The society people looked down their noses at the music people. Bankers wouldn't give them loans. Many landlords wouldn't rent apartments to them. It was hard for people in the music business to even get electricity without spending four times as much deposit money as somebody who walked in off the street."

Being a single mother with three kids was particularly tough on Wynette. Using the one word that most enraged her, one woman went as far as telling Wynette she just didn't rent to "hillbillies." She finally scored a place in a twelve-dollar-a-week motor court, but only after fibbing and telling the landlady she was working at a local beauty parlor. This was a desperate time in Wynette's life. She wrote home to Mildred asking for funds for shoes for the kids and received no answer. Relatives on the Byrd side say Euple sent her money. Sometimes she'd send it back.

Her children didn't have an easy time of it. Wynette was often in another world, the one of her dreams. Nancy Byrd took care of Tina for a few weeks while Wynette was off in Nashville. "The child's clothes were mildewed and wet. They had not been taken care of. It wasn't that Wynette didn't love her girls—I think she truly did, but that desire to make music was just eatin' her up and it caused her to make choices that most mothers wouldn't make. It just overrode everything. She wanted to sing that bad."

Don Chapel was smitten. "She was pretty, she was humble, she was sweet, she was innocent," said Chapel, who dragged her off to the dentist to have her teeth fixed. "She had twenty-two cavities," he claimed, noting that Wynette also had a high tolerance for painkillers. "Gave her five shots, it wouldn't numb her. For two or three months after, I'd kiss her and taste novocaine." And Don felt her coiffure needed work, beautician or no beautician. Wynette's hair was "bleached out, burnt, dead—it looked just like straw," said Chapel, who noted the end result left Wynette "lookin' butch. I said, 'I gotta go get you some *hair*!' I went to Zayre's and bought her a $9.95 hairpiece." The result is immortalized on the cover of Wynette's debut album, *Your Good Girl's Gonna Go Bad*.

Chapel paints a picture of a couple united to conquer the country music world. He describes a dramatic pact the pair made when they first met. "We cut our wrists and put our blood together," said Don. "She told me it was a blood oath—if one of us makes it, we'll help the other. We're gonna stick together. This was for life, and that's the way I meant it."

Although Chapel was no match for Wynette vocally, they worked up a few popular numbers of the day that they could sing together, such as "Jackson." And he got them gigs, meager as they were. "I had put Tammy on the road as my girl singer before she ever signed," said Chapel, who claims their first booking together was a one-room schoolhouse in the middle of nowhere with a potbellied stove and no sound system. "We had an awful time finding it," he said. "I think twenty people showed up. They passed the hat, took up a collection." The take amounted to about thirty bucks. "We spent more than twice that to get there."

Chapel has fond memories of driving through the mountains on the Pennsylvania Turnpike in his powder blue Pontiac convertible, Wynette tucked in the passenger seat, her head covered with curlers. "There we are in the boonies. She's fixin' her hair at a roadside park and we're cookin' out in a barbecue pit. In her mind, she was probably goin', 'Is this the big time? Is this the way it is?'"

Frank Scarborough was the one booking the gigs. He was one of the men behind the Dixie Jamboree, a country show at the Roosevelt Theater in Jefferson, Georgia. Scarborough had booked a number of country stars, including both Martha Carson and Jean Chapel, and that led to taking a shot on Don and Wynette. He paid them a hundred bucks a show, rented their motel room, and enlisted a band of local pickers known as the Cherokee Cowboys to back them up. "Don said they needed bookings so Tammy could feed her three daughters. They were totally broke," recalled Scarborough.*

Wynette was a big hit with the audience, according to Frank's brother

---

*Frank and his brother Glenn both insist that Chapel had already renamed her Tammy Wynette at the time. "She was booked as Tammy Wynette," said Frank. Producer Billy Sherrill is the one credited with coming up with the name, but Don says he was the one inspired by the popular Debbie Reynolds *Tammy* movies. "I knew then that she would need a good 'show' name," he said, adding that Wynette protested at first, wanting to keep her real name. "Her face got red," said Don. "That kind of bugged her—that I had admired somebody else female." When Don made these claims in a tabloid interview, her then-husband George Richey, speaking for Tammy, denied them, saying Sherrill had given her the name. Producer Kelso Herston, who knew Tammy shortly before she was signed by Billy, said she was still using the name Wynette Byrd then.

Glenn. "They didn't know anything about her, never heard of her before, but when she got up and started singin', they loved her." Frank was impressed by the devotion Chapel had for Wynette. "Don treated Tammy like a princess. He did everything that she wanted. She told me she would've given up on life if not for Don." Frank was very fond of Wynette, but almost dropped her after an incident during their second Dixie Jamboree appearance.

Scarborough was backstage when he stumbled upon Wynette sneaking some moonshine with the comedian of his show, Happy Harley. Don was nowhere in sight. "She was wearin' overall britches and an ol' plaid shirt. They were passin' the white lightnin' and both about drunk. He'd take a drink, hand it over to her, and she'd take a drink and just shiver." Scarborough told the pair he ran a family show and would have to terminate the both of them. "She begged me not to fire her. Because if I did, Don would drop her, and she would have no way to feed her babies." Scarborough relented, and didn't reveal to Don what had happened.

According to Frank, Wynette was "different, she was just strange. She stayed melancholy 'bout twenty-three hours a day. Didn't want to talk much. If you set her down in a restaurant, she'd turn away from the crowd, look at the wall for as long as she was there, and wouldn't speak a word to nobody. If you went to the bathroom and come back, she'd still be starin' at the wall. When you looked in her eyes, she was lookin' a million miles from you. Just like she was lookin' for somethin' on over the next hill. Like she was wantin' to climb some stairs."

Nashville was the one and only thing on Wynette's mind, and Frank remembered her gossiping incessantly about one up-and-coming female country star who was being hotly pursued by a lesbian songwriter. Everything and anything to do with Music City, USA, fascinated Wynette. "Stardom was something she had to have one way or another. Tammy just didn't have a lot of responsibility about her. She was a lot like Patsy Cline. Patsy was a person that was pretty much for Patsy. And that was Tammy. She was gonna climb that ladder, it didn't make no difference whose head she had to mash in the quicksand to do it. I admired that kind of guts."

In July 1966, Chapel and Wynette did some down-home campaigning for Zell Miller, then running for Congress to represent the state of Georgia. Miller, a Democrat, would cause controversy in 2004 not only for his support of George Bush, but also for his keynote speech at the Republican convention bashing the current Democratic candidates. (In the aftermath an angry Miller got into an argument with the host of MSNBC's *Hardball*, during which he lamented the fact we no longer lived in an age when a man could challenge an opponent to a duel.)

Frank Scarborough booked the gig and provided the stage: a two-ton flatbed truck, plus a tent borrowed from a local funeral home so the summer afternoon heat wouldn't "bake your brains out. Fifteen minutes before Zell was to show, Don and Tammy would climb up on that truck, start singin', and he'd come drivin' up in his car. Don would introduce him—'Here is your next congressman of the Ninth District, Zell Miller!'"*

After the show, Miller gave Wynette a check for $150, which she promptly took to the bank. "I guess she was makin' sure it was good," said Miller, chuckling. "She was all business. She had entertained your audience and she wanted to be paid for it. The teller happened to be my wife, so she kind of got a chuckle out of it. For years afterward any time Tammy would be in the area, I'd go see her and say, 'You trust me now?'" Wynette would campaign for Zell again in 1990 when he ran for governor.

Miller was so taken with Wynette that afternoon in 1966 that he attended an outdoor show she and Don gave the same night in Shoal, Georgia. "It was obvious this was a woman that had been knocked around in life," he said. "She was tough yet extremely vulnerable at the same time. The audience loved her, too. Her voice was so strong, so emotional, and came just so straight out of her soul that you felt she was just spillin' her guts to you. You felt the intimacy of her."

Since she had first started going to Nashville in October of 1965, Wynette had been scheming and dreaming to get her foot in the door. One fact she had to face: female singers were simply not offered as many opportunities as men and weren't considered as financially viable. "Female singers just really won't sell," Capitol Records producer Ken Nelson told Hank Thompson back in the early fifties when he was trying to get Jean Shepard a deal.

During those days the country charts amounted to "twenty-nine guys and Kitty Wells," as Bobby Braddock put it. Wells hit it big in 1952 with her answer to Hank Thompson's tale of an unfaithful spouse, "The Wild Side

---

*Miller recalled only one gig; Scarborough says there were ten and that Don and Wynette were paid $450.

of Life." Thompson tells of an "anybody's baby" deserving of a husband's ultimate insult: "I might've known you'd never make a wife." Kitty, in that inimitable, unexcited, and plain-as-a-pair-of-white-cotton-socks voice, gave it right back in "It Wasn't God Who Made Honky Tonk Angels": "Too many times married men think they're single / That has caused many a good girl to go wrong." She goes on to blame every broken heart on the opposite sex. The song might sound quaint nowadays, but at the time it was hot stuff— hot enough to be banned from both the Grand Ole Opry and NBC Radio. Hell, women weren't supposed to talk back!

Thirty-three years old, mother of two kids, and married to country singer Johnny Wright, Wells was "the most unlikely recording star in the history of music," wrote Michael Kosser. "There was nothing, absolutely nothing, theatrical or spectacular about her." Indeed, Kitty looked like some nice lady one might encounter behind the register at a church thrift store or selling a cupcake at a craft bazaar. But the lack of pizzazz and sex appeal only un- derscored the sincerity of Kitty's message, and she was a huge hit, not to mention a major influence on the singers that followed in her wake. (Tammy, Dolly, and Loretta would pay tribute to Wells by performing Kitty's signa- ture hit alongside her on their 1993 trio album, *Honky Tonk Angels*.)

Feisty Jean Shepard hit it big on Capitol, produced by the very man who had turned her down, Ken Nelson. Listen to what she sang in 1954: "The women ought to rule the world, because the men ain't worth a [hiccup] . . . I hope they croak, it ain't no joke, they're the lowest thing in town." Two years later she recorded what is regarded as country music's first "concept album," *Songs of a Love Affair*, a collection of numbers telling the story of a marriage doomed by adultery. The late fifties saw the ascendance of that megaton bomb of talent known as Patsy Cline, a sublime torch singer whose meticulous Owen Bradley productions were as much pop as they were country. Patsy, whose high-contrast, hard-boiled features could've been sto- len off some wisecracking dame inked by Milton Caniff, was a live wire with an attitude somewhere between devil-may-care and sorry, Charlie. Patsy could drink you under the table, trump your dirty jokes, and success- fully arm-wrestle a sailor.

All these women (not to mention Charline Arthur, Wanda Jackson, Goldie Hill, Connie Smith, and others) were tiny islands in a sea of cowboy-hat testosterone. Loretta Lynn and Dolly Parton both arrived in Music City be- fore Tammy, although Dolly would hit just months after Wynette. Loretta's first hit came in 1960 with "I'm a Honky-Tonk Girl." She moved to Nashville that same year, signing with Decca, where Owen Bradley crafted her hit after hit. Lynn's songwriting would cover everything from personal auto-biography to marital fidelity to birth control. Her plainspoken delivery had the casual intensity of a next-door neighbor who really doesn't want to start any trouble but just *has* to lean over the fence and inform you that your significant other is down at the Mouse Trap drunk off his ass and in the arms of a stranger. There is something very noble about Loretta, if a bit lik-ably screwloose.

Dolly Parton first appeared on the Grand Ole Opry at age thirteen, moved to Nashville fresh out of high school to sign with Monument in 1965, but she wouldn't hit until 1967 with "Dumb Blonde," the record that caught Porter Wagoner's ear and put her on TV as his duet partner. Dolly's irresist-ible combination of sex, humor, and heart enables an outrageous persona unique in country music, and she's a versatile performer who can effort-lessly deliver a factory-made pop number like "9 to 5" or imbue a song like "Jolene" with the chilling intensity of an old murder ballad from the Ken-tucky hills. She's had a pop star's knack for morphing along with the times. "For a long time, drums were not allowed on the stage of the Grand Ole Opry . . . before that it was black people, or women, or anything or anybody else that somebody thought was a threat to tradition," she wrote in her au-tobiography. "I love to hear Bill Monroe sing 'Muleskinner Blues' as much as anybody, but I also love to hear Garth Brooks. . . . Change is not always bad. Nor is it always good. But one thing is certain: change is inevitable."

Unlike Loretta or Tammy, Dolly possesses an added talent for being ut-terly ruthless in business. "If I catch a man who is not looking into my eyes as he talks to me, I have scored two really big points with him already. Many an old boy has found out too late that I look like a woman but think like a man. Just like the first prostitute who realized she was 'Sittin' on a gold mine,' I know what I have to sell, and nobody goes prospecting in my gold mine without first buying the mineral rights." Dolly has also been an incred-ibly prolific writer, with 607 song credits listed at BMI as of 2008. (Loretta has 176 and Tammy racked up 75.)

But that kind of success was unimaginable when Tammy came to town. "When I started out, radio stations were told not to play two women singers' records back-to-back," said Wynette. "We were not supposed to travel with a male band." That she was a divorced woman with three kids was another strike against her. "One booking agent just refused to book me," she said. There were also the occupational hazards that came with the gig. "I used to work clubs, and often the attitude was, if they booked you, they owned you as a woman," said Connie Smith. "They bought you to play the club. They bought you. Period."

One record company executive, hinting that he might be interested in signing Wynette, closed his office door and unzipped his pants. "He looked at me and he said, 'You take care of me, and I'll take care of you,'" recalled an angry Wynette. "I was gone like a bullet." She wound up out in her car, crying. Don Chapel said that she confessed that one trip to Nashville before she'd met him had resulted in "meeting" a producer at the Anchor Motel. Wynette returned to Alabama dejected.

But Wynette hung in there. Don Chapel tried to get Pappy Daily at Musicor Records interested. (Apparently Daily didn't remember this after she hit it big, because he asked her why she hadn't come to him. Wynette had the pleasure of reminding Pappy: "You turned me down.") Hickory Records told her they were looking for a female Don Gibson, so she went home and studied his records. It came to nothing. Paul Cohen at Kapp Records actually said he'd record Wynette, but warned her that it might take a couple of years for her music to be released. Producers Owen Bradley and Jim Vienneau also said no.

One somewhat constant figure in all this was Kelso Herston. An Alabaman who'd played on many a George Jones record, Herston was now producing for United Artists. Wynette had met Herston when she'd first come from Birmingham with Charles Colvin, and he had tried to encourage her, get her appointments, and even slipped her a few bucks to keep her afloat. "I wanted to sign her but I already had three female artists, and they wouldn't let me sign another," said Herston, who was not just impressed by Wynette's talent. "Man, when she first came to Nashville she was a good-looker. It was like Elvis—you'd do a double take. She was a beauty." Herston had just signed Billie Jo Spears, whom Herston described to Wynette as "the female George Jones." (The fact that Nashville thought in terms of an artist as a female version of this or that male singer drove Wynette 'round the bend.)

There are few country singers who can give Tammy a run for her money in terms of no-holds-barred emotional delivery, but Spears, who would not hit big until the seventies with "Blanket on the Ground" and "I'm Not Easy,"

was one of them, and Herston said Wynette hung around his office study-
ing her records. "I still think that she was influenced some by Billie Jo. She
really did like her."*

Herston remembers Wynette's frustration with the way things were
going for her in Nashville. "Just about everybody passed on her," he admitted. "One day she said, 'You're from Alabama, I'm from Alabama, Billy
Sherrill is from Alabama . . . can you set me up with him?'" At the time Billy
Sherrill was a new producer over at Epic Records, and he'd just hit big with
"Almost Persuaded," a number one smash for David Houston. Epic, as Herston instructed Wynette, was a subsidiary of Columbia Records. ("I remember trying real hard to learn how to say that word, 'subsidiary,'" she recalled.)
"Billy and I would send each other these people that couldn't sing, no-
talented people, as jokes. He used to send me everybody that walked in with
a cowboy hat on. I called him about Wynette, he thought it was a joke. But
she went over there the next day."

It was August 1966, and what happened next was, as reporter Eve Zibart
put it, "country music's version of the Lana Turner/Schwab's drugstore legend." It is a tale that has been told many times with many variations. In
some versions Wynette said she met Billy Sherrill in the lobby of his building. In some tellings she played him a tape; in others played a few songs on
his guitar. "I didn't know what a tape was," she claimed at other times, despite having cut demos with both Fred Lehner and David Vest in Birmingham. To further confuse the matter, Don Chapel insists that he was the one
that took her to Billy Sherrill, and can recount the songs she sang as well
as wax eloquent on the details of Billy's "thrift store desk." Kelso Herston

---

*The very first single Herston cut on Spears was UA 50092: "You're Too Much Like Me"
backed with "Not Enough of You to Go Around," and I must confess that I have waited
my entire career to tell the world of this vinyl double whammy. Like much of Tammy's
early work, these songs deal with the troubles facing a country gal trying to navigate
big-city life, and Spears just sings the hell out of both of them. Listen to Billie Jo belt
out "As I walk the streets of evil / Searching for you" on the A-side, and if the way she
gasps out the word "searching" doesn't reduce you to ashes, a heart transplant might
be in order. If Spears sounded even a fraction more desperate, they'd have locked her
away.

I have bought every copy I've ever encountered of this 45 just to give the damn thing
a home. Why no one has written about it or reissued it along with her other excellent
early UA singles remains a mystery to me. Truly one of the greatest honky-tonk singles
of all time—and get this, it wasn't a hit. Spears "didn't get a lot of airplay," said Herston.
"At that time it was hard to sell a chick singer. Tammy really kind of broke it in for the
girls."

maintains Chapel was never around for any of his meetings with Wynette.*

At any rate, Wynette made her way over to Billy Sherrill's tiny office at 812 Sixteenth Avenue South. At the time his secretary had just relocated to the West Coast, and Sherrill had yet to replace her. Wynette said she wandered unannounced into his office. There was Billy Sherrill, leaning back in his chair, boots up on the desk. A compact, unflappable fellow, "he didn't look much older than me," Wynette recalled. "And he didn't even seem curious about why I was there." She looked at him and announced, "I'm Wynette Byrd and I'd like a recording contract."

The way Sherrill usually tells it is that Wynette plunked herself down outside his office and, as he had no secretary to inform him she was present, spent the afternoon there. He was embarrassed to discover her still there at the end of the day. "A pale, skinny little blonde girl who looked like she was at rope's end," said Sherrill. "Caked with hair spray and wearing these huge fake eyelashes."

Sherrill says she wanted work as a writer. She had no tapes, so he handed her his guitar. Wynette did a few of the songs she'd recorded back in Birmingham with Fred Lehner. Billy "was leaning back in his chair and never said a word till I finished, and he said, 'You know something else?'" Wynette didn't know what to make of this strange little poker-faced creature. "No expression on his face a-whatsoever," said an exasperated Wynette. "I didn't know if he liked my singin'. He never did say."

Although he might've said nothing, it was the voice that impressed Sherrill, not the material, and he told Wynette that while he didn't have the time to look for one, if she came up with a good enough song, maybe he'd record her.

Wynette was shown the door, and Billy saw the weary resignation on her face. "She didn't believe me," he wrote later. "She was about half right. We both knew that I was graciously trying to say, 'Don't call me, I'll call you.'" But for some reason Wynette stayed on his mind. "Somethin' said, 'Don't turn this chick down.'"

As she remarked many times over the years, the fact that Sherrill was

*As I was finishing this manuscript I found contemporaneous proof backing Chapel's claims. In the May 1968 issue of *Country Music Life* magazine there is a long profile of Tammy by Ruth Charon. She quotes Tammy as saying, "Don is totally responsible for going to Epic."

brand new at his job, had only one hit to his name, and was too busy for her was extremely irksome. "Now here he's some hot big producer—you know, don't have time to look for material, one artist," she snorted. Which only fueled her to find some material. "I started hitting the streets for publishing companies, listening to all these songs."

In the meantime Billy happened to hear a number on the radio that moved him, "Apartment #9," by Bobby Austin.* It had been released on Tally Records, a small independent West Coast label run by Merle Haggard cohort Fuzzy Owen. Sherrill felt that with Epic behind it the record could be a smash. He tried to lease it from the label and was told in no uncertain terms they weren't interested in his offer. It pissed him off, and he decided to give Wynette a ring.

Billy says he reached her back at the Anchor Motel, where she was staying one last night before returning to Alabama for good. Wynette maintained she was living at her one-room efficiency apartment and was too embarrassed to tell Billy she didn't have a phone, so she gave him her landlady's number. "Total lie," insists Don Chapel. "She never had her own place, ever."

Whatever the particulars, Sherrill got Wynette on the horn and "asked her if she'd like to make a record. She said, 'When?' I said, 'Tonight.'" Wynette thought he was joking and told him to quit. Sherrill told her to come to the office.

It was there Billy played her "Apartment #9." "I knew instantly that it was my song," she recalled. "You can get a feeling like that about a song the same way you can about a person—that it was just meant to be." Sherrill gave her a portable record player, telling her to learn the song they'd be cutting that night.

Tom Sparkman, who was to engineer the session, said Billy had an additional motivation for cutting Wynette—she'd confessed to him that some of the producers she'd seen had tried to get her in the sack. "He came to me one afternoon and asked me if I would stay until six o'clock and do a session," Sparkman recalled. "I said, 'Billy, I gotta get home, man. I get off at five.' He said, 'Please stay. There's a young woman who came into my office that's got a lotta talent, she's been to a half dozen different producers in

---

*Paycheck, who also cut the song, usually gets credit for writing it. According to those who knew Austin, Paycheck only contributed one couplet to the lyric, albeit a great one: "Loneliness surrounds me / Without your arms around me."

Nashville, and all of 'em wanted to get her on the casting couch. I want to prove 'em wrong. I want to let 'em know she's got talent. Will you stay?' I said, 'If that's your attitude, you're damn right I'll stay.' What had happened to her really ticked him off. Billy was being honorable."

Wynette said that the period before Sherrill rescued her had been one of her lowest. Despite the gigs Don had gotten them, she had no steady income to keep her kids afloat. "We had been living on corn bread, milk, and pinto beans for weeks when I met Billy Sherrill. I was on my last leg, just about ready to give up and go back to a steady job in a beauty shop."

"I really think I was Tammy's last hope," said Sherrill.

Don't Burn the Beans

I cannot understand a song that becomes successful without emotion,
without happiness or sadness or love or hate in it.

—Billy Sherrill

One thing about Billy: he did it his way. He just didn't give a damn, and
if you didn't like it, well, let the door hit ya where the dog bit ya.

In the heavenly kingdom of ballads there sits a king's golden throne that
awaits Billy Sherrill. Back in the day he was the Little Caesar of Music City,
USA, because from the late sixties to the early eighties Sherrill had a phenomenal run of more than fifty number one singles, plus a stack of gold
and platinum albums. Chances are you can hum a few of them: "Stand by
Your Man." "Behind Closed Doors." "The Most Beautiful Girl." "Take This
Job and Shove It." "Delta Dawn." (He'd also cowritten many a hit, Tammy's
in particular.) Then there are the recordings that might not have been
smashes, but will live forever anyway: Charlie Rich's "Life's Little Ups and
Downs" and "Set Me Free." Tammy's "You'll Never Walk Alone," "True and
Lasting Love," and "It's My Way." The boozy version of "You Better Move
On" by George Jones and Johnny Paycheck. Jones doing "I'm Not Ready Yet"
and "Someday My Day Will Come."

I brought up that last number the day I met Billy. I was nervous as hell.
I'd been obsessed with Sherrill and his records for much of my life. "When
I die, I've requested they play 'Someday My Day Will Come' at my wake,"
were the first words I blurted out. I knew every note of the song, one of the
very saddest he'd cut with George Jones, but Billy appeared unmoved. "I'll
stick with 'Amazing Grace,'" he muttered.

Of all the people I've interviewed—thousands—the one I'd most like to
spend more time interrogating is Sherrill. His thought process seemed random and reckless, like a quirky little pinball of unedited thought that rico-

cheted indiscriminately between the good, the bad, and the ugly. One minute he's telling you the foulest racist joke imaginable, the next he's waxing poetic about the artistry of George Jones, then suddenly he's musing over what the head of a Fox News anchor looked like when it passed through the birth canal. (Throughout our interview Sherrill kept an eyeball glued to a TV set tuned to Fox—said Billy, "I'm one notch right of Attila the Hun.") But Sherrill doesn't seem all that interested in reliving the glories of the past. He left the record business behind long ago. "I've turned doing nothing into an art form," boasted Billy. Fifty bucks says he misses the action, although he'd deny it. Sherrill has that curious look of a man who won all the battles, got bored with the results, and then didn't know what else to do with his life.

Because he sometimes used strings on his productions, Sherrill's sound was often reduced to the ridiculous label "countrypolitan." "A lot of these country music critics who go for the purity, the integrity of country music, they were sayin' that the stuff he did was schmaltzy and slick," said songwriter Bobby Braddock, coauthor of what may be Sherrill's greatest achievement, the majestic Jones ballad "He Stopped Loving Her Today." "Lookin' back on it, the truth is Billy Sherrill produced some of the greatest traditional country records of all time. So the arrangement didn't sound like 1950, it wasn't 1950. Billy brought a little bit of pop music."

Sherrill made some very extreme records, pop-tainted or not. "He Stopped Loving Her Today" begins starkly, only George's voice leading the way as clouds start to gather with the guitars of Pete Drake and Phil Baugh. It builds to an operatic crescendo with that cosmically weary recitation by Jones, Millie Kirkham's ghostly background wail sailing over him, the mournful strings just below. The amount of drama Sherrill packs into this one song would've caused Douglas Sirk to blush. Billy was particularly taken with the late Bill McHilhiney's string arrangement. "When he went up another third on the second go-round, I thought that was the greatest thing I ever heard. You hear the guy in the song go right up to heaven. Nobody liked it. I didn't get one positive word from the big powers that be. They called down from New York—'That would've been a heck of a better record if you hadn't covered it with all those strings.'" But Billy was right, and they were wrong, as was often the case in his illustrious career.

"Billy was thinkin' about the song, what the song was sayin', and how the singer was singin' it," said his longtime engineer Lou Bradley. "If you listen to all the records he made, the Tanya records are different from the

Tammy records and the Charlie Rich different from the Paycheck." The song, the song, the song—this was Billy's mantra. "The song is so much more important than the artist, the producer, or the record company," he said. "If I believe in a song I'll go after it 'til hell freezes over."

In the case of "He Stopped Loving Her Today," it took about a year and a half for hell to freeze over and for Jones, who'd been on a cocaine/alcohol rampage, to dry out. Charlie McCoy, who counts his five-note harmonica solo as the best work of his recording career, remembers how Sherrill sat at the piano before they cut the song, telling the various pickers on it what he wanted. "Billy started walkin' to the control room and all of a sudden he realized he hadn't included me. He just stopped, looked over at me, and said real quick, 'Get somethin' on the second verse,' headed for the control room, and that was it. Billy was smart. He hired musicians he trusted and let 'em be creative."

Among Nashville producers, Sherrill was the wild card. Nashville has never known what to make of him, and perhaps that is one reason he never quite got his due in town. "It's a travesty Billy's not in the Hall of Fame," said musician Harold Bradley. *Billboard* went so far as to compare Billy to Howard Hughes. "Some people feel the only difference between the two is that Sherrill's nails are shorter," wrote Gerry Wood. "Mr. Sherrill is an impatient man with an overwhelming interest in purchasing speedboats," wrote Elvis Costello, a serious fan whose 1981 misfire *Almost Blue* was a well-intentioned attempt to bathe himself in the Sherrill glow. Costello admitted his only "uneasy moment" came when Sherrill and his engineer Ron "Snake" Reynolds were "discussing the merits of their handguns across the mixing console." He noted his previous producer "had never come to the studio bearing firearms."*

The country singers he produced found him equally formidable. "I think the artists in a way feared him," said songwriter and longtime crony

*As far as Elvis Costello is concerned, "I never was a fan of his," said Sherrill. "I thought he was the worst singer I ever heard in my life." When the idea of Billy producing was first broached, "I said, 'No way, I'm not gonna be grilled and tortured doin' an album for a guy that sounds like he's sittin' on the commode when he's singin'.'" When informed Costello's last record had sold seven hundred thousand copies, Sherrill thought to himself, "Well, maybe I can suffer a little with him." The sessions were grim. "I had my mind on goin' to the lake on every cut," said Billy, who couldn't even escape the singer on water. "I finally got to the lake, got on my houseboat, and, lo and behold, there's a little boat—and there's Elvis Costello."

Glenn Sutton. "You never knew if he liked it or not. And he was very, very strong that way." Bob Allen, perhaps the only Nashville reporter who had regular access to Billy back in his glory days, witnessed some primo Sherrill moments, such as a party where a guest arrived at Sherrill's Nashville home to be greeted by a well-oiled Billy pointing a loaded .38 in his face. Wrote Allen, "When the last visitors leave Sherrill is still moving restlessly around the house, sipping a drink, listening to *Tales from the Vienna Woods* on his stereo and watching a videotape of *The Triumph of the Will.*"

There have been few producer-artist matches as perfect as Billy Sherrill and Tammy Wynette. Both hailed from small Alabama towns, were raised in the church, and were solitary figures who gave their all to music. "I put my gut and heart into every record," said Billy, but the words could've just as easily flowed from Tammy's lips. And beneath Sherrill's sarcasm and studied indifference and Third Reich proclivities lurks, dare I say, a stone romantic. How do I know? Oh, just a sad glint in his eye. Said Mr. Sherrill once, "I love to record love songs. Like, 'You're the greatest thing on earth, man, and I can't tell you enough and I'm gonna tell you on the *next* record and the *next* record . . .'" And that is exactly what he did in an extremely unrelenting way with Tammy Wynette.

Billy Norris Sherrill arrived in the world on November 5, 1936, in Phil Campbell, Alabama, a three-stoplight town twenty-five miles north of Red Bay named after an English railroad engineer settler. He was raised in nearby Haleyville, home to gospel great Jake Hess, became interested in piano around age six, and was soon playing in church. "Billy grew up in a different world," fellow producer and friend Rick Hall told Peter Guralnick. "His father was an evangelist, one of those hellfire-and-damnation preachers that traveled in tent revivals."

"Clyde Sherrill," remembered cousin Dianne Sherrill. "Big man. We used to go to church every Sunday mornin'. Billy'd be playin' piano, his daddy'd be preachin'." Billy took his Bible straight, no chaser. In 1973 *Time* magazine would report that Sherrill "does not attend church because he cannot find one that teaches a literal enough interpretation of the Scriptures." Gospel was the big influence on Billy. "I think that's the most all-encompassing music there is," he said, raving about the harmonics involved and dropping such esoteric names as LeRoy Abernathy, Vep Ellis, and Virgil O. Stamps.

"I stole from a lotta those guys," said Sherrill, chuckling. "Mostly the melodies and chord structures."

His first actual gig came at age ten playing a funeral for ten bucks. Billy chose a rather pointed send-off piece for the deceased—"Bye Bye Blues." Clyde, who sang and played piano himself, recognized the ditty and was not amused. "My daddy kick my butt after it was over with." Did Clyde encourage his interest in music? "No," said Billy. "He encouraged me to keep playin' piano because I was *free.*

"I was kinda sneaky. One time they were takin' up collection for the preacher. I played a slow piano tune—sounded like a hymn, but it was a real slow version of 'That's Where the Money Goes.' I looked at my daddy and thought, uh-oh, I'm gonna get another ass-kicking when this is over with."

Like Wynette, he'd been exposed early on to the glories of shape-note singing. "We'd go to all-the-day singin's . . . They had brand-new books, they smelled new, all these new songs, and nobody ever saw 'em before—'Okay, let's go to page one.' Everybody could just sight-read the song. It was beautiful. It was like they'd been practicin' for years. I wish some of those things had been recorded. It would amaze me how a sixty-five-year-old farmer would open a book and he and his wife and kids would sing it right off the bat."

As a teen, Sherrill turned to secular music out of "starvation. My dad was being paid in cabbages and pigs, milk and fruit." He played VFW square dances with local favorites Benny Cagle and the Rhythm Swingsters ("the worst name for a band I ever heard," said Sherrill). "Billy was a fabulous sax player and piano man and could sing good, good harmony," said singer Tony Couch. "The man had great ideas."

Even then Sherrill was a tough nut to crack. He would lose both his father and mother early on, but spoke little about his background. "Billy never did want to talk about his family," said Couch. "When we first started, he had this one little ol' one-bedroom apartment there in Hamilton, and he lived by himself. Billy was probably eighteen. I couldn't get over that—I thought, 'Good grief, that must be so lonesome to live by yourself and not have a family around you.' Billy was on his own. I never knew him not to be.

"Billy was shy, standoffish, just a different kind of guy. He could skip further than anybody, he could do one-arm pull-ups and push-ups, he could do all kinds of crazy things. And he was so funny. I loved bein' around him." Not that Sherrill was any sort of rock and roll animal. "We were womanizers, Billy was not," said Couch. "He didn't go in for that kinda stuff. He did not participate in our orgies."

Sherrill and band member Clement Hall went up to Florence one night to meet a couple of girls. Local toughs didn't cotton to the idea of out-of-towners from Haleyville hitting on their women. "They got after 'em and, boy, they was gonna do 'em bodily harm," said Couch. "Billy was drivin' this ol' '48 black Buick, he called it 'the Tank.'" When the other car caught up with them "Billy just flipped 'em the bird, didn't bother him a bit. He was cool under fire, man."

And Sherrill had plans. Ray Barger recalled Sherrill driving him back home from a Tennessee gig in his 1960 T-Bird and telling him, "I'm gonna be a millionaire by the time I'm thirty-five years old."

"We were just too country for Billy," said Couch. "I think he was kinda ashamed of us. We were country bumpkins, we didn't know doodley-squat. Billy wanted to be big-time. He had a real burnin' desire to go to Nashville. He talked about it a lot. He just knew he was gonna make it. He *knew*."

It was in Benny Cagle's band that Sherrill met Rick Hall, a fiddle player who'd previously been with Carmol Taylor and his Country Pals. Hall had grown up "poor white trash" in north Mississippi and went to school ten miles away from Billy. Like Sherrill, he'd been exposed to gospel music early—his father had taught shape-note singing in church. "Both of us had lost our fathers," said Hall. "We got very close." At the time Sherrill hated country music. "He made fun of it," said Tony Couch. Rick's love was country. "He was a country hoedown fiddler, and I was the bluesman," said Sherrill. "Both were very opinionated," said Couch of the competitive, ambitious duo. "But Billy was the mastermind of everything. Anything we did, it was, 'Is Billy gonna approve?'"

Hall told Peter Guralnick that Billy "was the kind of guy, I never cussed around him; if I took a drink, I'd hide it from him. He never condoned it and used to sulk with me for a week if I got drunk. . . . Very conservative, very mild mannered, sophisticated, isolated from the world, had very few friends and didn't talk a lot." Rick Hall was just as eccentric as Billy. "Back then there were a lotta mistakes made on radio cause it wasn't polished," said Tony Couch. "We'd be drivin' along listenin' and if some disc jockey made a mistake, Rick would just pull a *fit*. He'd beat on the radio and cuss and raise hell that somebody had made that mistake. . . . He did some funny things. Rick chewed on his tongue. He was so country."

Rick and Billy went on to form the Fairlanes, a rock outfit that played hits of the day like "Sea Cruise" and "Tossin' and Turnin'." "One of the best bands I've ever seen," said Dan Penn about the Fairlanes. "They just had this incredible sound, a heck of a presence." In addition to Sherrill and Hall, the Fairlanes' sound was revved up by guitar ace Terry Thompson, and Tony Couch belting out the vocals. "Tony was cool, y'know what I mean?" said Penn. "Tony had the black ducktail. He was Fonzie before Fonzie ever was."

In 1956, James Joiner and Kelso Herston, two Alabama boys who'd played guitar together in the service, formed Tune Records with a couple of partners in Florence. Joiner's family ran a local bus company, and Tune's first recordings were done in the restaurant of the bus station. ("I thought, 'What a great place to have a studio,'" enthused Penn.) They could record only on the weekends when the restaurant was closed. The following year Tune scored a local hit with Bobby Denton's "A Fallen Star," which spawned top-ten covers by country heavyweights Ferlin Husky and Jimmy C. Newman. Alabama's first record company was on the map, and, as Joiner told Richard Younger, musicians and songwriters "started coming out of the woodwork and the farms."

Herston remembers the day he met Sherrill. Rick Hall had brought by a song Billy had written, as Sherrill was too shy to come in himself. Herston went out to the car to meet Sherrill, who was all scrunched up in the backseat. "You couldn't even see his head. I stuck my hand in to shake hands, Billy wouldn't even look up. He just stuck his hand out. . . . His father and mother had died, and I think he was pretty much still in shock at that time."

Sherrill and his bandmates became regulars at Tune headquarters, playing on demo sessions and writing. "Young and Innocent," a Sherrill and Hall song, was the B-side of Denton's next single, which led to a Roy Orbison cover. (Fifteen years later Donny Osmond's version went to number 7 on the pop charts.) The very first time Sherrill heard a song he'd written on the radio was in 1958. Billy had been dating some chick, and they'd "parked in some old cemetery. I'd been pawin' at her. She was kinda stuck on the idea I was a songwriter. She asked, 'Do they ever play your songs on the radio?'" Magically, a song he'd written with Hall—Marlin Green's "Ballad of Love"—came wafting over the airwaves and, *presto*, off came the girl's top. Thus Sherrill discovered the power of pop music.

Within a few years Sherrill and Hall would have their own publishing company, FAME: Florence Alabama Music Enterprise. They began to get songs cut by Homer and Jethro, George Jones, the Browns and Brenda Lee. The third partner in the company was a strange and mystical figure in Alabama music history named Tom Stafford.

A hunchbacked, asthmatic hipster who had a penchant for abusing cough syrup, Stafford kick-started the Muscle Shoals music scene, not to mention a few Nashville careers. "Tom had kind of a deformed look," said Dan Penn. "He was a short guy, dark hair, real piercin' eyes, very intense, smoked Pall Malls constantly. He knew how to talk to musicians, writers, people like that. Tom just had a way about him. He could make you believe. He'd sit there and smoke them Pall Malls, fold up like a bat, and tell ya, 'Oh, yeah, we can have a hit record.'"

Besides Hall and Sherrill, songwriters Dan Penn, Spooner Oldham, and Donnie Fritts and musicians such as Earl "Peanutt" Montgomery (author of many a song for Tammy and George Jones), Roger Hawkins, Norbert Putnam, Marlin Green, Kelso Herston, Jerry Carrigan, and Hurschel Wiginton were the major talents who among their endless credentials would play on many a Sherrill session once he hit it big in Nashville.

The musical match for all this fire was Arthur Alexander, a tall, elegant-looking black man sporting otherworldly Occidental features beneath a compact, processed conk. Alexander had a one-of-a-kind knack for turning a phrase, and he created a small but highly influential body of work, a landmark mixture of R & B and country, delivered by a Roy Rogers and Eddy Arnold–loving Afro-American backed by a band of hillbilly hepcats who swooned over the greasy sounds of John R's WLAC broadcasts.

Alexander created such Stones/Beatles favorites as "You Better Move On" and "Anna (Go to Him)," as well as such weird and luminous globs of soupy Alabama sludge as "The Girl That Radiates That Charm," and it all began right there in Stafford's funky homemade studio. "To me Arthur was like Hank Williams," said Dan Penn. "He was a very simple and cotton-patchy type deal. He wasn't big-city, he was a small-town-type writer—but he was very authentic . . . we all learned so much from Arthur. I don't think he gets enough credit. You go down to the Alabama Music Hall of Fame, they just got a little bitty picture of him. They should have his picture all over it, because he's what started the whole Alabama/Muscle Shoals deal. Arthur actually stepped out there, got a hit record, and showed a bunch of country boys how to write songs."

Sometime during the very tail end of the fifties Hall and Sherrill answered a newspaper ad Stafford had placed looking for songwriters to run a publishing company. They both ended up working for him, but it was Sherrill with whom Stafford really clicked. "He and Billy hit it off," said Tony Couch. "Tom saw Billy's potential, and him and Tom set up that studio together over this drugstore." There above City Drug Store (co-owned by Stafford's family) was a lone room without plumbing that had been deserted by a podiatrist and which now became home to Spar Music Company.

A plethora of characters hung out in the studio, and a few lucky ones managed to live there. Sherrill and Hall had previously been catching shut-eye under a bridge in a '42 Mercury. "Tom kept us all alive there for a while," said Sherrill. "A bunch of us paid no rent. We'd go down and steal candy bars from the drugstore." The friendship with Tom Stafford spurred Billy's growth. To Sherrill, Stafford was "everything rolled into one, from a dope addict to a philosopher to a guy who ended his life preaching against drugs. . . . We'd sit and talk for hours . . . all the other guys were boring, all they wanted to do was make music, make records, get drunk, and go to bed."

One wonders if Sherrill is referring to Rick Hall here. Tom Stafford ran the Florence movie theater and would let his cronies in for free, an idea that particularly appealed to Sherrill, a movie nut whose big favorite was *Shane*. "Rick wanted to work in the studio all the time, and Billy wanted to go watch the movies," said Kelso Herston. "Rick didn't like that." Hall was in a hurry to get somewhere, while Sherrill was lethally nonchalant, the type who clocked miles on the career odometer without even bothering to check if there was gas in the tank. The inscrutable one claims to have had no plan. It was just "one day at a time, as the old song goes."

Dan Penn encountered Sherrill, Stafford, and the rest of the mob for the first time as a teenager, when he sat in with Benny Cagle's band at a Sulligent, Alabama, square dance. "*Rural* square dancing," Penn clarified. "You'd do-si-do 'round and 'round, just a big circle in a big room. Not any intricate, *real* square dancin'. Everybody was sippin' that wildcat whiskey. Billy Sherrill was playin' electric saxophone—he had it run through an amp and a little ol' mic fixed up on it."

When Tony Couch quit Cagle's band, Penn became their singer. One night after a gig Sherrill mentioned he'd heard Penn had been writing songs, and Dan sat down and played him a few. "Why don't you come up to Florence," Sherrill suggested. "We got a little studio up there, we might cut a record on you."

Penn, accompanied by Tony Couch, headed to Florence and Tom Stafford's studio. "It's twelve o'clock in the day," recalled Penn. "We knocked, ain't nobody answerin'. Finally somebody come to the door. There was four grown men in there asleep—Rick Hall, Billy Sherrill, Hurschel Wiginton, and Earl 'Peanutt' Montgomery. They got up slowly and wiped the sleep from their faces. Four grown men there still asleep at noon! I said, 'This is the life for me.'"

"Spar was the first studio I'd ever seen. It had this particular smell— studios just all smell that way, it don't matter how big or how little. It's still that same thing, just a sensation that it gave you—kind of like, 'I'm gonna record you and play it back.' It was one room, hardwood floors, all these egg crates on the wall, a really good-soundin' upright piano, a couple of mics on a stand, maybe three at the most, and a little bitty ol' mixer goin' into a Berlant Concertone tape recorder." Penn paused. "'Course, nobody down there knew what in the world they was doin'.'"

That day they cut a few of Penn's songs, and one of Billy's, "Crazy over You," which would be the A-side of Penn's first single on Earth Records, released in 1960. (Dan's birth name was actually Pennington; it was Sherrill who'd suggested he shorten it for showbiz.) As far as I know, it is Billy Sherrill's first production credit. Penn returned home to Vernon, Alabama, unaware that one of the songs he'd demoed for Sherrill, "Is a Bluebird Blue?," wound up being cut by Conway Twitty. "A month later Tom Stafford called me and said, 'Dan, do you know you got a song goin' up the charts? It's not only on the charts, it's got a bullet. You've got to join BMI.' I said, 'What's that?'" Penn's first check went to the purchase of a souped-up '54 Chevy from his uncle. "That was my introduction to the business of music. I seen right quick you could buy a car if you got lucky."

Sherrill's confidence in the studio made a big impression on Penn. "He told somebody to do somethin', they did it. Most of us back then, we were green and dumb, didn't know nothin' about music. Billy was the same way, except he was quite a few steps quicker than everybody else. I didn't think anybody in that part of the country could get anywhere or do anything. I had no faith. But you had a sense *this* guy could."

Around this same time the Sherrill-Hall partnership suffered its inevitable bust-up. Hall claimed he was fired by Tom Stafford and Billy; Sherrill's version is he got tired of Rick's pushy ways and sold him his share of FAME for a dollar. "Rick just took things too seriously," said Sherrill. According to one friend who knew them both, "I think there was a little jealousy there. Friction."

Sherrill the R & B fan headed to Nashville and the world of country; Hall remained in Florence, abandoning his love of the hillbilly hit parade to record soul music. "I was kind of thought of as the guy who was hangin' on to Billy Sherrill's coattails in order to make it," Hall told Barney Hoskyns. "I was pissed off about that." He'd first score with Arthur Alexander's 1962 smash "You Better Move On," which paved the way for FAME Studios' productions of such singers as Wilson Pickett, Joe Tex, Candi Staton, and Clarence Carter, not to mention such lesser-known but spine-tingling singles as "I Worship the Ground You Walk On" by Jimmy Hughes. Just as Billy would rise to the top in Nashville, Hall would produce some of the greatest soul music ever, records that were every bit as deep and gut-wrenching as any of Sherrill's Nashville ballads.

Nashville, a strange place. Whenever I'm there I detect no vibe whatsoever other than "bland." Imagine that you're at the dry cleaners, they've lost your pants, and you're expecting them to be found. Then imagine you've been standing there waiting for forty-seven years. Country music historian Robert K. Oermann points out that the town was dry until the late sixties. "I find it ironic that the music business settled here because Nashville is such a brown-shoe town. People don't know how to dance in Nashville. It's so funny, because everything on the face of it in terms of the complexion of the city is not fun, and music is fun. . . . Pittsburgh is more fun than Nashville!"

It was a four-grand royalty check that brought Billy Sherrill to Music City. "Your Sweet Love," a song he'd written, wound up as the B-side of a 1962 hit by Bob Beckham. Sherrill thought no more of it until he went to the mailbox one day. "All of the sudden four G rolls in," said Sherrill, who was so shocked at the amount he called Buddy Killen of Tree Publishing, who'd sent the loot. "I said, 'What is this, a mistake?' Each member of the Fairlanes was makin' about thirty-five a week. That was it. I said, 'I'm in the wrong place, doin' the wrong stuff. I'm goin' to Nashville.'"

At the time Nashville was a hotbed for recording, and not just country. Roy Orbison, Buddy Holly, Bobby "Blue" Bland, and Gene Pitney were but a few of the acts who had cut hits there. In Music City the producer was the star. He came up with the songs, picked the players, and created the sound. Just as Hollywood had Hitchcock and John Ford, Nashville had its own auteurs, and in the fifties and sixties men like Owen Bradley, Chet Atkins, Don Law, and Bob Ferguson were at the top of the heap.

Music Row—the cluster of blocks where the country music industry took root—started when Owen and Harold Bradley built a studio at 804 Sixteenth Avenue South. Originally they recorded in a duplex, adding out back a Quonset Hut, an arched-roof, military-style prefab structure they'd bought for $7,500. Initially the Quonset Hut was used as a film studio, but the house in front of it proved too cramped for recording. The Bradleys souped up the Quonset Hut with the exacting attention to detail of some hot-rodders tricking out an old Caddy, enabling them to, as Michael Kosser put it in his essential history *How Nashville Became Music City, USA*, "turn a corrugated metal building with no acoustic merit into a studio that would be the home of hit records for more than two decades." Billy Sherrill would record nearly all of his Tammy sessions there.

"I loved everything about the studio," said Tanya Tucker. "The seedy-looking carpets, overflowing ashtrays, and Coke cans strung throughout the place." When asked what was so special about Studio B, bassist Bob Moore gave a one-word answer he'd copped from Owen Bradley: *spizzerinctum.* "Here is how Owen described it: You've been drivin' down the road out in the country, it's springtime, and a horse has just had a little baby colt," said Moore. "That colt is about a month old and just kinda walkin' around. And all of a sudden it will jump up in the air and kick and run for no reason—just do it. That's called 'spizzerinctum.' That's what we had in that studio. And that's why all the musicians knew what each other was going to do without it ever being said. Spizzerinctum was not necessarily just the room. It was the whole combination—the songwriters and the engineers and the musicians and the producers. Every now and then you'd jump up and click your heels."

Owen Bradley, of course, was there first, cutting hit after hit on Ernest Tubb, Patsy Cline, and Brenda Lee. Another sometime piano player, Bradley developed a spartan, uncluttered sound that was a big influence on Billy Sherrill. "Somebody asked me one time who was my favorite country producer. I said, 'You mean *besides* Owen Bradley?' He could produce a record in 1954 that sounds like it was produced last night. None of his stuff is ever dated. 'I'm Sorry' by Brenda Lee, Patsy Cline's 'I Fall to Pieces'—his stuff just slays me. They're just beautiful, timeless records. Owen was it."

Yes, Billy had changed his mind about hillbilly music, all because of a little ditty he'd heard on the radio coming home from a Fairlanes gig in his yellow and black '57 Chevy. The song was "Seasons of My Heart," and the singer was George Jones. "I thought, 'This is the damnedest thing I ever heard—this guy makes a five-syllable word out the word "church."' . . . Turned me on to country." Little did Sherrill know that less than ten years later he'd be recording Jones himself.

Not that country and R & B were the only sounds flooding Billy's cranium. He dug Johann Strauss. And the equally dramatic Phil Spector. "I loved the way he had all these instruments together. He'd have this little black girl singer surrounded by what sounded like a thousand people. And he made the drums sound like they were ten feet across. *Dumdumdumdum pow, dumdedum pow,* 'The night we met . . .' You could barely hear her, she was almost drowning in a sea of music."

Sherrill built and ran a small independent studio on the third floor of the old Masonic Lodge in downtown Nashville that was also home to the offices of recent Alabama transplants Kelso Herston and Buddy Killen. When it looked like the studio was going under, Sherrill prodded Herston to rope his then-boss Sam Phillips into eyeballing the joint. Phillips wound up buying the place, and Herston then convinced him to keep Sherrill on as engineer. "Sam didn't want to hire him," said Herston. "He thought Billy was too young."

Phillips relented and paid Sherrill a hundred bucks a week to engineer sessions for the likes of Jerry Lee Lewis and Fats Domino. Working for the grand pooh-bah of Sun Records was a watershed event for Billy. "Sam probably helped me more than anybody. He never pressured me. The biggest thing he ever taught me was, don't worry about every little mistake, that you're probably the only person in the world that will ever hear it anyway. He taught me not to obsess over things that weren't totally perfect. One of his favorite sayings was when I'd be mixing something and he'd be standing background. He'd say, 'You got it really loud, Billy boy? You got to have everything up loud. It's gotta sound good when you take it home and play it on your little kitchen radio.' His whole philosophy of music helped me. Sam let me do what I wanted to do in the studio after hours, all free, 'cause

I was his engineer," recalled Sherrill. "I'd make records and sell 'em to various labels make ends meet."

The most successful of these was "Tipsy," a 1963 instrumental tribute to alcohol, complete with pouring booze and popping cork sound effects. Concrete evidence that Sherrill had gotten over his disdain for drink, he played all the instruments on the record, as "I couldn't afford to hire anybody else." He was the first person to overdub in Nashville, which swiftly brought him to the attention of the Musicians' Union, who demanded he stop as it robbed musicians of a live session. "I kept right on overdubbing. I would do it all hours of the day and night because I knew they couldn't watch me all the time." Nashville was to learn quickly that no one could tell Billy what to do.

The Fairlanes' handful of off-the-wall singles are well worth seeking out as they display the irks and quirks of a man in search of some very strange sounds. The year 1960 begat the rollicking "If the World Don't End Tomorrow," a self-penned number inspired by the Coasters. Two years later came "The Dagwood," a lowdown dance inspired by the comic strip character that featured a panty-removing vocal by Tony Couch (during which Sherrill can be heard exclaiming, "I lost my twist radio"). It was a hit in such outposts as Shreveport and Oklahoma City, enabling the Fairlanes to rock the frat circuit.

On these crude early singles Sherrill's talent is already in evidence: inventive arrangements, great harmonies, not to mention odd touches that could only come from a demented mind. Listen to his ghoulish 1961 solo single "Rules of the Game," a slow-drag, echo-drenched tale of love gone wrong featuring doo-wop zombie backing vocals and the whap of a wet-sock drum. The Fairlanes' swan song on vinyl—released under the moniker "The Rainbows"—is the truly cuckoo "Gonna Go Down (To See My Baby)," a smutty paean to oral sex awash in skin-crawling, pistonlike percussion. With lyrics extolling the virtues of "the little man in the boat," it was not destined to be championed by the likes of Dick Clark. Sherrill soon quit the band, got married, and concentrated on studio work.

It was during this period that Lillian Evans, Sherrill's new mother-in-law (and financial advisor—she would make Billy a fortune in real estate), talked a powerful song publisher by the name of Al Gallico into paying Sherrill a visit. As Billy recalled, "She said, 'You gotta hear this guy play—he writes songs, he makes records all by hisself.' And she brought him down." Gallico, who had been in the business since the days when swarms of song pluggers would lurk outside the studio hoping to pitch songs to Bing Crosby, was to be one of Sherrill's most powerful allies.

An abrasive, heavyset Italian, Gallico was a fish out of water in Nashville and beloved because of it. "Al was a New Yorker—he'd come down here and bitch about the food," said producer and songwriter Norro Wilson. "He should've been Fred Flintstone. That's the way he talked—he growled. Al was a one-man band. He got really interested in Nashville and Nashville music."

For kicks Sherrill told his longtime secretary Emily Mitchell to ask Gallico why he never wore sunglasses. "He said, 'Because I look like I'm Mafia'— and he did!" said Mitchell. "He coulda been the Godfather." To the Sherrill crew he practically was. "If you had the greatest song on earth, he'd find a way to buy the publishin' from you before he walked out the door," said songwriter Glenn Sutton. "He was a deal maker, he could get anything done. I loved Al. He fucked me several times, but a lotta guys did. It's the music business. You gotta walk with a lead pair of shorts on."

"We kinda became buddies," said Sherrill. "He helped me a lot. He knew everybody in the world. If I had a little master, he'd take it to the record companies. I gave him the publishin'—he didn't do it for nothin'. Introduced me to a lot of people—like Clive Davis, back when Clive was a mere human."

In 1964 Sherrill was hired as a staff producer for Epic Records. He cut R & B for the OKeh subsidiary, producing such acts as Major Lance, Ted Taylor, Obrey Wilson, and a tremendous live-in-church album of the Staple Singers. (He tried to talk Mavis Staples into doing a secular record, but Pops put a stop to that fast.) "For eight grand a year I'd produce anything they would let me produce. But everything was kind of mediocre until 'Almost Persuaded' sold forty thousand records in one day in Atlanta."

Which is where a highly entertaining scallywag with a world-class pompadour of white named Glenn Sutton slips into the picture. Sutton had been writing songs since the days when he'd ask his mother to grade his initial efforts at age ten. He'd cut a few rockabilly records and written for Starday before Al Gallico hired him in mid-1964 as a fifty-dollar-a-week songwriter. Sherrill's office was right down from Gallico's, and Billy and Glenn started hanging out at lunch, playing pinball. Sutton said he turned Sherrill on to a lot of country music. Sherrill might've already experienced a George Jones epiphany in his old Chevy, but by his own admission he "knew as much about country as the Shah of Iran."

Sutton—a sometime wrestler, a full-time prankster, but first and foremost: a great songwriter. In 1968 he'd pen the Jerry Lee Lewis country smash "What Made Milwaukee Famous (Has Made a Loser Out of Me)," a title he conjured up in a moment of desperation one day when Al Gallico called during a mixing session.

"Gallico would call ya at the weirdest times," Sutton recalled. "He said, 'Jerry Lee's comin' in, ya gotta have somethin' for him.'" Sutton had already bullshitted Gallico previously that he had a song written. Now it was two weeks later and, as Sutton recalled, "I ain't got shit." Glenn told him he'd bring over the thus-far-nonexistent song in the morning. He figured he was momentarily off the hook, until Gallico asked, "Wait a minute—what's the title of it, so I can tell Jerry?"

Now Sutton was in a panic. Jerry Lee was one of his heroes, and he had to deliver. At that moment inspiration struck in the form of a newspaper on the floor that one of the engineers had tossed. "As God is my witness, I look down at the paper, and there's a full-page ad with a Schlitz beer can on it. It said, 'The Beer of Milwaukee.' And I told Gallico, 'It's called "What Made Milwaukee Famous."'" Al said, 'That's a GREAT title, kid.' I went home, stayed up all night 'bout half drunk, and wrote it. They cut it two days later in one take."

Sutton had a way with a country lyric. In ten pared-down-to-the-nub lines he'd create a little universe the listener could live in and return to, all by merely dropping a nickel in a jukebox. He knew how to hit it and quit, and his words fit the artist recording them as snugly as a low-cut frock stuck to Sophia Loren. You haven't lived until you've heard Jerry Lee drawl out the line "Payday nights and painted women, they do strange things to me" in the Sutton masterpiece "She Still Comes Around (To Love What's Left of Me)." Sutton would follow Sherrill to Epic and become a producer there, cutting the 1971 monster crossover hit "(I Never Promised You A) Rose Garden" for his then-wife Lynn Anderson.

"Glenn Sutton was a maniac, a total wild man," noted engineer Ron "Snake" Reynolds. "He was pretty much drunk all the time, and he had the mind of a sixteen-year-old." Glenn kept a gorilla suit in his office and amused himself by sending out office memos to all the secretaries that they were to submit to a mandatory physical exam by a doctor whose last name happened to be Sutton. At night the cleaners had to steel themselves before entering Glenn's office. "They'd come in and find him naked," said Reynolds. "Passed out on the floor with his head in a trash can."

Sutton plus Sherrill—now there was a depraved combo. "They were amazing together," said Steve Popovich, then a vice president of promotion at CBS. "Billy and Glenn were so against the grain. They never took it real serious. That was left to New York or Los Angeles." Billy was the kind of guy who, as he walked away from you, might mutter anything under his breath; Glenn was the type who didn't mind repeating it for you—and embellishing it if it wasn't crude or rude enough. "We just laughed ourselves through life," said Sherrill. "Glenn had the weirdest, quickest sense of humor of everybody I've ever known."

This was not songwriting produced by appointment books or quota, as is the case in current-day Nashville. After everybody had left for the day Sherrill and Sutton would grab a bottle of what Billy liked to call "the nectar of the gods"—J & B scotch—and write. "Glenn wasn't all that good with melodies," said Sherrill. "I was a better melody man. He just had that knack—lyrics. Sutton always amazed me, the way he came up with lines."

"Lotta times Billy would have nearly a whole melody and I'd put lyrics to it," Sutton confirmed. "His office was upstairs. He'd come to me and say, 'What about this line?' I'd work on it, come up with two or three more. I don't remember us ever sittin' down and writin' one all the damn way through. We worked on songs lazily . . . we might write a line a month." They were a ferocious writing team, one who delivered the goods right up through Johnny Paycheck's 1978 "Outlaw's Prayer" and were responsible for such Tammy Wynette classics as "I Don't Wanna Play House," "Take Me to Your World," "Your Good Girl's Gonna Go Bad," "Kids Say the Darndest Things," and "The Ways to Love a Man."

"Almost Persuaded" came about one night after Sherrill and Sutton had gone out for chow with Gallico. "We went to dinner, it got late, and we went out to Billy's house to write. Damn Gallico wanted to go with us. Billy said, 'How the hell are we gonna write with *him* lookin' at us?' Gallico just sat there and stared at us as we piddled with piano and guitar."

"We spent all night writin' that song," Sherrill continued. "We'd write a little bit, go have a scotch, eat somethin', come back, write." Finally a song took shape, but it wasn't complete until Sherrill raided the hymnbook. "We still didn't have a title to it or bridge—we had the verses," said Sutton. "There was a Broadman hymnal book layin' there on his piano. Billy was just thumbin' through it. He opened to the old Albert E. Brumley song. He said, 'What the hell's wrong with 'Almost Persuaded'?"

Ripping off a gospel title was the icing on the cake. As Sherrill would point out many times over the years, "Almost Persuaded" clashed with many a Nashville guideline at the time: it was a waltz, it was over three minutes, and the title phrase came late. "The punch line was at the ass-end of the song," said Sherrill. "We broke all the rules." Proud of their work, they went in to share it with Billy's wife, Charlene, who was fixing breakfast. "We sang the whole thing to her. She said, 'You're kidding. That's the silliest thing I ever heard.' We didn't know whether to shit or go blind."

The song was intended for honky-tonk singer Charlie Walker, but he was on the road, so Sherrill cut it with new artist David Houston. There in Studio B, Hargus "Pig" Robbins laid down those brief, stuttering notes on the piano that define the record. This would be one of Billy's great strengths— adorning songs with quizzical little licks that burrow straight into the brain.

Not that Sherrill had any real confidence in the song his wife had laughed at. He slapped the song onto the B-side of a number called "We Got Love" and promptly forgot about it. And then the phone started ringing. Atlanta ordered forty thousand copies of the single. Curious, Sherrill called up Mac Curtis, the disc jockey and ex-rockabilly singer who'd broken the record, asking if "We Got Love" was indeed that popular. Curtis didn't know what the hell he was talking about. It was the flipside—"that song that's got the piano goin' *deedle-dee-dee*"—that had lit the switchboards up. "It was people—with a capital P—that turned that record over," said Sherrill.

The song shot to number one in mid-August 1966, and remained there for nine weeks. It went on to become a country standard cut by hundreds of singers, including such unlikely candidates as Louis Armstrong and Jim Nabors. The fact that Billy had co-opted a spiritual didn't sit well with some. "I got hate letters," said Sherrill. "'You have desecrated that great old hymn.' Well, I'm gonna cry about that all the way to the bank."

After the Houston hit came Tammy, and then the rest of the mob. "The seventies became the Billy Sherrill generation," said Steve Popovich, who was vice president of promotion at CBS. "At that time we were kickin' everybody's ass in country." For a decade every note Sherrill touched turned to gold. How much corporate ass did Sherrill have to kiss? "Very little," he admitted. "I was good at what I did, and they couldn't do any better. And I knew that *they* knew that I knew they couldn't do any better . . . it's a very comforting thing." The vibe to the Sherrill compound was laid-back. Where the rest of Music City, USA, execs and artists sported suits, either business or Nudie, Billy favored Sansabelt slacks augmented by silken polyester shirts festooned with tigers. "A lotta times the secretaries would wear these white short-shorts and black boots," said art director Bill Barnes, who also noted that security guard Ed Grizzard could often be found "eating fried chicken in the waiting room. We weren't that corporate."

"I never felt like I was workin' for Epic," said Emily Mitchell. "I was workin' for Billy Sherrill. We were in our own little isolated world." Not a world easy to gain admittance to, mind you. Outside of a special secret hotline Sherrill kept in a wooden box behind his desk, he never answered the phone and admitted few people into his inner sanctum. "That was the worst part of my job," said Mitchell. "I had to be the bulldog at the door. I will never go to heaven—I have lied so much, even to the artists." At one point Sherrill had a line installed from Studio B up to his office so he didn't even have to attend the recording in person if he didn't want to. About halfway through a Paycheck session, a distraught Johnny went up to his office. "Aren't you even gonna come down? It's like you don't even give a shit!"

It appears Sherrill didn't give a shit about much. Eminently quotable, he gave few interviews, and didn't take it too seriously when he did. Lou Bradley recalled the day a scribe from *Rolling Stone* came by to pick Billy's brain. "Has anything changed since your success?" asked the writer. "Yes, the word 'love' has gone out of my vocabulary," Billy replied. "Boy, the guy's pencil got really sharp," said Bradley. "He got up on the edge of his chair, he had a scoop here. He said, 'Waddya mean, the word "love" has gone out of your vocabulary'? Billy said, 'I used to say, "I'd *love* to go to Hawaii, I'd *love* to cruise the Greek Islands." Now I do it.'"

"One day Larry Gatlin came in the office and sat down," Glenn Sutton recalled. "He was on the label. Gatlin said, 'Y'know, Billy, you haven't really cut any of my songs. Have you listened to this song on my new album, "The Heart"?' Billy said, 'Larry, contrary to what you might think, I just don't sit around here listenin' to your fuckin' albums.' I about fell out! Larry Gatlin just kinda . . . walked out."

Nobody was immune and nothing was sacred. One day old Alabama pal Carmol Taylor—who'd recently cowritten a Joe Stampley hit with Billy and his cousin Mark, "Red Wine and Blue Memories"—walked into Sherrill's office sporting a grave look on his face. He sadly announced, "I got some bad news. I just got back from the doctor yesterday. I've got lung cancer." Even Billy seemed shocked as he recalled his response. "I said, 'Then can I have your third of "Red Wine and Blue Memories"?'" Taylor thought about it for a moment and, luckily for Billy, started to laugh.

Of course, not all were amused by Sherrill's ways. Sometime in the eighties Glenn Sutton appeared on a TV show with then-ex-wife Lynn Anderson. He stopped by her dressing room to say hello and to inform her that Billy had undergone open-heart surgery. "Bullshit," said Lynn. "He hasn't got a heart."

Billy's personality, people will tell you, had some dark nooks and crannies. String arranger Bergen White recalled heading over to Sherrill's home one day for a meeting. Surrounded by tall fences and a "great big monstrous gate," the house "looked like Fort Knox." Once he'd cleared security, White mentioned to Sherrill that some kids had done some wheelies in his yard and torn down his basketball goal. Apparently one of the juveniles in question had dated Sherrill's daughter. "Billy said to me, 'Just put up another goal. Get you some electrodes and attach 'em on that sucker. The next time one of them goes out and grabs it, you'll find 'em hangin' out there like a piece of bacon.' He was dead serious. He said, 'I'll hire somebody, I'll take care of this.' He was talkin' about havin' this person eliminated!"

Sherrill's interest in Hitler and all things Third Reich raised an eyebrow or two. Back in the seventies George Jones, who seemingly has bought a car about every ten minutes throughout his professional life, wound up with a 1938 Steyr that had belonged to a Nazi bigwig. It wasn't long before Sherrill snatched it away. "I got it for a real good price, and Billy beat me out of it," said Jones. "He was a fanatic on Hitler." Sherrill spent a fortune and at least five years having the vehicle restored. Eve Zibart, then a young reporter Billy had taken under his wing, was in his office one day when Sherrill rubber-stamped her hand with a red swastika. Zibart, who is Jewish, was somehow amused, but her parents weren't. "It caused a lot of discussion that night at the dinner table."*

Glenn Sutton recalled one outing when he and Billy were taking their wives out to Sherrill's boat. "Damn if he didn't tell the entire story of *Mein Kampf* all the way to the lake. Forty-five minutes! He said, 'Lemme tell you, Hitler was a great man.'" Sutton said that during meetings Sherrill would sometimes muse, "What would Hitler do?"

Who knows how much of this was for effect, because underneath it all lurked something of a softie. Sherrill told Emily Mitchell that he hated cats, but the minute a stray showed up around the offices, he worried until the feline found a home. If he saw a drunk out in the alley he'd send Sutton out with food. "Billy has the greatest respect for old people," noted Mitchell. When his mother-in-law was in the hospital, "Billy would go up there and brush her hair for hours on end." When Steve Popovich's assistant was hospitalized with chest pains, "Billy Sherrill sat there every day in the waiting room. The man has a real heart of gold."

The riddles never end with Billy Sherrill. "He was so contrary," said Mitchell. "There's just too many facets to him. It's just impossible to explain Billy. I never figured him out." Jerry Kennedy felt the same way. "He's one of the strangest little people I've ever worked with in my life, man." Kennedy laughed. "You would think he was the last person in the world who needed anybody. That's the only way I know how to describe Billy." Even Glenn Sutton, who knew Sherrill better than most, found him inscrutable. "You couldn't get close to him."

"We are manufacturers of songs," songwriter, producer, and Sherrill crony Norro Wilson proudly announced to *Billboard* in 1975. These days the Nashville songwriting machine operates with the bland efficiency of a McDonald's drive-through. Writers carry appointment books, collaborate in cowriting teams that have all the sizzle of an arranged marriage, and generally acquiesce to the seemingly endless input and interference of artists,

---

*It appears Billy had a penchant for rubber stamps. Producer Steve Buckingham inherited Sherrill's office when he left CBS, and Billy gave him a pair of the ones he'd sometimes use to stamp rejected demos before returning them. One inexplicably said only GOON; the other was a map of Texas with a star illustrating the location of the appropriately named city listed above it: EL PASO. After bequeathing Buckingham with these gifts, Billy "puts his arm around me, walks me to the door, and says, 'I've just got one piece of advice: artists, they're all crazy.'"

producers, and label executives. Back in Tammy's era it was already heading in that direction, but it was a lot more down-home—a mom-and-pop diner with many an open stool.

Songwriter Bobby Braddock, part of the posse at Buddy Killen's Tree Publishing, recalled the days when you could mosey into fellow writer Curly Putman's office, see who was hanging out, and write a song if the spirit hit you. "Nashville was very, very loose in the old days. You had a lot more characters, writers that were hangin' out in bars and writin' songs while they were drinkin' beer. You'd light up a joint, pass around a bottle of wine, listen to each other's songs. Everybody who had a song recorded knew everybody else who had a song recorded. There are so many writers now, I don't know who they all are. You go into a publishing company, and what other writers are doin', nobody knows or really cares. It's very corporate at every level. At Tree, I could sit down with the guy who owned the company."

The hunger for a hit was ever present, but in those days it often coexisted with a deep need to spill your guts. "Songwriting was this thing you did late at night," Bill Anderson told Philip Self. "You closed the door and saw how miserable you could get and wrote a song . . . Songwriting was a lonely thing." That sort of mood would permeate many a Tammy cut, including such gripping works of despair as Red Lane and Larry Henley's "'Til I Get It Right" and Mickey Newbury's "I Don't Think About Him No More."

If you had a song to pitch, Billy Sherrill was the man with the golden ears. "I was able to get in and see him," said Bobby Braddock. "Not a lotta people did." Braddock, along with Curly Putman and Jones crony Earl "Peanutt" Montgomery, were allowed an audience, as was Sherrill's own personal posse of writers at Epic: Glenn Sutton, Norro Wilson, George Richey, and Carmol Taylor.

The finished product did not always adhere to the songwriter's lyric. "Billy is one of the few producers who can add a line to a song himself and get by with it," said Braddock, who learned after the fact that Sherrill had changed a lyric in Tanya Tucker's 1975 hit "I Believe the South's Gonna Rise Again" and inserted the couplet "the Jones and Wynette set / Aint' the flamin' Suzette set" into the end of George and Tammy's "(We're Not) The Jet Set." "He just added it on the fade-out," said Braddock. "Maybe the best line in the song. He'd do it without askin' me. That was Billy . . . that's somethin' I wouldn't let *anybody* do. But Billy was so good at it that it didn't matter."

If Sherrill didn't have a hand in writing the hit himself, he found it else-where. "A good song lasts three hours in this town," he told John Grissim in 1970, and like a big-game hunter whose prey lurked somewhere in the mountain of tapes and acetates crowding his desk, he was determined to bag them all. "Hiring somebody else to listen to your songs for you is like hiring somebody to make love to your wife," Sherrill mused.

It didn't hurt that Billy was pals with two of the most powerful publishers in town, Buddy Killen and Al Gallico. "Buddy was probably my closest friend," he said. "We traveled all over the world together." But he was well aware they needed him as much as he needed them. "Check and see how many Tree songs were cut by Billy. Killen took good care of Billy," said Glenn Sutton, who would watch in amusement as both Killen and Gallico would try to curry Sherrill's favor. "Gallico would go to the garment district and give everybody expensive shirts that we didn't have around here. He gave Billy three. Sherrill said, 'Man, you oughtta see the fuckin' *car* Killen bought me.' You know what Billy's nickname for Gallico was?" asked Sutton, laughing. "The Greaseball. I'd come in the office and he'd say, 'Greaseball just called.'"

"If Billy believed in a song, son, it was damn the torpedoes, full speed ahead," said Lou Bradley, who likes to point out that when promotion men declared Ray Price's "For the Good Times"—a Columbia single Sherrill didn't even produce—a stiff, he instructed them to ship it again. And again. Finally, it was a hit. "Fifth time," said Bradley.

"If someone brings in a hit song to me, I know I'm ninety-five percent home," said Sherrill. "Going into the studio to record is the other five percent." Nearly all the musicians who worked for Sherrill say one reason for that was the fact that Billy often had a vision of the song before he went into the studio. "He knew what he wanted," said drummer Jerry Carrigan. "Billy could take the same group of musicians that had just worked for another guy, put them in the studio, work with them, and make them sound totally different, and better."

"Billy was very knowledgeable musically, where a lot of producers would think triplets were three babies," said Bergen White. Plus there were the places he'd been—band member, engineer, songwriter. "He knew all sides of it," said Hargus "Pig" Robbins. "That's what I thought was so unique about him."

During the Tammy era, sessions were three hours long and you were usually expected to capture at least the same amount of songs in that time.

The lead singer, the band, and backup singers were usually all recorded live, excluding strings, although on occasion they, too, were cut live. Glenn Sutton said that they often didn't even have a demo to play the pickers. And he or Billy would play it for them on either piano or guitar. There was no written music like you'd get in Los Angeles or New York City—musicians utilized the Nashville Numbering System, a shorthand for chord progressions that can be easily adapted to changing keys.

Sessions were generally at ten a.m., two p.m., six p.m., and ten p.m., Monday through Friday.* Weekends meant overtime, an unpopular concept in Nashville, a place where you could cut a record fast and cheap by people who knew what they were doing. "Scale for a player then was $51.50," said producer Jerry Kennedy, who moonlighted on guitar for Sherrill sessions. "Studio time was forty-five an hour, plus tape. Three hours' time, a couple of rolls of tape, six or seven players—it cost twelve or fifteen hundred bucks for some of these sessions."

When rock publications like *Rolling Stone* mocked the assembly-line nature of Nashville recording, it irritated people like Charlie McCoy. "We're in the music business here. This is not an art center, you know—it's business." The idea of spending months and millions on one album like they did in the rock world was, at least in Sherrill's era, an unimaginable pretension in Nashville.

"Me and Sherrill went to an Eagles concert one night—CBS gave us tickets," said Glenn Sutton. "Here these guys got a mixing board as big as a hotel room in the center of the auditorium. After every number there's a guy who just *tunes all the guitars.*" Billy stared at all this parade rock grandeur for three or four numbers and, musing on Nashville's place in the hierarchy, muttered to Sutton, "We ain't even on the edge of the fuckin' record."

Lacy J. Dalton thought she'd doomed her recording contract with Columbia because the first time she met Sherrill they wound up at a restaurant "practically screaming at each other about Bob Dylan. He was saying the only good song Dylan ever wrote was 'Blowin' in the Wind.' And I said, 'Oh, you're just an opinionated old ass.'" According to Dalton, the evening ended with her "sticking a fork in his shoulder."

Dylan, of course, made the trek to Nashville, leading a bunch of fellow

*Sherrill had a permanent lock on the two o'clock time in Studio B. The time "had always been real lucky for me," he said. Luck had nothing to do with it, said Pig Robbins: "He didn't like to get up early!"

rockers to do the same, but Billy paid little attention to it. "I never was a fan of all that stuff," said Sherrill. "Somebody asked me my all-time favorite? I said Mel Tormé."

A major element of the Billy Sherrill magic: a group of Music City musicians known as the "A-Team." It's usually an exercise in futility asking a Nashville player what they remember about cutting song A or song B. The sheer volume of songs these musicians were involved in works against the memory. "You'd begin to get a little stir-crazy after you'd worked in the studio so many hours," said background singer Dolores Edgin. "We saw more of each other than we did our families. Sometimes on a break we'd get out and just run around the parking lot." "We had 'cancel buttons,'" said bassist Bob Moore. "When we walked out of a session and we were goin' to another one, we'd take our thumb, put it to our temple, and hit our cancel button. A lot of music that we did we had to forget so we were fresh for the next session."

The mighty six-foot, three-inch Moore played bass on many an early Tammy session. (Henry Strzelecki came later.) Surely one of the most recorded musicians in the history of Nashville, Moore has played on everything from Patsy Cline's "Crazy" to Elvis Presley's "A Fool Such as I" and Roy Orbison's "Crying." "Bob Moore was my absolute hero," said Jerry Kennedy, who had the nerve-racking challenge of producing Jerry Lee Lewis's country material for Mercury and counted on Moore to lead the band. "Jerry Lee never played anything the same way twice. Bob would sit on a stool and look over Jerry's shoulder and watch his left hand to know what kind of bass line to play."

You had Harold Bradley and then Tommy Allsup on tic-tac bass for Sherrill's sessions. Billy usually used two acoustic guitars and one electric on a date, drawing from a stellar pool that included Jerry Kennedy, Pete Wade, Billy Sandford, Phil Baugh, Jimmy Capps, Bobby Thompson, Chip Young, Kelso Herston, and Mac Gayden, not to mention Ray Edenton, famous for playing his "high third" on such Everly Brothers hits as "Bye, Bye Love" and "Wake Up, Little Susie." "Ray is one of the old heads that gave you what you wanted without you knowin' you wanted it," said Bob Moore. "He made *a sound* on the record."

These guitarists had played so many sessions together they knew who was to play what without anybody uttering a word. "If Billy Sandford walked in, he wouldn't bring any guitars in from his car until he saw who all was there," recalled Lou Bradley. "If he saw Jerry Kennedy, he'd bring in his acoustic; if no Jerry Kennedy, electric. If Pete Wade walked in and didn't see Jerry Kennedy or Billy Sandford, he'd go get his electric. They just kinda knew the peckin' order." According to Bob Moore, who sometimes produced his own sessions, such telepathy could also work against you in the studio. "I would always be lookin' out for the bass player and the drummer that I had hired. If they smiled at each other, you were gonna get a good session. If they didn't, you were in trouble."

On drums came the masterful Murray "Buddy" Harman. "He was the guy when I first came here, he was still the guy twenty years later," said Charlie McCoy. "Buddy could play any kind of music and play it with the right style rock and roll, country, jazz. And he could play soft—we'd have to beg him to play louder so we could stay with him. Vince Gill called him the 'Shuffle King.' Nobody had the country shuffle down like Buddy. The record felt good." Later came Sheffield, Alabama, native Jerry Carrigan, who added a bigger and sometimes bluesier drum sound to Sherrill's records. "Billy dared to be different. Some days I'd walk in there and he'd say, 'Carrigan, no drumsticks today. Play 'em with your hands, brooms—but no drumsticks.' Listen to George and Tammy's 'Golden Ring'—I'm usin' my hands." By the same token, Sherrill shunned fancy licks that might get in the way of the song. "If I was playin' little ghost notes between the beats, he'd say, 'Carrigan, save that stuff for Miles Davis.'"

There are two names that you hear repeatedly when you ask musicians about the Sherrill sound: steel player Pete Drake and pianist Hargus "Pig" Robbins. "The music started from the piano," said Lou Bradley. "That was the anchor." And there was no heavier weight on the 88s than Hargus Melvin "Pig" Robbins, the blind keyboardist whose playing graced such Sherrill productions as Charlie Rich's "Behind Closed Doors." What exactly did Pig add to the music? "Taste," said Bob Moore. "Pig put taste all around the room." "Pig is the greatest session man I've ever known," said harmonica player Charlie McCoy. "He's played the same set of chord changes so many times, because a lot of country music is very similar, but he always comes up with somethin' different, somethin' new. When Pig's on a session everybody else plays better."

Born in 1938, Robbins lost his sight at age three when he stuck a knife in his eye. He said his left-handed style came via the Carter Family: "I stole it from Mother Maybelle and the way she bent notes together." From Grady

Martin he learned it was "cool to play in between the lines and not on top of it." According to Harold Bradley, when the blind pianist first tried to join the Nashville Musicians' Union, "the president of the union tried to get him not to, he didn't think he'd get any work." But once Robbins's licks were featured on the George Jones 1959 number one smash, "White Lightning," his handicap was forgotten.

Pig, other players will tell you, has a phenomenal memory. Once Shelby Singleton was cutting an album of show tunes, and one number in particular was causing the pickers grief. "My chord chart on one song took three music stands, and it had three or four different tempos, and it modulated to this, that, and the other," recalled Ray Edenton, who said the band fumbled through the song until somebody asked Pig how it went. *"Blam, blam, blam*—he played the whole damn thing through on the second take and never made a mistake. If we ever wanted to know what a chord change was, we'd holler at Pig and those golden ears."

Bob Moore on bass, Pig on piano, and Buddy Harman on drums was a particularly lethal combo. "Pig was the best shuffle piano player in the world, and Bob Moore had the greatest swing," said Harman. "The three of us would groove like you wouldn't believe."

And then there is Pete Drake and his Talking Steel Guitar. "We kind of looked at the country band as an orchestra, not as a small little individual group," said Lou Bradley. "Pete Drake was Billy's horn section." You can hear Drake on "(I Never Promised You A) Rose Garden," Charlie Rich's "Behind Closed Doors," Bob Dylan's "Lay, Lady, Lay," and countless other hits. "I reckon ol' Pete was on more sessions than any other steel player," said Ray Edenton. "Ain't no tellin' how many number one records he's on. Pete could put it in the right spot. He just made the records sound different." There are those who say that his licks are simple and corny. Maybe so, but that made him perfect for country music. Listen to Drake's playing on Frankie Miller's unsung classic "It's Not Easy," and see if his slow, rolling notes of regret don't demolish you. Buddy Emmons might be the Jimi Hendrix of steel players, but Pete Drake is the Jimmy Reed.* "He didn't overdo," said Sherrill. "He knew when not to play."

---

*Bobby Braddock has an amusing anecdote concerning Emmons and Drake. Once they were in the studio together and Emmons said, "Hey, Pete—can you do this?" He then let rip some mind-boggling steel run. Said Braddock, "After the session they were both at the union and Pete went and picked up about 256 checks, flashed 'em, and said, 'Hey, Buddy—can you do *this?*'"

Augusta-born Roddis Franklin "Pete" Drake was, like Billy, a preacher's son. He had an ashtray screwed into his Sho-Bud steel, alongside a piece of rubber tubing attached to a parking meter–like gizmo that enabled Drake to "talk" through his guitar. He even had an open-stringed rigging on his steel he called his "Tammy Wynette pedal." Pete was "150 percent pro-Nashville," said guitarist Bill Hullett. "If you didn't love country music, you didn't belong here." The day George Harrison called to ask him to play on his *All Things Must Pass* album, Drake asked his secretary, "What company's he with?" "The *Beatles*," she responded. "The name just didn't ring a bell," admitted Pete. "I'm just a hillbilly."

When Bill Hullett was trying to break into the Nashville session scene in the late seventies and early eighties, Drake was his mentor. He tried to educate Hullett as to what sort of initiation rites he might expect in the studio, regaling him with tales of when he first started recording in the Quonset Hut alongside guitar great Grady Martin. "Pete said if Grady realized no one was really lookin' out of the glass at him, he might go over, put his foot out, and just kick Pete's steel right in the middle of a fill, and just grin, like, 'Waddya gonna do now, big boy?' They'd just screw with him. So he learned early on, don't ever let them see the fear in your eyes or you'll be like the little black chicken in the hen yards and they'll peck you to death. These guys all had that same eye of the tiger."

When Hullett finally got booked for a Billy Sherrill session, Pete practically put the fear of God into the young player, prepping him as if he were about to get in the ring and go head-to-head with Joe Frazier. Drake drilled the gospel of recording with Billy Sherrill into Hullett's head, which went something like this: "Billy never writes charts ahead of time, so when you get there get a paper and pencil. The second you hear music comin' over the loudspeaker, don't screw around and visit, write the stinkin' chart. And without even saying anything they're gonna rewind that cassette and play it again.

"Then we're gonna run the song down. Billy will probably come out the door and suggest, 'Why don't we do this going into the turnaround?' Or he may plink out two or three notes on the piano. Don't be screwin' around. Listen to every word he says, because when he says something, that's what he wants. Otherwise he's just leaving it up to the band. Don't question it or say, 'Billy, what if we do this instead?'

"Then we're gonna run it down again. That second time he's recording, and that's what he hopes to be his record. If someone screws up on the second take, he'll probably go that third run-through. Do *not* be the guy that screws up on the third run-through, because he'll probably say, 'Y'know what? I don't think this song is makin' it today,' and he'll move on to another. And George Jones or whoever is gonna remember that *your* mistake cut him out of that hit and next week Johnny Paycheck got it."

Guitarist Chip Young recalled the trial by fire that was his first Sherrill session. He had played on a 1965 demo of a song called "What Color (Is a Man)?" Somehow the song made its way to Sherrill. "Billy heard the song and heard this thumb-pickin' intro on a gut string I played. His office was next door to the publishing company I had done the demo for. Billy told them, 'I'll cut that song with Bobby Vinton—*if* you give me the guy who played guitar on the demo.'"

Young showed up at the studio only to find a half dozen of Nashville's heaviest guitarslingers, including perhaps the most formidable one of all, Grady Martin. And they had heard the tape of the song. "Billy Sherrill said, 'We got the guy who played on the demo, and he's gonna play on the record.'

"Grady Martin said, 'Who is that?'

"'This guy—Chip Young.'

"Grady looked around at me. 'Did you play that?'

"'Yessir.'

"'Let me hear you play it.'

"Boy, y'know, Grady was a like a bear in the studio, a big ol' bear. He made me get down, sit in front of him, and play that little lick. He said, 'You little son of a bitch, that's *good*.' We was best friends in the whole world after that. And Billy started usin' me on everything he did."

And that's just how fast it went in Studio B. "You had to have a song finished about every thirty-five or forty minutes," said Bill Hullett. "When you got there that morning, you'd never heard any of the songs, and when you left that evening, you'd have played on a whole album."

"Today the whole process crawls by; back in those days things moved at lightning speed," said engineer Ron "Snake" Reynolds. "We would literally cut a session in the morning, say, on George Jones. Billy'd say, 'That's the single, mix that.' I'd mix it at two, they'd take it downstairs, cut a demonstration record or a dub, send it over to the local radio station, and that night on the way home I would hear what I cut that day." Said Chip Young, "There was an expression in Nashville in those days: 'Don't leave it on too long, you'll burn the beans.'"

As was the fashion at the time, the musicians never had any credits on the back of Sherrill's albums. "Produced by Billy Sherrill" was all that the world needed to know. Sherrill had a reputation for being a dictator in the studio, and he encouraged such ideas by boasting to the press, "The guys I use are *machines*. They do *exactly* what I tell 'em to do and they don't stray from it. They never ask questions." As recently as 2007 esteemed country music historian Rich Kienzle referred to Sherrill as "the ultimate control freak" with a reputation for "not allowing even A-Team studio players the creative freedom Chet Atkins, Owen Bradley or Don Law encouraged." Bill Hullett said Sherrill's nickname among some of the players was "Little Hitler," and not just because of his fondness for Nazi memorabilia.

"Billy has one way of doing things: his way," said David Houston, who noted that the one time he made a creative suggestion in the studio, Sherrill announced he was going to the restroom and didn't return for hours. Houston then went on to compare Billy to General George S. Patton.

The great honky-tonk singer Lefty Frizzell, who'd been on Columbia for years, was supposed to be produced by Sherrill, but Billy dumped him on Sutton. "The only reason he gave him to me was Frizzell didn't want to cut a song he wanted to cut on him, 'Borrowed Angel.'" Frizzell's session with Sutton would be his last for the label. "That's the way Billy was," said Glenn. "When they dropped Lefty, he said to me, 'Hell, I guess I shoulda cut 'Borrowed Angel.'"

Most of those who worked with Billy paint a different picture. Sherrill "knew how to get the best out of his musicians," said Billy Sandford. "He was the best I ever saw about leavin' the musician alone. He was a champ." Buddy Harman agreed. "Billy would listen to you. He pretty well let you do what you wanted to if you had an idea." More than one picker compared him favorably to the ultimate of country music producers, Owen Bradley— but with one difference. "Owen Bradley could intimidate a telephone pole," said Tom Sparkman. "Sherrill was not that way at all. He'd go out and make suggestions, and before they got through they'd think what they were doin' was their idea."

Lou Bradley agreed. "The kiss of death for an engineer or a bunch of musicians is for somebody to walk in and throw a record down and say, 'I want my record to sound exactly like *that.*' Billy had the greatest tact—if the musicians were barkin' up the wrong tree, he would go out, sit down at the piano, and say, 'Guys, what if we did it this way?' Not 'Here's how we're gonna do it'—'What *if* we did it this way.'"

"When a guy can set in a control room, and you've got four guitar pickers—two rhythm, one electric, and one bass guitar goin'—and he can hit that talkback and say, 'Son, your third string is flat,' they've got a helluva ear on 'em," noted Tom Sparkman. And while he knew the technical intricacies of recording, he had learned from Sam Phillips not to get caught up in them. As Sherrill deadpanned to one reporter, "I've never heard anybody yet say, 'You know, I would've bought that record had he put a little 12,000 cycle on the sizzle cymbal.'"

Sherrill's main concern was the singer. He wanted them comfortable and focused on the task at hand. In order to keep the material fresh, he didn't let them rehearse much, and if a song wasn't working within a few takes, he'd move on. "Billy never did like to spend a lot of time," said guitarist Chip Young. "He wanted it to feel good. If there was a little mistake, it didn't wear him out, y'know. It had 'human' in it." Lou Bradley explained that Billy was a master at editing a performance together out of bits and pieces from a number of takes, rather than have the singer overdub a line there or a word here and risk draining the emotion out of a performance or making a singer "feel like they had this big mountain to climb. Billy would just have 'em sing the whole song, and keep track of what he needed."

Every once in a while you'd get a glimmer of what the music meant with Billy, but it vanished just as quickly. According to Tom Sparkman, "Kiss Away," a ballad cowritten with Sutton which he recorded with Tammy among others, was one that cut the deepest with Sherrill. "I have actually seen the guy put his head down on the desk when they're playin' that song back. And he'd leave you there, because he was relivin' what happened to him somewhere prior to that in his love life or whatever. That made such an impression on me, his reaction when he listened to somebody singin' that song. I'll remember it all my life because I could tell this guy has been hurt. 'Kiss Away' was written from his heart. He had lived that." Of course when I asked Sherrill about the song, he just shrugged as if it were just another number.

Sherrill's eternal poker face didn't fool Jerry Carrigan. "Man, he's one of the most emotional men I've ever known. You could tell when somethin' was botherin' him in the studio. He'd mope, he'd hang his head down, pace, and twirl that cigarette—roll it from side to side in his mouth—and say, 'Wait a minute, I know what it is. Pig, get up just a minute. This is what's buggin' me.'" Sherrill would sit at the piano, tinker with a riff or change this or that about the arrangement, they'd play it again and nail it. "From the heart and soul, that's what Billy wanted," said Carrigan. "Real human emotions that would well up in people and come out through their hands, through their instruments."

So now that you've met Billy and the boys, imagine it's 1966. You're stand-ing in a nondescript room with lots of wood on the walls and big heavy curtains at the back. You don't know why, but it strikes you as a comfort-able, warm place. And in that room are the finest musicians Nashville has to offer, instruments at hand, ready to do battle. Stepping up to the mic just right of the center of that room is one scared, skinny stick of a singer, an Alabama gal sporting some big, likably fake blonde hair. At the head of the room is a glassed panel allowing you to see inside the control room, where a terminally nervous Billy Sherrill sits with his engineer. He's got a song, and he wants a hit, or maybe even something a little more durable than that.

   "You're trying to pull a little moment out of forever with every record," he once said, and little ol' Wynette Pugh was just about to start helping him pull a whole lot of moments out of that forever.

Deeter-minded

I wrote more and sang better when I was sad.

—Tammy Wynette

"Just follow . . . the stairway . . ."

Looking on from the control room, Billy Sherrill listened as Wynette sang those four words and nearly swallowed his cigarette. "When I heard the first note outta her mouth, I thought, 'My God,'" he recalled. "I didn't know until I got her in the studio she was great."

The song "Apartment #9" happened fast, as a track usually did with Sherrill producing. He'd played the Bobby Austin record for the pickers, figured out the best key for Wynette, voiced his suggestions, and let 'er rip. "It was easy," he said. "Tammy is probably the quickest study I ever worked with. Sing it to her once, she knows it."

As she waited to lay down her first vocal, Wynette was clearly "scared to death," said Kelso Herston, who was watching from the control booth. "She was a nervous wreck."

But once she swooped into the number, "it floored the pickers," said Billy, adding that the players on the session—Bob Moore on bass, Jerry Kennedy on guitar, Pete Drake on steel, and Buddy Harman on drums—exchanged wordless, amazed glances at each other during the recording, just listening to Wynette sing. "Everybody just sorta stopped. I'm getting goose bumps now just thinkin' 'bout it. I never heard anything like her voice."

Jerry Kennedy's first impression of Wynette was of "a quiet little mousy lady, so humble. In a way I kind of felt sorry for her. She wanted it so bad, y'know. She was just kinda pitiful." After the session Kennedy called up Al Gallico, raving over the new voice in town. Gallico would soon become her publisher and her most important ally after Sherrill, but right now in Studio

B she was still another nobody. Billy recalled that Tammy was wearing "a pink sweater with a hole in it" and had his wife, Charlene, take her out to buy her some clothes.

After the track had been recorded, Sherrill had Wynette lay down a harmony vocal. "Billy told me we have to overdub," she recalled. "I thought, 'What in the world is that?' But I wouldn't dare ask." Once she actually sang along with herself on tape it occurred to her that this was how Skeeter Davis had recorded one of her favorites, "The End of the World." "When she got through singin' the guys didn't wanna leave," Sherrill said. "They just wanted to play it over and over again." But Wynette somehow remained unaware of their admiration, and, as Billy was his usual inscrutable self, she had no idea what he thought. Wynette left the session feeling unsure of it all.

It was around this time that Sherrill—Don Chapel's claims aside—gave his new singer her name. Wynette Byrd wasn't a snappy moniker for a star; Wynette Pugh was considerably worse. As she sat in his office one day in her $9.95 ponytail, Billy thought of the blonde, backwoods country bumpkin Debbie Reynolds originally played in *Tammy and the Bachelor* and announced, "You look like a Tammy to me." And thus Wynette Pugh became Tammy Wynette. "I sensed it was more than a new name," she wrote in her book. "I felt I was also about to start a new life."

The very first Epic publicity shots taken by James J. Kriegsmann show a radiant, tanned Tammy gazing heavenward, her eyes lined by heavy mascara. She looks stunning, almost regal, a Nashville Nefertiti. And that new life of hers was about to take off like a rocket. One day Tammy stopped by Sherrill's office to find him throwing darts at a map of Alabama on the wall. When she asked just what he was doing, he threw a dart at one little city, then another, and announced, "I'm gonna put Red Bay and Haleyville on the map." It was no idle boast.

"Apartment #9," the very first single by Tammy Wynette, was released in October of 1966. I don't know if there has ever been a more perfect debut. Bobby Austin's original version is a respectable country record, but Tammy just kills it. While Austin's fine delivery is by comparison a bit bombastic and obvious—he trills the final notes of the song as if to say, "Dig this trick"—Tammy holds the ending line, leaving a mournful little question mark at the end of the song. She takes what Austin did, boils the fat off, and adds a pinch of mystery. He merely sings about being lonely; she *is* lonely. To compare the two reminds me of what jazz clarinetist Tony Scott said when talking about Billie Holiday and Ella Fitzgerald. "When Ella sings 'My man, he's left me,' you think the guy went down the street for a loaf of bread. But when Lady sings . . . he's got his bags packed and he ain't *never* coming back."

Tammy sings the song quietly and doesn't linger on the notes, except in weird, unexpected places where she chooses odd words to pull on ("sta-a-a-airway"), which only adds to the drama. Wynette exhibits great restraint as she pulls back on some of the phrases, cutting them off precisely, letting the silence between words hang in the air. Her delivery is softer, subtler, but much more dramatic. She makes little choices throughout the song that add to the tension, and if there's one thing Tammy the recording artist is about, it's tension. And the harmony vocal she adds to her own voice! Austin does likewise on the original but can't dovetail his vocals the eerie way Wynette can.

Sherrill's arrangement is tighter, more polished, but just as spare as the original. Pete Drake's steel guitar changes the melody ever so slightly, resulting in a sadder atmosphere for Tammy to drown her sorrows in. It's a tiny, desolate world, this Apartment #9, right across the street from the dusty fairgrounds where the carnival has packed up and moved on. The idea of a woman singing such a number in that day and age adds another dimension: it suggests the disintegration of country values, the corruption brought by city life. Why, no "good" woman would be waiting manless and alone in Apartment #9. She's a prisoner, and the pain in her voice says she'll never be free.

"Apartment #9" stalled at number 44 on the country charts. Epic executives informed Tammy that truckers helped break the record initially—no doubt it sounded good on a deserted highway at three a.m. So what if the record wasn't exactly a smash hit. "Apartment #9" announced to the world Tammy Wynette had arrived, and a lot of the country singers Tammy most admired took notice.

Loretta Lynn was out on the road, her brother Jay Lee Webb at the wheel of their Chevy. "I was in the backseat sleepin', and Tammy come on singing 'Apartment #9.' I knew she was great when I heard that song. I said, 'Oh, my God, little brother, I have some competition now!'" Dolly Parton, who was struggling to make it in Music City herself at the time, was similarly moved. "I just remember turning on the radio one day in my little junky apartment and I heard this unbelievable voice singin' out—'Just follow the stair-way.' It was 'Apartment #9.' And I just thought that was the greatest thing I ever heard."

Out on the West Coast, Merle Haggard was also impressed. "She didn't try to sound like Patsy Cline or Loretta. She had her own style. Tammy stood alone."

Even George Jones took notice. "Her voice, it was different. She didn't sound like the other girls. She had a lotta heart, a lotta soul . . . That was the kinda stuff I thrived on." Within a few months Tammy and George would be sharing the same stage, with much more to come.

In October 1966 Tammy attended the Nashville DJ convention, but now, instead of singing on a flatbed truck for passersby in the street, she was a guest of honor. Wynette had no dress to wear for the occasion and no money to buy one, so Don Chapel's sister Jean, who'd sew a lot of Tammy's early stage clothes, made her an outfit. Tammy and Don had moved into the Graystone Motel trailer park in Goodlettsville right next door to Jean and her family. Wynette said that during this time she occasionally sang in church in a trio with Jean and Martha Carson, and also did some demo recordings of Jean's songs. "Martha and Jean were the sweetest human beings," said Frank Scarborough. They both helped Tammy with everything that they could. Don and Tammy were rentin' an eight-by-twenty-five for about ten dollars a month. You couldn't hardly stand up in it. There was no room whatsoever."

Tammy might have had a recording contract and a song climbing the charts, but she was still flat broke. (Not to mention the fact that, according to her, Euple had heard she'd signed to a label and sicced his lawyer on her in a failed attempt to get some money.) Sherrill sent Wynette to fabled booking agent Hubert Long, who agreed to represent her. Shortly thereafter the phone rang in Tammy's trailer. Long had a gig in Atlanta—the Playroom, five hundred dollars for a week, five shows a night. By the time Wynette paid the house band and her expenses, she returned home with just eighty-two bucks, but this was her first real stand as a solo artist. Tammy was touched by the fact that CBS Atlanta promotion man Joe Casey showed up on opening night with three dozen roses—the first roses she'd received in her life. Tammy was getting encouragement everywhere she turned. "Finally someone was listening to my voice and they seemed to like it."

In February 1967 came Tammy's second single, "Your Good Girl's Gonna Go Bad," about a woman who's tired of her man's bad behavior and decides she'll show him by doing a little carousing herself. No longer was the wife staying home lamenting that it wasn't God who made honky-tonk angels; it was time for a little revenge. "If you like 'em painted up, powdered up, you oughtta be glad," Tammy informs us menfolk. It is that rare item in Wynette's catalog: an up-tempo song, the sort of revved-up number Loretta Lynn was famous for, but Tammy just ain't that feisty. "I'll even learn to like the taste of whiskey," she threatens, but one imagines she'll hold her nose as the rotgut goes down. You just know Tammy's not gonna be *that* bad. What a great performance. She already sounds fully in command, jumping in slightly ahead of the beat, adding a subtle tension to the rubbery twang surrounding her.

Glenn Sutton, who cowrote the song with Sherrill, maintained that nobody thought much of the number and that it was cut almost as an afterthought at the tail end of a session. Billy was so particular when it came to songs that often when Tammy would meet with him in the morning before a two p.m. session, he didn't have enough material for it. "Lightning will strike," he'd tell a mortified Tammy. Somehow he'd pull a song out of the air. "Most of the writing I've done has been out of panic or a last resort," Sherrill told Bob Allen, as in the studio downstairs he had "an acre of violins already hired and sitting there waiting."

"Your Good Girl's Gonna Go Bad" came out so well that Billy put it out as a single, and it shot to number 3. The song was the title cut of her very first album, released in April, which, besides her two singles, was mostly a collection of Tammy doing her versions of various hits: "Don't Touch Me," "Don't Come Home A-Drinkin' (With Lovin' on Your Mind)," "There Goes My Everything," and "Almost Persuaded." (Sherrill was shameless—just about everybody he produced cut this song at one time or another.)

At the time country albums were generally haphazard affairs consisting of a single or two, a few cover versions of hits past and present, plus whatever else the producer could come up with to fill a side. The closest Sherrill got to a unifying theme for Tammy was a gospel album, a Christmas album, and 1973's *Kids Say the Darndest Things*, the "concept" of which was as obvious as the title (and which Sherrill had to get permission to use from ultra-square family entertainment superstar Art Linkletter, author of a book by the same name). In this book therefore I will concentrate on her single performances rather than the steady stream of albums, which in the Sherrill period (1967 to 1980) resulted in at least two Tammy albums a year (sometimes three). Add to this constant touring, television appearances, and press interviews, and you have one incredibly busy dame.

When Tammy recorded, musicians just played better. "They'd move up on the front of the chair—you could see them thinkin', 'That lady's over at the mic really puttin' in there, I better do my part,' Lou Bradley recalled. "You could just feel the snap. I guarantee I seen the hair stand up on the back of Pete Drake's head when she'd go for those high notes." When Tammy sang in the studio, said Bradley with a chuckle, "lightning bolts would go through the air."

"When she was singin' her lungs out, you wanted to beat the hell out of that piano," said Pig Robbins. "It made you want to play." Jordanaire Ray Walker recalled that "Tammy didn't make any emotion, she just stood there and sang. You'd think, 'Man, this is gonna be high, she'll never reach that note,' and she just went on up and *got* it." Wynette was friendly and kind to the musicians, not a diva in the slightest. "There wasn't a time when you walked in to do a session that she wasn't gonna give you a hug when you came in and a hug when you left," said guitarist Harold Bradley, adding that Tammy's warmth and openness made the pickers feel like "we were all in it together."

Unlike some artists Tammy was "always very appreciative for what we did," said Gordon Stoker of the Jordanaires. When bass player Roy Husky, who had played on many a Tammy session, died, she "really took that hard," said Stoker, who was impressed by how much Wynette cared. "Tammy loved all those musicians." The feeling was very much mutual. "She was so easy to work with," said guitarist Ray Edenton. "Everybody loved Tammy."

In June 1967 Wynette recorded her first duet. "My Elusive Dreams," a song about a struggling couple that could've been penned directly for Wynette and Euple, had first been pitched to Tammy by Curly Putman right after she first met Billy Sherrill and was frantic to find a hit song to record. "I had just started it," said Putman. "She said, 'Y'know, that would be good for Peter, Paul, and Mary.'" Sherrill helped Curly finish the song, and Putman decided to cut it himself for ABC records. Then Billy recorded it as a duet with David Houston and Tammy. Singing in her lowest register, Tammy provided just the right counterpoint to Houston's angst-ridden Irish tenor. This is the first time we hear her entrancing speaking voice during a short recitation. She is the epitome of Southern charm, and it's not hard to imagine Wynette whispering sweet nothings in the ears of her men, reducing them to puddles in the process. "My Elusive Dreams" shot up the charts, hitting number one on September 16, 1967.

And now we arrive at "I Don't Wanna Play House," released in July 1966 and Tammy's first solo number one. It is hard to contain my excitement over this one, for it is Tammy, Billy, and the boys from Studio B at their best. This is what the Sherrill sound is all about: dynamics, or to put it in terms we-who-can't-carry-a-tune types can understand, *softLOUDsoftLOUD*. Tammy could go from a whisper to a wail in the bat of an eyelash, and Sherrill made sure she took the whole band with her. Boy, is it thrilling to hear. Lou Bradley insists that Wynette influenced Sherrill as much as the other way around. "I think the dynamics Billy got evolved from Billy makin' the band play to Tammy. She'd sing the verses soft, and when she belted, he'd make the musicians play to that. That was just her way of singin'.'"

The song begins with just a couple of notes from Pig on piano, a perfect stepping stool to sad little Tammy's voice, which already sounds on the edge of a breakdown: "Today I sat alone at the window, and I watched our little girl outside at play." Talk about drama! Just the space Tammy leaves between the first and the second word alone contains enough room to park a car. As she describes watching her daughter about to unleash the dreaded chorus on her tiny playmate, Wynette sings softly and conversationally, until the jaw-dropping second line of the second verse, when she suddenly and unexpectedly belts out the bit about starting to cry with a lacerating power and emotion she seems barely able to contain. She drops back down to a murmur, then kicks the volume back up for her double-tracked chorus, Pete Drake's steel guitar sounding particularly punchy as he'd just gotten the gizmo he'd dub his "Tammy Wynette pedal" the day before.

Wynette had lived this song, giving her vocal the sort of authenticity that seems almost prehistoric in this era of computerized pitch correction and melismatic overdose*. Sherrill and Sutton crafted a simple and heart-

---

*Just how different are things in modern-day Music City? Auto-Tune, the pitch-correcting software responsible for the android-perfect vocals so omnipresent in rock and pop these days, proved so popular with late-nineties country stars that it was originally nicknamed "the Nashville Plug-In."

breaking lyric which Tammy sings with such utter conviction that you see it all in your mind: a worn-out housewife hunched over a sinkful of dirty dishes, a crying baby parked on her hip as she looks at the kids out the window and wonders how it all went so wrong. When she sings "hung my head in shame," the condemnation from Mildred and other family members over her own divorce must've been front and center in her mind.

"I Don't Wanna Play House" zeroed in on the bleaker side of married life. "It's a soft-focus world with a hairsprayed blonde, a hard drink, a big man in work boots, a child nearby, and lots of tears," noted filmmaker Anna Biller. In Tammy's world women are "raging inside with a turmoil of feelings, yet pretty and sweet on the outside. Wearing a mask of composure and false eyelashes in a never-ending need to please and satisfy that elusive man . . . it's not exactly uplifting material. There's not really a catharsis. It's more like you want to hit the bottle and cry."

Tammy confided to one old Red Bay friend that it hurt to stand so nakedly before a microphone. After a show in Fayetteville, North Carolina, Wynette caught up with Holly Ford, who was living there at the time. As they lay on the bed in her tour bus reminiscing over old times, Holly asked Wynette if there were any songs in particular that got to her emotionally. "'I Don't Wanna Play House,'" Tammy confessed without hesitation. Sometimes she just couldn't face singing the song. "There's been many a time I've almost had to stop it," she admitted.

Tammy Wynette had gone from nobody to somebody in a flash. In 1967 alone, four of her singles would go top ten, three of them to number one, and her debut album would make it to number 7. She was also voted Most Promising Female Artist by *Country Song Roundup, Music City News*, and *Record World*. Plus she'd win a Grammy for "I Don't Wanna Play House."

On April 7, 1967, Tammy tied the knot with Don Chapel in Ringgold, Georgia, a popular spot for country stars seeking quickie marriages. "You could literally get a blood test at a roadside stand," wrote Dolly Parton. "And getting a marriage license was as easy as a drive-through."

The couple bought a fifty-thousand-dollar home out on Imperial Point in Hendersonville by the lake. Tammy said she made the down payment from the bookings she was getting; Don said he scraped up the three-thousand-dollar deposit himself. Don's three children from a previous marriage came to join Tammy's kids: Gwen, almost six; Jackie, who was a year younger; and little two-year-old Tina. "It was like the Brady Bunch, only with music," said Don's daughter from a previous marriage, Donna.

Donna came to visit in the summer of 1966 and instantly became Wynette's backup singer. "I didn't know he had married anyone, he hadn't told us yet," said Donna, laughing. "It was like, 'Get in the car, here's your new stepmother.'" Only fourteen and fresh out of junior high, Donna was a black-haired beauty with a great set of pipes, and her apparent maturity was definitely a burden while out on the road with a bunch of lonely male musicians.

A typical teenage Beatles fan, Donna recalled riding along in the backseat of the Pontiac while Wynette was up front singing along to the country songs wafting out of the car radio. "I had never heard this honky-tonk stuff, traditional country. I was making fun of it, holding my nose. She turned around from the front seat, got real stern, and said, 'Don't you *ever* make fun of country music!' And that was the last time I did. She was real serious about it." Perhaps Donna was green when it came to the sound of a steel guitar, but she had an uncanny ability to harmonize with Wynette. "I could phrase and match her voice almost instantaneously. We only had one microphone, everybody crowded in. We were two and a half inches apart, singin' together mouth to mouth. I could look in her eyes and tell what she was gonna do before she was doin' it. I just read her face."

Donna did Wynette's hair before she went onstage, stood in for her at band rehearsals, and shared outfits, since they were the same size. "She was a very independent kind of person. Very strong-willed. She was an only child, so she always wanted to have her way. 'Domineering' may not be the correct word, but she wanted to be the leader, to push things her way. Instead of the word 'determined' she used to say, 'I'm deeter-minded. Very deeter-minded. That's the way we say it where I come from.'" Donna would watch success engulf Tammy and experience firsthand just how ruthlessly "deeter-minded" she could be. "You could see the change happening in her whole personality," said Donna. "She just became, for lack of a better word, harder. That sweet little country girl was leaving quickly, heading to the city."

"I think success came too quickly," said Jan Howard. "It didn't take long before Tammy had all these other people around her that were takin' care of things." Bassist Bob Moore agreed. "Tammy never knew what hit her.

She never expected what she got. She never expected to be big. She was always a hairdresser."

The first real Tammy Wynette touring band, dubbed the Countrypolitans by Don, consisted of Joe Ridings on guitar, Roy McCoy on steel, Calvin Crawford on bass, and Jimmy Halfacre on drums. Donna would come out and do a few numbers, Don would join her and do his own set; then came Tammy, followed by Tammy and Don together on a few duets like "Jackson." Wynette was still green when it came to the stage, said Halfacre. "She was not real familiar with workin' the mic," he said. "Like a lot of girl singers, Tammy played rhythm guitar. It was a hindrance more than a help." Her erratic timing on the acoustic tended to throw off the rhythm section, and Halfacre was relieved when Don coaxed her into putting the guitar down. Originally Donna had opened the show by singing the Buck Owens hit "Act Naturally." When the crowd went wild, she'd do it again. "I only knew one song," she said. "I was just a kid!" Donna often spotted Wynette in the wings, "clenching her jaw. She didn't quite like it when I'd get a little more attention."

Donna felt a close bond with Tammy, but trod softly in her presence. "She was a tense kind of a person." Abram Richman, a thirteen-year-old neighborhood kid enlisted to babysit the children, felt Wynette "seemed pretty brittle. There was a lot of attention paid to Tammy's mood. The whole atmosphere around the house was always very tense. There were almost freaky rules about keeping quiet when Tammy was home."

Health problems, both real and imagined, were already starting to plague Wynette. "She had stomach trouble all the days of her life," said Donna. "We were always stoppin' at emergency rooms . . . I wonder sometimes if she didn't just want the drugs." Wynette was abusing medication even at this early stage in her career. Preludin, an amphetamine-like appetite suppressor favored by the Beatles in their Hamburg days (and taken off the market in 1965), was her drug of choice. Don said that throughout their time together Tammy was doing Preludin "heavily." "That's why she got so thin," said Donna. One gets the feeling from talking to those who knew her at the time that Tammy had serious problems with anxiety. As Donna saw it, "the calming effect of the medication was almost more beneficial to her than anything else."

Other conflicts brought on by success troubled Tammy. She felt Don pressured her into asking Billy Sherrill to record both himself and Donna. (Epic released two Don Chapel singles, but Donna's recordings never saw the light of day.) The tour bus was painted to read THE DON CHAPEL AND TAMMY WYNETTE SHOW, which the headliner quickly began to resent. Promoters were complaining there was too much family onstage and not enough Tammy. The demands of stardom were already having an effect. "Don and Tammy fought pretty vociferously," recalled Abram Richman. "You could hear it down the street."

Wynette frequently butted heads with Don's son Michael. "Mike's pretty headstrong, independent—and guess what? Tammy was, too," recalled Donna. "But he was a child. She just didn't want him there." Wynette would detail her troubles with Michael in her autobiography, causing him great embarrassment. "She was unmerciful to my son," said Don. "After we divorced I asked her, 'Why were you always after Michael?' She told me, 'Because he looked like his mother, and I couldn't stand that.'"

Lost in the confusion were Tammy's own children, who, Richman felt, were "somewhat neglected. They were often dirty, and the house was a pigsty." Tammy was so self-involved at times that she seemed unable to connect with her daughters. Said Donna, "To be honest, Tammy sometimes would walk by, pat the kids on the head like they were little doggies—and *keep* walkin'. It always killed me to see that, because they would look at her with their big eyes, just dyin' for her to run up and grab 'em, and she was just so tired from everything. It was sad."

In December 1967, Don, Tammy, and Donna left the country for a few weeks for Wynette's first overseas dates in Germany and the United Kingdom. "I had never flown anywhere in my life," said Donna. "The Bee Gees were on the same plane—that was so exciting. We were all in first class together." First stop was Frankfurt. "We entertained the troops for a couple of weeks," said Donna. "The guys were grabbin' at us, so they had to take us outta there. They hadn't seen a woman for a while." Handbills from London, which Donna saved, misspell Tammy's name as "Wynett." They'd soon get the name right, however, as Tammy would return to the UK on a regular basis throughout her career, earning her a large and dedicated British fan base.

That same month saw the release of her fourth single, the magnificent "Take Me to Your World." A Sutton-Sherrill number, the song had originally been cut by Glenn with a singer by the name of Beverly Byrd. Sherrill wrote and overdubbed prominent skating-rink-organ strings on the track, then decided he wanted it for Wynette. At first Tammy feared that her first single with strings might "ruin" her. "Everyone will think I'm going pop," she shuddered. Hot on the heels of "I Don't Wanna Play House," the record shot to number one on March 9, 1968. It was another song about a woman lost in the neon jungle of city life, this one a stained-by-sin barmaid who can't bear to "hear another dirty joke." Tammy's singing was growing more extreme by the minute—listen to the way she slow-drags the word "dirty" into a murmur of pain and regret.

January 1968 brought the arrival of Wynette's third album, the imaginatively titled *Take Me to Your World/I Don't Wanna Play House.* This collection had a few extra killers, however. From the opening bubba-boos of the Jordanaires to Pete Drake's away-in-the-darkest-night wailing steel, "It's My Way" is a real heartbreaker, with Sherrill's spare but rich arrangement providing an immaculate showcase for Wynette's genius. There is a beautiful take on the old Johnny Ray smash "Cry," which provoked one of her few clashes with Sherrill, who wanted her to do the song almost as a spoken recitation. "I really disagreed," said Tammy, who had a "mental block" when it came to the noncountry song and its melody. But Wynette couldn't argue with the end result. "Billy was right. In the studio he really is always right."

And in "Good," another Sherrill-Sutton composition in which the country woman with the scarlet letter confesses her sins, you can literally hear the turmoil churn within Wynette as she sings, "I'll never be good / like I used to be." The lost years and many penny-ante tragedies between Red Bay and Nashville had branded Wynette, but it was valuable suffering. This music was more barren and lonely than a church bell tolling for nobody in some ugly little Midwest town without a bus stop. Most of us want to be good; most of us fail sooner or later. That's what's so powerful about Tammy. She validates those feelings, lets you know it's no crime to shed a tear over the frequently tawdry and disappointing misadventure that is life. It's a great release for us listening. Singing these sad songs over and over and over, one has to wonder: was it always that way for Tammy?

Don and Tammy hit the road in style, commandeering a navy blue 1967 Cadillac Brougham they'd bought off of Ray Walker of the Jordanaires.

"Tammy looked so good in blue," Walker recalled. "I saw them pull up one day to a recording session. Don has blue eyes, too—they got out of that car, and damn if they didn't look like a bandbox. I said, 'Have mercy.'" That was replaced by a drafty old Flxible bus Donna called "the rolling casket." Sometimes Tammy took the wheel, much to the amusement of passing truckers peering in. "She liked to drive at night," said Halfacre. "She'd have her hair up in rollers. People wouldn't know it was Tammy Wynette."

They had bought the "Flex" for two grand from none other than the Possum himself. The first time Tammy had encountered George Jones was back before she had a record deal. "I had a pretty strong image of him before we met because of his music and all I'd read about him," she said. "I expected him to be quiet and shy, a loner, and he turned out to be all those things." Don had to deliver some songs to Jones, so off they went to knock on the door of room 127 at his then-favorite Nashville crash pad, the Biltmore Motel, where a little party was in progress. There was king George in silk pajamas, watching TV as he held court from a huge bed, some tarted-up trollop by his side. Tammy was completely tongue-tied, unable to utter anything clever. "He didn't even notice me," she'd complain. "Didn't even speak to me." Tammy sulked for days.

He remained on her mind, because bassist Bob Moore remembers Tammy suddenly showing up at his door one day asking if he could direct her to George's house, somewhere in the same neighborhood. Nothing apparently came of that, because the first real encounter took place when she arrived at Billy Sherrill's office one day and he informed her that Jones was down below in Studio B cutting "Apartment #9." Panicked that he was going to release it as a single—"I knew I couldn't handle *that* kind of competition my first time out"—she calmed down once she found out it was only to be an album cut. Still, Jones seemed unimpressed by her presence, which miffed Tammy even further.

Then came the fateful gig in Canada in March 1968. Don and Tammy were doing some dates with David Houston, and Jones was also on the bill. Wynette usually opened the show, followed by Houston, then Jones. Tammy came back out during Houston's set to do their duet. One night, either in Calgary or Winnipeg, depending on who's telling it, Houston had to leave early, and his manager, Tillman Franks, wanted David to open and Tammy to come out and do the duet cold, without having done her set first. "Tammy blew up," said eyewitness Don Chapel. As Wynette and Tillman got into it over "who was the biggest star," Chapel and Houston, who was tuning a guitar, sat mute. "We were all too embarrassed to enter into the argument," said Chapel. The exchange grew more heated by the second, and at some point Tillman smirked and made his infamous, unfortunate remark: "We all know how girl singers get ahead in this business."

Franks might as well have poured gas on Tammy and thrown a match. She told him she wouldn't sing with David Houston again if he was the last artist on earth, which was followed by the sound of high heels scraping concrete as she stormed off down the hall of the venue. In his autobiography the late Tillman Franks denied that he made the comment, stating that not only had he "never said anything negative to Tammy" but he hadn't talked to her that night, period, and she ditched Houston as a duet partner simply because she "wanted to sing with George." He also claimed somewhat ominously that late that evening somebody crept out to their tour bus and "put sand in our gas tanks." At least three people on hand dispute his version of the events. Wynette would keep her promise and never recorded nor sang with Houston again. (The news didn't trouble David too much. He later told Donna Chapel that he "didn't like Tammy—and he hated the song 'My Elusive Dreams.'")

Wynette now had a big problem—no duet partner to perform her hit. News of the Tillman-Tammy brouhaha traveled backstage to Jones, however, and during his set he suddenly announced to the audience he was inviting her out to sing "My Elusive Dreams" with him. Tammy, who watched George's set religiously every night from the wings, was stunned. Out she stepped onstage to sing with Jones, who didn't know a word of the song and had to be prompted by Wynette whispering the lyrics in his ear. "I was on cloud nine," said Tammy. Her husband was less than impressed, claiming that the reason Jones stumbled through the song was because he was stewed to the gills.*

According to Wynette, the promoter wasn't happy, either, demanding that Tammy continue to perform with Houston. Tillman continued to pitch a fit as well, but Wynette stood her ground, pointing out that the contract didn't specify her singing a duet with anybody. The rest of the dates she sang with Jones.

---

*Amusingly, during an interview he did a few years later alongside his then-wife Wynette, Jones referred to Houston as "this foreign singer that Tammy recorded with," apparently because of Houston's proclivity for yodeling. "George can't yodel like David," countered an embarrassed Tammy, trying to downplay the insult.

———

Jimmy was talking to his bandmates on the bus when George barged in on the conversation "with a milkshake cup full of bourbon and coke. He says, 'Have a drink, boy.'" Halfacre didn't care for firewater—"I took pills," explained Jimmy—and politely declined the offer. Jones persisted, and his menacing tone told Halfacre he'd better take his medicine, so down the hatch it went. "I just stayed away from him," said Halfacre. "He was notorious for havin' parties and shootin' buses and whatever."

At first Jones seemed particularly fond of Donna Chapel, whom he called Dody, and whom he called at odd hours of the night. "He kept sayin', 'When you grow up, I'm gonna marry you.' He tried to break into my room one time, beating on the door. He was really drunk . . . I was so terrified, all the time." But the show must go on. Jones would call Donna out to sing "We Must Have Been Out of Our Minds"; then Tammy would come out and sing "Rollin' in My Sweet Baby's Arms." (I doubt Jones ever bothered to learn "My Elusive Dreams.") "George is just one of these people, if he wants something, he's gonna try to get it, and that's what he did. As time progressed, he was just too much around," said Donna. "Too much around."

Complicating matters was the fact that Donna's dad was busy pitching songs to Jones. He'd cut four songs by Chapel (Tammy herself would record four of her husband's numbers), the biggest of which was "When the Grass Grows Over Me," a mournful ballad by Don that would provide George with a number 2 country hit in 1969. For the rest of her career Tammy would claim that she'd written the song and that credit had been stolen from her. Bullshit, says Don. "It was written way before I ever met Tammy Wynette," insisted Chapel. "She actually hated this song, because she knew that I had written it about my wife, before I ever met her. Tammy was very jealous!"

It should be noted that Tammy claimed authorship for other songs she didn't write. Bobby Austin's wife, Fern, remembered attending a concert in Vancouver, Washington, where Wynette announced to the crowd she'd written "Apartment #9." Earl "Peanutt" Montgomery said Tammy took credit for his song "Stayin' Home Woman" on a daily basis, while he was standing there next to her, playing in the band. "I wrote every bit of that song myself, and Tammy got onstage every night and said, 'George had been out all night, and I was settin' there about three o'clock one mornin' and I'm tired of waitin' on that man to come home. So I wrote this song.' She never helped me write one word. I'd tell people, 'If she wrote it, her name woulda been on it.'"

Back to Don Chapel, who was in a bit of a pickle. He wanted to promote his wife, and his own songwriting. George Jones was a big, big star with unlimited juice to help them both. "The thing that really got me is that I trusted George," said Chapel. "And Tammy—I thought we had a blood oath. Here I am puttin' her in his hands . . ."

Literally, it appears. Jones drove to his shows by car, accompanied by his road manager Billy Wilhite. He says Tammy started traveling to shows with them as her band—and her husband—trailed behind in the old Flex bus. "If I had been him, I wouldn't have let her run around with me," said Jones. One night George and Tammy even shared a motel room bed in Wood-bridge, Virginia, as Wilhite slept on the next mattress over. All innocent fun, says George. "We weren't doing anything wrong—except falling in love," he wrote.

As if this story weren't fraught with enough tension, now comes the time to discuss the "dirty pictures," and like so many other events in Wynette's life, there is no shortage of conflicting testimony. Tammy relates the story of how she found out about the photos rather dramatically in her autobiography. She was appearing at the Edison Hotel in Toronto when a creepy bald fan in green pants who'd been hovering at the front of the stage handed her an en-velope. After she finished the show she opened it, only to find a nude picture of herself stepping out of the shower. She got on the bus and confronted Don, who she claimed told her that he swapped photos with other men around the country. "It was a sickening, lowdown thing to do," she said. Chapel made a blasé promise to burn the evidence. Tammy tore up the photo and let him have it. "Our marriage was never the same after that," she said. In his memoir, Jones claims that he ended up buying the pictures, although he didn't know he was doing so at the time. It was only years later that Billy Wilhite informed him that, to spare George and Tammy the embarrassment, he bought the negatives off Don Chapel and destroyed them.

Chapel, who gets very testy when the subject is raised, insists they were instant photos (thus no negatives) and that it was his ex-wife who made them public to have him look bad. "That was concocted in her mind," he hissed. "Pictures—might've been two or three Polaroids. Polaroids, big deal. Who hasn't done that? Everybody takes pictures, if you got a girlfriend or wife. She picked up one and said, 'Y'know what I'm gonna do? I might even frame this,' and she kept it. We had 'em of each other. They was put in a locked bag with a key. She took that bag with her and said, 'I may have to blackmail you someday.' By showin' her own photo of *herself*!! She wasn't even pretty! She was bowlegged." And that's Don Chapel's version. After Tammy's death he went to the Ryman Auditorium to see the play *Stand by Your Man* and was mortified by the role he'd been reduced to in the stage version of her life. "When they said I sold nude pictures of her, the crowd went laughin'. They didn't know I was sittin' in the audience. What kind of a man would do something like *that*?"

Daughter Donna sticks up for her dad. "If anything bad was done, Tammy did it right with him. There wasn't nothing done bad against her that she wasn't partaking with, and I'm talking private issues. Tammy was just as much a part of that as anybody—she was pretty open to walk around without clothes on half the time. I *know* that."*

◆

"I hated myself for not writing that song," said Tammy of her next single, "D-I-V-O-R-C-E," released in April 1968. "It fit my life completely." Bobby Braddock said the song started out as "I L-O-V-E Y-O-U" but then morphed into its familiar title. "I wrote it, and nobody bit," recalled Braddock, who asked Curly Putman, then plugging songs at Tree Publishing, what was wrong with it. "I think the melody around the title is too happy for such a sad song," Putman replied. "It sounds like a detergent commercial." After Curly added a little sad to the melody, Billy Sherrill bit right away. The odd keyboard lick derives from Braddock's demo. "Bobby had it kinda bouncy," said Putman. "Bobby did a lot of weird piano licks on the song because he played piano. They used a little bit of that in the intro." The song is also notable as one of the few Sherrill-produced Tammy records to feature the great Lloyd Green on steel instead of Pete Drake.

Unbearably catchy and irredeemably hokey, the song is written from the point of view of a mother trying to spare her little "J-o-e" the hurt of divorce by spelling out the "hurtin' words." Only Tammy could invest such feeling into a novelty number. There's some wild singing here, like the way Wynette bends the letters during "he thinks C-U-S-T-O-D-Y means fun or play" (an

---

*Chapel later told a tabloid that he and Tammy "even took movies of one another in the nude, but they were not obscene. She was involved in that just as much as I was."

awkward line if there ever was one). As Roy Blount, Jr., put it, "Lord, can't Tammy sing a letter of the alphabet." The song was her fourth number one smash, and the title of her fourth (and first gold) album, released in August, which also featured the roof-raising "Come on Home" and a particularly melancholy (and beautifully arranged) version of "Lonely Street."

The title song made an impression on George Jones. One day he moseyed on over to Don and Tammy's house and began singing "D-I-V-O-R-C-E." After seventeen years of marriage to his second wife, Shirley, they had called it quits, and, just like in the song, his divorce had indeed become final that day. It was a bit of information Jones just had to plant in Tammy's brain.

In late summer of 1968 Tammy returned to Red Bay to do a benefit concert for the Jaycees in the local high school gym. According to Jane Williams, her relatives knew very little of what she had been doing the last few years. As far as Wynette's having a recording contract, Jane just thought it was one of "those fly-by-night deals. I just didn't take her seriously." But then one day Jane's father and brother were having breakfast in a Mississippi roadside café when "Apartment #9" came wafting out of the jukebox. And then Wynette—now Tammy Wynette, of course—returned home, to Jane's shock, sporting a big new hairdo. "She had it really, really blonde. I mean as blonde as you could get it, swept up in the back, all the way to the front. I thought, 'Well! We just don't know about this.'"

Tammy encountered a surprise herself when their bus pulled up to the school. There sat a brand-new burgundy Cadillac Eldorado, and out of it stepped George Jones. "So this is Red Bay, Alabama," mused George. Back on the road Tammy had mentioned the benefit in Red Bay, and he took it upon himself to show up unannounced. "I introduced the sumbitch onstage," said Don ruefully. "He says, 'Can I sing one with her?' I said, 'Well, sure.' She was lookin' at him goo-goo eyed the whole time. That he drove down there all the way from Nashville to see her—that registered all right. Here's her Elvis, comin' to see *her*?"

Jones "seemed lonely," admitted Tammy. "I was lonely. I thought, 'Gosh, if I could just get close to him, I can change him. I can make him happy.'" Her friends certainly noticed she was smitten. During a trip to Panama City with Birmingham DJ Fred Lehner and his wife, Jane, she sang George's praises to the hilt. "We were sittin' on the beach, and she says, 'Jane, you've got to meet George Jones. He is just *fabulous*.' I thought, 'Well . . .' It wasn't long after that she was no longer with Chapel."

———

"For years people have whispered that I took Tammy Wynette from behind Don Chapel's back," said George Jones in his book. "That's a lie. I did it in front of his eyes." The fateful day Tammy Wynette left Don Chapel for Jones is a milestone in Tammy's mythology, and it's a story that's been told and retold for years. It appears a bit of the truth somehow got left behind in the telling. In her version Wynette maintained there was no romance with Jones before the day he showed up at her home and announced to both Tammy and her husband he was in love with her. George "never so much as touched me," she wrote. Jones pretty much said the same. "We had never even been alone, much less dated or anything."

But Don Chapel told a different story, as did George's sometime road manager, the late Bill Starnes. When journalist Pepi Plowman interviewed Starnes for a Jones profile in *Texas Monthly* magazine, he told her that he'd distract Don so Jones could sneak off with Tammy. He claimed at least one of those meetings was at a motel.* Recalled Chapel, "Bill Starnes would call me and say, 'Don, I want to go look at a new bus, will you go with me?'" Off he'd go, unaware that Jones was swooping in. "He violated my trust in my own home, with my wife. A number of times I found out. One time I come back in with Bill, and Jones was sittin' on the couch with his arm around her."

One night Tammy's kids were in the throes of food poisoning and had to be taken to the hospital. Wynette claimed that Chapel was nowhere to be found. ("Malarkey," said Donna.) Sometimes when Wynette told the story she said Don was drunk; in other tellings she claimed that she'd "found him with somebody else." Chapel denies the charges and insists that it was Tammy who was doing the philandering. "We did shifts in the hospital, Tennessee Christian. She took the night shift, I took the day. My spirit was troublin' me, man. I drove down to the hospital and I saw George Jones's ol' maroon Cadillac settin' in the back of the parkin' lot." He claims that Tammy was inside the car with George. "The nurse told me she had left with George Jones. When I left, I drove past the parking lot totally ripped apart." Wynette didn't deny the Possum's three a.m. hospital arrival—"I looked up, and there was George"—but she maintained he was only there to help with the kids.

———

*One detail (perhaps apocryphal) Plowman left out of the story: according to Billy Wilhite, when Jones returned from the motel, he told Billy, "You know what that girl done? She sucked my toes!"

The next day Jones, accompanied by Starnes, paid a visit to the Chapel household. According to Bill Starnes, Tammy had been playing George's version of "When the Grass Grows Over Me" over and over, irritating her husband. George, who had been hitting the sauce, walked in on a tense situation. They all sat down to dinner, Don and Tammy continuing to fight and Jones continuing to imbibe. Chapel, according to Jones, "was yelling at the kids," and Tammy asked him to stop. That's when Don "called Tammy a bad word," and all hell broke loose. "George flew into a fury," said Wynette. "It shocked me because he'd always been so quiet." Jones proceeded to overturn the dining room table. (Tammy claimed he also threw a chair through the dining room window, an embellishment no one else remembers.) "Ruined our dinner," complained Chapel, who maintained the only reason the table fell over was because George was trying to get up. "He was drunk on his ass."

As the plates and silverware went flying, Jones, who was only a few inches taller than Wynette and probably didn't weigh a whole lot more, told Chapel not to talk to Tammy that way. "What's it to you?" barked Don. "Because I love her," muttered Jones. "And Tammy loves me, too. Don't you, Tammy?"

Time stood still for a moment there in the Chapel home. Even George was shocked by the words coming out of his mouth. "I don't know who was more surprised to hear me say it—me, him, or her . . . But when a man's in love he's got to be willing to go all the way."

That was an attitude Tammy could appreciate. Yes, she admitted to her soon-to-be ex-husband, she did love him. "I guess from the first moment I saw him . . . I was in love with him. Had been for years, I just didn't know it." And with that his wife walked out the door with George Jones, Starnes scooping up Gwen, Jackie, and Tina behind them.

Wynette would never return. Donna Chapel recalled being awakened the following morning by her distraught father, who asked, "Do you know where Tammy is? I think she's gone." "Dad was like a lost little person, he had a bewildered look. He let the tears roll down his face, and for a man to do that . . . He walked around in a state of shock. He didn't speak some days."

Unfortunately Tammy and Don had some Northeast concert dates to fulfill. The first show was at Henry's Pub in Brooklyn, New York. "Tammy didn't even show up," said Jimmy Halfacre. "Here we are, we had bookings to do," said Donna. "And she's not there, so I went and stood in her place. I had to do her songs, and it was rippin' me to pieces." Halfacre was amazed at how Donna held her own against an audience hungry for Tammy, but once word got out she was gone, the tour was doomed. "We finished a few of those dates, and they canceled the rest," he said.

In hopes of getting some bookings on their own, Don and Donna went to see Hubert Long. "I can't book you," Long told them. "This would aggravate Tammy Wynette, and she's a major account. I'm sorry. When you get a record in the top ten, come see me."

Meanwhile, Jones had hidden Tammy and her kids away in a motel so she wouldn't be at his house when the cops came looking for her, which they did. Before leaving for Mexico to obtain a quickie divorce, George felt the coast was clear enough for Tammy and company to spend the night. The next morning, lacking an official engagement ring, Jones plucked a huge rock off his hand and gave it to her, along with the keys to a brand-new Lincoln Continental in the driveway. "She had the car keys in one hand, the ring on the other, me on a string and Don in a rage," wrote Jones. "Friends, it was a romance straight out of Shakespeare."

When Don went to serve divorce papers on Tammy, she was at Studio B. "The Epic security guard wouldn't let me in," said Don, who said she was inside recording a new song. Ironically enough, it was "Stand by Your Man."* Chapel also filed a hundred-thousand-dollar civil suit against Jones, infuriating Tammy, who got on the wire and gave him a piece of her mind. "I was the one who filed for the divorce, because of her adultery," said Don. "That is when she telephoned me and said, 'I'll see that you never make it in this business, because no one will want you when I'm through.'"

After the phone call Chapel went to see Ray Walker, his friend in the Jordanaires. "He was absolutely devastated by the breakup," said Walker, who maintains the main thing on Chapel's mind was how vulnerable Wynette was. Don was worried she'd be taken advantage of. "When they broke up, he wasn't angry, he was afraid for Tammy." Walker insisted that

---

*Chapel had cut a Glenn Sutton song, "In a Phone Booth on My Knees." The lyric was from the point of view of a man begging to come back to his wife. In light of the breakup, Epic—this is according to Don—felt they could squeeze some juice out of it as an answer record to Tammy's "Stand by Your Man." "They'd play hers, they'd play mine," said a disgusted Chapel. "I said, 'I'll be damned if I'm gonna get laughed at the rest of my life.'" Al Gallico said, 'Don't do that, it's gonna be a hit song,'" but Chapel walked out of Epic for good, and "In a Phone Booth on My Knees" was never released.

Chapel deserves a lot of credit for helping Wynette through the early days of her career. "Don Chapel earned more than he ever got. Because he was absolutely devoted to her. He did nothing else but Tammy." Frank Scarborough agreed. "If not for Don Chapel's generosity and love for Tammy, she and her daughters would've starved."

Donna Chapel concurred. "Dad worked so hard promoting her. He waited on her hand and foot. I was so shocked when she left. He truly thought he found his soul mate with Tammy. They had a real compatibility, a real spark. They were very affectionate to each other, hugged all the time. Mushy. He used to rub her feet. Dad was crazy for her, and they were always together. I've got a picture of their heads together all loved up. It wasn't very long after that when she left."

And Tammy, agreed Don and Donna, cleaned out all the bank accounts upon leaving. "When she left, she took everything with her," said Donna. "She took all the money and left. We had nothing." "She burned my credit cards, all of them," said Don, who claims the damage came to over twenty thousand dollars.*

Donna remembers having to accompany her father to the next disc jockey convention in Nashville. For the Chapels it was a grim event. There was Tammy across the room with George. "All of our eyes met, and she looked distraught," Donna recalled. "She didn't want us to look at her, you could tell. It was a very uncomfortable feeling. Dad just hung on to my arm."

The wounds were reopened when Tammy published her autobiography in 1979. Chapel was outraged by the book and filed a multimillion-dollar lawsuit, but it went nowhere. "She made such a public spectacle of him, she could've just as well shot him and made it easier," said Donna. "I never saw somebody shrivel up and die from the inside out like my dad did. He was just destroyed, his life stopped. Nobody can know what that man felt." The one thing that seemed to alleviate his pain after Tammy died was when Donna took him to Woodlawn Cemetery, where Wynette's body is interred. Her father "put his hands on the marble and talked to her quiet. He loved her and probably still loves her all these years later."

In Tammy's defense, she maintained she left Chapel the house, the fur-

---

*Credit cards were a favorite means of revenge for Tammy. George Jones told his girlfriend Linda Welborn that Wynette had done the same thing to him after they split. "She took every credit card they had and maxed it out," said Welborn. "She took everything he had."

niture, and the car, "which later I was sued for . . . and he let the house go back." Don, said Tammy, "created a lot of his own problems." Wynette was unusually candid in discussing the breakup with *Country Song Roundup* in 1978. "I'll take a lot of the blame for it," she said, admitting she was no good at facing problems head-on. "I don't mean to leave anybody mad or hurt. I will go out of my way to avoid a confrontation or an argument. I cannot stand it. That's why I have stomach problems. I don't yell and scream like I should."

And for George Jones to swoop in and "rescue" her the way he did was just too irresistible for a romantic like Tammy. "I never regretted leaving with him that night," she told Dolly Carlisle years later. "It was just fantastic."

Throughout the years Donna Chapel managed to stay friends with Tammy, and when Chapel relocated to Iowa, she'd go see Wynette when she performed in the area. Tammy, by then a superstar, was playing the big venues* but was as down-home as ever, addressing Donna from the stage (as she often did when old friends were in the audience), inviting her to come see her after the show. During one such visit Chapel brought a copy of Wynette's book along for her to sign. "I could always just talk with Tammy. I never had words with her, ever.

"She took me back in the back of her bus, pulled her little door shut in her bedroom there, and then she said, 'How is your dad?' And she said it in such a way to infer that she still had a care for him. And I said, 'Well, how do you think he is?' And I just looked at her. I believe at times she felt a lot of guilt for what she did. I truly do. And I felt really sad, because she didn't look happy. I could tell looking at her face. I know she was more successful as far as the outward things, but she was not happy emotionally.

"I showed her the book and said, 'Tammy, you know all these things that you put in here aren't right, don't you?' Here's what she said, and I quote: 'Well, when you're leavin' one husband and goin' to the other one, that's the way you have to write it up.' I just shook my head."

---

*One thing Donna immediately noticed was that success had bought Tammy a new set of bosoms. "She leaned over onstage and they almost fell out—I almost had a heart attack," she says. "They weren't there when I was around!"

Dear Tammy,

You must've been feeling like the cat that ate the canary right about now. I doubt you gave leaving Don Chapel a second's thought. Oh, I don't think you intentionally wanted to hurt anybody, but you were just one of those people who couldn't wait to get to the next page of the romance novel. Especially your own.

When I was a kid, I was obsessed with slow, sad music. Therefore you and George Jones became my surrogate parents, although thankfully I never had the hots for my actual mother. Boy, those album covers, Tammy. I know many a man driven crazy by just staring at that big, beautiful (and deeply tanned) forehead of yours.

We have this thing called eBay now. You'd love it. Anything you can dream of, you can buy, and you don't have to get off the couch. For a biographer it's a gold mine. I've found records, pictures, and even those little Tammy figurines that Richey was hawking on TV just after you died, which I'm glad you didn't live to see, because they look about as much like you as a Tammy drag queen with very limited funding.

I buy tons of Tammy magazine clippings on eBay. Every few weeks this lady in Pennsylvania sends me another battered manila envelope with your name handwritten in ink along the top, and stuffed inside are clippings from newspapers, gossip mags, country music monthlies, and all those tabloids you so loved/hated.

Last time I was emptying the current envelope, about to throw it away, when a tiny black-and-white picture I'd never seen before fluttered out. It was of you and Jones and Little Richard, backstage who knows where and who knows when. Just a strange little paper comet shooting down from the celebrity ether. Besides all those wild rockers, Richard cut what may be the most devastating soul ballad of all time, "I Don't Know What You Got (But It's Got Me)," a record I'd know you'd appreciate, Tammy. There you are, the King and Queens of sad. With your hair piled high, the three of you are like golden gods, and you look so radiant standing there next to Jones.

George told me he went to see Little Richard at some casino this past New Year's Eve. Richard didn't do "Long Tall Sally" and it made him mad, but Nancy danced up a storm.

You and Jones were doomed from the start, weren't you?

Beneath Still Waters

You bet against me?

—Fighter Louis "Mountain" Rivera to his manager Maish, *Requiem for a Heavyweight*

Let's let Tammy provide the proper introduction for George Jones: "When it comes to singin', no one can touch him. They never have been able to and they never will."

Few would be foolish enough to disagree. Jones can cut to the black heart of a ballad quick as an old fisherman guts a trout. He opens his mouth, and the sad comes out. George Jones has had a recording career that now spans fifty years plus. He holds the record for most charted country singles—140—and 78 of those made the top ten.

Ray Charles, Bob Dylan, Frank Sinatra have all sung his praises. Once Jones has cut a song, forget it. Said Earl "Peanutt" Montgomery, author of many a Jones number, "I never had a lot of covers on my songs with George, because when George recorded a song nobody wanted to cover it." Elvis Costello valiantly plodded his way through "A Good Year for the Roses," and I'm sure he'd be the first to admit his performance wilts in comparison. Emmylou Harris recorded a respectable version of "Beneath Still Waters," but it is the Jones recording that will have you on your knees praying for sunrise in the wee hours of night. Even Ray Charles couldn't top Jones doing "Just a Girl I Used to Know." And while Hank Williams himself might've written "I Can't Escape from You," the stark and skin-crawlingly slow demo George cut is the one that puts your head in the oven.

If I had the jitters meeting Billy Sherrill, I was terrified facing Jones. I've always looked up to him, even in the dark, demented days when he was quacking like a duck. There I sat in his den. And in his favorite spot on the couch, I might add, which the housekeeper luckily had me vacate moments before these words filled the air: "Did I hear somebody say they were *nervous*?" I'd have recognized that low rumble of a voice, honeyed and mischievous, anywhere. Suddenly a compact little figure toddled across the room, and—oh, brother—there was that face, its two-dots-and-a-slash features as minimal as an Internet emoticon. The glassy, close-set eyes suggesting the roadside critter that provides his nickname, that perfect soft-serve swirl of snow-white hair, the comical upturned nose above a slightly crazed grin . . . Jones could've waltzed right out of an old *Henry* comic strip. He has always been one of the oddest-looking fellows ever to walk upright. But then every last thing about Jones is a bit off center.

There's a lotta miles on this particular speedometer—Jones is seventy-eight as of 2009—and the face seems to be pulled a bit tight, regrettably the showbiz norm in these high-def days. But here's the rub: Jones has the mischievous energy of a kid who's misplaced his slingshot. That childlike quality you encounter in most creative types? George has it in spades. That said, I wouldn't want to be around when Junior pitches a fit. I'm certain Jones can still be a terror when things don't go his way.

George lives pretty much the life of Riley these days. He lives in a big, beautiful mansion a safe distance from Nashville and buys cars the way most people change socks. A big day consists of a trip to the nearby mall, a bite to eat, and endless hours of TV. (*The Jeffersons* and *Gunsmoke* were longtime Jones favorites; current contenders are *24* and *Lost*.) Although he hasn't had a hit in years and loves to grouse about what passes for country music these days—"shit," as George gleefully calls it—he lords over his own record label, tours constantly, and hawks a number of products bearing his name, such as George Jones dog food, breakfast sausage, and spring water. (Billy Sherrill suggested a new addition to the lineup—George Jones sanitary napkins, and even came up with a slogan: "Two little beady eyes between your thighs." The Possum was mortified.)

Never far from reach is wife Nancy, a spiffy, shrewd brunette from down Louisiana way whose charm is a slipcover for what has to be a resolve of steel—after all, she has stood by her man through years of drug addiction, humiliating poverty, mental cruelty, physical violence, and all-around general madness. To say nothing of the drug dealers who used to hover around Jones, threatening to carve him up along with anybody else unlucky enough to be in the way. In nearly every interview these days, he credits his wife with saving his life. George and Nancy bicker back and forth in that play-ful, occasionally cutting fashion only those who truly love each other can abide. Georgette—George's one child with Tammy and now a singer herself—informed me that one country music channel wanted to do a real-ity show featuring the couple à la *The Osbournes*, but thankfully the Joneses have spared themselves that burden. Nancy would, however, like to see Jones cut a duet with Cher. "What she thinks we'd do, I don't know," mused George.

Jones is frequently hilarious company. He nicknamed Evelyn Shriver and Susan Nadler, the executives of his current label, Bandit Records, "Shug" and "Paul," after two of his most notorious managers, Shug Baggot and Paul Richey, both harbingers of doom from the bad old days. I thought Jones might resist discussing those grim years, when he was so far gone on the booze and coke that he frequently engaged in three-way conversations be-tween himself and his alter egos, DeDoodle the Duck and the Old Man. But he managed a weary chuckle about his past, even going so far as to happily belt out a version of "He Stopped Loving Her Today" in full duck voice.

It was much harder to pry anything out of Jones about Tammy. As senti-mental a character as he is, I got the picture he'd rather poke his pecker in a beehive.

A few months after I spoke to him Jones put on a show in Portland, Oregon. It was old-school country in its presentation; no lasers, flying cow-boys, or pneumatic dancers, just a crazy old singer doing the only thing he knows how to do. He ran through the hits, dedicated a number to "our boys in Iraq," sailed through some gospel, and failed to remember the governor's name, even though he'd just met the man backstage. Behind Jones hung a large video screen showing the requisite visuals from his life (including the infamous TV footage of George looking completely deranged and ready to attack during his 1982 highway arrest, proving once again everything in a real country star's life is grist for the mill) as well as a low-rent video mon-tage accompanying his old hit "A Picture of Me (Without You)" that com-bined footage of an empty church, a mushroom cloud, and, inexplicably enough, clips from *On Golden Pond*, *Pretty Woman*, and *Walk the Line*. He danced a jig, extolled the virtues of George Jones spring water, and, as usual, threatened to play all night, which he never, ever does. George's voice was shot, apparently a common occurrence of late, and he spent as much time on his shtick as he did singing, but it mattered not one iota to this gathering of devoted fans. They were just glad the Possum was alive.

And that is what is most striking about Jones these days: how relaxed and at peace the guy seems. This was a man who never seemed comfortable in his own skin. I can recall nights when (if No-Show even managed to show), he prowled about the mic like an unchained animal anxious to shuffle back to the confines of his cage. Addiction, arrests, bankruptcy, guns . . . it was more than just for a year or two that the Grim Reaper clutched George's phone number in his bony fingers. Never the most expansive personality even when in good spirits, this happy-go-lucky incarnation of recent years is not only miraculous but invigorating. Nearly all of the artists I've written about have kicked the bucket, and not that long after they qualified for an AARP card.

There are writers who have portrayed Jones as some sort of idiot savant, a blank slate who happened to be born with pipes of gold. "If George wanted to know if it was rainin' he'd have to call the dog in to see if he's wet," said songwriter and friend Jerry Chestnut. "God gave him a great talent to sing— and that's *all* he gave him." I don't know about that. Jones has survived a long run in a ruthless business with both talent and dignity intact. And nobody but nobody who knew both George and Tammy way back when would've placed a nickel bet on Jones outliving Wynette. But she's long gone. And here stands Jones. "There ain't no way I'm supposed to be here," he's admitted. And at least a small part of him remains unrepentant. "Truth be told, I would probably do it the same if given the chance."

Jones was born in Saratoga, Texas, on September 12, 1931, the youngest of eight children. He was raised in Kountze, then Beaumont. All three towns lie within a grim industrial zone of east Texas known as the "Big Thicket." "The asshole of Texas" is how one former resident of the Lone Star State described Beaumont. "All the fumes and debris flowed down there and spewed out in a staggering mess. And with the refineries the smell was frightening. If you really wanted to be mean, you'd call someone a Beauhole." Jones grew up dirt poor. "Only thing my seven brothers and sister and I ever had under our Christmas tree was fruit."

George's mother, Clara, played piano and organ in church, and his father, George Washington Jones—a logger and sometime moonshiner—could

manage a bit of what his son called "square dancin' guitar." George Sr. became a heavy boozer after losing Ethel, his seven-year-old daughter, to illness. "You never would see my dad smile or laugh about anything," said
George. "You could tell a joke and he'd be just as solemn." Until payday
rolled around, that is. George Sr. would meet Clara at the H & H hardware
and grocery store in Kountze and hand over enough loot to pay the bill and
buy groceries. "While she was doin' that, he'd sneak across the street and
get him a beer. Just the thought of it, he'd start smilin'."

Ask George's friends where some of the sadness in his voice comes from,
and they will point to his father and what he inadvertently taught his son
about the strange power of music. George Sr. would stumble home from
the bar in the midnight hour, then shake George and his sister Doris awake,
demanding they sing for him. Doris would make her brother "sing the high
tenor," he noted. "We'd sing gospel songs—'Precious Jewel' and 'Wreck on
the Highway,' stuff like that. As a kid you was dreadin' it. Nobody likes to
be woke up in the middle of the night." George Sr. took the rest of his frus-
trations out on Clara, sometimes physically. "I always hated my daddy for
drinking," admitted George, who would head down the same path with a
vengeance. "You would think he wouldn't have went that way," said Nancy
Jones. "But that was the only life that little boy knew."

As with Tammy and Billy Sherrill, gospel music was George's first love.
"My mother had a beautiful voice. She could sing them gospel songs. As
children, we were very devoted to church, especially the singin' part." One
way or another, the Bible has always loomed large in George's mind. Jones
"has a lot of religion in him," said Nancy. "People will probably never believe
that, but whenever George was really, really, really bad, I'd say, 'Y'know,
Jesus is lookin' at you,' or put on some gospel music, and I could always
calm him down."

George's father bought him a guitar—"a shiny Gene Autry guitar with a
horse and a lariat on the front"—and it never left his side, except at school,
where Jones would hide the guitar in a pile of leaves outside the building.
Picked on due to his half-pint stature, Jones "just wanted to go out in the
woods and hide and play guitar." He got no further than seventh grade. "It
seems like he was in a dream world," said his oldest sister, Helen Scroggins.
"He was just a loner."

At age eleven, playing to a crowd of passersby from a shoe-shine stand
outside a penny arcade on Pearl Street in downtown Beaumont, George

earned his first payday playing music. Twenty-four dollars and ninety cents, in fact, all of which he promptly blew in the arcade. Right from the get-go, Jones had a rather majestic sense of irresponsibility. As an adult, one of his favorite banks for an impromptu deposit seemed to be any commode that happened to be in the vicinity. Countless witnesses have relayed tales of a shitfaced and trigger-happy Jones flushing a fortune down the john.

Little George soon joined forces with Brother Burl and Sister Annie, a local Pentecostal preacher and his wife. He'd harmonize with Annie inside an old car, a cheap speaker broadcasting their gospel down the dusty Texas streets. At fourteen he was earning $17.50 a week plus room and board as a guitarist for Eddie and Pearl, another husband-and-wife act who had a popular radio show on Beaumont radio station KRIC. It was on that show in 1949 that George came face-to-face with Hank Williams for the first and only time. "I was just startin' to play at some of the honky-tonks. I'd have to stay back in the kitchen except when I did some singin'. Every weekend I couldn't wait to get out there to see if the jukebox operator had put on the new singles yet. I'd be out there early, lookin' up and down those records, tryin' to find a new one by Hank Williams. It kindly got me away from gospel a little bit."

Jones was seventeen when he married his first wife, Dorothy. His father-in-law insisted George get a job painting houses. Jones says the stress of living with in-laws and working day jobs did the marriage in. He failed to make child support payments and was thrown in jail. His sister Helen felt this was the first time George began to drink heavily. He joined the Marines. "It was better than goin' back to jail," he told Nick Tosches. According to one band member, Jones wept the night before going into the service. "He didn't want to go on account of his music," said bandmate Dido Rowley.

Just months after he left the Marines, Jones cut his first record for the scrappy independent label Starday in February 1954, a song he wrote entitled "No Money in This Deal." ("And in that deal, there wasn't," said Jones of Starday.) The session took place in the living room of label honcho Jack Starnes. Jones began recording a dozen years before Tammy Wynette would walk into Epic, when conditions were much cruder, to say the least. Egg crates were stapled to the wall to deaden the sound, and Jack's son Bill, manning the tape recorder in another room, let the band know they were rolling by switching a light on and off. "Eighteen-wheelers would go by, and we'd have to do another take or two," said Jones. "When I heard myself back,

Lord, I thought it was terrible. I thought, 'Boy, can't y'all get a better sound than that?'" Jones admitted in an interview on the *700 Club* that he'd literally prayed for a hit. "I want one so bad. I would pray to the Good Lord all the time, 'Let me just get that one record to see how it feels.'" But George said he was embarrassed by "Why Baby Why," his first Starday release to chart in 1955. "My harmony was way off, not together, and the guitar didn't come out right. What the hell, it went to number 4."

One of the partners in Starday was Harold "Pappy" Daily, a Houston jukebox potentate who would function as George's manager, producer, and (some say) surrogate father. He was the one constant in his career until Tammy lured Jones away to Epic after their marriage. "Pappy Daily was a colorful guy," said Kelso Herston, who led many a George Jones session in those days. "He smoked cigars and loved to gamble at the dice table." Pappy was an old-school record maker: he cranked them out fast and cheap, utilizing as many numbers he held the publishing rights to as possible. ("Some of the publishers would split publishing to get a George Jones cut," said Herston. "A lot of this was done in secret, but happened frequently.")

Pappy was the one who gave Jones an astute piece of advice during his very first Starday session. George had spent the first few hours imitating his favorite singers: Hank Williams, Roy Acuff, and Lefty Frizzell. (Of the three, Jones said Lefty is the most present in his phrasing—"I love all them wiggles and what have you"—and anybody who's heard Frizzell worry his way through a lyric would have to agree.*) "We've heard you sing like everybody on the Grand Ole Opry, I think," said Daily. "Can we hear you sing just one time like George Jones?"

Beyond that, Pappy knew little about the art of making music. Unlike today, however, where the artist has to deal with a vast horde of record executive interlopers anxious to tinker with the product, Daily let the singer and the musicians create in peace. "His artists picked most of the material to record," said Herston. "I never heard the man make a suggestion. He wasn't a producer, even though he got credit for being one." The one thing

---

*Jones would befriend Lefty near the end of his life, when Frizzell's alcohol intake had caused him to be banished to the basement of his own home by his churchgoing wife, Alice. "It was really sad," said Jones. "Lefty, he crawled in a shell. He had all that big success at once and it seemed like it stopped all at once, too. And he got to think he was losin' his voice. It was weird. I'd go to his house, we was gonna write a song, I wouldn't be there ten minutes and he'd be talkin' about losin' his voice. And then he'd take another drink of vodka."

Pappy cared about was quantity. The standard quota for a three-hour Nashville session during those days was three songs, but Daily "was disappointed if he didn't get six sides in three hours," said Herston. "One day we recorded two George Jones albums in four sessions—twelve hours. That would be impossible in today's world." When I asked Jones what Pappy contributed as a producer, he was succinct: "a stopwatch." George said it was Pappy who talked him into cutting a handful of lead-footed rockabilly sides (under the alias "Thumper" Jones) he is rightfully ashamed of.

In 1957 Jones moved to Mercury, cutting his first top ten ballad (unlike Tammy, Jones scored numerous up-tempo hits), the self-penned "Just One More." Significantly enough, it was a paean to the memory-demolishing powers of the bottle, and while Jones expertly draws out the syllables, it only hinted at the exquisite havoc he'd soon wreak upon a lyric. This was what George did best: the ballad. "I'm a fool for a sad song," said Jones. "We just fit." Engineer Lou Bradley once asked Jones how he could tell a song was right for him. "It's gotta make fire come out of my ass," responded George, and he must have left quite a trail of scorch marks, because the hits kept right on coming: "White Lightning," "The Window Up Above," and "She Thinks I Still Care."

In 1962 he moved to United Artists, and it was there he cut the bluegrass-tinged duets with Melba Montgomery that made such an impression on Tammy. The strangely creepy 1963 hit "You Comb Her Hair" featured one of George's odder deliveries and would remain Wynette's number one Jones song (her favorite line: "I finally met a girl who turns me inside out"). George was hanging around ace songwriters Hank Cochran and Harlan Howard down in Howard's basement music room when they penned the song. "Hank Cochran got on the phone for a minute and was callin' his girlfriend or wife. And she must've evidently asked him, 'Who do you love?' and he said, 'Well, you know who I love—you comb her hair every mornin'. And put me to bed every night.' Harlan heard him say that and they set down and wrote that thing right off."

Jones cut nearly all of his sessions at the studio Tammy would record in with Billy Sherrill, the Quonset Hut. Jones had understandably developed a rep as a singer's singer, and the whole world wanted in when Jones came to town. "He drew a crowd," said Herston. "All the writers came by. It was almost like a cocktail party." And you never knew what to expect from Jones, which was part of the excitement. "Everybody loved George," said Bob Moore, who in 1970 produced the extra-baroque Jones hit "A Good Year for the Roses." "Just because he was pitiful. Nobody could sing like George. It didn't make any difference what song it was, he just sung the shit out of it. Then you'd start hearin' these stories—'Well, Jones got sloshed last night and gave his boat away.' Fifty-thousand-dollar boat. He *owed* forty-five on it."

Ironically enough, while alcohol might've been a destructive force in his personal life, in terms of his singing, it had a beneficial effect—at least to a degree. "When he had a few drinks, he could just sing his ass off," explained Pig Robbins. "But there was a point when he'd go over the line and get kind of . . . feisty." Bob Moore agreed, explaining it thusly: "If you're playin' in a dance band and you go back, play the second set, it's always better because you done had a beer or two. George was kinda like that. He'd come in and do real good, it was letter A. Then letter B, he'd start singin' *real* good. And then at letter C, he's getting sloshed."

The trick was to strike when Jones was still at letter B, which was no easy task. "I remember the day we cut 'The Race Is On,' " said Kelso Herston, who led the session and played the bass guitar lead. "George was drunk. He mispronounces some of the words—he says, 'Ray right down and die' instead of 'Lay right down and die.' We just barely got through it. I had to take him back to the motel after." Bob Moore said there was a telltale sign when George was heading south: "One eye'd start crossin' a bit."

In 1965 Jones moved to Musicor, source of many of his tackiest album covers, hitting right away with Leon Payne's dirgelike inventory of domestic catastrophe, "Things Have Gone to Pieces." Later that year came the screw-loose "Love Bug," soon to be followed by the even more demented "I'm a People," one of George's more idiotic novelty numbers, which is saying something.* During the period that George started doing shows with Tammy, he was on top of his game, enjoying a number one smash with the ever so hopeful "Walk Through This World with Me."

Besides the singing and drinking, just what sort of fellow was Wynette going to spend the next seven years with? One whose inner workings were

---

*Jones has always balanced out ballads with cosmically moronic throwaways. Masochists are urged to search out 1988's "The King Is Gone (So Are You)," a song that delineates a conversation between Jones, a Flintstones jelly bean jar, and an Elvis decanter.

at least as complex as her own. Here is a man who could weep openly while singing "House of Gold" in front of friends, then turn and run if the raw emotions of loved ones were unleashed. "You can cry in front of him all day long, he's not gonna get up and hug you," said Nancy Jones. "Now, he'll hug you if you're not cryin', but if one of my children is cryin', and I'm up there huggin' and kissin' 'em, he'll go out of the room. He can't handle that, that cryin'." Jones admitted as much himself in a 1981 interview with Mark Rose. "I don't show a lot of affection. I have probably been a very unliked person among family. Like somebody who was heartless. I saved it all for the songs."

But just because Jones was reticent and reluctant to reveal doesn't mean he wasn't taking notes. "He knew people," said ex-girlfriend Linda Welborn. "George don't want you to know how smart he is. He sets back and he watches. George might be cuttin' up, havin' the biggest time in the world, but he's checkin' you out." She said sometimes he'd go so far as to feign being blotto just so he could eavesdrop. "George would act like he was passed out, so he could lay there and listen to what was bein' said about him."

George's endless idiosyncrasies could fill a set of encyclopedias. "I do crazy things when I'm not drinking, too," Jones told Joan Dew. "Like I might leave here tonight with every intention of driving to Alabama and end up in Texas. I don't know why, never have understood it. Just restless, I guess." Linda Welborn said the only way she knew for certain Jones wasn't about to amscray was if his shaving kit was in its customary place in the bathroom. If it was anywhere else—propped up against the couch, say—she could count on the Possum pulling a disappearing act, usually without much of a good-bye. The other dead giveaway that Jones was plotting something was when he started making little noises by sucking air through his teeth. "I didn't put anything past him," said Earl "Peanutt" Montgomery. "Hanging around George you might wind up in South America tomorrow. You never knew what he'd do. He mighta bought two houses, or a motel. He'd do anything that come across his mind."

Like Tammy, Jones hated to be alone and kept a little entourage of friends around him. Chief among them were Earl and his wife, Charlene. A Florence, Alabama–born musician who dates back to the Fairlanes and Arthur Alexander, Earl was Melba Montgomery's brother. Beginning in 1961, he wrote some classic songs for George, played in his band, and even ducked a bullet from George's gun on one infamous occasion. Until their estrangement in the eighties, George and Earl were practically inseparable. Montgomery said Jones once told him, "Peanutt, if we were any closer, we'd be gay."

When it comes to any kind of game—billiards, marbles, bowling, cards—Jones loathes losing. "He'd call it 'getting stomped,'" said Peanutt's wife, Charlene. "If you beat him in a game of anything—getting stomped. When we was playin' volleyball, I'd always tell 'em, 'Miss the ball, let George win, keep him in a good mood.' He takes it serious." Linda Welborn recalled Jones getting on a bowling kick. They went out and bought new bowling balls, gloves, and shoes. "First game I beat him," said Linda. "Second game I beat him. In the middle of the third game, he gets mad—'We're goin' home. I'm not playin' no game with no woman that can beat me.'" They drove behind the bowling alley and George deposited all the gear he'd just bought in the Dumpster. "We didn't go back bowlin' no more," said Linda.

Linda picked Jones up at the airport one day. Her son Dale was in the car, as was his box of cassette tapes. "When George got in the car, he got to flippin' through these little tapes. He didn't see any of his in there." Jones asked Dale if there were any of his albums in the collection. Not at the moment, replied Dale. "George said, 'I can't believe you don't have no tapes of me in here.' And out the window the whole bunch went. He told Dale, 'Son, that's what you get for not havin' some of *me* in there.'"

Jones was fastidious about his appearance, particularly his hair, which, said Linda, "had to be done just about every day." But even in this area Jones could throw a curveball. One night Jones was hanging out with Peanutt, Charlene, and songwriter "Wild" Bill Emerson and his wife. For some unknown reason Jones decided it was time for an Afro. His friends tried to talk him out of it, which only made George more adamant. As Linda recalled, "He's sittin' there, he's not gonna have it no other way—'I said I want an Afro and I'm gonna *have* one! You'll have one, too! We're *all* getting Afros!'" As it was already evening, George summoned a hairdresser to unlock a local parlor. "We all go marchin' down there and we all get Afros," said Linda. "George gets up the next mornin', looked in the mirror, and said, 'Oh, my God. OH, MY GOD! What am I gonna *do*?'" As Jones had a show to do that night, he put in an emergency call to his Nashville hairdresser. ("I looked like a Keekadoo from Kookamoo," said George when I reminded him of the tale.)

Jones wasn't a controlling personality, but it should come as no surprise that the author of "The Window Up Above" could be a jealous one. One day

out on the road Linda was summoned to the tour bus. George was sitting
there with Hank Williams, Jr. "I want you to meet somebody," Jones said to
Linda. "'This is Hank Jr.' I said, 'Hi, Hank, nice to meet you.'" After a few
pleasantries were exchanged, Linda exited the bus. "When we get home,
George says, 'You better be proud of what you done today.'" Linda inquired
as to what it was, exactly, that she'd done, and George repeated himself.
Finally he blurted out, "You know why I brought you out to the bus to meet
Hank Jr.? I want to see if you'd ask for his autograph, because when you
met me, you didn't ask for mine. I just wanted to see if you'd ask *him* for
his autograph." Linda was nonplussed, a frequent reaction to the behavior
of George. "I just looked at him and said, 'My goodness, George, you beat
all I ever seen.'"

George is known to be incredibly generous, impulsively giving away cars,
guitars, jewelry, and cash—and not just when soused. "We was drivin' down
the road one day, and there was this elderly black couple settin' on the porch,
just a small little frame house," said Linda. "George slammed on his brakes."
Jones pulled two hundred dollars from his wallet and put it in Linda's hand.
"I want you to take this money and give it to 'em," said Jones.

Linda was afraid she might offend the strangers, but George insisted.

"Somethin' tells me to give them some money," he said.

Linda did as she was told. "If I get in trouble, you better come and rescue
me," she said.

"I told the lady, 'George Jones the country singer is out there in the car.
He said he had a feeling he wanted to give y'all some money. I hope that's
okay.' The man didn't say nothin', he was just lookin' at me. The woman
reached out, took it, and said, 'That's plenty okay! We need it! This is the
answer to our prayers!'"

Linda returned to the car, telling Jones, "George, they didn't kill me, and
they really appreciated it."

"Good," said George as they drove off.

There are countless stories like these. Just before his near-fatal wreck in
1999, Jones encountered some poor unfortunate at a rest stop driving a
vehicle with bald tires. He plucked off some bills from his bankroll and told
her to buy a new set. "He's got a heart as big as Texas," said Peanutt.

What a quizzical entity Jones had grown into circa 1967. Some sort of flat-
top alien Huck Finn in a Nudie suit. If that wasn't weird enough, George's

mouth barely moved when he sang. It cut through you, nonetheless, my friend. Once a ballad got its hooks into him, night fell and the fun was over. For here was a voice that "quivers with a suppressed tension that makes pleasantries sound uncertain and turns weepers into small-scale tragedies," wrote Jon Pareles in the *New York Times*. "His singing dwells on betrayal and loss with a calm fatalism."

When asked about what he does, Jones makes it sound easy. "If you start singin' a sad song or a good love song, you're naturally gonna start feelin' that song. I know when I go in to record or I'm onstage singin' each song I sing, I'm actually livin' that two or three minutes. I put my heart and soul in it. I see this person, I see this happenin'. I live the words, the idea, the story of the song." And refreshingly enough, he offers no lame excuses for what comes with the territory. "It's a shame to say this, but the booze, the wild life, the women—that's all a part of country music."

Writers have long searched for some well of regret, some defining moment of despair that might shed light on the Jones enigma. But, as with Tammy, something impenetrable remains. I doubt the Possum himself could tell you what it is, even if he bothered to try. "He's got a mystery about hisself," Nancy Jones, the one person who should know all the secrets, confessed to me. "You think you can read him, but when I think I've got him figured out, I really don't."

"Beneath Still Waters," a Dallas Frasier song that surely ranks as one of George's most hypnotic performances, says it all: "Beneath still waters, there's a strong undertow / The surface won't tell you what the deep waters know." Great as the lyrics are, they lie on the page like roadkill. You have to hear Jones *sing* them. For all his craziness, there is a great warmth to George. He's an analog being, not digital. And Jones knows the abyss is never far away. Listen to his music, it's the one thing George has never run from. He steps right out to join us on the ledge, calming us with a lullaby, however melancholy it may be.

By the time Jones met Tammy, he'd already had an astonishing run of more than fifty hits, been in the business a dozen years, and was already widely recognized as the greatest ballad singer of his time. He was ten years older than Wynette, had just divorced his second wife, Shirley, and had seen it all and then some. Jones must've intimidated the hell out of her. Nor was Tammy one who liked to have things sprung on her, and Jones was a surprise a minute. It must've been thrilling at first, but she'd soon find his brand of chaos more exhausting than her own inner turmoil.

George and Tammy were two great artists, each capable of plumbing the absolute depths of a sad song. Recording together, they'd create genuine husband-and-wife art in one of few art forms hokey enough to embrace it: the country duet. And both were incredibly stubborn creatures. "George did what George pretty much wanted to do," noted Billy Sherrill. "You can't push a rope." Back in the eighties when everybody was fed up with George for blowing shows, recording dates, and his career in general, he told Billy Sherrill, "Look, as long as I can go into Holiday Inn with a guitar and make a living, nobody's gonna push me around."

In Tammy, George had finally met someone who was just as intent on getting her own way. "Hard head" is how Tammy once described herself. There was just no way this romance was going to be a smooth ride.

"She wanted her way and he wanted his way," said George's sister Helen. "They was too much alike."

We Got Married in a Fever

We never were friends when we were married.

—George Jones

There is this great shot of George Jones in the December 1975 issue of *Country Music* magazine. A two-page color spread of Jones standing by the fireplace in his office. I never tire of gazing at it. Among his many talents, Jones loves to decorate, and there's no question he's overseen every quizzical detail. Standing there, plucking away on his guitar and staring off into space, George looks like a wax figure in his very own Spanish Colonial diorama. A faux gold coat of arms/clock with matching lions sits above the rock fireplace, an ornate pendant lamp (also gold) hangs from a ceiling chain, a bold painting of a bullfighter adorns one wall. There are also potted ferns, fat candles on stands, and a shiny statue of a leopard. It's all quite fancy, but a closer look reveals the open can of Coors at George's feet.

This was the strange universe Tammy Wynette had willingly entered, and on their first official night together George and Tammy closed the black velvet drapes in the Possum's bedroom, tiptoed across the bloodred carpet, and plopped down on his massive four-poster bed, turning on the TV to watch Anthony Quinn and Jackie Gleason in *Requiem for a Heavyweight*. The film tells the bleak tale of an over-the-hill prizefighter. Sold down the road by an overextended manager, he eventually winds up on the wrestling circuit in an Indian headdress, whooping and hollering like some carnival geek. It plays out not unlike the downhill spiral of George's own life over the next few decades. Forty years later, when asked if he had a favorite movie, it was the first title he named.

As Jones wept watching the movie, Wynette, who'd been feeling apprehensive over their first actual night in the sack, melted. Only one small detail tainted this romantic reverie: the bottle of whiskey on the nightstand. This scared Tammy. "I did not understand alcohol," she admitted later. "I didn't know how to cope with it."

The next day the couple flew to Mexico City for Tammy's quickie divorce from Don Chapel. They returned to Nashville only to find that Tennessee didn't recognize Mexican divorces and that the Tammy, George, and Don triangle was now front-page fodder for the *Nashville Banner*. But Wynette would prevail. A legal loophole allowed her to have the marriage to Chapel declared null and void: Alabama law requires that parties who remarry within a year of their divorce have to seek permission from the judge in their case. Tammy had married Don two months before her exit from Euple was final. Although George thought such an outright fib was a bad idea, Tammy insisted that they tell the world they'd tied the knot while in Mexico on August 22, 1968.

Paranoid that the press would find out there had been no actual nuptials, Wynette wanted to slip away from Music City, and since Jones had a residence in Lakeland, Florida, they decided to relocate there. For the time being, though, they moved into a house Tammy had bought on Old Hickory Lake. She watched in amazement as Jones went into a redecorating frenzy, transforming their home into some sort of gloomy, macho hacienda. "I had never seen one room with all the same kind of furniture in it," said Wynette. "He taught me an awful lot."

"It was a really stormy marriage from the beginning," said Tammy, and it was during her first trip to Lakeland that things began to get ugly. Some friends of George's paid a visit to his room at the Holiday Inn (a couple who were actually leasing his Lakeland home at the moment), and Jones drank himself into a stupor. When Tammy tried to reel him in, he threw a punch at her, smashing a whiskey bottle against the wall. Terrified, she ran out into the night in her pajamas, Jones in hot pursuit. George tripped, landing facedown in a flower bed. Tammy sprinted down the street to the Blue Egret Motel. She returned to a sullen Jones nursing a broken wrist. The next day he was back to his jolly self. George Jones, Tammy confessed, was "the only person who could get me so mad I could scream one minute and then sing me a song that was so sad I'd cry my eyes out."

As far as country music fans were concerned, the Jones-Wynette romance only stoked the coals of their popularity. George's next hit was "I'll Share My World with You," a ballad written by a middle-aged Florida maker of seashell art who'd been inspired to take up songwriting after reading about George and Tammy's romance in the fan rags. Now their very lives were song fodder, and it was only the beginning. "The relationship was acted out in the material," said country music authority Robert K. Oermann. "How cool is *that*? It's fascinating to me that Tammy and George would make their music mirror their lives. That is *so* country."

Recorded in early November 1968, "I'll Share My World with You" stalled at number 2 on the charts. A monster hit was blocking its entry to the top spot, and it was by Tammy: "Stand by Your Man." This particular record was to become her signature song and, for better and for worse, define her image for all time. It would thrust Wynette out of country music's insular bubble and subject her to close scrutiny by the world at large.

The song would also outrage many a feminist. Sue Tyrell, analyzing Tammy and the song in a provocative 1975 article entitled "Tammy Wynette: Peroxide Politics and the Counter-Revolution," saw "Stand by Your Man" as "a protest song" for right-wing America. "Figurehead of the counter-revolution," Wynette was "spearheading the inevitable backlash to the women's movement." Tyrell found the Wynette-Sherrill productions to be diabolical manifestos in which "womanhood is packaged, promoted and sold as not only the most fulfilling occupation, but the *only* occupation.... What keeps women going is the urge to first get a man and then struggle to keep him and her happiness in life is dependent solely on how successful she is doing it . . . stuck up on a pedestal, out of harm's way, Woman is defined totally by her man."

Wynette would often joke to the press that she and Billy spent twenty minutes writing "Stand by Your Man" and she'd spent twenty years defending it. "I'm gonna have to sing 'Stand by Your Man' 'til the day I die," she told her hairdresser Barbara Hutchison.

"And she did," added Barbara.

"I thought 'Stand by Your Man' was incredibly great—so well written, so well done. Tammy was singin' it with great conviction. It rubbed a few people raw, but I never was into that women's lib thing. I believe if you got a man worth standin' by, you should. And I think if you got a man ain't worth standin' by, kick his ass out—and Tammy did that enough times. So she didn't really stick by her song, either, did she? HA!"

—Dolly Parton

"'After all, he's just a man.' [laughter] Well, he can't help it. He's got that . . . thing."

—Allison Moorer

"I wanted to do a video of 'Stand by Your Man' but do it all beat up. Have my arm in a sling, with a black eye, and I'm limpin'. 'Sometimes it's hard to be a woman . . .'"

—Roni Stoneman, *Hee Haw* comedienne

"She is not the victim. She is singin' this as a total heroine—and it's that contradiction that makes that record one of the best records ever made."

—Bill Drummond, KLF

"I think you ought to stand by your man if he's standin' by you. If he ain't standin' by you, move over!"

—Loretta Lynn

"I'm not sitting here as some little woman standing by my man like Tammy Wynette."

—Hillary Clinton, 1992

"Hillary missed the point. The lyrics echo a recurring theme in country music, that of the moral superiority of women who stand by their men not because they're hopelessly enthralled, but because they know the boys can't help it. 'After all,' as the song says, 'he's just a man.'"

—Julia Reed

"Tammy was a doormat, according to these feminists? 'Stand by Your Man' is a beautiful song. She's a hypocrite, Hillary. Hillary stood by her man long enough to get points to run for senator and now for president. If she had any true balls she woulda left the guy, for God's sake."

—Robert Duvall

"I like the idea of sayin', 'I know I'm a jerk, but love me anyway.'"

—Lyle Lovett, who recorded the song in 1989

"I will stand by my man."

—Amy Winehouse, speaking outside of a courthouse in 2007
after her husband had been thrown in jail

"The ambivalence expressed by the song is, after all, a deep and troubling one, and the song exudes a sense of sadness. . . . For these tens
of thousands of women who made 'Stand by Your Man' the biggest-
selling song in the history of country music, the song may have been
the quintessential expression of their ambivalent and pathetic experience in conflictual and unequal relationships with men."

—Kenneth E. Morris

"It was just a pretty love song."

—Tammy Wynette

1968. Brother, what a year. It really seemed like America was coming apart
at the seams. Vietnam was an ongoing nightmare, Kennedy and King were
mowed down by assassins, three black students were shot to death and
thirty were injured by police on a South Carolina campus, angry youths
rioted outside the Chicago Democratic Convention. Even poor Andy Warhol
got shot. As "Born to Be Wild" blasted out of transistor radios, turmoil lurked
everywhere. Lording over our world by the year's end was Richard Nixon,
and if you wanted to design a being that a vast majority of young people
were destined to hate, you couldn't do better than this guy. A dark and
ridiculous figure that bellowed on like some befuddled, hungover parent
who's finally decided to confront his kids about that damn marijuana, Nixon
was humorless, authoritarian, and paranoid. The man had it all, and Music
City embraced him. The night of its 1974 relocation to Opryland, the Grand
Ole Opry greeted a Watergate-weary Nixon with open arms as Roy Acuff
none too successfully instructed the president on his yo-yo technique.

I doubt if Tammy paid much attention to any of the above. Consumed
by her career, she was either on the road or in Nashville making records.
But during this period there was one subject Wynette commented on frequently in interviews: the women's movement. Nineteen sixty-eight was a

banner year for feminists. Members of the National Organization for Women took to the streets, demonstrating against the war, abortion laws, and even the Miss America beauty pageant. "Women's lib" was the phrase on everyone's lips. But in the Jones-Wynette household, "George is the boss," Tammy told Ralph Emery in 1971. "There's no mistakin' that Tammy Wynette is not one for women's liberation."

Tammy was far from alone in such sentiments, particularly among Nashville peers. "I just really believe what the Scripture says," said Connie Smith. "The head of a house is a man." Jean Shepard: "Country entertainers have a tendency to let the man wear the pants." Jody Miller: "Man is usually a little wilder. A woman should be better. You bear the children." Wynette's contemporaries tended to regard feminists with distrust, seeing them as sullen, man-hating gorillas in the mist that burned their brassieres and swung through the trees with furry legs. They were unladylike. Antichurch and antifamily!

However, there were certain issues on which Tammy wholeheartedly agreed with the movement. Back in Alabama she'd seen where "a woman couldn't make a third of what a man could make doing an identical job. . . . It's very wrong. A woman should be equal to a man for anything she's capable of doing." Wynette herself had risen to the top in a very tough, male-dominated business, and, according to her daughter Jackie, "when she and Jones were married, *she* ran the place, *she* did the books. I remember her comin' in the kitchen and she said, 'We've toured a million dollars.' That's because Mom took care of everything." Tammy felt she was winning the battle where it counted most. "Sometimes I think that the ladies makin' the most noise are the least liberated," she said. "I didn't have time to go 'round squawkin' about some cause, because I was too busy workin'."

When it came to anything that threatened to blur the lines of her "old-fashioned" concepts of gender, however, Tammy was turned off. "Personally, I'm not particularly fond of the thought of digging ditches or climbing telephone poles. I'd rather stick with something a little more feminine. I wouldn't want to lose the little courtesies that we've always been extended, like lighting cigarettes and opening doors . . . I guess I just enjoy bein' a woman."

Billy Sherrill agreed with that point of view, and made it clear that this particular song was a direct response to the women's movement. He told Dorothy Horstman in 1981, "After being barraged by women's lib and the

Equal Rights Amendment, I wanted it to be a song for all the women out there that didn't agree, a song for the truly liberated woman, one who is secure enough in her identity to enjoy it. To some skeptics it may hint of chauvinism . . . they can like it or lump it. Because 'Stand by Your Man' is just another way of saying 'I love you'—without reservations."

"Women are very sympathetic creatures," explained Sherrill. "I make records for women. I write songs for women. They sell." Early on in their association Billy and Tammy saw the results of a survey that would influence the content of her music. "Epic Records did a poll to see what age group bought records," said Wynette. "And the results were that 55 to 65 percent of country records were bought by women between the ages of twenty-two and forty-five. . . . That's one thing that helps us determine what to record."

Sherrill went after this market with a vengeance, creating tailor-made songs "so skillfully," wrote Jack Hurst, "the titles might've been borrowed from the pages of *Cosmopolitan* magazine." It should be pointed out that even taking into account Tammy's contributions, the bulk of her songs were written by men, although I'd hazard a guess that just about anything Wynette sang was something she personally believed in. This is what created "Stand by Your Man": the personal beliefs of Sherrill and Wynette, plus a dash of down-home marketing. Don't let it define the meaning of this very unusual song.

It was the night of August 28, 1968. Billy and Tammy were recording in the Quonset Hut. "We were in the middle of a lackluster recording session," recalled Sherrill, who told the pickers to take a twenty-minute break while he took Tammy up to his office in the hopes of dredging up a worthy song. Although Wynette later felt she knew Billy "like the back of my hand," at this point he still remained inscrutable: "I was very intimidated by him."

Billy was not one to pal around with his artists after hours or even attend their shows. "I didn't want to. I don't like to go to damn concerts. I'd rather see a movie. Only time I ever saw Tammy was in the offices or in the studio." But he and Wynette had a different bond from the one he had with other artists. It certainly wasn't combative, such as the relationship Patsy Cline had had with Owen Bradley, or even the one Sherrill had at times with little upstart Tanya Tucker. One day in the studio Tanya was chattering away to Pig Robbins in between takes, and it began to irritate Billy, who was instructing Billy Sandford. "All of a sudden Billy turned around and said, '*Shut up!*'" Tucker recalled. "Everybody just got real quiet and I said, '*You* shut up!' Oh, my God, you coulda heard a pin drop. They couldn't believe that I would say that to him. 'Course, I was thirteen years old! Billy just stood back looked at me and just smiled."*

Wynette, on the other hand, followed orders without complaint. As Sherrill boasted to *Rolling Stone*, "If Tammy walked up right now and we were recordin' tonight and I said, 'Your next record is "Three Blind Mice,"' she'd say two words: 'What key?'" As he discussed Tammy with me, Sherrill's voice got a bit quiet. "Tammy was very, very down to earth, extremely humble. She believed in me, and I believed in her. We just hit it off.† It was a pleasure recording her. Unlike the Possum, she was a very quick study. She'd learn the song and she wouldn't question anything." When I asked Sherrill what drove Tammy, he paused. "I don't think she was ever driven. Tammy was just so unique that she didn't have to be driven. Everything just kind of fell in place for her. She was lucky to write well enough—and be the recipient of some damn good songs."

"Stand by Your Man" is credited to both Sherrill and Wynette. What isn't widely known is that this particular collaboration (according to Sherrill) was about 90 percent Billy and 10 percent Tammy. Sherrill has since donated the original lyric sheet, handwritten in pen and complete with chord changes, to the Alabama Music Hall of Fame. Originally called "I'll Stand

---

*Tanya Tucker on Wynette and Sherrill: "Tammy had a real close relationship with Billy. I was always jealous of Tammy Wynette because Billy always wrote songs for her." Tucker says the only song Sherrill ever penned for her was "I Guess I'll Have to Love Him More."

†Wynette told an amusing story concerning rumors over her relationship with Sherrill to author Holly George-Warren in 1994. "It was all over Music Row that Billy was having an affair with me . . . I got so upset and aggravated over being accused—Billy was just like my brother. . . . I don't know what made me do it, but I guess I had thought about it for so much it had bothered me 'til I went to the hospital for something, I was sick. And I was feeling real groggy, and I remember picking up the phone and I called Billy Sherrill and he said, 'How are you doing?' Lord, this was about three years into our relationship working together. I said, 'Well, I'll tell you one thing, if you want to have an affair with me, you better get over here right now, 'cause this is the last chance you'll ever have.'

"Well, I just heard a chuckle and I laid the phone down. It dawned on me what I had said. I came to my senses and said, 'Oh, my God!' And Billy laughed. He laughed, and Charlene, his wife, thought that was the funniest thing she'd ever heard. That was as close to a relationship, an affair, as we ever got."

by You, You Please Stand by Me," the song was started by Billy in 1965. "It was inspired by 'Stand by Me,' by Ben E. King," he admitted. "Sneaky little devil, ain't I?" (The melody came by way of a Johann Strauss waltz.) Glenn Sutton then read what he'd written and added a second verse in pencil. "I decided not to use it," said Sherrill, who later wrote a replacement (which is not present in the lyric sheet on display).* It was on the day of the session, some three years later, when he and Tammy "collaborated on the last two lines of the song."

So there they sat in Billy's office on that August night, trying to conjure up a hit before they went back to face a roomful of musicians. The clock ticking away, that old song Billy had never completed came to mind. As Wynette recalled, "He said, 'Do you like the idea of "stand by your man"?' And I said, 'Yeah, I do. With the old-fashioned Southern Baptist upbringing that I've got, I like that idea.'"† That was it. Tammy helped him finish the last lines of the lyric; then they went back downstairs and cut it. "We wrote it so fast," said Wynette.

Guitarist Harold Bradley recalled working with bassist Bob Moore on the turnaround—the *babababababubum* right before Tammy belts out the chorus. "It worked out where it didn't end up where I was on tonic, so it was a little tricky," said Bradley. "We didn't usually get to play that much on records. It was outstanding that we would get to play something that busy. Those little licks on there are just perfect. If you took out any of those licks it would weaken the song, and I don't ever want to hear anybody in some bar band play it any different."

The one detail on the track Sherrill didn't like was Pete Drake's steel guitar intro, which sounded too whiny to his ears. So he got ahold of ace guitarslinger Jerry Kennedy, then producing records for Mercury, who'd missed the original session due to an A and R meeting in Chicago. Sherrill brought him into the studio on a Saturday. "He knew what he wanted," said

---

*In 1990 a play based on Wynette's life opened at the Ryman Auditorium. Glenn Sutton attended the premiere, and at the cocktail party afterward ran into Sherrill, whom he hadn't seen in years. After exchanging hugs, Billy said, "Y'know, your life woulda been a whole lot different if I'd have put your verse in 'Stand by Your Man.'" Sutton was momentarily stunned, although he laughed in recounting the tale. "The one thing about Billy is he will never stab you in the back, he'll *look* at you and stab you. And love it!"

†Another version of the tale has Billy discussing the original 1965 lyric while still in the studio, with one of the session players calling out the idea to change the title to "Stand by Your Man" as Tammy and Billy headed up to his office.

Kennedy. "I was overdubbin'. He needed an intro other than the one he had and some harmony on the chorus. I never heard the song front to back." As Sherrill recalled, "I said, 'Let's just do a riff, Jerry—don't play melody. So that was Mr. Kennedy's idea—*dum de-dum dum, dum de-dum dum.*" Jerry felt that it might have come to him while tuning his guitar, which certainly sounds right.

"I have to feel a song to do it best," Tammy once said, and, boy, did she feel this one right down to the marrow. Yet Tammy was less than confident over the result. She didn't care for the melody. She was worried that the record wasn't in keeping with the "kid-type" songs ("D-I-V-O-R-C-E," "I Don't Wanna Play House") that she was known for. She especially hated the last note she hits, which was right at the roof of her range and, to say the least, provides a song that is all drama with a stirring crescendo. "'Stand by Your Man' is a lot harder to sing than the national anthem," noted Emmylou Harris ("Better song, too," she added). Perhaps it was the nearly out-of-control emotion in that one note, which Tammy compared to "a pig squealin'," that made Tammy cringe. "I sounded like a rhythm and blues singer," moaned Wynette.

Things went from bad to worse when she took a dub of "Stand by Your Man" home to play for Jones, with whom she'd been living for only two weeks.* When George informed Tammy he didn't particularly care for the story the song told, she burst into tears. Jones tried to make amends by saying he'd listen to it some more, but Tammy claimed she thwarted his attempts daily. "He'd put it on, and I'd slide the needle all the way across," she told Ralph Emery.

Jones readily admits he didn't care for what would be his wife's biggest hit but maintains it was because of the production. "I thought it was too pop. I said, 'I think it's a good song, but it's too far to the left. It's *pop.* It's probably gonna be a big record, but I don't like it that much.' And Tammy, she told it in magazines—this was after we divorced—that I was just jealous. Professional jealousy—'He was just jealous as hell of that song.'"

A panicked Wynette went back to Billy Sherrill and asked him to deep-six the record. "I begged him not to put it out," she told Burt Reynolds in a TV interview. "Pleaded." Regardless, the song shot to number one, cracked

*When Tammy told the tale in interviews, she said that she and Jones had been "married" for two weeks, but that is in reference to the Mexican marriage that never occurred.

the pop Top 40, and became a hit all over again in the United Kingdom in 1975. (The UK record executive Dick Sasher believed in the song so much he released it year after year until it finally hit.) It would become soundtrack fodder for numerous films and be covered by everyone from Bobby Vinton and the Blues Brothers to Roseanne Arnold, Tina Turner,* even Alvin and the Chipmunks.

"It became the biggest-selling country music single of all time," said Wynette. "Billy is always right. He's a genius."

"Brilliant recorded performances have often given lyrics a depth of meaning beyond their original intent," wrote Simon Napier-Bell, and that is certainly the case with the exhilarating and exhausting "Stand by Your Man." Structurally it's an odd song—two verses, then the chorus twice (hear it once, and it's stuck in the cranium forever). The lyrics are a little clunky— "understand" is repeated twice, as is "love him." But make no mistake: there's a fistful of drama packed into these two minutes and thirty-eight seconds.

Once again it's Tammy's reading of the song that makes the record so riveting, and her delivery here is particularly intense. Authors Robert K. Oermann and Mary Bufwack describe her "soul-piercing" vocal as sounding "like it came from a whitewashed holy-roller church in the full heat of Pentecostal fervor." I'd say. She also sounds ready to burst into tears throughout. To these ears there's a conflict in her voice: she wants her fairy tale to be true, but reality has already kicked her in the ass. I have no proof, no DNA, no men on the grassy knoll, but this is what I hear. Right in that devastating first line: "Sometimes it's hard to be a woman."

As Daniel Cooper has written, "The song's moral center is elusive." On the surface, it seems very straightforward: he's gonna do what he wants, put up with it, a woman must suffer. And then comes that line: "After all, he's just a man." It just stops you in your tracks. What exactly does she

---

*Tammy, who seldom criticized any artist, said, "Tina Turner's was the worst. I thought she did a horrible job." (Sherrill's old pal Rick Hall cut an R & B hit of the song with Candi Staton.)

Wynette herself did the song no favors when she recorded some "Stand by Your Man" radio spots in 1974 for Democratic candidate for governor of Tennessee Tom Wiseman. Tammy tailored the lyrics to fit his campaign: "Stand by your man / for your child's education / And let's show this whole big nation / Just how to stop inflation." Thankfully, there is nothing too shameless when it comes to country music promotion.

mean? Her delivery is so calmly aware. On the head of a dime, she turns from what seems to be a clueless, suffering creature into an all-knowing one. But knowing *what,* exactly? Men are to be pitied, not scorned? Men are children? Men are dogs? Men are to be loved unconditionally? There's no definite answer. It's a puzzle, this song, and all because of that one sentence. Without it, "Stand by Your Man" would possess no mystery. And it was an accidental mystery, as it turns out. "I didn't intend for it to be puttin' down men or anything," insisted Tammy when asked about that line. Obviously there are those who hear it as a critique, intentional or not. I think this was a big factor in its success—the song is vague enough to allow the listener to complete the meaning. Shake your head in disgust, or raise your fist in support.

Now that Sherrill and Wynette had seized upon the formula, they proceeded to beat the country audience to death with it. Incredibly, Wynette's next five singles would all hit number one, each of them some variant on the "Stand by Your Man" theme.* Tammy was the right woman for the job. She threw herself into these songs like a method actor. Over and over she goes for it without a net, and listening to these records back-to-back can be a draining experience.

First came "Singing My Song," released March 1969, and in terms of attitude and energy, this is one of the absolute looniest Tammy numbers, which is why I love it. Hey, "Stand by Your Man" haters, give this one a spin. Your head will explode! This is a song about desperation and duty, and that's just how Tammy delivers it. From the wacko opening line, in which Wynette references the song she has just begun to sing, to its over-the-top finale, this is a wild ride through one crazy idea of Woman.

She's clueless as to why her man sticks around, but oh so grateful, and when she sings, "I'll make sure he gets everything," the way Tammy pauses, splitting the last word in two ("every . . . *thing*"), lets you know exactly what she's delivering. Even more shocking is the line "I'll swing

---

*The most offensive reduction of the "Stand by Your Man" ethos Wynetteophiles all mention is "Don't Liberate Me (Love Me)," a real howler with none of the complexity of the original. The opening couplet, which Tammy delivers in a slightly sinister tone: "Today a group of women came to see me / To convince me women don't have equal rights." The song was never a single, however; just an album cut on 1971's *We Sure Can Love Each Other.*

when he feels like swinging." Whoa, Tammy! There isn't a whole lot of happiness on display, however. The attitude expressed is that of a resigned soldier heading off to combat, or maybe a reality show contestant about to be dropped in a vat of maggots, gritting her teeth for the win. But a newfound confidence presents itself. Like Tina Turner belting out her love for Ike, Tammy knows she's got what it takes and she'll gladly take on any comers. Wynette got a cowriting credit for this song, which certainly surprised Glenn Sutton, who wrote it with Sherrill. (Her next single shared the same triple credit.) "I don't know how her name got on there," said Sutton. "The only thing I could think was Tammy didn't like it—and maybe she'd like it *better* if she was in on it."*

Five months after "Singing My Song" came "The Ways to Love a Man," a potent distillation of the Sherrill-Wynette sound: the loud/soft dynamics, the key change, the extreme delivery and point of view. It's the same story we've been hearing, but with an added twist: the devious nature of the female psyche. Tammy tells us she will use "my child, my home, my soul, my mind" to keep her man. Yes, this scheming dame will use every weapon in her arsenal, boys, including controlling your very *brain*. This is a stronger, less desperate Tammy, but she still reminds us it's a very shaky world for a woman—if "one little thing" goes awry, the big lug's out the door for good. Burn that steak once and you've had it, ladies.

Penned by Sherrill with Norro Wilson, "I'll See Him Through" followed in December 1969. Again they hammer the formula, right down to the big belt-out at the end, and again it went number one. The agonized lyric could've come right out of one those nights Tammy waited up for her no-show husband: "He never tried to wake me and offered no excuse for where he'd been." But for once there's a reason to love a man: "He gave me love when I needed it bad." The vocal control Tammy exhibits on these records is a wondrous thing. From a little whisper to the heartrending exclamations, she makes it sound so easy, so conversational.

April 1970 brought the Sherrill–Norro Wilson–Carmol Taylor composition "He Loves Me All the Way," a breezy up-tempo number that finally breaks the "Stand by Your Man" formula: we're back to an actual verse-

---

*Glenn said he never wrote a single song with Tammy. According to Sutton, the powers that be "didn't ever let me spend any time with her by myself. I'm sure they were afraid I might write songs with her—and they might have to *cut* 'em." Very few people got the opportunity to write with Wynette, and Sutton felt it was intentional.

chorus-verse song. Tammy surprises us by utilizing an understated delivery here, telling the world that she's getting what she wants, she's never caught her man cheating, and while things may not be perfect, she can live with it. It's not that Tammy sounds exactly happy here—does she ever?—but perhaps she can allow herself to feel a little smug.

"Run, Woman, Run" from August of that year is perhaps the greatest testament to Tammy's power at the time, because this sketchy nothing of a song, featuring Wynette dispensing the usual cautionary advice to her fellow females, also shot to number one.

Tammy's winning streak on the country charts was finally broken by "The Wonders You Perform," a slice of Christian mysticism that only (*only?*) hit number 5. In terms of delivery, this is Tammy's "Subterranean Homesick Blues"—she talks the lengthy song poem-like lyric of this nearly tuneless number.

This rather unusual song was written by Jerry Chestnut, author of (among many others) "Trouble" for Elvis as well as "Another Place, Another Time" for Jerry Lee. He was putting up some paneling in his home at the time. "While I was doin' this, I kept thinkin' about my grandfather, who was a Pentecostal preacher. He was the closest thing to a prophet I ever seen. When we would go visit him, he wouldn't say, 'It's good to see you,' he'd say, 'Praise the Lord.' He believed 'in all things give thanks,' because that's what the Bible said, and he followed the Bible right to the letter.

"So if you had a baby die, he might send you a congratulations card. I'm exaggeratin' a little—he would just say, 'It's gone to be with the Lord, hallelujah.' And he wouldn't cry about it. The day he died, I was standin' at his bedside. He said, 'Praise the Lord, I believe I'm goin' home.' It was the happiest day of his life!

"Well, I got to thinkin' about him and I couldn't get him off my mind. I was puttin' up that panelin', I kept havin' these thoughts. Like about a baby dyin'—and the church people who don't understand. If they go to church every Sunday and still have a baby die, they just think, 'How could the Lord do this to me?' Well, 'The Wonders You Perform' explains it. So I get to writin' it down and I think, 'Now who in the God's world would ever cut a song like this if I made a song of it? Who in the world would you even pitch that to?' They'd think you were nuts!"

That same week Chestnut also wrote another song, "A Good Year for the

Roses." And then George Jones called. He was at the Ramada Inn and he needed some new songs pronto. "George used to do that every time he was in town. He said, 'Bring a hit down here and sing it to me. I'm fixin' to cut, I ain't got a damn hit and I need one.'

"So I just got my guitar and went. Well, Tammy was in the bathroom washin' her hair, so I sat down there and started talkin' to George. Tammy never even came out. I played him 'Good Year for the Roses.' He said, 'By God, that's what I'm lookin' for! Have you written anything else lately that you think is a hit?' I said, 'George, I've written a thing and I don't know *what* it is. I think it's great, but I don't think you or anybody would ever record the damn thing.' George said, 'Well, play it for me!'"

Chestnut did. The only reaction Jones could muster was, "Damn!" "'Bout that time Tammy came out with these rollers in her hair. And she said, 'Would you play that again?'" Chestnut played it again. "Tammy said, 'Get me a copy of that. And if Billy Sherrill will let me, the first time I get in front of a microphone, I'll record it.'"

Wynette delivered on her promise. The song remains special to many a Tammy fan. Close friend Jan Howard toured with Wynette in the early eighties and sang backup. No stranger to tragedy herself, having lost two of her sons, Howard would watch Tammy sing "Wonders" from the wings, and it invariably tore her to pieces. "It's a fantastic, unbelievable song," she said. "Put that together with Tammy's heart, my God—I can't listen to it. I literally cry. It touches home too much."

"'The Wonders You Perform' ain't made a million or even three hundred thousand. It's a different ball game," said Chestnut. "It's inspirational, it's not religious. It's not somethin' you'd sing in church. Porter told me when he heard it, 'Son, that's the damn greatest song that's ever come out of Nashville.' Elvis was learning it when he died." But it is Wynette that Chestnut credits with unleashing it on the world. "Son, Tammy was wide open. There weren't no airs to it. Just an ol' rawboned country girl raised in an Assembly of God church in Alabama tryin' to get ahead. There wasn't nothin' about her singin' that was false. She didn't try to be anything she wasn't. She was just Tammy."

In addition to the singles just discussed, Tammy released *six* albums of original material from 1969 to 1970, plus her first *Greatest Hits* album in November 1969, which was the first country album to go gold (and then platinum), earning Wynette the moniker "First Lady of Country." (Some insist it was Loretta Lynn; details are in the source notes.)

Two of Tammy's albums from this period were definitely more than just the usual collection of current hits plus random songs of varying quality. March 1969's *Inspiration* was a riveting collection of gospel numbers (Wynette frequently named it her favorite of all her albums), central among them being "You'll Never Walk Alone." Listen to the way Tammy comes in ever so quietly on the opening line. The voice is so forlorn, yet at the same time *so* empathetic, it never fails to stop my clock. A stirring "Just a Closer Walk with Thee" displays Tammy at her most relaxed and confident. "Most country artists who sang gospel songs in that period got all churchy and inhibited with it," said her old piano player David Vest. "It's probably the music Wynette was into earliest in her life, so it would've touched the oldest chords." The fall of the following year brought *Christmas with Tammy*, a collection of holiday songs. Christmas was Wynette's favorite time of the year, and she delivered once more on songs like "Blue Christmas," not to mention one by Jones, "Lonely Christmas Call."

The awards poured in for Wynette. She won a Grammy for "Stand by Your Man"; was named Most Programmed Female Artist by *Cashbox* magazine and Top Female Artist by *Record World*; NARM declared her Bestselling Female Artist; and the Country Music Association awarded her Top Vocalist of the Year three years in a row, 1968 to 1970. In 1969 Wynette's work began turning up on movie soundtracks. Her first exposure to Hollywood came via contributing a title song to *Run, Angel, Run*, a low-budget biker picture produced by cigar-chomping exploitation mogul Joe Solomon. Stu Phillips, who did the score, was a bit friendly with Billy Sherrill, who he said "desperately wanted to write a song for the movies." Phillips and Sherrill cowrote the decidedly poppish "Run, Angel, Run," and Tammy cut it, but not before Phillips, frantically awaiting delivery of the recording, discovered what a tough customer Billy was when it came to a deal.

On the eve of the session, "Billy hit me with a brick," wrote Stu Phillips in his autobiography. "He wanted to have 100 percent publishing on the song. Billy wanted it all." And Sherrill got it, much to Joe Solomon's fury. (Amazingly, Tammy was paid only five hundred bucks for performing it.) He also said "Run, Angel, Run" would not be the single, as promised, as the song was felt to be too strong competition for Tammy's next Epic single. According to Phillips, Solomon took revenge by running a "starring Tammy

Wynette" credit on Deep South versions of the movie poster even though she'd only contributed a song. (A year later Sherrill apologized to Phillips and stuck the song on Tammy's *Greatest Hits* album. "I earned a nice piece of change from that song," said Phillips. "Thank you, Billy.")

Typically nasty late-sixties drive-in fare, *Run, Angel, Run* still manages brief topless nudity, a gang rape, and a hint of miscegenation, all acted out by hairy biker characters with names like "Space" who punctuate nearly every line of dialogue with the word "baby." It mortified George and Tammy, who caught the picture at a theater in Lakeland. "Jones got so embarrassed he made me get up and leave," recalled Wynette.

Tammy's music reached a new audience via a much artier film the following year, Bob Rafelson's grim classic *Five Easy Pieces*, which featured four Wynette songs, among them "Stand by Your Man." Rafelson said when he and screenwriter Carole Eastman were discussing the script, Tammy Wynette was already on their minds. Rafelson decided to use source music for the score, choosing classical pieces as background for the Jack Nicholson character. For Rayette Dipesto, Karen Black's character, they wanted "the kind of music she listens to, and she was as country as can be," said Rafelson. "Carole said, 'What about Tammy?' The script hadn't been written yet—we knew it was gonna be an abusive relationship between Nicholson and the girl, and I suppose that better suited Tammy Wynette thematically than Loretta, Patsy, or Skeeter Davis. It just seemed that Tammy was writing songs about a high-heeled, overly made-up country girl like Rayette— bold, sweet, and ingenuous, who hung on to Nicholson and was basically left stranded in every situation she's in with him. Unable to get a full commitment, but ready to stand by him one way or another." For Rafelson, Rayette Dipesto and the music of Tammy Wynette "just seemed like a perfect marriage."

When the movie was completed, Rafelson invited Tammy out to see a private screening. "At this point in Hollywood nobody knew who the hell Tammy Wynette was," he noted. "The idea of her attending a premiere would have given us no bonus points." When she saw the picture, "She didn't much like it. I think the movie was kind of an art movie—and 'art movie' she was not."

George and Tammy performed live shows together from the start, although at first they were more or less "surprise" gigs, as they both still had solo dates to fulfill. "She would just show up," said band member Charlie Carter, who remembers Tammy waltzing onstage in Dallas shortly after their trip to Mexico. "George sang a few songs and then he said, 'I got somebody here I want y'all to meet.' Tammy came out and the people just went wild." In February 1969, they started being booked as a unit, but they would not record duets until 1971, once George was free of his contract with Musicor. "We tried every way in the world to record a song together," said Tammy. "I'd sing background on some of his singles so my voice would be on there."

Although Tammy didn't sing on it, George proudly exhibited her on the cover of his next album. Dressed in a neon yellow frock with matching headband and looking skinny as a rail, Tammy joined George for an unannounced appearance on the Wilburn Brothers' TV show, duetting with Jones on "Milwaukee, Here I Come." They also appeared together in the 1969 no-budget country music spectacular *From Nashville with Music*, a beaming George introducing her as "the sweet and tender part of our show, Mrs. Hitmaker, Tammy Wynette!" The thrill they got by singing with each other is palpable in just about any clip of the couple. "When we were onstage we were in our own little heaven," said Jones.

On February 16, 1969, George and Tammy officially tied the knot. This was during their first booking as a couple at the Playroom in Atlanta, Georgia. On opening night Jones had gotten drunk, tottered offstage, and boarded a Vegas-bound Learjet with the club owner, leaving Tammy to face the hostile crowd on her own. George returned a few days later in a sour mood, telling Tammy he'd never marry her. The next morning an upbeat Jones told her to put on a nice outfit, as this was the day they were getting hitched. By now Wynette's head was spinning. Jones, noted Tammy, "was not a great talker and he wasn't one to apologize, ever." Off they went to—where else?—Ringgold, Georgia. "Tammy took George Jones to the same courthouse where we took our ill-fated vows," said Don Chapel. "Wonder if she ever told George that?"

In March George and Tammy moved to Lakeland, Florida. Next door lived Cliff and Maxine Hyder, a couple who'd become their close friends. "We was country," said Maxine. "So we was gonna get along fine." Cliff was sidelined by Lou Gehrig's disease, and George was instrumental in getting him out of the house for some physical therapy. Maxine bonded instantly with Tammy. "I loved Tammy more than my own sister," she said. "She tried to do the right thing by everybody she touched." Maxine was struck by Wynette's never-ending generosity. One day she commented on a picture she liked in Tammy's home, and the "next thing I know it was out there in my garage."

Maxine found out quickly what a devil George could be. Early on in their friendship George and Tammy invited the Hyders to fly with them to a show in nearby Pensacola. "I said, 'We've never flown,'" recalled Maxine. "Oh, that tickled George to death." Jones arranged for a flight that went first to Miami, then back to Tampa, hopped over to Jacksonville, then finally landed in Pensacola. Maxine soon became ill, asking George, "Why can't we fly directly instead of having to fly up and fly down?" "Well, I wanted to break you in," said the Possum. "He does them things," explained Tammy. "You'll have to get used to it."

Success enabled a Tammy/Mee-Maw reconciliation. When the first money from her hit records starting pouring in, Wynette "called my mother—they were farming—and I said, 'Mother, hang it up.'" She moved Mildred and Foy to Nashville and later bought them a house in Lakeland. Wynette would support her mother and stepfather for the rest of their lives. "She got great satisfaction out of it," said her friend Joan Dew. "There was a feeling of, 'You didn't think I was gonna amount to anything and look what I did.' Mee-Maw didn't stand up to Tammy anymore. She knew where her bread and butter was." Mildred and Foy would often travel with Tammy on the road, and Mildred would even run the George and Tammy fan club for a spell. While mother and daughter still managed to bicker from time to time, Mee-Maw was crazy about George, which Tammy found a little irksome. One day when they were buying Mildred furniture, "she found a sofa she liked and asked my opinion," Wynette recalled. "I told her it was perfect, and she said, 'Well, I'd really rather talk to George about it. I think I'll wait and see what he says!'"

Those early days in Lakeland were happy ones for George and Tammy. Jones could make Wynette laugh. One day coming into the Nashville airport from the road they spotted a country music tabloid with the cover headline: TAMMY WYNETTE RUNS OFF WITH WAYLON JENNINGS! "Jones thought that was the greatest thing," said Tammy. Waylon was a friend of theirs, and George summoned him to the house, showed him the scandal sheet, and "acted real angry," recalled an amused Wynette, who said Jennings "was stutterin' and stammerin'" before Jones let him in on the joke. George was one of the few people who could tease Wynette. He'd scrunch up his nose and make fun of her smell-bad birth name: "Pugh." "He's always makin' fun of my name," complained Tammy.

George went ape over his wife's cooking. She'd make him biscuits and gravy from scratch, serve him chocolate pie in bed. Tammy got George to abandon his buzz cut and grow his hair into a carefully sculpted do that one wag dubbed his *Planet of the Apes* haircut because of the oddly scalloped front.* They went to the dog races, fished (which Wynette loved to do), and played the marble game Aggravation incessantly with Cliff and Maxine. And they fought like cats and dogs. "I never have met a woman with such a temper!" confessed George. "They'd get into it over who had the best song out at the time, or who made the most money," said Peanutt Montgomery.

The biggest battles were over George's alcohol intake, which led to Tammy's oft-repeated quip: "He nipped and I nagged." Jones was more liable to disappear than duke it out, however. "He ain't a fighter," maintained Peanutt, although he conceded Jones "might shoot ya if he gets drunk." The maddest Charlene Montgomery ever saw George get followed a trip she and Wynette made to Kmart. "I'll never forget it. Tammy bought him some blue jeans, and on the back side they had one orange pocket and one purple pocket. She bought him two or three pairs. We come home, and George got so mad when he saw them britches. He said, 'Damn, Tammy, what the hell do you think you're doin'?' She said, 'Well, waddya mean, George? You said you wanted some everyday pants.'" Reaffirming his Anglo-Saxon roots by way of a racial slur, George refused to accept them. "And then Tammy got angry," said Charlene.

The Montgomerys felt as if they had to walk on eggshells around Wynette. "Tammy was not a fun-lovin' person," said Charlene. "You had to be careful takin' pictures, doin' somethin' out of the ordinary. She played a higher-class

---

*Tammy fixed the Possum's hair every day. "He said that's the reason he married me," she told Ralph Emery. "He always wanted a travelin' hairdresser." When it came to his appearance, Jones was "very particular," said hairdresser Jan Smith. "Tammy had to fix his hair. I couldn't do it." Wynette was far looser when it came to her own locks. "You'd do it and she liked it. Tammy wasn't real picky about anything."

role, more upsy-dupsy. She'd get down to earth, but she still had that reserve about her. You couldn't just cut up and have fun.

"This is how you can't clown with Tammy. I found one of those little toy windup mice. I thought, 'I'm gonna fix her up good.'" Charlene wound up the toy and set it under the covers on Wynette's side of the bed. "George knew about it. Come bedtime, she got her pj's on, pulled the covers back, crawled into bed, and that thing went off. She didn't know it was a toy. She jumped out of bed a-screamin', climbed up on a chair, got one of her wigs, and was just a-flingin' her wig at it, beatin' at this mouse, yellin', 'Kill it! Kill it, George! Kill it!' George nearly died laughin'. He was bent over double, and it made Tammy mad. Finally she came out—'Lord, don't you ever EVER do nothin' like that to me again.' You couldn't play with Tammy like that."

Jones could irritate Tammy just by being George. The couple went on a cruise to the Bahamas. Along for the ride were the Montgomerys and the Hyders, plus backup singer Patsy Sledd and her husband Bill. "All the men decided they were gonna go shoppin'," recalled Charlene. "Well, it was Valentine's Day. Tammy said, 'Oh, I know why the men wanted to go by themselves today—it's *Valentine's Day*!' I said, 'Tammy, they won't *one time* think of us.'"

"George better!" said Tammy.

"He probably won't, him on a holiday. They're not thinkin' 'bout us," Charlene said.

"Well, he better."

Charlene had an idea. "'Let's go on down to the cafeteria on the ship, and tonight when we go to eat, we'll have 'em bring a cake to our table in the shape of a heart.' Well, we didn't tell the men. I told the girls, 'Let's don't tell George or Peanutt or nobody. Let's see who takes the credit.'"

That night at dinner, out came the cake. "Tammy says, 'My Lord, look—it says, *"To the Ladies"*! We didn't think you'd think about us *at all*!'

"I said, 'Well, now which one of you men did this?'

"Peanutt says, 'I didn't do it.'

"Bill says, 'Not me.'

"Cliff: 'Well, I didn't, either.'

"Ol' George, he kind of perked up, squared them shoulders back, and he said, 'Y'all thought we forgot you, didn't ya?'

"Tammy was infuriated. She come down with her fist and hit the table.

'George! Don't you make like you did this, because WE did this ourselves! 'Cause y'all didn't even think about us for Valentine's Day!'"

Often it all came down to who won at marbles. "We played a lot," said Maxine Hyder. Unlike everybody else, Tammy refused to let George win, and losing only riled him up. "Then he would drink," said Hyder. "So he and I got to be partners." One day they made plans to go to a rib joint in nearby Auburndale after Aggravation. "George and I lost two games," said Maxine. Jones calmly got up and said he was going back home for a minute. Despite losing, George seemed to be fine, but Tammy knew better.

"He's goin' in there and he'll mix him a stiff drink. And then he'll leave," she told the Hyders. This didn't sit well with Cliff, who was counting on dinner.

"He can't do that! George promised me he'd go to the barbecue," he moaned.

"Well, you just wait," said Tammy. "I'll count, I might get to twenty. Before that you'll hear him start up the car."

"She started countin'," remembered Maxine, and sure enough, before Tammy hit twenty they heard Jones drive away. Cliff asked Wynette where she thought Jones was headed. "Either the Holiday Inn on Memorial or Buddy's Oyster Bar," she said. Cliff took off after him, found George's red convertible outside Buddy's, and, insisting he keep his dinner promise, dragged George back home. Jones said he just had to step inside his house for a minute before they left for the barbecue. Tammy was already over there. Cliff and Maxine sat outside in their car and waited.

"All of a sudden we heard a noise. We didn't know what it was," said Maxine.

"Then George come out carryin' a drink." Tammy got in the back with Maxine. "As we were drivin', she whispered to me, 'He broke the marble board. I think he broke the table, too.'" Such violent antics scared the bejesus out of Wynette. "Tammy was a strong person to put up with some of the stuff he did. She loved George with all her heart, but her nerves would not take it. He was so unpredictable."

It was that fear of the unknown that routinely put Tammy in knots. Was Jones going to show up for the gig? Would he be drunk? "We were up and down with engagements," she said. "We would miss one and be sued. Things were so crazy. I was very frightened." She never knew what state he'd be in when he returned from one of his benders. As Jan Smith recalled, "Tammy would say, 'George is drunk, he's gonna come home, and he's probably gonna drive through the front doors.' That was the big fear of hers—'He's gonna crash through the front door with the car.'"

One day Tammy's kids showed up at Maxine's door in a panic. "Jackie, Tina, and Gwen came over here runnin' one afternoon cryin', and one of 'em said, 'My dad's maybe gonna kill my mother.' Said George had a knife in his hand." At a loss for what to do, they waited until Jones left, then went over to check on Wynette. "And he had hit Tammy. But she said, 'I deserved it because I swung at him.' That's all she said. 'It's my fault, I swung at him.'" Maxine felt bad for the children, because "they saw George do things to their mother." At the same time, Jones was very good with Tammy's kids, legally adopting them. When Tammy dispensed a spanking, George would bolt from the room, unable to handle it. "Deep down he had a heart of gold," said Jackie. "He wanted to provide for us. He never treated us any different than he did his kids. I never had any bad things to say about him. I just wish that things would've been different for Mom."

Tammy's relationship with the Montgomerys was an uneasy one. While she liked the couple (her nicknames for them were "Cherlene" and "Poonut") and recorded a number of Peanutt's songs, their presence filled her with apprehension, because when they'd appear, the booze would flow and George would get wild then disappear. When Jones went crazy, everybody was a witness to it. (Hell, the whole world knew, as his drinking was the subject of so many of their solo songs.) Tammy's dark side was far less visible. During one of the Montgomerys' visits to Lakeland, Charlene was jolted awake one night by noises coming from outside the house.

"All of a sudden the dogs started havin' a fit. I went and knocked on George and Tammy's door." They all went outside and nervously peeped around. "When Tammy started back in she yelled out, 'Oh, my God, George! Somebody's been here—and they wrote "Pig" on my back door in lipstick!'" The men went out to search further while Tammy and Charlene huddled in the house. "'Bout the time we got in the bedroom and got the door locked, the ice maker dropped a load of ice and it scared the fool out of me." Charlene found it odd that Tammy didn't seem scared in the slightest. "Tammy never did get upset, even though I was scared to death. 'Course, they never did find nobody. She did it herself. I *knew* that Tammy did it."

The most incriminating evidence for the Montgomerys was the book on the Manson killings Wynette had been toting around. "Tammy had just got through readin' it," said Charlene. "She was tellin' me, 'Oh, I just read this Charles Manson book, it was somethin' else.'" Charlie's followers had used the blood of their victims to scrawl messages on the wall before fleeing the scene of the crime, including the word "Pig." Both Peanutt and Charlene were convinced Tammy had concocted the threat herself. "She wanted attention," said Charlene. "Part of it was to get her way about somethin'. She didn't want George to go off, so she wanted to make him afraid to leave her by herself. Tammy had her motives for the things she did."

Remember Bob Eubanks, the incessantly exuberant host of that innocent smutfest *The Newlywed Game*? It just so happens that he also booked rock and country acts in the seventies. He much preferred the latter. "The country guys had no demands! When I came in and offered them food and a dressing room and a limousine from the hotel to the facility, they thought I was the second coming. They were used to playing high school auditoriums. I took the rock and roll way of doing things and took it to country music. That kind of forced some other promoters to do the same thing." (Not that Eubanks was popular because of it: "I used to check in to the Nashville Hilton hotel and get a call in the middle of the night—'Get your Hollywood ass outta here.' I was hated in Nashville.")

Eubanks booked George and Tammy for a West Coast tour. At the time George's backup band, the Jones Boys, consisted of Charlie Carter on guitar, James Hollie on bass, Freddy Haws on drums, Charlie "Grumpy" Justice on fiddle, and Sonny Curtis on steel guitar. Patsy Sledd, a brunette about the same size as Tammy and with hair twice as big, sang backing vocals. (She was also a seamstress and made most of Tammy's outfits, and a few of George's.) The band might've belonged to George, but the Jones Boys quickly grew devoted to Tammy. "They would have crawled through cut glass and fire for her," said hairdresser Jan Smith. "Every one of 'em." Charlie Carter would last through all the personnel changes, staying with Tammy until the bitter end.

They traveled in a hundred-thousand-dollar custom-made bus that, as Mildred pointed out in the fan club newsletter, came "complete with electric stove and oven for cooking the pinto beans, taters, and corn bread." George might've craved Tammy's cooking, but the band didn't like the aftermath.

"They'd have to take the pans and pots to the motel room to wash them," said Patsy Sledd. "They hated it with a passion when she'd cook."

Eubanks, a big fan of the music, was a little nervous the first time he stepped onto the bus. "The interior was decorated in a Spanish style—from the drapes and upholstery to the wrought-iron lamps," wrote Eubanks in his autobiography. "Tammy sat in a breakfast booth with Patsy Sledd. Both had their hair in rollers." George started grilling Eubanks on the ticket sales. He assured them of full houses. Jones and Wynette never made more than five thousand dollars a night in those days—peanuts compared to the astronomical amounts country superstars make now.

The nonchalant manner in which Wynette and Sledd delivered their background vocals during George's solo set dumbfounded Eubanks. The pair would sit out of view of the audience backstage and chatter away to each other, then stop suddenly, pull the microphones they were each holding close to their lips, and belt out a harmony line for "The Race Is On" or some other George number; then down would go the mics and on went their conversation until the next chorus came.

Jones earned a reputation for being a slacker when it came to live shows. One review of an August 1971 performance at California's Oakland Coliseum, entitled "Fans Saw Little of the Joneses," complained about their brief forty-minute set. The review said that Jones, who "speeded onstage . . . left the distinct impression that he, his wife, their kids and the whole production had to catch an eleven o'clock bus back to Nashville." Such criticisms mortified Tammy. "She was always tryin' to get him to do more," maintained Patsy Sledd. "She had to fight him to do thirty minutes. George never wanted to do any more than what he had to." Jones had other things on his mind, such as *Gunsmoke*. "Tammy would say, 'Hurry up and get to the hotel,'" said Jan Smith. "George loved to get in bed and watch television."

Not surprisingly each had their own style when it came to their followers. "Tammy would go out of her way for fans, more so than George," said Maxine Hyder. "He'd say, 'I've done my show, I don't have to sign autographs.' If he had too much to drink, he'd tell Tammy, 'You sign 'em!'" Wynette would stand out in the pouring rain to meet fans. "She never hesitated to sign autographs, hug a baby, stop for a picture, I mean *never*," said Jan Smith. "I don't care how bad she hurt, I don't care how bad she felt. She loved her fans. Tammy knew they made her who she was."

Wynette was intimidated by her husband's talent and experience, but as an artist definitely she held her own. "Tammy was the most gracefullest person I've ever worked with onstage," said Peanutt Montgomery. "She was like a queen." When Tammy stood there at the mic and belted out a tune, said Peanutt, "You just felt somethin'." And so did George, no matter what they were bickering about at the time. Joan Dew noted that when Jones talked about his wife in the professional sense he'd refer to her by "her full name, even in her presence." It was the Possum's little way of paying respect. "Nobody in the world sounds like she does," he'd say.

One day in Lakeland Jones took Maxine Hyder for a ride down state road 540A to show her a decaying sixteen-room colonial mansion. "Tammy's always wanted one of these," he told Maxine. The house came with forty-three and a half acres, upon which Jones would build a country music park. Tammy tried to talk him out of the hundred-grand purchase, but once George had his mind set on something, forget it. "A little boy in men's clothes" is how Wynette once described him, and as Jones threw himself into the project, even she got caught up in the excitement. He refurbished the run-down mansion, imported exotic vegetation for the park's landscaping, and had guitar-shaped ponds built. Jones was at his best when he had a project to occupy his mind, and this one kept him busy for months.

Wynette was busy with a little endeavor herself. One night after a show in early 1970 George lit up a cigarette back at the motel, and the smoke made Tammy sick. She knew from past experience that that could only mean one thing—she was, to quote one of her song titles, "with child."

Tamala Georgette arrived that October. Jones had just recovered from a weeklong drunken bender in Texas that had a very pregnant Tammy apoplectic over his whereabouts. She nudged George awake in bed one night to tell him the baby was on the way. First Jones had to get dressed, but he couldn't find the avocado green trousers that went with his matching green and white shirt. ("The only man I ever knew who wore coordinated tennis outfits to mow the lawn," noted Tammy.) They made it to the hospital, where George left the car running. The staff buzzed over Lakeland's only celebrity couple. Nobody was more thrilled than the Possum. "He blew the car horn all the way from the hospital to the driveway next door," said Maxine Hyder. "I thought, 'Well, that baby's come into this world.'"

Wynette arrived home to find a gift Jones had made for her hanging above the bed. It was a big Spanish plaque. On a red velvet background hung color pictures of Tammy, George, and Georgette. Below each picture was a poem in bronze letters.

Beneath Georgette's picture was a bit of verse announcing the date of her birth and hoping her future love was as crazy about her as George was for Tammy. Under George's image he asked if Wynette would still love him when he was old and gray (a favorite question before they drifted off to sleep at night). And there below Tammy's picture was written:

This bedroom holds lots of old memories
There are good ones and bad ones I fear
But from now on they'll only be sweet memories
Because my darlin' Tammy sleeps here

No one knew better than Tammy that Jones was a man of few words. "It's very hard for him to say, 'I love you,'" she said. "He'll try to buy you somethin' to tell you he loves you." When Wynette saw the plaque, she wept. "It's my prized possession," she told Ralph Emery in 1971. "George is the greatest."

A country music park being built, a new baby in the home—things in the Lakeland home were peaceful and happy. For a little while, anyway.

Happy Never After

How can anybody really believe what I sing about, knowin' what a mess
I've made of my life?

—Tammy Wynette

The country duet, one of the odder art forms. Author Joyce Maynard
described it as "a musical dialogue between a man and a woman, low
voice and high . . . the contrast of two enormously different but compatible
voices as a kind of metaphor for the continuing tension in relationships between
men and women." During the George and Tammy era you had numerous male-
female duet acts. There were Johnny and June Carter Cash, a real married
couple (although "Jackson" came before they were even a known item, let alone
betrothed) that were loose and fun, but only one of them could really sing.
Conway Twitty and Loretta Lynn, both top-notch vocalists, belted out tales of
illicit romance that somehow didn't sound all that illicit. People often forget
how omnipresent Porter Wagoner and Dolly Parton once were. They spent nine
and a half years recording together, releasing twenty-one hits off fourteen
albums. But there is little heat to their performances together and (forgive me,
Dolly) something a bit inbred about the pair. I mean, look at them together!
Brother and sister from some deep, dark holler?* There are others: the slightly
lurid ultra-seventies appeal of Jeannie Seely and Jack Greene, both great singers
but projecting a vibe one might encounter in the paneled lounge of some ill-lit
suburban rumpus room; the innocent perversity of father-daughter honky-
tonkers the Kendalls; diminutive Hank Snow and towering blonde Kelly Foxton
in their eyesore rhinestone suits.

*To say nothing of actual brother-sister act Jerry Lee and Linda Gail Lewis. Their highly
idiosyncratic, wigged-out performance of "Jackson" on a 1973 episode of the *Midnight
Special* is a slab of unsavory tent-revival lunacy that will have you bookish types reaching for the Tums, or maybe a bar of soap.

For my money George and Tammy were the most intense of the duets, their vocal blend just beyond compare. George is such an on-the-fly singer—you can practically imagine him belting out a tearjerker while putting on his shoes—and Tammy so controlled, it made for a dynamic combo. If you watch old footage of them performing, you'll see them standing nose to nose when they perform, often singing very softly, and the effect is certainly intimate. Outrageous characters on their own, together they resembled king and queen of some strange and faraway intergalactic empire, swathed in neon as they pacify their subjects with an endless stream of sad, sad songs. The records they made together, although they amount to only a handful of hits, remain unsurpassed. "They were fantastic, them duets," said Loretta Lynn. "George and Tammy, how could you beat 'em?"

It wasn't until April 1971 that George was finally able to record with Tammy. It didn't come cheap—he had to buy his way out of his contract with Musicor, which cost him a hundred grand and the rights to a pile of songs, not to mention his relationship with Pappy Daily, whom his wife was never crazy about in the first place. (Remember, he turned Wynette down.) The move to Epic couldn't have come at a better time for Jones. As his Musicor sessions sank beneath the weight of increasingly bland songs and haphazard production, he must've been impressed (perhaps a bit jealous) of the career trajectory Billy Sherrill had set for his wife.

For once Sherrill was nervous. "You can't stay enamored of people you produce, but that's the closest I've ever been to just shakin' in my boots. Later Jones told me, 'Hell, I was a nervous wreck. All the damn hits you've had, and I was cold as Elvis's nuts!'" Theirs was not the instant fit that Billy and Tammy had been. George had never worked with a real producer. For the most part he'd chosen his own songs. And there were those . . . strings. "When I first came over to Epic, Billy was riding real big on the Tammy kick," said Jones. "Billy was a little more on the poppish side, I'll be honest with ya. I come off the old country twang thing. Billy tried to mellow me down. He tried to do those strong arrangements that I hadn't been used to a little too quick. 'We Can Make It,' that wasn't George Jones. I thought 'Take Me' wasn't George Jones, either. But it was."

Interestingly it is this song, cut before his work with Sherrill, where Jones sees a change in his style developing, which might surprise those critical of his work with Billy.

"Take Me" was a 1965 hit he'd written with blind country songwriter and singer Leon Payne. It was a smooth ballad, somewhat unlike others Jones had cut before. "I had to finish just a little of that song and I said, 'Leon, does this sound like a George?' Meaning like a George Jones song. He said, 'You can sing anythang if you set your mind to it.' I didn't hear the song like a hard-core driver like I'd been doin', but I got into it. That's one reason I started doin' more songs like that. Usually I love the song before I go in there. You do have those songs where you know there's somethin' there, but you're not really that thrilled with it. You haven't sung it yet, I guess. 'Take Me' was one of those. I said, 'Well, this is like nothin' I've done before.' And durin' the process and once you hear it on the playback, damn, you start fallin' in love with the song." ("Walk Through This World with Me," a 1967 number one for Jones, was another he saw as "too pop.")

Jones found Sherrill a mighty confusing individual to work with at times. "If Billy *believed* in that song, he was there every second. If it was what we used to call an 'album cut'—a good song, but it wouldn't make fire come out of your butt, he wasn't interested. I'd go in the studio, he'd get the parts, we'd do a little rehearsal, and once he thought that everybody knew what they were supposed to do, he would go up to his office! Lou [Bradley, the engineer] would tell us, 'Okay, let's put one down.' And you wouldn't know what to do next. I'd say, 'Hell, boys, let's go ahead and work out another song.' I kept seein' that year after year—'What the hell's wrong with him today?' Finally it hit me—'Well, shit, it's the song. He just don't like the goddamn songs I brought.' I wish he'da told me that. I woulda tried to find better songs!"

As a person, Jones found Sherrill even more obtuse. "He was like a loner. I thought I would never get to know him. Hell, it was hard to *talk* to him. I was so damn scared. I started goin' up there to try to get to know him. He'd say, 'Come in,' I'd sit down, and he'd walk out. He was a short fella like me and took those little fast steps, walkin' like Hank Snow. (Bless his heart, if Billy heard me say that he'd kill me!) And he'd be talkin' to somebody else at length. Hell, I done sit there thirty minutes. Well, I got the hint. I thought, 'Well, shit, he's not very polite or he's weirder than hell.'

"I finally got to know him. It took me years. He's just ol' Billy. Lord, to me he was almost like an Owen Bradley. Billy was one of the great producers and one hell of a songwriter."

One of the first things Sherrill did was to persuade Jones to sing in a lower key. "I thought everything he cut with Pappy Daily was too whiny, too high," said Billy. As Jones recalled, "I'd get in there, get carried away, have a few drinks, and I'll wanna put 'em in that high card that I can really throw it out there." George agreed to try the low road. But he wanted something in return. "It was hard to ask Billy anything. I still didn't know him. I said, 'You got to turn me loose with the steel and fiddle and let me be me, do it like George.' From there on we came out with our best stuff." (For the record, when it comes to his work with Sherrill, I hear a lot of songs where Jones sings in a lower register—and very few with a fiddle.)

If Tammy was a quick study when it came to learning new material, Jones was the opposite. "The laziest one of all is the Possum," groused Sherrill, who maintained the biggest challenge was "getting him to learn songs. If he didn't like something, he didn't learn it. It had to hit him. Some ol' Mickey Mouse nothin' song—if he liked it, he'd learn it real quick. So many times I'd say, 'If you'd just do the right melody, this thing would be good! Learn it, dammit!' He'd go home, sleep, smoke ten cigars, and finally you'd just have to *drag* it out of him. And when he does it, it's done. But he's lazy."

The big challenge for anybody singing with George was trying to follow the man whose lips never appeared to move. "It would give the vocal group nightmares," recalled engineer Ron "Snake" Reynolds. Dolores Edgin, a member of the Nashville Edition, the background outfit Sherrill used on many a Jones session, explained how the group was positioned in the studio so they could see George up close. "We watched his face the whole time," noted Edgin. Sometimes Dolores would go over and ask Jones how he was going to phrase something, as the group could then add "little marks where he pushed a note or strung it out by phrasing behind the beat." But there was no guarantee the Possum was going to repeat himself.

"Tammy was in awe of him, absolutely in awe," said Jordanaire Ray Walker, who sang background on many of their sessions. But George's impromptu vocal acrobatics drove her nuts. "They argued and fussed every time we tried to do somethin' together," said Sherrill. "She couldn't phrase with him." As engineer Lou Bradley recalled, "One time Tammy turned to George just tryin' to figure out his phrasin' on somethin' and she said, 'George, it's a wonder you have more than one kid. You don't ever do the same thing the same way twice.'" Billy finally decided to do it one singer at a time. George would lay down his vocal; Tammy would listen, then overdub her part. "It was easier for all of us," said Sherrill. However the duets were cut, no one could argue with the results. George and Tammy had a devastating vocal blend. "Their voices were so compatible that it was unreal," said Ray Walker.*

The first single Sherrill cut on Jones and Wynette was a duet version of "Take Me" recorded on April 29, 1971. (It wouldn't see release until December of that year, after George's contract with Epic was finalized.) It is a tender performance by both singers, soft as a gentle, slow-moving stream. Compared to the bombast Tammy had been delivering song after song, it's very understated, and free of the melancholy that marks so many of her records. Perhaps because she had to overdub many of her vocals with George, she usually follows his lead. But how beautifully she does the job. Her performances on the duets are less adventurous than her solo work, but so sincere: she really loves this guy, and the music they make together.

Seven George and Tammy albums were released while they were together, and if Tammy solo albums are haphazard affairs, the duet albums are equally random. It was hard enough to find a song worthy of one voice, but to find material two singers (and singers who specialized in sad songs at that) could join forces on was a particular challenge. Aside from the hit singles, their albums are largely filler, although there is the occasional unexpected gem, such as their 1973 cover of the Louvin Brothers classic "When I Stop Dreaming," as well as "A Lovely Place to Cry" (a sad little picture of suburban isolation and disappointment, written by Peanutt and Tammy), "It's So Sweet," and "Never Grow Cold" (both penned by George and Tammy). One also cringes listening to Wynette trying to pull off a Loretta Lynn–style delivery on an old-school honky-tonker like "After Closin' Time." Wild and wooly ain't her style. What is great is the opportunity to hear Tammy singing more in a pure country vein—there are way more numbers in three-quarter time with the duets—and as I doubt much time was spent on the

---

*It is interesting to compare their individual performances on the same songs. "Lovin' You Could Never Be Better," a Peanutt Montgomery composition, was a number 2 hit in 1972 for George and an album cut for Tammy the same year. Jones kind of sexes up the romantic attitude (well, as sexy as Jones ever is) while Wynette as usual serves up the sorrow. Her performance cuts deeper to these ears. Tammy got the first crack at Tom T. Hall's "I'm Not Ready Yet" in 1979, but George's version released one year later blows hers away.

arrangements other than for the hits, Sherrill goes for simple, spare charts that showcase the mesmerizing interaction of George and Tammy.

Interestingly the Wynette and Jones pairing didn't exactly set the charts on fire at first. "Take Me" only reached number 9 and their next single, the truly unbelievable "The Ceremony," only hit number 6. Out of the seven singles released while they were together, only one would hit number one, 1973's "We're Gonna Hold On." Their other two number ones—"Golden Ring" and "Near You"—came in 1976, after they'd broken up.

But back to "The Ceremony," which was written by Alabama songwriter Jeannie Russell (formerly Strickland) and Carmol Taylor, with some final help from Billy Sherrill. (On any vinyl/CD copies I've seen, the song is credited only to Sherrill. All three are credited at BMI.com). Said Russell, "I'd write the lyrics and Carmol the music. They wanted a love song for George and Tammy. What I originally named it was 'Until Death Do Us Part.'" It was a simple affair—a call-and-response with both singers exchanging lifetime vows. Sherrill loved the song but didn't want any reference to the Grim Reaper in the title. He changed it to "The Ceremony" and added a local DJ who played the part of "the minister" on the record, "marrying" the couple in the space of three minutes and five seconds. In case you missed the point, the song opens with a cheesy organ playing a slightly off "Here Comes the Bride." Such shameless exploitation of the George and Tammy phenomenon! Impressive.

There is a gleefully voyeuristic 1972 performance of the song taped at the Ryman for the show *That Good Ole Nashville Music.* Lurking before the minister is a sad, scary Tammy at her most bewitchingly Gothic, sporting a big ol' blonde wig, Magic Marker eyeliner, and a strange amulet-like copper necklace she must've lifted off a Druid. Man, does she look *hot.* And in a slightly cubist Western suit, there's George, looking more resigned than agitated, his gleaming eyes staring at some offstage ghost. This is one of those classic "happy" country records that manages to sound quite the opposite. A deathly serious business, marriage. "'The Ceremony' goes to a whole 'nother place," said singer Laura Cantrell. "It was so crazy. Like watching Romeo and Juliet."

Old Plantation Country Music Park opened in Lakeland on April 4, 1971, with Conway Twitty and Charley Pride among the headliners. It was a family affair. "I sold tickets to every show," said Maxine Hyder. Her husband,

Cliff, "sat on the gate to keep any outsiders goin' back to where the stars were." Tammy, who'd cook up a big meal for the performers back at their house, got a kick out of watching George haggle over the phone with their booking agent Shorty Lavender* over the fees he'd have to pay an act. On June 12, 1972, ten thousand people would flock to Old Plantation park to attend a fund-raiser for George Wallace, who'd just survived an assassination attempt a few weeks before in Laurel, Maryland, that left him crippled for life. Wallace was Wynette's kind of guy: powerful, oddly charismatic, with something dark and foreboding pulsating just below the surface. "I like a man that speaks out the way he does," she told a Tupelo paper in 1973. "He's a really fine man." As far as the rest of it, well, "this business with the black people has been exaggerated."†

The Lakeland concert featured Del Reeves and Ferlin Husky in addition to George and Tammy, who'd been on the road with Wallace just days before he was shot. The *New York Times* dubbed the event "Wallace's Woodstock." For the next few years there'd be a big show at Old Plantation at least once a month.

Wynette made her debut in Las Vegas at the Landmark Hotel on May 5, 1971. Jones was on the bill with her, but failed to show opening night. George, who often got the heebie-jeebies playing tony venues outside the South, disappeared into a casino and drank. Tammy wound up carrying the show alone on her birthday.

An avid slot machine player, Wynette got hooked on a one-armed bandit

---

*Shorty Lavender, another legendary Music City character. Author Scott Faragher, who worked for him back in the seventies, describes him thusly: "Shorty was short, had a hat that was five times too big for his head, and he guzzled Maalox. He actually had his desk on a pedestal so he could look down at people." Lavender was "just nuts about George Jones" and knew how to be scarce when Jones was at his no-show worst. "Friday afternoon he'd get the hell outta there, go fishin' and leave us holdin' the bag. I'd get a call from some woman I'd sold a date to, cryin', 'I've lost everything I own. Where's George?' Shorty knew the whole time he wasn't gonna make it." Working for Lavender, Faragher said, "made a man of me quickly."

†As far as civil rights went, Wynette wasn't too interested. "It was like the way it was in the South when I grew up: black people did their thing, white people did their thing, and, yeah, if a white person mistreated a black person, that was not good—but you'd better believe you're not bringin' somebody home for dinner," said Joan Dew. "There wasn't gonna be a black guy in her band, nor would there be a black boyfriend, no matter how much she loved Charley Pride. That was the way Tammy was raised, and she never looked beyond that."

by the name of Big Bertha. "It was a huge machine, dominated the room," said Jan Smith. "We played this slot machine literally for days. They gave us fifteen minutes off to go to the bathroom. Tammy would do a show and I would stay there while she was singin' and play the damn slot machine."

But Bertha wasn't turning a profit, and Wynette didn't have a lot of patience. "On the third or fourth day she just got furious. She said, 'I'm over it!'" Smith continued. "There was a Sears down the road and she said, 'I'm gonna go buy me a petticoat,' and she did. An old Mexican woman walked in, put three quarters into Big Bertha, and hit it for eight thousand bucks. The band was relentless. We called it Tammy's eight-thousand-dollar petticoat. It probably cost ten dollars. And then she was so pissed. She was havin' to walk by Big Bertha in the lobby, and she'd go, 'Uh! I HATE that thing!'" Added Patsy Sledd, "You did not mention Big Bertha—ever. Tammy would have a fit."

Other artists fell under the George and Tammy spell. Tanya Tucker ran into the couple in the hallway outside the Quonset Hut studio and was stopped in her tracks. George was barely taller than tiny Tammy, but the pocket-sized couple loomed larger than any movie stars to Tanya. "They looked so good together, man. They were the perfect pair." Rosanne Cash remembered a visit Wynette and Jones paid to her father's home. "I sat slack-jawed and transfixed as they sang '(We're Not) The Jet Set.'" Tammy "sat on the plush blue antique sofa, hair poufed out to here, with nails, makeup, and outfit perfectly coordinated. She looked like a lotus blossom."

George vibrated with chaos; Tammy radiated power. Raeanne Rubenstein photographed the couple at the Country Music Awards. "Tammy was definitely the queen bee backstage," said Rubenstein. "She was amazingly popular. It was like the entire backstage area kind of circled her in this big vortex. She didn't really have to get up and circulate because all the other artists—Minnie Pearl, Eddy Arnold, Tanya Tucker—gravitated to her."

Now that Tammy had money, she refined her image. Off came the little go-go dresses and white boots; out came bigger blonde wigs and glitzy, extravagant gowns. Wynette created a new sort of country music elegance, bringing a wacky class to ensembles that could compete with any neon sign. For more than a decade much of her wardrobe would be designed by Harvey Krantz, who also dressed Liberace, Ike Turner, George Foreman, Don Ho, Oral Roberts, Hank Snow, and Isaac Hayes. ("All his capes and chains," boasted Krantz, who created the wild mink tuxedo Hayes wore to pick up his Oscars in 1972 for "Theme from *Shaft*.") Tammy was a favorite client. "She liked high fashion," Harvey noted. "A lot of rhinestones, embroidery, glitter." (Krantz was less crazy over dressing George, who was "a little difficult, extremely picky" about how clothes fit.)

Wynette was "more a beauty icon than Dolly or Loretta," said Laura Cantrell. "The look of the sixties really suited her—big hair, eyeliner. But Tammy was not a cartoon character," stressed Cantrell, who saw her as "an incredible mixture of being a sexy woman and having this restraint to her. Almost like Dusty Springfield." Cantrell was so taken with the look of Tammy's albums, she paid homage with the cover of one of her own releases, 2002's *When the Roses Bloom Again*.

Ah, yes, the Tammy album covers. So powerful. They had a lot to do with creating the image Cantrell called "Domestic grief goddess," and one man is largely responsible. "I was the first art director for any major label in Nashville," said Bill Barnes. Previously covers had been designed via the New York office, who'd send down a photographer, but "they just didn't have the rapport. I was hired specifically because I was from the South. Billy thought that by being a Southerner I would understand country music." Barnes made the most of the LP format's twelve-by-twelve canvas, each cover serving as a seductive trailer for the musical stories contained on the vinyl within.

Bill Barnes came up with iconic images of Tammy that really pack a punch. After all these years, I can recall them from memory: there's melancholy porcelain doll Tammy with yellow bow tie (*Another Lonely Song*); floral pantsuit Tammy in straw hat and beige high heels at the old-timey piano (*'Til I Can Make It on My Own*); blurry close-up glamour Tammy (*You and Me*); woman of the world Tammy in scarf-festooned hat, lace shawl, and under a parasol (*Woman to Woman*); sad onstage Tammy in white jumpsuit (*One of a Kind*); and let's not forget devoted mommy Tammy (*Bedtime Stories*). The Bill Barnes Tammy album covers *are* the seventies. Roll them up, smoke them, and visions of Naugahyde Barcaloungers dance in your head. There is something so muted and elegant about their often misty, late-afternoon look, albeit with a touch of brown corduroy.*

---

*One stunning cover Barnes didn't shoot was 1978's *Womanhood*, a Norman Seeff portrait that was also used for Tammy's autobiography. Melancholy in tousled blonde hair and a low-cut black spangled dress, Wynette looks magnificent here.

For George and Tammy's album art to blossom, Barnes had to first ex-
cise George McClelland, a police photographer and family friend from
Lakeland whose cover shots Barnes felt were a little harsh. He told Sherrill, "Since we're using a police photographer, why don't we have Tammy
lay down, we can draw chalk around her, she'll get up, he can shoot the
chalk outline, and that'll be the album cover." Billy laughed but got the
point. Al Clayton and Slick Lawson were brought in to photograph covers,
although later Barnes wound up shooting many of them himself because
he was tired of paying kill fees due to no-show stars. "The music was their
focus," said Barnes. "Album covers were sort of a nuisance." Jones, who
missed many a photo session, was so bored during the three-hour shoot
for the *George & Tammy & Tina* cover, "he was gonna lay down and take
his shirt off. Tammy said, 'George! Get your shirt on, we gotta take these
pictures!'"

These shoots were low-rent affairs consisting of Barnes, his camera,
and a makeup person (sometimes his wife). Many were shot in Tammy's
backyard. The entire budget was usually a few hundred bucks. At times
they had to be done at the last minute, with Barnes flying out to meet
Wynette on the road somewhere. The highly memorable cover of *Let's Get
Together* shows a sexed-up Tammy barely contained in a low-cut white
pantsuit with matching rhinestone headband. Little did people know that
the photo was shot in the dank basement of a Holiday Inn near Pittsburgh,
with Barnes grabbing a space blanket from the trunk of his car to use as
a backdrop.

Barnes found working with Wynette a breeze. "Tammy wasn't one of
those people that play to the camera and have these moves. She would get
in a mood, then turn, look at you, and just kill you with her eyes. Tammy
was communicating a feeling. It wasn't a put-on. She was just real."

In the sixties and seventies Nashville functioned as a kind of low-rent version of the old Hollywood studio system. Producers were the moguls of the
studios, the boss just about everybody answered to, including the artist.
You were expected to toe the line with seemingly incessant recording, touring, and promotional appearances while the record company concentrated
its energies on career longevity. In return it was much easier to absorb a
dud, as the stakes were much lower. "They used to keep an artist forever.
We would do four albums a year on them, one single out of the album," said

Glenn Sutton. "Now they do one album every three years, put all singles on there, and just work it to death. We had an unbelievable party when Tammy sold fifty thousand albums. Now if an artist don't sell four to five hundred thousand, they drop 'em."

One requirement was to be on call for interviews. Unlike the world of rock, where reclusiveness and unavailability could be salable commodities, country stars had to be accessible to the *Boise Daily Register* as well as for the *New York Times.* When it came to charming reporters, Wynette was a femme fatale. Ralph Emery—Music City's answer to Merv Griffin— had Tammy on his radio and TV shows countless times. "I learned in the beginning I was treated a lot better by the press if I was honest with 'em," Wynette told Robert K. Oermann in 1982. "I may be a singer, but I'm a plain human being." She would wow the media to such an extent that— more power to her—they were pretty unquestioning of the myth she presented. Not that she was deceitful—far from it. She so believed in the version of her life she told and seemed so "real" telling it that the rest of the world believed, too.

Tammy came along at a time when the attitude in the press toward country music—particularly Nashville—was changing. Jack Hurst, one of the first reporters to write seriously about country musicians, clearly remembers the response when he told his editor at the *Tennessean* that he wanted to cover country in 1969. "He looked at me like I'd just dropped onto his desk from Mars."

Once again it had to do with the divide between the classes that made up Nashville. "In the same sense there's Beverly Hills and there's Hollywood, there was Music City, USA, and there was Nashville," said Eve Zibart, a young reporter who took over Hurst's beat in the mid-seventies. The music industry was not viewed as an asset but an embarrassment. "The people who started showin' up down at the Opry when it was on lower Broadway were showin' up in cars that barely made it to Nashville from Opp, Alabama, places like that," said Hurst. The old-line Southern wealth "looked at it as somethin' that reflected badly on the town." Reporter Huell Howser agreed. "In those days country music was considered hillbilly music. It was looked down on in the same way you would've looked down on people who had tattoos or chewed tobacco. There were whole groups of people who were born and raised in Nashville who wouldn't be caught dead goin' to the Grand Ole Opry."

When country stars did merit coverage in the paper, it was concerning "every time they got drunk or shot somebody," said Hurst. "That's all that ever made the paper, so it always made 'em look like the lowest-class people in the world." Hurst felt country music "hadn't been regarded in Nashville as a serious art form, and that's the way I looked at it. At that time country was much more of a music comin' from people at the bottom of society. This was the voice of the voiceless."

Hurst's in-depth, carefully researched profiles started running on the front page of the *Tennessean*, his pieces there and later in the *Chicago Tribune* showing country in a new light, and the artists appreciated it. "It came across that I was takin' these people seriously and that the *Tennessean* was takin' 'em seriously. I was not an enemy of the music." Even usually reticent Nashville figures like Billy Sherrill and George Jones granted him an audience. Hurst profiled Tammy many times, even contributing liner notes to her 1977 album *Let's Get Together*. "You were always struck by how forthcoming she appeared to be. It seemed like she was always tryin' to be very cooperative, very gracious without being 'on' or anything. Tammy seemed to be respectful of me as an interviewer. She acted like she was grateful for the attention."

"I found her to be the quintessential old-line country star that hadn't forgotten where she came from," said Huell Howser. "The last generation of real superstars who came from that kind of background and were really proud of their struggles—they were part of who they were. I never, ever saw her put on any airs or pretend to be anybody except who she was." Robert Oermann, who would interview Tammy later in her career, was similarly smitten. "By the time I met her she was a star, but you never, ever thought that. She never acted like it. Tammy was fascinating. Her speaking voice was just fantastic. She spoke in this beautiful honeyed Alabama way that was just almost seductive as her singing. I introduced her to a writer friend, and she kissed him on the cheek. He was beside himself! She just had a wonderful effect on people."

Oermann was also struck by Tammy's candor. "She didn't pull back anything. Tammy just kind of threw herself at your mercy. She opened her life like a book and said, 'I hope you like it.' It was hard not to respond to that. It was just so genuine it was hard not to love her. She was tragic, beautiful, and glamorous—all of those things. I always thought she was like Barbara Stanwyck."

No surprise that Jones was the exact opposite in many ways. He wasn't comfortable giving interviews and blew many of them off, yet Jack Hurst found him to be "an absolutely unbelievably exciting person to be around, because you just never quite knew what was gonna happen." Picking George's brain was a challenge. "You had all these questions about what was goin' on inside with him, and he didn't want to fool with it. There were a lot of yes and no answers, not much amplification. It wasn't like he was tryin' to be uncooperative. He couldn't put into words what he wanted to say. He had his own demons."

Hurst was fascinated by the dynamic between George and Tammy. "Now Tammy is seen as one of the prototypical country voices, but at that time she was not. Hers was from the Billy Sherrill country pop sound, whereas Jones was just from the dirt road, the Big Thicket." Hurst saw their relationship as similar to the one between Carrie and Hurstwood in Dreiser's *Sister Carrie.* "They started off in exactly opposite places—he was at the very top of their level of society, and she was at the very bottom, and by the time the book ends their positions had just reversed, like they had traveled in a big X." Tammy's massive success quickly eclipsed George's, and his personal problems would be his undoing for many a year. What Hurst found most interesting, however, is that, unlike in the Dreiser novel, the tables would turn yet again for George and Tammy near the end of their lives, and Jones would rise to the top once more.

Throughout 1971 to 1973 Tammy's solo career continued to burn brightly. During this period she had five number one hits and two just one notch below. "We Sure Can Love Each Other" was a song Sherrill had written with Wynette after hearing Johnny Cash read the line "We sure can hurt each other" off a greeting card on a late-night talk show. (Listen for the great rhyme pitting "compassion" against "old-fashioned.") Tammy is at her best here: neither on her knees weeping nor hitting you over the head with a rolling pin, but singing with a quiet double-tracked beauty. You believe every word. Sherrill's sophisticated arrangement—light strings, a touch of vibes—only underscores the power.

"Good Lovin' (Makes It Right)" is a rare solo writing credit from Sherrill, who wasn't proud of the ditty. ("It's not exactly 'Moon River,'" sayeth he.) This is conversational Tammy, giving advice, warning of the usual impending doom if the good lovin' ain't delivered: a man-stealer waits "around every corner wrapped in furs."* It's a classic Nashville soundtrack: acoustic guitars and brushes on the drums mesh into a truckin'-along rhythm so square it's cool (as is the self-explanatory non-LP B-side, "I Love You, Mr. Jones"). "My Man" (with that classic, peppily sung, wince-inducing line "He holds me in the palm of his hand . . . and I like it") was another jaunty number from the Sherrill-Wilson-Taylor factory, and "Kids Say the Darndest Things" was a Sherrill-Sutton song revisiting the "look what we've done to the children" battlefield of "D-I-V-O-R-C-E."†

To these ears the stunner of this period is "'Til I Get It Right," a graveyard-tempo ballad written by Red Lane and Larry Henley, the latter a former member of the Newbeats and of "Bread and Butter" castrato pop infamy. Opinions differ over how the song arrived on Sherrill's desk, but Henley claims neither Billy nor Tammy was that impressed with it—Jones happened to be present when it was pitched, and they cut it because "*he* liked it." (Said cowriter Red Lane, "George was jumping up and down over that song.") Well, Jones picked a killer, because I'd rank this one in Tammy's top five. Her spot-on phrasing is the perfect blend of restraint and emotion. After listening to this one, anyone who accuses Sherrill of overproducing should be beaten with a rubber hose. There is a wondrous television performance of the song from *That Good Ole Nashville Music* televised June 24, 1973. Caught at the height of her statuesque beauty, Tammy is Greco-Nashvillian elegant in a black gown, wearing enough turquoise to sink a battleship and sporting eye shadow to match.‡ The line "My door to love has opened out more times than in" always makes me chuckle, until

---

*"Tammy had some songs that encouraged women to look at us men as I guess what it is we are," said Charlie Louvin, a big fan of "Good Lovin'." "A woman is supposed to put up with that. In other words, if you don't make love to your man, you're turnin' him out on the street to hunt for what he can find—when all it would've took to keep that marriage together was just a little lovin'. I thought that was one of the best songs Tammy ever did. Because it is so true. As true as the Good Book."

†To give an idea of just how on the fly this music was created, Sherrill went down to Sutton's office during the session and said, "I'm cutting a track on this thing, so finish a verse and a chorus." Sutton did as instructed, took it to the studio, and Tammy overdubbed the missing lyrics.

‡Marshall Fallwell, a photographer and antiques appraiser friend of Wynette's, said: "Back in the seventies Tammy and George and everybody in Nashville had hundreds of thousands of dollars' worth of turquoise—big hunks of turquoise hangin' around their neck. Paid thirty, forty thousand for it. Wasn't worth a nickel."

Wynette's delivery makes me weep. (George and Tammy do a rousing duet of "We're Gonna Hold On" on the same show, with Jones in a pretty unforgettable orange pants and Flintstones vest ensemble.)

The day of the session for "Bedtime Story," Wynette walked into Sherrill's office to find Billy and Glenn Sutton stretched out on the floor perusing stacks of children's books. Boiling down the archetypes to a castle, a king and queen, and a little princess, they managed to craft a saga of infidelity that was decidedly unfairytale-like. When one of the session players expressed concern over the length of the four-minute-plus track, Sherrill said, "I don't care if it's ten minutes long—I like it." The single shot to number one in January 1973.

As success mounted, Wynette's health crumbled. First she was hospitalized for an appendectomy. Days after Georgette was born, Tammy had to undergo an emergency hysterectomy, and that left her shattered. "I have a complex, something that bothers me more than anything else in my whole life," she said in a mid-seventies interview. "The thought of marrying somebody and not being able to give him a child really disturbs me." Even worse, she had to go back on the road without properly healing. This caused a condition of recurring scar tissue—adhesions—that would have a grave effect on the rest of Tammy's life. In October 1971 Wynette passed out at the wheel of her car, taking out a pair of palm trees in the process. Blood sugar was blamed. Little by little she was using drugs on the road. "Tammy would take Valium, or a little pill called a 'Miltown,'" said Charlene Montgomery. "She tried to get me to take it." Author Bob Allen claims that during a nine-month period in 1973 Tammy had "undergone nearly a dozen hospital stays." There were maladies of somewhat vague origin. One night Wynette "passed out onstage," said Patsy Sledd. "I don't know if that was for real. She pulled ones sometimes." Sledd laughed. "Anything for attention."

Jones had pretty much managed to stay sober for a period in Lakeland. But one day it ended with a bang. Depression would hit him "like a woman going through her monthly cycle," said Tammy. And then came the booze. According to Tammy, Jones drove home one day bombed out of his mind. She tried to put him to bed, he swung at her, then pointed a gun at her as she fled, firing and missing. George emphatically denies this. (As recently as 2005 Jones insisted, "I never shot a gun at Tammy Wynette.")* Wynette claimed he then went on a drunken rampage, demolishing the contents of their home. George denies this as well.

One enters very murky waters trying to report George and Tammy blowouts with any hope of accuracy. It is he said–she said on a grand scale, repeated, embellished, and forgotten over decades of interviews, books, and documentaries. Tammy insisted that George went into her closet one day and cut all the heels off of her countless pairs of high-heeled shoes so she couldn't get away from him. Never happened, said Jones. There is the old lawn mower story everyone's heard—how Tammy hid the keys to all their vehicles to keep Jones on the wagon, so he hopped on the riding mower and puttered miles down the road to the nearest bar. George admits that one's true but maintains it happened back in Texas when he was married to second wife Shirley. With the many depraved things Jones cheerfully admits to in his autobiography, you'd think firing a gun at his wife and demolishing the house wouldn't raise an eyebrow. At the same time, Tammy was obviously known to embellish a story or ten. In her autobiography Wynette tells of serving George moldy food left over from a weeklong drunk with the Montgomerys. They insist the offending morsels never existed. Said Peanutt, "Tammy would lie, man. She'd fabricate, just make somethin' up."

Whatever the particulars of that day in Lakeland, both husband and wife agreed that the net result was George being carted off in a straitjacket by men in white coats to a nearby facility with a padded room. Tammy had to leave for a tour of Canada the next day. Jones had the hide to complain she didn't visit him during the ten-day stay.

The Joneses returned to Nashville in late 1972. City officials had thrown various wrenches into George's plans for his Old Plantation Country Music Park, and now that the challenge of creating it had been met, he had grown a bit tired of it. The couple had been on the road so much, there was little time to spend in Lakeland. They returned to Music City, moving first to their old home on Old Hickory Lake, then to a swanky French Regency

*Peanutt Montgomery, one person who's definitely faced the wrong end of George's barrel, concurred: "He didn't try to shoot her. I don't remember any story like that until her book come out."

manor at 1813 Tyne Boulevard. They also bought a 340-acre farm about a half hour outside of Nashville, which George stocked with Black Angus cattle.

George and Tammy's unending activity didn't hide the turmoil beneath, however.

"They both had too many dollars and not enough sense," said Patsy Sledd. "They'd buy a house, tear it all apart, and fix it all up, just spend money— that was their happiness together, the money they had to spend—and as soon as they get it fixed up, they'd move to another one. There was always somebody around, company all the time. Their friends went with 'em everywhere. I never known 'em to go anywhere alone and share each other's love or sit and talk about things."

When conflict came up, they'd run. "Most people have to sit and fight it out, work it out, get over it," Patsy maintained. "If you have a problem, you talk. One of 'em would take off to Acapulco, the other one would fly somewhere else. Then in a week or two they'd get back together, nothin' solved, nothin' talked about. That's the way it went. There was never any resolution to the problem."

When Jones disappeared with the Montgomerys on a trip to Alabama, Wynette went berserk. "When we got back Tammy had parked her van crossways of our driveway where we couldn't get into our house," remembered Charlene Montgomery. "George was lookin' to see if he could find a set of keys in the van. He couldn't find no keys, but he found those divorce papers." Wynette later said she did it only to scare Jones. "I told my attorney, 'If he signs these papers, I'll die. I'm just tryin' to shock him.'" George was shocked—so much so that he showed up at the Quonset Hut bombed out of his mind and got into a tussle with security guard Ed Grizzard, which resulted in Jones putting his fist through a glass window, ripping up his arm, and being dragged off to the hospital.

Wynette also accused George of being interested in Charlene Montgomery. The Montgomerys claim other songwriters in the Sherrill clan were envious of the amount of songs Peanutt was getting cut. "On one album George and Tammy cut six of Peanutt's songs," said Charlene. "Well, Carmol and George Richey and Norro Wilson would only get one song on an album, and their cut was only a third of that. It created a jealousy. That's when Tammy started turnin' on us. They done planted the seed." Wynette called up Charlene and started hurling accusations. "You and

George were seen by yourselves comin' up to the Tyne Boulevard house in your white Cadillac," she hissed. Charlene denied it, making the point that she and Peanutt were friends with Jones years before Tammy entered the picture.

"She didn't back off," said Charlene. "Tammy knew better, and *I* knew Tammy knew better. It was just her aggravated at George, and she had to have somebody to blame." The Montgomerys felt Tammy's new hairdressers were whispering in Wynette's ear as well. "Nan was there, mouthin' off in the background," said Charlene. "I been doin' Tammy's hair on the road. Jan and Nan—they didn't want me in the picture."

Patsy Sledd didn't care for the hairdressers, either. "Tammy was pretty gullible. She would listen to what anyone would tell her instead of her own feelin's. Jan and Nan had their nose up her bottom. Stuff like that caused a lot of problems with George and Tammy. I think Jan was the biggest duck in the puddle in George and Tammy's divorce—'I'd do this, I'd do that.'"

The angry phone call from Tammy ended with Charlene telling her she was going to put their Nashville home on the market and move back to Alabama. Perhaps realizing what the outcome of that might be, Wynette panicked and instructed her not to. "The house sold in two weeks," said Charlene. "Tammy was pleadin' and beggin', 'Don't do it, don't do it.'" The Montgomerys returned to Florence, Alabama, and the result was George spent more and more time away from Tammy at their new home.

Hairdressers on one side, songwriters on the other, the air around George and Tammy was thick with spies, ass-kissers, and infidels, all of them jockeying for position. Said a woeful Wynette, "If ever a home was broken up by outsiders, it was ours."

Despite the divorce threat, Jones and Wynette reconciled, but it was an uneasy truce at best. Peanutt, who played rhythm guitar in their band at the time, recalled a squabble one night after he and George had returned from a lost week of boozing in Alabama.

"They were into it over the money," said Peanutt. "George was sayin', 'Look, I was makin' more money when you was doin' hair.' After a while I heard Tammy say, 'I tell you what, George, we ain't gonna make it. We're just not gonna make it.' George said, 'Honey, we're just gonna have to hold on.'" The phrase clicked in Montgomery's mind. "I thought, 'That'd be a good song.'"

The tour bus rolled into Jamestown, Pennsylvania. As Peanutt had been off on the drunk with George, he was in the doghouse with Wynette. "I'd kid Tammy about things and picked at her a lot," said Montgomery. "I guess that's why she didn't like me." Peanutt saw no reason to change his MO now, so he decided to go down to the Holiday Inn bar, ring up a three-hundred-dollar tab, and have it billed to Wynette's room.

"The next mornin' I'd written like a verse and a chorus of 'We're Gonna Hold On.'" Montgomery got out the old guitar he played on the bus and headed for George and Tammy's room. "I walked in—boy, was Tammy mad. She was in there doin' George's hair. 'I heard about that bill up there at the lounge.' George, he was laughin' about it because it was somethin' like he'd do. I took that old guitar, sat down on the bed, started singin' 'We're Gonna Hold On.' After a little bit, why, Tammy wasn't mad anymore."* Jones helped Peanutt finish the last verse. The original tempo was busier. "I did it fast," said Montgomery. "Billy Sherrill slowed it down."

Recorded on March 28, 1973, "We're Gonna Hold On" was to be George and Tammy's first number one hit. And what a record. Sherrill did indeed slow Peanutt's song down to a perfect shuffle, with drummer Jerry Carrigan's *knock-knock-who's-there?* dragging drum beat inserting a sublime tension into the chorus. The tempo is perfect for the steadfast attitude expressed in the lyrics. The singing here is really stunning—Tammy's ascending on the tail of the chorus, George descending, both in perfect harmony. And when he lifts off on the final lap, it's a knockout. George and Tammy were sharing the crisis in their marriage and their desire to stay together with the whole world. You had to root for them.

When asked about divorce rumors on Ralph Emery's radio show, Tammy dismissed the idea of leaving George. "There's no way he's gonna get away from me," she insisted. "He's here to stay."

The Joneses moved once more in 1974. The Franklin Road home, mere minutes from the Quonset Hut, was the most opulent yet—17,600 square feet, twelve bedrooms, an Olympic-size pool, tennis courts, and a personal merry-go-round—all situated on nine and a half acres.

The houses might've gotten more and more expensive, but the tastes of

---

*Tammy recalled the "We're Gonna Hold On" lyric as originating with Jones: "George picked up a guitar and he went over that line and over that line and over that line."

the owners stayed gloriously the same. Tammy's antiques appraiser friend
Marshall Fallwell, rather sensitive to style, dubbed the look of George and
Tammy's latest manse "Redneck Gothic."

"The décor was awful. Tammy's private bedroom—everything in it was
pink, including the walls and the bed. She had something like three hundred stuffed toys on the bed, all pink. There was a French chandelier in the
foyer—Tammy just gave it to one of the workmen. We're talkin' about a
fifty-thousand-dollar antique French chandelier." Then there was the coffee
table: "the size and shape of a coffin surrounded by Naugahyde poufs." Sitting in "a living room big as an airplane hanger," it had "a velvet interior
with some sort of Spanish-looking scabbards in there, so it was also a display case." Tammy announced, "That's not all it is," and "she pulled out a
secret drawer underneath. There were George's favorite games—dice, a
croupier stick about a foot long, and a tiny little roulette wheel."

One can practically visualize Fallwell reaching for the smelling salts.
"People of her generation, they had no feelings about natural beauty," he
maintains. "They associate that with being dirt poor. Once I asked Dolly,
'Why all the pink sequins?' She said, 'Well, you didn't live in the country
and nearly starve to death.'"

"George had a more forgivin' spirit about him than Tammy did," claimed
Charlene Montgomery. "She was not a very forgivin' person. Tammy would
hold a grudge." The perfect example of this was Wynette's strange obsession with Melba Montgomery, George's old duet partner whom Tammy
always thought she could better vocally. Once she was married to Jones, she
undoubtedly discovered that George had once had strong feelings for Melba,
even considering marriage at one point.* The mere mention of her name
would send Tammy into a tirade over the singer, whom she nicknamed "Ol'
Melber."

"*Whooo-hooo*," said George, shaking his head at the memory. "I was fin-

---

*Apparently Melba took the Possum's idiosyncrasies in stride. Larry Fullam, a member
of Connie Smith's band in the sixties, recalled a gig they did with Jones in Cincinnati.
Jones Boy Charlie Carter, using Melba's guitar onstage, experienced all sorts of technical
problems with it during George's set. Once they got backstage, Jones took the offending
instrument and flung it across the room. The guitar "took three leaps across the floor,
hit the wall, and smashed into a million pieces," said Fullam. "Melba was sittin' there
reading somethin'. She barely looked up and said, 'George, I always did want that little
ol' Martin you got.'"

ishin' an album for Musicor, and Melba was supposed to come in and over-dub with me," Jones recalled. "I hadn't told Tammy about it—hell, I was gonna try and keep it quiet." Melba called the house only to encounter a very frosty Tammy on the other end of the line. According to George, the conversation went like this:

"Is George there?"

"No, Melber, George ain't here."

"What's wrong, Tammy?"

"Not a goddamn thang."

"I'm supposed to go into the studio and overdub with George."

"You're WHAT?!"

That was the end of that. "I don't think I got to finish that overdubbin'," said Jones, chuckling.

Tammy's vendetta continued. As Charlene Montgomery recalled, "Tammy used to tell me on the road, 'Melba Montgomery will never have another hit record. If she should come out with somethin', I'll cover her, and you know me bein' the artist I am, they're gonna play mine over Melba's.'" But in 1974 Montgomery returned to the charts with "No Charge," a Harlan Howard mother's-point-of-view recitation addressed to a child who wants to get paid for doing chores and homework. Remark-able if only for the guilt it intended to provoke in offspring everywhere, the song went to number one.*

"Tammy ran into the studio and covered Melba just like she said she'd do—and demanded that Billy release it," said Charlene. (Daughter Tina was enlisted to perform the role of ungrateful child on the record as well.) The song was released only on an album, not as a single (except in the UK), but that didn't stop Wynette from sweet-talking DJs trying to get it played. "You would not believe what she went through to try to knock that song out of the saddle," said Patsy Sledd. But there was no stopping Montgomery's smash hit, and, according to Charlene, it drove Tammy into a meltdown. Charlene remembered Wynette "jumpin' up and down on the middle of the bed because they wouldn't play her version. She pitched a fit." Friends knew

---

*If you're the sort of sadist who gets chuckles out of child exploitation set to a steel gui-tar, check out "The Telephone Call." George calls home for Tammy, but little Tina mangles his messages to Mama and alleged hilarity ensues. The song went to number 25 on the country charts. Both that and "No Charge" are on the album *George & Tammy & Tina.* Weren't their other kids a bit jealous?

better than to bring up her name. "She was jealous of Melba, just because George went with her," said Patsy. "She didn't like Ol' Melber."

"Tammy was kind of a split personality," insisted Charlene. "She could be a real sweet person or she could be a very vindictive person. If she got it in for somebody, she got it in for 'em all the way—and did things that was contrary, things that would hurt their careers. On the other hand, if she liked you, she'd just go plumb out of the way to help. She would just overdo for you."

A moment of levity as the dark clouds gathered: January 1974's "(We're Not) The Jet Set," a sly Bobby Braddock number set to a grumpy-duck guitar riff, is one of George and Tammy's finest. A hillbilly (sorry, Tammy) protest record, this is a celebration of all things country ("Our steak and martinis / Are draft beer and wienies"), everything the better-thans cringe over, right down to pronouncing Chevrolet with a hard *t*. That summer saw the release of "We Loved It Away," a mawkish George Richey ballad and the last George and Tammy single to be released during their marriage. (Their next single, in April 1975, was undoubtedly their all-time worst, the execrably cute "God's Gonna Get 'Cha (for That)," an inventory of offenses punishable by the man upstairs set to the manufactured "joy" of a faux gospel track.)

A newer, darker Tammy was unleashed in the recording studio in 1974. Steeped in the delirium of her daily existence, her voice had mellowed, the phrasing growing a touch more extreme. Dare I say she sounds more womanly? And if it's humanly possible, sadder? There was something increasingly noble and more than a bit crazy about her dedication to unrealistic romantic ideals. Perhaps because every country songwriter on earth was slobbering to get a Tammy cut, her albums were improving in terms of content. Nineteen seventy-four's *Another Lonely Song* had knockout renditions of "Help Me Make It Through the Night" and the Jeanne Pruett hit "Satin Sheets," a song Wynette was known to tear up in concert. Released that same year, *Woman to Woman* had the Mickey Newbury stunner "I Don't Think About Him No More," and 1976's *'Til I Can Make It on My Own* had Wynette reaching back to her childhood for a stirring rendition of the Louvin Brothers' "If I Could Only Win Your Love." (Engineer Lou Bradley swears that's Billy Sherrill himself singing uncredited harmony.) "Easy Come, Easy Go" sure sounds like a hit as well, but by this point Wynette was churning out so much great material it's easy to see how it got lost in the shuffle.

"Another Lonely Song," a collaboration between Sherrill, Wynette, and Norro Wilson, went to number one in January of 1974. The title came about when Wynette nonchalantly said, "Let's write another lonely song" in Billy's office, and it was Tammy's first single to deal with adultery from the perspective of a guilty partner who cheats to alleviate the pain caused by her unfaithful man.* It's a breezy number, almost Carpentersesque with its fluffy, cotton-candy strings. Norro Wilson was Billy's new favorite, a much poppier guy than stone-country Glenn Sutton, and he admitted the arrangement was "a little slicker than what we usually wrote." Wilson maintained he and Sherrill were thrilled whenever they could expand the confines of a country song. "Billy was an ol' pop guy, and so was I. I didn't listen to country music growin' up. Hell, I listened to Nat King Cole and Rosemary Clooney. The Four Freshmen is my favorite sound in the world." I love the nonchalant weariness in the way Wynette sings, "The night goes on and on." And the heartbreaking way she admits to being "weak." The fact that Tammy uttered the word "damn" in the song was the subject of much discussion with George, and she tearfully wanted to change the line after cutting it. A meeting was called with Billy Sherrill. After a playback Jones had to admit that his wife's usage of such an unladylike expression was "in good taste."

That fall's "Woman to Woman" was Sherrill attempting to take Wynette in a new direction. Yet another mere wisp of a song (with the intimacy of her previous recordings, do we really need Tammy to tell us she's "singing straight to you"?) where Wynette warns the women of America of the harlots lurking in every corner—"She can do things to a man you never dreamed a woman can do"—the jazzy arrangement, with funky electric piano, female backing chorus, and Pete Drake's inebriated little corkscrew steel fills, wasn't exactly "Stand by Your Man."

Wynette could've cut a fantastic album of R & B standards—skeptics should search out her versions of "Cry" and "It's Just a Matter of Time"—but such experimentation scared the bejesus out of her. "'Woman to Woman' was a bluesy kind of song, the kind of thing that Charlie Rich does, and I don't consider him really country . . . I don't want to be known as anything but country," she maintained. "I started out as a country singer, and all I

---

*Despite the fact that a number of her late-seventies singles were cheatin' songs, Wynette admitted, "I don't particularly like to do songs that talk about cheating . . . I prefer something more positive."

want is a country hit." Tanya Tucker recalled Sherrill being so unsure of the tune he asked her opinion. "Billy said, 'Man, what do you think of this song?' Here's Billy askin' me this when I'm fourteen years old! I said, 'I think it's a *hit!*' 'Course, I don't guess it was." A number 4 Tammy Wynette record didn't qualify as a success in Nashville, and no doubt Tammy noticed.

Although it wasn't a single, Wynette's 1974 recording of Newbury's "I Don't Think About Him No More" ranks among her finest. "Tammy was one of the biggest fans of songwriters there ever was," said band member David Sloas. "She listened to a lot of music on the bus. One of her biggest pleasures was sittin' on the bus, turning the lighting down a little bit, and listening to Mickey Newbury." The Newbury song that really got to Tammy was "San Francisco Mabel Joy." "She would listen to that song and cry." Newbury could receive no greater tribute than Wynette's recording of "I Don't Think About Him No More." Millie Kirkham's ghostly wail kicks off this dreamlike elegy to a long-gone love whose memory haunts Tammy "like poison red berries that cling to the mind." Wynette's wistful, plain-spoken delivery plays like she's next to you in the passenger seat during a midnight Greyhound ride to nowhere. Morbid romanticism, ain't it grand? This one reminds me a little of the Ray Davies solo piano demo of "I Go to Sleep." Or maybe it's an embryonic version of George's "He Stopped Loving Her Today." There is just as much spook lurking in the shadows here. Sure, the arrangement is florid and weird, but so are the obsessions being expressed. Listen as Sherrill stops the Symphony of Melancholy on a dime so Wynette can strut her stuff.

"You can say as much with a blank space as you can with a space that's all jammed up musically—where, if you shine a light, nothin' comes through, there's no holes in it," explained Lou Bradley. "Billy understood the importance of a little daylight in the music."

George Jones kept vanishing. Jan Smith remembers a day in the summer of 1974 when they were all playing Aggravation, Jones outfitted in shorts, tank top, and ball cap. "That mood came over him," said Smith. "He got mad, shoved the board aside, and said, 'I'm through,' and left." George tore off in Tammy's car.

After a few days Tammy got antsy. She decided Jones had run off to the Sunshine State. She called Jan and Nan and said, "Let's go to Florida." They packed the kids into George's new black Cadillac convertible and began the Possum hunt. Jan and Nan drank beer on the way down, giving one to Tammy, who drank the occasional margarita at most. Tammy drove all night, and when Jan and Nan woke up the next morning, they were at the beach. "Tammy still had the can of beer that we had given her right there between her legs. It was boilin' hot. She poured it out there on the beach and said, 'Don't ever give me a beer again—that stuff tastes like piss!'"

They failed to locate George, but since the kids were along, they stopped "at every alligator farm and every snake farm. We'd watch 'em milk the snake for the venom." Tammy loved to see the kids' excitement every time they spotted a sign for another reptile farm.

The women also wandered into a roadhouse one night, "just three girls yukkin' it up, havin' a good time." Wynette, who usually wouldn't be caught dead in a bar, was dressed down with a scarf wrapped around her head in hopes she wouldn't be recognized. The owner cottoned on to the fact there was a superstar in his joint and asked her to do a number.

Tammy said she wouldn't do one of her own hits, but if he turned the lights out onstage she'd get up and sing "Help Me Make It Through the Night." Apparently no one figured out who she was, and as soon as she finished she wanted to hightail it out of there. As they made their escape, Wynette was cornered. "This drunk girl at the bar slapped Tammy on the back and said, 'Hey, honey, you sounded pretty good up there. You might oughtta make a career out of this.'"

The women had a big laugh over that one. The man she loved nowhere to be found, Tammy was starting to realize there was life beyond George Jones.

George and Tammy fought constantly during the fall of 1974. Wynette tried to keep him away from the Montgomerys, to no avail. "One day a cab pulled up in front and it was George," said Charlene Montgomery. Jones had taken a taxi all the way from Nashville. "Couldn't get no keys," said the Possum. "Nobody's gonna keep me away from y'all."

Particularly Tammy, according to Charlene. "She'd call the house and talk to George. He'd go up there to try and work things out with her. They'd get into it every time they got together."

That December George and Tammy planned to take the kids to Acapulco for a Christmas vacation. Wynette hoped it might provide a fresh start for the new year. But Billy Sherrill called, summoning them to the studio on December 12. He wanted to cut the old pop chestnut "Near You," which had been a number one hit for Francis Craig in 1947.* Neither Tammy nor George was sold on the idea. "I always felt bad about recording a song that's so well known," said Jones. "I can't do this thing like Guy Lombardi [*sic*]." Regardless, Sherrill coaxed beautiful performances out of the couple, and although the song wasn't released until two years later, it was another number one hit. The session was a bumpy one, however. When Wynette arrived at the studio to find the Montgomerys already lurking, she began to cry, fearing Jones would vamoose with the dastardly duo once more.

To her surprise George returned home with her after the session, but it was a rocky evening. "Tammy kept me awake all night, bawling about her career," said Jones. Wynette had scored only one number one hit at the beginning of that year: "Another Lonely Song." It couldn't have helped matters that George's partnership with Billy Sherrill was skyrocketing that year with two number one singles, "The Grand Tour" and "The Door." If there ever was a wrong person to express career paranoia to, it was Jones. He never gave a shit about anything other than wanting to sing, and Tammy's hysteria drove him up the wall. "I think she wanted to drive me back to drinking," said a rather uncharitable George.

The next morning Tammy and daughter Jackie had dental appointments. Jones was in his pajamas, planning to putter around the yard. Just another day. But when Tammy called home from town, George was gone. Mildred told her she'd seen him staring out the kitchen window, watching Foy work in the yard, when she heard him mutter to himself, "It's just not gonna work. It'll never work out." When Wynette got home, she checked to see if his "getaway bag" was there. It wasn't.

Jones had walked out on her for the last time. She spent the night crying, consoled by Jan and Nan. George did later come to his senses, but it was too late. "I went to Alabama and I was afraid to come back," said Jones. "And so I wanted to straighten up. I called the next mornin', I said, 'I messed up.'"

---

*Glenn Sutton suspected Billy had an ulterior motive for cutting "Near You." The cowriter of the number was Kermit Goell, a crony of Sherrill's, and he was a German. Apparently Goell had a considerable collection of Nazi memorabilia Sherrill coveted. "Shit, lamps with swastikas . . ." said Glenn.

Tammy informed her husband that he was no longer welcome. "She said, 'You son of a bitch, you messed up good—and don't you EVER step foot back in this house.' Well, that told me right there that she was waitin' for that chance, she was ready for an excuse. You just don't throw somethin' away that easy. With a little baby we got together. She was unhappy. Ready for a new stud, I guess."

Two great artists, two complex people, two intense souls, each of whom, unfortunately, was a walking haunted house. Together they were great; together they were destructive. They had tried and tried, but they just couldn't find a way to "hold on." At some point Tammy found herself staring at the plaque George had hung over their bed. "That was the first thing to come off the wall," she said.

On January 8, 1975, Tammy filed for divorce. Each of them got a house; George kept the houseboat; Tammy got the bus and even "custody" of their band, the Jones Boys. Tammy wrote a gut-wrenching song about the wake Jones left behind: "Your Memory's Finally Gone to Rest." Her answer to George's "The Grand Tour," it was an inventory of all the possessions he'd abandoned: "By mistake the Goodwill people took your desk." When she hits that chorus, it's devastating.

Fans mourned. "A country music legend had died, too," Tammy realized later. "The fans loved us as a team." Wynette would be unsettled by concertgoers shouting "Where's George?" at her shows.* Jones exhibited ghoulish humor about it all later by sneaking his ex-wife's name into familiar onstage favorites: "If drinkin' don't kill me / Tammy's memory will," he'd sing, a gleeful grin on his face. That's Jones: always ready to give the fans what they want, no matter how perverse.

Tammy spilled her guts to the tabloids. "George is one of those people who can't tolerate happiness. If everything is right, there's something in him that makes him destroy it. And destroy me with it." It almost seemed as if she was trying to talk her way into some peace of mind. The sight of Sonny and Cher choked her up. When the glittery, goofy duo "broke up it just broke my heart, because I identified with them."

---

*In the nineties, when Wynette toured Australia, an Aboriginal woman came up to her clutching four George and Tammy albums demanding to know where Jones was. Wynette tried to explain they'd divorced back in the seventies. "I couldn't convince her. Finally I said, 'I'll tell George you asked about him.'"

Jones retreated to Alabama, near the Montgomerys. A big, bad downward spiral had begun. Nowhere near as adept at dealing with the press as Wynette, George found it hard to discuss the separation. "I never, not once, put Tammy down onstage or anything after all these things happened and we got divorced. I always spoke highly of her. I felt in my heart that I was probably overbearing because of drinking and things like that." Other times there were flashes of anger, hurt. "I don't think she tried to understand me and help me understand her," he said years later. "I think she took the quick way out." How George could think seven years in the land of the Possum is the quick way out baffles the mind, but the interior of the Jones cranium is a unique and bewildering place.

Some nights Jones would show up in Nashville just to circle her driveway before slipping off into the darkness. There would still be the occasional duet, concert, or tour together, and George refused to give up. "There will never be anyone else for either of us," he muttered to the press in November 1976, arriving at a London airport to be by an ailing Tammy's side.

Nineteen seventy-five was a lost year for Tammy Wynette. Only two singles were released and no new albums outside of the duet collection *George & Tammy & Tina*. "(You Make Me Want to Be) A Mother" bit the world on the ankle in March 1975, making it all the way to number 4. This egregiously catchy little offense is a wowser only in that it is Tammy at her most shameless. Here she admits to being a manipulative, game-playing hussy ("Playin' with 'em like a toy, then leave 'em like a little boy / With teardrops on his face") who can only hold her head high when impregnated. Funnily enough we learn nothing about the man she's singing to—he seems incidental to the song outside of his role as sperm donor.

In October came "I Still Believe in Fairy Tales." A return to the short verse–chorus "Stand by Your Man" school, the lyrics are full of the anguished details of the doomed love story country music fans everywhere had breathlessly followed, down to the "dragon in the bottle" that was slaying King George. "It was almost like he was reading our minds," said Tammy of songwriter Glenn Martin. The way she belts out "And we all lived happy never after / For we just put the castle up for sale" just chills my blood. But Tammy the dreamer still believes.

It wasn't until 1976 that George and Tammy cut what many believe is their finest track ever, "Golden Ring." "I don't think there's a better song written," said Peanutt Montgomery—high praise coming from another songwriter. Bobby Braddock had been inspired to write the song after watching a documentary on the different phases in the life of a handgun. From that he decided it would be "a good idea to write a song about a ring." Bobby was a fan of the old gospel group the Chuck Wagon Gang, so he wanted the feel "kinda churchy, almost Pentecostal." And he knew who he wanted to sing it. "Usually if I write a song, it's not for a specific artist, I just write it for the sake of the song. In this case I specifically wanted to write somethin' for George and Tammy." He couldn't quite finish the number, so he headed over to Tree to look for his frequent partner in crime, Curly Putman, who was off on his farm. "Rafe Van Hoy walked in," remembered Braddock. "I said, 'Hey, you wanna help me finish a song?'" Van Hoy's mother worked in a jewelry store, so they consulted her for technical assistance. Bobby took the finished song, cut a demo tape, and took it to his boss at Tree, Buddy Killen. Killen was producing Bill Anderson at the time and wanted him to do the song. He couldn't find Bill that day, so he called his pal Billy Sherrill, who scooped it up for George and Tammy. "It was cut within a day or two from when it was pitched and immediately came out as a single," said Braddock. That sort of thing doesn't happen anymore. "Today, from the time you write a song to it being on the radio, you're talkin' a couple years, probably."

From the opening line "In a pawn shop in Chicago . . ." you know you're in for a succinct, evocative narrative, the story of a wedding ring "with one tiny little stone" as it goes from love to hate and back to the pawnshop. Author Aaron A. Fox describes it as an "epic narrative of working-class romance, moving from naïve young love through impulsive marriage to a final bitter and disillusioned breakup." He notes that in this song, the ring, the ultimate symbol of wedded bliss, "also signifies darkly: entrapment in poverty and a hasty and loveless marriage." Then Jones sings the part where the wife throws the ring down and says, "I don't love you anymore," and it just gets to you, particularly given the history of George and Tammy. The session featured gospel pianist extraordinaire George Richey and the Gatlin Brothers on backing vocals. (Jones overdubbed the final bass note, as the Gatlins had no bass singer.) The bluegrass feel brought out the best in George and Tammy's harmonies—her performance in particular is full of fire, and there's no taking a backseat to Jones here. She matches George lick for lick.

Merle Haggard loves the song. "It's as religious as can be without sayin' 'Jesus,'" he said. When I asked him to clarify that observation, he explained, "It's about matrim ony—matrimony's supposed to be the highest gift of God." As far as the vocals go, Haggard hears "two people that have high respect for each other—you can hear it in their voice. And they're singin' somethin' they believe in, somethin' they've experienced." Sadly, something they no longer had.

George Jones hovered in the shadows. The first year after the split Jones "kept coming around just like he always did," said Tammy. "There was no romantic love left for George," said Wynette's attorney, John Lentz. Jones was a man used to getting what he wanted, and it hurt. "He was like a schoolboy in love with some girl who didn't want him." He'd visit the kids or stop by to indulge in his favorite drunken pastime, flushing money down the commode. One night he showed up and headed for her bedroom. No, she informed him, that's *my* bedroom. She turned down the covers for him in an upstairs guest room, but when she awoke at three a.m. she knew Jones was gone. For good. "It was finally ended. It was over and done."

On December 15, 1975, Tammy entered the studio to record a song she'd written with George Richey and Billy Sherrill. Entitled "'Til I Can Make It on My Own," it said everything there was to say about the pain she'd been through. The line everybody loved was Tammy's: "Let me keep on using you / 'Til I get over losing you." This was Tammy's favorite of all her songs, and for good reason. It is a magnificent performance. Sherrill swathes her in a velvet production that shows her off like Marilyn in a mink coat. There's an epic sweep to the number, and she just sings the hell out of it. On the surface it seems like a rather modern point of view for Wynette, but listen to the way she sings the chorus. This is not something she wants to do, or finds empowering. In her heart, Tammy knows she will never "make it on her own." The sadness over her lost marriage bleeds from every note.

"I remember it being played back at the session, and no one really said anything," said Tammy. "They all knew my private life . . . they knew the song was about Jones."

Wynette Pugh, already looking about ready to belt out a sad song. "I loved an audience from the time I could walk," she said.

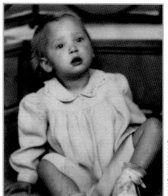

Mother Mildred Pugh, Wynette, her grandfather Chester Russell, and his mother, Margaret Mayhall Russell. "Wynette was rich as far as we were concerned," said friend Agnes Wilson. "Chester would give her anything she wanted."

Rare shot of Tammy's father, Hollis Pugh, who died when Tammy was still an infant. "My father inspired me and gave me the hope, but I don't remember him," she said.

Wynette's childhood home, not far from the Alabama/Mississippi state line. "There weren't but eight hundred people in all of Itawamba County," said Mildred.

Early yearbook photos of Wynette. When she arrived at Tremont High, "it was like a great wind came through," said classmate Holly Ford. "She was born to be a star."

Hopewell Elementary girls basketball team (Wynette is second in on back row left). Chester wouldn't let Wynette wear the shorts the rest of the girls wore unless they were fitted close to the leg with elastic bands. "I can see up the legs of them britches," he said. "I ain't havin' that."

Wynette looking sullen (back row right) at her friend Holly Ford's (far right) senior class graduation slumber party, 1960 (note Elvis 45s). Shortly after this picture Wynette disappeared to rendezvous with much older paramour D. C. Byrd. Holly panicked, thinking she'd get them all in trouble, but admitted, "You could forgive Wynette for anything."

Wynette cut school one day so she could pose for glamour photos shot by her friend Linda Cayson. "Oh, she was just like a movie star," said Linda.

A grim family portrait of Wynette, Jackie, Gwen, and Euple from July 1963. "Euple did the best he could," said friend Agnes Wilson. "There was no controllin' Wynette."

Tammy and husband number two, songwriter/singer Don Chapel. According to Don, the couple cut their wrists and mixed blood. "She told me it was a blood oath—if one of us makes it, we'll help the other. We're gonna stick together. This was for life."

Songwriter Glenn Sutton just prior to his marriage to Lynn Anderson, getting his tie adjusted by Wynette's long-time producer Billy Sherrill (seen here sporting a rare mustache). Together Sutton and Sherrill wrote many a hit for Tammy. "We just laughed ourselves through life," said Sherrill.

A forlorn Tammy stands behind a shabby motel door to publicize her first single, "Apartment #9." "The greatest thing I ever heard," said Dolly Parton.

Early publicity shot of Tammy sporting the infamous ponytail. "I said, 'I gotta go get you some *hair!*'" recalled Don Chapel. "I went to Zayre's and bought her a $9.95 hairpiece."

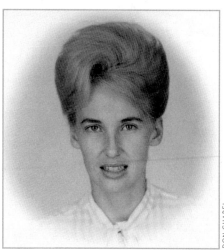

Wynette's passport, August 1967. Booking agent Frank Scarborough thought Tammy "was just strange. She'd turn away from the crowd, look at the wall . . . wouldn't speak a word to no-body."

Tammy on her bus. The folks back home were shocked by her new hair. "She had it really, really blonde. I mean as blonde as you could get it," said cousin Jane Williams. "I thought, 'Well! We just don't know about this.'"

Tammy, DJ Bennie Kaye, Don and Donna Chapel, and George Jones at the American Legion Hut in Red Bay after Wynette's 1968 benefit concert. "I trusted George," said a woeful Chapel. "Here I am puttin' her in his hands."

Tammy and her band, Lavonia, Georgia, 1971. Left to right: Wynette, James Hollie, Patsy Sledd, Charlie Justice, Charlie Carter, Sonny Curtis. "They would have crawled through cut glass and fire for her," said hairdresser Jan Smith. "Every one of 'em."

Tammy surrounded by fans in Lavonia. "She never hesitated to sign autographs, hug a baby, stop for a picture, I mean *never*," said Jan Smith. "I don't care how bad she hurt. She loved her fans. Tammy knew they made her who she was."

Wynette exhausted after the show. Health problems had her relying on painkillers to keep going on the road. "Everything was a catch-22 with Tammy," said Jan Smith. "More operations . . . more drugs."

Contracts with different labels would prevent George and Tammy from recording legitimate duets the first few years of their marriage, but that didn't stop Jones from putting Wynette on the cover of his latest album.

George, Tammy, and Tamala Georgette at Niagara Falls. Jones, said Wynette, was "the only person who could get me so mad I could scream one minute and then sing me a song that was so sad I'd cry my eyes out."

Jones and potential duet partner, late seventies. "I didn't put anything past him," said friend Earl "Peanutt" Montgomery. "Hanging around George you might wind up in South America tomorrow."

George and Tammy. "When we were onstage we were in our own little heaven," said Jones.

A Jones family Christmas (the kids, left to right: Tamala, Georgette, Tina, Gwen, and Jackie). Tammy's children loved George. "Deep down he had a heart of gold," said her daughter Jackie. "I just wish that things would've been different for Mom."

Relatives Hazel Hall (left) and Jane Williams (right) pose with George and Tammy in front of their Lakeland, Florida, mansion. After one particularly bad bender, Jones was carried away from the home in a straitjacket.

Jones and Wynette cutting it up on a Florida fishing trip. "Son, Tammy was wide open," said songwriter Jerry Chestnut. "Just an ol' rawboned country girl raised in an Assembly of God church in Alabama tryin' to get ahead. She didn't try to be anything she wasn't. She was just Tammy."

OLD PLANTATION
MUSIC PARK
CENTRAL BARN RD. S 540A
LAKELAND, FLA.
HOME OF
GEORGE JONES & TAMMY WYNETTE

George and Tammy (with friends Cliff and Maxine Hyder in the backseat) go for a spin in one of the Possum's fancy rides. "They looked so good together, man," said Tanya Tucker. "They were the perfect pair."

George and Tammy in England, 1976. The couple continued to record and perform after they'd broken up, although Jones found it agonizing. "There will never be anyone else for either of us," he told the press.

Charley Pride, Wynette's hairdresser Jan Smith, and Tammy at the Opry in the seventies. "Tammy was definitely the queen bee," said one photographer. "She was amazingly popular. All the other artists gravitated to her."

Wynette, mainstream superstar. Tammy with Ethel Merman and game show host Peter Marshall to promote her appearance on *Hollywood Squares.*

"Tammy wasn't one of those people that play to the camera and have these moves," said one photographer. "Tammy was communicating a feeling. It wasn't a put-on. She was just real."

Wynette works the crowd at a 1976 Ramsey, New Jersey, show. Photographer Stephanie Chernikowski recalled that when Tammy "was finished, she was rushed out the back door to an awaiting ambulance and carried away."

Tammy backstage at the Ramsey show. Wynette was known to hide painkillers in her makeup kit.

Tammy and George Wallace and his wife, Lisa, at a campaign rally. Wynette was known to plant a kiss or two on Wallace. "Right on the mouth," noted Lisa. "It embarrassed George. He said, 'Lord, it's gonna lose me votes.'"

Tammy at the Opry.

Husband number five George Richey stirs the sauce, smokes a cig, and keeps an eye on the wife. "I think George Richey was among the greater things that ever happened to Tammy Wynette," one employee insisted. Another declared him as "phony as a two-dollar watch."

Tammy (wearing her infamous red peace sign earrings) and Mee-Maw. "Mildred was strict," said friend Linda Cayson. "She wanted Wynette to be perfect."

Jan Howard, background singer Paula Poe Murrell, and Tammy raise the roof during London rehearsals in November 1979. "Jan, what happened to our music?" Tammy would ask Jan shortly before her death.

Burt Reynolds, Tammy, and pianist Mike Maiocco in 1991. Wynette and Reynolds had a mid-seventies romance and remained pals forever after. One reason they broke up, according to Tammy: she didn't want to "share the mirror."

Tammy at the christening of the Tammy Wynette Highway in Red Bay, Alabama, in 1990. "I kept thinking, 'Oh, Tammy, if you don't slow down we're gonna get a ticket,'" said hairdresser Barbara Hutchison. "Sure enough, we got pulled over twice—on *her* highway."

Tammy and childhood pal Linda Cayson. "It was like there was always a void in her life," said Linda. "Like she was searchin' for somethin' that she couldn't find."

Tammy's daughters: Gwen, Georgette, Jackie, and Tina. "They weren't prima donna kids, they loved her," said Richey employee Michelle Broussard Honick. "And I know they loved her for herself. The star thing was a drawback to them."

Tammy onstage with her devoted guitarist Charlie Carter, who was with Wynette nearly three decades. "You couldn't talk bad about Tammy in front of him," said drummer Charley Abdon. "He would correct you on it."

Tammy and Killer. Wynette spoiled the pooch. By the time pianist Van Abbott joined the band in 1996, he'd note that Killer had "eaten filet mignon for a year and a half, his front feet were stickin' out at forty-five degree angles and he couldn't take a crap."

Tammy shows off those famous gams in a 1990 portrait by Scotty Kennedy.

George and Tammy at a press conference to promote their 1995 reunion album, *One*. "When she talked about him, her countenance changed," said backup singer Karyn Sloas. "Almost like a schoolgirl, her eyes would brighten."

Tammy belting out a gospel number as Richey tickles the ivories (relatives Jonathan Williams and Hazel and Dan Hall join in on the left). "In my mind she was thinking about her own death," said Linda Cayson. "She'd talk to me about the hereafter. I'd say, 'Aw, let's not talk about that.'"

Wynette leaves the stage in Birmingham, 1996. Said Tammy, "The sad part about happy endings is there's nothing to write about."

―――――

"I don't think she was ever content," said George of Tammy. "It seemed like one moment she was happy, another she wasn't. She was a lonely person, that I'm sure of. She lacked satisfaction of somethin', and she couldn't get it all her life."

Tammy was a lost soul after the split. At one point Wynette wound up in the hospital due to an overdose of pills she insisted was accidental.

"After Jones, I thought it was just all over, I've ruined everything," said Tammy. "I really just didn't care for a while." It took little Georgette to finally snap her out of it.

One night when the house was quiet, dark, and lonely, Tammy and her daughter "were walkin' down the hall, and I didn't turn the light on. All of a sudden she looked at me and said, 'Gosh, Mommy, it's dark since Daddy left.' It just hit me—'I have to get my life together.'"

Tammy on the Run

Favorite colors: peach/apricot/salmon

Favorite beverage: iced tea

Favorite books: Tammy is an avid reader and is particularly fond of
Sidney Sheldon's books and the writings of Rod McKuen

—a late seventies Tammy bio

✣ "Tammy was a basket case," recalled Wynette's old childhood friend
Holly Ford. "We had to help her off the bus. She had taken so much
stuff tryin' to prepare herself to get up there onstage, we just didn't think
her legs was gonna hold her up. She couldn't quit cryin'."

Tupelo, Mississippi. February 1975. Tammy was thirty-two. She'd been
through three marriages and a world of hurt. Now she was attempting her
first solo dates without George and she was terrified. "They kept comin' to
the door sayin', 'Tammy, you've gotta come on, you've gotta come on,'" said
Ford. Somehow Wynette made it onstage. Holly and some of Wynette's
other old friends went into the venue and nervously awaited her entrance.
They were mortified by what they saw. "She did not do a good show at all,"
said Ford. "She was just in a fog, like somebody havin' a mild nervous
breakdown." Wynette sat on a stool and, seemingly in a trance, talked about
Jones, then did a song, then talked about Jones again. "She kept bringin' it
up, basically sung and talked about him the whole time," said Ford. "I just
kept thinkin', 'Oh, if she makes it to the end of this, it's gonna be nothin'
short of a miracle. She's either gonna fall off the stool or burst into tears
and just have to run from the stage.' That's the worst shape I ever, ever saw
Tammy in, bar none. That woman's heart was broken. She *loved* George
Jones."

Watching Wynette sing "'Til I Can Make It on My Own" that night, Linda
Cayson burst into tears. "I couldn't hardly stand it. Cold chills just went all

over. Then when we got in the bus Wynette cried and cried. She said, 'I hated to let him go so bad.'"*

There was plenty at stake here. When George and Tammy divorced, Shorty Lavender had called promoters promising either one or the other would make up their scheduled appearances. But they wanted the package deal, and dates were being canceled left and right. Wynette had to make $35,000 a month to stay afloat, and that required she play twenty dates every month.

Here she was in Mississippi, stumbling around onstage, besieged by hecklers yelling, "Where's George?" Jones had always handled talking and joking to the audience. All Tammy had to do was stand there and sing. "I didn't find out I had a personality until I went out on my own," she said.

Drastic measures were taken. Billy Sherrill instructed her to update her act. Tammy fired backup singer Patsy Sledd and Harold Morrison. "Harold and I was too country," said Sledd. "They were plannin' her career for her. She had to turn to somebody because she was very insecure." In their place she hired the Gatlins, a family of singers who had come up through the church in Texas. Tammy named them "Young Country." The Jones Boys became the "Country Gentlemen." She bought new outfits and polished her stage patter.

Her Country Gentlemen grew very protective of her. They were the usual characters—the drummer with an anger management problem, the steel guitar player who left his motel key hanging off his instrument with the room number visible just in case there were any lonely women down front. The only rules on the bus were no drinking, no girls, and no cussing. What you did on off hours was your own business. "Tammy just wanted everybody to be happy," said Nan Crafton. "She didn't give a shit. She did not care who you slept with." That was a good thing for Nan, because she was involved for years with Wynette's bass player, James Hollie, who just happened to be married. A tall, good-looking Texan extremely devoted to Tammy, James was known to be popular with the ladies.

---

*Not everybody in Tammy's entourage was touched by her nostalgia for Jones. According to Nan Crafton, after one of these solo shows, "We got back on the bus goin' down the road, and Tammy said, 'I miss him. Do y'all miss him? I miss him.'" Harold Morrison, the comedian who opened for Tammy (and George) responded, "Well, I guess if somebody hits you in the head with a hammer every day for seven years and they quit, you'd miss it."

("James Hollie would fuck a snake if somebody would hold its head," claimed Nan's sister Jan.)

Talk to Tammy's old entourage about any of her road musicians, and the first name uttered is Charlie Carter. From the time Wynette joined up with Jones until she died, Carter was onstage behind her every single night, making sure she had her stool, her glass of water, and whatever she needed. "He was the heart and soul of that whole deal," said fiddle player Bobby Napier. "Charlie Carter could read Tammy like a book. Charlie could take one glance at Tammy and know exactly how she was feelin'. Those two had a bond." Another Texan, Charlie was nicknamed "Superstar" due to his Elvis pompadour. "He had star hair," enthused keyboard player Van Abbott. "He'd be in the hallway of the band bus workin' on it way before showtime. It took a lotta hair spray to get that up." (Former hairdresser Wynette was always after him to let her bring his coif up to date. "I put them damn perms in it," said Carter. "Tammy wanted me to cut it off because the ends of it would get all burned up from that ol' dryer.")

Carter was the type who'd "come on the bus with a truck stop tuna sandwich, and he might have half of it in one hand and a salt shaker in the other hand. At the same time he was talkin' to you, just pourin' a ton of salt on the tuna, he'd be sayin', 'Well, the doctor's got me on a strict diet. I really gotta watch myself.' A gentle soul, Carter was loved by all. He knew every old country song in the world and had a prodigious capacity for drinking beer. "Charlie wouldn't get in nobody's face," said drummer Charley Abdon. "He could work with Satan." And he would've taken a bullet for Wynette if need be. "You couldn't talk bad about Tammy in front of him," said Abdon. "He would correct you on it."

Many of Tammy's associates maintain that Carter was in love with Wynette. "Charlie Carter told me at one time he could've married Tammy," said steel player Rusty Pence. "According to Charlie, she actually asked him. Maybe he thinks about it every day of his life." Said fiddle player Tim Watson, "When he'd get drunk, he'd tell Georgette stuff like, 'I should be your dad.'" When I asked Carter about the rumors, he was ever the gentleman. "That's just stuff that I'd rather not talk about. We were close for a while, I'll just put it that way."

Now that Tammy was single, she had a little trio of outspoken, eccentric, and very entertaining women who often traveled on the road with her. There was author Joan Dew, who had profiled Tammy and was working with her on her autobiography.* Dew lived with Wynette for a spell and cowrote a terrific ballad with her, "Love Doesn't Always Come (On the Night It's Needed)." And then there were the terrible twosome of hairdressing sisters, Jan and Nan. Jan, the older one, was funny as hell, and told it like it was. Her sister was the wild one. "Nanette, what a pistol," said Joan Dew's son Cliff. "She was an unbelievable Tennessee gal, hot as she could be. That Southern charm, y'know? She would always say and do the right things for Tammy. Tammy really depended on Nanette for emotional reasons, and Nanette depended on Tammy for financial reasons."

Once again, everyone stressed that Wynette was incredibly generous to friends and employees. "One time we were all layin' around the pool, and Tammy had left for the jewelry store," said Nan. "She came back, threw me a box, threw Jan a box. She bought Jan a ring, me a ring, bought her a ring. On Worth Avenue in Palm Beach she'd shop all day long buyin' stage clothes. 'Okay, now, Nanette, buy you somethin'.' 'I don't want anything, Tammy.' 'Buy you somethin'. We bought for me all day, now we're buyin' for *you*.'" (Added Joan Dew, "If she heard some sad story about one of the band members or somebody she knew, Tammy would help them out financially. Not loan them money, *give* them money.") Then there were the shopping sprees out on the road. "We would hit a town, and if Tammy didn't have a DJ interview or anything for a couple of hours before the show, the first thing she wanted to do was hit the mall," said Dew. "She had a big paper bag of cash. That's how they collected their money on the road. In grocery bags!" Afterward, Wynette would "put on a fashion show and try everything on. We'd just giggle and have just as much fun as you could imagine."

The house on Franklin Avenue was a world of women—Tammy, Jan, Nan, Joan, and Tammy's daughters. "It was like a girl's dorm," said Nan.

---

*When it comes to the other country stars she interviewed, Joan Dew tells some uproarious anecdotes. "First time I ever met Loretta, I got on the bus to go with her, she had never seen me before in her life. We were talkin' for not even five minutes and she said, 'I want you to tell me somethin'—she whispered—'I want you to tell me about lisbon.' I said, 'Lisbon?' 'Yeah, I want to know about *lisbon.*' I thought she meant Lisbon, Portugal. 'I've never been to Lisbon.'"

It became apparent Loretta was trying to ask about lesbians. "I want to know what they *do*," she asked Dew, who happens to be straight.

"Tammy would've never done that. Tammy would've never shown that she was that ignorant even if she had been. Loretta was very uneducated, very naive, but very shrewd. Loretta could spot a phony a mile away and wouldn't mind tellin' the person that they were. She had no sense of diplomacy whatsoever. None."

"Everybody had fun." That, and the little scene out on the road constituted Tammy's hermetically sealed universe. "It's the wildest thing, travelin' on that bus," said Nan. "You're in a capsule. I didn't have a phone, didn't read the newspaper. You're with a star, and nothin' can touch you. If somethin' went wrong, Tammy'd fix it just like that. We'd get on that damn bus, listen to songs, tell jokes and laugh, and have the best time in the whole wide world. That Silver Eagle was our *world*. Nothin' else existed. They were all my best friends. If I murdered somebody, they'd help me hide the body. Life on the road was so unrealistic. Can you imagine a life like that?"

By the mid-seventies Tammy's little brood of girls was starting to grow up. Gwen, the oldest, was a serious soul, responsible for looking after the rest. "Gwen was mama," said Cathye Leshay. "Gwen pretty much ruled the roost." Jackie, who looked the most like Euple, was quiet and easygoing, and gave her mother the least trouble. "I just kinda wanted to roll with the flow," she said. Georgette, runt of the litter, started singing onstage with her mother at the age of three, performing "Delta Dawn." And then there was Tina, the child Tammy had almost lost as a baby. "Tina was the black sheep of the family. She was the rebel," said Cathye Leshay. "Tina Denise should never have made it. She made it fightin' and she hasn't stopped yet. We got right up in each other's faces on a regular basis. I just loved her." (Tina, said to possess a fantastic voice, would also tour with her mother in the eighties.)

Cathye Leshay was Tammy's governess in the late seventies and early eighties. At first she barely saw or spoke to Wynette, who was on the road constantly. She found the kids a rather unruly mob who knew every trick in the book when it came to the hired help. "Finally Tammy called," said Leshay. "She was talkin' to the girls. I said, 'Is that your mother? Give me that phone!' I said, 'Tammy, this is Cathye. Excuse me, but you have never told me what your rules are for these girls, what your limitations are. And if I had an emergency with one of them, I do not have any paper sayin' that I can take them to the hospital. And I need a phone number where I can reach you anytime—'

"Tammy whispered, 'Cathy, if you need me, call my lawyer.'"

That sent Leshay through the roof. "'Your lawyer? Is your lawyer gonna raise these girls, or are me and you gonna raise 'em?' I was furious. And I could hear her kind of chuckling." Leshay's directness endeared her to Wynette, and she was given a free hand to raise the girls. She would also be one of the very few people that Tammy confided in during the years ahead.

As Wynette was mostly single in the mid-seventies, she had more time to spend with her kids. "The seventies were great because Mom wasn't sick then. She was a lot of fun," said Jackie. "She'd put us in the car and say, 'Girls, we're goin' to the beach.' And she'd put her little bikini and her rhinestone headband on. The guys would just be lookin' at her. Me and Gwen would be goin', 'Okay, how about *us*?'" Tammy loved to take the girls bowling or join them on the trampoline in the backyard. "In the summertime when Mom played the fairs, she was the first person to get the tickets and take us on all the rides," said Georgette, adding that her mother was happiest when she was "in her pajamas hangin' around the house just chitchattin' and cookin', havin' a good time just bein' one of the girls." In those days Wynette loved activity of any kind. "It was never boring around the house. Never," maintained Jackie. "I think Mom liked chaos. She liked having things goin' on even if they were bad. She just had a passion for life."

Wynette suffered unending remorse over the fact that her career had deprived her children of her presence, so when she came home, she was a "Disneyland mom," said Leshay. "She wasn't there havin' to go through the daily trials and traumas of raisin' kids, so when she came home all she wanted was for things to be really, really happy. They pretty much had anything they wanted, they pretty much got to do whatever they wanted." But Tammy still felt it wasn't enough. "There was a lot of guilt," said Jackie. "I would always tell her, 'Mom, it's okay.'" Georgette said her mother's guilt occasionally came in handy. "As teenagers we learned, 'Okay, if I'm gonna try to get away with somethin', I need to do it the first day Mom gets home, because she'll be feelin' guilty.'"

Not that Wynette was a pushover when it came to her kids. "When it was time to lower the boom, Miss Tammy could lower the boom like you wouldn't believe," said Leshay. "Mom was definitely strict," said Georgette. "She didn't take any mouth. Boys were never at any time ever allowed to go near anybody's room. That was a big no-no. And we had to be at home in bed by ten o'clock every night." As Tammy was fond of repeating, "Anything that you want to do after midnight is just trouble anyway."

"Nobody had the guts to talk back or be disrespectful to Tammy—except Tina," said Leshay. "Tina wasn't afraid of her." Mother and daughter would have screaming matches on a regular basis. "When the two of them would lock horns, it was really ugly," added Georgette. "Neither one of them wanted to give." Tammy was known to give a spanking or two, and when Tina was the recipient, she refused to acknowledge the pain. "There was no way in the world she would've cried," said Georgette. "I can vividly remember her turnin' around to Mom and goin', 'Are you done yet?' You didn't do that with Mom. I knew better—if I got a spanking, I was ready to drop to my knees and cry so I could get it over with. Tina would just rather pass out from it than have to admit it hurt in any way." More than one of Wynette's friends made the same point: Tammy and Tina were a mirror image of Tammy and Mildred. "But I never would've told Tammy that," confessed one confidante.

Wynette had not kowtowed to Mildred, nor would Tina give in to Tammy. "I've taken her horse away from her, I've restricted her from the phone, I've spanked, I've used a switch," confessed Wynette to Jack Hurst in 1977. Exasperated over Tina's bad report cards, she had Epic deep-six a Christmas single her daughter had recorded solo.

Tammy wrote a song for her children on a long solo drive from Nashville to her Jupiter, Florida, home. "Dear Daughters" was an album cut on the 1977 *One of a Kind*, and although never a single, it was a staple of Tammy's live shows. A spoken recitation, Wynette addresses each of her daughters by name and lists all the milestones in their lives—first date, homecoming queen, graduation day—she missed because of her career. The last line says it all: "I wish I could have been there, but I was gone." Mothers in the audience would weep whenever she performed the number. "What makes that song so good and so powerful is that it's so honest," said Georgette. "She's not makin' excuses for herself."

"That song came from every fiber of her body," said Cathye Leshay. "Tammy loved her girls as much as any mother on this earth, but she couldn't be with them. It just ate away at her."

Yet no one doubted the devotion Tammy had to her children. "I suppose I just know it's always going to be me and the girls," she said. A year later she said the same thing, adding, "I have to support them. I always will." These words would come to haunt Wynette when her final husband entered the picture.

In the wake of Jones, Wynette started dating. Between 1975 and 1978, she'd be involved with New England Patriots lineman Tommy Neville (introduced to her by George Wallace), backup singer Rudy Gatlin, Burt Reynolds, a married country singer, a married politician, and a football coach, not to mention a fling or two. "Tammy loved 'em all," said Nan. When asked if men responded to Wynette's charms, Nan shot back, "Well, hell, yeah! What's not to like? Tammy was gorgeous and sexy and filthy rich! She had it *all*. She had the world by the tail!"

Wynette's love life was complicated, to say the least. The Gatlins were singing backup on a session right after she'd dated Rudy, and during that recording an ex-husband was trying to get her on the phone. As Billy Sherrill told Michael Kosser, Tammy "was singing and telling the engineers not to put Don Chapel through on the phone—she wasn't gonna talk to him. I said, 'Tammy, you need to slow your love life down a little bit.'" Wynette confessed that the attention her romances received in the press embarrassed her. "I can't bear to see my name in print linked with this man or that man. It goes against the grain of my upbringing, somehow."*

If Tammy had her sights set on a man, look out. It wasn't hard to deduce when she was in the midst of some feverish crush. "The way she flirted, she might as well have had a neon sign across her forehead," said Joan Dew. "We have a saying in the South, when a woman wants to get something from a man, that she 'gets little.' Now, that doesn't mean she gets physically little, but she gets kind of helpless and real feminine. Here is this incredibly strong woman, I mean really strong—you never would've wanted to be her enemy. But Tammy could get little with the best of 'em."

Wynette's passions could change with the wind. "In an odd way Tammy had a masculine kind of thing, in the sense of what she liked was the conquest," said Dew. "She liked getting the guy to fall in love with her. Whether he was married or not. The proof of love was the proposal of marriage. That's how you proved to Tammy that you loved her—you married her. And if there was no marriage—or even if there was—she very soon lost interest and was onto another conquest. If she wanted you she was obsessed with you, if she wasn't obsessed with you she didn't want you."

There was something endearing about Wynette's romantic obsessions,

*When Tammy's friend Martha Dettwiller was about to enter into what Wynette thought would be a disastrous marriage, "she sat me down, she said, 'Now, Martha, you don't have to marry everybody you sleep with.' I said, 'What do mean? You married everybody you ever slept with.'" "Well . . . not *quite*" was Tammy's response.

as well as something a little troubling. "Tammy had a very childlike quality about her—I don't mean this in a negative way—like a little girl excited at the fair," said Dew. When it came to men, Wynette was "like a junior high girl who gets crushes and thinks about and talks about the guy she has a crush on 24/7. And she's gonna *die* if she doesn't get a date with this guy. It's very junior high. But it's like she didn't grow out of it. Arrested development. Arrested from adolescence."

It didn't concern her one iota if the man she was interested in was already attached. "I don't like to say this about Tammy, but if she wanted a man it didn't matter," said Nan. "I was dating Johnny Rodriguez, she slept with Johnny. And then Michael Tomlin—I was datin' him, *she* started datin' him. And then she'd have to get mad at me to make it okay. It was just Tammy. That was her MO." Nan even claimed Wynette slept with her longtime beau James Hollie. "I said, 'James, why did you do it? You could've been the one that *didn't* sleep with Tammy Wynette.' He said, 'I just want to see what it felt like to sleep with a star.'"

At one point in the mid-seventies Wynette went out on the road with a very popular group that had roots in the church. She fell for one of the members, a married man, and the affair had tongues wagging all over Nashville. Bus driver Steve Hoker, who drove for Tammy in the early eighties, said she relished reminiscing over the scandalous romance. "She'd come to life when she told me the story," he said. According to what Wynette related to him, she had instructed the tour manager to make sure her bus and his bus kept in sight of each other en route. In the wee hours of the morning, when everybody was asleep, the buses would pull into a rest stop. "The tour manager paid the bus drivers to walk away and smoke," said Hoker. Then Wynette would rendezvous with her lover. "Tammy said, 'He would sneak out of his bus and slip into the back room with me. Ohhh, we would be so *deceitful*. It was so thrilling, so exciting! You know, he'd stay a little while . . . we'd pull over, he'd get back on his bus, no one would be none the wiser.'"

Tammy was fanatical about keeping tabs on her paramour's whereabouts. "If we lost sight of that bus, she would kick our ass," said Nan. One night while Wynette was sleeping the bus stopped in Vegas so the band could gamble a few hours. Her boyfriend's bus went AWOL because of the stop, and when Tammy found out about it, she hit the roof. "God almighty, hell knows no fury," said Nan. "I thought she was gonna kill every one of us."

The affair went on for over a year. "In her mind, he was gonna get a divorce and marry her," said Joan Dew. "He never told Tammy that. It just kind of petered out. He backed off big-time. It made her very unhappy—and threw her into the arms of the next best man that came along." She'd get one song out of the romance: "That's the Way It Could Have Been." Wynette told backup singer Karyn Sloas that Mr. X "came to get her off the bus one night, put his hand out, and said, 'I'm your Prince Charming, I'll take you away.'" Tammy responded, "That's the way it could've been." Before long she was scribbling on her legal pad.

"Thank God for my music," wrote Wynette, maintaining that writing helped her get over the loss of Jones. "Now when I can't sleep, I just go to the piano and start writing." She always kept a pad on the seat of her car or on the bus in case inspiration struck. Although none of the songs were released as singles, the mid-seventies would see some classic numbers written by Tammy: "That's the Way It Could Have Been," "Dear Daughters," "Let Me Be Me," "We'll Talk About It Later," "The Bottle," "Your Memory's Finally Gone to Rest," and "Love Doesn't Always Come (On the Night It's Needed)." All but the last were solo writing credits, a first for Wynette. She'd also cowrite two songs for Jones, the fine 1975 single "These Days (I Barely Get By)," a number 10 hit for George—"The way he does it broke my heart," said Tammy at the time—and "I Just Drove By (To See If I Was Really Gone)," a song that came into being in November 1976 after Wynette fell to the floor from exhaustion in a London dressing room, bruising her face and earning her a three-day stay in yet another hospital. Jones rushed to her side and, while making small talk as Tammy lay there in the bed, mentioned he'd driven by their old home "just to see if I was really gone." Wynette told him she'd have to steal that line for a song. "Well, half of it's mine," insisted George. Even apart, they managed to transform their lives into music.

The year 1976 was a big one for Tammy—four number one singles in a row: "'Til I Can Make It on My Own," "You and Me," and two duets with Jones, "Golden Ring" and "Near You." But these would be the last number one country singles of Wynette's career. There were some fine offerings in the next few years, including the touching "One of a Kind," the Bobby Braddock–penned "Womanhood," and the highly underrated "No One Else in the World," which features a steamy recitation ("Last night there was no holding back / I gave it all, I gave it all to you") and which the *Village Voice* declared "the most sensual song Tammy has ever done." Yet only two of her next seven singles would make number 5 or higher. For another artist this would constitute a successful showing, but after Tammy's unbelievable run it was clear the downhill slide had begun. The pressures must've been intense—both outside and within. Years later, when Wynette's health was failing, Linda Cayson would implore her to quit singing. She told Cayson, "Lin, you just don't know what it's like. Once you have a number one song, I don't think you ever get over tryin' to get another one. You get on a high, y'know. You're always tryin' to get another one."

It must also be said that Tammy encountered a more complex kind of pressure than what her male counterparts faced. "If you are a strong woman in this business, you're a bitch," said Lorrie Morgan. "Tammy fought demons to be a smart businesswoman and a great mother and a wife—and still remain beautiful. A man can get on the bus, he can travel for eight days straight, and he can take a shower—one shower—or he don't have to, because no matter how he goes onstage, women are going to think he looks hot. If you're a woman and you're on the bus for eight days and you try and hit that stage without the correct makeup, freshenin' up, whatever, you know the first thing they're gonna say? 'She looked terrible! She looked *just awful!*' And you get the young people comin' in right behind you, always a little bit younger, prettier. Those things weigh on your mind."

Somebody like Jones could go on a bender, commit all sorts of egregious offenses, and it would only add to the legend. The First Lady of Country didn't have that option, especially in those days. She internalized her feelings. No wonder Tammy had so many problems with her stomach. There was no place for all that frustration, fear, and pain to go—other than into another sad song.

Nan Crafton recalled being in London with Tammy very early one groggy morning. "We'd been playin' all night, they took us straight to a studio." In preparation for some taping, a makeup artist starting working on her face. "It was so cold, so sleepy in London. Tammy looked over at me and said, 'Y'know, Nan, it's not all sunglasses and autographs.'"

Strange things were happening at the house on Franklin Road. Weird phone calls. People walking on the roof. Rocks thrown through windows. Death threats in the mailbox. Someone breaking in and stuffing up the sinks and bathtubs, flooding the place. In a weird replay of the incident in Lakeland, an intruder "had come in through the skylight and written filthy words in lipstick all over my walls and mirrors," said Wynette.

Then there was the fire. Tammy was in bed; her grandmother and her daughters, plus two of their friends, were home at the time. "I tried to call the fire department, but my wires had been cut to the telephone," said Wynette. "The burglar alarm system had also been cut." She called then-boyfriend Rudy Gatlin to stand guard. Fire destroyed three rooms in the house, causing thousands of dollars in damage. Curiously, years later Wynette would blame the blaze on "a little time bomb of some sort."

The police investigated. "They insisted it was done by someone on the inside," said Tammy. "We all took lie-detector tests." For a while Rudy Gatlin was a suspect. "They put him through hell," said Wynette. Rudy was ten years younger than Tammy, and, according to her, "he made me feel like a kid again." His brother Larry was against the relationship. "Tammy was a lot older and had a bad reputation with guys," said Joan Dew. "Larry was protecting his younger brother."

The fire and the resulting bad publicity were the last straw. "The relationship with Rudy was never the same," said Tammy, who lost not only her boyfriend but her backup singers. "The Gatlins ended up going to work for Larry." As far as the fire, "we still don't know who did it or why," said Wynette. "No one was ever caught."

"There are a lot of theories about it," said Joan Dew. "Including that Tammy did it herself."

Let's let a woman explain the heterosexual appeal of Burt. "Burt Reynolds is the quintessential 70's sex object," wrote cultural critic Kim Morgan. "First off, he had that much-imitated high pitched laugh; it flowed easily but was abrupt, almost bizarre. And then there was his face—Cherokee cheekbones made his dark features almost exotic, especially with those thick eyebrows that appeared charming and amused one minute (watch any frame of *Smokey and the Bandit*) angry and insane the next (check his very believable domestic fight at the beginning of *The Longest Yard*).

"He's of a time when men were men, but in their Coors-drinking, shit-kicking way, somewhat dandy in their manliness. These guys wore crotch-tight jeans, enormous belt buckles, cultivated thick mustaches and drove muscle cars without a hint of irony. But it was his easygoing charm, his confidence, his continual amusement at the loony world and his apparent down-to-earth nature that captivated the public—like he was one of them, only a lot better-looking and enjoying a lot more sexual conquests. . . . Women wanted to have sex with him (remember that nude *Cosmopolitan* center-fold?) and men not only wanted to be him but be his best friend as well."

The First Lady of Country and the King of the Drive-Ins: Burt Reynolds and Tammy Wynette were a potent pairing. The relationship, which they tried to keep secret at first, sent the tabloids into a frenzy. "We Find Burt Reynolds and Tammy Wynette in Their 'Love Hideaway'—Dinah Bitter Over Their 'Sneak Affair'!" shrieked the January 1977 cover of *Screen Stories*. Wynette had been in the gossip rags before, but this romance would gain her the dubious status of tabloid queen, and for the rest of her life they'd keep tabs on her.

Tammy met Burt through his friend Jerry Reed. After appearing on a Reed TV special in September 1975, during which she performed a wrenching "'Til I Can Make It on My Own," she joined Reed and Reynolds for dinner. Then Burt called her during a recording session at the Quonset Hut. Wynette had to endure the hoots and catcalls of the pickers when they heard who was on the line. Reynolds and Wynette had a few things in common: Baptist upbringing, a love for country music and the state of Florida, not to mention pinto beans and corn bread. Tammy had her maladies, and Burt suffered from panic attacks. "At least I know he doesn't want to become a singer, or want me to record some song he's written, and he sure isn't after my money," said Wynette. They would see each other off and on the next few years and remain friends for life.

Tammy was completely smitten by Reynolds. As Joan Dew recalled, "He'd say to her, 'You'll never know when you're on the road, the house is dark and you look out there, I may be standing in the back watching you.' She thought that was *so* romantic. She really believed Burt was in love with her." When Reynolds suggested she buy a place of her own in Florida, Tammy found a stunning oceanside estate in the town of Jupiter where her neighbors included Perry Como and Mike Douglas. The residence would be her favorite hideaway for years. The house curved around a swimming pool, and you could see the ocean from every room. Tammy would sit out in the sun for hours with Nan. "The big thing was to get there, run up the stairs, peel off your clothes, and jump in the pool," said Nan. Jan Smith recalled the drama of Tammy's bedroom. "She loved nothing better than to open her sliding glass doors as the tides were comin' in and there was a huge wind. I seen those drapes stand straight out from the wall, the wind would be gusting so hard. She loved that. Tammy loved the ocean."

Burt and Tammy, a slightly kooky couple. Once when Wynette was staying at the swanky Beverly Wilshire hotel in Beverly Hills, she planned a surprise for Reynolds. Burt loved her Southern cooking, and Tammy enlisted the help of Joan Dew. "We went shopping for what she wanted to make for him, which was pork chops, mashed potatoes, gravy, and greens—a full meal, including the banana pudding," said Dew, who assisted Wynette in preparing it at her Los Angeles home. "We put it in containers you could transport to the Beverly Wilshire, and they agreed to keep it warm for her." But Reynolds, in the midst of a movie shoot, failed to show up on time. Said Dew, "Tammy kept calling me about every twenty minutes—'I don't know when he's getting here! The food's gonna be ruined!'" Burt finally showed up at midnight, immediately suffered a panic attack, and sat there breathing into a paper bag to calm himself down. "It didn't turn out to be the romantic evening Tammy had hoped it would be," said Dew.

During one visit to Florida, Reynolds had been mysteriously ill and seeing various doctors. Tammy ran a hot bath for him and left him to relax. She thought she heard a voice calling out and finally realized it was Reynolds. She ran into the bathroom to find him unconscious and underwater. "It absolutely scared me to death," said Tammy. "Finally I got into the tub with him trying to get him out. It never once dawned on me to pull the plug and let the water out." Reynolds was rushed to a hospital, where it was discovered he was hypoglycemic. He spent three and a half weeks convalescing. When he was released, on Christmas Eve, Wynette had a present waiting for him—a white 1957 Lincoln Continental. Burt was so excited he tossed Tammy into the air and demanded they go for a drive. Wynette had been suffering from a twenty-four-hour bug and immediately got sick. She bravely went for a second go-round and got ill again. Reynolds was "dying laughing," recalled Tammy. When they got back to his house, Tammy nodded off. "He looked at his mother and said, 'Boy, that says a lot for Burt Reynolds, don't it?'"

Reynolds would name a character after Tammy in his 1977 smash *Smokey and the Bandit*. He invited an excited Wynette to the premiere and told her to listen real close for her name. In the movie Jerry Reed announces to his wife he's going out for a beer run. As Tammy recalled, "She came to the door with rollers in her hair, a sloppy old housecoat, a cigarette danglin' from her mouth, and he says, 'Wynette, I got to . . .'" Tammy, who was mortified, "just slid down in my seat," she said. (Reynolds would cast Wynette as another downtrodden housewife in his 1985 movie *Stick*, but her cameo was apparently cut from the movie.)

They'd both see other people during the relationship, and Tammy maintained that this was fine with her. "I never checked up on him when we were together, and he never checked up on me," said Wynette. "We'd have a good time and say good-bye with no promises." When it came to marriage, this time she claimed to know better. She said she told Burt, "If you and I walk down the aisle and a pretty girl waved at you, you'd be looking back over your shoulder and blowing her a kiss." Her friends paint a different picture. Jan Smith felt Tammy's insecurities undermined the relationship. "Burt was too big an achievement for her. He was a big star, and she never realized that she was, too." Joan Dew felt that Wynette was dreaming of the same old fairy tale. "I think she really believed Burt was gonna marry her. It was very sad, really."

One day Tammy returned to the house on Franklin Road to find a gaggle of uninvited reporters from the *National Enquirer* at her doorstep, trying to ferret out the latest on the romance with Burt. Well, she had a scoop for them. There was no romance with Burt Reynolds, because she was going to marry local real estate developer J. Michael Tomlin. Her daughters standing inside the house were stunned. "Gwen and I were speechless," wrote Jackie. Mom hadn't said anything to *them*. Nor did Burt know anything about it. Miss Tammy was full of surprises.

Tomlin, who had dated Nan Crafton, was a smooth operator—drank Dom Pérignon, traveled by Mercedes and Learjet. He appeared to have money. "I don't want to be known as Mr. Tammy Wynette," he claimed. According to Joan Dew, Tomlin "was the first successful, well-to-do socially climbing man to come on to her. Before that it was country music and low class. . . . Tomlin was educated, he was supposedly turned out. It was all a facade. The furniture in his office was rented." Tammy's friends tried to warn her, but she refused to listen. "Nothing is sadder than a jaded lady," she maintained. "When I married Michael I thought this was the fulfillment of a certain emptiness in my life. I thought I had found my Prince Charming."

Mildred, highly upset over this latest Prince Charming, thought Tammy was making a terrible mistake and reached out to George Jones. "Mildred called me the day before she got married in that tent to that ol' Tomlin. She said, 'I wish you would give Tammy a call. You probably won't do any good, but just say somethin' to her. This man is after what she's got.' Well, I did it. I called Tammy and said, 'None o' my business, you're as free as the breeze, but—and I'm not sayin' this for me, I'm sayin' it for you—you're fixin' to get in trouble again with a guy that's only got dollar signs ringin' in his ears.' That's the worst thing I coulda *ever* done. That put the seal on it!" According to Maxine Hyder, Jones showed up at Tammy's house for the ceremony "but he couldn't get enough courage to come into the wedding."

The nuptials took place at Tammy's home on July 18, 1976. Her first ceremony not to occur hastily at some courthouse, it took place "out in the monster front yard of her mansion," said photographer Marshall Fallwell. "Hundreds of her so-called closest friends." Orchids everywhere, the grounds were done up like "the movie set of a Polynesian paradise," said Tammy, who'd foot the bill for the extravaganza. (Best of all was the irresistible pillow-talk version of "Hawaiian Love Song" she'd recorded just for the service and which wound up on her 1976 album *'Til I Can Make It on My Own*.) The atmosphere only turned more carnival-like when the minister came out on behalf of the husband and bride-to-be to ask her band members "to refrain from selling albums and T-shirts at the reception."

An inebriated Nan Crafton tried to talk Tammy out of the marriage right up until the last minute. "Just hop on this golf cart, and we can make a run for the street before it's too late," she told Wynette. Marshall Fallwell felt sorry for Tammy. "Everybody told her what a wonderful life she was living. She was sort of bewildered."

Ominously, when she'd gotten into the car to head for the ceremony, what should come on the radio but her and Jones singing "Golden Ring." The marriage was to last a mere forty-four days. As Tammy had to perform at the White House for then-president Gerald Ford, bride and groom left the reception in a helicopter. Jan had been out on the road with neighbors of Wynette—Minnie Pearl and her husband, Henry Cannon. As they drove down Franklin Road they looked up in the sky to see the chopper floating away. "Minnie said, 'Oops, we missed Tammy's wedding.' And Henry, who had the driest sense of humor in the world, said, 'Oh, that's okay. We'll catch the next one.'"

Tomlin and Wynette honeymooned in Hawaii, and already the bickering began. Tammy, now having trouble with her gallbladder, wound up in the hospital pumped full of drugs. She claimed Michael racked up bills left and right. Back in Nashville, Wynette had gallbladder surgery, then headed to Jupiter to recuperate. According to Tammy, Tomlin fired off a pistol on the beach, scaring her kids. She told Michael it was over. On her way back to Nashville, her incision opened, oozing fluid during a layover in Atlanta. She was taken to a local hospital. She called Burt Reynolds, who was in town filming *Smokey and the Bandit*, and asked if he could recommend a physician. "I think she wanted to see Burt as much as she wanted to see a doctor," noted daughter Jackie.

Reynolds came to check up on her. It was an emotional visit. She'd never told Burt about the marriage and was too humiliated to confess it was already over. "I guess you know it should've been you and me," Tammy told him. She'd hang on to that line, asking Sherrill to craft a song out of it, resulting in the delicate "You and Me." (Sherrill's cowriter and Wynette's next husband, George Richey, offered a different story, saying the song was inspired by Richey's then-secret love for Tammy.) Told from the point of view of a woman who's with one man but thinking of another, Wynette sings most of the song in a highly intimate whisper, belting out a line here and there just to stand your hair on end. There is a great clip of a tanned and very blonde Tammy doing the song on a Burt Reynolds TV special. He interviews her beforehand, and she seems so smitten by Burt she can barely answer the questions.

The aftermath of the Tomlin marriage was a gruesome affair. Tammy wanted the marriage annulled; Tomlin held out for a divorce. "Michael was strictly after my money," said a crestfallen Wynette. "He said that he would give me a divorce but first he wanted a three-hundred-thousand-dollar cash settlement. I said, 'You'll get it when hell freezes over. You've already gotten plenty of money from me.'" (Tomlin denied the charges in an interview with the *National Enquirer*.) Wynette said she finally paid him fifteen grand to go away.

The situation deeply embarrassed Tammy. "The worst thing about the marriage to Michael was what it did to me mentally. I'm beginning to really get paranoid and bitter . . . I'm beginning to lose faith in myself, and I'm hurt by the talk it's brought—'Four marriages? What's she trying to do—set some kind of record?'"

It was during this chaotic period that prescription painkillers entered Tammy Wynette's life.

Following her hysterectomy, she had been having constant problems with her stomach. Adhesions kept developing in her intestines, wreaking havoc on her digestive system. "It would look like there was a grapefruit protruding from her abdomen," said Joan Dew. "She was always talkin' about how painful it was." Jan Smith remembered heading over to a late-night pharmacy on Twelfth Avenue in Nashville to pick up the first narcotics Tammy ever had. Wynette was suffering severe stomach cramps, and, said Smith, a doctor "innocently prescribed" Demerol, an extremely powerful and highly addictive painkiller. Tammy's adhesions kept returning, which necessitated repeated operations—and more and more painkillers to enable her to work. Thus began a terrible cycle. "Everything was a catch-22 with Tammy," said Jan. "More operations, more keloids, more drugs, more obstructions."

Unfortunately Wynette started taking the drug even when she wasn't in pain. "She wasn't like a person who went out into the street to get high," said Joan Dew. "Tammy wasn't even the kind of person who really drank. She was one of those people—this is not uncommon in her era—that if the doctor gives you the prescription, it's okay. He's not gonna give you somethin' that's gonna harm you in any way. The doctor's word is law."

Not only that, but physicians are prone to the same sort of celebrity worship as anybody else. Georgette Jones, who worked as a nurse, noted that her mother's addiction was not unlike what "happened to Elvis. Doctors want so badly to impress and make friends with celebrities that they prescribe things that they wouldn't necessarily prescribe for just their average patient. And it's a terrible thing, because it makes the person feel like it's appropriate when it's not."

The end result was that one way or another Wynette had easy access to narcotics and she quickly developed a tolerance. "I have seen her go onstage and do a show with enough Demerol in her to knock a two-hundred-pound man out during surgery," said Dew. "She started needing Demerol shots because the pills weren't working anymore. So we would go into a town, and usually James Hollie would find a doctor for her, explain what was going on, and the doctor would come on the bus and give her Demerol. That would keep her for the night, and we'd go on to the next town." Her entourage aboard the Silver Eagle kept her secret. "I can tell you, everybody on that bus has given her a shot," admitted Nan, who said a Nashville doctor "took me into his office and taught me how to give her a shot. He would give us thirty cc's of Demerol and thirty cc's of Valium every time we went on the road."

As Wynette's need for the painkiller intensified, it became harder and harder to get the drug in her hometown. "The doctors in Nashville all caught on, and they would not give her any more prescriptions for Demerol," said Joan Dew. But she found one in Atlanta that would. And one in Vegas. "She had doctors all over the country." Many a sleepless night on the road was spent hunting down emergency rooms so Tammy could get medicated. "Sixty-milligram stop at one, then another—get another sixty milligrams," said Nan. "The magic number was 250 milligrams," said Jan.

It was at a concert date at an Iowa racetrack when Joan Dew realized just how grave the situation was. "Tammy was in pain that day, and James hadn't been able to find a doctor. She hadn't done a very good show and she was almost doubled over in pain." Joan and Nan were helping her down the steps backstage when Tammy mysteriously acquired a sudden surge of strength. "She pushed us both aside with such force it almost knocked Nan over. Tammy wanted to prove how much pain she was in. She threw herself down the steps on purpose." Wynette got her a doctor, and her Demerol.

"There were a lot of times Tammy wanted the drugs, and the pain wasn't there," said her governess, Cathye Leshay. "She'd do all sorts of little tricks to make you think she needed 'em." One Christmas Tammy was entertaining some friends and "she went back in the bathroom and got bath powder, put it all over her face to make her look pale, came out, and said, 'I don't feel well. Do I look pale?' And you could see that she had put powder on her face." According to songwriter Jerry Taylor, Wynette once stuck a pencil in her ear to get drugs.

"I know that Tammy would fake pain," said singer and friend Jan Howard. "She called, had a bad toothache and asked who my dentist was. He told me later, 'Jan, your friend has a problem. There's nothing wrong with her tooth. I'm not prescribing anything because there's nothing wrong with her.'" Wynette stormed out of a hospital in San Antonio because doctors wouldn't give her painkillers without a full diagnosis. Joan Dew said that working on Tammy's autobiography became more and more of a challenge as Wynette fell deeper into drugs. "It would go in cycles. She'd be fine for a few days, really in pain for a few days, then really out of it a few days."

Yet Wynette never complained. She was of the school that the show must go on, and often it went on when she was in agony. "Tammy could knock twenty-five thousand people out of their chairs with the best show you've ever seen in your life and then just pass out from pain comin' off the stage," said Cathye Leshay, who noticed that Tammy had a little trick where she'd hold the mic in one hand, letting the cord stretch across her stomach, which she'd then press on "to get a little bit of relief. It was just so sad. Because you felt so helpless. There wasn't anything you could do. I would just cry. We all would."

"I'm by no means a swinging single," confessed Tammy to *Gallery* magazine in 1976. Despite the many romances, Wynette did not enjoy being husband-less. "Mom's compulsive gallivanting was not so much a pursuit of amusement as it was an escape from the void that always consumed her when there was no man in her life," wrote her daughter Jackie.

"It really used to get to me as I headed back to Nashville after each tour," said Tammy. "I dreaded knowing that nobody was waiting at home for me, that there would be no welcoming arms to hug me, or a warm hello kiss . . . That's when the real pain set in."

Wynette was lonely. She had a myriad of health problems and was cultivating a serious drug addiction. Her recording career was slowly losing steam.

Tammy was in a very vulnerable state. Which is where George Richey enters the picture.

Ask people about George Richey and you'll get some curious responses. Merle Haggard toured with Tammy and had briefly utilized Richey as a producer, but when I inquired about him, Merle simply said, "I'm gonna take the Fifth." What kind of guy was George Richey? I asked Billy Sherrill. "Weird. Just out of it . . . way out there somewhere," he said, not wanting to linger on the subject. When George Jones was asked if he thought Richey had had Tammy's best interests at heart, he paused uncomfortably and said,

"I believe a lot of things went on that shouldn't have went on. Let me put it that way." When I quizzed Lorrie Morgan on what she thought drove George Richey, she said, "Money," and then let loose with a smokey chuckle. Patsy Sledd found Richey as "phony as a two-dollar watch." A few people even entertained me with their Richey impressions, which consisted of reading glasses perched way down on the nose and intoning commands in a sonorous, somewhat regal tone.

George Richey is easily the most controversial character in Tammy Wynette's life. After she died her daughters took both Richey and Tammy's last doctor, Wallis Marsh, plus UPMC Presbyterian and University Health Center of Pittsburgh, to court over allegations concerning her final years and demise. (Richey was later dropped from the suit, which was settled out of court.) Jackie Daly's 2000 book, *Tammy Wynette: A Daughter Recalls Her Mother's Tragic Life and Death*, painted a highly unflattering picture of Richey, which was only amplified in the media, particularly in the tabloids.

While they are certainly in the minority, Richey does have his defenders. "I think George Richey was among the greater things that ever happened to Tammy Wynette," insisted bodyguard Steve Chapman. "He looked after her every need." Sue Richards, who sang backup for Wynette for fifteen years starting in 1977, said that Richey "pulled me through some tough times. . . . In 1984 I lost a child. It devastated me so bad I didn't know if I'd come out of it. And Richey just insisted that I come back to work. If it wasn't for Richey I don't know exactly where I'd be today. He was good to me."

It should be noted that Tammy not only never criticized Richey publicly but regularly praised him to the skies. To hear her tell it, Prince Charming had finally arrived.

1983: "This is it for me. I could never find anyone who would love me the way Richey does."

1984: "I look on the time Richey and I have had together as the most contented I've known since I was a little girl, when Daddy was always there to take care of me. No man has ever done for me as Richey has."

1989: "He's very easy to live with and he makes me talk things out when I get mad and want to yell and scream. He's taught me a lot of patience, a lot of endurance. I'm lucky I found him."

1997: "He means everything to me. I love him to death and I'm so thankful I found him. I finally got it right."

On the rare occasions Tammy felt strong enough to discuss him in private, she told a different story, at least according to friends and family. "I think Richey played the role of the good guy for a very long time in front of people," said Georgette Jones. "It wasn't until he was behind closed doors that he did what he did. Which was manipulate and control."

Wynette had odd taste in men—there seems to be no common thread when you put them all in a line—but George Richey was definitely the oddest. Add up the cockeyed grin/sneer, the permed hair, mustache, and beard, plus the open shirts, gold chains, and gaudy rings ("He'd always twirl this ring on his finger," noted Cliff Dew. "It was like he was conniving, thinking, scheming all the time"), and the persona is more that of a third-rate magician holding on to a lounge gig in Reno than any sort of Music City legend.

George Baker Richardson aka George Richey came into the world on November 30, 1935. The son of a Baptist preacher, Richey was born in Promised Land, Arkansas, and raised in Missouri. Barbara Hutchison recalled joining Richey and Wynette on a trip to see the house where George grew up in Malden, Missouri. "He took us ridin', got down into dirt roads. We came upon this shack." Barbara was shocked, noting that the broken-down house where Tammy lived with Euple was "a mansion compared to Richey's. This place was like a shantytown. I think they were seven of 'em in this little two-room shanty house, didn't have wallpaper in it. They must've been very, very, very poor. Lord, no wonder Richey was desperate to make it to the top."

Richey left school at age fourteen for the world of gospel music. "My favorite gospel singers were James Blackwood, Jake Hess, and Denver Crumpler," he said. A formidable gospel pianist, he played with the Foggy River Boys on Red Foley's *Ozark Jubilee* TV show. "I then moved into country music for two reasons. I had started to love country music and I couldn't make a living in gospel. Gospel music is still my first love." Two of his other brothers went into the music business, Paul—a mediocre singer and songwriter who'd be deeply involved behind the scenes—and Wylie McPherson, who put out a single or two as a solo artist.

Richey also worked at a mortuary in 1962. During one of Tammy's hospital stays, Barbara Hutchison heard Richey tell a nurse how he had "started out in the undertakin' business." She claims he went on to relate "how he locked his brother Paul, who was extremely afraid of dead people, in a room with a corpse. He was screamin' to let him out." Richey found it amusing. "That gave me the willies," said Barbara. "Just sent chills down my spine."

After a stint in the army, Richey entered the world of radio, working as a DJ at KMOP in Tucson, KAYO in Seattle, and KGBS in Los Angeles. He then went to Capitol records as head of A and R, beginning a long career as a producer. "He's produced the greats—Burl Ives, Tex Ritter . . . ," said Tammy. "I can't begin to name them all." Not everyone was thrilled to have Richey in charge. Charlie Louvin, who worked with Richey at Capitol, re-called a session where the producer spent the first forty-five minutes or so talking to some woman. "We had the Jordanaires in the studio, six or eight musicians," said Louvin. "All this expense comin' out of my hide." To avoid wasting any more time, Charlie proceeded to start work on his own.

"And almost at that exact second George turned on the mic so he could hear what was goin' on in the studio. He jumped up, ran in, and said, 'Who changed the arrangement on my goddamn session?'" Louvin informed him no arrangement had been changed, as thus far there wasn't any. "He re-peated one more time—'Nobody changes the arrangement on my goddamn session.' Finally I handed him the words to the song and said, 'If it's your "goddamn session," here's the words, *you* record it. I'm outta here.'" Louvin called Ken Nelson, head of Capitol, and asked to record with someone else. Nelson informed him Richey was in charge. Charlie told him, "If we go in the studio again together there'll be a killin'.'" Louvin actually left the label over it.

Along the way Richey had a brief and unsuccessful career as a singer. "When I was quite young I really wanted to be a recording artist," he wrote on his Tammy Web site. "I found out much to my dismay that I wasn't a great singing talent." He had a handful of singles on Hickory and Ascot, most notably the truly abysmal "Jimmy Brown the Newsboy," in which Richey sings in a flat, nasal monotone but which actually charted. He said he cut the record as a joke: "It occurred to me that if it did become a hit, that I would have to sing through my nose the rest of my life." His frustrated desire to become a star might explain some of his behavior during his mar-riage to Tammy. "Richey was . . . *different*," said Nancy Jones. "I think Richey loved the limelight more than Tammy did."

In 1967 Richey moved to Nashville and landed at Epic with Billy Sherrill, working as a staff writer and sometime producer. It was there that George first encountered Tammy. Richey started cowriting songs for her, beginning with the beautiful "Come on Home" from Wynette's 1968 album *D-I-V-O-R-C-E*. "He's written I guess half the things I've done in my career," said Wynette in a 1980 interview. (I only count about a dozen cowriting credits for Richey from 1966 to 1980, including a pair of songs for George and Tammy. All were album cuts, save for "'Til I Can Make It on My Own," "You and Me," "Let's Get Together (One More Time)," and "We Loved It Away." He also cowrote "A Picture of Me (Without You)," "The Door," "The Grand Tour," and "The Battle" for George Jones.

Richey also had a successful publishing company, which held the rights to such moneymakers as the Billie Jo Spears hit "Blanket on the Ground," as well as the Kenny Rogers smashes "Coward of the Country" and "Lucille." From 1970 to 1977 he was musical director of *Hee Haw*. In his book about the show, producer Sam Lovullo wrote that Richey left *Hee Haw* "under less than perfect conditions," but he didn't care to elaborate much when asked. "Without getting into the personal aspect of why he was gone, George was very, very much involved in his publishing company. He was forever promoting songs . . . It was a case in point of absentee once in a while, okay?"

Richey's first marriage was to Dorothy Ann Tippitt, with whom he raised two children, Deirdre and Kelly, before divorcing her and then marrying Sheila Hall in 1974. Hall had worked as a secretary for Kelso Herston. "She was a good-lookin' dame," said Kelso. "She had that vulnerable look about her," added singer Dianne Sherrill, cousin of Billy. "She was a lovely person, befriended me when I came to town, opened her home to me. She was a great gal."* Through Richey she got to know Tammy and the rest of the crew. Sheila "was very submissive," said Jan Smith. "She always was doin' laundry."

The Richeys were extremely close to Tammy Wynette. When Tammy overdosed on pills during the demise of her relationship with Jones, it was Richey that came to the hospital. Joan Dew thought it strange that whenever Wynette broke off a relationship, George would suddenly appear. "Every time she'd be between men in her life, you'd look out the back door, and

---

*Sheila was a bit of an odd duck. According to her friend Diane Jordan, "she took photos of her mother in the casket and would show them. She'd say, 'You haven't seen Mama's picture.' No one would expect it was of her in the casket. People didn't know what to say."

here comes George Richey. I swear to God, it was like he had a Tammy de-
tector, some kind of homing device to let him know she was between men."
During the many weird break-ins and threats at the Franklin Road house,
she turned to the Richeys for help.

Sheila Richey was "one of Tammy's very best friends, and would travel
with her on the road a lot of times," said Dew. "She was around all the
time. Sheila was funny—she was one of those kind of people who enjoys
being a celebrity's friend but wasn't obnoxious about it. She always carried this huge purse. It was always a joke on the bus—anything you could
ever want from a Band-Aid to I don't know what, she had in that
purse."

"Tammy didn't have a lot of people surrounding her that she could
trust," said Sheila's brother Jerry Hall. "My sister was one person she could.
At one time they were like sisters. Sheila knew Tammy's secrets." Jerry
said Sheila was so loyal to Tammy she rarely shared anything she knew
even with him.

George and Sheila's marriage was a turbulent one. They "used to fight
like cats and dogs," said Hall, who alleged Richey "would take her formal
dresses and he'd throw 'em in the fireplace and burn 'em." In June 1975,
Sheila filed for divorce, alleging "cruel and inhuman treatment." She maintained she was "dreadfully afraid" of Richey, who she claimed threw her
out of the house in her underwear one winter night. Sheila showed up at
the door of neighbor Nan Crafton, wearing only a pair of loose-fitting pants
she'd pulled up over her chest. "She had come through the woods barefoot,"
Nan recalled. "Richey was mean. *Mean.*" The divorce was dropped, and the
allegations were never proven in court. Friends say Tammy was well aware
of such stories.

At Wynette's wedding to Michael Tomlin, Sheila was Tammy's matron
of honor, and George played keyboards. "I thought, 'Well, I'm history now—
the only thing I can hope for now is she divorces him.' "

According to what Richey told Ralph Emery, he was "drinking heavily
with two women" one mid-seventies night when he stopped by the studio
to visit Tammy. When she went to kiss him hello, Richey "just pulled her
into my lap. I had had just enough sauce to have enough courage to say
whatever I wanted." He confessed his feelings, and after the session, off into
the night they went. The next day Joan Dew received a "guess what I did
last night?" call from Wynette. "Tammy told me she'd slept with him after

a recording session one night—they went to the 'No-Tell Motel.' I said, 'How was it?' And she said, 'Wonderful!'—which she said about every guy she slept with. Sex was important to Tammy the way it was with my aunt who was married five times. It wasn't about really loving the act of sex, it was about feeling a man wanted you."

Richey wanted Wynette with a vengeance, and some of her friends were suspicious. They found him arrogant, controlling, and sporting a false air of spiritual superiority. "He always pretended to be very religious," said Joan Dew. "He didn't go to church or anything." Once Richey took over Tammy's affairs, he'd call any band member on the carpet for swearing. "He didn't like foul language—or pretended not to," said Dew, who maintained it was fine for George or his brother Paul to cuss. When it came to "bad language," said Charlene Montgomery, "George Richey was one of the worst. Richey was rough, rough talkin'." Dew found Richey to be "very two-faced and hypocritical. I wouldn't have trusted him behind a screen door with my grandmother."

The affair worried Dew, as she knew Richey wouldn't be as easy to shrug off as Wynette had her other flings. "I was concerned and fearful. He had been waiting for years for an opportunity. Oh, my God, had he been waiting! If Richey got her, I knew he would do whatever it took to stay with her. To *keep* her." George Jones was stunned when he found out. "Of all people, I would never dream she'd marry Richey," he said.

Complicating matters was the fact that Richey was still married to Sheila at the time.* "When George moved in with Tammy, his wife didn't know it," Joan Dew continued. "Sheila didn't know they were quote-unquote separated. Much less that Richey was seeing Tammy." When friends informed Sheila her husband was seeing Wynette, she was devastated. She considered Tammy a best friend. Wynette, however, was intoxicated by the illicit affair. As she admitted in a 1981 interview, "We slipped out of town and hid out for a few months. It was all so romantic. Just that feeling of, 'It's the two of us and nobody else knows.'"

"That's the kind of thing Tammy would do with absolutely no qualms," admitted Dew. "No sense of, 'Hey, maybe this isn't the right thing to do.'" Not only that, but friends have accused Richey and Wynette of cruel be-

---

*George Jones had his own suspicions about Richey during his marriage to Tammy. "He started sneakin' in seein' her when we wasn't even divorced."

havior toward his soon-to-be ex. "They would call Sheila all hours of the night, hang up on her, do mean things to her," said Nan Crafton. Some feel Richey was to blame for such shenanigans. "Tammy was led by the person she was in love with pretty easily," said Jan Smith.

Others have admitted that Wynette had a troubling side to her. "There were a few things that Tammy did when I was with her that were horrendous, and I would never tell what they were," said Joan Dew. "They weren't illegal or anything like that, just things you would do if you wanted to get even with somebody. It didn't happen often, but it gave you a picture that Tammy was someone you wouldn't want to mess with." And yet her friends forgave her for such behavior. How did she get away with it? "Because she was Tammy Wynette!" said Dew.

Sheila filed for divorce once more in October 1977, alleging adultery. Everybody in Nashville knew who "the other woman" was. "If you were writin' about Tammy, this would be the dark pages," said one friend of Sheila's who shall remain anonymous. "It wouldn't be a pretty chapter. When you have a woman steal another woman's husband—and that husband is this woman's life—then you got a reckless triangle, and somebody's gonna get hurt really bad. In this case it was Sheila, because George and Tammy fell head over heels in love. And that's when Sheila was left at home all alone. I'd never seen her take a drink or smoke a cigarette until all that happened. It really did drive her to drinkin'."

"It broke her heart when George said, 'That's it, I'm leaving you for Tammy,'" said her brother Jerry. "She was brokenhearted over Tammy doing what she was doing. They were doing this behind her back. She just went downhill from there."

Friends say Sheila Hall never got over the betrayal. One night Sheila was driving back from seeing Dianne Sherrill perform at Printer's Alley. She was drunk and ran into a telephone pole. The accident left her with a severed Achilles tendon, crippling her. "She couldn't walk, and many times she fell," said Dianne. "She said, 'That's the end for me.'"

On October 16, 1981, Sheila Hall was found dead in her Nashville apartment at 514 Doral Country Lane. By her side was her pet poodle, Elsie, given to her by Richey, and the pooch had no pulse either. Sheila's death was ruled an accident, although an unnamed Nashville cop assigned to the case told a tabloid that Hall "took an overdose of drugs. It seems she killed her dog, then killed herself." Her brother isn't so certain. "I won't say she took her own life," said Jerry. "I say there was the possibility that it occurred." Others have whispered for years that foul play was involved.

Nan Crafton insisted that even if Sheila had committed suicide, she would've never let the world see her in the disheveled state she was found in. "I knew Sheila well, and she didn't let anybody see her unless she was absolutely to the nines—false eyelashes, full makeup. Her hair would be done—always, always. They said she killed herself and she killed Elsie. I just never have believed that. Never, not one second." When Jerry Hall was cleaning out his deceased sister's home, George Richey called. There were two possessions he wanted back: Tex Ritter's hat, and a rifle. "He never showed up," said Jerry. "I think he was afraid to see me."

Seven years later author Randall Riese wrote about the Richey-Tammy-Sheila affair in his compendium of Music City scandal entitled *Nashville Babylon*. Hairdresser Barbara Hutchison had innocently bought the book while she was on the road with Tammy. Back on the bus she mentioned the tome she'd purchased to Richey, who, with one eyebrow cocked, picked it up and flipped through the pages. "I got back into my bunk that night and read the stuff about Tammy telling all about Sheila," said Barbara. "I went, 'Oh, my God.' I thought, 'Ooooh, I don't want Richey to read this book.'" When they got to the next venue, Hutchison left the copy of *Nashville Babylon* with her other belongings on her bunk. "I came back from the concert that night and that book was gone—and never did reappear!" Barbara was certain Richey had gotten rid of it. "He knew that book was out and didn't want anybody to discuss it openly on the bus."

"I always said I would never live openly with a man with my children around," said Tammy in 1978, failing to take into account that she'd lived with both Don Chapel and George Jones before heading to the altar. "It was against everything we have ever been taught . . . But his divorce wasn't final, and we needed each other."

When Richey and Wynette marched into Sherrill's office to tell him the news, he was his typically irreverent self. "Your boobs are bigger," he pointed out to Tammy. She informed him that she'd just been sick and lost weight. Then she dropped the bomb: she and Richey were tying the knot. "Oh, my God. I just told you your boobs were bigger," he said, cracking them both up. Billy had one other pronouncement to make that day, albeit a more serious one. "There will be no more sad songs written," he told Tammy. He was only half right. Once Wynette married Richey, there would hardly be *any* songs written, sad or otherwise.

Richey's divorce was finalized in May 1978. George and Tammy married on July 6 of that year, on the beach in Florida. Some have felt that Tammy's aunt Carolyn Jetton, who'd been like a sister to Tammy, had a lot to do with the wedding's taking place. Carolyn was dying of cancer and had one last wish. "Tammy promised Carolyn she'd marry Richey," said her old Florida friend Maxine Hyder. "I think she did it because she knew that Carolyn was gonna die, and Carolyn didn't like 'em livin' in sin."

The fact that Jetton was desperately ill didn't stop Tammy from wheedling some drugs out of her the day of the wedding. "Carolyn was on Demerol for pain," said Joan Dew. "Carolyn really *needed* Demerol." On the day of the ceremony, Wynette proceeded to finagle some of the painkiller out of her dying aunt. "That day when she got married to George Richey, Tammy was stoned out of her mind. That's the kind of thing that in a million years the old Tammy would never have done. That's how desperate she was."

Once George and Tammy were married, big changes occurred. Richey called Cathye Leshay into his office and told her, "I cannot start a life with and build a relationship with Tammy and her girls when I'm livin' in a female dormitory . . . I guess I gotta get rid of everybody." And over the next few years, get rid of everybody he did. Gone was Tammy's longtime lawyer, John Lentz. Save for Charlie Carter, one by one the band departed. As for her friends, "Richey ran us all off," said Nan Crafton. "George Richey got rid of everybody that Tammy liked," said Joan Dew. "So he could be totally in control. She wouldn't have any other confidants."

The marriage to Tammy "creates no problem for me," boasted Richey to the press, adding proudly that he was "often referred to as Mr. Wynette." He'd state repeatedly how he felt that Wynette had been victimized before he'd arrived on the scene. "I felt she was being used by a lot of people," he said. "I was determined to make certain . . . it wouldn't happen any longer." He "weeded out the bloodsuckers, leeches, and joyriders" from around Tammy. There are those around Wynette who find such comments darkly ironic.

"When Tammy married George Richey, she married that entire friggin' family," said songwriter Jerry Taylor, who wrote for Tammy and worked with Richey. "So what happens? The first thing we do is start a Cadillac dealership in Malden, Missouri. Who's runnin' it? The Richardsons. We start a publishing company, First Lady Songs. Who's runnin' it? Paul Richey."

Tammy was no longer in charge of her finances, her friends, or her life. Now came years of illness, drug addiction, and isolation. Even Jones was cut off from her. "When Richey married her, you had to go through channels—you couldn't even call direct to Tammy anymore. I couldn't even call and check on my *daughter*—'Well, Miss Wynette will call you, Mr. Jones. When the time is right, we'll get back to you.' You'll get back to me?! Richey took over her business, everything that pertained to money. He took over the bank accounts, bookings, everything. *Everything.*"

Dear Tammy,

So now we get to the kidnapping. For the first time the world doesn't believe you. Changed everything, didn't it?

You know what I think? You were tired. After you married Richey, you gave up on romance. The obsessions that drove your art had worn you down. Over and over, searching for this crazy ideal. Reality had smacked you in the face a few dozen times. You couldn't take it anymore. And the kind of misery you were trapped in now produced no artistic dividends. There was nothing to sing about. So you just checked out.

And nobody was going to tell you what to do. Jones, Jerry Lee, Hank . . . sometimes I think you were more hard-core than all them bad boys.

There is this song of yours from 1979, "Let Me Be Me." It has been on my mind constantly as I've been writing this. It's a simple ditty, at least on the surface. Let me be free, let me be me. *Truly beautiful, the slow and deliberate way you sing it. Then comes the jaunty little middle eight where you ask to be molded, fitted, hammered, and welded into the Perfect Wife.* Let me be *versus* Whatever you want. *It's two completely opposite points of view car-crashed together into one song. I can appreciate the split personality, Miss Tammy. It's you in spades.*

I never let a woman "be" in my life. But I keep trying. Part of the reason is because of something I hear in your voice. What to call it—kindness?

Last night I had a dream. We were starring in a remake of that old black-and-white melodrama Something Wild. *I was playing the Ralph Meeker part, you the Carroll Baker. And I locked you in that cheap apartment until you answered every question* and *solved every riddle in this book. A love story, in other words.*

There we were riding down Highway 23 in your yellow Lincoln, you looking like a million bucks in a yellow pantsuit and matching headband. Listening to the country station, you were staring out the window, feeling blue. Turns out I didn't make you happy, either.

Did anybody ever just let you be you, Wynette?

Mr. Tammy Wynette

I'll take care of you better than you'd ever imagine.

—Sam "Ace" Rothstein, Casino

I don't know what he does. All I know is, he provides.

—Victoria (Mrs. John) Gotti

It was around seven p.m. on October 4, 1978. Twenty-one-year-old Bobby Young was on his way to pick up his brother Jimmy from deer hunting when he drove by his family's home off Route 65 about ten miles northeast of Pulaski, Tennessee, and noticed a stranger staggering up the driveway. Their house wasn't far from exit 31A, and it wasn't the first time they'd had unwanted company. "I thought, 'Well, I wonder who this drunk is,'" said Young, who drove around the back entrance intent on rousting the intruder. He was soon face-to-face with a bedraggled little blonde with a stocking tied around her throat who told him, "I'm Tammy Wynette and I need help." "I didn't believe her," said Young. "She didn't have her wigs on or all her makeup—she was just plain."

Bobby sat her in his car while he ran to get his mother, Junette. "He come in the house sayin', 'Mama, come out right quick.' I said, 'Son, I'm busy.'" Bobby insisted, whereupon Junette "saw these pink legs hangin' out of his car. My heart just went to my throat. I just knew it was my son who had been bow huntin' and had hurt hisself. Then I realized he didn't have on pink britches! So I ran to the car right quick, and she said, 'I'm Tammy Wynette and I've been kidnapped.'"

Junette's eyes nearly popped out of her skull. She was a big fan. "I wanted to say how I just love her and George Jones together, but it wasn't the time or place to talk about her ex-husband," she explained to *People* magazine. The first order of business was to get that stocking off Wynette's neck. "She was gaspin' for breath, it was really tight. It was all I could do to get my finger between the pantyhose and her neck."

243

Junette had Bobby fetch a paring knife from inside the house; then she cut away the panty hose. "I carried her in the house. She was shakin'." Wynette asked Junette for a glass of water and some aspirin. "I gave her a bath rag to put on the sore places and she said, 'Oh, that hurts, that hurts,' so I took it away." Tammy had a big scrape on her cheek.

When Wynette asked Junette to call her husband, Wynette's maid answered, who was skeptical until she told Junette to ask her boss what kind of car was she driving. "A yellow convertible," said Tammy. Convinced that this was no crank call, the maid said that Richey wasn't there and she'd have him ring back. "Wasn't but a few minutes 'til he called," said Junette. "He said, 'Keep her there 'til I get there.'" Still shaking, Wynette sat quietly on the couch. "She didn't do a whole lot of talkin' to us," recalled Bobby.

Details would soon be spewing forth from every television, newspaper, and tabloid. Tammy had been shopping alone at Nashville's Green Hills mall in search of a present for Georgette's eighth birthday. She had left her Cadillac unlocked, and when she returned to the vehicle there was a man in the backseat. "I saw an arm with a pistol . . . he had a stocking on his face," she said. The man commanded her to drive, then took the wheel about fifteen miles later. The pair "drove around in circles" before he pulled off the freeway into a field near the Youngs' home. Her assailant "dragged me out of the car. Then he hit me with his fist. I thought, 'Oh, God, I'm gonna die.'" Wynette told Junette Young she "played dead" until her attacker fled the scene with another masked man at the wheel of a blue and white station wagon. It was then that Tammy stumbled up the road to the Youngs' house.

By this time Junette's son John had awakened and wanted to know what all the commotion was about. When she told him that Tammy Wynette had been kidnapped, John said he thought they should call the sheriff. But Wynette didn't want the authorities. She said her husband would call her friend and neighbor Governor Ray Blanton. Meanwhile John had slipped out the door to hit a nearby pay phone. "John David called the law," said brother Bobby.

"Tammy Wynette is at our house, she's been kidnapped and y'all need to come out," he told the Pulaski police, who told him to call the county sheriff. John responded, "YOU call the county sheriff. I don't have another dime." Said Junette, "They didn't believe him. Nobody believed him."

In the meantime Junette was concerned that all this ruckus might wake her graveyard-shift husband, who, as was his habit, would then mosey out in the living room in his underwear. She went into the bedroom, woke him, and told him, "If you come into the livin' room, make sure you put your britches on, because Tammy Wynette has been kidnapped and she's layin' in there on the couch." Her husband just looked at her. "I don't know what in the hell you're talkin' about," he said. Junette repeated her request and walked out of the room. Pants on, he soon came into the living room to see the jaw-dropping sight for himself.

About this time the law arrived. Recalled Junette, "The two deputies came in and very sheepish-like, said, 'Are you Miss Wynette?'" Tammy confirmed indeed she was and that she had just been kidnapped. The officers wanted to take her to the hospital; she wanted to wait for Richey. While Junette was on the phone dealing with a reporter who had somehow managed to find out Wynette was there, the officers managed to slip Tammy out the door to a nearby Giles County hospital where, according to the *Chicago Tribune*, she was treated in the emergency room for "cuts and bruises." Wynette later claimed her cheekbone had been broken in the attack.

It was in the hospital that TBI (Tennessee Bureau of Investigation) agent Jerry Eubanks first spoke to Wynette. "I couldn't see anything that wrong with her. She had a little abrasion, a small-lookin' red spot. The abrasion wasn't that bad, should've been cleared up in a couple of days." He helped hustle Tammy out of the hospital while evading the throng of reporters that had gathered outside. Next to the exit was George Richey, who, noted the *Tennessean*, "paused long enough to make a vulgar gesture toward reporters, then repeated the gesture."

A day or two later Eubanks went to Wynette's Nashville home to interview her. "Walter Cronkite and the news media were there. When I saw the abrasion had been painted with dark makeup, I figured then it was a publicity stunt. That's what I thought personally, that's not official. Show business, man, show business!" Eubanks got the distinct impression that Tammy had zero interest in having the incident investigated. "There was no cooperation, as far as I was concerned. We were treated like we didn't belong there." He laughed. "That's why we left—she was so busy with Walter Cronkite, I didn't have a chance."*

---

*Curiously, while Wynette may have been more than forthcoming in the press, the kidnapping was a verboten subject at home. "It was something we didn't talk about," wrote her daughter Jackie. "Whenever I asked Mom about it, she would dismiss the subject."

———

Michelle Broussard Honick, who worked in the office for Richey, pooh-poohed the idea that Wynette was cosmetically accentuating her bruises. "That wasn't makeup. Tammy was terrified. I saw her the next morning. She was beaten very badly. She was extremely shaken up. She was so afraid she made me spend the night there."

Two days after the episode, more bizarre details were unearthed in the *Tennessean*. Days before the abduction someone had called Wynette's office and whispered, "Where is Georgette?" Minutes later Tammy got an anonymous call that "someone else is going to pick up your kid today." Georgette, who attended Franklin Road Academy, was fine. Nothing added up, particularly when it came to Tammy's kidnapping. Lieutenant Sherman Nickens of the Nashville police appeared baffled. "We have no motive, no nothing . . . They didn't try to rape her. She had a million credit cards, and they didn't take those." George Richey, putting his two cents in, noted Tammy "wasn't exactly treated like she would if she got a standing ovation."

Wynette appeared in concert October 6 in Columbia, South Carolina. Photos of a bruised and haunted-looking Tammy at the mic made the papers. "He could possibly be here, I just don't know," Wynette whispered to the audience, her eyes scanning the crowd. A battalion of fifty bodyguards surrounded the tiny singer.*

Despite the massive security, a crumpled, threatening note was found backstage: "I'm still around, I'll get you." Another handwritten threat appeared stuck in the gates of her home on October 24: "We missed you the first time, we'll get you the next time." Both were turned over to the FBI.

Due to the Georgette subplot, some suspected George Jones, who frequently traveled the same highway between Nashville and Florence, Alabama. But the idea of Jones as the criminal mastermind behind any kidnapping struck those who knew him as utterly ludicrous, and police didn't even bother interviewing him. "Maybe whoever did it didn't like me . . . Maybe if they'd've brought her a little closer to Florence, they'd have

---

*Glenn Sutton thought the security around Wynette was ridiculous. "They treated it like Marilyn Monroe was comin' on—who in the fuck's gonna jump Tammy? Richey would walk along with a walkie-talkie like the CIA: 'Yes, she has left the bus.' Tammy had more people than the president!"

made it look more real," he said at the time, laughing. "It's a sad thing. And it don't make no sense to me."

Decades later, in his autobiography, Jones was much more succinct: "The whole affair was bullshit." George's coauthor, Tom Carter, interviewed an officer involved in the case, Red Smotherman, who expressed skepticism over the incident, noting that Wynette refused to take a lie-detector test. (Richey apparently did and passed it.) Jones declared the event "a hoax. Somebody beat the hell out of Tammy, that's for sure. But I don't think it was a kidnapper."

The alleged kidnapping became the talk of the town, a lot of the talk less than favorable to the First Lady and her new husband. One theory: it was a publicity stunt—after all, the CMA Awards were happening on October 9, and for once Tammy wasn't nominated for anything. The other speculation was much darker: Richey had beaten her up. Singer Diane Jordan was on a show with Minnie Pearl, and even she was speculating about the kidnapping. At one point Pearl turned to Jordan and said, "Well, what do you think really happened?" Jordan responded, "A lot of people think George Richey had something to do with it." Even little old Minnie concurred. "That's kind of heavy," said Jordan. "Minnie Pearl?"

If it was all a ruse to get publicity, Tammy got plenty, but not necessarily the kind she wanted. Just two days after the incident, the *Tennessean* ran an editorial entitled "Miss Wynette's Troubles." It quoted Tammy "as saying the kidnapping was 'mysterious'—which is putting it mildly. . . . Miss Wynette's many fans throughout the country—as well as her home community—are perplexed by her continuing troubles." San Francisco punk band the Maggots put out a single entitled "Let's Get Tammy Wynette." The picture sleeve was an outrageous image of her bruised face they'd lifted from *People*. "The whole situation was so bizarre," said Raeanne Rubenstein, who took the photographs. "Everywhere Tammy went she had a police escort and four armed troopers."

"People were already saying this is kind of a trumped-up thing, it was faked, and I'm sure Tammy knew that," said veteran Nashville reporter Alanna Nash, who attended a press conference Tammy gave in Nashville the first week of November. "She was really layin' it on thick—she was all bruised and she wanted to make sure people saw that."

In Nash's next interview with Wynette, she discussed the situation in detail. "I think the press has been very, very lenient with me, and very good to me . . . other than with the kidnappin' situation. . . . I picked up a couple of papers, and it said, 'Was this a publicity stunt?' Well, if they had seen the broken cheekbone, the terrible knots on my throat, my neck swollen, my face beat all to pieces, I don't think they would have thought it was a publicity stunt." She added, "The thing that hurt me the worst, was . . . I was a suspect."

Tammy went on to accuse the cops of bungling the case ("I lost a lot of respect for the Nashville Police Department") and complained that she and Richey "were the only two that took a handwriting test to prove that we didn't write" the threatening notes handed over to the FBI. However, in a report filed November 18, 1978, the FBI said only that their findings were inconclusive, because the notes "contain apparent distortions, possibly the result of an attempt to disguise normal writings. No opinion can be reached whether Tammy Wynette . . . did or did not prepare any of the questioned hand printing on these specimens."

Wynette would elaborate on the abduction story in years to come, and it only got weirder. She'd tell *Oui* magazine in 1984 that the day before the kidnapping she'd called home from Atlanta, mentioning she was going shopping for Georgette's birthday present the next day. "We found out later there were seven wiretaps on the phone," she said. She revealed to *Penthouse* in 1980 that police had discovered it was "all preplanned. . . . Three people in Nashville knew four hours ahead of time that I was going to be kidnapped" and that a listening station had been set up in the woods near her house. Yet no one was ever arrested for the crime. "It was just kind of put on the back burner," said TBI agent Jerry Eubanks. "We couldn't prove anything either way."

In May 1984 Wynette felt compelled to bring the incident to the attention of the press once more. She'd received a letter from a prison inmate who stated his cellmate had confessed to the crime. "He knew inside information that we had never made public," said Tammy, who admitted the missive "made my blood run cold." Nothing came of this revelation.

Even after Tammy's death, the plot continued to thicken. In her 2000 book, daughter Jackie revealed that in the early nineties she found her mother sitting on a suitcase at the end of the driveway. There had been an argument with Richey. In her agitated state, Wynette brought up the kidnapping, confessing to Jackie, "It didn't happen . . . it was all made up." She admitted it was a cover to explain away bruises she'd gotten from the hands of her husband. "Richey had knocked her around," wrote Jackie, who went on to suggest he might've been involved in the fires, threats, and general weirdness that led up to the kidnapping. "Based on what my mother told me about the kidnapping, I can't help but wonder if Richey was responsible for our year of terror."

Jackie isn't alone here. Tammy's hairdresser Jan Smith maintained Tammy told her the same thing. Carolyn Neal, an overseas fan whose entire family grew close to both Tammy and Richey, said that in June 1993 Wynette laid out the same scenario to her as well. Neal also recalled that Tammy's then-housekeeper Cleta told her that Wynette had admitted to her that she was the one who'd written the threatening notes.

Richey has denied any involvement. He told *Country Weekly* in 2000 that such "hideous allegations" left him "sickened." He pointed out that Tammy had been shopping "for a number of hours" before the attack. "If the allegations were true, she already had the bruises, didn't she? Does that all add up? No, it doesn't. It's ironic that Jackie never made any such claim while Tammy was alive and could refute her."

Whatever had actually taken place on October 4, 1978, it left a troubling impression in the minds of many. Alanna Nash interviewed Wynette several times over the years, and while she admired Tammy, she also felt sorry for her. "'Gracious' is the first word that always comes to mind when I think about her. She was very decent to members of the press. On the surface she seemed to be this kind of nice, normal person—this beauty who could sing a little bit and got lucky. Tammy was always kind of downplaying her abilities.

"But underneath that was obviously somebody who was very self-destructive—a person who needed to cause a lot of chaos in her life, a lot of drama. Her life was always one horrific thing after another—violence or the threat of violence, people beating her up, breaking into her house, fires, illness . . . Nothing was too extreme. She would talk about it pretty openly and willingly, as if she wanted you to say, 'How could all this happen to one person?' I think she kind of liked the drama of it."

Nash talked wistfully of the easy access writers had to the personalities in those days and of "this Southern thing that stars of yore would do—they would kind of bond with you." A writer could have an intimate, one-on-one dialogue with a star without the interference of managers or publicists. "Country music has always suffered this kind of inferiority complex. The

Nashville people kind of banded together as a family, because they were in a sense outcasts of the entertainment industry. Now it's all controlled, managed . . . That's the problem with country music today, there aren't any characters left."

But Tammy inevitably took the bonding a step further. She was forever showing reporters, fans, and friends the various wounds and incisions on her body from her many hospital stays. It happened to Nash during a 1980 interview at Wynette's home—in her bedroom, in fact. "I was almost quite literally in bed with her, because she was in bed. Tammy had just got out of the hospital, and she just pulled her nightgown down, showing me her backside and the bruises on her rear. It just struck me as very strange.

"I think part of that was an attempt to get sympathy, but there's also something just psychologically bizarre about it, particularly doing it to a reporter that she didn't really know. It was obvious this woman was unstable and needed a lot of attention—more so than most people that go into the entertainment business. Any relationship with Tammy would have to be complex, I think. She had to be difficult, just because she was so unsettled. This was someone who had deep psychological needs that were not being met."

"I got Richeys comin' outta my ears," Wynette complained to Cathye Leshay in 1982 when she called to coax Leshay back into her employ. George's family had by now engulfed Tammy. His parents lived with them. Brother Paul ran Wynette's publishing company. Paul's then-wife Sylvia ran the office. A sister ran the fan club for George Jones. Back in Richeys' hometown of Malden, Missouri, brother Carl took care of their car dealership, Richardson-Wynette Motors. Much to her chagrin, Tammy was roped into Fourth of July festivities in Malden year after year.

Richey's two children got the red-carpet treatment; Tammy's kids got something far less. "I saw the difference," said backup singer Yvonne Abdon, who recalled a tour date in California. "Here come Deirdre and Kelly in their BMWs and Mercedes." Tammy's kids "were drivin' Chevrolets." When it came to Wynette's children, Richey nickeled and dimed. "She wanted to buy Georgette a washer and dryer, and he threw a fit," said Abdon. "I mean, why should he control what she does? Tammy made all the money." But apparently Wynette saw very little of what she earned. Tammy told Yvonne she "got an allowance of five hundred dollars a week."*

While Wynette was very fond of George's son, Kelly, daughter Deirdre was another story. No one in Tammy's corner seemed very enamored of her. "She was the whitest girl you ever seen," said Jan Smith. "White, white hair, white, light skin, and she wasn't 'purty.' We kind of hated it when she was comin', adults *and* kids. Deirdre wasn't lovable. She was always antagonistic towards Tammy, and Tammy was a very loving human. She just couldn't get a break from Deirdre."

An odd couple at best, Tammy and Richey chain-smoked "Marlboro 100s in the gold pack," noted fiddle player Bobby Napier. "Long, harsh cigarettes . . . it took a long time to smoke one of those." Said Cathye Leshay, "Tammy and Richey didn't buy cigarettes by the carton, they bought 'em by the case—cases that were waist-high."

The couple often wore identical floor-length mink coats and matching hats. "It looked good on Tammy," said Karyn Sloas. "It just looked completely ridiculous on him—Sonny Bono!" Loretta Lynn recalled the time Tammy and Richey showed up just as her mother's funeral had begun. "Here they come through the door, and they had their long mink coats. Those dadgum coats were draggin' the ground, I thought that was the funniest thing. The funeral stopped until they got set down. Tammy knew how to make an entrance."† Many felt Richey was hungry for his own stardom. "I mean, why does George Richey need a fur coat?" said songwriter Jerry Taylor. "She was the Diana Ross, not him."

Despite her endless proclamations of love and devotion in the press, Wynette gave many a friend the impression that her marriage to Richey was "strictly business," as childhood friend Holly Ford explained. "She told

---

*Wynette had her methods of revenge. "She loved to shop from catalogs," said Yvonne. "Sometimes she would just do this to spite Richey. She would call, pick out everything in the world, and soon all this stuff's comin' to the house." Office manager Sylvia Richey would call George up to complain about the expenditures. Said Yvonne, "Tammy *loved* doin' that."

†Wynette had to climb steep terrain in her high heels to get to the service, which took place back in some Kentucky holler. "You couldn't get up there by car, so that was the only way," Tammy told Patsi Bale Cox. After the service, Wynette helped Lynn sing her sorrows away. "Richey started playing the piano, and Loretta began singing old-time gospel songs . . . We must have sung every hymn we knew by the end of the night."

me from her own mouth that they had a business relationship." When Agnes Wilson and her husband worked for her, Tammy mentioned she and Richey were going on vacation to some island and they were thinking of taking the Wilsons. "You need to go and enjoy each other," Agnes told Tammy. "We don't enjoy each other. We're not in love. We have great times together, but we're not in love."

The end result, claimed daughter Jackie, was a Tammy who "was more lonely than ever. Mom could make herself miserable, she didn't need somebody else doin' it for her. If Mom hadn't been on any kind of medication, Richey would've been out the door. He would've never have lasted as long as he did."

Medication. Wynette had plenty of it. As her health continued to deteriorate, she took more and more drugs. More than a few people say that this was Richey's main role in her life: finding the doctors who would take care of Tammy's pharmaceutical needs. One anonymous source said Tammy once informed Richey, "You will have this for me—or you won't be here." Jets were chartered. FedEx packages came and went.

According to Charley Abdon, "There were two things the tour manager had to get: the money and the bag of medicine. I'd hear on the radio, 'Has the package come in yet?' And we'd go, 'Oh, shit,' because we'd know if there's a package comin', we're twelve or eighteen hours away from cancelin' a show somewhere. *Virginia's* fixin' to come out."

Stanley Harman admitted that, in addition to being a bodyguard and a road manager, "I had another purpose, too. Anytime we crossed the border George would hand me the drugs to get 'em across. Tammy kept them in her black makeup case. Prescription stuff, supposed to be legit—but I don't know how legal it is in different countries. So they would always give it to me and let me worry about gettin' it across."

You never knew when Wynette was about to go under. "She'd get on the bus feelin' fantastic, and all of a sudden two hours later she was dyin' in pain," said Bud McComb. "Richey sayin', 'Find the nearest hospital, roll the marquee to private coach, and take her name off it'—like nobody knows who this bus belongs to with an American flag forty feet down the side of it. At two o'clock in the mornin' she'd wrap that ol' gold rag round her head, put on sunglasses, and we'd go find a hospital." Sometimes all it took was knowing there was a hospital in the vicinity. "If you were goin' down the road and saw one of those hospital signs, in ten minutes you had to be there," said Jerry Taylor. "It wasn't all George's fault.

"Bless George's heart, I'm tellin' you half of his time was spent in finding new ways of getting that stuff and keeping her where she could work. Because if you didn't get it, she couldn't—and if she couldn't work, they were going to be broke."

Jane Williams, Wynette's cousin, recognized the seriousness of the situation when Tammy came down to Alabama for her grandfather's funeral in the early eighties. Wynette had an obstruction in her intestines and was in agonizing pain. A local doctor recommended surgery.

Williams, who worked at the hospital as a registered nurse, saw firsthand what the countless surgeries and repeated bouts with adhesions had done to her cousin's body. "It took us two hours to get through the adhesions just to get down to the obstructions," recalled Jane, shaking her head. "It was just like glue in there. Like somebody had opened Tammy up and poured in glue."

It was after the operation that Williams realized just how dependent Wynette had become on pain medication. "There's one thing about a hospital: a nurse can pick out in a minute the people that want the pain shots like clockwork." According to Jane, Tammy's "hips were like leather" and her body already resembled a pincushion. Although they didn't discuss the matter, Williams felt certain that Wynette was aware of the gravity of the situation. "She knew—and she knew *I* knew." She tried to discuss it with Richey but felt all she got was lip service. "He would agree with you," but not with "an intention to do anything about it."

And so Wynette just got worse and worse. "It was always, 'Mama's not getting up today, she's not feelin' good,'" recalled Cathye Leshay. "So we would talk to her from her bed a lot of the time or the couch. It was just so sad. Tammy wanted so bad to feel good and to be healthy. We would be getting ready to go someplace and she'd say, 'I gotta go home, I gotta go home. My stomach is just really hurtin'.' But she would try . . ." Leshay felt that Tammy's deteriorating condition "also hindered the relationship with her girls. When she was home, she just needed her rest so desperately. When you're in bed and so exhausted and in such pain you can't move, you don't feel like goin' shoppin' and to the movies and havin' lunch and goin' to a school program."

Jan Smith was perhaps the only person Tammy confided in about the situation. "This was early on in the George Richey siege, when I knew things were getting bad with the drugs," said Smith. It was one of those very rare occasions out on the road when Richey wasn't around. "Tammy and I had rooms across the hall from each other. She came over and got in bed with me."

"Jan," asked Tammy, "are people in Nashville talkin' about me?"

"Yes," admitted Smith.

"Do they think I'm a drug addict?"

"Yes," she said.

"Do you think Billy Sherrill knows?"

"Yes," said Smith for the third time.

"Then I want to go check in a hospital," said Tammy. "I want to get off of this."*

Smith said she was all ready to escort Tammy to rehab when George Richey showed up. Jan claimed Richey told Wynette, "You're not a drug addict."

On and on it went. Tammy continued to abuse drugs, and everybody continued to worry about her. Cathye Leshay said she never knew when she awoke in the morning "if you were gonna find Tammy on the floor with a needle in her arm. Or dead."

Out on the road Richey ruled with an iron fist. No longer did Tammy have the comfort of her band around her, which now went by the name "Young Country." (In private the band was often known by the nickname Charley Abdon concocted—the Wynettetones.) There were now two buses, Tammy One and Tammy Two. Tammy Two was for the band and the crew; One was just for Tammy, Richey, the backup singers (now known as "Sunshine"), and the hairdresser. Richey had stars and stripes painted down the side of both. All the bus drivers wanted to drive the band bus, which was relaxed and fun. Nobody wanted to pilot Tammy One, the rolling mausoleum. "No

---

*Billy Sherrill couldn't mask his sorrow when I repeated this story. "Pain'll do that for you. I can't fault anybody for takin' drugs to stop the pain. It's one thing to take drugs to get high, it's another takin' 'em to quit hurtin'. She pulled up her shirt one time and her belly looked like a road map, there were so many scars on it. All these damn doctors and all those drugs." He sighed. "You know the story. Out-of-town doctors. Richey'd go get 'em and bring 'em in."

one ever spoke above a whisper," said driver Steve Hoker. "The girls and Richey, no other guys allowed on there. They'd sit and play cards all night. That's about it." Bodyguard Stanley Harman climbed aboard Tammy's bus one morning and bellowed a good morning to the women on board. "They just panicked—'*Shhhhh*, George is still asleep.' Everyone was tiptoein' like they were walkin' on eggshells. If they woke him up early he went through conniptions."

At least as far as Tammy's career was concerned, Richey had his strong points. Despite the fact that Wynette was recording less and less hit material, he demanded top dollar for her appearances. "I thought he was a genius," said Steve Hoker. "Richey kept Tammy in the limelight. He kept Tammy relevant. She was still makin' huge bucks, and she could work as much as she wanted—until her health started failing."

When it came to Tammy's booking agents, Richey was unrelenting. "He would hammer you every day, two or three times a day," sighed Tony Kincaid, who represented Wynette in the late eighties and the nineties. "Richey's day began—'At ten in the morning I'm gonna call my agent, and at four in the afternoon he better tell me he got somethin'.' He'd call you at the house on the *weekend*."

Whatever the offer was, it wasn't good enough, Tony explained. "You'd always be honest and tell him, 'Okay, George, here's the tour, and here's what I got laid out.' And he would say, 'Well, you gotta go back and get more money.' Richey had a standard line on every offer we'd get, didn't matter how much the money was: 'Well, go back and see if you can bump it up a little.' Always. *Always*. He would never say, 'That's a great offer, we'll take it, confirm it.' It was always, 'Well, Tony, go back and see if you can bump it up a little.'"

Richey upgraded Wynette's live presentation, and when she sang with a string section, he'd do the conducting himself. When it came to performance evaluation, Richey had, as Steve Hoker put it, "the ears of a bat." No detail of Tammy's show escaped him. He was particularly critical of piano players, being one himself. Charley Abdon admitted that, when it came to harmonies, Richey knew his stuff. "If one of the girls hit a note that wasn't the note he'd wanted to hear, he'd pick it out, which is hard to do live. He'd go over it, obsess about it, and want it a half a step flatter—and bring somebody to tears to get the part right."

For Richey, touring was not unlike some sort of covert military operation. Chosen members of the crew carried bulky Motorola walkie-talkies. Recalled fiddle player Tim Watson, "When Richey walked in somewhere, if nobody was payin' him any attention, he'd immediately whip that radio out and start in like he was some kind of secret agent."

It was all part of the ongoing espionage. "Those radios were like an appendage," said Steve Hoker. "And God help you if he called and you didn't answer. Because there was nobody who could chew you out like Richey."

No doubt about it, George Richey waited on Tammy hand and foot. He made it clear to everyone that whatever Wynette wanted, she got. "George had one rule: when it comes to Tammy Wynette, the word 'no' doesn't exist," said bodyguard Steve Chapman. "I was told that, with Tammy, there was never a criticizing word. Because criticism would've done no good. She needed encouragement, help, love, and all of us tried to give her that."

And what exactly did Tammy require on the road? There was a stop at the video store before every tour. "They would find a movie they would like, and we would watch it continuously from the time we left until the time we got back," said Karyn Sloas. "I've seen *Casino* twelve times. That was a favorite. Then we had a satellite dish, and Richey became a huge fan of Court TV. That's all we watched. He loved Nancy Grace." Charley Abdon, who besides playing drums drove Tammy One for a while, added, "Richey would fall asleep watchin' movies at killer volume. It would end, you'd think, 'Thank God, the movie's over'—but that would wake him up. He'd rewind the movie and watch it again."

Wynette "loved Westerns," said hairdresser Barbara Hutchison. "Anything to do with a cowboy she loved. John Wayne, Jimmy Stewart. *Matlock*, that was a favorite. Andy Griffith." Added Karyn Sloas, "Tammy loved Court TV, too. The Menendez brothers, JonBenet. She liked a real-life mystery more than anything. Tammy would be in heaven with all this reality television."

Tammy also had to have her tabloids. "She'd send you in to buy the *Enquirer, Star*, all of them," said Steve Hoker. "You had to buy one of each, bring the whole stack out. And she'd sit there in the middle of the bed and go through each one." Wynette confessed, "I enjoy the stupid stories—until I'm in it. Then I say, 'The nerve of them putting me in this thing!'"

Although she ate like a bird, food played a big part in her needs. "Tammy had an addictive personality," said David Sloas. "Everything that she did was to the max. Even eating was like an art to her. If something wasn't perfectly done, she would not eat it. Eating was an event. It had to be perfect."

"Tammy loved loads of sugar in her iced tea. If it was unsweetened iced tea, she'd put, like, five packages of sugar in it," said Michelle Broussard Honick. Wynette loved Twinkies, and had a special craving for fair food, the more deep-fried, the better. "If there was a corn dog within a fifty-mile radius, the woman had to have it," said Karyn Sloas, who remembered standing in line for a midway ride at some nameless state fair with tour manager Donnie Lewis when the corn dog command wafted over the Motorola. Lewis raced to the concession stand on the other side of the fairgrounds to find it closed, so he got them to open back up just for Tammy. "Poor Donnie," said Karyn. "By the time he got back, she was asleep and out of the mood."

Wynette's other weaknesses were the Cracker Barrel ("You know how crowded Cracker Barrels are?" muttered driver Bud McComb. "I had to squeeze that bus in!") and Steak n Shake chains. When Tammy lusted for a single with cheese, fries, and a shake, you had to deliver. "We've had to drive a *looong* way out of the way to go to a Steak n Shake," said Steve Chapman. "I mean fifty miles. Fifty miles! You didn't question it." Once Wynette had to have her cheeseburger after a gig in Branson, Missouri, at the end of one three-week tour as the buses were heading home. "Forty minutes south the wrong way!" Bobby Napier recalled. "And they didn't even *buy*. The guys in the band were just so livid we didn't even go in."

But was it all for Tammy? Wynette craved the corn dogs, but many felt her husband was the one demanding caviar. "Richey was really the star," insisted Steve Hoker. "By being married to Tammy, he was living a dream that he had never been able to realize. It was all about him—the jewelry, the suites, the whole deal. Makin' sure that Tammy was taken care of, that's what he always said. It was as much takin' care of himself as it was takin' care of her."

"My question is, what would've happened to George Richey if he hadn't married Tammy Wynette?" said Jerry Taylor. "I'll tell you what would've happened to George Richey—absolutely zero. He wasn't running record companies anymore and he wasn't writing songs anymore. He'd be playin' piano at a church."

A slippery character, Richey. Take the time Wynette was doing a show at the Circle Star Theater in San Carlos, California. To tell the story, Marty

Lewis (aka Mongo*) needs an introduction. A rabid Tammy fan, Lewis was homeless when Wynette and company first encountered him. "He used to eat out of Dumpsters," said Steve Hoker. "We'd go under a certain bridge down in Florida, and he'd say, 'That's my bridge! I used to live right behind there in a refrigerator box.'" Richey invited Marty onto the bus after a gig, and he soon became Tammy and George's personal gofer.

Lewis had many quizzical habits, such as spooning coffee out of the can and eating it raw. "It would be all around his lips when he woke up in the morning," said Bobby Napier, who spoke for many on the crew when he confessed Lewis "never really was much of a groomer." Lewis unnerved a few members in Tammy's entourage. "Marty was like Lurch," said Susan Nadler, Tammy's publicist in the late eighties. "I was terrified of Marty." Jan Smith's son Cannon was also spooked by Lewis. "Marty with his scary curly hair and bad teeth and crazed eyes . . . If you told me that, yes, Marty killed somebody and buried them because Tammy offhandedly said, 'I want them dead,' it wouldn't shock me in the least."

Lewis was never without his Motorola, and it was always on for the inevitable "How about you, Martha?" which meant George and Tammy had some strange task in mind, such as fetching Wynette that two a.m. Twinkie. As Steve Hoker recalled, there was another facet to Lewis's raison d'être. "Marty was the snitch—'Richey, you know what I heard today?' That was part of his job—he was the plant, and everybody knew that if you didn't want something to get back to Tammy and George, you better not let Marty find out."

Which brings us to the show in San Carlos. No live sound mixer was present, so Richey took over at the board. "George Richey is as much a sound man as a Chinese jet pilot," said David Sloas. "He had it loud." A member of the audience complained to Richey. And complained again. Said Sloas, "As I understand, there was an altercation." When it was discovered that the man intended to press charges, Richey "concocted a fairy tale to try and make him look good in the situation." Good old Marty came to the rescue, allowing himself to be roughed up enough that it looked like he had been accosted by the accuser and Richey had rushed to his defense. "I saw that," said Sloas. "Marty even scarred up his knuckles on the bend of the door

---

*For some unknown reason Richey referred to Lewis as "Martha." Curiously, years later Marty married a woman named Martha.

outside. He had blood coming out of his knuckles. You can't make this shit up, buddy! They took him to a clinic to validate it." Nothing ever came of the charges. Richey "got out of it scot-free," claimed Bobby Napier.*

Life was but a game to George Richey. "He'd just as soon beat you out of ten dollars as he would the promoter out of thirty thousand," said Charley Abdon, who recalled Richey chewing out one such promoter. "I'm thinkin', 'Richey's gonna have a heart attack, man. He's mad as he can be.' And about that time he looks over at me, grins, and winks. Richey likes seein' the horror in people's faces because he's got their head in a noose."

Richey "had a cruel and mean streak in him," said Jerry Taylor. "I've seen him put a guy off that bus, leave him out in the middle of nowhere in the middle of night, and say, 'Get home the best way you can.'" George cultivated his reputation as a thug. "Richey loved anything to do with the Mafia," said Karyn Sloas.† "We believed that he had Mafia connections—he led you to believe that he did. Richey liked the image that he was a bad guy. He'd look at me and say, 'You're scared, aren't you?'" During one dispute with Charley Abdon, Richey boasted, "I don't give a fuck about the law."

According to Karyn Sloas, Richey considered the band "a necessary evil." His affectionate nickname for them was "the maggots." Piano player Steve Samuels? "Richey referred to him as the 'token Jew,' constantly called him 'Jewboy,'" said Charley Abdon. When it came to fiddle player Wade Landry, Richey had a special term of endearment. "Because I'm a Cajun from south Louisiana, he called me his 'pet nigger.' He meant it jokingly. There were times I didn't want to hear it. His jokes were not too funny." Fiddle player Bobby Napier—who once woke up on the bus to catch a snickering Richey videotaping a close-up of his bald spot—said that George once helpfully explained to the band, "The only difference between what you guys make and what I make is a bunch of zeros."

---

*Although a well-known tale among Wynette's band members, it should be noted that Sloas was the only one I spoke to who admitted being present for the alleged Marty Lewis "rough-up." Richey didn't talk to me and I was unable to locate Lewis. Band members Bobby Napier and Rusty Pence said that Marty Lewis himself told them the story on different occasions out on the road. "I was floored," said Pence. When I asked then–tour manager John Paule to confirm the story, all he said was, "No comment." (Paule declined to participate in an actual interview.)

†Richey was also "very obsessed with Howard Hughes," noted Karyn Sloas. "He was like him in some ways. As soon as he got on the bus, the man *lived* in a bathrobe."

Richey's second-in-command when it came to the band was bassist Rick Murrell, and opinions vary wildly on the bandleader. Some say he was extremely devoted to Tammy and did an excellent job in a difficult situation, i.e., executing orders for George Richey. "Rick was the glue that held us all together," said Van Abbott. Others saw him as Richey's henchman. His nicknames among certain band members were "Company Man" and, as he never seemed to bear the wrath of Richey, the "Golden Child." "Rick Murrell really, really, really liked bein' the boss. He really, really, really liked it too much," said Bobby Napier. "He would cling onto that gig with the last cold dead fingers, and was there until the last day. But he was hangin' on for a different reason than Charlie Carter. Rick was just hangin' on for himself, what he could get out of it."

At one point Richey was planning to give Tammy's backup singers a hundred-dollar-a-day raise. A meeting was called, and the women found out their raise had gone down to half of that. "We found out Rick is the reason we didn't get the raise," said Yvonne Abdon. "Rick told Richey we didn't need to make as much as the guys did. Rick was motivated by the dollar." Sometimes Murrell's thriftiness worked against him. "Rick was a great guy, but he was the cheap cat," said Van Abbott. "Rick was always getting your french fries. He got one of Marty Lewis's donuts and said, 'Boy, Marty, those are really good. Where'd you get these?' Marty said, 'Over in that Dumpster.'"

In 1979 Tammy cajoled Jan Howard into joining her tour. "It was a very low point in my life," Howard recalled. "In fact, I was going to quit singing because I didn't have any music left in me." Wynette, who was heading out for a tour of Europe, knew that Jan was down and called her. "She said, 'I'd like to have my buddy with me. Come go with me. I get lonesome.' But Tammy was doin' it for me. She said, 'You don't have to sing.'" Within a few days Howard was singing backup for Tammy as well as doing her own numbers. "When I'd go onstage, she'd say, 'Yes, I know that's Jan Howard. She's gonna sing for you, but you're gonna have to put up with me first.' That's how gracious Tammy was. She probably saved my life."

Howard was one of the few people around Tammy who was not afraid of Richey. ("Jan and Nan would put Richey in his place, too," noted daughter Jackie.) She was in the lobby after a show one night when she saw a woman crying. When Jan asked what was wrong, she pointed to her tourbook and said she'd asked Tammy to sign it. "Richey wouldn't let her," said Howard. "Richey had told this woman, 'You paid for a ticket, not for her time or an autograph.'"

Howard took the woman's book and stormed up to Tammy's suite. "Richey answered the door. I said, 'Richey, I would like Tammy to sign this book.'"

"She's not signing anything," he said.

"Bullshit, and you're a son of a bitch," Jan told him, pushing her way past him to snag Tammy's autograph for the fan.* "Oh, he was furious. That wasn't Tammy, that was Richey. He would control her every move."

Strangely enough, Jan Howard seems to be the only one Richey went to for advice when it came to Tammy's drug addiction. "He came right to my kitchen table and asked what he could do," said Howard, adding that George was well aware that her deceased son David had been involved in drugs. "I said, 'Richey, anyone who is addicted to drugs will never admit they're addicted. They can't be helped until they *want* help.'"

Stand by Your Man, Tammy's autobiography, was published in 1979 and then turned into an Emmy-nominated TV movie in 1981. Producer Robert Papazian found Wynette delightful to deal with, once he got past George Richey, who kept referring to the project as a "feature." "I kept saying, 'This is not a feature, this is television. There is no such thing as box office gross. You get the money, go home, and cash a check—it's not going to do two hundred million like *Coal Miner's Daughter.'*" Standard TV movie fare, the film is most notable for the fact that the two leads—Annette O'Toole and Tim McIntire—did their own singing. Wynette was a little troubled by some of the liberties taken. "At one point they had George Jones's mother

---

*As Tammy's health deteriorated, getting her actual autograph was something of a rarity. According to Karyn Sloas, just about everybody on the Tammy One bus could fake Wynette's John Hancock, along with her trademark "Love Ya!" greeting. "We were *all* taught to sign her name," Sloas recalled.

"After a show Tammy would go to bed and there'd be a line from the bus all the way to the street," said Cathye Leshay, who maintained that she and hairdresser Wanda Williams would then "sign names as fast as we could go." Leshay was a little too effusive in her work. When Wynette went out to local shops, she'd see her eight-by-ten behind the counter covered in what was supposed to be her scrawl. "Tammy would get so mad at me," said Cathye, laughing. "She'd come home and say, 'Did you have to write *a book*? Just sign my name!'"

saying, 'Hell, I don't know.' I told Richey, 'Ooh! That poor Pentecostal woman! She would turn over in her grave!'"

At first the Nielsen ratings were unexceptional, but when the final tally came in, it went up ten points. "It was the highest-rated movie for that year," said Papazian. "Grassroots mid-America really supported her, as opposed to the big cities." Papazian recalled Tammy being very happy with the results, but afterward she admitted to an interviewer, "It was kind of sad they didn't get it right."

Coauthor Joan Dew got into a dispute with Richey over the autobiography revenue. Dew had written a large check for a hospital stay, which then bounced as Richey had held on to a payment that Dew thought had been deposited into her account. Joan paid a visit to Tammy's estate and found her in bed and George in the bedroom with her. "In front of Tammy, he said the reason he had held up the check—because I was spreading rumors all over Nashville that Tammy was a drug addict. That's absolutely not true. Richey said that because he could make Tammy believe that." Dew, who had been worried about Wynette, expressed her concern to a few people, including Minnie Pearl, whose autobiography she was working on. "I had talked to several people about Tammy's problem, it was not anything that was not known in Nashville.

"I said, 'George, that's a lie, you know it's a lie. I would never do that.' And he said, 'I'm sorry, but you did do that and you're not getting the money.' I said, 'You know, of course, I'm going to sue you for the money.' He said, 'Well, are you going to sue Tammy?' Tammy never said one word in this conversation."

Joan's son Cliff rose to her defense. "I went right into his office, busted right through the secretary, and I just said, 'Look, you owe my mother money, I want it right now.' He wrote me a check on the spot. Richey was a weasel, man. Just a weasel of a guy."

His mother's friendship with Tammy was all but over, however. "I did see Tammy a few more times backstage at the Opry. She was always very, very friendly, but cool friendly. Richey was always around. I never saw her again that George wasn't by her side."

In 1980 Tammy Wynette made the biggest blunder of her career: she left Billy Sherrill. None of her four solo singles from 1979 to 1980 had cracked the top five, and the last two produced by Sherrill, "He Was There (When

I Needed You)" and "Starting Over," both only hit number 17. After fourteen years with Billy, Wynette felt it was time to make a change. "We were getting stale, because we weren't looking for material as much as we had before. I was on the road too much, and he had too many other people to record."

Wynette likened the split to her least favorite subject: divorce. "I walked into his office one day and said, 'Billy, I need to talk to you, it's serious.' He looked up at me and said, 'I know a good producer.' That got to me. The tears started."

"Tammy didn't say, 'I want another producer,'" recalled Sherrill. "She'd die and go to hell before she said that to me. I just knew it. It's somethin' I really wanted to happen, because I burned out with her. I burned out with Possum, I burned out with everybody. She needed fresh blood, fresh ideas."

Not everybody was convinced by Sherrill's acceptance of the situation. As Charlene Montgomery recalled, "Billy told me one day, he said, 'I'll tell you what, there's three people I cherish as artists: Tammy Wynette, Tanya Tucker, and George Jones. It liked to have killed me when Tanya left. I don't know what it would do to me if Tammy left.' Well, Tammy did leave him. It did hurt him. Hurt him bad."

There were other factors in Wynette's exit. Those close to Sherrill feel a central one was her new husband. "I think Billy was disappointed when George Richey got too involved with her," said Sherrill's secretary Emily Mitchell. "George just had the attitude he was gonna take over Tammy. Maybe that's another reason Billy just decided to let her go. Because he didn't want to put up with the Richeys anymore." Lou Bradley also feels that Billy would've stayed with Tammy had Richey not entered the picture. "I think he knew Richey was gonna be in charge more or less at that point." The back cover of Tammy's last album with Sherrill, 1980's *Only Lonely Sometimes*, features a Norman Seeff shot of Tammy with her arm around Richey, who is wearing bib overalls and the usual assortment of flashy ice and gold, not to mention sporting an umbrella. Just one more album and George Richey would be Wynette's producer.

Wynette's success had opened the doors for plenty of competition. Throughout the seventies and eighties came a plethora of female singers: Jessi Colter, Barbara Fairchild, Jeanne Pruett, Lynn Anderson, Barbara Mandrell, Crystal Gayle, Billie Jo Spears, Margo Smith, and a host of others, not to forget the exquisite Sammi Smith, whose cigarette-stained vocal cords and worn visage suggested a dame who'd just finished washing out a pair of dimestore panties in a truck stop restroom before stepping up to the mic.*

The country music business was getting much more highfalutin'. Billy Sherrill had enjoyed an incredible run, but the inevitable downhill slide had begun. Billy's old writing partner Glenn Sutton had drifted away. He felt the problems had started back in 1971 when he cut a number one smash at Epic on his then-wife Lynn Anderson, "I Never Promised You a Rose Garden." "If you had a hit, you were gone, you were fucked," said Sutton, who maintained Sherrill didn't care for any competition at his label. "He didn't mean any harm, that was just the way he was." Glenn also felt that everybody got greedy. Vast sums of money were being made in Nashville, and it was serving to demolish creativity, not to mention long friendships. "When it got to be bread—money stuff like that, it just got to where everybody couldn't get along," said Sutton. "It pulled everybody apart."

Sherrill remained inscrutable to most. With all his success, was he a happy guy? "I'm not sure that Billy knew what he was," said bassist Bob Moore. "I think that he got to a place where he would've liked to have been happier, but he couldn't find it. Like he wanted to have the biggest boat on the lake. Then Buddy Killen bought another boat ten feet longer than his."

Country music itself was struggling to change with the times. Music City, USA, was beginning its great ascendancy into a second-rate factory for third-rate soft rock. In 1977 producer Jimmy Bowen left Los Angeles and crept into town, determined to fix "what was wrong with Nashville." In his autobiography Bowen seems to relish the pain he caused Music Row's old guard. "The great Billy Sherrill was famous for picking songs out at two o'clock for a session at four. Fine, but I couldn't work that way." A self-described "gruff Yankee" who "had never developed a taste for" country music, Bowen "was determined to shake things up." Shake things up he did. Bowen felt the A-Team players "all repeated their licks," and he brusquely instructed them how to do their parts and to "try something different." He

---

*Loretta Lynn likes to tell a funny story concerning Tammy being at an awards show next to an unnamed rising young songstress. "Why don't y'all that's been in the business a few years move over and let us new singers get in?" this young singer complained to Wynette. "Move me," said Tammy. "That's my girl," said Loretta, laughing at the memory.

told Conway Twitty, "What you're doin' is old." He found the state of such legendary rooms as RCA's Studio B "awful and antiquated."

Bowen declared that "Nashville was stuck in a technology time warp a full decade behind New York and L.A." He was determined to cut one or two songs instead of four in three hours of studio time and "make use of all the gadgetry." Bowen told one engineer, "You dumb-ass hillbilly, get the drums out in the studio, where they can breathe." He was pushing the town into an era where the track was as important as the song, heresy to somebody like Billy Sherrill. And while Bowen insinuated that the Nashville pickers were past their prime, all he did was replace their sound with the kind of expensive rock wallpaper that was churned out on a daily basis in Los Angeles and New York. "I put fifteen mics on one set of drums, and people again thought I was crazy," he boasted. Sherrill certainly found such activity to be overkill. "There's no reason to take an hour to get drum sounds," he told Dan Daley. "It's like killing a fly with a sledgehammer."

Any spontaneity was a thing of the past. Hours were spent doing take after take after take on vocals. Rhythm tracks were subject to microscopic scrutiny. Replacing the intimate down-home studios like Pete Drake's, where, as guitarist Bill Hullett put it, "you could literally look right into the eyes of the guy playin' steel," came an era where "everybody started buildin' the big multimillion-dollar rooms where you'd be thirty-five feet from the next guy. You couldn't hardly even see his facial expression, much less what he's playin'."

Before Bowen, a Mel Tillis album had cost $15,000 and sold forty thousand copies. The first Bowen-Tillis production cost $36,000—and sold three and a half times what his previous album did. Not good enough for Bowen: "Anything under five hundred thousand is bullshit," he told Mel. "If you spent more money, you made better music, sold more albums, and made more money." Old-guard producers like Jerry Kennedy were turned off by such excess. "Right before I quit doin' it they were askin' me to spend $150,000 on an album, and I couldn't find a way to do it. At that time producers would look bad if we turned in an album for sixty or seventy grand."

Bowen had phenomenal success with artists like George Strait and Hank Williams, Jr. He paved the way for the Nashville megastars of the nineties like Garth Brooks (himself a "secret" rocker; check out his work under the alias Chris Gaines, the most ludicrous alter ego since Thumper Jones) and cyborg chanteuse Shania Twain. The reference point for such characters was rock, despite whatever old-school allegiances they might have given lip service. Sherrill engineer Ron "Snake" Reynolds, who worked on Twain's sessions, witnessed the recording process taken to ridiculous extremes. "We would start in the morning," Reynolds recalled. "By one o'clock we had the intro worked out. Usually by seven at night we'd have the basic track for one song done. We cut ten songs in ten days."

As they were making double and triple scale, session players were certainly fat and happy. But unlike Sherrill's sessions, nobody said it was fun. "It's almost slow-motion madness because it just takes *so long*," said Bill Hullett. "You run it down and people want to *talk* about it and the producer wants to talk about it and the artist puts in his two cents and they *change* it and you're thinkin', 'We're beatin' this stinkin' thing to *death*. It was a hit thirty minutes ago and now it's dyin'.'"

Of course, to bemoan such developments is pointless—time marches on, and nothing lasts forever, not even country music. Nashville had been slobbering for the pop/rock money for decades. "We were always thinking of how to get our records to a broader audience," said producer Owen Bradley in 1994, admitting that Patsy Cline's string-laden "Crazy" was a response to New York executives angling for maximum pop appeal. This is the American way: one man's hamburger stand becomes tomorrow's McDonald's. Nashville is no exception to capitalist rule. But for fans of handmade country ballads that eschewed perfection to preserve emotion, the writing was on the wall. Wynette's last album with Sherrill ended with "Ozark Mountain Lullaby," a lilting bluegrass-tinged number that left one wishing that she'd cut albums of the stuff. It was a beautiful way to say good-bye. Before Tammy left Billy, though, came one last album of duets and a tumultuous tour with her ex, George Jones.

George Jones had spent most of the last five years hiding out in Florence, Alabama, where he was slowly unraveling. Instinctively Jones understood exactly what was required of a tragic country star, and he viewed the collapse of his marriage to Tammy as an occupational hazard. "You hear a lot about country artists getting divorced," he said in 1977. "They gotta stay sad. They get married and they get happy and they can't sing. After three or four bad records they've got to do something about it."

Jones was staying sad, and with the help of Billy Sherrill, making some of the greatest music of his life, including such devastating numbers as "I Just Don't Give a Damn" and "Hit and Run."* In 1976 he recorded one of his best albums, the exquisitely morose *Alone Again*. Sherrill pulled forth a quieter, more mature Jones, deep and dark as molasses, showcasing a voice that, after a few songs, could put you in that place where one walks out the door and leaves no forwarding address. It is the kind of melancholy you can wallow—no, *drown*—in.

Unfortunately Jones had also discovered cocaine. His then-manager Alcy Benjamin "Shug" Baggot boasted to George's friends that a surefire antidote to getting a drunken George Jones to perform onstage was a Jones with a snoutful of toot. The Possum's manager was also his dealer, leaving him not only crazy but broke. Baggot would eventually do three years in the pen for selling two pounds of coke to undercover cops. (These days he's a preacher.) George was far from being the only artist snorting his career away in Nashville at the time. The drug "ruined a lot of voices," said Billy Sherrill, who grew to recognize that "high, wispy cocaine sound."

"With alcohol, we knew how to handle George—pamper him, keep him under control," said Peanutt Montgomery. "But, buddy, once he got on cocaine, he was paranoid, he was vicious. George became ugly." Jones got weirder and weirder, developing a pair of rather unusual alter egos. First came the duck. The duck initially appeared on the scene when his then-girlfriend Linda Welborn refused to bicker with him.

"If he wanted to argue, he wanted to argue," said Welborn. "He'd set in the living room and say, 'Daffy, she's mad at us, she's not gonna talk to us. Waddya think about that?' Then he would talk in Daffy's voice—'Ask Donald what *he* thinks about it.' He'd carry on a conversation for hours like they were there. It used to drive me up the wall, settin' here listenin' to one person supposed to be three people, talkin' about me! I'd just look at him and shake my head, but that didn't bother George. He just kept right on talkin'."

George's web-footed alter egos eventually coalesced into DeDoodle the Duck. And to keep DeDoodle company was a grouchy Walter Brennan–style codger simply called "the Old Man." When George morphed into the Old Man, George "got crazy, he got scary," said Peanutt, shaking his head.

---

*On the sly from Epic, Jones would also cut two as-yet-unreleased albums with Peanutt Montgomery producing: a fantastic set with Roy Acuff and his band, plus a collection of Little Richard covers recorded in Muscle Shoals.

"The Old Man almost caused me a wreck." Jones went on Ralph Emery's radio show one day and, with the world listening, broke into both De-Doodle and the Old Man. Funny, but not to those around Jones, who shudder at the memory. "I hate that duck," said wife Nancy. "I hate that old man, too."

Lou Bradley recalled what a trial it was attempting to record Jones during this period. "When he was on the cocaine, he'd come at ten o'clock in the mornin', try to sing a couple of lines, and start singin' like Donald Duck. We'd just quit and go home."

Jones had big plans for DeDoodle. "He wanted to do a whole album as the duck," said Ron Reynolds. "Jones was serious, man—*he wanted to do an album singin' like the duck.* He could really do that duck thing well." (Sherrill disagreed. "He wasn't even a real duck. I know a lot of guys who can do duck better than Jones.") There was no telling where old George might quack next. Jerry Carrigan was doing a session for Kenny Rogers when an emaciated Jones stumbled in. "George was about as big around as a pencil. He was supposed to do a guest appearance and he came in there, got on the microphone, and sang like a duck!"

Jones even performed live shows as DeDoodle. One day while out on the road, a deranged George showed up at the doorstep of his old Florida friends Cliff and Maxine Hyder. "We didn't even go to the show in Orlando because we heard he sang like Donald Duck," Maxine recalled. "George was always neat as a pin—everything had to match and be perfect." Not today. "He had on a shirt, it was buttoned wrong. Hair hadn't been combed. He was in bad, bad shape."

Under a full head of snow, the rapid-fire gibber-jabber flying out of George's mouth became completely incomprehensible. "I couldn't talk to him," said Maxine. "I sat down on the floor and I said, 'Y'know, we didn't go to your show, and I want to find if you done what I heard you done.' I said, 'Shake your head yes or shake your head no, because I can't understand you.'"

Maxine asked George, "Did you do your regular show?"

Jones shook his head no.

"Did you sing like Donald Duck?" inquired Maxine.

George smiled and enthusiastically nodded.

Maxine said, "Cliff didn't want to go and see you get onstage and make a fool out of yourself. He would cry."

Jones lost it. "George set his head down and just cried like a baby. Cliff asked me if I would get the camera and take a picture. He figured we would never see George alive again."

George Jones was losing his mind. "You saw things that weren't there," he told Nicholas Dawidoff. "People in Halloween costumes." Everywhere George turned gremlins lurked. "I got to where I saw ghosts, saw things all the time. It just seems like you was in a big, long movie, one that just never did end. The damn ending never come."

"He'd think there were people on the curtains," said Linda Welborn. "He'd want me to take the curtains down. He'd say there were people standin' there laughin' at him. Once he come flyin' in like he was just scared to death—'Monsters all over the top of my car! They got on the hood, they was beatin' on the windows! They're tryin' to get me! Lock the doors, lock the doors! Hurry, hurry!'" Linda had to stand at the window and convince Jones that there were no creatures outside waiting to get him.

Guns entered the picture. "George had the demonic spirit," said Montgomery. "I think he was possessed, I really do." Jones was furious that Peanutt had found the Lord and quit drinking.* "He became jealous of Jesus," said Montgomery. George taunted Peanutt. He'd come by and leave booze and cigarettes on Montgomery's doorstep, hoping to lure him back into the fold. Things came to a head on September 13, 1977. Mad at Peanutt over a financial matter, Jones had put word out that his old pal's days were numbered. Montgomery called him, and they agreed to face off at George's favorite little spot, under the bridge on the muddy west bank of the Cypress Creek River. ("He'd set down there, have him a drink," noted Montgomery.) It was an hour past midnight, and Peanutt didn't know what he was in for. "I was very messed up in my mind," said Jones. "I was boiling over ... Peanutt just picked the wrong night to call me."

Montgomery spotted George's tan Town Car sitting there in the dark by the river's edge and pulled his silver Trans Am in beside it. The two men got into it over religion. Montgomery told Jones he'd go to hell for his wicked

---

*Nashville wasn't exactly cheering Peanutt on, either. One day when Jones was cutting a gospel number Montgomery had written, Sherrill "took me into the control room and said, 'Peanutt, why don't you write some good country songs—why write this s-h-i-t?' Somethin' came over me—I thought, 'I don't have to put up with this, bein' humiliated by people over religion.' So I came home and wouldn't go back."

ways. "I was witnessin' to him. He called me 'Little Jesus'—I had a beard, y'know." Montgomery's proselytizing sent George over the edge. He whipped out a .38 Smith & Wesson and, before pulling the trigger, bellowed, "I'm gonna see if your God can save you now, you son of a bitch!" Luckily the bullet lodged in the car door and not inside Peanutt. "I wasn't scared 'til after it was over. He could've shot me in the head." Jones insisted he only fired over the roof of Peanutt's car, although that didn't explain the bullet hole just below the driver's side window. ("*Supposed* hole," declared George in his book, who to this day refuses to acknowledge the evidence.)

Peanutt happened to be armed as well. "I just set there a minute, started to reach for the gun, and somethin' just said, 'Don't do that.' Legally I could've shot the man and killed him." Montgomery sped off into the night, and Jones was later charged with assault and attempted murder. "My friend was a DA—he told me, 'I'll send him off for fifteen years.' I said, 'Scare him, but don't do that.'" (The charges were later dropped.)

One way or another the Man Upstairs always managed to torment George. "He was layin' in bed one night," recalled Welborn. "We were talkin', watchin' TV, and he was cryin'. I said, 'What's wrong, George, why are you cryin'?'" He said, 'Y'know, Linda, I'd love to be a preacher.' He was serious as he could be." When Welborn encouraged the idea, Jones grew sullen. "Are you kiddin' me? People would laugh at me tryin' to preach."

One day Jones had tossed a Bible out into the yard. Apparently still smoldering, George now pointed his .38 at Linda. "He took the gun and he put it right at my head."

"Tell me you don't believe in God," demanded Jones.

"George, why are you doin' this?" responded Welborn, who refused to comply.

"*Tell me* you don't believe in *fuckin'* God!" George snarled.

Linda asked if she could say something before he fired. "He still had the gun right there, settin' on my forehead.

"I said, 'If you shoot me just 'cause I won't tell you I don't believe in God, I will go to heaven—and you will die and go to hell for it. So if you're gonna do it, go ahead and get it over with.' And I didn't take my eyes off of him. When he was in that kind of state of mind, you couldn't let him know that you was afraid. It would only make him worse. I just took one little step forward and braced myself, because I thought, as messed up and upset as he was, he might do it."

Things took a comical turn when Jones suddenly decided he was having a heart attack. "All of a sudden he grabbed his heart and fell to the floor," said Welborn. "He was hollerin', 'Oh, oh, oh'—just a-groanin'. And I knew he was fakin', I could tell. I used to be a nurse myself. So I got the gun and put it on top of the refrigerator." Linda then grabbed the phone and pretended to call 911. ("Oh, Lord, if you put this in the book, George is gonna know what I done," she interjected.)

Jones immediately recovered. "He come off that floor real quick. He didn't want no ambulance comin' and getting him." "What the hell are you doin'?!" barked George. "Put the damn phone down!"

Jones. A one-way ticket on the highway to hell.

"I think he contemplated commitin' suicide many times," said Peanutt, who ran into Jones in Nashville and was shocked at the sight of him. George looked like death on a hot plate. He weighed less than a hundred pounds and, according to one friend, had creases so deep in his cheeks "you could've set quarters in 'em." He and Peanutt went to grab a bite. "He got down on the table, he was eatin' food like a dog." (According to George's own book, doctors would later place his IQ during his drugged-out days at seventy-four.)

Montgomery couldn't stand to see Jones this way. "I just went down to a judge, I told him, 'George is a danger to himself and other people.' They committed him." In mid-December 1979, Jones was put in Hillcrest, a private rehab hospital in Birmingham, Alabama. Which is where Tammy Wynette enters the picture once more.

All this time Tammy had been on George's mind. "For months I had no longer been able to lie to myself about Tammy and me someday, somehow getting back together," wrote Jones. He was about to be reunited with her, but for purposes of money, not love.

Peanutt had attempted to get in touch with Wynette, but, like the rest of the world, could only reach a Richey. "Tammy had told me, 'If George ever needs help, Peanutt, don't you hesitate to call me. I'll always help him.' I called and I couldn't get Tammy. I got Paul." Paul was a sometime singer, songwriter, and, in the words of writer Bob Allen, "a purported born-again Christian." After a quick exit from Hillcrest in January 1980, it was announced that Paul Richey would now manage George Jones under the leadership of his brother. George and Paul Richey "were thick as thieves," said Larry Fullam, then a member of the Jones Boys.

Secretary Michelle Broussard Honick felt that the Richeys treated Jones poorly. "George would come to our offices. He was very nice, wasn't egocentric, didn't want anybody waitin' on him. He would sit and sing to me. They would always keep him waiting—not Tammy, but Paul and George. It was a power trip—'One of the greatest singers in the world is here, so let's make him wait and show him we're more important than he is.'"

Cliff and Maxine Hyder had visited Jones in Hillcrest. "George had lost a lot of weight, didn't seem like his normal self," recalled Maxine. "He said, 'They're gonna let me out tomorrow. I'm gonna go do a show with Tammy.'" The Hyders were shocked. "They shouldn't have let him out," said Maxine. The Richeys had already lined up a reunion album and tour for George and Tammy. Jones had his own way of preparing—he went right back to booze and coke.

In the midst of this chaos, on February 6, 1980, Jones would record the final vocal for what would become his anthem, "He Stopped Loving Her Today," a Sherrill production masterpiece. Maybe the ultimate country ballad of tragic love, the song was written (and at Billy's insistence, rewritten) by ace songwriters Bobby Braddock and Curly Putman.* The track had been kicking around for a year, but George couldn't get the melody right; he kept singing it to the tune of "Help Me Make It Through the Night." (Glad that Jones had finally stopped quacking and started singing, Lou Bradley told Billy Sherrill he was glad to have George back. "Ninety percent, but I'll take it," responded Sherrill.) Tammy had lucked into her theme song after just a couple of years in the business. George's came well over two decades into his career. While Nashville had been busy preparing his obituary, the Possum had triumphed again. The irony wasn't lost on him.

"The more anguish I went through in my personal life, the more my career flourished."

---

*Over the years Braddock has told a story relayed to him by songwriter L. E. White, who claimed to be at the sessions for "He Stopped Loving Her Today." White told Braddock that Wynette and Richey dropped by the studio the day he cut the song, and as Jones sang the lyric, he was looking right at Tammy. Hell of a tale, but apparently untrue. Neither Richey, Sherrill, nor engineer Lou Bradley can recall Tammy being present. "When he finally sang the song, it was me and him in the studio—he was singin' to a track," recalled Sherrill. "He might've been lookin' at me—maybe he was in love with me."

———

Reuniting Wynette and Jones for any purpose wasn't the easiest affair. Linda Welborn loved to hear George and Tammy sing together, and, during a duet performance at the Opry, she clapped along a little too loudly, which irked Jones. Said Linda, "I know why you're mad at me—because I enjoyed you and Tammy's singin'."

"Yeah, why do you? Why do you take up for her?" George asked.

Said Linda, "I don't take up for her, George. The woman's never done nothin' to me. Why should I dislike her?"

Now Jones was on a mission. "Well, you think she's so good, you think she's so sweet—I'm gonna show you what she's like!" George instructed Linda to pick up the receiver in the other room while he called Wynette.

"He calls her, and started out talkin' nice. Then he got a little rougher, and started callin' her every name in the book. Tammy says, 'George, you know I didn't run around on you, I didn't cheat on you. You know that's not so.' But he just kept on and on and on. He made her mad—that's what he wanted to do. And all of a sudden she fired up, and, buddy, she came down on him! I just hung the phone up. And after I hung up, he hung up.

"He said, 'Now what do you think of Tammy?' I said, 'My goodness, George, you was callin' her everything in the book.' And he jumped up and said, 'I shoulda *known* you'd take up for her!'"

While Richey's marriage to Tammy had thrown a wrench into Jones's communication with his ex, he didn't help matters by not paying child support for Georgette—or at the very least not making sure it actually got to her. According to Linda Welborn, "what happened was that George owed some back child support, it was forty thousand dollars. So George paid Shug the money." Linda told Jones to get a receipt from Baggot. "He said, 'Linda, I don't need no receipt.'" Somehow the money never went to Tammy, and a few years later she took George to court.

When Jones called Tammy to check up on Georgette, Richey told him not to call anymore. Jones said he just wanted to speak to his daughter. "He said, 'Yeah, that's another thing—we want you to stay away from her, too,'" Jones told Bob Allen. "I said, 'I'll die and go to hell!' And I hung up the phone . . . Just because he marries my ex-wife, he hates me." Then Tammy called George and gave him an ultimatum: either pay the forty G or let Richey adopt Georgette. "Boy, George came unglued," said Welborn. "It devastated him. Oh, he could not believe that they even asked the question. Because George does love his children." Jones wound up paying Tammy another forty grand.

Don't ask me why, but this George and Tammy exchange from a press release for some grand eighties event called "Jamboree, USA" rather poetically conveys the feeling still left between them:

"You like my fingernails, George? They're gold. They're just glued on, though, with Krazy Glue."

"You still play the guitar?"

"Of course I do, silly."

Old-school country music loves a song in which mundane inanimate objects are central to the story (or even *tell* the story—ever heard "The Carpet on the Floor" by Stonewall Jackson?). "Two Story House," George and Tammy's 1980 single, was firmly rooted in that daffy tradition. "An interrogation of the trash piled high around the house, the beer joint, and the mind," wrote Aaron A. Fox. "Moments of verbal poesis become the virtual walls and ceilings of the collapsing structure of a 'Two Story House.'"

The song has an interesting history. Tammy claimed the day before the session that all she had of the song was the his-and-her couplet of the chorus—"I've got my story / I've got mine, too." "The title had come from two guys. They got credit for the song, even though I wrote it," she maintained and said she got Richey on the piano at two o'clock in the morning to finish the lyric. "I knew exactly what I wanted," said Wynette, who saw the song as the story of George and Tammy. "We climbed to the top, but we couldn't make it, because success really destroyed us."

But the "two guys" Wynette credited only with the title have their story, too. Dave Lindsey and Glenn Tubb first pitched the song for George and Tammy in 1977. "They told us they intended to record it and make it the follow-up release to 'Southern California.'" Nothing came of it, and then three years later they got a call from their publisher. George and Tammy wanted to release it as the first single of their reunion. However, the lyric had been reworked, and if Tubb and Lindsey accepted the new version, the writer's credit would be split, according to Lindsey, "to give 25 percent credit to each of us—Jones, Wynette, Tubb, and myself. We accepted the deal, and three days later the song was on the radio, but with Tammy credited with

50 percent, Glenn and me 25 percent each, and Jones nothing." (Somehow Richey's publishing company had the lion's share of the songs on the reunion album—Tammy cowrote the single plus another song; Paul Richey contributed another; and three others were written by members of Nightstreets, a group the Richeys managed and published.)

"Two Story House" hit number 2, Wynette's last top five country hit ever. Meanwhile, "He Stopped Loving Her Today" shot to number one. (Two other singles from the same album, *I Am What I Am*, "If Drinkin' Don't Kill Me [Her Memory Will]" and the magnificent "I'm Not Ready Yet," also made the top five.) Jones, who had spent the recent past seeing nonexistent poltergeists, quacking incessantly, and living out of a beat-up car, was hot once more. "George was getting big, big money—ten thousand dollars a day," said band member Larry Fullam. But that didn't prevent him from skipping out on "probably half the shows. He was still in love with Tammy, didn't want to be around her, and he didn't like George Richey at all."

At the time, being a Jones Boy could seem akin to doing a tour of military duty.

Larry Fullam recalled a date in Pennsylvania where George was tinkering with his reel-to-reel recorder and "wouldn't come off the bus." The audience began to riot. "They were throwin' bottles, and there were a bunch of deputies tryin' to restore order." The steel player was packing up his instrument when a glass hit the wall behind him, lodging a shard of glass in his hand. He retreated to the bus bleeding. "Paul Richey was ready to quit that night and was bitching about George," said Fullam. Little did Paul know that the Possum was behind the bunkhead door listening to every word. Jones threw the door open, and, wearing only "a pair of bikini underwear with his little tummy hangin' over, he said, 'I'll tell you sumbitches one thing: Jesus never walked on ropes of twine!' And with that Jones turned and walked to the back of bus."

The George and Tammy footage from this period is a thrill to watch. Wynette's fashions in the early eighties ignored taste completely, and she was in the middle of one of her more garish looks, the Jazzercise cowgirl—Farrah Fawcett helmet-hair wig, ornately plumed cowboy hat, a fringe-laden top, and neon red spandex tucked into big white boots. Jones, who appears absolutely unhinged in this period, barrels through their songs like an uncoupled caboose picking up speed, going downhill fast but enjoying the ride. During their UK appearance at Wembley Stadium, you can feel the tension onstage as all eyes are on a wobbly, vibrating Possum, wondering what he'll do next, and his duets with Tammy threaten to collapse into utter chaos at any moment. The sadder the song, the more upbeat he seems. Determined to unsettle Wynette, Jones inquires about her love life: "You happy, Tammy?" Yes, she responds, then asks him the same. George shakes his head no, grinning at the same time. He is in his element here, and he knows the best way to get to his ex is by doing what he does best: open his mouth and sing. Top that, George Richey!

Best of all is George's 1981 HBO special, which absolutely wallows in Jones-Wynette mythology. Tammy comes out and talks about the birth of Georgette and the plaque Jones had made for the bedroom. She sits there silently morose in the background as George sings "He Stopped Loving Her Today." If that wasn't grim enough, Tammy belts out "'Til I Can Make It on My Own" as Jones watches from the wings. Even little Tamala Georgette gets in the act, coming out to join Daddy for the tear-jerking "Daddy, Come Home."

Jones and Wynette fly through "Golden Ring" as if it were a magic carpet ride, albeit an unwieldy one. I could listen to George and Tammy sing this song forever. Since they had long split up, the song had only grown more cosmic, and maybe it's not exactly wisdom we're hearing, but bloody, hard-won experience. The battle long over, here they stand, united again to spill their guts in song. "Golden Ring" evokes something so timeless and deep about the male-female union: the beauty and the tragedy, not to mention the folly.

At the end of the George and Tammy tour, Jones complained he had only $237 in his bank account. "They lied again and stuck the money in their pockets," he said of his management. George admitted to a local TV reporter he was "scared to death of 'em. . . . They're stealing my money. They came to my house twice and beat up on me." The Richeys refused comment at the time, but at least one band member thinks it's possible. "One time in Knoxville Jones had a white shirt on," said Larry Fullam. "He had bruises on his back—you could see through the shirt where they just beat the hell out of him. George Richey said, 'That's the only thing he understands, treating him like a dog.'"

But Jones knew how to exact a little revenge. At a show in upstate New York he decided he was too drunk to go on. George was cajoled into performing and told he had to open the show. (In those days the "girl singer" always went on first.) He was also informed that Tammy had a rented plane waiting for her after the gig and he wasn't to let his set go over forty-five minutes. "I didn't like the idea of opening for my ex-wife. I went onstage and sang every song I could remember." Two and a half hours later, Richey, going berserk at the side of the stage, unplugged George. Undaunted, Jones continued with his acoustic guitar. When Tammy finally took to the stage, Jones happily reported, "She spent a lot of her slot bitching about me."

That was the end for George and Tammy for this round. They would not do another album or tour together until the mid-nineties.

The first post-Sherrill Tammy solo album was 1981's *You Brought Me Back.* It was produced by Chips Moman, a Memphian who'd started his career at Stax recording such soulful numbers as William Bell's "You Don't Miss Your Water" and, with Billy Sherrill's old bandmate Dan Penn, cowriting such soul standards as "Dark End of the Street" and "Do Right Woman." His lush, layered productions were hits for Elvis Presley, Willie Nelson, and Waylon Jennings, for whom he'd written "Luckenbach, Texas." To varying degrees these artists lent themselves to a more pop approach. Tammy did not.

The first single off the album was the hopeless "Cowboys Don't Shoot Straight (Like They Used To)": "They'll look you in the eye and lie with their white hats on . . . It's 'wham, bam, thank you, ma'am' and they're gone." The leaden *Urban Cowboy* lyrics are welded to a pointlessly ornate guitar solo (wasn't Wynette supposed to be the one to "wail" here?), heralding her downward slide into eighties country Muzak. This was one of those numbers Wynette would defend as "cute." Oh, Tammy. (The song was cowritten by Moman, as were three others on the album.) Somewhat easier to digest was "Crying in the Rain," previously a number 6 pop hit for the Everly Brothers, which Wynette puts her heart into despite an overblown track that threatens to topple onto her. Undoubtedly an expensive record to make, neither of *You Brought Me Back*'s singles cracked the top ten.

Toni Wine, married to Moman at the time, sang backup on the record, and she recalled Wynette's excitement over being "given the opportunity to try something new." After it was over, however, Tammy was uncharacteristically critical of her own album. "I think Chips saw me as being more pop than I am. I'm not pop, I'm country. And I think I held back a little bit."

At a loss for what direction to take next, Wynette pouted. She told Jack Hurst in 1982 that Richey had informed her, "I've made up my mind—*I'm* gonna do your next album. If anybody knows you it's me." Tammy claimed she'd been after him to do just that for the past five years. "For a long time he said, 'No, that's what Nashville expects me to do—marry you and step into Billy Sherrill's place.'"

Unfortunately George Richey was no Billy Sherrill.* Ron "Snake" Reynolds, who engineered for both men, described the Richey sessions as "pretty bland. Not a whole lot of gunfire goin' on." Richey would produce Wynette's next three albums—*Soft Touch* and *Good Love & Heartbreak* (both 1982) and the following year's *Even the Strong Get Lonely*—and they are the dullest of Tammy's career. At least one person agreed with me—Tammy's mother, Mildred. As Wynette's childhood pal Linda Cayson recalled, "Mildred told me one time the reason Wynette didn't have any hit songs in those few years is because Richey was producin' 'em—and that nobody in Nashville had any kind of respect for him."

Only one Richey single made the top ten—1982's painfully jaunty "Another Chance." The best single from this period, Bobby Braddock and John Prine's "Unwed Fathers" didn't even crack the Top 40, perhaps because of the unsparing lyric: "Unwed fathers can't be bothered / They'll run like water through a mountain stream." Jerry Crutchfield produced her next single, another forgettable up-tempo number called "Lonely Heart," but it only made number 40, and the album's worth of material he cut went unreleased. Post-Sherrill Tammy reminds me of one of those little birds with a bum wing you come across in the city sometimes. You want them to soar, yet they barely manage to teeter over the traffic before crashing into the sidewalk—or in Wynette's case, the musical mediocrity that surrounded her.

Wynette's career was adrift. Unlike, say, George Jones, Wynette had crossed over into the mainstream and achieved that peculiar station of celebrity where one is famous for being famous. Her souvenir tourbooks were now lined with snapshots of Tammy with such luminaries as Engelbert Humperdinck, Norm Crosby, Evel Knievel, Charles Nelson Reilly ("my buddy"), O. J. Simpson, Jim Nabors ("a wonderful friend"), Tom Jones, Ethel

---

*Apparently Richey had quite the Billy Sherrill fixation. After Sherrill had open-heart surgery, so did Richey, leading Billy to send him a get-well card that said inside, "All these years, George, you've been trying to be exactly like me, but this is ridiculous."

Merman, and Wayne Newton (with whom she'd record an almost bearable duet in 1989, the oddly understated "While the Feeling's Good"). She traded recipes on a cooking show hosted by Florence Henderson. Wynette even cut a version of "Stand by Your Man" with the Chipmunks. Richey still squeezed all takers for the big bucks when it came to her live performances, but Tammy was in the unfortunate position of being a legend with no hits.

Wynette turned to Tinseltown big shots for help. Manager Stan Moress, then of the Los Angeles–based Scotti Brothers, had engineered the careers of Leif Garrett, Susan Anton, Gloria Estefan, and Eddie Rabbitt. Moress, said then–Columbia executive Mike Martinovich, was the one responsible for transforming Wynette "from the Tammy of old to the more classy, sophisticated Tammy." He was hired in April 1983 for 10 percent of Wynette's gross. "She was an unusual lady," said Moress. "Tammy never had an air about her. She was never antagonistic, never mean-spirited. She always took people for what they said they were."

Richey, in the midst of his heart trouble, agreed to step aside—at least initially. Moress went to work, making drastic changes. "There are certain artists you work with that you have a vision about, and I had a vision about Tammy. The first thing I thought she should do was cut her hair." Tammy Wynette without big hair? The idea seemed sacrilegious, even to the wearer of the wigs. Moress suggested Wynette "do like Barbara Mandrell and do a reverse frosting," she said at the time. "I was petrified. I cried for weeks that I didn't want to be a brunette. Being a hairdresser I have seen some reverse frostings that didn't work out and I didn't want to be one of those casualties." When Moress finally put the hairdresser on a plane to Florida, "Tammy called me in tears—'Is it too late? Has he left? I can't do it, I can't do it!'" Luckily she loved the new do.

Designer Jef Billings, now famous for outfitting figure skaters Kristi Yamaguchi and Nancy Kerrigan, was called in for wardrobe. Exit the homespun dresses and wacky hats. "They said to me, 'We want to make her look hip,'" Jef recalled. "Tammy had a pretty big bustline, and no one had ever figured out how to dress it without making her look dowdy and sort of frumpy."

Billings flew to New York to meet with Wynette at the Plaza Hotel, and the pair hit it off immediately. While he was checking out a display case in the hotel lobby, he casually said, "'Oh, wow, that looks like the necklace that

Felicia wears on *Another World*.' Tammy said, 'You watch *Another World*?' At which point we went up into her room, watched *Another World*, and talked about *Another World* for three hours." ("Felicia was Tammy's favorite. She loved Felicia's flamboyance—feather boas, padded shoulders, and beaded gowns. She was the hostess with the mostess, like Auntie Mame.")

During the visit Billings showed Tammy five sketches he'd done for potential stage wear. "She looked at them and said, 'I want 'em all.'" Jef was infamous for, as Martinovich put it, "thirty-pound dresses" of intricate bead-work that showed off Tammy's knockout figure, including her great set of gams.

When it came to designing for Tammy, "the catchphrases were 'classy' and 'elegant,'" said Billings, but her husband's sartorial splendor inevitably clashed with Wynette's newfound sophistication. "George could always play golf in whatever he was wearing and not look out of place. I would show up when Richey was conducting, and he would be wearing a short-sleeved lace tuxedo jacket. I'm serious—a short-sleeved lace-up Beatle jacket. Who could even *invent* that? Apparently it was short-sleeved to conduct. But then you can't explain the lace. And I think he had them *in different colors.* He didn't have the best taste in the world. White patent leather shoes, I think, says it all."

Like so many others, Jef found Tammy to be unpretentious and open. If she had some new plastic surgery, "she couldn't wait to show me." Richey was balding in the back, and when he got back from "having his scalp made smaller," Wynette was all excited. "She said, 'Look what Richey did!' I know Tammy was payin' for that."

Ace photographer Harry Langdon was brought in to shoot Tammy's next album cover and publicity shots. "They were coming to me to get a kind of a glamour superstar look—bigger-than-life Hollywood glamour," said Langdon, who would photograph Tammy until her death.

The final piece of the revamp was perhaps the most extreme. Hollywood choreographer Kevin Carlisle, who'd worked with Barry Manilow, Debbie Reynolds, Rich Little, and Jerry Lewis as well as creating the infamous *Solid Gold* dancers, was brought in to overhaul Tammy's show and teach her some fancy footwork. Injecting a little *Solid Gold* pizzazz into Tammy and the Wynettetones was a daunting challenge, but Carlisle was used to such a reaction in Nashville. "When they were told I was coming to work with them, they all just panicked that I was going to try to turn them into Liberace." (Kevin knew he'd broken the ice with the male country acts when they gave him a cowboy hat. "I have a collection," he noted.)

Carlisle was "the one who got Tammy to move," said Charley Abdon. "Before, she'd just stand there in one spot. It was Charlie Carter who said, 'Tammy's got the rhythm of a dishrag.'" For six weeks they rehearsed the new show. "It felt like forever—'No, Tammy, do this. Move that, Tammy,'" Abdon recalled. Tammy loved to kick off her shoes and do the set in her bare feet. No more. This was serious, Las Vegas–style show business, and Carlisle was an intense taskmaster. "Kevin kept telling me a song was like a play—you had to act it out," said Tammy. Standing "about a foot in front of me," Carlisle would have her sing. "He watches how I say things and how I feel them. Now that's tough."

The rest of the band "got all new clothes," said Sloas. "Brand-new professional hillbilly outfits—grays, wools, vests. For once it didn't look like Porter Wagoner threw up on 'em." Funnily enough, the one person to voice criticism of the new show was the terminally easygoing Charlie Carter. He thought (quite rightly) that Wynette was watering down her set, covering songs that belonged to other artists, like Dolly's "Nine to Five." When Carter voiced his opinions he was told to butt out. He'd never speak up again.

The show debuted at Harrah's in Atlantic City in May 1984. Wynette "was definitely nervous," noted Sloas. "There was a lot of money ridin' on it." Tammy pulled it off, and Kevin Carlisle loved her for it. He also detected a certain melancholy, seeing similarities between her often tragic past and that of another artist he'd worked with—Judy Garland. "There was tragedies in their lives that they could not divest themselves of. It was there and it wasn't something they were ever free of." Jef Billings noted that it was a "very rare occasion when Tammy wasn't in some kind of excruciating pain." Wynette sang a rousing version of "Climb Ev'ry Mountain" during the 1984 Olympics. Although you'd never know it from looking at the performance, Tammy was "doubled over as we were walking her to the stage. We had to practically carry her on."

Those around Tammy felt it was inevitable that Richey would come to consider Stan Moress a threat. "Stan was wonderful," said Jan Smith. "Stan Moress would've had Tammy in bigger, better, greater venues, but George Richey got jealous and fired Stan. He couldn't stand not to be in control, plus he didn't like payin' Stan money." Moress would end up leaving

Tammy in 1985 and filed suit over $192,000 left unpaid on the management contract. "I had my issues with George—and they weren't all pleasant—but it was made up for by her," said Moress. "I could put up with him because Tammy made it worthwhile. She made everything worthwhile."

Sometimes When We Touch was the album that introduced the new Tammy to the world in 1985. There she was on the cover in all her reverse-frosted glory, wearing an off-the-shoulder cable-knit white angora sweater, photographed against a fuchsia pink background and looking every bit the eighties diva. "Keeping up with the musical times while still being true to my musical roots is an exciting challenge," wrote Wynette on the back cover. Translation: The title single is a little pop, I hope you can live with it.

For that single Tammy had a new duet partner. Wynette had wanted to cut an album with Merle Haggard—they'd toured together, and Tammy would join him onstage to belt out "Today I Started Lovin' You Again." "Merle Haggard is my hero," said Tammy in 1984.* After Jones, Haggard would've been a fitting and worthwhile choice, but Nashville in its infinite wisdom decided otherwise.

It was time for the "let's dust off the old legend so they can add a little luster to an unworthy up-and-comer" ploy. Thus Tammy was teamed up with Mark Gray, whose angst-ridden vocal stylings lacked any of the subtlety of her own. They cut a duet version of that grotesque pop anthem that had been a 1978 number 3 pop hit for its performer and cowriter Dan Hill, "Sometimes When We Touch." (Admit it, you know that repellent line that comes next: "The honesty's too much.") "People got upset," confessed producer Steve Buckingham. "It wasn't a country song." The single hit number 6, however, pumping new blood into Wynette's career.

Outside of Tammy tearing it up on a heartfelt rendition of "It's Hard to Be the Dreamer (When You Used to Be the Dream)," the album is pretty nondescript. "Precious Memories," the best thing cut at the sessions, wasn't released until Wynette's 1992 box set, *Tears of Fire*. The song came about due to an after-hours gospel session featuring Tammy, Richey, and two of

*According to Merle's daughter Kelli, Tammy told her that Haggard had made a play for Wynette back when he was married to Bonnie Owens. "He hit on her and she jumped all over him," said Kelli. "She chewed his ass one side and down the other because she had the greatest respect for Bonnie."

the background singers on the album, Pam Rose and Mary Ann Kennedy. The studio was the Bennett House, a big old residence in Franklin, Tennessee. "Richey sits down and starts playing piano in this big Victorian living room," recalled Buckingham. Tammy started just singin', Pam and Mary Ann singin' harmony. It was all very impromptu."

Buckingham was so taken with what he was hearing that he grabbed a boom box and recorded it. Tammy resurrected an old song from her childhood that night—"Precious Memories." Steve had her sing it again in the studio, accompanied only by Richey. White gospel heavyweights the Masters V (James Blackwood, J. D. Sumner, Jake Hess, Rosie Rozell, and Hovie Lister) were then overdubbed on vocals. It must've been a great satisfaction for Wynette to cut a record with her childhood heroes. She more than holds her own, for "Precious Memories" is a stunner, one of Tammy's absolutely greatest performances. Buckingham wisely kept everything minimal, letting Wynette shine. "It wasn't easy to record the dynamics of her voice," confessed Buckingham. "It literally went from a whisper to a scream. Boy, she was loud."

When it came to Richey, Steve had a different experience than others. "All I can tell you is what I saw, and he worshipped the ground Tammy walked on. He called her 'Mama.'" And he gave Buckingham freedom to produce however he saw fit. "It could've been a nightmare—he's a musician, a songwriter, a producer. Richey could not have been more gracious. He never questioned me." As far as Wynette, she always delivered in the studio. "Did Tammy take a lot of drugs for pain? I guess she did. Did it ever affect anything she did with me? No. Tammy never complained."

Wynette felt a great kinship with Buckingham, who would go on to a long association with Dolly Parton. "After we had done this first album at the Bennett House, Tammy said, 'Please don't ever leave me.'" Steve, a bit startled, asked what she meant. "There's very few people you ever connect with creatively," explained Wynette. This exchange would come to haunt Buckingham.

Next, though, he'd record Wynette's last great masterpiece—and maybe her finest album of all time—*Higher Ground*. Before Tammy could ascend to *Higher Ground*, however, there would be a lot more sorrow, sickness, and an aborted trip to the Betty Ford Center.

"Don't Ever Get Married"

Fragile? Good Lord! Fragile I am not.

—Tammy Wynette, 1982

The phone rang at around two a.m. at James "Bud" McComb's place. It was Tammy.

"I could tell she was real messed up. Her voice was real slurred. I don't know what she was on. Tammy was cryin'. She said, 'Bud, I need you to come down here. I need to talk to you.'"

Bud asked where Tammy was. "I think I'm at the Hee Haw Inn . . . Me an' Richey's had a fight." McComb, Wynette's bus driver at the time, knew the joint. The Hee Haw Inn was a no-frills Music City motel behind a Waffle House. Bud woke up his wife, Maria, and told her to get dressed. "It sounded like she might OD or somethin', and I didn't want to walk in and find her dead by myself."

Driving a pickup Bud had bought from Tammy, the McCombs drove over to the Hee Haw Inn. McComb sat in the truck while his wife knocked on the door of Tammy's room. "She just cracked the door open and saw Maria," said Bud. After a few minutes his wife came back and told him to come in. "She said Tammy didn't have no clothes on or nothin'. Just wanderin' around the room like she was out in space."

They got her in bed, and Bud fetched her a Coke. He asked what was wrong.

"I'm just tired of it," said Wynette.

"Do you need to go to a hospital?" asked Bud. "You haven't OD'd on anything, have you?"

"No," said Tammy wearily. "I'm just sick of everything." According to McComb, the main thing Wynette was sick of that night was George Richey.

"She couldn't make him happy, no matter what she done. He was never happy. He was just money-hungry . . . greedy." Bud and Maria stayed by Tammy's side for a few hours, "got her calmed down, and she finally went to bed." Unfortunately they didn't know what else to do, other than make sure Wynette made it home safe the next morning.

Many on Wynette's road crew agreed—when George Richey was out on the road, "everybody was tense," said McComb. "If he wasn't with us, everybody had a ball." Tammy, crew and band members concurred, was more relaxed on the rare occasions when Richey wasn't around. "She was much lighter, a lot of fun," said Karyn Sloas. "She would sit up and talk a lot. And she would actually say, 'Let's go shopping.'" Steve Hoker said, "Richey would never let her get off and go into a restaurant and be real. He always thought she had to be a certain way, be the Tammy character. She just wanted to be Wynette from Red Bay, Alabama."

If Richey wasn't around, Wynette looked for company. "She confided in all the men around her," said Barbara Hutchison. "She'd talk to all the bus drivers about Richey." In the wee hours Tammy would come up to the front of the bus, sit in the buddy seat, and regale the driver with "stories from the Jones days," said Steve Hoker. "She'd tell the same stories over and over, and I'd just sit there and act like that was the first time I'd ever heard it." Wynette just "couldn't get over him," said Bud McComb. "We'd set up there and listen to George Jones tapes all night long. It was one of them deals. That was her soul mate."

Although it has been over twenty years since McComb drove for Wynette, she still visits him in his sleep. "'Bout once a week I still dream about drivin' for Tammy. She was just a great lady. Downright country. The funniest thing that ever happened is when she flashed them girls. We were doin' some shows in Canada, and this car come up behind us, kept flashin' their lights." It was a carload of unrelenting female fans. "They kept flashin' their lights, flashin' their lights. Tammy said, 'Reach up there, flip that switch, and dump the toilet on 'em.'"

Bud did as instructed, and as he looked in the rearview mirror noticed that the car's windshield was covered in the blue water from the bus toilet. It didn't deter this bunch. "They come up beside us with their wipers wipin' off toilet dump. And the girls pulled their T-shirts up."

Wynette was not to be outdone. "Tammy said, 'Watch this.' She got up in the six-foot-high windshield of that big ol' Silver Eagle bus, turned the light on, pulled her shirt up, and said, 'I'll show 'em somethin'.' Boy, did she ever! Tammy was hilarious. She was made miserable, but other than that, she loved life."

If a driver had to go to the restroom, Wynette would "come over, take the wheel, and get on the CB radio." McComb explained, "I'd come back, and she'd be on the CB talkin' truck driver stuff."

Tammy seemed particularly enamored of Marty Johnson, a tour manager who'd come by way of Burt Reynolds. "Young little guy, thought he was hot stuff—Marty thought he was going to be the next George Richey," said Barbara Hutchison, who watched Wynette flirt shamelessly with Johnson when Richey wasn't around. "Tammy went onstage one night really stoned and she had this see-through lace body catsuit she wore with a jacket and no bra. She had big boobs, and without the jacket, it looked like she had her nightgown on—you could see everything that the woman had."

When Wynette got back on the bus, Marty said, "Oh, I like that outfit."

"You don't think it's too risqué?" a coy Tammy inquired.

Johnson told Wynette she looked hot. "He was just all over her, telling her how great she looked. Oh, Tammy just loved it." Barbara told Wynette she had to put on the jacket before she went onstage. "And Marty says, 'Don't wear the jacket, wear it like that.'"

Barbara was mortified, as was the rest of the bus. "Everybody told her, 'Wear the jacket,' but not ol' Marty," said Charley Abdon.

"It was a Sunday afternoon, bright sunshine outside," continued Hutchison. "I thought, 'Oh, no, don't you dare go out there with that thing on, Tammy!' Well, she went out.

"When Tammy came onstage, all the guys dropped their teeth. Everybody was just standin' there goin', 'I don't believe she's gonna sing to these people like this.'" Due to her many surgeries, "Tammy was very self-conscious about how she looked.* That shows you how high she was. She'd believe anything anybody told her, especially a man."

---

*Karyn Sloas said just the opposite. "Tammy wasn't ashamed of her body in any way. She was very open about the plastic surgery that she had. You name it, she'd had it. We used to joke because she'd had a butt implant, and it didn't really take, so she still had to wear padding to make her look like she had a butt. She'd say, 'Hand me the butt pads!'" On the bus Wynette could look ready to keel over, but by showtime, she'd pull off a miraculous transformation. Said Karyn, "No matter what, when she got ready to hit that stage, the woman looked incredible."

Wynette was known to smoke a little pot occasionally.* According to Jan Smith, the first time Tammy ever lit up was during a trip to Vegas with Richey. "She called me and said, 'Now I know why you smoke marijuana. I can't ever tell my children this, but I am as high as a kite and I am havin' a real good time.' When she'd get stoned, Tammy was the funniest human you ever saw in your life! She always had to have a fried egg sandwich, and it had to be cooked until it was rubber. You could bounce it off the floor." The other thing that Wynette craved when she was under the influence was white bread. "You always knew when Tammy was going to get stoned because she would say to the bus driver, 'Stop and get a loaf of bread.'"

Jan recalled one of her more memorable road trips with Wynette. "One time, after George had fired me, Tammy called and said, 'I need you to go to Kentucky to the Executive Inn with me.'" Richey was sick, and her road manager was unavailable, so Smith accompanied her. "That was one of the few times ever we were away from George Richey and he wasn't controllin' everything.

"After the show every night we'd smoke a joint, and then we'd get the munchies. We made friends with the bellman, tipped him real good. One time it was about two or three in the mornin'. Tammy said, 'I *got* to have some sherbet.'"

And what flavor did Tammy want? asked Jan. Every kind they had, Wynette informed her, and she instructed Jan to call room service pretending to be Tammy herself. "You use my name a lot better than I do!" said Tammy. "So I did. And I could sound just like her. Called and said, 'This is Tammy Wynette. And I am *dying* for some sherbet.'"

A big bowl of sherbet immediately appeared in their suite, and the women devoured it.

"Tammy and I put our cigarettes out in that sherbet," said Jan, laughing. "It looked like crack whores lived in that hotel room. Room service finally called and said, 'When y'all are at the show tonight, could we please take the dishes out of the room?' We were havin' the best time. Playin' Hank Williams songs, dancin' all over the livin' room . . . Tammy had her

*In interviews Wynette was usually honest when it came to the subject. "I've tried marijuana several times," she told an interviewer in 1982. "It's not something I would want to do every week or every month . . . I told my children I tried it. I didn't want to be hypocritical . . . I can't say that I won't try it again."

hair pulled back in a ponytail and had on a pair of pink baby doll pajamas. I don't know where the hell she got 'em, they were from the sixties—with some knee socks she'd gotten in high school. And we were pretty stoned.

"It started snowin' like hell, and the river was right outside the window of our suite. Tammy loved the snow. She came runnin' through the room just skippin' and said, 'The First Lady's havin' a *real* good time.'"

Wynette continued to campaign for George Wallace throughout the 1980s. As usual, people say Wynette had no interest in politics, just in the man himself. "On his feet or in the wheelchair, I don't think it mattered," said his last wife, Lisa. At the end of a rally Tammy would serenade George with "Stand by Your Man," then give him a great big smooch. "Right on the mouth," said Lisa uneasily. "Seemed like forever to me. It embarrassed George. He said, 'Lord, it's gonna lose me votes. I don't know what to say to her. I don't want to hurt her feelings.' George liked Tammy. He felt sorry for her. She was just like a little wounded animal."

During one rally Tammy wore a red Southern belle number with big ruffles "cut low as it could be," according to Lisa. Somehow the outfit got caught under George's wheelchair. "She walked offstage, that dress unraveled layer by layer, and nobody would go and tell her. George is there in a wheelchair, lookin' down, and there's her dress."

The Wallaces spent a night in Jasper, Alabama, with Tammy and Richey. Wynette asked Lisa if she had anything for a headache. Lisa handed her a big bottle of Empirin 4s. The next morning the bottle was nearly empty. While Wynette convalesced, Richey amused himself by "playin' the piano," said Lisa. "After everybody left, he takes off his clothes, runs around in a little red thong. He's an ugly man anyway—and thinkin' he was gonna get me?"

Lisa Wallace found George Richey a little unnerving. Once George was out of office, "you never heard another word from him. He wouldn't have anything to do with you if you had no power or money."

Tammy's daughter Jackie—then married to Wynette's sometime tour manager John Paule—gave birth to a daughter in 1983. Tammy was over the moon. As Karyn Sloas recalled, "We were in an airport somewhere. She had called to talk to Jackie. I was standin' right next to her—all of a sudden

Tammy threw the telephone way up in the air and she started jumpin' up and down at the gate. I thought, 'My God, somebody's gotten killed! What in the world's goin' on?' Tammy yelled, 'I'm gonna be a *grandmother!*'"
Jackie had twins in 1988, as did Georgette in 1993. Tina, ever the rebel, had two kids out of wedlock. ("Tina's first child's father was—well—a Yankee," said Martha Dettwiller. "Illegitimate child by a Yankee?! It couldn't have been much worse.")

Now forty, Wynette was crazy about her grandkids—undoubtedly these relationships were fraught with fewer complications than with her own daughters. "Every time we'd get on the bus, first thing she'd talk about—the grandchildren," said Karyn Sloas. "We would get an update immediately. Tammy was very proud of them."

Wynette's relationships with her daughters were as melodramatic as any others in her life. "She would not talk to you—that was the hardest thing" said Jackie. "She was awful stubborn. If Mom didn't feel like it was her fault, she would not be the first to pick up the phone and say, 'I'm sorry.' She would pout. At times she'd make you feel like you'd just broken her heart. She'd lay it on you. We all went for months without talkin' to her."

Richey's defenders will tell you that Wynette's daughters were all on the payroll and only took advantage of her. When Kelli Haggard-Patterson's brother sold some stories about their dad, Merle, to a tabloid, she said Tammy called her and told her to tell Merle she had four children just like him at home "and they've called me everything but the Antichrist." "She loved her daughters, and they treated her like crap," said Haggard-Patterson. "Tammy told me, 'My daughters want nothing but my money.'"

Wynette's friends say that was just Tammy blowing off steam, like she did with just about everybody close to her. "They weren't prima donna kids, they loved her," said Michelle Broussard Honick, who worked for Richey. "And I know they loved her for herself. The star thing was a drawback to them."

"The girls and Tammy had a lot of friction from time to time," said Martha Dettwiller. "Tammy was very sorry that she wasn't around for her girls like she needed to be, and also understood that they depended on her to make a living. Of course, like any other child that's born to that kind of privilege, they don't understand it. And they never, ever were grateful—like any other kid. Her children and grandchildren were truly the focus of her life. That was what was most important to Tammy—their well-being, their happiness."

It's apparent that George Richey drove a wedge between Wynette and her daughters like he did with anybody around Tammy that he viewed as a threat. His detractors will tell you that not only did he prevent her from providing for her children, he could be cruel. "George used to sit around and say how dumb Jackie was," said Jan Smith. Not all the kids took it lying down. "Tina was a spitfire," said Barbara Hutchison. "She'd tell her mother, 'Hey, he's just a freeloader, he's letting his people do this and do that, and you're lettin' him get by with it.' Tammy didn't want to hear it because she knew it to be true."

Things came to a head in the fall of 1984 when an agitated Tammy called her daughter Gwen. She was at the Florida house, concerned because Richey was setting up lines of credit in her name at local banks. "I'm scared," she told Gwen. Thus began yet another bizarre caper in Wynette's life.

Gwen soon showed up in Jupiter, along with then-husband Zack. Over lunch Tammy told her daughter she wanted a divorce. She also wanted Gwen to break into Richey's locked briefcase to see what was happening with her money. She instructed Gwen to make it look like a burglary. Jackie and Tina were called in as backup. They were about to do the deed when Tammy and Richey pulled up to the house. She'd revealed to George what was going on, and he went ballistic, pushing Tina over a sofa and charging into the bathroom after Jackie, who hissed "I hate you!" at him.

Richey called the police. "Mom stood beside Richey and ordered all of us out of the house," wrote Jackie. Her children weren't even allowed to take their belongings from the house without a police escort.

"This was to form a pattern in the years to come," wrote Jackie. "She would muster the courage to defy Richey and then, fearful that she couldn't get along without him, she would crater." Her daughters didn't talk to her for months.

"We all felt that she had set us up, and then betrayed us," said Jackie.

In March 1986, Tammy had a small recurring acting role as waitress Darlene Stankowski on the afternoon soap *Capitol*. "I've lived my own soap opera for forty-three years," she quipped. Old-guard Hollywood cowboy Rory Calhoun played her love interest.

That same year Wynette shot footage for a fine documentary aired on the BBC in 1987, the aptly titled *Stand by Your Dream*. Cameras followed Tammy as she returned to Itawamba County to wander through her deserted childhood home and to sing in church with friends Linda Cayson and Agnes Wilson. Particularly haunting was a shot of Tammy in the back of a limo, riding through the streets of Los Angeles looking very melancholy. Director Rosemary Bowen-Jones was another who saw Wynette as "a restless soul, someone who was forever going to be searching and had never found the place that she was looking for. Nothing was really right."

When Bowen-Jones met Richey, he "had a hospital intern uniform on, and that was kind of a joke between them, because he obviously gave her medication." Like so many others, she found Richey—and his relationship with Tammy—to be somewhat inscrutable. "They didn't seem to have much intimacy. It was like he was her attendant more than anything else."

Bowen-Jones filmed Richey at home alone while Tammy was out on the road. "He really appeared quite lonely playing on his pinball machines. Just a big kid in a house with all these toys."

In 1986 Tammy reunited with Billy Sherrill for one last single, the rousing if slight "Alive and Well." It failed to crack the top twenty, and the rest of the album they apparently recorded never saw the light of day, although one of the songs crept into Tammy's live set: "If I Had Someone to Leave, I Wouldn't Go." Although Sherrill and Wynette never worked together again, Billy continued to worry about her.

"I don't think Tammy was ever very happy. Just one bad relationship after the other . . . She always hooked up with people that mistreated her and used her. I don't think she was really truly happy 'til the day she died."

As the eighties dragged on, Wynette's drug intake steadily worsened. Not that it was ever acknowledged out on the road. "It was never talked about," said Steve Hoker. "Part of the reason I left was because I started findin' these little needles under the mattress when she'd sleep in the bunk by herself. I went to Richey and told him that I thought that Tammy might have a problem—that's how stupid and naive I was." Richey "looked totally shocked, like he'd never heard that before. He told me, 'You're wrong, you don't know what you're talkin' about. Everything she takes is because of her stomach, it's all prescribed, you shouldn't worry about stuff like that. Tammy thinks of you as a son. If she knew you were talkin' about her like that, she would be so disappointed.' I felt like a total idiot." When she got out of her bunk one morning, one of Tammy's backup singers nearly stepped on a used hypo.

Her daughters attempted to help. "We had interventions," said Jackie. "That was horrible." All this accomplished was to make Tammy furious, but that fall she begrudgingly agreed to check in to the Betty Ford Center in California. "I only stayed one night. I said, 'No, this is not for me. I'm goin' home,'" she admitted to Larry King. "Tammy didn't want to get off of it," said Jerry Taylor. "You have to want to. You weren't gonna make her."

Two weeks later Wynette, apparently trying to kick her Valium addiction on her own, was about to depart for a casino gig in Laughlin, Nevada, when she began to hallucinate. "She started telling the house staff, 'Go get some food and take it out to the Vietnamese kids that are livin' in the bushes outside the house,'" said David Sloas, who maintained Wynette also mentioned seeing Elly May and Jethro from *The Beverly Hillbillies* lurking in the underbrush.

Despite Tammy's condition, everybody forged ahead to Laughlin. The first show was a disaster. Tammy rushed the tempos for all the songs. "She kept wantin' everything faster—even songs like 'D-I-V-O-R-C-E' and 'I Don't Wanna Play House' she wanted a third faster," said Sloas. "It was almost comical." Tammy couldn't finish the second show. "I just fell apart," she told Larry King. "I just left the stage." Sloas watched as tour manager Bill Simmons and a security guard poured a dazed Tammy into an old wooden chair and swept her off to a hotel room.

Wynette agreed to return to the Betty Ford Center on November 4, 1986, making it public with a press release. Mrs. Ford herself requested that Tammy be put into a four-person room nicknamed "the Swamp." She had to be up at six a.m., have her bed made by seven thirty, then attend meetings all day. "They keep you really, really busy," she told King. "They just pound away at drug abuse."

The Ford program can last anywhere from four to six weeks to months longer for more involved cases. Unfortunately, on November 21, a little more than three weeks in, Tammy collapsed with a life-threatening bowel obstruction. Wynette later claimed she lay in pain for hours at the Ford Center, denied even an aspirin. She had surgery at the Eisenhower Medical Center, then five weeks later underwent an eight-hour operation at the Mayo Clinic, during which a quarter of her stomach was removed. She remained at the hospital from January to March 1987, "put back on the very drugs she sought to escape," as one reporter noted. While Wynette was in the hospital, Mrs. Ford brought her the medallion that signified that she had completed her treatment, but the fact remains she had spent only three weeks to treat a decade-plus problem.

During interviews Tammy would discuss how wonderful the Betty Ford Center was; in private, said Barbara Hutchison, "she talked about how she hated it. Tammy blamed the Betty Ford Center for nearly causin' her to lose her life." Whatever lip service Wynette gave to her addiction now that it was public was just that, according to Hutchison. "Tammy never admitted that she had any problem. She was so stubborn. *She* could handle it, and she didn't like anybody telling her what to do with those drugs. It was because Tammy enjoyed the feelin'. I know she did."

When Barbara Hutchison showed up at Tammy's house one day to do her hair before a trip to Malden, Missouri, Georgette's then-husband Billy suggested she wait before entering, as Wynette's daughters were inside attempting an intervention. Richey was off in the bedroom. "He didn't wanna be involved," Billy told her. "Well, a lot of good that's going to do unless Richey's sittin' there with 'em," Barbara replied.

That night, when they arrived in Malden, Richey demanded to have a meeting with Hutchison. "He gets right up in my face and says, 'I wanna tell you one thing: You stay out of my family's affairs.'" At first she didn't know what he was talking about, then it occurred to Barbara that somebody had repeated her remark about the intervention being useless without Richey present. "He knew that *I* knew that he didn't participate."

By this time Richey was "just screamin', his neck was bulgin'—he was just a wild man." Finally Richey left. Hutchison then proceeded down to Tammy's room to attend to her coif. "I go into the room, Richey's sittin' there drinkin' his coffee and reading a newspaper like nothin' happened. I'm doin' Tammy's hair and I'm startin' to tear up a little bit. Tammy looks up and says, 'Why are you so upset, Barbara?'" Hutchison said nothing. "I thought, 'I ain't letting George Richey know he got to me.'" It was never discussed, like so many other problems. "Tammy would always say, 'Y'know, we're all family.' Yeah, a dysfunctional family."

Hutchison said it became routine for Tammy to say she was over and done with Richey, only to turn around and praise him during some TV interview. "They'd have a big argument, Tammy would be cryin', she'd end up havin' to get her makeup on, go on Ralph Emery talking about 'Richey this, Richey that, Richey was the love of her life.' I thought, 'Whoa, it takes a strong person to go on television letting the people know that you love your husband—and then come off screamin' that you want to divorce him.'"

Any analysis of the Richey-Wynette dynamic at this stage of the game is to submerge oneself in a fog of ambiguity. Richey controlled her, friends tell you. He only wanted her for a meal ticket, say others. Richey adored her and took care of her every need, insist his defenders. Tammy loved him. She didn't love him. He enabled Tammy. She made sure he did. There are those who maintain that underneath it all, Wynette ran the show. "Wasn't nobody that was Tammy's boss," said Bud McComb. "Tammy had a will," insisted Steve Chapman. "After she'd made up her mind, that was the way it was going to be, end of conversation. She wasn't this monotone dweeb walkin' around under the control of George Richey. That's bull."

Richey's gig certainly wasn't easy. "The whole time I was there, the only thing he had to do was everything she wanted," said Barbara Hutchison. "That was his main job. The gofer. I know he hated it. She treated him like he was a waterboy. She belittled him a lot." Richey would dutifully get off the bus, get Tammy whatever she wanted to eat, bring it back, "and she'd say, 'No, that's not what I want.'

"'Well, Tammy, what do you want?'

"'Richey, just leave me alone. I don't want any of that.'

"They would do that constantly," said Barbara. "Back 'n' forth, back 'n' forth. It would unnerve you, sittin' there listenin' to that. Finally he'd shut up and she'd tell us girls, 'I get so tired of him, he just gets on my nerves . . .'"

Their battles could be comical. "Every time they got into an argument, he'd have an angina attack—he'd grab his chest like Fred Sanford—'It's the big one,'" said Bud McComb. "We were out in the Mohave Desert, and I could hear Tammy yellin' in the back, 'You son of a bitch, I got along *without* you before I met you and I can get along without you *now*.' And she called me on the intercom and said, 'Bud, stop this bus and put him off right now.'

"I said, 'Tammy, honey, we're in the middle of a desert.'"

"I don't give a damn where we're at, I want him *off* my bus!" screeched Wynette.

"I'm not going to put the man off the bus in the middle of the desert," argued Bud. "We're two hundred miles from anything." In times like these Richey would invariably "have to put one of those little pills under his tongue, have an angina attack, and make her feel sorry for him."

"I don't remember Tammy standin' up to him," countered Yvonne Abdon. "I thought it was very ironic that people would say, 'Tammy, you're such a strong woman.' All of her songs were about bein' a strong woman, every interview was about her bein' a strong woman. She'd made her fortune and made it on her own, but with George Richey she wasn't a strong woman. I've seen him make Tammy feel horrible and make her cry. And she didn't fight back."

There is one Tammy/Richey story that I just can't shake. It was November 1997. Wynette was out on the road in Wheeling, West Virginia. There were only three people on the bus at the time; one of them's no longer with us and another isn't talking. That leaves Barbara Hutchison, and she wept as she told her version of the events. Tammy had finished her first show and was on the bus preparing for her second performance. Richey was on the couch reading. Barbara was lost in a magazine. Tammy was getting ready to hit the stage. Just another day on the bus, but suddenly things went seriously awry when Wynette started screaming. Says Hutchison, Tammy "got her makeup halfway on and all of the sudden I hear, 'NO, Richey, NO! Don't do it, I don't want it!'"

Hutchison looked up from her gossip rag to see the couple tussling over a line of tubing that provided Wynette's medication.* According to Hutchison, Richey got up, and without uttering a word, cornered his wife against the wall of the bus, "grabbed that line," and started "insertin' that stuff in her." Tammy was "wailin' like a hurt animal. She said, 'Richey, please don't give me anymore. I can't go onstage, I won't be able to sing, my mouth'll be dry.' He just grabbed her arm and did it again." Hutchison wanted to help Tammy, but was frozen in fear. Barbara watched as Richey appeared to be giving her more drugs.

---

*Medication that Wynette no doubt had a prescription for and that Richey may well have been administering in accordance with doctor's orders.

A now-docile Tammy "sat there a few minutes, and then she said, 'I love you, Richey.' He didn't say anything. She said, 'Did you hear me, Richey? I said I love you.' She got upset and went on into the back. He sat down and was putting all her medication back in his briefcase. I was just petrified. He didn't even look up at me. Just business as usual." The show was canceled. "Tammy was in halfway normal spirits that day," said Hutchison. "It was close to showtime, she was ready to go on and he completely sank it."

There are others who experienced a completely different couple. Kelli Haggard-Patterson, Merle's daughter, got close to both Richey and Tammy in the eighties. To her, they were just "Ma" and "Pa." They loved to pull pranks on Kelli, like dragging her over to the booth of her father's ex-flame Leona Williams one year at Fan Fair. "Not only did I hate Leona, she hated me with a passion. Well, George and Tammy knew this. Luckily she wasn't there. I got back to Tammy's booth, she was dyin' laughin'. She goes, 'Richey took you to Leona's booth! I *love* that.' They just messed with me."

Their nickname for Kelli was "Squirt." "I might add I'm five foot seven and a half," she said. "Tammy is about the size of a minute, and they call *me* Squirt?" Haggard-Patterson admitted she was lonely staying in the cavernous wing of Wynette's home. Some fans were staying there as well, so "Tammy and George said, 'You can go stay over with the girls. It'll be a sleepover!' Well, they were all lesbians. They didn't tell me, though. Their big song was 'Stand by Your Man' and none of 'em wanted a man." Said Tammy with a chuckle, "Is that too cute, Squirt?"

According to Kelli, Wynette loved it when Richey acted like a pit bull on her behalf. "One time I was at their house and somebody said somethin' nasty in a local paper. I remember Tammy sittin' in her pretty little sweats, and she looked at George and she said, 'Get 'em, Richey,' and he said, 'Okay, baby.'" (When Hillary Clinton attacked Wynette on television in 1992, Richey told Kelli, "Tammy just looked at me and said, 'Get 'em, Richey.'")

Richey, Richey, Richey. How I wondered about this strange being. Of course I wanted to talk to him. After endless machinations with his "media representative," I submitted fourteen pages of questions to be answered via e-mail. Given the raw nature of my inquiries, I was not surprised when he declined. This was a project completely out of his control, and, judging from the comments Richey has made in interviews and on the Richey-run Tammy Wynette Web site, he wants only the most idyllic portrayal when it comes to his relationship with Wynette. "There is no one on this earth that loved Tammy the way that I did," he wrote on the site. "Not only did I dedicate my entire life and career to her, I truly was madly in love with her. She felt the same way about me. There will never be another Tammy. I adored each breath that she took. I still love her today."*

Friends say that, whatever the bond was with Richey, it wasn't one of passion, and I have often wondered if Richey suffered from what Terrence Rafferty called "the pure panic that is sometimes the secret source of cruelty." What George Jones was for Tammy, Tammy might have been for Richey, but even Kelli Haggard-Patterson admitted it was not vice versa. "Richey worshipped the ground she walked on. He would've bowed down and got on his knees for that woman, and he so wanted to be everything to her and he . . . couldn't. She loved him but she wasn't *in* love—there's a difference." Kelli said Richey was painfully aware of this fact. "It hurt him very bad. And I think that's one of the reasons he did everything for Tammy—all she had to do is blink her eyes, and he was right there. But I don't think she ever felt that feeling of true love. All you had to do was touch her hand. It was empty—totally empty."

Others insist that when it comes to Wynette, all roads lead back to George Jones. Barbara Hutchison often accompanied Tammy in the car on trips back to Red Bay. "As soon as we'd get out of the driveway, she'd say, 'Get out my new CD I got of George.' And we'd play George Jones CDs all the way there." Wynette would then go on to point out every minute detail of his phrasing. "One time I said, 'Tammy, what about you and Jones?' She told me, 'I'll always love George. George is the love of my life.'" So what about Richey? asked Barbara. "'Well, Richey is kind of like a brother to me. Jones, he'll always be the person I love.' Then she said the love of Richey's life was his second wife, Sheila. I was just stunned. And Tammy wasn't high then, either. I just thought, 'That's so sad.'"

The Tammy Wynette International Fan Club kept growing over the years. There were state representatives all over the country, overseas chapters, a

---

*Richey has threatened to write his own book over the years. "There have been so very many lies spread . . . I would like to set the record straight," he wrote on Tammy's Web site. "Unfortunately, that would mean selling Tammy out, and that I cannot begin to imagine doing." While taking the high road, he does add, tantalizingly, "I have, however, recorded hundreds of hours of my experiences on tape."

monthly newsletter with words of wisdom from Wynette herself (who always signed off with the words "Love Ya!"), and in June, during Nashville's Fan Fair event, often a get-together for the club right at Tammy's home.* It wasn't unusual to find a couple of club members staying at Wynette's place. A small core of members became extremely close to the star. "There was a group of about ten of us—Tammy knew us all. If she saw us in the audience, she'd point us out," "Super" Judy Vleck said proudly.

So it was no surprise that during Wynette's 1987 Mayo Clinic stay, two extremely devoted fans from Pennsylvania—Evelyn Resch and Beverly Clark—went out to visit. Wynette later confessed to Beverly and Evelyn they had been the only ones to pay their respects besides Conway Twitty. Her daughters were no-shows. "Them girls never came out to see her," noted Clark. "Richey was there every second of every day." It was a rough time in Tammy's life, but you'd never hear a complaint from her lips. She had a sense of humor about it all. This was a woman who nicknamed her IV unit "Oscar."

"The lady was given no chance of survival," said Clark. "When they first brought her in, she was as near to death as you could be. I know her pain was excruciating. Even with all the medication she was on, the pain would be so severe she would let out a scream every now and then. That was heart-breaking. The tears would roll down our faces." Beverly and Evelyn sat and played cards with Richey. Tammy would join in for a while, then totter off to her bed, Oscar in tow.

"Her and that Oscar," said Beverly with a sigh. "She never said, 'Oh, woe is me.' Tammy was just a tough girl."

Dolly Parton paid a visit during another of Wynette's many hospital stays. "I'd just climb up in bed, fix her hair and makeup. She didn't want people to come in and see her without it—I know, I'm that way. She'd try to paint her lips—she was all drugged up by that time—and have it all over her face. I'd say, 'Hey, girl, you can't put on your own damn lipstick, let me have that. You're lookin' like Bozo the Clown!' We would laugh and I would fix her up."

---

*In 1997, for just fifteen bucks (only ten for those fourteen and younger), a fan club member could go to Tammy's home for her thirty-years-in-showbiz celebration and not only meet Tammy, Richey, and their Pomeranian, Killer, but enjoy an "award-winning" buffet of baby-back ribs, smoked turkey breast, smoked loin of pork, specially blended barbecue beans, Southern potato salad, and coleslaw.

When Tammy resurfaced following the Betty Ford–Mayo Clinic ordeal, she was a revitalized woman. Even though they had to cut through her diaphragm during her operation, her voice remained intact. Wynette's stomach was now divided and much smaller, but she could digest better. "I find myself getting up every couple of hours and eating a snack," she said at the time. "Kind of like a baby on a schedule!" And for the first time in a long time she had an album's worth of songs worthy of her talent—*Higher Ground.*

Producer Steve Buckingham escorted Tammy into the modern era with grace and dignity, in the process obliterating the many turkeys Wynette had cranked out in the eighties. Not unlike what Billy Sherrill had done with George Jones, Buckingham unleashed a quieter, more reflective, and, if possible, deeper Tammy, one who might not be engulfed in the fires of love any longer, but one whose soulful embers were still aglow. Eschewing the bombast, melodrama, and masochism so characteristic of her seventies work, Buckingham paired Tammy with simple songs of sophisticated emotions, framing them in an equally understated bluegrass-tinged setting that only emphasized her utter sincerity. From the new generation of studio pros surrounding her came the sad, keening fiddle of Mark O'Connor, perhaps the best foil for Wynette since Pete Drake's sobbing pedal steel. "We wanted it to be very rural, very earthy . . . Like I am, just plain country," explained Tammy.

For once some thought was given to a coherent Tammy Wynette album of songs instead of singles plus filler. Each track featured a different guest artist: Vern Gosdin, Ricky Van Shelton, Gene Watson, Vince Gill, the Gatlins. (Tammy's original title was *Out with the Boys,* but that idea was deep-sixed once Emmylou Harris came aboard.) The concept of older legends plus (mostly) younger admirers could've easily stank up the room—a few years later Wynette herself would prove just how bad a duet album can be with the turgid *Without Walls*—but Buckingham wisely went for a more subtle approach: letting Tammy shine as the vocalist and letting her guests excel as her accompaniment. The half-spoken "Talkin' to Myself Again," in which Wynette "talks" to an absent paramour, manages to sound simultaneously old-school classic yet fresh—no small trick. And the ballads are killers. Paul Overstreet and Don Schlitz, who'd together or separately written hits for Randy Travis, George Jones, Alabama, Tanya Tucker, the Judds, and Pam Tillis, contributed two first-rate songs, "There's No Heart So Strong" and "I Wasn't Meant to Live My Life Alone," the latter of which features one of Wynette's all-time greatest vocals. "All Through Throwin' Good Love After Bad," a tremendous Guy Clark–Richard Leigh composition, is another stunner, with O'Connor's violin setting a grave-deep elegiac tone for Wynette's eerily calm vocal. You just want the album to go on forever. Even the up-tempo songs, "Higher Ground" and "Your Love," ooze class instead of cuteness, the latter boasting electrifying vocal accompaniment by Ricky Skaggs, who, noted an admiring Wynette, "added those little turns like a steel guitar." Skaggs laid down two harmony parts, then "came up with a third part that was so high we couldn't believe it," said Buckingham. It is a tragedy that Wynette wasn't able to do more records like this one, and a crime that *Higher Ground* isn't readily available on CD.

Wynette actually went back to pounding the Music Row pavement with Buckingham to find the songs, and it is a testament to Tammy's stature that nine of them were nabbed the first day out. The last, "Higher Ground," was written by Buckingham himself during a late-night dog walk, although he refrained from admitting authorship until after Tammy committed to doing the song.

The sessions went quickly, utilizing, Buckingham noted, "mostly live recordings with as few overdubs as possible." Seven tracks were recorded on March 26, 1987, the initial day of recording, with the three remaining captured the following day. The next month was spent chasing down guest-star vocalists, with the mixing finished May 18.

The adoration Tammy received in the course of making this record must've been a real shot in the arm. "Everybody was awestruck by her," said Buckingham. The O'Kanes were so nervous recording vocals for "Talkin' to Myself Again," they requested that Wynette wait outside the studio. "But I still see her foot moving," one of them whined.

Released in June 1987, *Higher Ground* was greeted with great acclaim. Of the three singles released, "Your Love" went to number 12, "Talkin' to Myself Again" number 16, and "Beneath a Painted Sky" number 57. Wynette did countless interviews and television to promote the album, including a memorable appearance on Dolly Parton's show, where Dolly joined Tammy for a medley of her hits. For the first time in interviews, Wynette had to address her addiction to painkillers, and she was fairly honest about the matter, although she always linked her problem with the pressures of the road. Said Tammy, "When you miss a show with one guy, you hate to do it to him again. . . . I was getting like Jones used to be!" She admitted addictions to Esgic, Valium, and Demerol. "Not always together . . . sometimes one, two, sometimes all three." She also owned up to indulging "when I wasn't hurting bad enough to have to," as well as routinely hitting hospital emergency rooms to score. "I would demand a shot—and I usually got it."

For a period Wynette seemed to be more or less free of drugs, and her band certainly noticed the difference. "She was top of her game," said David Sloas. "It was a very encouraging time." *Higher Ground* should've served as the foundation for a new artistic direction for Tammy, but it was not to be.

During a meeting at Sony for her next album, Steve Buckingham confessed he just hadn't been able to come up with another concept, and suggested she work with Sherrill protégé Norro Wilson instead. "Tammy didn't say anything, but I saw her deflate," said Buckingham, who hadn't forgotten Wynette's plea never to desert her after their first project together. "I felt like I let her down. It broke my heart, just ate away at me, but honest to God, I did not have an idea." Buckingham and Wynette would not work together again until 1993, and then only for a trio album with Dolly and Loretta.

For an artist of her stature Wynette just didn't get the consistent creative support that she should've been entitled to. Part of the problem was that Tammy failed to speak up for herself when it came to record company politics. Evelyn Shriver, Wynette's publicist in the nineties, recalled attending a meeting with Sony when Tammy's *Without Walls* duet album was in the planning stage. "Tammy was hesitant to ever express what she wanted, because it wasn't her position to have any ideas. She was never of the mentality to be the artist and say what she wanted. I had just moved down from New York and I was used to handling Diana Ross, who would tell the record company if they were allowed to come backstage and say *hello* to her."

Wynette wanted to do a duet album with pop stars, but "the label said, 'Well, Tammy, that's a good idea, but we'd really like you to do a duet album with some of our newer acts,' which was a whole thing just to bolster their acts." Wynette also wanted to sing live in the studio with the band, but the executives told her she couldn't. "I'm watching Tammy agreeing and I said, 'Tammy, that's not what you wanted to do, is it?' The way Tammy and George Jones were brought up, the record company was always the boss. They'd always tiptoe around the label people. They never get the fact that the record company doesn't exist without them."

Nineteen eighty-eight brought a new calamity. On September 21, U.S. marshals showed up at the door of 4121 Franklin Road to seize control of her home. Tammy and Richey had invested in some Florida shopping centers and had gotten involved in some shady savings and loan deal in the process. Now the government wanted $750,000. Richey swiftly filed bankruptcy papers to thwart the seizure, but the attendant publicity mortified Tammy. "Tammy Wynette, the teary-voiced country singer who broke hearts with 'D-I-V-O-R-C-E,' added B-A-N-K-R-U-P-T-C-Y to her repertoire Tuesday after U.S. marshals seized control of her Franklin Road home," began the article in the *Nashville Banner.* Court records accompanying the filing revealed her debts to the world, as well as the value of her personal possessions, including Richey's mink coat ($9,000), two mink hats ($480), and a Pac-Man game ($60). Most embarrassing of all was the listing of a $50,000 loan from Burt Reynolds. According to Jackie, Tammy had "confided in me that Richey had asked her to borrow money from Burt" and she hadn't wanted to do it. "Now it was public record."

Wynette was under the impression she was completely destitute. As her sometime lunch companion Martha Dettwiller told it, "Our usual place was a 'place to be seen' in Nashville, Sunset Grill. We'd go down there, get all dressed up, sit out on the patio, and people would come by." One day Martha came by to pick her up. Wynette took forever to leave the bedroom and get out of the house, not an uncommon occurrence. "Finally I got her in the car and I said, 'Tammy, what in the world is the matter?'" Wynette announced that instead of Sunset Grill she wanted to go to Krystal Burger drive-through, where hamburgers are even cheaper than McDonald's. "Tammy's all dressed up and she wants to go to Krystal!" A bewildered Martha asked why. "Well, we're really, really broke," an embarrassed Tammy eventually admitted. Instead of buying presents for her granddaughters, Wynette started making outfits herself for gifts. "Richey would play on her and let her believe she had no money," said Dettwiller.

There would be only two more Tammy solo albums, and neither set the world on fire. Norro Wilson produced 1989's *Next to You*, but other than the superb Curly Putman–Don Cook–Max D. Barnes song, "If You Let Him Drive You Crazy (He Will)," the material was forgettable, particularly one of the singles, the execrable Paul Richey–Ed Bruce authored "Thank the Cowboy for the Ride." The Bob Montgomery–produced 1990 release *Heart Over Mind* was no better. "Let's Call It a Day Today" boasted a video directed by her old flame Burt Reynolds, but failed to dent the top twenty.

Linda Cayson, Tammy's old childhood pal, still lived in Itawamba County, and Wynette always kept in touch. Sometimes she wouldn't hear from Wynette for months, then the phone would ring at midnight. "You'd never know when to expect a call from her," said Linda, who would visit Tammy a couple of weeks every year. "The thing that I was always so proud of was that we were always just as close when she got big as we were when we were little girls. She didn't change, not to me. Sometimes she'd have tours here 'n' yonder, and we didn't talk for maybe six months. And then I'd get a call—'Lin, you've got to come up.' Even though we'd been apart, we'd go right back to where we were. We were always so happy to see each other. It was like we'd never been apart." Invariably, when Cayson came to visit, they'd hop in Tammy's car and "get to ridin'. She'd say, 'Let's see if we can still harmonize.'" They'd dip back to the old songs, singing one after another. "Oh, Lordy, we had fun," said Linda.

Wynette loved to return to Alabama. "I'd come off the road after bein' on the road nearly a year with her," said Barbara Hutchison. "She'd call me as soon as she got home—'We're gonna have to go to Red Bay and put Mee-Maw's curtains up.' I'd think, 'Tammy, we just got home!'" They'd hop into Tammy's Cadillac, put some Jones on the car stereo, and tear down Route 24, which had just been christened the Tammy Wynette Highway. "Tammy was a great driver, but she sped down that road as fast as she could. I kept thinking, 'Oh, Tammy, if you don't slow down we're gonna get a ticket.' And sure enough, we got pulled over twice—on *her* highway."

Once they got to Red Bay, the fun really began. Wynette would call in a food order to her aunt Hazel before they hit the road. "I mean, they'd have a spread for her," said Barbara. "Tammy would say, 'Be sure to leave enough of those green beans to take on the road.'" Then they'd round up Mildred— in the front seat with "her feet popped up on the dashboard"—and make the rounds. "Tammy loved bein' the center of attention when she'd get there. It was like she'd make a parade around town. The preacher'd be out on the front porch, Mee-Maw would be waving at everybody, Tammy'd be honkin' her horn. We'd stop at the little general store, and Tammy'd go in talk to everybody. Goin' around that town was a big deal for her and Mee-Maw. That was the real Tammy."*

Richey was conspicuously absent for many of these trips. "Richey hated Red Bay," noted Hutchison. There was no love lost between Richey and Mildred, either. "He'd make snide remarks about Mee-Maw to his family." When Barbara remarked to Mildred that Tammy needed rest, she said, "That's that ol' George Richey keeping her workin' to the bone." According to Hutchison, Mildred "hated him."

Starting in 1989 Tammy did four benefits for the Red Bay school raising fifty thousand dollars. "I think she would've done even more if it hadn't been for Richey," said her cousin Jane Williams, who described dealing with him as "a nightmare in Technicolor." Tammy would happily agree to do the concert, then Richey would put them off, answering one out of seven calls. He said Wynette would require a real stage, so one was built. "I think he actually thought we couldn't come up with it," said Williams. Richey would dangle a carrot, promising a great supporting act. "He'd say this, he'd say that, he'd just string us along. He'd name somebody, we'd get excited, then we'd find out he didn't have anybody."

Foy had passed away in 1988 and Mildred, suffering from diabetes, was not a well woman. In 1989 she had five bypass surgeries. At the end she stayed at Wynette's home with round-the-clock care. Tammy spared no expense taking care of her mother, even if Mee-Maw stayed ornery 'til the very end. "One time Wynette had been out on the road, and when she went in to see Mildred, her mother just looked at her and more or less bawled her out," said Linda Cayson. "Told her, 'I don't even want to *see* you. I don't *like* you.' Wynette said, 'I had my gown on and I went runnin' out of there cryin' and couldn't hush.' I tried to tell her that Mildred's mind was gone then. Not to take it personal. But Wynette sure did."

---

*Not that Wynette wasn't up to her old tricks in Red Bay. "Tammy knew the drugstore people down there like they were her best buddies," said Hutchison. "She'd call 'em at twelve o'clock at night and they'd open up for her." On one trip she scored Ambien sleeping pills. "Tammy chugged that whole bottle that night. Thirty pills. I thought she was gonna go into a coma. She got up the next day like she hadn't taken the first pill. We ate and drove home. Her body was unbelievable when it came to drugs." (Hutchison had no knowledge if a prescription was on file.)

On June 24, 1991, Wynette was hosting her annual Fan Fair fan club party and was scheduled to do an interview with TV host Leeza Gibbons. Mildred had been teetering between life and death, and her daughter was beside herself. "Tammy hadn't done her hair in days, and her roots were all showing," said publicist Susan Nadler. "She looked like a crazy lady in a halter top."

"Tammy was hysterical," said Evelyn Shriver. "Her mother had basically been revived several times. It was time to let her go." Leeza Gibbons offered to step in and host the Tammy fan club party. Wynette reluctantly agreed, then attempted to introduce her barely conscious mother to Gibbons. "There was Mee-Maw expectorating in Leeza's face as Tammy's going, 'Mama, this is Leeza Gibbons,'" recalled Nadler. At the same time, some burly, more aggressive female members of Wynette's fan club "were all guarding the door, not letting people in," added Nadler. "It was just one of those weird Tammy experiences."

Amidst all this chaos Mildred finally passed away. Scotty Kennedy attended the funeral. "Tammy was devastated. You could hear her crying during the whole thing, loudly." Wynette's gospel hero James Blackwood sang at the service, and Richey, who had undergone open-heart surgery just three weeks before, accompanied him on piano. "At the end two people had to help Tammy walk out," said Kennedy. Suddenly Richey "also had to have help walking, him crying and carrying on."

Richey's despair was short-lived, however. He angered Tammy's aunt Hazel by making a comment suggesting that now that the "matriarch" of the family was gone, things would be different. Indeed, Wynette would not return to Red Bay nearly as often, and she canceled her last benefit concert there the night before. "She never did another after that," said Kennedy.

Tammy and Mildred had had their battles, but they were still mother and daughter. "Mee-Maw was so strong she could be Mom's worst enemy or best friend," said Jackie Daly. "But I think Mom knew when push came to shove, Mee-Maw was always there, no matter what Mee-Maw thought about Mom." Most of Wynette's friends and relations agree: when Mildred passed away, something within Tammy died, too. "The wind went out of her sails," said Hutchison. "I think Tammy just gave up completely when Mee-Maw died. She'd stay halfway sober, try to not take so much medication when Mee-Maw was alive. When she passed away, Tammy kind of let herself go. She just gave in to self-medicatin' more and more."*

"She kept a lot of things private and hidden there towards the end," said daughter Georgette. "As strong and as headstrong as she was all her life—and I hate to say this—after so many years, I think that just kind of got beaten out of her. She was so tired and didn't want to fight anymore, didn't want to face those kind of battles, and she was so worried about what the public and the world would think about her as a person that she just kind of gave in to a lot of things that she never would've given in to years before."

The late eighties and early nineties brought Tammy a new team of devoted insiders. Susan Nadler, a smart, caustic ex–New Yorker handled her publicity, only to be replaced by her incredibly astute pal, Evelyn Shriver. And over at the label was Mike Martinovich, vice president of marketing and a serious Wynetteophile. "Mike Martinovich worshipped at the altar of Tammy Wynette," said Nadler. "We would go over to his house, and he'd have what he called 'Tammy Time.' And Tammy Time was when all of us would sit around and look at old videos of Tammy in Boise. We could do every song that Tammy did—we knew all of her moves. We could go down with her and up with her—because we watched it *a thousand friggin' times.*"

Martinovich, pushing hard to expose Tammy to a wider audience, faced an uphill battle in Nashville. "I was told by everybody here, 'Her career's over with.' I said, 'No, it's not.'" For the first time Wynette played the Bottom Line in New York City. "Nobody's gonna know me," worried Tammy, more accustomed to playing state fairs in upstate New York. "Two shows sold out

---

*The same year Mee-Maw died, Tammy recorded "If I Could Only Hear My Mother Pray Again" as a duet with Charlie Louvin for the ultra-obscure Playback Records, and it is worth searching out as a raw slab of Tammy gospel. Wynette arrived at the studio "straight from the hospital," said Louvin. "Her bein' raised in Alabama as I was, I knew that she would know exactly how to sing the tenor part on that, and, lo and behold, she did. I didn't know if I could do the harmony under her high lead, but her part was so good I couldn't let her down." The producer was inexperienced with syncopated harmony. "The guy cut the mics off. I said, 'What's the problem?' He says, 'Tammy's not singin' the same thing you are.' I said, 'You poor man. That's the way the song goes!'"

Louvin's old nemesis George Richey "waited in the car. He didn't even have the decency to come in the studio and support her. Tammy never disappointed me. She was one of the finest ladies I ever knowed."

in five minutes," noted Martinovich. The same thing happened when Tammy played the Roxy Theatre in Los Angeles nearly a year later. The packed house included movie and TV stars, not to mention rockers Tom Petty and Jeff Lynne, who kibitzed with Wynette after the show. "I was so dadgum nervous backstage I wished for a Valium the size of a half-dollar," Tammy confessed.

Nadler and Shriver, who was then Randy Travis's publicist, often traveled on the road with Tammy and Richey. Susan had first encountered Richey during a Tammy stay in Nashville's Centennial Hospital. She was amazed by the setup Richey had arranged for himself within the hospital. "It was like a suite! He had on black silk pajamas and a black silk robe, he was smoking, and there was a black guy serving a drink."

"I have tremendous affection for Richey," said Shriver. "He treated me like a princess, he treated Tammy like a queen. They were so much fun to travel with. Tammy had this tiny little stomach, so you would order room service about every two hours. There was never a second's thought given to money or expense. You'd just sit there and think what is your fantasy to have. Richey would get it and it would be gotten with great flourish. You'd just laugh the whole time.

"The one thing I'll say about Richey is, he demanded you treated Tammy like a superstar. You wanted Tammy, you provided hair and makeup, and they flew in a private jet. Tammy was always treated like a superstar, and consequently, to the day she died, she was a superstar."

In 1989 George Richey pulled off what might've been his biggest coup ever. For a year and a half Tammy hosted a country package sponsored by GMC trucks. "She was getting as much sponsorship fee as her concert fee," said booking agent Tony Conway, who gave Richey credit for the deal. "Randy [Travis] was the headliner, but it was Tammy's tour. Richey made millions of dollars. He had 'em payin' for sound and lights and trucks, the support acts . . . It was like a dream tour. It was like forty G a day to them, plus the guarantee." On the bill with Tammy were the Judds and Travis (later it was Shenandoah and Clint Black), and as the self-described "grandma of the tour," Wynette only had to do a thirty-five-minute set, then introduce the other acts. Tammy grew very fond of Wynonna, seeing more than a little of the Tammy–Mee-Maw dynamic in Wynonna's tempestuous relationship with her mother, Naomi. Wynonna would "get mad and pitch fits at her mama behind the stage," said an amused Wynette. "She'd come to my dressin' room, cool off, and go back." (Wynonna also had a pig she'd named Tammy Swinette.)

Wynette was a big fan of Randy Travis. Kelli Haggard-Patterson recalled being in the car with her one day when his hit "Diggin' Up Bones" came on. She had them pull over and stop just so she could listen. "Randy is responsible for bringing country music back to traditional country," enthused Wynette, who later cut one duet with Travis, "We're Strangers Again." Tammy was protective of him. During a television taping of the March 1991 special *A Festival at Ford's*, director Joe Cates "yelled at Randy on the stage. He was really, really nasty, and I got into it with him," recalled Evelyn Shriver. "And out of the back comes Tammy. She had on a red sweater with these big white poufy snowballs all over it, really tight pants, and high heels. She said to Cates, 'You *back off.* How *dare* you speak to Randy Travis like this? I've worked with you for twenty years, and you're nothing but *a hack.*' She leveled that guy. Tammy went wild, she was like a little tiger cub coming to life. We all stood there with our mouths open, because you never saw Tammy be rude to anybody. Tammy loved Randy."

In September 1991, Tammy was the beneficiary of extraordinary good luck: an international pop hit that dropped into her lap from out of nowhere. The gift came by way of UK musicians Bill Drummond and Jimmy Cauty, aka the KLF, a crackpot outfit known for dance hits and absurdist antics.

In early summer of that year, the duo were in a London studio trying to revive a track that had been kicking around in one form or another since a fragment appeared on their 1987 debut album in a song entitled "Hey, Hey We Are Not the Monkees." Cauty wanted to replace the singer, randomly suggesting Tammy Wynette. Drummond, a fan of not only country but of Wynette, got on the phone and a week later was being picked up at the Nashville airport by none other than George Richey. "Driving a powder blue Jag," Richey, recovering from open-heart surgery, sported "snakeskin boots, fresh-pressed jeans, a wet-look perm," wrote Drummond. "I liked him."

Bill met his idol back at First Lady Acres as he stepped into the First Lady's pink beauty parlor. "Her fingers were being manicured by a young man as a woman teased her hair into some feathered concoction. Her free hand was flicking through the pages of *Vogue*." Tammy had a question for her new friend. "'Bill, you're from Scotland? Can you tell me why I have such a large lesbian following there?' I had no answer, but promised to look into it."

Drummond was well aware of the inescapable pitfalls of the Tammy Wynette–KLF collision, which by its very nature was, as he described, "an evil and corrupt exchange . . . the young artist wanting to tap into the mythical status and credibility of the has-been, the has-been wanting some of that 'I'm still contemporary, relevant, will do anything to get back into the charts' stuff." But that didn't stop Bill from playing the number for Tammy on her white grand piano. Wynette gamely warbled along. "She couldn't find the key, let alone get it in pitch," worried Drummond.

Into a local studio they went later that night, Tammy attempting to lay down a vocal on a thunderous dance track that certainly featured no down-home fiddle (although there was steel guitar buried in the murk, along with a Jimi Hendrix riff), not to mention nonsensical lyrics about a place called Mu-Mu Land which contained the couplet: "They're justified and ancient / and they drive an ice cream van."

About as far out of her element as Mu-Mu Land was from Music City, Tammy was hopelessly adrift in this electronica wasteland. "She could not keep time with the track for more than four bars before speeding up or slowing down," said Drummond. Richey entered the booth and attempted to coach her. "A complete disaster" was Bill's pained appraisal. "How do you tell the voice you have worshipped for the past twenty years, one of the greatest singing voices of the twentieth century, a voice that defines a whole epoch of American culture, that it sounds like shit?"

Drummond whisked the track back to London and dumped the bad news on his partner, Jimmy. Cauty told him to relax—the latest digital technology they'd just purchased would allow them to take Tammy's words and "stretch them, squeeze them, get them all in time." (According to Mike Martinovich, Wynette recorded another verse missing in the final recording.) The end result was surely the most synthetic and tricked-out concoction Wynette had ever been involved in, and it was a total gasser. "Justified and Ancient (Stand by the JAMS)" was a phenomenon. It shot to number one in eighteen countries. It stalled at number 2 in the UK only because a reissued "Bohemian Rhapsody" lodged at number one in the wake of Freddy Mercury's early demise.

Best of all was the nutty video, an $850,000 extravaganza shot at London's Pinewood Studios, where many a James Bond film had been lensed.

There was Tammy, high on a throne surrounded by Zulu dancers and Asian chicks in blonde wigs, wearing a "skintight mermaid outfit with a bustier like Madonna wears. And I had this crown on. I don't know what the meaning of that was." (George Jones dubbed it Tammy's "voodoo video.")

Wynette appeared on *Top of the Pops* with Cauty and Drummond, who were dressed as twelve-foot-tall guitar-playing ice cream cones. "These guys are crazy," enthused Wynette about her young collaborators. Maybe so, but Drummond and Cauty had successfully updated Tammy's image, gaining her a new legion of fans in the process. Early on in her career a reporter from *Country Music Life* asked Wynette how she felt about the hit singles and many awards she'd gotten so early in the game. "Tammy in wonderland!" she exclaimed in response. After hit records, failed marriages, kidnapping attempts, illness, and addiction, Tammy was still in wonderland, albeit a darker and stranger one, and "Justified and Ancient" captured the vibe beautifully.

Understandably, the song never became part of Wynette's usual stage repertoire, but that didn't stop the other Wynettetones from unnerving Charlie Carter on the bus one day by telling him Tammy wanted them to learn the number for their next gig. "That song definitely has no country in it whatsoever, and Charlie Carter is old-school country head to toe," said Rusty Pence. "He was goin', '*How* in *the world* are we *ever* gonna play this onstage?!' He eventually realized we were jerkin' his chain."

Unfortunately drug abuse had once more crept back into the picture. Stanley Harman, who served as a bodyguard and road manager for Tammy in 1991, recalled an overseas tour during which Wynette, who was a big collector of crystal, was invited to a special tour and presentation at the Waterford plant in Ireland. "We were there for them to present Tammy a bowl." Wynette was in no shape to attend. "Tammy couldn't move, so I had to pick her up and put my hand up under her fur, up under her armpit, and pull her next to my body and walk with her. That's the only way Tammy could walk. She was out of it."

According to Harman, Richey trailed a safe distance behind. "I'm sure people were wonderin', 'Well, why is this guy walkin' so close to Tammy and her husband's back there?' But George always did that. When she got too messed up to really be in public, he'd stand about fifteen feet behind and let me walk with her.

"There were times she'd be rollin' in the floor of the bus, and Richey would just sit there and watch her. Tammy lyin' on the floor, writhin' in pain . . . and I'd wonder, 'Why isn't he pickin' her up and puttin' her on the couch?' I'd put her on the couch, we'd have to call emergency, and then they'd come haul her to the hospital. That happened a couple of times. I just thought it was so strange."

Along with fellow celebrities Ben Vereen and Ann Landers, Tammy was invited to Washington, D.C., to speak to the Senate about conquering drug addiction. Unfortunately she was still very much on them. As Tammy went off into the Senate, she slipped Barbara her little black cosmetic bag. Hutchison knew what was inside. "When we'd go off to the venue sometimes, she'd have her needle and her Dilaudid in a bag, and I'd have to hold it. She didn't want too many people around her when she was takin' drugs. At the end of the night that was just a regular thing she did. She did slowly start to do it in front of me—one night she just injected herself, and that just kind of threw me back, the way she just picked up and put the syringe in, just poked it in her leg. I was like, 'Oh, Tammy.'"

And so, Dilaudid in hand, Barbara waited as Wynette lectured Washington on the evils of drug abuse. "Tammy was feelin' real bad that day. She had the shakes because she hadn't had anything, she had to stay straight. She had to talk to all these Senate people, had to stand up in front of everybody and give a speech, tell 'em how drugs were bad, and take pictures with Ann Landers. . . . Oh, she was hurtin', I know she was hurtin'. And then as soon as she finished and everybody adjourned, she went to me and said, 'Find the nearest bathroom, *I have to go to the nearest bathroom.* Have you got that bag?'" Next thing Hutchison knew, they were parked in the ladies' room and Wynette was shooting up. Was the irony of the situation apparent to Tammy? "It didn't matter to her," said a blasé Barbara. "She did her part in the show."

On January 26, 1992, Bill and Hillary Clinton appeared on *60 Minutes.* In the course of being asked about her husband's then-alleged infidelities with Gennifer Flowers, Hillary said, "I'm not sitting here, some little woman 'standing by my man' like Tammy Wynette." Thus began perhaps the ultimate face-off over "Stand by Your Man." It was a flip, ill-considered remark, particularly since it appeared that that was precisely what Hillary was doing. Many critics felt that the comment suggested both snobbishness and superiority. Not only was Hillary attacking Tammy, she was putting down country music, and by extension its fans. And they were mad. "The fallout was instant and brutal," wrote Clinton in 2003. "I regretted the way I came across."

Wynette, who'd been lying in bed watching the broadcast, was not amused. Her first response, reported by *Entertainment Weekly*, was unusually salty for Tammy: "How dare that bitch say that about me!" George Richey, ready to milk this brouhaha for all it was worth, reported his wife was "mad as hell and she probably will be for some time." The First Lady of the White House versus the First Lady of Country: the press, hungry to see two powerful women go at each other, only seemed sorry they couldn't be coaxed into mud wrestling.

Tammy fired off an angry letter to Clinton (one which to these ears sounds more like Richey than Tammy): "With all that is in me I resent your caustic remark. Mrs. Clinton, you have offended every woman and man who love that song—several million in number . . . and every person who has 'made it on their own' with no one to take them to the White House. I would like you to appear with me on any forum including networks, cable or talk shows and stand toe to toe with me. I can assure you in spite of your education you will find me to be just as bright as yourself." How very unfortunate that particular tête-à-tête never occurred.

Clinton did call Tammy, who refused to speak to her until Burt Reynolds intervened. And Hillary did apologize publicly. "I didn't mean to hurt Tammy Wynette as a person. I happen to be a country-western fan. If she feels like I've hurt her feelings, I'm sorry about that." The remark has dogged Clinton throughout her career. "She's had to eat them words . . . how many times?" noted a pleased Loretta Lynn. "Shall we count the ways?" As Wynette fan Laura Cantrell pointed out, "the people were with Tammy."

Not only did Wynette get a truckload of publicity out of the brouhaha, Sony later rereleased "Stand by Your Man." "Hey, she used me," said Tammy. "I'll use her now." Sometime later Wynette was invited out to Barbra Streisand's Malibu home to be the surprise guest at a Clinton fundraiser. When Hillary saw Wynette onstage "her jaw dropped," said Mike

Martinovich, who was present. Wynette would later claim to Martha
Dettwiller that when she went to shake Clinton's hand backstage, Hillary
refused it.*

Early in 1992 Wynette toured Europe, then Australia. Her previous tour
down under had been a short one, but a great success, so plans were made
for an extensive Australia jaunt to last six weeks.† Ticket sales for the tour
went "absolutely through the roof," said promoter Wally Bishop. "Then it
fell off the rails."

The first alarm bells rang when Richey canceled her press after three
interviews. Tammy was not feeling up to it. Then came a show in Mackay,
North Queensland. As opening act Johnny Chester did his set, Tammy
arrived dressed and ready to go onstage. There was suddenly an emergency. "Her tour manager, Marty Johnson, came to me and said, 'I think
you better get an ambulance, because Tammy's gone down.'" Wynette's
musicians were eating with members of Johnny Chester's band when
paramedics rolled Tammy by on a gurney. The Australians were in shock,
even more so as it seemed her band was rather blasé about Wynette's
condition. "I never will forget that," said David Sloas. "I guess we had
seen it to the point where we were used to it, and kind of hardened. It
was sad."

Wynette spent several days in the hospital. "At this point we thought we
were covered with insurance—however, such was not the case, because
with insurance you have to disclose any preexisting illness. And there was
preexisting illness." Bishop had no idea how sick Tammy was. Unbeknownst
to him, Wynette had already collapsed on the European leg of the tour.
Plans were made to reschedule the canceled dates at the tail end. Shows in
Darwin and Cairns were added as well.

---

*Tammy also told Dettwiller and others that when she "walked up to Barbra Streisand
and said, 'You're my idol,' Streisand turned around and said, 'You're *my* idol.' Tammy
said that floored her—'I never even thought she knew who I was.'"

†One memorable meeting of the minds occurred on that first Australian tour: Phyllis
Diller happened to be touring as well and joined Tammy Wynette's entourage for dinner.
Diller told one dirty joke after the other, and as each gag got bluer and bluer, Wynette
grew more and more squeamish. Diller, said Wally Bishop, "was obviously gauging
Tammy's reaction. I remember the last gag she said: 'What's black and hairy and sleeps
on the wall?' And she said, 'Humpty cunt.' Tammy put her hands over her face and shook
with disbelief. And Phyllis just roared that raucous laugh of hers. Poor Tammy near
died."

Then, at the Burswood Casino in Perth on March 29, after eating supper at one a.m., Tammy fell ill again and returned to the hospital. The rest of the dates were canceled. Wynette and company, David Sloas confessed, "just flew home with our tail between our legs." English promoter Dennis Smith had underwritten the tour, and Bishop had to call him on his fiftieth birth- day and tell him the bad news. "It sent him to the wall. He lost everything. Richey said during that period of time to let him know what our losses were, and he would make it up to us. Never happened."

Back in North America came another health crisis. Out on the road in Canada on May 5, her fiftieth birthday, Wynette suffered a bile duct infec- tion that sent her to St. Louis Hospital for a fourteen-hour operation. A new doctor had entered her life, Wallis Marsh. Tammy called Martha Dettwiller and told her that Dr. Marsh was going to be the answer to her prayers. "She thought he was going to fix her up, wean her off the drugs, and then she could be free. Well, Marsh didn't turn out to be quite the answer she thought he would be." Wallis Marsh would be Tammy's physician until the very end. Marsh and members of his family came along on tours and received lavish gifts. Tammy told Karyn Sloas that she liked Marsh because he looked and sounded "just like Gomer Pyle." Richey told Barbara Hutchison that Marsh had designs on a show business career.

According to Hutchison, Marsh allowed Richey to dress up in scrubs and be present in the operating room for his wife's operation in St. Louis. "He wore those scrubs everywhere," said Hutchison. "Everywhere! He wore 'em on the bus. He's got to be sick to want to go in there and watch Tammy bein' operated on."*

In 1992 Tammy and Richey paid $422,500 for a new home at 4916 Franklin Road. Built in 1949, it had been the home of Hank Williams. His first wife, Audrey, had died there. According to Barbara Hutchison, Wynette wanted a house in another subdivision, but Richey insisted on the Williams home, boasting to Barbara's mother that the house had been put in his name. They spent a year remodeling the twelve-thousand-square-foot property, which included a waterfall pond and covered pavilion, not to mention a twenty- five-thousand-dollar ivory and gold toilet. Wynette put in a hot pink beauty parlor. "Her bedroom and bath area looked like a little girl's fantasy," gushed

*Since Marsh and Richey declined to be interviewed, I could not verify this tale.

Lorrie Morgan. "It was almost like being in the queen's palace, but yet feeling like you could wear your sweatpants and eat on the carpet."

Despite the overhaul "Tammy never liked that house," said Hutchison, who said that, because of its enormous lobby, the house felt like a funeral home, and Wynette sometimes called it "the mausoleum." One day while doing her hair, Barbara asked Tammy if she was superstitious, mentioning that Audrey had died in the bedroom and that previous owners claimed to have seen her ghost. "She looked at me kind of strange and said, 'I don't let those things bother me,' and walked off. But after I told her that, she never did sleep in that bedroom. She always slept on the couch." The walk from Wynette's master bedroom to the kitchen was about twenty-five yards, and Tammy, who was often hooked up to a portable IV unit in her final years, got tuckered out. Said Ruben Garces, "It was a good long walk, and on not-feelin'-good days, she'd say, 'I wish we'd get rid of this house and get a little house.' But you can't be First Lady and drive a Hyundai."*

Her spot on the couch in the kitchen was where Wynette watched TV into the wee hours. Tammy was a sucker for late-night infomercials. "We'd get somethin' new three or four times a month," said Garces. Tammy would proudly announce she'd gotten the new Ginsu knife or a weed whacker, and her housekeeper, Cleta, would just "roll her eyes," said Garces. Wynette watched the country music cable channels religiously. "Not being able to sleep, she stayed truly informed," said Evelyn Shriver. "Tammy knew who was good, who wasn't good, she knew what everybody had out at any given moment." Wynette never stopped listening to music. She was a big fan of songwriter Skip Ewing, and when Sony sent her a copy of Doug Stone's first single, she'd play it over and over on the bus after her shows.

One singer Tammy definitely didn't care for was Reba McEntire, who had trumped Wynette's record of winning the CMA's Female Vocalist of the Year award three years in a row with her fourth consecutive win in 1987. Karyn Sloas started doing a Reba song during the show, and Wynette "shut me down real quick on that one. I was told I wasn't to sing like Reba or sing anything by her."

Toward the very end of her life Wynette became enthralled with a Hank

*Garces served as Wynette's unofficial chauffeur. They'd get in Tammy's Lincoln, and Ruben would drive them to Corky's, a BBQ joint about five miles away, where she coveted the barbecue sandwich. "Tammy always made me laugh, because anytime we'd be out, she'd say, 'Ruben, you got any money?' I'd say, 'I got money, Tammy. I got you covered.'"

Williams boxed set. On one particular tour "that's all we listened to for the whole trip," said Sloas. "Just one haunting melody after another! That's how Tammy was about anything in her life. If she was interested in food, we would eat that food until she was burned out. An actress—she'd get every movie that there was with her and watch them one after another. And then we would go on to somethin' else."

A spoiled little Pomeranian named Killer was Tammy's new buddy in the nineties. Killer would join her on the kitchen couch for TV time and come on the bus for road trips. It wasn't unusual for Richey to send road manager John Payne into a supermarket for three filet mignons—one for Tammy, one for Richey, and one for Killer. Recalled Ruben Garces, "They'd get in trouble all the time with the vet, because they'd feed him crazy stuff. Tammy just wouldn't listen to the vet." By the time pianist Van Abbott joined the band in 1996, he'd note that Killer had "eaten filet mignon for a year and a half, his front feet were stickin' out at forty-five-degree angles and he couldn't take a crap." The Pomeranian pretty much ruled the roost. "Whenever that dog had to shit, buddy, both buses would hit the shoulder of the interstate, and they'd call for Marty Lewis to walk him," said David Sloas. "Marty was dogshit captain."

Tears of Fire, a three-CD anthology of Tammy's career, was released on November 10, 1992. While it benefited from several unreleased tracks, most notably her version of "Precious Memories" and a knockout Sherrill-produced version of Harlan Howard's "The Deepening Snow," it was a predictable selection of the hits with a thrown-together booklet, lightweight notes, and not enough of the album cuts that were sometimes more potent than the singles. As usual, Tammy deserved better.

Next Wynette went into the studio to cut a trio album with Dolly Parton and Loretta Lynn. *Honky Tonk Angels* would be her last gold album. Parton, who coproduced the album with Steve Buckingham, was the driving force behind the project. "I just kind of cracked the whip," admitted Dolly. "She kept sayin' all the way through the record, 'This is important, I don't care if it sells five copies, we gotta do this,'" Parton told Buckingham. "I need to do it before one of us dies." The three singers met at Dolly's Twelfth Avenue office in Nashville to pick songs, and recording began February 1, 1993. Buckingham, who taped everything including between-song conversations, was fascinated watching these three forces of nature work together. Parton had "more creative input into music"; Wynette, more concerned with her singing, was determined to "nail it on the scratch vocal"; Lynn was the absentminded but lovable clown. Wynette's vocal abilities earned high praise from Loretta. "She knew her harmony lines. Tammy was the greatest. Kind of like bluegrass harmony, y'know."

"It was like visitin' with sisters," said Dolly. "We were country people—we're not that different in age, and so we knew all the same people, and we had our own take on everybody, so we were good to gossip, we carried all the tales. So we had belly laughs." Wynette's sense of humor was "sorta like her singin'—she'd sneak up on you. It would just come out of nowhere when you weren't expectin' it. Very dry sense of humor. Very witty and very smart. I used to just die laughin' at her."

The album opens with a romp through the old chestnut "Silver Threads and Golden Needles," Tammy charging ahead on lead. That set the tone for this pleasurable but hardly earthshaking endeavor, with the ladies sailing effortlessly through such oldies as "Wings of a Dove" and "I Forgot More Than You'll Ever Know." (There is said to be an album's worth of outtakes from the session, including the Louvins' "When I Stop Dreaming.") As reviewer Alanna Nash pointed out, this was a trio that, unlike the serious-as-death Dolly-Emmylou-Linda triumvirate, felt "more at home with campy recitations than hip, new songs." Chief case in point is an update of Tex Ritter's beyond-corny laundry list of deceased country stars, "Hillbilly Heaven," in which Dolly has the hide to pronounce Tammy's name "Wine-ette," which must've had Mildred turning over in her grave. The down-home camaraderie was palpable and, as Parton explained, unlikely to be seen among their modern counterparts. "There's a lot of jealousy and competitiveness among a lot of the new singers—it's more like the rock 'n' roll business," she noted.*

The trio paid respect to the woman who had inspired them all, Kitty Wells, who joined in on "It Wasn't God Who Made Honky Tonk Angels." They also dubbed their voices to a 1960 Patsy Cline recording of "Lovesick Blues," the shameless sort of trick that makes one want to take a sledgeham-

---

*When it came to Dolly, some felt Tammy still had a chip on her shoulder. "There was a bit of jealousy there," said Karyn Sloas. "Dolly was an incredible businesswoman, very self-sufficient—she didn't need a George Richey. That pushed a few buttons with Tammy. She loved Dolly but you could tell there was a little rivalry."

mer to digital recorders everywhere (although it is worth a laugh to hear Parton ad-lib, "Good Lord, that's Floyd Cramer, he's older than we are").

Honky Tonk Angels was released in November 1993. (Dolly informed the press that the original title was *Hot Flashes*.) Music City had gotten a preview of the project on September 29, when the trio, all dressed in white, appeared on the CMA Awards and brought the house down singing "Silver Threads." (The fact that Loretta completely stepped on Dolly's part during the performance only made it all that more endearing.) Lynn wore an old-timey lace gown; Parton, a bodacious low-cut number; Wynette a stylish pantsuit. Their larger-than-life, utterly distinct personalities radiated out of all that white to remind the glossy new interchangeable country superstars and potentates how human the music used to be, even if radio no longer played them: "Silver Threads" went no higher than number 68 on the charts.

In June 1993, Tammy's fan club friends Den and Carolyn Neal and their son (and Wynette's godson), Darren, came to Nashville and visited Tammy, who was just getting settled in the Hank Williams house.* Den went off with Richey, helping him get some furniture out of storage. Carolyn and Darren sat in the kitchen watching TV when Tammy—"all tousled, bare feet, she just had a satiny wrap around her"—came out to join them. They shared a hello hug. "All of a sudden there were big tears rolling down her cheeks," said Carolyn. "I went over to her and said, 'What's the matter, darlin'?' And she started sobbing. She said, 'I don't know how I can cope with it any longer.'"

Then Tammy "just opened her robe up and showed us this scar—I swear it was an inch wide, raised, bright pink—it went from her breastbone down to her navel." Wynette pointed out an egg-shaped lump above her left breast where tubes had been stuck in her. "It itches incessantly," Tammy complained. "It drives me mad. I scratch it when I'm asleep. I make myself bleed." "'No problem,'" recalled Carolyn, "'I'll go into town and get you boxing gloves.' She did laugh at that." Then, according to Neal,

---

*It was Carolyn who came to the rescue when, as part of her act, Tammy recited "Changes," a poem she'd written after staring at her aging figure in the mirror. "And that onetime cute little fanny now needs braces to hold it up" went one line. Over in England, "fanny" is slang for a woman's front—not rear—end. The reaction of the audience, said Carolyn, was one of "stunned horror. Everybody just sat there and looked at her." Afterward, Wynette asked her what she'd said wrong. "You were about two inches out, hon," said Carolyn. A mortified Tammy then changed the line to "cute little butt."

she showed them bruises at the top of her leg and hip, which, Wynette claimed, came from no operation. "Tammy said, 'He's told me that if I leave him, I'll never appear on the stage again. He'll make sure of that.' And she really believed it."*

Wynette immediately regretted her confession. "Tammy kept saying, 'Don't tell him I've told you this, don't tell him I've told you this—he'll kill me.'" Carolyn promised she wouldn't. "She was sitting there crying and I was handing her paper tissues, and she must've dropped one that went just a little bit underneath the couch."

When Richey and Den arrived, "she just sat there, and the best way I can describe it: her eyes followed him, and it was like a whipped puppy looking for a kind word from its owner." Richey ignored her, only talking to the Neals. "He totally, totally cut her dead."

Richey and Den got more furniture, then were off in another part of the house. Carolyn convinced Tammy to eat something, and then she wanted to take some cake to the men. "She was very shaky, and she dropped the cake. It fell onto the carpeting on the stairs.

"And she looked petrified. At that moment my husband ran around the bottom of the stairs to come up, and she thought it was Richey. She just sank down onto the stair and started sobbing, 'He'll kill me, he'll kill me!'" Den helped her clean up the mess and assured Tammy nobody was going to kill her.

When Den went off again with Richey, Carolyn asked if she'd told her daughters what was going on. "I've told them, but they don't want to know," said Tammy. "If they acknowledged it, they might have to do something," mused Carolyn aloud. This disturbed Wynette. "She sprung around at me and said, 'Is that how you feel?' 'No darling, we're always here for you,'" assured Carolyn. "And she kind of relaxed again."

Richey then came into the room and told Tammy it was time for her to go lie down. After she left, his eyes fastened on that paper hanky under the couch. "Whose is this?" asked Richey. "Without thinking, I said, 'Tammy must've dropped it.' He picked it up, it was sodden with her tears. And he asked us whose it was, *waiting* to see if we would tell him that she talked

---

*The other reason Wynette often gave for not leaving Richey was that Tammy just couldn't take the public humiliation of another failed marriage. Recalled Jan Smith, "She'd say, 'My fans can't take another divorce.' I said, 'Oh, my God—your fans *love* it when you get a divorce!' It was part of her whole legend."

to us. Of course we didn't." Suddenly Richey's demeanor turned ice-cold. "He changed," said Carolyn.

When the Neals were ready to leave, they asked to say good-bye to Tammy. Richey said she was asleep, and he'd tell her good-bye. "At that moment Tammy walked out." Seeing Tammy's obviously upset face, Den distracted Richey by asking George to take him where their coats were. "He went, surprisingly," said Carolyn. "Tammy came to me, hugged me and held tight and said, 'Don't go, please don't go.' The tears were rolling down her cheeks. It tore me apart. I think she was frightened of being left with him."

The following February, Wynette called the Neals sobbing, maintaining Richey was still trying to wheedle out of her what she'd told them. Once again she begged them not to utter a word.

For a brief moment in 1994, Wynette hosted a seven-episode show on country cable, *The Legends*. Backed by her own band, Tammy interviewed guests like Ricky Van Shelton, Doug Stone, and Loretta Lynn. Wynette beamed with happiness as she devoted a show to her favorite gospel greats. There was old Jake Hess, fiendishly cheerful beneath the familiar toupee, belting out one of Wynette's favorites, "Death Ain't No Big Deal." It should come as no surprise that Tammy rose to the occasion, joining her guests on "Precious Memories" and "How Great Thou Art." She looked neither tired nor sick, and sang her butt off.

Barbara Hutchison accompanied Tammy and Richey on a trip to California. Tammy was flying out to Los Angeles to meet Melissa Etheridge and needed her hair done. It was a journey Hutchison would just as soon forget. When Barbara arrived at the house, it became apparent that Tammy and Richey had been fighting. "We got into the car goin' to the airport and Tammy started cryin'. He didn't say anything and she didn't say anything." When Richey went to get the tickets, Hutchison asked Tammy what was wrong. "And she says, 'Oh, it's Richey. He won't let me get anything for Georgette.'"

Georgette needed either a washing machine or stove, said Barbara; Richey refused to give Tammy a cent. "He tells me he's not gonna let me have any money for her to get those things," said Wynette, sobbing.

"Barbara, don't ever get married," Tammy continued. "Why?" she asked.

Wynette said she had no control over her finances, and that any purchases had to go through either Richey or Sylvia, his sister-in-law, who ran the office. "It has gotten to where I can't even write money for myself," she moaned.

"Tammy, that's money you make," said Barbara.

"Barbara, you don't understand. Everything from a pair of pants to nail polish I have to get approved through Sylvia. My life is not my own."

In Her Room

The sad part about happy endings is there's nothing to write about.

—Tammy Wynette

On Monday night, December 27, 1994, Wynette was back in the hospital. She'd spent the day recording a duet with Aaron Neville. That night she'd woken up three times in pain and, at four a.m., was having trouble breathing. Tammy finally decided she could take no more. Richey put her in the car and took her to the hospital, like so many times before. "I had no reason to think it was life-threatening," he said.

Wynette said she arrived at Baptist Hospital in "excruciating pain." Tests were run to figure out what was wrong. At six p.m. Tuesday, Richey noticed her blood pressure plummeting. Her feet were elevated to increase the blood flow to her brain. Wynette was rushed to intensive care, where a ventilator was put in her throat. Otherwise, said Richey, "she would have been brain-damaged." Evelyn Shriver was called to the hospital and told to prepare Tammy's obituary.

"I told Richey, 'I'm really getting frightened,'" recalled Tammy. "I looked at one of my doctors and said, 'Am I gonna be okay?' And there was no answer." Wynette's blood pressure sank to 42/16. She lost consciousness and would remain comatose for days. Doctors gave Tammy a 30 percent chance of surviving. "They told my family I wasn't gonna make it," she said, maintaining at one point that she had expired on the operating table, saw a bright light, and felt as if she were floating. "I felt no pain, no fear, no anything." Quoting Jake Hess, she added: "I think it's God's way of telling me death ain't no big deal."

Tammy had another infection in her bile duct, and even after surgery that Thursday doctors were telling Richey it was "too late" to save her.

Somewhat miraculously, Wynette pulled through.* Wallis Marsh performed another operation in Pittsburgh, and a few days later, on January 15, Tammy was doing her first date in Arizona, backed by the Tucson Symphony Orchestra.

Fifteen minutes and four songs into the performance, Wynette threw in the towel. "I'm not going to be finishing this show," she said. "I'm very sorry."

Tammy would spend most of the rest of her life hooked to a portable IV that pumped drugs through a portacath that was placed first in her chest, then in her back. Recurring problems with blood clotting sent her back into the hospital. Her voice sounded thin and weak, at times off pitch. Only fifty-one, Wynette looked at least two decades older. She'd lost a tremendous amount of weight, which left her with sunken cheeks and the bug-eyed look of some ancient vaudeville comic. Wynette may have survived the infection, but she was never to be the same. Said Karyn Sloas, "She wasn't Tammy after that, really."

The tabloid vultures smelled blood, and they hovered nearby, cameras in hand. One hospital clerk sold her records to a scandal sheet; Tammy sued and won. Richey got so fed up that at one point he told *Star*, "Yes, she's dying. She'll be dead at two fifteen this afternoon, why don't you print *that?*"

On April 9, 1994, Tammy made a triumphant appearance in New York City at Carnegie Hall to take part in a rain-forest benefit, in which she shared the bill with no less than Elton John, James Taylor, Sting, Whitney Houston, Aaron Neville, and Luciano Pavarotti. But as *Rolling Stone* would point out, "Tammy received the night's most thunderous applause." Taylor, who performed a duet with her, would graciously note that it had been "the lifelong dream of all the performers to share a stage with Tammy Wynette." It was a career milestone for Tammy, who spent a good deal of the day on her bus worrying over a Crock-Pot. "We're parked out there in front of Carnegie Hall, and all she cares about is that she has to get the pinto beans and corn bread ready," said Karyn Sloas. "That's Tammy—beans and corn bread."

---

*Out of the many guests she received in the hospital, the first person to make Tammy laugh was Billy Sherrill, who leaned down and asked her about the session with Aaron Neville, who has a rather distinctive birthmark on his forehead. Inquired Billy, "When you were singin' together, were you lookin' at his lips, or that stain up there on his head?"

———

Wynette finished work on her duet album in 1994. It was a glitzy project: duets with Cliff Richard, Wynonna, Lyle Lovett, Joe Diffie, Elton John, Aaron Neville, Smokey Robinson, and Sting. (Melissa Etheridge, Tom Petty, James Taylor, and Bonnie Raitt were other names that had originally been bandied about.)

Without Walls was produced by Birmingham, England–born Barry Beckett, who had an impeccable list of credits as keyboard player for the Muscle Shoals Rhythm Section, gracing everything from "Tell Mama" by Etta James and "I'll Take You There" by the Staple Singers to Dylan's 1980s gospel recordings. He also produced a few hits for Hank Williams, Jr., including his faux "duet" with Dad, "Tear in My Beer," not to mention that egregious soft rock offense from 1976, Mary MacGregor's "Torn Between Two Lovers." With Tammy, Beckett rolled snake eyes. Compared to the sturdy house of music Sherrill always built around Wynette, *Without Walls* was a prefab digital condo thrown together with phased guitars, processed vocals, and sucker-punch drums. For all her belting, Tammy was a master of restraint, unlike the vibrato all-stars that burn the beans on cut after cut here. The worst track was picked as the single, "Girl Thang" (just typing that title hurts), a blues workout wholly inappropriate to and completely undignified for Tammy, which is only made worse by Wynonna's sea lion caterwauling. The rest is almost as cringe-worthy: Does the world really need to hear Wynette singing "Every Breath You Take" with Sting? Or "I Second That Emotion" with Smokey Robinson? The most memorable thing about Tammy's duet with Elton John was what he scribbled when asked to autograph her sheet music: "To the Queen of Country from the Queen of England." "I never went in for the crossover song," boasted Wynette in 1988. Apparently she had changed her mind, but to no great effect.

All is redeemed, however, on the final cut, which is thankfully unpolluted by any superstar hoo-ha. The simple, stark "What Do They Know" is the territory Wynette knew best: the sadness of love and life. This was to be her final solo recording, and Tammy just knocks it out of the park. "They say life goes on / I'll find true love again," she muses, an ocean's worth of sorrow in that battle-scarred voice. "But what do they know?" Not much, it turns out. Here lies the sad riddle of Wynette, because it is all too apparent there was so much about Tammy we will never unravel, and so much that—

for whatever the reason—she couldn't bear to share. Permanently earth-bound, this little bird was staring into the black and starry night, yearning for one final flight.

Wynette's next trip to New York City to promote the just-released *Without Walls* was something less than her Carnegie Hall triumph. She flew from a Branson, Missouri, gig to do the *Late Show with David Letterman* on October, 24, 1994. Tammy was scheduled to perform her new "Girl Thang" single, with Karyn Sloas filling in for a curiously absent Wynonna Judd. Wynette augmented Letterman's house band with a few members of her own outfit, and they knew just how unprepared she was to do the song. "We were a little bit shocked," said steel player Rusty Pence. "We did not do this song in our show. We were in the process of learning it—the band knew it—but we hadn't done it with Tammy. Until you have played the song in front of people, to do this song on Letterman was kind of a mistake."

Wynette was extremely jittery about doing the Letterman show. "Tammy never got his sense of humor, and she was scared, because she knew she was going to have to go over and talk to him," said Karyn Sloas. "I could tell Tammy was nervous. Before we went out she grabbed my hand and about squeezed it off." Just how ill-suited the number was for Tammy became immediately apparent. "It was a song out of her element," said Sloas. "We were singing live on television, and Tammy jumped time." Nobody but a musician would've heard the error, and Wynette managed to limp through the number and chat with Letterman, only to face George Richey's wrath backstage.

"We go back, Richey comes barrelin' down the hallway," recalled Sloas. "He's so mad because he thinks she's messed up and made a fool out of herself. I couldn't hear everything he was sayin', but he was throwin' things and he was *mad*. I'm thinkin', 'Who's gonna hear this?'" The next morning Wynette performed on the *Today* show. Karyn shared a limo to the studio with Tammy's hairdresser, Mackie Pettus, who told her Richey and Tammy had continued to fight long after the Letterman taping was over. "Mackie said that you could hear 'em all night long."

Tammy sang "Girl Thang" once more on the *Today* show and screwed it up worse. After the show a sobbing Tammy called up Martha Dettwiller, moaning about how awful her appearance had been. According to Dettwiller, Wynette told her that she "had been ready to go onstage, and Richey had come up behind her and said, 'You look terrible! You look awful! I cannot believe you are going to go onstage the way you look.'" Richey's remarks "crushed her—I mean *crushed* her. She said, 'I was cryin' before I ever hit the stage.'"

That night Wynette gave a rousing concert at Town Hall, backed by the New York Philharmonic string section. "She blew the hair off of everybody's head," said longtime fan Laura Cantrell, who was reduced to tears when Tammy tore down the house with a showstopping "How Great Thou Art." The show was also notable for a colorful contingency of downtown denizens outfitted in gender-bending couture. According to Mike Martinovich, "The label got a call from the drag queen association of New York asking if they could cosponsor a party for Tammy. She goes onstage, here come streams of Tammys in drag, laying roses on the stage. She was a little frightened. People were storming her."

After the show Wynette and company were whisked off by bus to the Metropolitan Club for a private party attended by Melissa Etheridge,* quizzical television nonentity Larry "Bud" Melman, and an endless sea of men in big, blonde wigs. "That was the weirdest bus I've ever ridden on in my life," said Martha Dettwiller. "There were drag queens dressed up like Tammy Wynette, more than one. Can you imagine a size 12 pump?" Tammy's band members were somewhat dumbfounded by the affair. "I didn't go in," said a disturbed Rusty Pence. "How we ended up there, I don't know." One clownish-looking fop from a local cable access show in big pink hair and six-inch lashes had the nerve to stick a mic in Tammy's face and inquire, "Are we both drag queens?" Another angry queen parked his legs under the wheels of Wynette's bus, threatening to sue Wynette if she didn't give him an autograph. The bus driver looked ready to run over him when police arrived on the scene. "It was unbelievable," said pianist Mike Maiocco. "He looked a lot like Tammy—he had the hair, the jewels, and the gown." This tempest in a teapot ended when Wynette agreed to come out and sign a picture. "She was a good sport about it," noted Maiocco.†

---

*"The biggest Tammy fanatic I ever saw was Melissa Etheridge," said Karyn Sloas. "Oh, she just thought that Tammy walked on water. She came to three different shows while I worked for her. She would just be awestruck when she would come on the bus, like a giddy fan of some sort."

†"My large following of gays and lesbians thrills me," said Wynette in 1993. "I don't really care what anybody is. When I like somebody, I like them—whether they're black or white or whatever."

One unexpected guest had shown up when Tammy was in Baptist Hospital in 1993—George Jones. Still in a haze, she had thought she saw Jones at the foot of her bed and said to herself, 'I've already been to hell and back, I don't want to go again!' But there was the Possum, telling her she had to get better so they could record one last album together. It hadn't been easy to get George there.

"He didn't want to go," said Nancy, who was determined that the two of them make peace. "I knew that she was at Baptist, and Richey had told me that he didn't think she would make it. I said, 'I'm gonna go see Tammy.' He said, 'Well, *I'm* not.' I said, 'I think it's so wrong. You can set there and pout or make up your mind and go, but I'm goin'.' So I got dressed and I pulled the car out and I went back in and I said, 'Are you gonna go or not?'" That was it. "George said, 'Oh, hell yes, I'll go. And when he went he was so happy. He said, 'Y'know, I shouldn't dislike her, I shouldn't be actin' the way I am.' So then they ended up bein' friends."

As did Tammy and Nancy, which was even more unexpected. Nancy had first met Tammy back in the early eighties when she and Jones had driven up from Alabama to pick up Georgette for a visit. "When we got there, she was just really rude to me. She was like, 'No, you can't have her because I don't know who you are.' I said, 'Okay, that's fine, but I'm not anything like what maybe you've seen him with before.'" Tammy still refused to hand over George's daughter. "I thought, 'Golly, how could she be so cruel?'" Jackie Daly said the reason for her mother's animosity was simple: jealousy. Unlike Tammy, Nancy had gotten Jones straightened out. "Nancy took care of him. I know Mom had wanted to." It didn't help matters that Wynette had named her in the press as the obstacle preventing any more George and Tammy duets. "I don't believe Nancy wants us to," she said in 1989.

The ice was broken when Georgette, expecting twins, invited Nancy to her baby shower. Now Tammy was in a panic. She rang her old friend Linda Cayson and said, "You have *got* to come up here." "I can't," said Linda, "I have to work." "Get time off. I need moral support!" Wynette kept telling Georgette, "I hope she doesn't come, I do not like her, I hope she doesn't come!"

"We weren't gonna like Nancy," explained Tammy's friend Martha Dettwiller. "Tammy told us, 'Now, Nancy's comin' over here, but we're not gonna like her.' About fifteen minutes into the shower, Tammy calls us over—'Y'know, Nancy's a real good girl.'"

On October 11, 1994, George and Tammy reunited in the studio, rerecording a respectable if superfluous "Golden Ring" for George's all-star duet album *The Bradley Barn Sessions*. "It was real snowy that day," said Tammy, who worried that Jones would want to sing it in the high key of the original recording, as her voice was "not that high anymore." When she got to the studio, it was Jones who suggested lowering the key. Said Tammy, "I was real tacky—I said, 'Well, George, if you need to lower the key, go ahead.'"

The stage was now set for a full-scale reunion album, 1995's *One*, produced by Norro Wilson and label head Tony Brown. Not only did Wilson have to work around Wynette's health problems, but Jones had just endured triple-bypass surgery. "That was a hard project to do," admitted Norro. "Both of 'em were really sick." Lazybones Jones had to be cajoled into sticking around to finish sessions. "He wanted to quit early," said bassist Harold Bradley. "Norro Wilson would sit out there and tell jokes, try to keep him interested. We were hired for three hours—nobody ever comes in and does one hour and leaves!" Bradley, who hadn't worked with Tammy in years, was shocked at her condition. "This lady came up on me from behind and said, 'It sure is great to have you on the sessions again.' She looked so gaunt I didn't know who she was until I looked into her eyes. She really looked twenty years older than she was. It was frightening."

Wilson did a masterful job completing what would be the final creation in the Jones-Wynette legacy. Although a bit heavy on the strings even for a Billy Sherrill protégé, *One* was a class act, and included a number of fine duets, particularly the title track—the way Tammy and George match harmonies on the word "one," with Jones bending the word with a melancholic wistfulness, just breaks your heart.

George and Tammy did a ton of press for the album, cut a video for "One," and on November 7 gave a moving appearance on the CMA Awards show,* where they were nominated for Vocal Event of the Year. (They did not win.) Expectations were high. "Bruce Hinton at MCA paid them a lot of money to do that album together," said Evelyn Shriver.

But all the effort was to no avail. George and Tammy were no longer a

---

*Listen closely as the camera pans up on the photos of the couple in the background and you can hear George whisper to Tammy, "You look beautiful tonight"—all the more touching given the frail shape Wynette was in.

potent commercial commodity amid all the Garths, Rebas, and Billy Rays. Music City's conversion to a soft-rock assembly line was now complete. Cable stations like CMT subsisted on music videos aimed at the all-powerful "younger demographic." Which led to an inevitable skew toward the visual, which led to a bland assembly line of hot bodies, pretty faces, and big hats. Hard-won experience was no longer a required part of the package. "I don't understand how a young person of twenty-one can sing about walking out and hearing the baby cry . . . how they can put their heart and soul into it, because it's never happened to them," said Tammy. "It happened to us."

"They got dollar signs goin' all through their little brains . . . they're so pop and rock, it's pitiful," bitched Jones, Music City's loudest and most frequent critic. "They're screamin', they're up in the air . . . the soul and heart is gone. This new so-called country music is nothing but rock stuff for kids."

"There's only a handful of us old-timers still making records," said Tammy. "Country radio is a thorn in our sides. But they're not going to get rid of me."

The George and Tammy *One* tour began in Tupelo, Mississippi, on June 10, 1995, and got off to a disastrous start. Although few knew it at the time, Jones was at the tail end of his drinking, and as unpredictable as ever. He skipped his final solo song and went into the first duet while Wynette was still getting ready aboard Tammy One. As Evelyn Shriver remembered, "We're on the bus, and they have a monitor where you can hear what's goin' on onstage, and Tammy says, 'That's our music!' And George says, 'And who's a no-show here tonight?' It was just awful. They got her on a golf cart from the bus to the theater. Tammy heard her part and she started singing from the parking lot." Worst of all, a network TV crew was there to record the sorry affair.*

Despite the bumps in the road, the tour was a special one. Jones had a magical effect on Wynette. "Tammy was giddy," said Charley Abdon. "I never saw her giddy around people—she was giddy around Jones." Karyn Sloas agreed. "When she talked about him, her countenance changed.

---

*Jones was a beast that night. "He was so wild," said Shriver. The next day they were supposed to do *60 Minutes,* which would've meant instant sales for the album. "Well, he just blew that off. George just drove away. The producer called me and said, 'I just saw his bus leave! You gotta stop him!' I said, 'There ain't no stoppin' him, because, truthfully, George doesn't give a shit.'"

Almost like a schoolgirl, her eyes would brighten." Not that the Possum wasn't still capable of pissing her off royally. One night George broke into his Little Richard impression onstage, embarrassing Tammy to death. "He saw how much it got to her, and—oh, and it was every night from then on," said Sloas. "It actually was entertaining to see him jiggle and shake that way, but it really got to her." The bottom line was that even in her debilitating state, Jones brought out the best in her as an artist. "Tammy never sang better during my tenure there," said Charley Abdon, her drummer since 1985.

"We called it 'the tour from hell,'" said Nancy Jones, who played peacemaker on many occasions. "I'd be on our bus, and George was like, 'Go see what she's gonna wear. She better not wear them stupid short dresses, because she's too skinny for it.' And I'd go back, and if Tammy had one on, I'd say, 'Ohhh, but *this* one would look so good on you!' And I'd get her to change." The two singers clashed again during a gig in England. George is fiendishly punctual, and Tammy went over ten minutes. "And he was boiling. And when Tammy came off the stage, well, he said something to her and she started cryin'. After I got George, I ran in her dressing room and went, 'Now, you know damn good and well he's an asshole—you were married to him,' and I got her to laughin'.'"

Jones was particularly testy on the overseas leg of the tour. "Tammy's a bigger star than George over there," said Evelyn Shriver. "Tammy had always worked Europe. George never did. They didn't even know what he looked like. She was the big deal." Before one show Jones accidently got in Wynette's limo. The driver didn't know who he was and chased him off.

Maybe the biggest date on the tour was the Grand Ole Opry. Raeanne Rubenstein witnessed an amusing scene as she prepared for a photo shoot the day of the show. "They had a fight. Tammy was very cooperative—as usual, it was George who was more difficult. They were squabbling about the clothes." Under the impression the shoot was a casual one, Jones wore blue jeans and sneakers, only to find Wynette dressed to the nines. He was "charging all around the edge of the set, accusing people of not telling him. Finally he calmed down." Rubenstein, who had shot the couple over twenty years before, thought it was funny how easily they slipped right back into the roles they played in marriage. "It was the same dynamic. Nothing had changed."

Amazingly, George and Tammy had never played Music City together, and both were even more nervous that Billy Sherrill was actually venturing out to the show. Evelyn Shriver was worried about Wynette. "Tammy was so sick. She'd be hooked up to IVs everywhere—and they would unplug her to go onstage. Tammy hadn't worn high heels in ages because her feet were swollen. She wore this red satin suit, short skirt, and a little jacket, and somehow or another she shoved her feet into high heels. I don't know what the hell she did, but she went out there and gave one of the best shows of her life." Once again "How Great Thou Art" was the showstopper, earning Wynette one of many standing ovations. "Tammy was absolutely at her peak that night," said her steel player, Rusty Pence. "She was hitting on all twelve cylinders."

During the show Wynette mentioned how she had been signed to Sony Epic for thirty years, how grateful she was to them. "Meanwhile they had dropped her the week before and she didn't even know it," said Shriver. "There wasn't one person from the label there." Shriver was near tears after Wynette's performance. "Tammy came offstage and was standing there. She had nailed the whole show, but yet she could not even utter a word afterwards, and they hooked her back up to her machines. You'd think, 'How does this women do this?' It was the most heartbreaking thing you've ever seen in your life."

On August 11 George and Tammy were scheduled to do the *Tonight Show with Jay Leno.* Wynette had already canceled the appearance once due to her health, but when she arrived she was obviously in no shape to do the makeup date, either. Much to his chagrin, Jones had to go on alone and sing "He Stopped Loving Her Today," which he insisted on reading off of cue cards.

The scene on the Learjet (borrowed from Wynette's nemesis, Reba McEntire) traveling home from Los Angeles was a surreal one. Tammy, in her nightgown and hooked to an IV, was out cold with her head to the wall. A meal of chicken and rice was served, and when David Sloas looked over at Richey a bit later, he was facedown "in his Styrofoam plate." Sloas nudged his wife, Karyn, sitting across from him playing cards with Yvonne Abdon. Karyn looked back to sneak a peak at Richey, rousing him slightly and causing him to knock over his food, resulting in "chicken and rice all over the inside of that jet," said David Sloas, who will never forget the image. "A country music matriarch, sittin' there, just absolutely in pain, she's got some medication in her, she's out, and she's got chicken and rice all over her nightgown, face and hair."

Pianist Mike Maiocco, not used to seeing Wynette in such a condition, began to worry. "She was really out of it, against the window, barely breathin'. I thought, 'God, do we need to land this plane somewhere?' I'm thinkin' maybe we need to take her pulse. And I can't ask Richey, 'cause he's out." When he voiced his concern, Karyn and Yvonne, who had witnessed Tammy incapacitated on the bus many a time, barely looked up from their cards, saying, "Awww, she's fine." Maiocco was so disturbed by what he was seeing he lined up all the miniature Crown Royal bottles he could find. "I think I drank every one of 'em. When I walked down the steps of that plane, I thought, 'I can't believe what I just seen, I am hammered and I'm goin' to bed!'"

When Alanna Nash saw the video for the song "One," she was shocked. "Tammy looked ancient, like a plant that had withered up about to die. I thought, 'Jesus, this woman is dying—why isn't somebody doing something?'"

By now knowledge of Wynette's drug addiction was widespread. Charley Abdon recalled walking backstage into a conversation Nancy Jones was having with Karyn and Yvonne. Nancy was convinced that if something wasn't done, Tammy would soon be dead.

"I kick myself in the butt for not ever kidnappin' her," Nancy confessed to me. "I was gonna just kidnap her and hide her, get her off the drugs. And not let nobody know. I mean, who in the hell would've thought she'd have been with *me*? I could've done it. I told her, and one time Tammy said that I could, and then she called me and told me not to. Whenever I was going to do it, she pleaded with me not to."

Nancy had worked a miracle with George. She'd battled drug dealers, thugs, leeches, creditors, not to mention Jones himself. Although he wouldn't completely get off the sauce until 1999, George's career was thriving, he was healthy, and—hits or not—he recorded some of his finest performances in the nineties and beyond: "When Did You Stop Loving Me?," "You Can Tear Me Out of the Picture," and "When the Last Curtain Falls."

Tammy, on the other hand, was now without a label, not to mention plagued by various personal woes. "It seems like when I got my life straightened up, her life got as screwed up about as bad as mine was," said Jones. "With her problems of bein' sick and then all the other things that it led to,

Tammy was doped up a lot. She didn't know what was goin' on. She didn't really care, y'know. It's almost like she took over where I left off."

The comparison of George and Nancy versus Richey and Tammy was one that was noted many, many times by Wynette's family, friends, and associates. "You can't blame Richey for not bein' able to get Tammy off drugs, but what about Nancy Jones?" asked Jerry Taylor.

"That's the luck of the draw," said Wynette's old friend Nanette Crafton. "Jones got Nancy. And Tammy got Richey."

"I believe that George pushed Tammy," said David Sloas. "'Cause there were a lot of times I didn't think she should be onstage because of the way she felt. For the lifestyle they enjoyed, wanted to keep up, she had to work. Because you can't hire a Learjet at the drop of a hat if you're not makin' twenty-five K a night." As Wynette became more and more unreliable, the Wynettetones had a terrible time staying afloat. Since Tammy had gone into Betty Ford in 1985, Richey no longer kept the band on a retainer, but a day rate, and they'd only get paid if their equipment was set up. Wynette had canceled so many gigs her musicians were forced to take other jobs. "I had to start selling Chevrolets just to support my music habit," said Sloas.

Many people felt that Tammy Wynette was no longer in shape to tour. Dates would be scheduled; dates would be canceled. "Everybody in the industry knew that she was not well, and that also made it difficult for me to schedule dates down the road," said booking agent Tony Conway. "They didn't even have to ask me. They knew. A lot of shows I had to cancel week of." Plus, Richey still wanted top dollar. "He saw people pass Tammy up for Dolly or Reba and he felt Tammy should get equal to that. I said, 'Right now, it is not there. They're not gonna pay it. They're scared she's gonna cancel.' He didn't want to hear that. He wanted more dates and bigger money. Just because you want fifty thousand dollars a night doesn't mean somebody's gonna pay it."

At one state fair performance in Springfield, Illinois, Conway encountered an "exhausted and worn-out" Tammy, who told him, "I don't know if I can do the show. I just don't feel good." He was troubled that Richey would let her go onstage in that condition. "At times I think he did push her when she wasn't physically up to it. Let me put it this way: if I had been Tammy's husband or manager, at that point I wouldn't have made her go onstage that particular night. I felt sorry for her because I felt like she didn't feel like she could argue her position to George."

Conway eventually bowed out. "There towards the end it felt really bad— I felt like I shouldn't be bookin' these shows, because she was walkin' around with the little cart and the IV. She's hurtin', and you feel like you were part of puttin' her out there and makin' her hurt more. I couldn't do it anymore. I couldn't pound people and sell Tammy."

"In the later years of Tammy's life, when she should've been able to kick back, pick and choose dates, and do really special things as the icon that she was, I think Richey worked her to death," said Jerry Taylor. "She was married to and managed by one of the greediest people ever in this business. With all the money that was made, somebody should've taken care of Tammy Wynette."

Evelyn Shriver didn't think Wynette would survive the European leg of the reunion tour with Jones. "I was just hysterical that Tammy was gonna come back in a coffin. The tour was getting closer and closer, and she was just so sick." Shriver called Richey to confront him. "I said, 'This is gonna kill her—people think you're a leech. People think you're working Tammy to death.'" Richey started to weep. "He said to me, 'No one loves Tammy more than I do—and this will keep her alive.'"

All Tammy knew was to get on that bus and go sing her songs. "I'm afraid when I stop, everything else would stop," she confessed. Said employee Ruben Garces, "She'd go on the road for thirty days, she'd come back home, take a couple of days to wind down, and then within a week she'd be pacin' the floor again—'Richey, when are we goin' back out?'"

Kelli Haggard-Patterson saw Tammy after an Oregon date and was dismayed at the condition she was in. "Why is she still working?" she asked Richey. "George started crying. 'That's what I tell her—"Can you please stop working?"'" After a nurse tended to Tammy, Haggard-Patterson asked her why she didn't just stop. "She said, 'Kelli, when I die, I'm gonna be singin'. I do not wanna die in some bed. This is my choice. I will not go down quiet. I've always been loud. I will die loud.'"

"Now it's dark and I'm alone, but I won't be afraid," sang Tammy on one of her very last studio recordings, Brian Wilson's "In My Room." Originally recorded for the Beach Boys' Nashville album, *Stars and Stripes, Vol. 1*,

Wynette's performance appears only on the DVD—the actual track didn't see release until the posthumous *Tammy Wynette Remembered* tribute album in 1998. According to Jerry Taylor, Wynette's vocal needed massive digital tweaking. "Her voice was shaky. It was a shadow of who she was. We literally worked and worked on Pro Tooling until her voice sounded like Tammy."

And yet deep within that spectral, processed vocal something moves you. A dreamy song, but rather unsettling—does the singer ever leave her room? Not an odd choice of material for Tammy, when you really think about it. Brian Wilson knew a thing or two about drugs, illness, and refusing to grow up. Wilson, who joined her on the vocal, said she sang the words "as if they were written especially for her . . . and in a way they were."

Tammy certainly knew more and more about being in her room toward the end of her life. Few people could get past Richey even just to talk to her. Said Mike Martinovich, "When I'd call over there, he'd go, 'Oh, she's fine, pal,' and yet I knew she wasn't fine. That's the one thing I resented—that he wasn't really honest with me." Martha Dettwiller concurred. "If I called over there and I said, 'I'm gonna be in the neighborhood and I'd like to drop by,' well, Richey would put me off. 'Call tomorrow.' I'd call tomorrow. 'Call Wednesday.' It had to be what he wanted, not what Tammy wanted." If the two gals went shopping, Martha would hide the purchases in her car until they could sneak them into the house "because Richey would get upset that she bought them. She didn't have a checking account—he would leave a hundred-dollar bill on her bedside table every so often. That was her spendin' money."

Even if you got through the wall of Richey, there was no guarantee she'd emerge from the shadows. "Tammy always wanted me to be with her on the weekends, do her hair," said Barbara Hutchison. "I'd come to her house and have to spend half the day waitin' for her to come out."

"I think she was just off in her own world," said Yvonne Abdon.

People say something changed in George Richey in the last years of Tammy's life. "The first eight or nine years with Tammy I always had the feeling that George would take a bullet for Tammy, that he would truly do anything for her," maintained Rusty Pence. "But that last couple of years, I'm not sure. When she deteriorated to the point she had, I don't know if he lost his interest or had other things more important on his agenda."

The mood aboard Tammy One was grim. "Richey started this thing where all the curtains had to be shut, even the front curtain," said Yvonne Abdon. "You couldn't see out of the bus. I can say I've been here and there—and I don't even know what it looks like." At times, Richey seemed erratic, out of it. Creepily he watched the movie *Reversal of Fortune*—the tale of Eurotrash jet-setter Claus von Bülow, accused and acquitted of overdosing his socialite wife, Sunny, into an irreversible coma—over and over. "He played that tape from beginning of the morning until late at night for two or three days straight," said Barbara Hutchison. "Richey would be in a stupor, that tape would go off, and he would hit that button on the remote control, rewind it, and watch it again. There's somethin' sick about him wantin' to know every bit."

While Richey was conked out on the couch in the front of the bus, blasting his TV at all hours, Tammy would be back in the bedroom blasting hers. Wynette was particularly obsessed with the O. J. Simpson case. "The word 'obsession' is probably too light," said Karyn Sloas. "It was the delight of her life, the spectacle of it. She said, 'I can't believe that he did this, because I know him.' She alluded that they might have almost dated. You could tell she was a little enamored with him." But toward the end, Court TV gave way to TBN. Karyn Sloas had the bunk right next to Tammy's bed, and suddenly she was waking up to televangelists: Benny Hinn, Kenneth Copeland, Oral Roberts. "She was searching," felt Sloas.

Things were falling apart on the road. "They were burnin' bridges everywhere we went," said Yvonne Abdon. "They'd cancel shows in places we would play again and again over the years. Laughlin was one. Wheeling, West Virginia." Wynette was often out of it. The hairdressers had a terrible time. "You can't do somebody's hair when they haven't washed it in over a week, or they're so inebriated their head's bobbin' up and down," said Barbara Hutchison. "It got to where Tammy didn't want to get up 'til the last five seconds to go onstage."

The band could gauge how bad Wynette was feeling by the number of songs she let them sing without her. "She'd have a break in the middle," said Karyn Sloas. "She'd always let Charlie Carter sing a song, and Yvonne and I would trade out. It got to a point where she let the bus driver sing. We had to fill as much time as possible. We had a contract to fulfill."

As always there were conflicts with Richey. "Last few years of Tammy's life, every Christmas she'd get a face-lift," said Yvonne Abdon. "One day we were doin' a state fair somewhere. I got on the bus in the middle of the day, Tammy didn't have her makeup on yet, and I asked her what she wanted us girls to wear. There was nobody on the bus but her and me, and she started cryin'.

"She said, 'Yvonne, you're so beautiful. I'm so ugly. Richey won't let me get a face-lift.' And it broke my heart in two, because she was hurtin'. Tammy had the money to have anything done and to make herself look pretty, but Richey would not let her. I mean, why should he control what she does? Tammy made all the money."

On May 17, 1997, came Wynette's final appearance on the Grand Ole Opry. She was so sick at the time nobody was sure she would show. Giving the camera a weak thumbs-up sign, a tiny, skeletal Tammy insisted, "I'm feelin' wonderful" during a preperformance interview with Bill Anderson. Wynette then hobbled out onstage and, gasping for air, did "Your Good Girl's Gonna Go Bad." "Tammy came out onstage in her house shoes and she could not sing at all," said Lorrie Morgan, who had introduced her.* "I was standin' off the wings of the stage. Jan Howard looked at me and said, 'Get out there and help her sing that song.' I said, 'I can't, Jan, that's her song.' 'I'm tellin' you to *help* her.'" Wynette seemed a bit thrown but utterly relieved when Morgan came onstage to join her. Howard came out to add vocals to "Stand by Your Man." Then came an impromptu, bungled "Apartment #9" with Lorrie, and Wynette shuffled off. Tammy's second slot on the show was mercifully canceled. "They called an ambulance to come take her away," said Morgan.

What disturbed everyone particularly that night was the fact that Tammy, who had always been fastidious about her onstage appearance, had been allowed to go on with her black satin jacket clearly buttoned wrong. Before Wynette left, an angry Jan Howard went on the bus. "Tammy was sitting there, all these people on the bus, and her jacket was still not buttoned right. I said, 'Every damn person on this bus can see that that jacket isn't buttoned right. Why?' Nobody had an answer."

On June 14 Tammy appeared at Loretta Lynn's ranch in Hurricane Mills, Tennessee. This was Loretta's first show there since the death of her hus-

---

*Lorrie Morgan, who's recorded several Tammy songs, idolized her. Wynette approved. "She really thought that Lorrie hung the moon," said Karyn Sloas. "When a woman gets to be a certain age and sees a mini-me, she thinks, 'Wow, that's so cool, that's a younger version of me.' Lorrie made no bones about it—she wanted to *be* Tammy Wynette, and of course Tammy thought that was just too cool."

band, Doolittle, and Tammy came to support her, even if she and Loretta butchered "D-I-V-O-R-C-E" in the process. ("I can't spell!" blurted Lynn during the number. Accompanying them on piano, Richey was so disgusted he walked off the stage.)

"She was in bad shape, but she come down to surprise me, even though she wasn't feelin' good," said Lynn. "I don't think she should've come. She was skin and bones, that's what Tammy was. You know what she said to me? She said—and this was a hard thing to take—'Loretta, if you hear anything about me, if you hear that I'm dead, don't worry, because I think I'll be happy that way. I died on the operating table, and it really is great to go on. I was goin' toward the light. And it felt so great. I'm lookin' forward to it.' That's what broke me up, was her lookin' *forward* to goin'. She said, 'Don't you worry about me, because I'll be home. For one time I'd know I was home.' I said, 'Tammy, don't talk like that. I'm not ready for you to go.'

"It was awful. Tammy was ready to go, and that broke my heart. That's the last time I seen her alive."

Harry Benson had one last photo session with Tammy, a three-page *Enquirer* spread. The eight-hour shoot started at nine in the morning, and when Wynette began to fade around three o'clock, she was escorted into a side room. "I don't know if they gave her some injections or somethin' to try to get her through the rest of the shoot," said Benson. There were a few shots left to take out by Wynette's pool. "I noticed they really had to help her along. I started getting the guilties. About pushing this woman too far." But Tammy insisted on finishing. "She was one of those troopers that said, 'No, we gotta go on.' They were standing right out of camera range ready to catch her in case she fell over." What was striking to Benson—besides the O.J. trial blaring from every TV in the house—was the fact that in "every room of the house I saw an open Bible. It was kind of sobering."

Scotty Kennedy became aware of the sudden proliferation of the Good Book one day when Wynette was singing gospel songs at the piano with her aunt Hazel and cousin Jane. It was obvious Tammy was in bad shape. "Hazel and Jane were cryin'," said Kennedy.

Linda Cayson also took note of the Bibles, as well as a plethora of newly purchased angel figurines. "In my mind she was thinking about her own death. Wynette lived next door to a church. I know she was talkin' to a pastor more toward the end. She'd talk to me about the hereafter. I'd say, 'Aw, let's not talk about that,' and she'd say, 'No, I need to talk about it.'"

Tammy had decided to be buried in Nashville, not with her folks down near the home place, and she wanted to make sure Linda was okay with it. "She was just precious," said Cayson.

"I used to go up there, I'd take just tons of pictures, because my family always wanted me to. But those last few years I never took a picture of her. Unless she was totally made up, and then she still looked so bad." A beautician came over that day to put hair extensions on Wynette. "She had lost her hair, it just all came out.

"When he got through and left, Wynette was sittin' on the side of the bed just cryin' and shakin'. Just cryin' and shakin'. And she said, 'I am so sick.' She said, 'Just lay there by the side of me just a minute.' And I did. And she finally— well, she gave herself a shot and went to sleep. When I left there that day, we hugged each other and we both cried. When I started home, I was cryin' just for the longest time. I knew I would not see her again. And I didn't.'"

Christmas was Tammy's favorite time of year. Not the one of 1997, however. "I spent her last Christmas with her," said Barbara Hutchison. "She called just beggin' me and my mother to have Christmas dinner with 'em, because none of her children came." Wynette was upset that one of her daughters hadn't returned her calls for months and that another was dating a man of color. She seemed alone and melancholy. "I thought, 'Tammy's givin' up on everything.'"

Nobody saw much of Wynette in the early part of 1998. Richey "had her about as isolated as you can get," said Martha Dettwiller. "Those last months I didn't see her, from Christmas 'til she died. And every day that I would call, Richey would tell me, 'Well, maybe Wednesday.'"

On March 5 Tammy did a show in Plant City, Florida, filling in for Loretta Lynn.* It would be her last live performance. Her final TV appearance came on *Prime Time Country*, broadcast March 9. Wynette looked healthier than she had in a while and, perched on her ever-present stool, sang a creditable

---

*"I talked to her the night before she died," Lynn told author Tracy Pitcox. "She told me that she had gained a lot of weight. . . . She told me that when she had a little more fat on her, she was going to get a face-lift. I told her to wait on me."

version of "Take Me to Your World." She now looked and sang like a country version of *Lady in Satin*–era Billie Holiday. There was a gargoyle-like beauty present; scarred, disturbing, but moving nonetheless.

A few weeks before she died, Evelyn Shriver and Susan Nadler went over to Tammy's house for a visit. "Tammy and Richey were living in the kitchen on the sofas," said Nadler. "And Tammy was so weird-looking. I said to Evelyn, 'She must have on a mask or something.' She didn't—she was green." Richey's fingernails were all grown out. There was an unsettling vibe in the home. "It was so weird," shuddered Susan.

Tammy was recovering from surgery to remove her varicose veins, and her legs were swollen. "She wanted to show Evelyn her feet, which were popping open with pustules," said Susan, who fled the room. "I thought, 'This ain't for me, I don't want to remember Tammy this way.'"

As they left, Susan turned to Evelyn and said, "Tammy's dying."

Around that same time Wynette rang Jan Howard.

"Tammy always called me by my real name, Lula Grace—she'd call me and say, 'Lula Grace, what are we doin' this afternoon?' Lula Gra-*a-a-ace*, with that little growl in her voice.

"She called that day and said, 'Why don't you come over, and let's just talk.' And I went over. She had to take oxygen walking from the bedroom back to the kitchen. Heartbreaking. We went back in her bedroom and just talked girl talk for a long time.

"Tammy loved to be surrounded by pretty things. She deserved to be. She loved to buy shoes. She must've had five hundred pair."

Then came one of those strange little moments which happen before people die that seem to mean everything and nothing at the same time.

"I never will forget—that day she showed me this beautiful crystal bowl she just loved. I said, 'Tammy, it's just a bowl. Without you, it's just stuff. Yeah, it's pretty, but it's a damn bowl.' Wynette kind of laughed. 'Yeah, it's just a bowl.'" Miss Tammy and her crystal.

"Jan, what happened to our music? Everybody sounds alike."

Howard agreed.

"When we started, everybody had their own style," said Tammy. "You, me, Loretta, Dottie, Jeannie Seely, Connie Smith. When the music came on, you didn't even have to hear the voice—you knew who it was. What happened to our music?"

Jan didn't have an answer for that one.

In the course of conversation Howard asked Tammy if she had a will in place. "She said yes. Tammy had two insurance policies—one was supposed to go to the girls and one to Richey. Both were for a million dollars. Tammy also showed me a list of what was to go to each of her children and grandchildren."*

Howard heard Richey wheeling and dealing in the next room. "Richey was on the phone, and you couldn't help but hear him. He was yellin', tryin' to book a tour in Australia with Tammy and Kenny Rogers." Jan looked at the shape Wynette was in, and when Richey came in the room, she said, "What the hell are you doin'?"

According to Howard, his reply was "You gotta try to get it while you can."

Incensed, Jan turned to Wynette and said, "Come, go with me. Let's go to Florida, just you and me. We'll walk on the beach. No makeup, no worrying about hair. We'll wear our baseball caps. No fans, no publicity, no nothin'. Just us.

"Tammy said, 'Oh, I'd like to do that.' But I knew she never would." Howard got the impression that Wynette was well aware she was not long for the world.

"And she didn't seem afraid," said Howard. "Two weeks later she was dead."

Barbara Hutchison saw Tammy a week before she was gone. As she was coming back from a doctor's visit, something told her to stop at Wynette's home, even though she never had done so before without calling first. "I never seen Tammy so joyous," said Hutchison. "For Tammy to greet me like that was out of character. She said, 'I had you on my mind all weekend. I'd just love to talk.'"

---

*Numerous friends told me they saw this yellow legal pad list covered with Tammy's scrawl. "Tammy was right proud of the idea that she'd worked all this out," said Martha Dettwiller. "She had made notes in it for years—who was gonna get what, all written out. I mean, it was prominent in the house—you never knew what room you were going to find it in." "I saw it every time we went on the road the last few years," said Barbara Hutchison, who also noted that while at home Wynette "went around marking things, like her fine crystal. She'd take little bits of masking tape and put initials of who she wanted it to go to on the bottom."

The house was eerily quiet. "It felt strange, because she always had the television on in the kitchen. TV wasn't on. And the phone always rang at least one if not two or three times in thirty minutes' time. The phone didn't ring the whole three hours I was there." When the doorbell rang, Richey always appeared, "at least to see who had come in the house, see what Tammy was up to." The housekeeper said he was home, but "he never even came out once, the whole time I was there. I found that very strange."

Tammy told Barbara she was selling the house. "I just decided I'm going to downsize," she said. "I think I'll get a condo downtown, get rid of everything. I don't need this on me anymore."

Hutchison was a bit shocked. Tammy had maintained she'd always live in a house, not a condo.

Wynette had been working on her list of who was getting what and had it with her. "I've been workin' on things that I wanna give to the girls," she said.

And Tammy was going to take a break from the road. "I am going to cut back quite a bit. I don't know how much longer I can be on the road anyway. I'm going to really start enjoyin' my life."

Tammy move? Practically retire? "I thought that was really kind of unusual," said Hutchison. "I knew comin' home that day that somethin' was gonna go down. The way she spoke, things that we talked about that day in our two- or three-hour discussion . . . I knew that Tammy had come to the end of the line."

On the following Wednesday, Tammy threw Karyn Sloas a baby shower. "She was wonderful, she was tellin' jokes . . . one of the things Yvonne and I would laugh about was Tammy would tell the same stories over and over again, and we'd always have to laugh like we'd only heard them for the first time. She'd forget that she told us. But that night she told some new stories, and we were lookin' at each other, like, 'Wow.'"

"The old Tammy was back," thought Karyn.

Just five days later, on April 6, 1998, Tammy Wynette was dead.

Death Ain't No Big Deal

[Hank] was in too much pain to live. He discovered there is worse things than death.

—Billie Jean Jones Eshliman Williams Horton, last wife of Hank Williams

Tammy Wynette passed away quietly, her frail little body curled up in her favorite spot, a kitchen couch in front of the TV.

Sad to say, but the moment Wynette died she became an unsolved mystery. The cause of her demise, the circumstances surrounding it, even the time of death—all disputed. Suddenly Tammy had become fodder for the tabloid TV she and Richey so loved. Wynette's death had been grim enough. The unsavory machinations that followed proved even grimmer.

As Evelyn Shriver has remarked many times over the years, "I think Tammy deserved better than she got in life, and I certainly think she deserved better than she got in death."

April 6, 1998. Jackie had stopped to see her mother around noon. Both she and Richey were parked on the couches like zombies, with the television droning on as usual. Tammy appeared to be asleep. Richey, dressed in his familiar open robe, "was just sitting on the couch, just nodding his head." Jackie tried to ask Richey to tell her mother she had stopped by. "His eyes opened only halfway," said Jackie, who gave up on the conversation.

Richey's version of events, which he told to reporter and author Gerry Wood, is quite precise. "I had been up for two days and nights because Tammy had a very tough weekend. During the day, we were napping on the couch in the kitchen. I recall hearing Tammy say several times to the housekeeper, 'Please be quiet. Try to let him rest. He's had very little rest this weekend—he's been up with me.'"

Richey said his daughter Deirdre called at 6:55 p.m., and he told her he'd

343

call her right back, as he had to go to the bathroom. "I then noticed this note that was Scotch-taped to the glass-top coffee table in the kitchen." Cleta, their housekeeper, had run to the store. According to Richey, the note was written at 6:05 p.m.

"When I came out of the bathroom and sat down where I had been napping, I looked over at Tammy, and I thought, 'I'm not sure she's breathing!' I moved over next to her and felt her foot. It was cold—her legs were cold from the knees down. I immediately made a telephone call to her doctor, Wallis Marsh, in Pittsburgh." Richey says he made the call at 7:01 p.m. Despite Richey's recollection, Jan Smith says she got a call from an acquaintance at around five thirty telling her that Wynette was dead. Martha Dettwiller says she knew a half hour later. According to police reports, at seven p.m. Nashville police heard from the *National Enquirer*, which was already asking for confirmation of Wynette's death.

"She is gone, Wallis, she is gone," Richey told Marsh, who insisted he check her vital signs again. Richey came back with a confirmation. He claims Marsh instructed him not to bother calling 911, as it appeared Tammy was already past that.* "We thought that 911 was for the living, not the dead," George's spokesperson, Sylvia Richardson, later told the press. A plane was chartered to bring Dr. Marsh to Nashville. He'd sign Tammy's death certificate, then release the body to Woodlawn Mortuary, where she was promptly embalmed, destroying any possibility of knowing exactly what drugs were in her bloodstream at the time of her death.

Contrary to Richey's version, the police report states Wynette was discovered by both Richey and housekeeper Cleta Hillygus.† The day after Wynette's death, Barbara Hutchison asked Hillygus where she had been when Tammy passed away. Cleta quickly cut her off, informing her straightaway that she hadn't been present. "Boy, she just wanted to get off the subject right off the bat. Didn't want to talk about it." Groundskeeper Mark Crawford, who'd accompanied Cleta to the store, seemed equally agitated. "He was scared to death," said Charley Abdon. "Mark was very, very uncomfortable with the whole deal."

Sometime after seven p.m. Tammy's daughter Gwen was called, and she notified Tina and Jackie. Nobody had been able to reach Georgette,

---

*James Wallis Marsh declined to respond to several requests for an interview.

†Cleta Hillygus declined to respond to several requests for an interview.

who was working as a nurse. "I know Georgette didn't know anything about her death," said Loretta Lynn. "She went to work, and a nurse said to Georgette, 'I sure am sorry about your mama.'" Georgette learned the details of her mother's death from the TV. When Gwen and Tina arrived at their mother's house, Richey's friends and relatives were already trickling in. "It seemed everyone knew before her own children," Gwen said later.

At 8:55 p.m. Ralph Gordon, a lawyer who'd done work for Richey and Tammy but who said he was acting in the capacity of friend that night, finally called 911. By now the house was filling up with Richey's cronies. "Obviously a lot of people were notified of her death before the police department received the official word," their media representative noted later.

A little past nine thirty, Jackie arrived to find her mother lying on the couch in a fetal position. Tina, who was then four months pregnant, was rubbing her dead mother's foot. Friends of Richey's wandered "in and out, drinking coffee and smoking." Daly was deeply upset by their seemingly cavalier attitude, as were others arriving to pay their respects.

As guests mingled, no one appeared overly concerned that one of the greatest singers the world has ever known was dead on the couch, lying there, as Jackie put it, like "some kind of centerpiece for a ghoulish gathering." Tammy would remain there until two thirty a.m., when her body was finally taken to Woodlawn Mortuary. "All I could think was Mom would never want these people standing round staring at her in that shape," she said.

Meanwhile, all of Wynette's prescriptions, drug paraphernalia, and any medical records concerning her drug treatment were hustled out of the home to be destroyed. "Every drop of pain medication was removed without my knowledge," Richey would later state on national television, blankly declaring he had no clue who had done this or who instructed it to be done. I've spoken to the person who claims he was told to do away with the material. Unbeknownst to Richey, he informed me that he's kept it all these years. "I didn't destroy it," he told me. "I've still got the syringes and the records of every shot given her." Maybe one day he'll reveal to the public whatever information he has concerning the amount of medication Tammy had in her the day she died.

Two Nashville police officers arrived. Richey was off in another room, hysterical. "I could hear him screaming from the den," noted Detective Fuqua, who failed to interview him. Jackie says Richey kept wailing that there should be no autopsy.* Tina Jones told the detective her mother had been "sick for a long time from a degenerative disease," naming Wallis Marsh as her physician. "I saw no signs of foul play," noted Fuqua.

Officer Sam Roberts spoke to Dr. Marsh via telephone sometime before he left Pittsburgh. In his report Roberts stated that Marsh informed him that Wynette was only on four antibiotics and a blood thinner. No mention was made of her painkillers or her addiction to them, either that night or the next day when Marsh spoke to medical examiner Bruce Levy. Marsh also told Roberts that the reason for Tammy's death was a pulmonary embolism, meaning a blood clot. Contributing factors were "indwelling vena cava catheter" (the catheter in Wynette's back) and "small bowel dismotility" (blockage of the small intestine).

Noted pathologist Cyril Wecht, who was asked to look into the case in early 1999, found Marsh's actions rather curious. "I had never heard of a doctor getting on a plane and flying somewhere to declare a person dead. Second, I had a problem with Dr. Marsh opining that Wynette died of a pulmonary embolism without having performed an autopsy." As he would further reiterate in a television interview, "There is no way that anybody can look at a body and make a diagnosis of a pulmonary embolism. It is not possible."

At the time, Bruce Levy did not challenge Wallis Marsh's visual diagnosis, and Tammy Wynette's death was ruled one of natural causes. According to her book, the next day Jackie spoke to Marsh (who'd spent the night at Wynette's home), and he reaffirmed his diagnosis. He told her Tammy's vital signs were good before she passed and didn't indicate there had been any health issues in the days before she died. He'd change his assessment later.

Tributes to Tammy filled the newspapers, airwaves, and television in the days to come.

"The world has lost one of the most unique stylists in the music industry," said Dolly Parton. "The whole world will mourn Tammy Wynette."

---

*At a press conference on the day of the eventual autopsy, Richey outlined what he said were Tammy's wishes. "First, she did not want to be cremated. Secondly, she did not want there to be an autopsy on her body."

"This woman walked through so much crap and survived it," said Wynonna. "There was nobody like Tammy, period."

"Tammy Wynette was an American original, and we will miss her," said Bill and Hillary Clinton.

"Her voice had a husky center, with melancholy balanced by determination," noted Jon Pareles in a five-column *New York Times* obituary. "She sounded like an everywoman with unexpected reserves of strength and affection."

"We once made a record called *One of a Kind*," said Billy Sherrill. "There are no more words. The words have all been said."

"She was the epitome of a country star," said Lorrie Morgan, who felt her demise marked the end of an era. "It was kind of like the death of country music."

Back at Tammy's estate, plans were being made for her memorial. Some guests found the mood in the house disconcerting. "It just didn't seem like it was what I was accustomed to," said Nancy Jones. Barbara Hutchison described the scene as "joyous. They were havin' parties, they were all sippin' wine. I thought, 'Boy, these people are almost giddy.' They were all sittin' there laughin' and smoking and cutting up." Karyn Sloas sat on the couch, so stunned she called Yvonne Abdon over for a reality check. "I said, 'They're jokin'. They're tellin' *jokes*.' One minute Richey was cryin' and the next minute he was laughing, talking to whoever the celebrity was that was calling on the phone. Like he was planning a big show—the funeral. 'You get me as much coverage of this as we can, I want it on CNN.' It was just really weird, really macabre."

According to one witness, things became even more distressing during the open viewing of Wynette's body for the family and band members. "Tammy had her full jewelry on, a beautiful diamond necklace. We were all crying and goin' up one at a time to say good-bye" when one of the Richardsons "came in, took the jewelry, and left—with Tammy's daughters standin' right there."

Wynette's daughters were on their own. "When my mom passed away, Richey did not really offer any support to any of us," said Georgette. But one individual did rise to the occasion—George Jones. "My dad is the one who went with my sisters and me to the funeral home to talk about the arrangements and to do everything. Nancy sat outside, Daddy went inside the little room with us and talked about everything that we wanted and needed. He wasn't there to voice an opinion, but for comfort and support." (Richey wasn't present. "He was too distraught," said Evelyn Shriver.)

Jones attended both the private and public memorials. "My daddy absolutely hates to go to funerals," said Georgette. "He wanted to show his respect for Mom, and that meant the absolute world to me." It was the first time Jackie Daly had ever seen Jones cry.

After the service for Wynette at the Ryman, Martha Dettwiller was up on the stage, talking to Tammy's band members, when Jones walked up. "He'd been as strong as he could be for the girls. Helped them, done everything the right way. I was real proud of Jones. He looked at me and he said, 'Martha, our girl's gone.' He had this look in his face, just kind of lost it." Nancy had the bus ready, and she and George climbed aboard and got out of town. "Nancy said they just rode and rode and rode," said Dettwiller. "Him just sittin' there."

"I am just very glad that we were able to work together and tour together again," said Jones in a press release. "It was very important for us to close the chapter on everything that we had been through. I know Tammy felt the same way.

"Life is too short. In the end we were very close friends. And now, I have lost that friend. I couldn't be sadder."

On April 9 came the services. First was an hour-and-a-half private memorial at Judson Baptist Church, with a who's who of country music in attendance: Loretta Lynn, Vince Gill, Martina McBride, Randy Travis, and the Judds among them. Jake Hess sang Wynette's favorite, "Death Ain't No Big Deal." Dolly Parton was so overcome she had to quit singing "Shine On" two verses in.

Later that day fifteen hundred people attended the public service at the Ryman. Fans came from all over the country, lining up in the bitter cold weather to pay their respects. Covered live by CNN, it was the first funeral broadcast by the BBC since the death of Diana, Princess of Wales. "It was treated like a death of a head of state," said country music historian Robert K. Oermann. "It was very, very moving. Every star in the firmament was there. It was like a queen had died." J. D. Sumner and the Stamps did "Peace in the Valley" and "Angel Band." Randy Travis sang an a cappella "Precious Memories"; Wynonna, "How Great Thou Art." The Oak Ridge Boys, Rudy Gatlin, and Norro Wilson all sang or spoke.

But it was Merle Haggard who cut right to the bone. Unable to attend, he had had Tammy's old engineer Lou Bradley videotape him doing an acoustic number from home. Haggard delivered "If I Could Only Fly," a devastating choice of material, in his unadorned, direct style. "I feel so good and then I feel so bad / I wonder what I ought to do." What a bull's-eye to the heart. "Tammy liked that song," said Merle.

Backed by Tammy's band, Lorrie Morgan sang "Amazing Grace" and then, finally, "Stand by Your Man." "You won't hear any steel," said Rusty Pence. "I played not one lick—I was there, I was sitting onstage, but I couldn't make any sounds come out. I just couldn't do it." The Wynettetones would never play together again.

Before Morgan appeared, an unexpected eulogist hobbled to the microphone. Hunched over, weeping, speaking feebly, George Richey rambled on, thanking Billy Sherrill and several others before muttering a bit about the circumstances of Tammy's death. ("We were alone in the house on the couch when she died.")

Many of Tammy's friends were appalled. "I looked at Mike Martinovich," Martha Dettwiller recalled. "I said, 'Get him off the stage *now*, before he confesses.'

"There's a way that Southern people, especially Deep South people, handle grief. You don't go about shoutin' and cryin' and wailin' and makin' a to-do about it, you quietly mourn. Through the whole process, anytime anybody saw Richey—'*Waaaahhhhhhh*,' just this display that was so inappropriate and uncalled for. No decorum. White trash!"

Charley Abdon agreed. "The way he was actin', it was so full of crap—him goin' on and on and cryin' and wailin' like he was Arabic. He knew it was about over, so it was time to make his big entrance and stumble up onstage, the poor out-of-his-mind distraught husband. He was like that over at the house—one minute he'd be goin' on about, '*Ooooh*, I've *looost* her,' then start talkin' about the great numbers they had on CNN. Oh, he said that repeatedly. Then somebody would come into the room, and he'd go back into the wailing."

"What an act," said Wynette's former bodyguard Stanley Harman. "Oscar time."

In May Tammy's daughters (along with Richey's two kids) were summoned to a lawyer's office for an estate meeting. They were told that the executors of Wynette's will were to be George Richey and his brother Carl Richardson.

If either should pass away (as Carl did), Sylvia Richardson would step in. No member of Wynette's family would serve. Three trusts made up the bulk of Tammy's estate. One was specifically set up for her children.

The will itself contained the following instruction, supposedly from Tammy herself:

> I may prepare a written memorandum listing certain items of tangible personal property which I wish certain persons to have . . . if no such memorandum shall be found with this will, then it shall be presumed none exists.

But the yellow legal pad that had been omnipresent during Tammy's final years was missing. Richey couldn't find it. "It disappeared," said Tina Jones at the time. "He says he doesn't know where it is." According to Jackie's book, Tammy's will did not request an inventory of her estate, and none was taken (that leaves open the question of how the estate was evaluated for tax purposes), and although Tammy had told the children there was a million-dollar life insurance policy for their benefit, no such policy was ever located.

Lastly and most curiously, the will being addressed was not the original purportedly signed by Tammy in 1996, but a copy. Right there on the spot the children were asked to sign affidavits to affirm their acceptance of the copy as genuine. Incredibly, all but Tina did. For their trouble, each of them got a five-thousand-dollar "advance" against the life insurance policy. Except for troublemaker Tina, that is.

Not long after this meeting it was discovered that the second insurance policy taken out in Tammy's name in 1988 did *not* list her daughters as the beneficiaries. It was to go to "the estate of the insured." The result: both policies were under the control of George Richey.

According to Jackie, when questioned about the matter, Richey was evasive, saying Tammy had decided she didn't want her kids to get the money all at once. When Jackie showed up with a lawyer in tow, Richey appeared nervous, refusing at first to answer questions about the policies. He'd received $1.4 million on his policy and $1 million on the estate policy. Where did the million for her daughters go? Toward debts left on the estate. And how much was Tammy's estate worth? No idea, said Richey. Around in circles it went.

Tammy Wynette had literally worked herself into the grave. One reason for this, as all her friends and loved ones knew, was to provide for her children. Aside from Tina, Tammy's daughters each got five thousand dollars. The grandchildren were to receive ten thousand dollars apiece. Everything else was under Richey's control, including her property, tour buses, recordings, mementoes, photographs. The daughters got "nothing, not even family portraits," said a bitter Martha Dettwiller. "Not even pictures they had of the girls.*

"There's no honor in it, no honor at all. And the tragedy is that Tammy deserved honor. I feel like she should've been adored and honored in her death, and that man didn't do it. And, if guilty of nothing else, I find Richey guilty of that dishonor."

"Tammy's favorite saying used to be, 'I'll die and my kids won't get a penny and the Richardsons will get it all,'" noted Wynette's old friend Jan Smith. "Well, that's what happened. She died, they didn't get a penny, and the Richardsons got it all."

But as it happened Tammy's daughters wouldn't take these developments lying down. Many felt Richey had invited such an attack due to his flagrant disregard for them as well as for Wynette's other family members and friends. "A lot of it was self-induced on Richey's part," said Mike Martinovich. "I don't think he was fair. Had he been fair with them, I don't think they would have taken the hard line they took."

A relatively new player started making her presence felt in the days directly after Wynette's death. Sheila Slaughter, an attractive, thirty-two-year-old former Dallas Cowboys cheerleader, had served as executive producer of an extremely syrupy cable channel profile on Tammy that had aired in May 1997. She'd also helped Wynette put together a baby shower for Faith Hill the summer of the previous year. Martha Dettwiller had helped Tammy prepare such events for years, so she was curious to see what this new person was up to. The theme of the shower was "Hey, Diddle, Diddle, the Cat and the Fiddle," and Martha thought Slaughter had put together a rather lavish presentation. "Got to the shower and

---

*"Two years after Mom's death, Richey gave Gwen a ring," said Jackie. "Gwen was the only one who got anything. Richey did give my oldest Mom's car, a Lincoln. I'm not sure why. And he did give my girls each a piece of jewelry, not what Mom wanted anybody to have. Nancy Jones actually got us pictures. Maybe Richey was getting rid of 'em."

there was a man in a catsuit playin' a fiddle. I said, 'Tammy, this is impressive.' She said, 'I cannot tell you, she's about to drive me crazy.' That shower was so expensive—when we did things, we'd do Coca-Colas in a bottle with sandwiches we made. Sheila spent a lot of money puttin' that thing on, and Richey let her. Tammy didn't know until the very end how much this was costin'. She said, 'There's somethin' really weird about Sheila.' Tammy was suspicious. And after Tammy got suspicious, I got suspicious."

The next time Dettwiller encountered Slaughter, it was when she went to pay her respects at the Wynette home after her death. "As I pulled in the driveway, I could see somebody jump out of their car with the lights on, the motor runnin', and the door open. Here comes this Sheila, just runnin' and screamin' and cryin'. It was totally inappropriate. She wasn't that close to Tammy, so I thought, 'What the hell is she actin' like this for?' It was unnerving." Evelyn Shriver felt the same way. "Sheila jumped out of the car in her pajamas and came running up and started hugging us. I didn't even know who the hell this person was."

"I just thought it was always suspicious that Sheila showed up so fast," said Jerry Taylor. "What the hell was she doin' here? Was this thing goin' on *before* Tammy died? I know a lot of people think so." Kelli Haggard-Patterson said Slaughter "was chasin' Richey before Tammy died. She went after him like a heat-seeking missile." The documentary *Tammy Wynette: An American Tragedy* uncovered credit card bills that indicated someone was using Tammy's card to order "women's clothing in the week she died, on the day she died, and during the week after her death." (Richey denied he was involved with Sheila at the time.)

A close friend of Tammy's came to visit Richey that May. "They had this square table that sat in front of the very couch Wynette died on. I got to lookin', there was all these pictures of Richey and a real young-lookin' blonde woman." Richey saw her staring at the photos and told her, "I just can't make it by myself. That's Sheila. She's special to me." Cleta took the visitor's children on a tour of the house that skipped Richey's room. "I do believe that girl was there that day. I will always believe that. Because there was a car there I didn't know."*

Slaughter was soon seen driving Tammy's Rolls-Royce. Georgette would

---

*Shelia Slaughter Richey declined several requests for an interview.

tell *Star* that Sheila "would wear my mother's jewelry and her clothes." She found it all "just completely, utterly disrespectful."

Tammy had been dead less than a month.

On September 23, the Country Music Association voted Tammy into the Hall of Fame. Richey, looking slick in a typically garish black suit with tacky diamond piping, accepted the award on tape. "May you sleep peacefully until I see you again," he instructed Tammy, before God-blessing the watching minions à la the Pope.

The very next day the controversy surrounding Wynette's death was made public for the first time via a tabloid cover story. TAMMY'S KIDS DE-MAND NEW PROBE OF HER DEATH, screamed the headline of the story by Roger Hitts in *Star*. The daughters had hired private investigator Bobbye Casper, who began to dig around in the police records as well as conduct a few interviews with some of Tammy's friends and employees, which have unfortunately not been made public.

In September Sony released *Tammy Wynette Remembered*, a collection of her songs done by Melissa Etheridge, Elton John (a grotesquely over-wrought "Stand by Your Man" produced by Richey), and the usual Music City suspects. Unsurprisingly it is George Jones who pays Tammy the deep-est tribute with a somber reading of "Take Me to Your World." "It was always one of my favorite Tammy songs," he said. "I just always loved hearing her sing it. To be honest, it made me sad. To be in the studio singing one of her songs just brought it all back. I tried to . . . make her proud." The album ends with Tammy's eerie final recording of "In My Room."

On October 7 came an all-star tribute concert at the Opry House featur-ing many of the album's participants. Somehow Richey had neglected to invite Tammy's daughters, but they arrived in full force anyway. Richey and Slaughter had deigned to go public at this event, and at the preshow cocktail party, Tina Jones waltzed up to both of them and let them know what she thought. "You're a hypocrite . . . you pretend you're heartbroken, but you're sleeping with Sheila," she said loudly, silencing the assembled glitterati. "Richey and Sheila just stood there, looking like they wanted to be beamed up and out of the room," wrote a gleeful Jackie. Tina was promptly escorted out, but her point had been made, earning a page in the *Globe* complete with surreptitious photos of Richey and Slaughter. Later at the concert, tempers ran high. As photographer Raeanne Rubenstein noted,

"The drama was not onstage but in the audience. George Richey was there, and all the children, sitting in adjacent rows. It was so poignant to see all the characters in this Tammy Wynette drama sitting in the same three rows in front of the Ryman. It was really quite amazing."

Evelyn Shriver and Susan Nadler, two of Richey's longtime defenders, had encouraged his involvement in the tribute as a way of keeping his mind off his grief. But even they found the scene over at Wynette's former home rather unappetizing. As Shriver recalled, it was now "a house full of Dallas Cowboy cheerleader types running around with piña coladas and everybody in bathing suits." An appalled Nadler noted that even sixty-two-year-old Richey was in a "little spandex top and shorts! With his bandy little legs hangin' out!"

"We didn't want to be there," Shriver continued. "It's Tammy's house. You walk in, and there's all these bimbos you've never seen before in your life—blondes bouncing along with big tits, drinks in their hand. I just couldn't deal with it. This was not my idea of how Tammy's house should end. We stopped seeing Richey because it was too weird."

Carolyn Neal, the English friend Tammy had confided in back in 1993, admitted she still cares about Richey despite what she saw and what Wynette told her. In November 1999 she and her husband, Den, visited him, at one point joining him to listen to the Gaithers. As they sang, "Welcome home, my child, welcome home," Richey grew emotional.

"He just burst into tears, got up, came next to me, and just buried his face in my shoulder and sobbed," said Carolyn. "He totally, totally confuses me. He treated Tammy like shit, and he could still cry over things like this? I still can't work him out."

In December 1998, medical examiner Bruce Levy, Nashville Metro Police, and the district attorney all received letters from Jackie Daly, Tina Jones, and Georgette Smith imploring them to look into their mother's death and asking for an autopsy to be done. Their requests were denied. A lawyer representing the daughters contacted Levy again in January. Requesting a face-to-face meeting, they promptly got one on February 8. Levy told the daughters he'd look into the matter. He contacted Wallis Marsh, who confirmed that Wynette had been on previously unreported pain medication. Levy wrote on May 21, 1999, that Marsh "expressed regret that the complete list of medications had not been provided" the night Wynette expired. A miscommunication error, as Marsh put it. "This caused me to suspect there may have been an attempt to provide minimal information to the authorities that evening," wrote Levy.

Marsh also revealed for the first time that he'd been contacted the day before Tammy died and that he had been "extremely concerned" that Tammy was suffering from another blood clot "and urged that she be admitted to the hospital." Supposedly Wynette felt better the next day, and either she or Richey had decided against the hospital. Marsh told Levy "he was not surprised by her death due to the events of the last couple of days." According to Jackie's book, a few months later, in an informal meeting with a lawyer representing Tammy's daughters, Marsh was asked if Wynette would've lived had Richey taken her to the hospital as requested. He simply answered, "Yes."

The day after the meeting, Levy admitted to the *Tennessean* that "had we known about the medications" Wynette had been taking, "that may have raised questions in our mind about whether an autopsy needed to be held or not." Wallis Marsh declined to speak to reporters, but released a statement reiterating his autopsy-less diagnosis. "In my medical opinion, no doubt that her death resulted from the effects of blood clots in her lungs."

Despite the many troubling questions this new information raised, Levy held a press conference just two days after the meeting with Tammy's daughters to announce he would not perform an autopsy. After "a thorough review" of the case, he decided Wynette had been "terminally ill, and her death was due to natural causes." Terminal illness? This was news to her children.

The tale of Tammy Wynette's death took yet another strange turn as a result of the bird-dogging detective work of Jennifer Kraus, a local TV reporter. In sifting through the petitions of various parties of the estate seeking payment, she came across bills from Care Solutions, Inc., a local outfit that had been delivering pharmaceuticals to Wynette's home since February 1998. Among other prescriptions, they'd sent her two shipments of Versed, including one on the very day Tammy died. "Enough Versed went through her home to kill a bull," said George Jones.

Wynette had been on all sorts of medications, so what could be considered unusual about this one? First of all, it is a very dangerous drug that is only supposed to be administered, according to its makers, "in a hospital or ambulatory care settings . . . that provide for continuous monitoring of respiratory and cardiac function." There is a long list of possible adverse reactions: nausea, vomiting, blurred vision, respiratory depression, and respiratory arrest. One other rather strange side effect: it erases the memory. (I had this drug administered during a hospital stay and could recall nothing of the procedure afterward.) Tammy's friends wondered if she'd been given any papers to sign in her altered state. Incredibly, in a televised interview with 20/20, Richey claimed Marsh had never informed him of the danger of Versed.

One day short of the one-year anniversary of their mother's death, Jackie, Georgette, and Tina filed a $50 million lawsuit against George Richey, Wallis Marsh, and Marsh's hospital, the University of Pittsburgh Medical Center. Care Solutions would later be added to the suit. The suit alleged that "the Defendant, George B. Richardson, acting in concert and/or severally with the Defendant, James Wallis Marsh, M.D., was negligent and contributed to the death of Virginia Richardson, aka Tammy Wynette, in that he improperly and inappropriately maintained her narcotic addiction, improperly administered narcotics to her and failed to see that she would receive necessary emergency medical treatment at a time when he could have, and should have, known that his failure to do so would, or could, result in the catastrophic event of her death."

In a *Today* show appearance, Ed Yarbrough, lawyer for the daughters, put it in plain English for the TV audience: "We contend that Dr. Marsh was in effect enabling her addiction as well as Mr. Richey, and that's what killed her."

Wallis Marsh continues to decline all interview requests, including my own, but issued a statement via his lawyers. The charges had "no basis in fact," it insisted, and asserted that "when the facts become known" it would be apparent that Marsh had "provided extraordinary medical care to a person who suffered extraordinary medical problems."

Since the allegations had first been made public, the daughters had been pressing for an autopsy, to no avail. Bruce Levy maintained that Richey had not requested it and he didn't have enough cause to get a court order demanding one. According to booking agent Tony Conway, Richey was panicked by the request. "He called me to lunch and said, 'I don't know what to do, I don't know what to do—what would you do?'" Conway told him, "Well, George, if you were really innocent, why wouldn't you want them to do an autopsy?" Richey, said Conway, "was a wreck, he was totally stressed out."

Just days after the lawsuit was filed, Richey relented, formally asking Bruce Levy to conduct an autopsy. Tammy was exhumed on April 14, 1999. "They didn't even tell the lawyers until that morning. We found out from the television station," said Martha Dettwiller. "Jackie and I felt like somebody needed to be there, so we sat across the street in a car." They both felt Tammy's presence. "She was just everywhere," said Dettwiller, who became emotional reliving the memory. "Jackie and I sat there cryin' 'til it was over."

A smoldering but still imperious Richey, glasses resting low upon his nose as he read his statement, called a press conference that afternoon. Stating he had acquiesced to the autopsy "so we can all move on," he proceeded to blast Tammy's offspring. "I'm saddened that, out of frustration over financial matters, her daughters have been willing to work so hard to discredit their mother. And that's what they have done. I'm saddened that part of Tammy's legacy is part of this fiasco." Referencing his own experience working at a mortuary in 1962, he said, "I know exactly what's happening to Tammy today and I despise it."

Richey answered no questions after his public statement, but Sylvia Richardson addressed the lawsuit's accusation that Richey had declined to take Wynette to the hospital despite Dr. Marsh's wishes. It was Tammy who said she'd felt better and had refused to go, she maintained. "What you have to remember is that Tammy Wynette was a very strong woman, and mainly, she was in control."

On May 16, 1999, Bruce Levy issued a sixteen-page report based on the autopsy. Probable cause of death: "heart failure with cardiac arrhythmia" due to "chronic pulmonary emboli with pulmonary hypertension." As most people who die of natural causes experience cardiac arrhythmia, it was something of a safe, catchall diagnosis. "That's what *everyone* dies of," sniffed Nancy Jones. Levy felt that previous blood clots had damaged Tammy's arteries, enlarging the right side of her heart. Contributing cause: "intestinal dysmotility on pain management." Manner of death: "could not be determined."

Cyril Wecht noted that, contrary to Wallis Marsh's declarations, "the medical examiner found no acute, that is recent, blood clots in her system.

So that is not what caused her death." The contributing cause, "intestinal dysmotility on pain management," translates into problems such as blockages caused by chronic use of painkillers. "It was an interesting diagnosis, one I have rarely seen," said Wecht. Lab tests indicated the presence of two drugs in Wynette's system, Versed and Phenergan. Unfortunately there was no way to tell if Dilaudid had been in her body, because it was "one of the substances that dissipates during the embalming process," added Wecht. "The inference I drew was that perhaps the medical examiner wanted to get across that the drugs Wynette was taking to control her pain—Dilaudid and Versed—played a role in her death." Because there was no way to tell how much Dilaudid Tammy had in her system, if any, "Dr. Levy couldn't come right out and make such a statement."

Truly, though, the report was a victory for Wynette's daughters. According to Levy, their concern that pain medication had played a role in their mother's demise had more relevance than Dr. Marsh's diagnosis.

In 2000 came Jackie's book (cowritten with Tom Carter), *Tammy Wynette: A Daughter Recalls Her Mother's Tragic Life and Death.* While extremely sympathetic toward her mother and her many problems, it was a damning indictment of Richey. Jackie obviously had the support of George and Nancy Jones—Nancy was one of the agents for Carter's end of the book deal—and on June 2, 2000, George wrote an impassioned letter to Don Imus urging him to cover the story. "Why has not Richey been arrested for practicing medicine without a license?" asked the Possum.

Ignoring the fact that the book was critical of him, and not Wynette, Richey once again played the Tammy card, drawing comparisons to Christina Crawford's infamous Tinseltown exposé of her mother, Joan, *Mommy Dearest.* Finally granting the newsmagazine show *20/20* an interview, broadcast on January 14, Richey categorically denied the charges. Did he have anything to do with his wife's death? "The answer is unequivocally, absolutely, without question—no," he replied angrily. There he sat at the white grand piano, warbling "You and Me." He praised the treatment Wallis Marsh had given Tammy, but also admitted that Marsh had "personally showed me how to" inject Versed into his wife, insisting the doctor had not informed him of how dangerous the drug was. "No, I was not told that," he said.

George Richey wanted to make sure the world knew that he alone understood the wishes, dreams, and soul of Tammy Wynette. "I knew her better than anyone on this earth," he declared. "Better than her children, better than her relatives . . . she was the love of my life."

Sheila Slaughter, the new love of Richey's life, appeared before the camera for her fifteen seconds of fame, denying that she and Richey had been an item before Tammy's death. "In no way did we have an affair," she demurred. "It's ludicrous. It did not happen." Tastelessly referencing Wynette's trademark song in defending Richey, she added, "I will stand by him no matter what."

But George Richey had the last word, one final eerie statement about Tammy's death. "We will never know—will we?—what really happened."

Unfortunately it is extremely unlikely the facts *will* ever be fully known. Cyril Wecht laid the blame at Wallis Marsh's doorstep. "Much time and effort was spent and unnecessary anguish suffered by many people in this case," he wrote. "Much, if not all of it, could have been spared had Dr. Marsh provided a full accounting of the drugs Wynette was taking and had Dr. Levy ordered an immediate autopsy."

It is certainly possible that Wynette suffered an accidental overdose. Although the catheter was in her back, out of reach, she was known to inject herself with drugs she'd hoarded. Said Jerry Taylor, "I know for a fact that Tammy would hide it in that house, so if she wanted some more—and it wasn't time for her to get some more—she could *get* some more." Some have considered the most unpalatable theory for Tammy's friends and loved ones—the possibility that she herself had decided it was time to go. "Richey may never forgive me for saying this, but if Richey had anything to do with her death, it was at her wish, because Richey loved her," said Kelli Haggard-Patterson. "Maybe she administered something, and maybe he didn't revive her, worst-case scenario."

What is known is the appalling behavior of these parties since that event. Could George Richey really believe this is what Tammy would've wanted? Her wishes denied? Her children scorned?

"I think it was all wrong," said Nancy Jones. "Tammy loved her daughters and she loved her grandkids. I just think it's all wrong, because now I can see how hard it is for these girls. They're strugglin' really hard. I don't think Tammy would've wanted them to live a life like that—I know she spoiled 'em, she gave them just what she wanted when she was alive. I think maybe she's lookin' down with a little teardrop."

Others feel that Wynette's reaction to Richey's actions might not be so benign. "It is a possibility," said Tammy's cousin Jane Williams, "that she would've cut Richey's throat. Without even a second thought."

Richey was dropped from the daughters' lawsuit just weeks after the filing. In a bizarre irony, he himself, as Wynette's spouse, would've gained from any settlement. A judge threw out the case against Care Solutions. The remaining parties, Wallis Marsh, UPMC Presbyterian, and University Health Center of Pittsburgh, settled out of court in April 2002.

Yet another controversy flared when George and Nancy Jones requested that Tammy's body be moved from the main building in Woodlawn Memorial Park to a fancy, fan-friendly crypt on the Jones lot. When the Joneses visited her resting place, they considered the location unkempt and unsuitable for a legend. "The First Lady of Country Music and she's buried in a damn wall," Nancy told Julia Reed. Jones was upset that Tammy was interred among strangers. "She doesn't even *know* anybody over there where she is," complained the Possum.

"Tammy never wanted to be buried in the ground," said Evelyn Shriver. "Woodlawn doesn't really have aboveground crypts, but George and Nancy went there and convinced the cemetery to allow them to have an aboveground crypt for Tammy." There was one catch, however. She'd still have to be buried next to her husband. "One of the girls fought me and said, 'No, I don't want it, because Richey's going to be there,'" said Nancy. "Well, Richey's gonna be buried next to her no matter what." Unless Richey decides otherwise, the Wynette will states that he will be buried alongside Wynette—wherever she's interred.

"If the girls ever change their mind, I can promise the whole world there would be a huge monument for Tammy," said Nancy, who gave up on the plan once one of Wynette's daughters hired a lawyer. "So she's still, as I call it, stuck on the wall."*

"My life will be lived to perpetuate Tammy's music and her legacy for as long as I live," George Richey promised not long after Wynette's death.

---

*As moving Wynette's remains would cost in the neighborhood of $100,000, various powers that be were asked to contribute to the cause. "People who made millions of dollars off her—Sony Records, Sony Publishing, other labels," said Evelyn Shriver. "No one would give us a dime."

Richey went on TV to hawk a crappy miniature statue of his wife, helped produce a more or less lifeless tribute album, and, finally, a decade after her death, unveiled a refurbished Tammy Wynette Web site. Most of Wynette's albums remain out of print. One of the primary raisons d'être of the old Tammy Web site seemed to be to defend George Richey. When one visitor posted material critical of him, his name, address, and phone number were revealed, with the Webmaster urging Tammy's fans to harass the evildoer. "VIP" fans were invited to a "secret" tête-à-tête with Richey, accompanied by his wife and by former Wynette hairdresser Wanda Williams, in June 2007. At one point it was revealed that Tammy had written a letter to Richey suggesting that he get together with either Sheila Slaughter or Kelli Haggard-Patterson following her demise. What else was in this supposed missive, and exactly why Tammy felt compelled to communicate such an idea, makes one wonder if indeed she knew she was about to die.*

During the course of that 2000 *20/20* interview, Richey was asked if he had any plans to marry Slaughter. "Absolutely not," he announced. One year later in a secret ceremony at the Little Country Church outside Nashville, Richey did exactly that. Bride and groom arrived in his 'n' her vintage automobiles and were serenaded by Tim McGraw. "Tammy was one of my most cherished friends," the new Mrs. Richey boldly told the *National Enquirer.* "And I'm sure that she's blessing this marriage from heaven." Richey, then in his midsixties, went on to sire a child with Sheila, Tatum.

It appears that whatever funds were left in the Wynette bank may be long gone. Richey called Tony Conway out of the blue one day about six months after Tammy died. He wanted some comp rooms at a Tunica, Mississippi, casino that Conway used to book Wynette in. Conway did as asked. When one gets comped a suite, the casino expects you to gamble an amount worthy of the favor, as Conway found out when the irritated entertainment director called him a few days later. Richey had blown a mere three hundred dollars on the slots.

These days, Richey is said to be in poor health. He arrived at the one

---

*George and Sheila Richey seem obsessed with Wynette's daughters. During the Christmas season of 2006 they sent out a quizzical DVD of outtakes from the cable profile Sheila produced. It included unflattering interview snippets of each of Tammy's daughters intending to show them contradicting their later claims, alongside endless footage of Tammy praising Richey. This strange document concludes with a montage of slow-motion shots of Tammy and Richey, "Stand by Your Man" as the soundtrack, then a final shot of Richey at the press conference announcing the autopsy.

meeting of the VIP Tammy Wynette Fan Club in a wheelchair and with an oxygen tank. Before Richey moved to Midland, he was Tony Conway's neighbor for a while. "Honestly, the only times I ever saw him is when the ambulance would show up at two in the morning. The red lights would be flashin' in my window. I'd look out the curtain, they had Richey on a stretcher, he had on an oxygen mask and a little stocking cap. I'd see Sheila standin' there with the baby—'Okay, Richey, we'll see you tomorrow.' This happened five or six different times."

At least one witness reported him ferreting through the ashtray outside the Nashville apartment complex home he occupies when he isn't in Midland, Texas, searching for cigarette butts to smoke away from his wife's disapproving gaze. Richey told one friend, "I have bad days and I have worse days."

On March 6, 1999, almost a year to the day after Tammy's death, George Jones was piloting his Lexus SUV down the highway, talking to his stepdaughter while attempting to navigate the cassette player in order to locate a rough mix of his new single, the aptly titled "Choices." Jones lost control of the vehicle, and it plowed into a concrete bridge. Jones had made the choice to drink that day; an empty bottle of vodka would be found under his seat. He nearly died from a collapsed lung and torn liver. Afterward he'd say that it had been a rough past year; Nancy had been sick, and they'd lost Wynette. "I had just made friends again with Tammy . . . we thought we might be able to do some other things together down the road. Then she passed away."*

But Jones rose from the dead once more, vowing never to drink again. "It put the fear of God in me," he insisted. "It's a miracle I'm alive." Georgette, who's decided to pursue a singing career, helped her father return to the road sober by joining him onstage to sing her mother's parts in the old duets. She's recorded a song with Jones, a number she cowrote, about her relationship with her father, "You and Me and Time." The drama of the lyrics, not to mention the stop-start chorus, would surely win the approval of her mother.

---

*During an interview with two of the Possum's associates, they mused over his relationship with Wynette. One wondered if, despite his undeniable love and allegiance to Nancy, Tammy was the one that he thought of in the midnight hours. "No," insisted the other. "If anything, he's thinking of *a new car*."

"It's a great song," said Jones. "I was very proud of her. It was really heart-touchin'." And did Jones hear any of Tammy in his daughter? "Well, I do. She don't have that really bursting-out drive type singin' like her mother, y'know. Hittin' those hard notes. She sings smoother. I should say quieter. Georgette's got a beautiful voice. She does an up-tempo number good."

A new calmness seemed to have settled over Jones—well, as calm as the Possum can ever be. "He never gets mad no more," said Nancy. "He's a very sensitive guy. Good husband, too." Our interview was cut short because an impatient Jones was in the car, waiting, as always, to go to the local mall. "He loves to shop."

Only a fool would wish for the kind of destruction and depravity Jones has lived through, but he also understands that these were the cards he was dealt. *You have to live the song.* George has lived every last bloody drop and, amazingly, unlike so many others—Tammy included—he has survived. But, he notes, at a price to the music.

In the bad old days "we'd always have three, four drinks just to relax us good. And maybe one or two *extra*. And go in there, record, and get in a sad, sad mood right with that song. And then when you're on tour drinkin' onstage, you get those same feelin's singin' 'em.

"But when you quit drinkin' like I have, you calm down. You're happy, you're content, and in some cases"—he laughed a bit ruefully—"maybe that's not too good for the work that you do. That is why we may not sound today onstage and in person like we did on records.

"I seem to satisfy the fans, but I do know in my heart that I'm not cryin' like I used to in my songs," he admitted. When all the chaos left his life, he knows something else left, too. "You're feelin' *great*, and you lose a lot of that hurtin' expression in your phrasin' because you don't hurt anymore, y'know? You got nothin' to cry about. Everything's . . . happy. In other words, you want to sing gospel songs and happy songs. That's *it*.

"The only thing you can do is go forward, and thank God you're still *alive*."

Nobody would've predicted Jones outliving Wynette way back when. So I asked George: does he have any clue why he is still here and she isn't?

"No, I don't. Only thing I can tell you, I think He's let me stay for a reason." As usual, Jones was elusive on the subject of Wynette, so it didn't surprise me that he changed the subject to the singer that had been so important to both him and Tammy—Hank Williams.

"I think he was put here in this business for us to have somethin' to cry with. Help us cry, get rid of our misery. We only had Hank five years. Five years is all this man's career lasted. But I still play his music all the time. He was put here for a purpose, and he left for a purpose. Because I think God put him here to open our eyes to something good, and also to the bad. In the sad songs."

I wouldn't dare to put words in the Possum's mouth, but I think he was trying to say Tammy Wynette had been placed upon earth for a similar reason.

"What happened to our music?" Tammy had asked as she hobbled around in her end days. In its continual pursuit of the rock/pop dollar, Music City has only sunk lower, aligning itself with reality shows and goofball TV singing contests.

You don't hear Wynette much on the radio anymore. Or anything else that stays with you longer than the song itself. "In those years you could ride down the road, hear a country song play, and you'd have to stop your car, it'd touch you so much," said Norro Wilson. "It's hard to drive down the road today."

"You can't walk in with a heartfelt song anymore and say, 'Look, I lived this and I need to record it,'" said Lorrie Morgan. "'Is it radio friendly?' Who gives a shit if it's radio friendly?"

Gifted, complex characters like Tammy Wynette are one thing pretty much missing from American popular culture these days, particularly music. "Now everybody's famous," said that chilly arbiter of celebrity, Tina Brown. "And nobody's interesting."

As I've stated elsewhere, to shed tears over such inevitable developments is somewhat akin to bemoaning the fact that most of us no longer churn our own butter. This music belongs to a time and place that has vanished. Virtually every variation on three chords, a steel guitar, and a sad story has already been recorded, however. The formula was exhausted—and then some. "It's really a more narrow art form . . . it has limitations," Nashville Row executive Tony Brown once said of country. Amen to that. Yes, it may be elusive on radio or TV, but these days classic country is more accessible to the individual than ever before—all you need is a computer with a search engine. Want to learn more about Wayne Kemp, Cal Smith, Frankie Miller? Press a button. And though Tammy is gone, her music remains, and right about now one of her songs is getting some lost soul through a dark and lonely night.

There was no joy taken in telling the end of this story. Tammy's present only as a ghost. It's just a catalog of depair, the brutal aftermath. There was no way around it, really. I don't think Wynette would want the story sugar-coated. She might've been a teller of tall tales, but Tammy was an honest person. If you have any doubts, listen to her sing.

Late one evening I asked Jan Howard if Tammy's story had a moral.

"I don't know about a moral," she said. "Judge not, lest ye be judged. I'm just thankful that she was on this earth for as long as she was and was blessed with a talent that brought so much joy to so many people, not only with her music, but by her very presence.

"It makes me very sad to think about a lot of what she went through. Tammy is in God's hands now, God's care, and she is at peace. No more demons."

Dear Tammy,

I hope you got your heavenly crown. One with plenty of jewels.

Your friends all miss you. I look in their eyes and see a wreck on the highway. They never got to say good-bye, and they still feel guilty . . . guilty they didn't save you. I know you'd give 'em a big hug if you could. And then feed 'em some of that chocolate pie of yours. Boy, do they still talk about that.

Jones is going strong, singing, touring, and still bitching about how they've ruined your music.

Your daughters are hanging in there, although I hear one is cleaning houses. Really, Tammy, you should've given somebody that legal pad. Georgette would make you proud. She recently guest-starred on a cable comedy show playing none other than . . . Tammy Wynette. I bet you'd get a big kick out of that.

Richey . . . aaaaaaaaah, forget it.

Biographies. Do they ever sum up a life? I wish I could've written you a happy ending, Tammy. It just wasn't in the cards. Let's just play everybody "Apartment #9" and call it a day.

You know what your buddy Linda told me? She still has a little bottle of your perfume, Private Collection. And sometimes when she misses you, she opens it up, takes a whiff, and for a moment her old pal Wynette fills the room.

And then, like a distant train whistle, a firefly in the night, a song on a faraway jukebox, you're gone.

Acknowledgments

By saying the right thing at the right time, Kelly Berner, who happens to be my niece, provoked this book into existence. Thanks, Kelly.

John Kopf not only encouraged me to write this book, he provided many corrections upon reading the manuscript. I thank you, John. And Wayne Cochran's hair thanks you.

As with all my books, Charlie Beesley did his usual forensic edit, suggesting many great changes. Mr. Beesley is an indispensible ally. Dave Frasier has assisted me on research for both of my last books. If it exists somewhere in print, Frasier will find it. There is no one better. Sarah Heldman was an excellent detective when it came to finding the bodies.

Rick Kot proved to be the perfect editor for this book. He did a fantastic job and I can't thank him enough. The highly amusing Laura Tisdel did the heavy lifting. One day Tisdel will run her own publishing house, or be dictator of a third world country. Thanks to Gregg Kulick for a knockout cover, Carla Bolte for the classy interior design, Nicholas "The Rubber Hose" LoVecchio for his fiendish copyediting, Sharon Gonzalez for managing the handoff, Kate Lloyd for masterful publicity, and Gary Mailman for his thorough but relatively painless vetting.

David McCormick, the greatest agent on earth, has always been there for me. Thanks as well to Leslie Falk, P. J. Mark, Liza Wachter, Caspian Dennis, and the folks at Abner Stein. At Simon & Schuster UK, thanks to Angela Herlihy, Mike Jones, and Katherine Stanton.

Allow me to express my gratitude to the writers who covered the Nashville/Tammy/George beat before me: the fabulous Joan Dew, Jack Hurst, Michael Kosser, Dan Dailey, Alanna Nash, Holly George-Warren, Gerry Wood, Tom Roland, Holly Gleason, Bob Allen, Susan Toepfer, Tom Carter, Dolly Carlisle, John Gabree, Peter Guralnick, Stan Leventhal, Philip Self, Patsi Bale Cox, Ralph Emery, Robert K. Oermann, and Mary Bufwack.

Linda Cayson still lives in Wynette's old stomping grounds. She was a great, great help to me, and I felt Tammy's spirit nearby whenever I talked to her. I had a fantastic pair of guides in Red Bay, Alabama: Scotty Kennedy, one of Tammy's favorite photographers, and Jane Williams, who has all of her cousin's charm. This duo was instrumental in putting together the Red Bay Museum, and while their Tammy display isn't huge as of yet, I highly recommend you visit (www.redbaymuseum.org) to get a sense of the world Wynette came from. You can't have a better time for three bucks. Tell 'em Jimmy sent you.

Evelyn Shriver, Nashville's answer to Barbara Stanwyck, opened many doors for me in Nashville and made key interviews possible. A beautiful dame, inside and out. Her partner in crime, Susan Nadler, kept me laughing and suggested an interview or two herself.

For assistance in obtaining interviews, thanks to David Wykoff, James V. Roy, Betty Layton, Theresa Hughes, William Smithson, Jerry Grammer, Tresa Redburn, Nancy Jones, and Allan Rinde. For assistance with research, thanks go to Jim Diana, Nick Young, Colin and Paulette Fox, Dan Cutrer, John Morris, the Country Music Hall of Fame (particularly John Rumble), Debra Paris, Steve and Kimberley Thomas, Brian Ferrantino, Matthew Turi, and Robin Chen. Special thanks to my George Jones experts, Jim Marchant and John Morris. In Australia, thanks to Steve Newton and David Dawson.

Interviewees are listed in the source notes. I thank them one and all. Special thanks to Charley Abdon, Joan Dew, Martha Dettwiller, Maxine Hyder, Jan Smith, Nan Crafton, Barbara Hutchison, and Carolyn Neal. Thanks to Lou Bradley for giving me a tour of the Quonset Hut and putting me in touch with many of the Sherrill session musicians. Special thanks to two of Tammy's daughters, Georgette Jones and Jackie Daly. Glenn Sutton passed away during the writing of this book, one of the funniest people ever to walk the earth. I'm sorry that he didn't see the end result. Nashville should build Sutton a monument. Perhaps something that periodically explodes.

Lorraine Waser is the greatest country music fan there is in Amboy, Washington, and she was a great help to me during my years in Amboy, as was Ray Waser. Ray would pull his old truck into the farm, amble over with some fresh salmon, then proceed to educate me on what "a rat race" it was down in nearby Battle Ground. I really miss you guys.

Hair by Jerry Ripley, The Tonsorial Parlor, Portland, Oregon. Ford Falcon maintenance, John Wilson.

Thanks to: John Waters, Eliza Paley, Vicki Keller, Richard and Jessica Meltzer, Mark Linn, Brittany Karas, Philip Kenney, Bruce Kitzmeyer, Sally Mayrose, Liz Main, Mable and Buddy John, Lorena Lazheztter, Brian O'Hara, Victoria Landis, Leo Trombetta, Isaako Si'uleo, Margaret Doll Rod, Kim Morgan, Frank "Poncho" Sampedro, Kevin Kiley, Bill Bentley, Kent and Nancy Beyda, Anna Biller, and my Spanish translator for life, Elvira Asenzi Monzo. Belated thanks to Christine Karatnytsky and Dennis Dermody for help on past books. In Australia: Jaime and Aspasia Leonarder, Chris Ruhle, Kerry and Rita Wisdom, Carl Wurth, Martin Heales, Kate Wisdom, and Eleanor Bowen (Willie Nelson's Australian girlfriend, although Willie doesn't know this yet). Thanks, as always, to my brother, John McDonough. And a very special thanks to Clare Catner.

My friend and consigliere George Hedges passed away during the writing of this book. He protected me from the world and from myself. Not a day goes by that I don't miss him.

I have an obsession with stereo photography, and the reason for that was Lux Interior. Whenever I had a three a.m. 3D conundrum I could shoot off an e-mail to Lux and by morning there would be an e-mail (or five) solving the problem in minute detail. RIP, Lux. Thankfully Poison Ivy is still around to raise a little hell.

A very special thank you to Wendy Swanson, Kat Heldman, Mara Stevenson, Lindsey Malatesta, Jess Kreutter, Jessica Winn, Yumi Atteberry, Lucy Fur, Anna Hinterkopf, Jessica Wainman, Andrea Viviano, Ariana Altieri, and Annie Anyedy. They know why.

A good deal of the writing about music in this book was done in collaboration with Natalia Wisdom. Natalia knows far more about the subject than I ever could. She is the inspiration for everything.

—Jimmy M.

Discography

This is my humble attempt at a very basic Tammy Wynette discography. For the most part it concerns only American releases, and I'm certain it's incomplete. Everything post-1987 or so got a CD release; for anything produced before that I've tried to note any digital reissues. Not all the greatest hits–type packages are listed, nor every career overview like the 1983 Time-Life three-record set (no unreleased performances there). Radio shows, live concerts, and interviews aren't included; differences between single and album versions of songs haven't been identified. You will find that there is a lot of material here unavailable in legitimate digital form. If you really want to experience the music, track down the old vinyl albums. The records sound great and look fantastic. Plus it's fun to do and they can be had for cheap. As far as the CD releases go, anything mastered by Steve Hoffman or Vic Anesini is as good as it gets. I've heard rumors there is a considerable amount of Epic unreleased material in Sony's vaults. Maybe one day we'll hear it.

UNRELEASED EARLY RECORDINGS

DAVID VEST RECORDINGS, Birmingham, Alabama (1965/66). Unreleased.

You'll Remember My Name / Sing Me a Lonesome Song / Put Some Lovin' in Your Life / You Should Have Seen His Face / Matrimony

FRED LEHNER RECORDINGS, Birmingham, Alabama (1965/66). Unreleased.

Release Me / He Thinks I Still Care / The Way Things Were Going (duet with Sid Linard) / My Hurt's Bigger Than Yours / I Didn't Have a Change / I'm Coming Down with You / I Can't See Nothing Yet / Dark Time / She Went to My School / Hello, Old Friend

DON CHAPEL RECORDINGS, Nashville, Tennessee (1966–67). Unreleased.

You Can Steal Me / I'm Comin' Down / She Didn't Color Daddy / Together We Stand (Divided We Fall) / Put It Off until Tomorrow / Let's Get Together/ I'm Losing All Track of Me / If I Had Someone to Leave.

During the time Tammy was married to Don Chapel, he made some fascinating recordings of the two of them singing together and Tammy singing solo at home with an out-of-tune guitar. Great stuff, and I'm sure there's more than what's listed above.

TAMMY WYNETTE SINGLES (*indicates non-LP B-side)

Apartment #9 / I'm Not Mine to Give SP Epic 5-10095 (Oct. 1966)

Your Good Girl's Gonna Go Bad / Send Me No Roses SP Epic 5-10134 (Feb. 1967)

I Don't Wanna Play House / Soakin' Wet SP Epic 5-10211 (Jul. 1967)

Take Me to Your World / Good SP Epic 5-10269 (Nov. 1967)

Your Good Girl's Gonna Go Bad / Apartment #9 SP Epic 5-2264 (1968)

D-I-V-O-R-C-E / Don't Make Me Now* P Epic 5-10315 (Apr. 1968)

Stand by Your Man / I Stayed Long Enough SP Epic 5-10398 (Sep. 1968)

I Don't Wanna Play House / Take Me to Your World SP Epic 5-2275 (1969)

Singing My Song / Too Far Gone Epic 5-10462 (Feb. 1969)

Ways to Love a Man / Still Around SP Epic 5-10512 (Jul. 1969)

I'll See Him Through / Enough of a Woman SP Epic 5-10571 (Dec. 1969)

D-I-V-O-R-C-E / Singing My Song SP Epic 5-2285 (1970)

Ways to Love a Man / I'll See Him Through SP Epic 5-2286 (1970)

He Loves Me All the Way / Our Last Night Together SP Epic 5-10612 (Apr. 1970)

Run, Woman, Run / My Daddy Doll SP Epic 5-10653 (Aug. 1970)

Wonders You Perform / Gentle Shepherd SP Epic 5-10687 (Nov. 1970)

One Happy Christmas / We Must Be Having One SP Epic 5-10690 (Nov. 1970)

Stand by Your Man / He Loves Me All the Way SP Epic 15-2301 (1971)

We Sure Can Love Each Other / Fun SP Epic 5-10707 (Feb. 1971)

Good Lovin' / I Love You, Mr. Jones* SP Epic 5-10759 (Jun. 1971)

Bedtime Story / Reach Out Your Hand SP Epic 5-10818 (Nov. 1971)

Reach Out Your Hand / Love's the Answer SP Epic 5-10856 (Apr. 1972)

My Man / Things I Love to Do SP Epic 5-10909 (Aug. 1972)

Bedtime Story / Good Lovin' (Makes It Right) SP Epic 15-2320 (1972)

'Til I Get It Right / Bridge of Love SP Epic 5-10940 (Dec. 1972)

Kids Say the Darndest Things / I Wish I Had a Mommy Like You* Epic 5-10969 (Mar. 1973)

We Sure Can Love Each Other / My Man Epic 15-2326 (1973)

One Final Stand / Crying Steel Guitar Epic 5-11044 (Sep. 1973)

Another Lonely Song / Only Time I'm Really Me Epic 5-11079 (Dec. 1973)

Woman to Woman / Love Me Forever* Epic 8-50008 (Jul. 1974)

(You Make Me Want to Be) A Mother / I'm Not a Has Been (I'm Just a Never Was)* Epic 8-50071 (Dec. 1974)

I Still Believe in Fairly Tales / Your Memory's Gone to Rest Epic 8-50145 (Aug. 1975)

'Til I Can Make It on My Own / Love Is Something Good for Everybody Epic 8-50196 (Jan. 1976)

You and Me / When Love Was All We Had Epic 8-50264 (Jul. 1976)

Let's Get Together (One Last Time) / Hardly a Day's Gone By* Epic 8-50349 (Jan. 1977)

One of a Kind / Loving You I Do Epic 8-50450 (Aug. 1977)

Golden Ring / Near You Epic 15-2353 (1978)

'Til I Can Make It on My Own / You and Me Epic 15-2356 (1978)

One of a Kind / Let's Get Together (One Last Time) Epic 15-2357 (1978)

I'd Like to See Jesus / Love Doesn't Always Come Epic 8-50538 (Mar. 1978)

Womanhood / 50 Words or Less Epic 8-50574 (Jun. 1978)

They Call It Makin' Love / Let Me Be Me Epic 8-50661 (Dec. 1978)

No One Else in the World / Mama, Your Little Girl Fell Epic 8-50722 (May 1978)

Womanhood / They Call It Makin' Love Epic 15-2382 (1979)

He Was There (When I Needed You) / Only the Names Have Been Changed Epic 9-50868 (Mar. 1980)

Starting Over / I'll Be Thinking of You Epic 9-50915 (Jul. 1980)

Note: All the above singles produced by Billy Sherrill

Cowboys Don't Shoot Straight (Like They Used To) / You Brought Me Back Epic 19-51011 (Feb. 1981)

No One Else in the World / He Was There (When I Needed You) Epic 15-02158 (Jun. 1981)

Crying in the Rain / Bring Back My Baby to Me Epic 14-02439 (Aug. 1981)

Another Chance / What's It Like to Be a Woman Epic 14-02770 (Feb. 1982)

You Still Get to Me in My Dreams / If I Didn't Have a Heart Epic 34-03064 (Jul. 1982)

Good Night's Love / I'm Going on Everything* Epic 34-03384 (Nov. 1982)

I Just Heard a Heart Break / Back to the Wall Epic 34-03811 (Apr. 1983)

Unwed Fathers / I'm So Afraid That I'd Live Through It Epic 34-03971 (Jun. 1983)

Still in the Ring / Midnight Love Epic 34-04101 (Sep. 1983)

Lonely Heart / Candle in the Wind Epic 34-04467 (Mar. 1984)

You Can Lead a Heart / He Talks to Me Epic 34-05399 (Jun. 1985)

Alive and Well / I'll Be Thinking of You Epic 34-06263 (Jul. 1986) Note: Produced by Billy Sherrill

Your Love / I Wasn't Meant to Live My Life Alone 34-07226 (Jun. 1987)

Slow Burning Fire / Talkin' to Myself Again Epic 34-07635 (Oct. 1987)

Beneath a Painted Sky / Some Things Will Never Change Epic 34-07788 (Mar. 1988)

Next to You / When a Girl Becomes a Wife Epic 34-68570 (Dec. 1988)

Thank the Cowboy for the Ride / We Called It Everything but Quits Epic 34-68894 (Apr. 1989)

Let's Call It a Day Today / When a Girl Becomes a Wife Epic 34-73427 (Jul. 1990)

I'm Turning You Loose / Just for a Minute There Epic 34-73579 (1990)

Let's Call It a Day Today / What Goes with Blue Epic 34-73656 (Dec. 1990)

DUET, TRIO, AND COLLABORATION SINGLES

With David Houston

My Elusive Dreams / Marriage on the Rocks SP Epic 5-10194 (Jun. 1967)

It's All Over / Together We Stand (Divided We Fall) SP Epic 5-10274 (Nov. 1967)

With George Jones

Take Me / We Go Together SP Epic 5-10815 (Oct. 1971)

The Great Divide / The Ceremony SP Epic 5-10881 (Jun. 1972)

Take Me / The Ceremony SP Epic 15-2322 (1972)

Old Fashioned Singing / We Love to Sing About Jesus SP Epic 5-10923 (Nov. 1972)

Let's Build the World Together / Touching Shoulders Epic 5-10963 (Feb. 1973)

We're Gonna Hold On / My Elusive Dreams Epic 5-11031 (Aug. 1973)

Greatest Christmas Gift* / Mrs. Santa Claus* Epic 5-11031 (Aug. 1973)

(We're Not) The Jet Set / Crawdad Song Epic 5-11099 (Feb. 1974)

No Charge / Telephone Call Epic 5-11099 (Mar. 1974)

We Loved It Away / Ain't Love Been Good Epic 5-11151 (Jun. 1974)

God's Gonna Get 'Cha (for That) / Those Were Good Times* Epic 8-50099 (Apr. 1975)

The Ceremony / We're Gonna Hold On Epic 15-2339 (1976)

Near You / Tattletale Eyes Epic 8-50314 (Jan. 1977)

Southern California / Keep the Change Epic 8-50418 (May 1977)

Golden Ring / Near You Epic 15-2358 (1978)

Two Story House / It Sure Was Good Epic 9-50849 (Feb. 1980)

Pair of Old Sneakers / We'll Talk About It Later Epic 9-50930 (Aug. 1980)

Two Story House / Pair of Old Sneakers Epic 15-02159 (Jun. 1981)

Note: All the above singles produced by Billy Sherrill

One / Golden Ring MCA S7-55048 (Jun. 1995)

With Mark Gray

Sometimes When We Touch / Mark Gray B-Side Epic 38-04782 (Dec. 1984)

With Wayne Newton

While the Feelin's Good / Wayne Newton B-Side Curb CRB-10559 (Jun. 1989); also on Newton's 1989 album, *Coming Home*, released in 1995 on CD, Curb B0000081KP.

With Randy Travis

We're Strangers Again / If You Were the Friend Epic 34-73958 (1990); album version of "We're Strangers Again" rereleased on *I Told You So: The Ultimate Hits of Randy Travis*, Warner Brothers B001VFSNYS (Mar. 2009)

With the KLF

Justified and Ancient Arista 12403-1 (Jan. 1992); extended 12-inch version on CD 5, Arista 12403-2

With Dolly Parton and Loretta Lynn

Silver Threads and Golden Needles / Lets Her Fly Columbia 34-77294 (Nov. 1993)

It Wasn't God Who Made Honky Tonk Angels (adding Kitty Wells) Columbia unknown number (1993?)

With Wynonna Judd

Girl Thang, released as part of three-track promo CD single *Selected Album Thangs* Epic PR 6491 (1994)

THE ORIGINAL ALBUMS

YOUR GOOD GIRL'S GONNA GO BAD—Apartment #9 / Don't Come Home A-Drinkin' (With Lovin' on Your Mind) / Don't Touch Me / There Goes My Everything / Send Me No Roses / Your Good Girl's Gonna Go Bad / Walk Through This World with Me / I'm Not Mine to Give / I Wound Easy but I Heal Fast / Almost Persuaded. Epic BN 26305 (April, 1967); rereleased on CD, A 58922 (2003)

TAKE ME TO YOUR WORLD—I DON'T WANNA PLAY HOUSE—I Don't Wanna Play House / Jackson Ain't a Very Big Town / Broadminded / Cry / Phone Call / It's My Way / Take Me to Your World / Or Is It Love / Fuzzy Wuzzy Ego / Good / Ode to Billie Joe. Epic BN 26353 (Jan. 5, 1968); rereleased on CD by Koch, CD 7944 (1998)

D-I-V-O-R-C-E—Gentle on My Mind / Honey / Legend of Bonnie and Clyde / All Night Long / Sweet Dreams / Yesterday / D-I-V-O-R-C-E / Come on Home / When There's a Fire in Your Heart / Kiss Away / Lonely Street. Epic BN 26392 (June, 1968); rereleased on CD by Koch, B000001SMY (1997)

STAND BY YOUR MAN—Stand by Your Man / It's My Way / Forever Yours / I Stayed Long Enough / It Keeps Slipping My Mind / My Arms Stay Open Late / I've Learned / Cry Cry Again / Joey / If I Were a Little Girl / Don't Make Me Go to School. Epic BN 26451 (December, 1968); rereleased on CD in 1999 with two previously unreleased bonus tracks: I'm Only a Woman / There's Quite a Difference. Epic/Legacy EK 66018

INSPIRATION—You'll Never Walk Alone / Count the Blessings Instead of Sheep / Just a Closer Walk with Thee / I Believe / Battle Hymn of the Republic / How Great Thou Art / He's Got the Whole World in his Hands / It Is No Secret What God Can Do / Crying in the Chapel / He / May the Good Lord Bless and Keep You. Epic BN 26423 (March, 1969); rereleased on CD as *Inspirational Favorites*, adding Tammy's 1987 recording of Precious Memories Ranwood Records B000007RZ5

TAMMY'S GREATEST HITS—Stand by Your Man / Singing My Song / Take Me to Your World / Apartment #9 / D-I-V-O-R-C-E / I Don't Wanna Play House / Your Good Girl's Gonna Go Bad / Run, Angel, Run / Too Far Gone / Almost Persuaded / My Elusive Dreams. Epic BN 26486 (November, 1969)

THE WAYS TO LOVE A MAN—Ways to Love a Man / The Twelfth of Never / I'll Share My World with You / Enough of a Woman / Singing My Song / He'll Never Take the Place of You / I Know / Yearning / These Two / Where Could You Go / Still Around. Epic BN 26519 (December, 1969)

TAMMY'S TOUCH—I'll See Him Through / Love Me, Love Me / It's Just a Matter of Time / Cold Lonely Feeling / Divorce Sale / When He Loves Me / He Thinks I Love Him / Our Last Night Together / Lighter Shade of Blue / Lonely Days / You Make My Skies Turn Blue. Epic BN 26549 (March, 1970)

Note: The two previous albums have been released together on one CD by Australian label Raven Records, RVCD-237 (2006);includes bonus tracks Run, Angel, Run / Too Far Gone / Run, Woman, Run / My Daddy Doll

THE WORLD OF TAMMY WYNETTE—Walk Through This World with Me / Legend of Bonnie and Clyde / Don't Come Home A-Drinkin' (With Lovin' on Your Mind) / Where Could I Go / I Stayed Long Enough / It Is No Secret / I Believe / My Arms Stay Open Late / There Goes My Everything / Crying in the Chapel / Don't Touch Me / Good / Cry / Ode to Billie Joe / Honey / Cry, Cry Again / It's My Way / Joey / Kiss Away / Yesterday. Epic EGP 503 (March, 1970); rereleased on CD by Wounded Bird 503 (2009)

THE FIRST LADY—Run, Woman, Run / I Wish I Had a Mommy Like You / True and Lasting Love / I Never Once Stopped Loving You / Safe in These Lovin' Arms of Mine / Sally Trash / My Daddy Doll / Lovin' Kind / He's Still My Man / Buy Me a Daddy / Playin' Around with Love. Epic E 30212 (September, 1970)

CHRISTMAS WITH TAMMY—Silent Night / O Little Town of Bethlehem / It Came Upon the Midnight Clear / Joy to the World / Away in a Manger / Gentle Shepherd / Blue Christmas / (Merry Christmas) We Must Be Having One / White Christmas / Oh Happy Christmas / Lonely Christmas Call / Let's Put Christ Back into Christmas. Epic E 30343 (October,1970); rereleased on CD in 1991 and 1995 (Koch B000002YEB), but the former omits "Gentle Shepherd" and "Lonely Christmas Call."

WE SURE CAN LOVE EACH OTHER—We Sure Can Love Each Other / Joy of Being a Woman / He Knows All the Ways to Love / Make Me Your Kind of Woman / Don't Liberate Me / Bring Him Safely Home to Me / Only Thing / Longing to Hold You Again / Have a Little Faith / If You Think I Love You Now / Baby, Come Home. Epic E 30658 (April, 1971)

TAMMY'S GREATEST HITS VOLUME II—Good Lovin' (Makes It Right) / Run, Woman, Run / We Sure Can Love Each Other / You Can't Hang On to Lookin' On / Ways to Love a Man / When He Loves Me / I'll See Him Through / Still Around / Only Time I'm Really Me / Our Last Night Together / The Wonders You Perform. Epic E 30733 (August, 1971)

IT'S JUST A MATTER OF TIME—Don't Touch Me / It's My Way / Love Me, Love Me / All Night Long / It Keeps Slipping My Mind / Set Me Free / Run, Angel, Run / I'm Not Mine to Give / Singing My Song / It's Just a Matter of Time. HARMONY H 30914 (1971)

BEDTIME STORY—Bedtime Story / That's When I Feel It / Take Me Home and Love Me / If This Is Our Last Time / Tonight My Baby's Coming Home / Love's the Answer / I'm Gonna Keep on Loving Him / Just as Soon as I Get Over Loving You / I Got Me a Man / Your Love's Been a Long Time Coming / Reach Out Your Hand. Epic E 31285 (February, 1972)

MY MAN—My Man / Things I Love to Do / Hold On to the Love I Got / Loving You Could Never Be Better / 'Til I Get It Right / Walk Softly on the Bridges / Bridge of Love / You Can't Hang On to Lookin' On / Happiest Girl in the Whole USA / Gone with Another Man / Good Lovin' (Makes It Right). Epic KE 31717 (August, 1972)

THE FIRST SONGS OF THE FIRST LADY—Apartment # 9 / Don't Come Home A-Drinkin' (With Lovin' on Your Mind) / Don't Touch Me / There Goes My Everything / Send Me No Roses / Your Good Girl's Gonna Go Bad / Walk Through This World with Me / I'm Not Mine to Give / I Wound Easy / Almost Persuaded / I Don't Wanna Play House / Jackson Ain't a Very Big Town / Broadminded / Cry / Phone Call / It's My Way / Take Me to Your World / Or Is It Love / Good / Ode to Billie Joe. Epic KEG 30358 (Jan 1973)

KIDS SAY THE DARNDEST THINGS—Bedtime Story / My Daddy Doll / I Wish I Had a Mommy Like You / Listen Spot / D-I-V-O-R-C-E / Kids Say the Darndest Things / I Don't Wanna Play House / Too Many Daddies / Joey / Buy Me a Daddy / Don't Make Me Go to School. Epic KE 31937 (April, 1973)

ANOTHER LONELY SONG—Another Lonely Song / Crying Steel Guitar / What My Thoughts Do All the Time / Stayin' Home Woman / Satin Sheets / Homecoming / Help Me Make It Through the Night / Keep Me in Mind / Oh How I Miss Him / With Child / One Final Stand. Epic KE 32745 (March, 1974)

WOMAN TO WOMAN—Woman to Woman / Right Here in Your Arms / What's a Little Rain / This Time I Almost Made It / Please Come to Boston / I Don't Think About Him No More / For the Kids / Woman I Am / Touching Love / I've Been Loved Before. Epic KE 33246 (October, 1974)

TAMMY WYNETTE'S GREATEST HITS VOLUME III—Kids Say the Darndest Things / Bedtime Story / 'Til I Get It Right / My Man / There Goes that Old Steel Guitar / (You Make Me Want to Be) A Mother / Another Lonely Song / Love's the Answer / Woman to Woman / Reach Out Your Hand. Epic KE 33396 (February, 1975)

I STILL BELIEVE IN FAIRY TALES—I Still Believe in Fairy Tales / I Did My Best / Brown Paper Bag / I Just Had You on My Mind / Dallas / I'll Take What You Can Give Me / I'm Not a Has Been (I'm Just a Never Was) / Man from Bowling Green / Bottle / Your Memory's Gone to Rest. Epic KE 33582 (1975)

'TIL I CAN MAKE IT ON MY OWN—'Til I Can Make It on My Own / Just in Case / He's Just an Old Love Turned Memory / World's Most Broken Heart / If I Could Only Win Your Love / The Heart / You Can Be Replaced / Love Is Something Good for Everybody / Where Some Good Love Has Been / Easy Come, Easy Go. Epic KE 34075 (February, 1976)

YOU AND ME—You and Me / Every Now and Then / Funny Face / Hawaiian Wedding Song (Ke Kali Nei Au) / Little Things / Jesus, Send a Song / One of These Days / You Hurt the Love Right Out of Me / When Love Was All We Had / Dixieland, You Will Never Die. Epic KE 34289 (September, 1976)

LET'S GET TOGETHER—Let's Get Together (One Last Time) / If We Never Love Again / Loving You I Do / It's Gonna Take a Long, Long Time / You Could Be Coming to Me / Your Sweet Lies / Cheatin' Is / I Can Love You / No One Can Take His Place / I Can Still Believe in You. Epic KE 34694 (March, 1977)

ONE OF A KIND—One of a Kind / That's the Way It Could Have Been / Love Survived / That's Just the Way I Am / Sweet Music Man / What I Had with You / I'm Not That Good at Goodbye / Heaven's Just a Sin Away / I'll Be Your Bridge / Dear Daughters. Epic KE 35044 (November, 1977)

WOMANHOOD—Womanhood / That's What Friends Are For / You Oughta Hear the Song / What's a Couple More / One Song I Never Could Write / I'd Like to See Jesus / Mem'ries / Standing Tall / Love Doesn't Always Come / Fifty Words or Less. Epic KE 35442 (July, 1978)

GREATEST HITS VOLUME IV—You and Me / Let's Get Together (One Last Time) / Womanhood / I Still Believe in Fairy Tales / One of a Kind / 'Til I Can Make It on My Own / This Time I Almost Made It / Southern California / I'd Like to See Jesus on the Midnight Special / Dear Daughters. Epic JE 35630 (October, 1978)

JUST TAMMY—They Call It Making Love / We'll Talk About It Later / Somewhere / Mama, Your Little Girl Fell / I'm Not Ready Yet / No One Else in the World / You Don't Know the Half of It / I L-O-V-E Y-O-U / You Never Cross My Mind / Let Me Be Me. Epic JE 36013 (May, 1979)

ONLY LONELY SOMETIMES—He Was There (When I Needed You) / I'll Be Thinking of You / You Never Knew / Come with Me / You Needed Me / Starting Over / Out of the Spotlight / Only the Names Have Been Changed / When You Love Me / Ozark Mountain Lullaby. Epic JE 36485 (June, 1980)

Note: All the above albums produced by Billy Sherrill

YOU BROUGHT ME BACK—Cowboys Don't Shoot Straight (Like They Used To) / Crying in the Rain / Bring Back My Baby to Me / You Brought Me Back / Goodnight, Cowboy, Goodnight / Easy Street / I Don't Think I See Me in Your Eyes Anymore / Best There Is / Easy Come, Easy Go / He's Rolling Over and Over. Epic FE 37104 (June, 1981)

ENCORE—Your Good Girl's Gonna Go Bad / I Don't Wanna Play House / Woman to Woman / They Call It Making Love / Another Lonely Song / One of a Kind / Let's Get Together (One Last Time) / He Was There (When I Needed You) / You and Me / No One Else in the World. Epic FE 37344 (June,1981)

SOFT TOUCH—Old Reliable / She Can't Take My Love off the Bed / Being Gone / What's It Like to Be a Woman / I'll Still Be Loving You This Much / Another Chance / If I Didn't Have a Heart / You Still Get to Me in My Dreams / Sometimes I'm a Little Girl / Dancin' Your Memory Away. Epic FE 37980 (May, 1982)

BIGGEST HITS—Run, Woman, Run / Starting Over / Kids Say the Darndest Things / My Man / Crying in the Rain / Stand by Your Man / Cowboys Don't Shoot Straight (Like They Used To) / Bedtime Story / 'Til I Get It Right / D-I-V-O-R-C-E. Epic FE 38312 (October, 1982). Note: Liner notes by Tammy

GOOD LOVE AND HEARTBREAK—Good Night's Love / I Still Dream About You / Back to the Wall / Half the Heart / It's the Goodbye That Blows Me Away / I Just Heard a Heart Break / Somebody Hold Me / Time / I'm Going on with Everything Gone / I've Come Back. Epic FE 38372 (November, 1982)

EVEN THE STRONG GET LONELY—Unwed Fathers / I'm So Afraid That I'd Live Through It / Slightly Used Woman / Only the Strong Survive / With a Friend Like You Who Needs a Lover / Still in the Ring / Midnight Love / Love Overdue / Darlin', Take Care of Yourself / Even the Strong Get Lonely Sometimes. Epic FE 38744 (June, 1983)

SOMETIMES WHEN WE TOUCH—Sometimes When We Touch (duet with Mark Gray) / You Can Lead a Heart to Love / Breaking Away / Every Time You Touch Her / Between 29 and Danger / It's Only Over for You / Party of the First Part / It's Hard to Be the Dreamer / If It Ain't Love / He Talks to Me. Epic FE 39971 (February, 1985)

HIGHER GROUND—Your Love / Tempted / Some Things Will Never Change / Beneath a Painted Sky / I Wasn't Meant to Live My Life Alone / Higher Ground / Talkin' to Myself Again

/ A Slow Burning Fire / There's No Heart So Strong / All Through Throwing Good Love after Bad. Epic FE 40832 (June, 1987). Note: Last two albums produced by Steve Buckingham

ANNIVERSARY: TWENTY YEARS OF HITS—Apartment #9 / Your Good Girl's Gonna Go Bad / I Don't Wanna Play House / D-I-V-O-R-C-E / Stand by Your Man / Singing My Song / Run, Angel, Run / We Sure Can Love Each Other / Good Lovin' / Bedtime Story / 'Til I Get It Right / Kids Say the Darndest Things / Another Lonely Song / We're Gonna Hold On / Woman to Woman / 'Til I Can Make It on My Own / Golden Ring / You and Me / One of a Kind / Two Story House. Epic E2 40625 (1985), including brief liner notes by Billy Sherrill; CD release EKG 40625 (1987)

NEXT TO YOU—Next to You / I'm So Afraid of Losing You Again / You Left Memories Layin' / When a Girl Becomes a Wife / If You Let Him Drive You Crazy (He Will) / The Note / Thank the Cowboy for the Ride / I Almost Forgot / We Called It Everything But Quits / Liar's Roses. Epic FE 44498 (January, 1989)

HEART OVER MIND—Let's Call It a Day Today / I'm Turning You Loose / Suddenly Single / What Goes with Blue / Just for a Minute There / Half the Way Home / I'm Falling Heart over Mind / Where's the Fire / If You Were a Friend / One Stone at a Time. Epic FE 46238 (August, 1990)

TEARS OF FIRE—CD 1: You Can Steal Me† / Apartment #9 / She Didn't Color Daddy† / Your Good Girl's Gonna Go Bad / Walk Through This World with Me / My Elusive Dreams / I Don't Wanna Play House / Take Me to Your World / D-I-V-O-R-C-E / Sweet Dreams / Lonely Street / I Believe / He / Stand by Your Man / You'll Never Walk Alone / How Great Thou Art / Singing My Song / Too Far Gone / Ways to Love a Man / I'll See Him Through / Kids Say the Darndest Things // CD 2: When He Loves Me / We Sure Can Love Each Other / Deepening Snow† / Good Lovin' / Bedtime Story / 'Til I Get It Right / My Man / We're Gonna Hold On / (We're Not) The Jet Set / Another Lonely Song / I Don't Think About Him No More / No Charge / Woman to Woman / This Time I Almost Made It / Near You / I Still Believe in Fairy Tales / 'Til I Can Make It on My Own / Golden Ring / Did You Ever / You and Me / Let's Get Together (One Last Time) / One of a Kind / Southern California / Dear Daughters / They Call It Making Love // CD 3: Two Story House / Cowboys Don't Shoot Straight (Like They Used To) / Crying in the Rain / Another Chance / You Still Get to Me in My Dreams / Unwed Fathers / Candle in the Wind / Sometimes When We Touch / Between 29 and Danger / Alive and Well / Talkin' to Myself Again / I Wasn't Meant to Live My Life Alone / Beneath a Painted Sky / Your Love / Higher Ground / Liar's Roses / We're Strangers Again / Suddenly Single / It Could've Been So Good† / Justified and Ancient / Precious Memories†. Epic E3K 52741 (November, 1992)

COLLECTOR'S EDITION—There's No Use Hanging On† / Greener Than the Grass (We Laid On)† / Easy Come, Easy Go / What's Your Mama's Name, Child† / When He Loves Me / I Don't Wanna Play House / You Can Be Replaced / Your Good Girl's Gonna Go Bad† / D-I-V-O-R-C-E / Stand by Your Man†. Epic EK 69560 (1998). Pointless collection of Tammy rarities and inane overdubbed "new" versions of two of her classic hits; the album was initially released with varying speed problems.

Note: On the previous two titles, † indicates previously unreleased or rerecorded track

LOVE SONGS—'Til I Get It Right / Take Me to Your World / Help Me Make It Through the Night / Loving You Could Never Be Better / Right Here in Your Arms / No One Else in the World / I Stayed Long Enough / If You Think I Love You Now (I've Just Started) / Walk Through This World with Me / Forever Yours / Hawaiian Wedding Song (Ke Kali Nei Au) / The Twelfth of Never / The Only Thing / Stand by Your Man. EK 87150 (2003). Superb compilation produced by Gregg Geller and mastered by Vic Anesini.

THE ESSENTIAL TAMMY WYNETTE—Apartment #9 / Your Good Girl's Gonna Go Bad / My Elusive Dreams (with David Houston) / I Don't Wanna Play House / D-I-V-O-R-C-E / Stand by Your Man / He Loves Me All the Way / We Sure Can Love Each Other / Take Me (with George Jones) / 'Til I Get It Right / Bedtime Story / Kids Say the Darndest Things / Woman to Woman / 'Til I Can Make It on My Own. EK 90645 (2004). Superb compilation produced by Gregg Geller and mastered by Vic Anesini.

MISCELLANEOUS SOLO RECORDINGS

YOU CAN TAKE THE WINGS OFF ME—Lonely Heart / Touch and Go / If I Could Sing Something in Spanish / Love Never Sleeps / I Think I Could Love You / You Can Take the Wings Off Me / Small Two Bedroom Starter / I Just Called to Keep You on My Mind / After Dark / Candle in the Wind // BONUS TRACKS: Alive and Well / It Could Have Been So Good / Fun / The Music Box / There Goes That Steel Guitar (stereo and mono) / A Slightly Used Woman (stereo and mono) / I Will Love On / Hardly a Day Goes By (mono) / Love Survived / A Player, a Pawn, a Hero, a King. An unauthorized Japanese release of an unreleased 1984 Jerry Crutchfield–produced Tammy album, of which only "Candle in the Wind" saw release on *Tears of Fire*, plus rare cuts.

TAMMY WYNETTE: REMEMBERED—Stand by Your Man (Elton John) / 'Til I Get It Right (Trisha Yearwood) / D-I-V-O-R-C-E (Rosanne Cash) / Apartment #9 (Melissa Etheridge) / Woman to Woman (Wynonna) / Take Me to Your World (George Jones) / Your Good Girl's Gonna Go Bad (K. T. Oslin) / You and Me (Lorrie Morgan) / I Don't Wanna Play House (Sara Evans, Golden Ring, Emmylou Harris, Linda Ronstadt, and Kate and Anna McGarrigle) / 'Til I Can Make It on My Own (Faith Hill) / In My Room (Tammy Wynette and Brian Wilson). Asylum Records 62277-2 (1998). Posthumous Tammy tribute CD with liner notes by Evelyn Shriver; Tammy appears on only one cut, "In My Room."

DUET / TRIO ALBUMS

With David Houston

MY ELUSIVE DREAMS—My Elusive Dreams / I'll Take My Chances with You / Hey, Good Lookin' / Set Me Free / Together We Stand (Divided We Fall) / Something Stupid / Back in Baby's Arms / It's All Over / Clinging Vine / Marriage on the Rocks. Epic BN 26325 (June, 1967)

STRAIGHT FROM THE HEART—The Two of Us / Have a Little Faith / Take Me / Clinging Vine / The Ways to Love a Man / I'll Kiss the Baby / Too Many Daddies / If You Love Him (Love Him Right) / Tell Me Where I Stand / Baby, Come Home / Still Around. Columbia Musical Treasures DS 592 (1971). Two-record set, one of which is with David Houston.

With George Jones

WE GO TOGETHER—We Go Together / It's So Sweet / Something to Brag About / Never Grow Cold / You're Everything / Take Me / Just Someone I Used to Know / Living on Easy Street / Lifetime Left Together / When True Love Steps In / After Closing Time. Epic E 30802 (August, 1971)

ME AND THE FIRST LADY—We Believe in Each Other / Lovely Place to Cry / There's Power in Our Love / Perfect Match / Great Divide / To Live on Love / You and Me Together / Lovin' You Is Worth It / We're Gonna Try to Get Along / It's Been a Beautiful Life / The Ceremony. Epic KE 31554 (August,1972)

WE LOVE TO SING ABOUT JESUS—We Love to Sing About Jesus / Old Fashioned Singing / He Is My Everything / Me and Jesus / Noah and the Ark / Let's All Go Down to the River / Talkin' About Jesus / When Jesus Takes His Children Home / Everything's Gonna Be Alright / Show Him That You Love Him. Epic KE 31719 (October, 1972); mastered by Steve Hoffman and rereleased on CD, Razor & Tie RE-2118-2

LET'S BUILD A WORLD TOGETHER—Let's Build a World Together / World Needs a Melody / When I Stop Dreaming / After the Fire Is Gone / My Elusive Dreams / Your Shining Face / Touching Shoulders / Love Is All We Need / Help the People / Our Way of Life / This Growing Old Together Love We Share. Epic KE 32113 (February, 1973)

Note: *We Go Together* and *Let's Build a World Together* were rereleased on CD by American Beat 24612 (2007)

WE'RE GONNA HOLD ON—We're Gonna Hold On / When True Love Steps In / Never Ending Song of Love / Wouldn't I / Rollin' in My Sweet Baby's Arms / (We're Not) The Jet Set / Crawdad Song / If Loving You Starts Hurting Me / That Man of Mine / Woman Loves Me Right / As Long As We Can. Epic KE 32757 (1974)

GEORGE & TAMMY & TINA—We Loved It Away / Ain't Love Be Good / We're Putting It Back Together / It / Telephone Call / God's Gonna Get 'Cha (for That) / Number One / Closer Than Ever / Those Were the Good Times / No Charge. Epic KE 33351 (February, 1975)

GOLDEN RING—Golden Ring / Even the Bad Times Are Good / Near You / Crying Time / I've Seen Better Days / Did You Ever / Tattle Tale Eyes / I'll Be There / If You Don't Somebody Else Will / Keep the Change. Epic PE 34291 (August, 1976); rereleased on CD by Razor & Tie Boooo02ZBY (Nov. 1997) and American Beat BoooMMOKVU (Feb. 2007)

GEORGE & TAMMY GREATEST HITS—Golden Ring / We're Gonna Hold On / We Loved It Away / Take Me / Near You / Southern California / God's Gonna Get 'Cha (for That) / (We're Not) The Jet Set / Let's Build a World Together / The Ceremony. Epic KE 34716 (1977)

MY VERY SPECIAL GUESTS—George Jones, Epic (1977); rereleased on CD with bonus tracks (none including Tammy) by Legacy 776624 (2005). Tammy appears only on "It Sure Was Good."

PRESIDENT AND THE FIRST LADY—We're Gonna Hold On / Two Story House / Take Me / The Ceremony / Old Fashioned Singing / (We're Not) The Jet Set / We Loved It Away / God's Gonna Get 'Cha (for That) / Someone I Used to Know / Livin' on Easy Street / Golden Ring / After Closing Time / Something to Brag About / We'll Talk About It Later / Roll in My Sweet Baby's Arms / Near You / Southern California / Let's Build a World Together / After the Fire Is Gone / If We Don't Make It. Epic CSP P 15769 (1979)

TOGETHER AGAIN—Pair of Old Sneakers / Right in the Wrong Direction / I Just Started Lovin' Today / Love in the Meantime / We Could / Two Story House / If We Don't Make It / It's Not My Fault / We'll Talk About It Later / Night Spell. Epic JE 36764 (September, 1980); mastered by Steve Hoffman and rereleased on CD by Razor & Tie RE 2094 (1996)

GREATEST HITS VOLUME II—We Go Together / When I Stop Dreaming / Two Story House / My Elusive Dreams / Something to Brag About / Pair of Old Sneakers / Just Someone I Used to Know / Did You Ever / Lovely Place to Cry / World Needs a Melody. Epic EK 48839 (1992)

Note: All the above albums produced by Billy Sherrill

THE BRADLEY BARN SESSIONS—George Jones; CD release, MCA 08811 10962 (October, 1994). Tammy appears on one song, a rerecording of "Golden Ring."

ONE—One / It's an Old Love Thing / Whatever Happened to Us / Will You Travel Down This Road with Me / She's Just an Old Love Turned Memory / If God Met You / Just Look What We've Started Again / Solid As a Rock / They're Playing Our Song / All I Have to Offer You Is Me. CD release, MCA 11248 (June, 1995)

LOVE SONGS—The Ceremony / When True Love Steps In / To Live on Love / It's So Sweet / We Could / My Elusive Dreams / If Loving You Starts Hurting Me / When I Stop Dreaming / Even the Bad Times Are Good / We're Gonna Hold On / Near You / It's Been a Beautiful Life (Loving You) / Never Grow Cold. EK 90899 (2004). Superb compilation produced by Gregg Geller and mastered by Vic Anesini.

BURN YOUR PLAYHOUSE DOWN: THE UNRELEASED DUETS—George Jones, Bandit Records 79842 (2008). Tammy appears only on the previously unreleased "Lovin' You, Lovin' Me." Also features Georgette's duet with her dad, "You and Me and Time."

With Charlie Louvin

AND THAT'S THE GOSPEL—Charlie Louvin, Playback Records (1991). Tammy appears only on "If I Could Hear My Mother Pray Again."

With the KLF

THE WHITE ROOM—KLF, Arista ARCD-8657 (1991). Tammy appears only on "Justified and Ancient."

With Dolly Parton and Loretta Lynn

HONKY TONK ANGELS—It Wasn't God Who Made Honky Tonk Angels / Put It Off Until Tomorrow / Silver Threads and Golden Needles / Please Help, Me I'm Falling / Sittin' on the Front Porch Swing / Wings of a Dove / I Forgot More That You'll Ever Know / Wouldn't It Be Great / That's the Way It Could Have Been / Let Her Fly / Lovesick Blues / I Dreamed of a Hillbilly Heaven. Columbia CK 53419 (1993). Produced by Steve Buckingham.

With Various Artists

WITHOUT WALLS—If It's the Last Thing I Do (solo) / Woman's Needs (with Elton John) / Every Breath You Take (with Sting) / If You Were to Wake Up (with Lyle Lovett) / Glass Houses (with Joe Diffie) / Girl Thang (with Wynonna) / This Love (with Cliff Richard) / I Second That Emotion (with Smokey Robinson) / All I Am to You (with Aaron Neville) / What Do They Know (solo). Epic EK 52481 (1994). Note: The Elton John duet first appeared on his 1993 MCA album, *Duets*

Perfect Day—Tammy appears alongside Bono, Elton John, David Bowie, and Lou Reed on this BBC benefit single for the Children in Need charity. Chrysalis CDNeed1 7243 8 88784 0 (1997); rereleased in 2000

MISCELLANEOUS GUEST APPEARANCES

CHIPMUNKS IN LOW PLACES—Alvin and the Chipmunks, Sony CD B000028T3 (Sep. 1992). Tammy appears only on "Stand by Your Man."

THE CHRISTMAS ALBUM—David Foster, Interscope Records 92295 (1993). Tammy appears only on "Away in a Manger."

MERRY CHRISTMAS FROM LONDON—Lorrie Morgan, BNA 66282-2 (1993); rerelease, BMG Special Products 144580 (1997). Tammy appears only on "A Christmas Festival Medley."

SOUNDTRACKS

RUN, ANGEL, RUN—Epic BN 26474 (1970). Tammy sings only the title song.

FIVE EASY PIECES—Stand by Your Man / D-I-V-O-R-C-E / When There's a Fire in Your Heart / Don't Touch Me. Epic E 30456 (1971). The other cuts are non-Tammy tracks.

WHEN YOU COMIN' BACK, RED RYDER?—Tammy sings one duet with Freddy Fender over the credits, "No One Knows Better Than You," which was produced by Jack Nitzsche (1979).

Note: As far as I know, there was no soundtrack released to this film, which is currently unavailable on DVD. Which is too bad, because this psychotic little number also features the best use of a Tammy song ever in a film ("Kiss Away"), and her gospel favorites Hovie Lister and the Statesman rip it up in a high-voltage cameo.

HOOPER—Warner Brothers 3234 (1978). Tammy appears only on "A Player, a Pawn, a Hero, a King."

THE NIGHT THE LIGHTS WENT OUT IN GEORGIA—Atlantic Records P 11061 (1981). Tammy appears only on "Imaginary Arms."

SELECTED TAMMY WYNETTE ON DVD/VHS

SILENT WITNESS 2: A TRIBUTE TO COUNTRY'S GOSPEL LEGACY—VHS, Rainmaker Films, 877-790-0170 (1994). Tammy lip-synchs "Precious Memories" with the Masters V and is interviewed briefly concerning her faith.

NASHVILLE SOUNDS: MAKING OF STARS AND STRIPES—The Beach Boys, Intersound Records, E 37752 (1998) Image Entertainment (1998) and reissues by others. Tammy is seen singing "In My Room" with its author, Brian Wilson. The cut wasn't used on the Beach Boys' *Stars and Stripes* album and surfaced only in a reworked version for the *Tammy Wynette: Remembered* tribute album.

CONWAY TWITTY: ON THE MISSISSIPPI—Eagle Rock B0000JLLCW (2003). Release of a 1982 TV special in which Tammy sings only "I Just Heard a Heart Break" plus a few impromptu (and great) songs while sitting and talking with Conway.

TAMMY WYNETTE: IN CONCERT—My Man / Another Chance / Apartment #9 / I Don't Wanna Play House / Your Good Girl's Gonna Go Bad / D-I-V-O-R-C-E / Singing My Song / 'Til I Can Make It on My Own / Rocky Top / Alive and Well / Turn Around / What a Difference You've Made in My Life / Makin' Love / You and Me / Take Me to Your World / Womanhood / Crying in the Rain / I Still Believe in Fairy Tales / Amazing Grace / I'll Fly Away / Will the Circle Be Unbroken / I Saw the Light / Stand by Your Man. Rhino B00005NRNQ (2001). DVD rerelease of a 1986 live concert from Wheeling, West Virginia.

THE HEE HAW COLLECTION—Time-Life M18973 and 19808-9 (2005). Compilation includes a 1969 performance of Tammy singing "Stand by Your Man." In Time-Life 19943-9 (2005), Tammy does "Another Lonely Song" and George and Tammy sing "We Loved It Away." Great performances from *Hee Haw*. If only we could have them all.

OPRY VIDEO CLASSICS: LOVE SONGS—Time-Life 21910-9 (2007). Tammy sings " 'Til I Get It Right."

OPRY VIDEO CLASSICS: DUETS—Time-Life 21906-9 (2007). George and Tammy sing "We're Gonna Hold On" and "The Ceremony."

OPRY VIDEO CLASSICS: HALL OF FAME—Time-Life 21907-9 (2007). Tammy sings "Your Good Girl's Gonna Go Bad."

OPRY VIDEO CLASSICS: QUEENS OF COUNTRY—Time-Life 21912-9 (2007). Tammy sings "Stand By Your Man."

Note: A great series from Time-Life featuring vintage TV clips in excellent quality.

THE JOHNNY CASH SHOW 1969–1971—Sony Legacy/Reverse Angle Productions B000TLMWMY (2007). Tammy sings only "Stand by Your Man."

TAMMY WYNETTE GREATEST HITS LIVE—Quantum Leap B000JLQPVS (2007). Oft-repackaged 1981 concert from Church Street Station in Orlando, Florida.

TAMMY WYNETTE: LEGENDARY PERFORMANCES—Time-Life 82663-10976 (2008). Don't Come Home A-Drinkin' (With Lovin' on Your Mind) / Your Good Girl's Gonna Go Bad / I Don't Wanna Play House / D-I-V-O-R-C-E / Stand by Your Man / Reach Out Your Hand / We Loved It Away (with George Jones) / Woman to Woman / 'Til I Can Make It on My Own / Golden Ring (with George Jones) / You and Me / Near You (with George Jones) / He Was There (When I Needed You) / We're Gonna Hold On (with George Jones) / Cowboys Don't Shoot Straight (Like They Used To). Bonuses: Wynette's induction into the Hall of Fame and a vintage Nashville TV news report on her wedding to George Richey.

Note: This is a fabulous collection of Tammy TV performances (some of which are discussed in this book), put together by the Country Music Hall of Fame. Essential Tammy.

SELECTED GEORGE JONES CD DISCOGRAPHY

THE EARLY HITS: THE STARDAY RECORDINGS—Time-Life M19487 (2007). George finds his way in the recording studio. Includes Why Baby Why / Yes, I Know Why / Just One More.

CUP OF LONELINESS: THE CLASSIC MERCURY YEARS—Mercury 314-522-635-2 (1994). Two-CD set of George's Mercury recordings (and some Starday). Includes such killers as Mr. Fool / The Last Town I Painted / Tender Years.

SHE THINKS I STILL CARE: THE GEORGE JONES COLLECTION—Razor & Tie RE 2136-2 (1997). Mastered by Steve Hoffman, this rich collection from George's United Artists years includes Sometimes You Just Can't Win / A Girl I Used to Know / You Comb Her Hair (Tammy's favorite).

SHE THINKS I STILL CARE: THE COMPLETE UNITED ARTISTS RECORDINGS 1962–1964—Bear Family BCD 16818 EK (Germany, 2007). Great collection from the fiendishly thorough folks at Bear Family. All their sets are highly recommended.

RADIO JAMBOREE—I don't know what fan found and put out this 1963 collection (which is perfecto, right down to its faux United Artists cover), but I'd like to shake their hand. Twenty-three primo cuts of George live in the studio, and the only place I know to find a solo version of "House of Gold."

WALK THROUGH THIS WORLD WITH ME: THE COMPLETE MUSICOR RECORDINGS 1965–1971 (PART 1, five CDs)—Bear Family BCD 16928-5 EL (Germany, 2009). Jones recorded a lot of crap for Musicor, as well as some of his greatest material ever. Here you'll find Don't You Ever Get Tired (of Hurting Me) [unjustly maligned in the liner notes, by the way] / Things Have Gone to Pieces / My Favorite Lies / Walk Through This World with Me.

A GOOD YEAR FOR THE ROSES: THE COMPLETE MUSICOR RECORDINGS 1965–1971 (PART 2, four CDs)—Bear Family, BCD (Germany, 2009). More Musicor, including "Beneath Still Waters," "I'll Share My World with You," the Don Chapel–penned "When the Grass Grows over Me," and the first known recordings (albeit uncredited at the time) of George and Tammy.

GEORGE JONES: 40 YEARS OF DUETS—Time-Life M19330 and A704020 (2007). Want to compare George's duet partners? Here's a collection of them all, male and female, from the very beginning (Jeanette Hicks) through Melba Montgomery and right up his best post-Tammy duet partner, Patty Loveless.

THE ESSENTIAL GEORGE JONES: THE SPIRIT OF COUNTRY—Legacy/Epic D 207396-2 (1994). A fine two-CD collection of the Sherrill years, including "I'm Not Ready Yet" and "The Ceremony" (with Tammy).

THE ESSENTIAL GEORGE JONES—Epic/Legacy, 82796 92565-2 (2006). Excellent two-CD Epic compilation that includes "Take Me" (with Tammy), the Wynette-penned "These Days (I Barely Get By)," and "Someday My Day Will Come." Produced by Gregg Geller and mastered by Vic Anesini.

STEP RIGHT UP, 1970–1979: A CRITICAL ANTHOLOGY—Raven RVCD-292 (Australia, 2009). A strange collection of George that manages to rescue such dazzling obscurities as "I Love You So Much It Hurts" and "She Loves Me (Right Out of my Mind)." Not as strong as *Dispatches* but rewarding nonetheless.

DISPATCHES 1990–1999—Raven RVCD-199 (Australia, 2005). Definitive collection of George's recent work, including: When Did You Stop Loving Me? / I Sleep Just Like a Baby / When the Last Curtain Falls.

WAYS OF THE WORLD—Magnum CDSB 008 (UK, 1996). A collection of very spartan and somewhat drunken demos, listed here because it includes George's hair-raising interpretation of the Hank Williams "I Can't Escape from You."

Source Notes

Author interviews are listed below chapter by chapter and took place from 1995 to 1999. They were conducted and transcribed by the author. I reviewed countless hours of TV appearances and interviews, as well as thousands of pages of articles on Tammy. A lot of this material was obtained via fans or collectors and some of it is missing information, leading to less than complete citations. Apologies. Once again I must thank Dave Frasier for tracking down much of the source material. Scotty Kennedy of the Red Bay Museum in Alabama was an invaluable resource as well. Corrections and/or new information can be sent to jimmymcdonough.net.

BOOKS BY AND ABOUT TAMMY WYNETTE

Dal, Jackie with Tom Carter. *Tammy Wynette: A Daughter Recalls Her Mother's Tragic Life and Death*. Putnam, 2000.
Wynette, Tammy. *The Tammy Wynette Southern Cookbook*. Pelican, 1990.
Wynette, Tammy with Joan Dew. *Stand by Your Man*. Simon & Schuster, 1979.

Various issues of the ***Tammy Wynette Fan Club Newsletter*** (later known as *First Lady News*) were also consulted.

SELECTED TAMMY WYNETTE DOCUMENTARIES

Intimate Portrait: Tammy Wynette. Produced by Doug Arnold; executive producer, Sheila Slaughter. Lifetime, 1997.
Living Famously: Tammy Wynette. Mark Hill, executive producer. BBC Bristol, 2002.
Stand by Your Dream: The Tammy Wynette Story. Arena BBC documentary produced by Rosemary Bowen-Jones, 1987.
Tammy Wynette: An American Tragedy. Directed by Jelena Ilic, produced by Mike Parkinson. September Films, 2001. Shown in the UK on Channel 5 and in the U.S. on Bravo on the Bravo Profiles series.
Tammy Wynette: Biography, Biography Channel, 1998.
Tammy Wynette Talks to Shay Healy. Directed by Declan Farrell. Prism Leisure Video (UK), 1990.
'Til I Can Make It on My Own. Directed by Jill Nicholls. BBC, 2005.

SELECTED BIBLIOGRAPHY

Allen, Bob. *George Jones: The Life and Times of a Honky-Tonk Legend*. Birch Lane, 1984.
Amende, Coral. *Country Confidential: The Lowdown on the High Living, Heartbreaking, and Hell-Raising of Country Music's Biggest Stars*. Plume, 1999.
Amos, Edward. *Gravesites of Southern Musicians: A Guide to Over 300 Jazz, Blues, Country and Rock Performers' Burial Places*. McFarland & Co., 2002.
Blackburn, Julia. *With Billie: A New Look at the Unforgettable Lady Day*. Vintage, 2005.
Bowen, Jimmy and Jim Jerome. *Rough Mix: An Unapologetic Look at the Music Business and*

How It Got That Way: A Life in the World of Rock, Pop, and Country, as Told by One of the Industry's Most Powerful Players. Simon & Schuster, 1997.

Braddock, Bobby. *Down in Orburndale: A Songwriter's Youth in Old Florida.* Louisiana State University Press, 2007.

Brown, Jim. *George Jones: Why Baby Why.* Quarry Music Books, 2001.

Brown, Maxine. *Looking Back to See: A Country Music Memoir.* University of Arkansas Press, 2005.

Bruen, Ken. *American Skin.* Justin, Charles & Co., 2006.

Bufwack, Mary and Robert K. Oermann. *Finding Her Voice: The Saga of Women in Country Music.* Crown, 1993.

Cantwell, David and Bill Friskics-Warren. *Heartaches by the Number: Country Music's 500 Greatest Singles.* Vanderbilt University Press, 2003.

Carlisle, Dolly. *Ragged but Right: The Life and Times of George Jones.* Contemporary Books, 1984.

Chalker, Bryan. *This Is Country Music.* Paradise Press, 1976.

Chesher, Deborah. *Everybody I Shot Is Dead.* Cheshire Cat Productions, Inc., 2007.

Cockburn, Alexander and Jeffrey St. Clair. *Serpents in the Garden: Liaisons with Culture & Sex.* CounterPunch/AK Press, 2004.

Cornfield, Robert with Marshall Fallwell, Jr. *Just Country: Country People, Stories, Music.* McGraw-Hill, 1976.

Daley, Dan. *Nashville's Unwritten Rules: Inside the Business of the Country Music Machine.* Overlook Press, 1998.

Davis, Clive with James Willwerth. *Clive: Inside the Record Business.* William Morrow, 1974.

Dawidoff, Nicholas. *In the Country of Country: People and Places in American Music.* Pantheon, 1997.

Dellar, Fred and Roy Thompson. *The Illustrated Encyclopedia of Country Music.* Harmony Books, 1977.

Dennis, Allen. *James Blackwood Memories.* Quail Ridge Press, 1997.

Dew, Joan. *Mario Ferrari on Wine and Food.* Favorite Recipes Press, 1985.

————. *Singers & Sweethearts: The Women of Country Music.* Country Music Magazine Press/Doubleday Dolphin, 1977.

Dickerson, James L. *Goin' Back to Memphis: A Century of Blues, Rock 'n' Roll, and Glorious Soul.* Cooper Square Press, 2000.

————. *Go, Girl, Go! The Women's Revolution in Music.* Schirmer, 2005.

————. *Mojo Triangle: Birthplace of Country, Blues, Jazz and Rock 'n' Roll.* Schirmer Trade Books, 2005.

————. *That's Alright, Elvis: The Untold Story of Elvis's First Guitarist and Manager, Scotty Moore.* Schirmer, 2005.

Diekman, Diane. *The Faron Young Story: Live Fast, Love Hard.* University of Illinois Press, 2007.

Drummond, Bill. *45.* Little, Brown (UK), 2000.

Elliott, Carl Atwood, Sr. *One Hundred Years of Memories: An Oral History of Red Bay, Alabama (1888–1988).* Red Bay Civitan Club, 1995.

Emery, Ralph with Patsi Bale Cox. *50 Years Down a Country Road.* HarperCollins, 2000.

———— with Tom Carter. *More Memories.* Putnam, 1993.

Eng, Steve. *A Satisfied Mind: The Country Music Life of Porter Wagoner.* Rutledge Hill Press, 1992.

Erlewine, Michael and Vladimir Bogdanov, Chris Woodstra, Stephen Thomas Erlewine. *All Music Guide to Country.* Miller Freeman Books, 1997.

Escott, Colin with George Merritt and William MacEwen. *Hank Williams: The Biography.* Little, Brown, 1994.

———— with Martin Hawkins. *Good Rockin' Tonight: Sun Records and the Birth of Rock 'n' Roll.* St. Martin's Press, 1991.

Eubanks, Bob with Matthew Scott Hansen. *It's in the Book, Bob!* Benbella, 2004.

Faragher, Scott. *Music City Babylon: Inside the World of Country Music.* Birch Lane Press, 1992.

Field, Kim. *Harmonicas, Harps, and Heavy Breathers: The Evolution of the People's Instrument.* Fireside, 1993.

Fox, Aaron A. *Real Country: Music and Language in Working-Class Culture.* Duke University Press, 2004.

Frady, Marshall. *Wallace.* Random House, 1996.

Franks, Tillman with Robert Gentry. *I Was There When It Happened.* Sweet Dreams, 2000.

Frith, Simon and Andrew Goodwin (eds.). *On Record: Rock, Pop and the Written Word.* Routledge (UK), 1990.

Fuqua, C. S. *Music Fell on Alabama.* New South Books, 2006.

Goff, James R., Jr. *Close Harmony: A History of Southern Gospel.* University of North Carolina Press, 2002.

Grissim, John. *Country Music: White Man's Blues.* Coronet, 1970.

Guralnick, Peter. *Lost Highway: Journeys and Arrivals of American Musicians.* Vintage, 1982.

———. *Sweet Soul Music: Rhythm and Blues and the Southern Dream of Freedom.* Little, Brown, 1986/1999.

Haggard, Merle with Peggy Russell. *Sing Me Back Home: My Story.* Pocket Books, 1981.

——— with Tom Carter. *My House of Memories.* HarperCollins, 1999.

Hazelwood, Roy and Stephen G. Michaud. *Dark Dreams: A Legendary FBI Profiler Examines Homicide and the Criminal Mind.* St Martin's Press, 2001.

Hemphill, Paul. *The Nashville Sound.* Ballantine, 1975.

Horstman, Dorothy. *Sing Your Heart Out, Country Boy,* revised and expanded edition. Country Music Foundation Press, 1996.

Hoskyns, Barney. *Say It One Time for the Brokenhearted: Country Soul in the American South.* Bloomsbury, 1987.

Howard, Jan. *Sunshine and Shadow.* Richardson & Steirman, 1987.

Hume, Martha. *You're So Cold, I'm Turnin' Blue.* Viking, 1982.

Jensen, Joli. *The Nashville Sound: Authenticity, Commercialization, and Country Music.* Vanderbilt University Press/Country Music Foundation Press, 1998.

Jones, George with Tom Carter. *I Lived to Tell It All.* Random House, 1996.

Jones, Mrs. George [Nancy Jones] and Tom Carter. *Nashville Wives.* Cliff Street Books, 1998.

Killen, Buddy with Tom Carter. *By the Seat of My Pants: My Life in Country Music.* Simon & Schuster, 1993.

Kingsbury, Paul (ed.). *The Encyclopedia of Country Music: The Ultimate Guide to the Music.* Oxford University Press, 1998.

——— and Alanna Nash. *Will the Circle Be Unbroken: Country Music in America.* Country Music Hall of Fame/DK Publishing, 2006.

——— and the Staff of the Country Music Hall of Fame Museum. *Vinyl Hayride: Country Music Album Covers 1947–1989.* Chronicle Books, 2003.

Knight, Baker. *A Piece of the Big Time: My Songs, My Success, My Struggle for Survival.* Authorhouse, 2005.

Kosser, Michael. *Hot Country Women.* Avon, 1994.

———. *How Nashville Became Music City, USA: 50 Years of Music Row.* Hal Leonard Books, 2006.

Leamer, Laurence. *Three Chords and the Truth: Hope, Heartbreak, and Changing Fortunes in Nashville.* HarperCollins, 1997.

Lee, Brenda Lee with Robert K. Oermann and Julie Clay. *Little Miss Dynamite: The Life and Times of Brenda Lee.* Hyperion, 2002.

Lesher, Stephen. *George Wallace: American Populist.* Addison-Wesley, 1994.

Lewis, Jerry Lee and Charles White. *Killer!: The Baddest Rock Memoir Ever.* Century, 1993.

Lovullo, Sam and Marc Eliot. *Life in the Kornfield: My 25 Years at Hee Haw.* Boulevard, 1996.

Lynn, Loretta with George Vecsey. *Coal Miner's Daughter.* Bernard Geis Associates, 1976.

———— with Patsi Bale Cox. *Still Woman Enough.* Hyperion, 2002.

Malone, Bill C. *Country Music, USA.* University of Texas Press, 2002.

————. *Don't Get above Your Raisin': Country Music and the Southern Working Class.* University of Illinois Press, 2002.

————. *Stars of Country Music: Uncle Dave Macon to Johnny Rodriguez.* University of Illinois Press, 1975.

McCusker, Kristine M. and Diane Pecknold. *A Boy Named Sue: Gender and Country Music.* University Press of Mississippi, 2004.

Moore, Thurston (ed.). *The Country Music Who's Who,* 1966 edition. Heather Publications, Inc., 1966.

Nash, Alanna. *Behind Closed Doors: Talking with Legends of Country Music.* Knopf, 1988.

Obstfeld, Raymond and Sheila Burgener. *Twang!: The Ultimate Book of Country Quotations.* Owl Books, 1997.

Parton, Dolly. *My Life and Other Unfinished Business.* HarperCollins, 1994.

Phillips, Stu. *"Stu Who?": Forty Years of Navigating the Minefields of the Music Business.* Cisum Press, 2003.

Pitcox, Tracy. *Legendary Conversations with a Texas Disc Jockey.* Heart of Texas Country, 2007.

Pride, Charley with Jim Henderson. *Pride: The Charley Pride Story.* Quill, 1994.

Pruter, Robert. *Chicago Soul.* Illini Books, 1992.

Reed, Julia. *Queen of the Turtle Derby and Other Southern Phenomena.* Random House, 2004.

Reise, Randall. *Nashville Babylon.* Congdon & Weed, 1988.

Richards, Tad and Melvin B. Shestack. *The New Country Music Encyclopedia.* Fireside, 1993.

Riley, Jeannie C. with Jaime Buckingham. *From Harper Valley to the Mountain Top.* Chosen Books, 1981.

Rubenstein, Raeanne and Peter McCabe. *Honky-Tonk Heroes: A Photo Album of Country Music.* Harper & Row, 1975.

Self, Philip. *Guitar Pull: Conversations with Country Music's Legendary Songwriters.* Cypress Moon, 2002.

Shelton, Robert and Burt Goldblatt. *The Country Music Story: A Picture History of Country and Western Music.* Bobbs-Merrill, 1966.

Stoneman, Roni as told to Ellen Wright. *Pressing On: The Roni Stoneman Story.* University of Illinois Press, 2007.

Style, Lyle E. *Ain't Got No Cigarettes: Memories of Music Legend Roger Miller.* Great Plains Publications, 2005.

Sutton, Glenn. *Crazy Verse.* Lisa Music Productions, Inc., 1993.

Terrell, Bob. *The Music Men: The Story of Professional Gospel Quartet Singing.* Bob Terrell Publishing, 1990.

Tichi, Cecelia. *High Lonesome: The American Culture of Country Music.* University of North Carolina Press, 1994.

———— (ed.). *Reading Country Music: Steel Guitars, Opry Stars, and Honky-Tonk Bars.* Duke University Press, 1998.

Tosches, Nick. *Country: The Twisted Roots of Rock 'n' Roll.* Scribner's, 1985; Da Capo, 1996.

————. *The Nick Tosches Reader.* Da Capo, 2000.

Tucker, Tanya with Patsi Bale Cox. *Nickel Dreams: My Life.* Hyperion, 1997.

Wecht, Cyril H. with Greg Saitz and Mark Curriden. *Mortal Evidence: The Forensics Behind Nine Shocking Cases.* Prometheus Books, 2003.

Whitburn, Joel. *Joel Whitburn's Top Country Albums 1964–1997.* Record Research, Inc., 1997.

————. *The Billboard Book of Top 40 Country Hits.* Billboard Books, 1996.

Wolfe, Charles. *Close Harmony: The Story of the Louvin Brothers.* University Press of Mississippi, 1996.

Wootton, Richard. *The Illustrated Country Music Almanac.* Virgin, 1982.

Younger, Richard. *Get a Shot of Rhythm & Blues.* University of Alabama Press, 2000.

CHAPTER NOTES

Where publication information is not listed for the books below, please refer to bibliography.

Virginia's in the House

Author interviews: Dolly Parton, Joan Dew, Jan Smith, Jane Williams, Karyn Sloas, David Sloas, Yvonne Abdon, Charley Abdon, Chip Young, Holly Gleason, Lisa Miller, Michelle Broussard Honick, Jack Nitzsche, Mike Judge, June Zendt, Phoebe Gloeckner, Robert K. Oermann, Loretta Lynn, Georgette Jones, Jef Billings, Nan Crafton, Kelli Haggard-Patterson, Barbara Hutchison, Linda Cayson, Martha Dettwiller, Charlene Montgomery, Cathye Leshay, Don Chapel, Rosemary Bowen, Lorrie Morgan, Alanna Nash

3 "I believe you have to live the songs," Wynette on *Today's Country*, TNN, 1997
3 "My neck's too long . . . no rear end," Wynette to Alanna Nash, *Behind Closed Doors: Talking with Legends of Country Music*
3 "Tammy never had the movie star looks . . . ," Bill Drummond, *45*, Little, Brown (UK), 2000
4 "a tear in every word," Sherrill to anonymous, "Tammy Wynette Tops Country Music Field, But Don't Call Her Hillbilly," *Journal* [?], Tupelo, Mississippi, Mar. 29, 1973
5 "I didn't know it . . . say anything," Wynette to John Tesh, *One on One Show*, Feb. 20, 1992
5 "I had goose bumps," Reagan quoted by Adam Clymer, "Carter Says Reagan Has Failed to Accept His Responsibilities," *New York Times*, Oct. 1, 1982
5 "the more than 2,000 Republicans . . . ," "Reagan Says His Opponents Risk Central America Influx," *New York Times*, Jun. 21, 1983
7 "She went from bein' a beautician to the queen of country music," Emmylou Harris, "The Death of Tammy Wynette: First Lady of Country," MSNBC, Sep. 4, 1998
7 "I have big . . . everything big," Tammy Wynette, "I've Had All the Happiness Any Woman Would Want . . . and All the Tragedy You Could Imagine," by George Haddad-Garcia, *Country Music Scene Annual*, 1981
7 "It's honest music . . . sugarcoat things," Wynette to Rex Rutoski, "Wynette Gives her Best," *Tarentum* (PA) *Valley News Dispatch*, Feb 16, 1989
8 "In this song the male . . . it may have," Cenate Pruitt, "Stand by Your Man, Redneck Woman: Towards A Historical View of Country Music Gender Roles," master of arts thesis, Georgia State University, 2006
8 "The singer's perspective . . . uncaring ex-husband," Kenneth E. Morris, "Sometimes It's Hard to Be a Woman: Reinterpreting a Country Music Classic," *Popular Music and Society* 16:1, spring 1992, Bowling Green State University Press
8 "A conversational mezzo-soprano . . . ," Jon Pareles, "Tammy Wynette: Nashville and Glitter," *New York Times*, May 5, 1989
8 "She could just milk . . . sounded contrived," Harris on *40 Greatest Women of Country Music*, CMT, produced by C. J. Hicks, 2002. Wynette came in at number two.
9 "blend of dependency . . . working-class women," Stephen Holden, "Dependency and Determination," *New York Times*, Oct. 27, 1984
9 "She speaks for the woman . . . ," Sherrill to Jack Hurst, "The Queen of Broken Hearts," *Chicago Tribune*, Jan. 30, 1977
9 "Even the saddest songs . . . dealing with despair," Julia Blackburn, *With Billie: A New Look at the Unforgettable Lady Day*

10 "It's hard for me . . . without crying," Faith Hill, *Tammy Wynette: An American Tragedy,* 2001 documentary

10 "I listened to her . . . way I sing," Emmylou Harris, "The Death of Tammy Wynette: First Lady of Country," MSNBC, Sep. 4, 1998

10 "She made me . . . it was real," Harris, ibid.

12 "like two trained seals," Wynette to Stan Leventhal, "The Tammy Wynette Interview," *Country Rhythms,* Feb. 1982

13 "A hot dog is still my favorite food," Wynette to Veronica Visser, "Tammy Wynette: An Intimate Conversation," *Country Rhythms,* Sep. 1981

15 "hard enough to draw blood," Wynette to Joan Dew, *Stand by Your Man* (hereafter appears as *SBYM)*

17 "My life's not a fairy tale . . . ," Wynette to Neil Pond, "Tammy Wynette: Country's First Lady Celebrates Two Decades of Hit-Making," *Music City News* 24, Oct. 1986

Nettiebelle

Author interviews: Agnes Wilson, Nancy Byrd, Holly Ford, John Wilson, Gerald Jetton, Dan Hall, Martha Chumbley, Linda Cayson, Jan Smith, Nan Crafton, Charley Abdon, Betty Chasteen, Bobby Canup, David Vest, Jane Williams, Dan Hall, Jamie Cole, Lou Bradley, Jackie Daly, Hazel Hall

18 "The Southern air. It's filled with rambling ghosts and disturbed spirits," Dylan to Bill Flanagan, "Interview with Bob Dylan, Part 3," CBC radio blog (www.cbc.ca/radioblog)

18 "Oh, I wish daddy . . . lose your talent," *Whatever Happened to Baby Jane?* directed by Robert Aldrich, 1962

18 "She bought every single record George ever did," Wynette to Susan Toepfer, "Nashville's Own Cinderella," *Photoplay,* Oct. 1974

18 "I'm proud to be . . . country girl," Wynette, interview as shown posthumously on *Time and Again,* MSNBC, Aug. 27, 1997. Original date of broadcast unknown.

18–19 "you don't know anything," Wynette to Harvey Schoonover, "Country Music's Mournful Songbird," *Grit,* Dec. 29, 1974

19 "I hated pickin' cotton worse than anything in the world," Wynette to Reed, *The Jerry Reed Show,* 1975

19 "It was chicken . . . the worst life ever," Wynette on *Country Profile,* Westwood One radio show

19 "Country authenticity presumes . . . ," Paula Fox, "Recycled 'Trash': Gender and Authenticity in Country Music Autobiography," *American Quarterly* 50:2, 1998

19 "I don't want . . . hungry too much," Loretta Lynn with George Vecsey, *Coal Miner's Daughter*

19 "poor—very poor . . . cornmeal," Parton in *Dolly: My Life*

20 "I don't know if anybody . . . sackcloth dress," Wynette on *The Tammy Wynette Story* 1990 Sony music promotional CD produced by Ron Huntsman (Epic ESK 2251)

21 "Life was so 'Billy Joe'–ish," Wynette, undated Epic bio, circa 1967

21 "Everything we had to eat . . . it was all over," Wynette to Dew, *TWCB*

22 "We lived in . . . prayer meetin'," Wynette on *Country Closeup* with Glen Campbell, Aug. 16, 1982

22 "It was the only . . . place to sing," Wynette to Josh Castle and Bill Grine, "A Day in the Life of George Jones and Tammy Wynette, Part One," *Country Song Roundup,* Oct. 1970

22 "My father's people . . . Southern Missionary Baptist," Wynette to Stan Leventhal, "The Tammy Wynette Interview," *Country Rhythms,* Feb. 1982

22 "They really got cookin' over there . . . more like black gospel music," Wynette to Dew, *SBYM*

22 "Fa-so-la singin's," Wynette to Holly George-Warren, Sep. 1994 interview (partially unpublished), used with permission

22 "where they teach you to sing all the notes and never the words," ibid.

22 "lived and breathed music," Wynette on *The Tammy Wynette Story*, 1990

23 "I was taught . . . all I knew," Wynette to Dotson Rader, "Don't Tell Me I Can't Do Something, 'Cause I'll Show You I Can," *Parade*, Sep. 9, 1995

23 "There wasn't any . . . of Itawamba County," Wynette to John Gabree, "Tammy Wynette: Songs of Heartbreak, but a Happy Home," *Country Music 1:8*, Apr. 1973

23 "My top half comes from Mississippi and my bottom half from Alabama," Wynette to Harrison Wells, "Tammy Wynette," *Song Hits*, Jan. 1985

24 "I was spoiled," Wynette to Joan Dew, "Tammy Wynette," in *Country & Western Classics: Tammy Wynette*, Time-Life Books, 1983

24 "He was dying, and knew he was dying," Wynette, *The Tammy Wynette Story*, 1990

24 "Mother said that . . . thing when I'm gone," Wynette to Holly George-Warren, Sep. 1994 interview

24 "My father inspired me and gave me the hope, but I don't remember him," Epic 7-inch vinyl promotional interview (AS7 1040)

25 "I loved an audience from the time I could walk," Wynette to Dew, *SBYM*

25 "Every time we had company . . . granddaddy to death," Wynette to Stan Leventhal, "The Tammy Wynette Interview," *Country Rhythms*, Feb. 1982

25 "I hate being alone," Wynette, ibid.

25–26 "Mama and Daddy bossed . . . usually get it," Wynette to Joan Dew, "Tammy Wynette," *Country & Western Classics: Tammy Wynette*, Time-Life Books, 1983

26 "I wanted to quit . . . nobody would know," Wynette to Jerry Reed, *The Jerry Reed Show*, 1975

26 "I saw daddy . . . started runnin'," Wynette, ibid.

26 "I cut my knee and I thought, 'Maybe that'll help,'" Wynette, ibid.

26 "He wore me . . . awful!" Wynette, ibid.

27 "I can see up . . . havin' that," Wynette to Dan Miller, *Miller & Company*, CMT, date unknown

28 "I remember Carolyn . . . sings and sings!" Wynette to Holly George-Warren, Sep. 1994 interview

28 "I want to be a singer, or an actress," Wynette on *Country Profile*, Westwood One radio show, date unknown

29 "Oh, she was a good . . . from that radio," Mildred to Sarah O'Toole, "Tammy Wynette Dates Famous Football Player!" *TV & Movie Screen 22:12*, Nov. 1975

29 "I asked her what was wrong . . . ," Mildred Lee to Dwight Gentry, "Little Lass from Bounds Crossroads Atop Country Music," *Journal* [?], date unknown

30 "Mother's record collection influenced me a lot," Wynette on *The Tammy Wynette Story*, 1990

30 "I'd lie on my stomach . . . over and over," Wynette to Dolly Carlisle, *Ragged But Right*

30 "Those old songs . . . wouldn't have a voice," Wynette on *Silent Witness 2: A Tribute to Country Gospel's Legacy* videotape, Rainmaker Films, 1994

30 "Your dad was my hero . . . Always will be," Wynette to Hank Williams, Jr., *Hot Country Nights* TV show, 1991

31 "James Blackwood has . . . still in awe," Wynette to Allen Dennis, *James Blackwood Memories*

32 "She was fascinated by guitars," Moore to James Dickerson, *That's Alright, Elvis: The Untold Story of Elvis's First Guitarist and Manager, Scotty Moore*

32 "They just looked like teenagers . . . she just laughed," Wynette to Holly George-Warren, Sep. 1994 interview

32 "The carpet . . . just gorgeous," Wynette, ibid.

32 "I thought gosh, how neat," Wynette, ibid.

32 "The music teacher . . . what she hears,'" Wynette, ibid.

32 "I knew someday you'd make something of yourself . . . used to be brown," Ganus in *SBYM*

34 "My mother would let . . . we were something," Wynette to Holly George-Warren, Sep. 1994 interview

34 "We'd sing a while . . . sing some more," Wynette to Roy Blount, Jr., "Country's Angels," *Esquire 87:3*, Mar. 1977

35 "mousy," Wynette to Dew, *SBYM*

36 "to hear a girl called names for doing the same thing a boy will brag about," Wynette, ibid.

41 "I'm a Taurus . . . of a bull," undated Epic bio circa *Soft Touch,* 1981

42 "I'd lay awake at night . . . anybody tells me,'" Wynette to Reed Sparling, "Memories of Tammy," *Star,* Apr. 25, 1998

42 "I dreamed of being a singer, but I also wanted to be a housewife and mother like my girlfriends," Wynette to anonymous, "Tammy Wynette," *Country Hits,* fall 1981

42 "One side of me . . . I still believe," Wynette to James Neff, "Tammy: Despair-Ridden by Alcoholic, Money-Grubbing Husbands, Harassed by Irate Fans and Officials, She's Beginning to Wonder What's Wrong with Herself," *Country Style,* issue 12, Mar. 10, 1977

42 "I *will* love him," Wynette to Dew, *SBYM*

Euple

Author interviews: Linda Cayson, Agnes Wilson, Judy Allen, Diane Bruff, Nancy Byrd, Martha Chumbley, Holly Ford, John Wilson, Betty Chasteen, Gerald Jetton, Jane Williams, Dan Hall, Hazel Hall, Martha Byrd, Mary Forbess

43 "In almost every marriage . . . always giving way," Iris Murdoch, *A Severed Head,* Chatto & Windus (UK), 1961

43 "I say what . . . tells me no," Wynette to Susan Toepfer, "Nashville's Own Cinderella," *Photoplay,* Oct. 1974

46 "No soft music, no candlelight, no champagne, and no satin sheets," Wynette to Dew, *SBYM*

48 "I had no electricity . . . my fireplace," Wynette, *TWCB*

48 "My life was dull, drab and exhausting," Wynette, source unknown at press time

50 "I found it very disappointing . . . felt cheated," Wynette to Dew, *SBYM*

50 "They were horrible . . ." Wynette to Reed Sparling, "Memories of Tammy," *Star,* Apr. 25, 1998

50 "There was no such thing . . . work it out," Wynette to Dolly Carlisle, "Why Tammy Wynette, and Why She Still Matters," *Billboard,* Oct. 3, 1992

It's Country Boy Eddie *Time*

Author interviews: David Vest, Eddie Burns, Mark Colvin, Fred Lehner, Wanda Byrd, Diane Bruff, Martha Byrd, Jackie Daly, Linda Cayson, Jane Lehner, Lisa Wallace, Don Chapel

54 "Q: Are they two separate people. . . when I go out on stage," Alanna Nash interviewing Tammy Wynette in "Tammy Wynette Stands by Her Man," *Behind Closed Doors: Talking with the Legends of Country Music*

54 "I'm a goddamn image, not a person," Joan Crawford to Roy Newquist, *Conversations with Joan Crawford,* Citadel Press, 1980

55 "I thought, 'Well, if getting . . . wouldn't die," Wynette to Joan Dew, *Singers & Sweethearts: The Women of Country Music*

56 "had a badly crippled . . . to a fight," David Vest in e-mail to author

57 Debut on *Country Boy Eddie* from the waist up, Wynette on *A Conversation with Burt Reynolds,* 1997 TV show

57 "It was a center for gossip," Wynette to Roy Blount, Jr., "Country's Angels," *Esquire,* 87:3, Mar. 1977

57 "I knew the words . . . pickin' up," Wynette to Sarah O'Toole, "Tammy Wynette Dates Famous Football Player!" *TV & Movie Screen* 22:12, Nov. 1975

58 "a special appearance by the reigning Miss World," David Vest, "Sting of Stings?" *Counterpunch, Mar. 3, 2002.* Quoted with permission of David Vest.

58 "A stretcher appeared . . . suffered a heart attack," ibid.

58 "The show must go on . . . under the sheet," ibid.

58 "I believe that it's the soulfulness . . . or they don't," Ray Charles to Bob Costas, TV interview, Jul. 6, 1994

58 "The minute you heard her, she had you by the heart," David Vest, "Remembering Tammy Wynette," *Birmingham News,* Apr. 12, 1998

60 "made marriage sound like Devil's Island or Botany Bay," ibid.

62 "Was God punishing . . . the first place?" Wynette to Dew, *SBYM*

67 "Don't tell me I can't do something, 'cause I'll show you I can," Wynette to Julia Reed, *Queen of the Turtle Derby and Other Southern Phenomena*

67 "there was no turning back after that," Wynette to Gerry Wood, "Thirty Years of Hits for Tammy Wynette," *Music City News,* 4:12, Mar. 25, 1997

67 "He never said a word," Wynette to Reed Sparling, "Memories of Tammy," *Star,* Apr. 25, 1998

67 "depression turned to anger," Wynette, ibid.

67 "I'm the only one Porter helped by not helping," Wynette, source unknown at press time

67 "You wouldn't believe . . . in that car," Wynette to Ralph Emery, *On the Record with Tammy Wynette,* TNN, date unknown, circa Wynette's 1994 album, *Without Walls*

67 "brief, loveless affair," Randall Reise, *Nashville Babylon*

67 "Let's put it this way . . . Cain and Abel," Wynette, ibid.

68 "I had to prove to my mother I could do it," Wynette to Roy Blount, Jr., "Country's Angels," *Esquire 87:3,* Mar. 1977

68 "The most frightening . . . really desperate," Wynette on *Country Closeup with Glen Campbell,* Aug. 16, 1982

Country Boy Eddie's single "Hang in There Like a Rusty Fish Hook" (Reed RR1031) is prized by certain maniac collectors due to the B-side, "Fodder Fossil's Blues," which is an excuse of a song that allows Eddie to indulge in his mule impression.

Dear Tammy, p. 69

Makeup quote: *First Lady News,* Jul. 1979. Red Skelton info: *First Lady News,* Apr. 1982. Favorite actress/movies and "Misty": *First Lady News,* Jan. 1979. Tom Jones: *First Lady News,* Apr. 1979. Favorite soap opera: *First Lady News,* Aug. 1983.

Girl Singer

Author interviews: Don Chapel, Billy Sherrill, Nancy Byrd, Frank Scarborough, Glen Scarborough, Zell Miller, Kelso Herston, Eve Zibart, Fern Austin, Tom Sparkman

70 "I decided . . . kill myself trying," Wynette to Jani Walker, "Tammy Wynette's Story of Faith—I Lived with a Miracle!" *TV Radio Talk 8:5,* Feb. 1975

70 "Nashville's Only Uptown . . . Each Room," contemporaneous postcard for the Anchor Motel

72 "the tongues of stars . . . as the truth," Chapel, e-mail to author

73 "The ruling class preferred . . . off the street," Brenda Lee with Robert K. Oermann and Julie Clay, *Little Miss Dynamite: The Life and Times of Brenda Lee*

76 "Female singers just really won't sell," Nelson to Thompson via Jean Shepard quote, *Finding her Voice: The Saga of Women in Country Music,* Bufwack and Oermann; for

an excellent article on Jean Shepard, see "Jean Shepard: The Woman in the Asbestos Suit," by Robbie Fulks, *Journal of Country Music* 22.3

76 "Twenty-nine guys and Kitty Wells," Bobby Braddock quoted in Michael Kosser's *Hot Country Women*

77 "the most unlikely recording . . . spectacular about her," ibid.

78 "For a long time . . . is inevitable," Dolly Parton, *My Life and Other Unfinished Business*

78 "If I catch a man . . . the mineral rights," Parton, ibid.

78 "When I started out . . . male band," Wynette to Linda Redeffer, "Country Singer Donates $10,000 to SEMO State," Kennett Missouri *Dunklin Democrat*, Jul. 5, 1988

79 "One booking agent just refused to book me," Wynette, "The Big Speakout: Lil Darlin' Know the Score," compiled by Carol Offen, *Country Music,* Jul. 1974

79 "I used to work clubs . . . bought you. Period," Connie Smith quoted in ibid.

79 "He looked at me . . . a bullet," Wynette, *Intimate Portrait: Tammy Wynette*, produced by Doug Arnold, Lifetime, 1997

79 "You turned me down," Wynette to Ralph Emery, "Tammy Wynette Tribute Night," *Nashville Now,* 1992

80 "I remember . . . 'subsidiary,'" Wynette to Neil Pond, "My Last Conversation with Country's First Lady," *Country America,* Jul. 1998

80 "country music's version . . . drugstore legend," Eve Zibart, "Tammy on a Tightrope," *Washington Post,* Oct. 26, 1978

80 "I didn't even know what a tape was," Wynette to Holly George-Warren, Sep. 1994 interview

81 "he didn't look . . . I was there," Wynette to Joan Dew, "Tammy Wynette," *Country & Western Classics: Tammy Wynette,* Time-Life Books, 1983

81 "A pale skinny little . . . rope's end," Sherrill to Lucy O'Brien, "The Mad Life and Crazy Death of Tammy Wynette," *Q,* volume 155, Aug. 1999

81 "Caked with hairspray and wearing these huge, fake eyelashes," Sherrill to Reed Sparling, "Memories of Tammy," *Star,* Apr. 25, 1998

81 "was leaning back . . . something else?" Wynette to Peter Guralnick, "Tammy: The Only Time I'm Really Me," *Country Music* 7:5, Mar. 1979

81 "No expression . . . never did say," Wynette to Emery, *The Ralph Emery Show, day two of radio show,* Oct. 1971, Eugene Earle Collection, Southern Folklife Collection, University of North Carolina at Chapel Hill

81 "She didn't believe . . . I'll call you,'" Sherrill liner notes, *Anniversary: Twenty Years of Hits,* Tammy Wynette (Epic CD EGK 40625)

81 "Somethin' said, 'Don't turn this chick down," Sherrill to anonymous, "The Sherrill Sound," *Time* 102:17, Oct. 12, 1973

82 "Now here he's some hot big producer . . . all these songs," Wynette to Holly George-Warren, Sep. 1994 interview

82 "asked her . . . said, 'Tonight,'" Sherrill liner notes, *Anniversary: Twenty Years of Hits, Tammy Wynette* (Epic CD EGK 40625)

82 "I knew instantly . . . meant to be," Don Cusic, "Notes on the Music," *Country & Western Classics: Tammy Wynette,* Time-Life Books, 1983

83 "We had been living . . . a beauty shop," Wynette to anonymous, "Tammy Wynette," *Country Hits,* fall 1981

83 "I really think I was Tammy's last hope," Sherrill to Jani Walker, *TV Radio Talk* 8:5, Feb. 1975

Don't Burn the Beans

Author interviews: Billy Sherrill, Lou Bradley, Tom Sparkman, Bobby Braddock, Curly Putman, Millie Kirkman, Charlie McCoy, Harold Bradley, Ron "Snake" Reynolds, Glen Sutton, Norro Wilson, Dianne Sherrill, Tony Couch, Ray Barger, Dan Penn, Kelso Herston, Robert K. Oermann, Tanya Tucker, Bob Moore, Emily Mitchell, Steve Popovich, Ed Grizzard, Bill

Barnes, Bergen White, George Jones, Jerry Kennedy, Hargus "Pig" Robbins, Jerry Carrigan, Dolores Edgin, Murray "Buddy" Harman, Billy Sandford, Ray Edenton, Bill Hullett, Chip Young

84 "I cannot understand . . . hate in it," Sherrill to Eve Zibart, "Billy Sherrill: Music Row's Most Celebrated Non-Celebrity," *The Tennessean Magazine,* Oct. 19, 1975

86 "Some people . . . are shorter," Gerry Wood, "Nashville Scene" column, *Billboard* 98:19, May 10, 1986

86 "Mr. Sherrill . . . purchasing speedboats," Elvis Costello, liner notes to 1994 Rykodisc edition of *Almost Blue*

86 "uneasy moment," ibid.

86 "discussing the merits of their handguns across the mixing console," ibid.

86 "had never come to the studio bearing firearms," Costello, *Almost Blue* liner notes, Rhino edition, 2004

87 "When last the visitors . . . *Triumph of the Will,*" Bob Allen, "Billy Sherrill: Steward of His Own Talent," *Country Music,* Mar./Apr. 1984

87 "I put my gut and heart into every record," Sherrill to Walter Campbell, "Interview: Billy Sherrill," *Journal of Country Music* 7:2, May 1978

87 "I love to record . . . the *next* record . . . ," Sherrill to Michael Thomas, "Tammy Wynette: A Little Tear in Every Word," *Rolling Stone,* number 108, May 11, 1972

87 "Billy grew up . . . in tent revivals," Rick Hall to Peter Guralnick, *Sweet Soul Music: Rhythm and Blues and the Southern Dream of Freedom*

87 "I think that's the most all-encompassing music there is," Sherrill, undated print interview, Country Music Hall of Fame archives

89 "Both of us . . . very close," Rick Hall to Bill Williams, "Billy Sherrill Creative Spark Ignites Artists Everywhere," *Billboard,* Jul. 19, 1975

89 "He was a country . . . ," Sherrill to Dan Beck, "Producing the Country Everyone Wants to Hear," *Record World,* Dec. 8, 1973

89 "was the kind of guy . . . didn't talk a lot," Hall to Peter Guralnick, *Sweet Soul Music: Rhythm and Blues and the Southern Dream of Freedom*

90 "started coming out of the woodwork and the farms," James Joiner to Richard Younger, *Get a Shot of Rhythm & Blues*

92 "everything rolled into . . . go to bed," Sherrill, ibid.

94 "Rick just took things too seriously," Sherrill, ibid.

94 "I was kind of . . . off about that," Rick Hall to Barney Hoskyns, *Say It One Time for the Brokenhearted: Country Soul in the American South*

94 "I find it ironic . . . fun than Nashville!" Robert Oermann to Michael Kosser, *How Nashville Became Music City, USA: 50 Years of Music Row*

95 "turn a corrugated . . . than two decades," Kosser, ibid.

95 "I loved everything . . . throughout the place," Tanya Tucker to Patsi Bale Cox, *Nickel Dreams: My Life*

97 "I kept right on . . . all the time," Sherrill to LaWayne Satterfield, "'Talent' Best Describes Billy Sherrill's Success," *Nashville Banner,* Apr. 10, 1971

98 "For eight grand . . . day in Atlanta," Sherrill to Lani Rogers, "Billy Sherrill Says Good Songs Are Good Records," *Songwriters Review* 34:2, 1979

99 "knew as much about country as the Shah of Iran," Sherrill to Bob Allen, "Billy Sherrill: Steward of His Own Talent," *Country Music,* Mar./Apr. 1984

101 "It was people—with a capital P—that turned that record over," Sherrill to Gerry Wood, "Sherrill Owns Almost Persuaded, a Top-Selling Standard," *Billboard,* Jan. 31, 1976

104 "We are manufacturers of songs," Norro Wilson to Bill Williams, "Billy Sherrill Creative Spark Ignites Artists Everywhere," *Billboard,* Jul. 19, 1975

105 "Songwriting was this . . . a lonely thing," Bill Anderson to Philip Self, *Guitar Pull: Conversations with Country Music's Legendary Songwriters*

106 "A good song lasts three hours in this town," Sherrill to John Grissim, *Country Music: White Man's Blues*

106 "Hiring somebody . . . love to your wife," Sherrill, undated and uncredited print interview, Country Music Hall of Fame archives

106 "If someone brings . . . five percent home," Sherrill to John Grissim, *Country Music: White Man's Blues*

107 "We're in the music . . . it's business," Charlie McCoy to Michael Kosser, *How Nashville Became Music City, USA*

107 "practically screaming . . . opinionated old ass,'" Dalton to Alanna Nash, "From Hard Times to the Top," *Movie Mirror's Country Music Special,* summer 1982

107 "sticking a fork in his shoulder," ibid.

109 "I stole . . . notes together," Hargus Robbins to Walt Trott, "Pig Robbins Segues into Early Retirement,", *Nashville Musician,* Dec. 14, 2000

110 "cool to play . . . top of it," ibid.

111 "Tammy Wynette pedal," Drake to Doug Green, "Pete Drake: Everyone's Favorite," *Guitar Player,* date unknown

111 "The name just . . . a hillbilly," Drake, ibid.

113 "The guys I use . . . ask questions," Sherrill to Michael Thomas, "Tammy Wynette: A Little Tear in Every Word," *Rolling Stone,* number 108, May 11, 1972

113 "the ultimate control freak," Rich Kienzle in liner notes to *She Thinks I Still Care: The Complete United Artists Recordings, 1962–1964,* Bear Family BCD (Germany; 16818 EK)

113 "not allowing even . . . Law encouraged," Kienzle, ibid.

113 "Billy has one way of doing things: his way," David Houston to Tom Roland, *The Billboard Book of Number One Country Hits,* Billboard Books, 1991

114 "I've never heard . . . sizzle cymbal,'" Sherrill to Walter Campbell, "Interview: Billy Sherrill," *Journal of Country Music* 7:2, May 1978

115 "You're trying to pull a little moment out of forever with every record," Sherrill to Jack Hurst, "Nashville's Good Ol' Hit Man," *Chicago Tribune Magazine,* Oct. 24, 1976

ADDITIONAL NOTES: When I asked Sherrill if he had a favorite of all the records he produced, he said no. "Some I was ashamed of," he added. When pressed for an example, he gave "Grand Ol' Blues" by Troy Seals. "We were gonna write a song that was half country, half blues, and I had two sets of musicians. Did a blues thing in Memphis and a whole different set of pickers for the second half of the record. It was a total disaster. Didn't make sense." For more of the most over-the-top Sherrill, listen to "Dixieland, You Will Never Die," off Tammy's 1976 *You and Me* album.

Deeter-Minded

Author interviews: Billy Sherrill, Kelso Herston, Lou Bradley, Jerry Kennedy, Don Chapel, Donna Chapel, Merle Haggard, Loretta Lynn, Frank Scarborough, Ray Walker, Harold Bradley, Gordon Stoker, Curly Putman, Anna Biller, Jan Howard, Jimmy Halfacre, Abram Richman, Bob Moore, Bobby Braddock, Jane Williams, Jane Lehner, Pepi Plowman

116 "I wrote more and sang better when I was sad," Wynette, interview as shown on *Time and Again,* MSNBC, Aug. 27, 1997

117 "Billy told me . . . dare ask," Wynette to Neil Pond, "Tammy Wynette: Country's First Lady Celebrates Two Decades of Hit-Making," *Music City News* 24, Oct. 1986

117 "You look like a Tammy to me," Wynette to Roy Blount, Jr., "Country's Angels," *Esquire* 87:3, Mar. 1977

117 "I sensed it . . . new life," Wynette to Dew, *SBYM*

117 "I'm gonna put Haleyville and Red Bay on the map," Sherrill via Wynette to Shay Healy, *Tammy Wynette Talks to Shay Healy,* directed by Declan Farrell, Prism Leisure Video (UK), 1990

118 "When Ella sings . . . coming back," Tony Scott quoted in *With Billie: A New Look at the Unforgettable Lady Day,* by Julia Blackburn

119 "Her voice, it was . . . I thrived on," Jones, *'Til I Can Make It on My Own* BBC documentary, 2005

119 "Finally someone was listening to my voice and they seemed to like it," Wynette on *The Tammy Wynette Story,* 1990

120 "Lightning will strike," Wynette to Ralph Emery, *On the Record with Tammy Wynette,* TNN, date unknown, circa Wynette's 1994 album, *Without Walls*

120 "Most of the writing . . . last resort," Sherrill to Bob Allen, "Billy Sherrill," *The Many Worlds of Music,* issue 4, 1984

120 "an acre . . . there waiting," Sherrill, ibid.

123 "You could literally . . . a drive-through," Parton, *My Life and Other Unfinished Business*

127 "I really disagreed," Wynette to Gabree, "Tammy Wynette: Songs of Heartbreak, but a Happy Home," *Country Music 1:8,* Apr. 1973

127 "mental block," Wynette, ibid.

127 "Billy was right. In the studio he really is always right," Wynette, ibid.

128 "He didn't even notice me . . . Didn't even speak to me," Wynette to Susan Toepfer, "Nashville's Own Cinderella," *Photoplay,* Oct. 1974

128 "I knew I . . . first time out," Wynette to Joan Dew, "George and Tammy and Hank and Jeannie," *Country Music 3:5,* Feb. 1975

129 "never said anything negative to Tammy," Tillman Franks with Robert Gentry, *I Was There When It Happened*

129 "wanted to sing with George," Franks, ibid.

129 "put sand in our gas tanks," Franks, ibid.

129 "this foreign singer that Tammy recorded with," Jones to Josh Castle and Bill Grine, "A Day in the Life of George Jones and Tammy Wynette, Part One," *Country Song Roundup,* Oct. 1970

129 "George can't yodel like David," Wynette, ibid.

131 If I had been him, I wouldn't have let her run around with me," Jones to Tom Carter, *I Lived to Tell It All* (hereafter *ILTTIA)*

131 "We weren't doing anything wrong—except falling in love," Jones, ibid.

131 "It was a sickening, lowdown thing to do," Wynette to Dew, *SBYM*

131 "Our marriage was never the same after that," Wynette to Dew, *SBYM*

132 "I hated myself . . . life completely," Wynette on *Country Profile,* Westwood One radio show, date unknown

132 "even took movies . . . much as I was," "Bitter Mudslinging as an Ex-Husband Slaps Tammy Wynette with a $12M Lawsuit," anonymous author, unknown tabloid

133 "Lord, can't Tammy sing a letter of the alphabet," Roy Blount, Jr., "Country's Angels," *Esquire* 87:3, Mar. 1977

133 "seemed lonely . . . make him happy," Wynette to Shay Healy, *Tammy Wynette Talks to Shay Healy,* directed by Declan Farrell, Prism Leisure Video (UK), 1990

134 "For years people . . . of his eyes," Jones to Tom Carter, *ILTTIA*

134 "never so much as touched me," *SBYM*

134 "We had never . . . or anything," Jones to Joan Dew, "The George Jones Explosion," *Country Music,* Aug. 1977

134 "I looked up and there was George," Wynette to Dotson Rader, "Don't Tell Me I Can't Do Something, 'Cause I'll Show You I Can," *Parade,* Apr. 9, 1995

135 "was yelling at the kids," Jones to Dolly Carlisle, *Ragged but Right*

135 "called Tammy a bad word," Jones, *Same Ole Me* videotape, Hallway Productions (PC 104), 1989

135 "George flew . . . so quiet," Wynette to Joan Dew, "George and Tammy and Hank and Jeannie," *Country Music 3:5,* Feb. 1975

135 "I don't know who . . . all the way," Joan Dew, "The George Jones Explosion," *Country Music,* Aug. 1977

136 "I guess from . . . didn't know it," Wynette to Dotson Rader, "Don't Tell Me I Can't Do Something, 'Cause I'll Show You I Can," *Parade,* Apr. 9, 1995
136 "She had the car . . . out of Shakespeare," Jones to Tom Carter, *ILTTIA*
138 "which later . . . go back," Wynette to Valerie Ridenour, "No Sad Songs for Tammy Wynette," *Country Song Roundup,* Jan. 1978
138 "created a lot of his own problems," ibid.
138 "I'll take a lot . . . like I should," ibid.
138 "I never regretted . . . just fantastic," Wynette to Dolly Carlisle, *Ragged but Right*

Dear Tammy, p. 139

Little Richard, "I Don't Know What You Got (But It's Got Me)," Vee Jay 698, 1965. What a record. Available on various Richard CD collections but the original edited-with-a-hatchet two-sided 45 is still the best.

Beneath Still Waters

Author interviews: George Jones, Nancy Jones, Evelyn Shriver, Susan Nadler, Earl "Peanutt" Montgomery, Jerry Chestnut, Bob Moore, Hargus "Pig" Robbins, Kelso Herston, Lou Bradley, Linda Welborn, Charlene Montgomery, Billy Sherrill

140 "You bet against me?" *Requiem for a Heavyweight,* directed by Ralph Nelson, Columbia, 1962
140 "When it comes to singin' . . . they never will," Wynette, *Intimate Portrait: Tammy Wynette,* produced by Doug Arnold, Lifetime, 1997
142 "What she thinks we'd do, I don't know," Jones to Suzanne Murphy, "Not Ready for the Rockin Chair," *Woodstock Times,* Nov. 15, 2006
143 "There ain't no way I'm supposed to be here," Jones to Mary Huhn, "Jonesing for George: He's Back at Carnegie Hall, without Ducks," *New York Post,* Oct. 29, 2006
143 "Truth be told . . . given the chance," "George Jones," Internet article by Jeff McCord
143 "Only thing my seven brothers and sister and I ever had under our Christmas tree was fruit," Jones to Julie Bain, "20 Questions," *Playboy,* Nov. 1999
144 "square dancin' guitar," Jones to anonymous, unknown publication
144 "I always hated my daddy for drinking," Jones to Joan Dew, "The George Jones Explosion," *Country Music,* Aug. 1977
144 "a shiny Gene Autry guitar with a horse and a lariat on the front," I believe this is from an uncredited *Country Weekly* article in the 1990s.
144 "just wanted to go out in the woods and hide and play guitar," Jones to Dolly Carlisle, "The Rise and Fall of George Jones," *Penthouse,* Nov. 1980
144 "It seems like he . . . just a loner," Helen Scroggins to Pepi Plowman, "A Singin' Fool," *Texas Monthly,* Jun. 1982
145 "It was better than goin' back to jail," Jones to Nick Tosches, "The Grand Tour," *The Nick Tosches Reader*
145 "He didn't want to go on account of his music," Dido Rowley to Colin Escott, liner notes to *Cup of Loneliness: The Classic Mercury Years* (Mercury 314-522-635-2)
146 "I want one . . . how it feels,'" Jones to Cheryl Wilcox, "George Jones: Living to Tell It All," *The 700 Club* internet article, CBN.com
146 "I love all them wiggles and what have you," Jones to Julie Bain, "20 Questions," *Playboy,* Nov. 1999
149 "I don't show . . . for the songs," Jones to Mark Rose, "George Jones: Last Exit Off a Dark Highway," *Village Voice,* 26:39, Sep. 23–29, 1981
149 "I do crazy things . . . restless, I guess," Jones to Joan Dew, "The George Jones Explosion," *Country Music,* Aug. 1977

152 "quivers with . . . a calm fatalism," Jon Pareles, "Getting Just the Essence from a Country Singer," *New York Times,* Jan. 14, 1992

152 "It's a shame . . . country music," Jones to Jim Jerome, "George Jones: After a Sobering Brush with Death the Ol' Possum Shows the New Nashville He's Still King of Country," *People,* Nov. 23, 1992

153 "George did what . . . push a rope," Jones to James Hunter, "The Ballad of No-Show Jones," *New York Times Magazine,* Mar. 15, 1992

153 "Look, as long . . . push me around," Jones via Sherrill, ibid.

153 "Hard head," Wynette to Valerie Ridenour, "No Sad Songs for Tammy Wynette," *Country Song Roundup,* Jan. 1978

153 "She wanted her . . . much alike," Helen Scroggins to Pepi Plowman, "A Singin' Fool," *Texas Monthly,* Jun. 1982

We Got Married in a Fever

Author interviews: George Jones, Nancy Jones, Earl "Peanutt" Montgomery, Jerry Chestnut, Bob Moore, Lou Bradley, Linda Welborn, Charlene Montgomery, Robert K. Oermann, Dolly Parton, Roni Stoneman, Robert Duvall, Jackie Daly, Billy Sherrill, Tanya Tucker, Glen Sutton, Jerry Kennedy, Harold Bradley, Jan Howard, Bob Rafelson, Charlie Carter, Maxine Hyder, Jan Smith, Patsy Sledd, Bob Eubanks, Sonny Curtis

154 "We never were friends when we were married," George Jones (author), "It Was the Greatest Thing—We Finally Became Friends," *Country Weekly,* 1998, exact date unknown

155 "I did not understand alcohol," Wynette to Dan Miller, *Miller & Company,* CMT, date unknown

155 "I didn't know how to cope with it," Wynette on *Country Closeup with Glen Campbell,* Aug. 16, 1982

155 "I had never seen . . . an awful lot," Wynette to Shay Healy, *Tammy Wynette Talks to Shay Healy,* directed by Declan Farrell, Prism Leisure Video (UK), 1990

155 "It was a really stormy marriage from the beginning," Wynette on *Country Closeup with Glen Campbell,* Aug. 16, 1982

155 "the only person . . . my eyes out," Wynette to Ron Wheeler, "First Lady Tammy Wynette: The Life She Has Chosen," *Country People,* volume 4, 1976

156 "a protest song," Sue Tyrell, "Tammy Wynette: Peroxide Politics and the Counter-Revolution," *Spare Rib,* Dec. 1975

156 "Figurehead of the counter-revolution," Tyrell, ibid.

156 "spearheading the inevitable backlash to the women's movement," Tyrell, ibid.

156 "womanhood is packaged . . . by her man," Tyrell, ibid.

157 "After all . . . got that . . . *thing,*" Allison Moorer, *'Til I Can Make It on My Own* BBC documentary, 2005

157 "She is *not* the victim . . . records ever made," Bill Drummond, ibid.

157 "I think you ought . . . move over!" Loretta Lynn to Carol Offen, "The Big Speakout: Lil Darlin' Know the Score," *Country Music,* Jul. 1974

157 "I'm not sitting . . . like Tammy Wynette," Hillary Clinton to Steve Kroft, *60 Minutes,* Jan. 26, 1992

157 "Hillary missed . . . says, 'he's just a man,'" Julia Reed, *Queen of the Turtle Derby and Other Southern Phenomena*

158 "I like the idea . . . love me anyway," Lovett to Leno, *Late Night with Jay Leno,* 1989

158 "I will stand by my man," Amy Winehouse, "Amy Winehouse Sobs as Husband Is Refused Bail," TheInsider.com, Nov. 12, 2007

158 "The ambivalence . . . relationships with men," Kenneth E. Morris, "Sometimes It's Hard to Be a Woman: Reinterpreting a Country Music Classic," *Popular Music and Society,* 16:1, spring 1992, Bowling Green State University Press

158 "It was just a pretty love song," Wynette to Colin Irwin, "Stand by Your Record Producer," *Melody Maker,* Sep. 16, 1978

159 "George is the boss . . . women's liberation," Wynette to Emery, *The Ralph Emery Show,* day three of radio show, Oct. 1971

159 "I just really believe . . . is a man," Smith on *Hairdos and Heartache: The Women Of Country Music,* directed by Morgan Neville, AETV, 2006

159 "Country entertainers . . . the pants," Jean Shepard to Carol Offen, "The Big Speakout: Lil Darlin' Know the Score," *Country Music,* Jul. 1974

159 "Man is usually . . . bear the children," Jody Miller, ibid.

159 "a woman couldn't . . . capable of doing," Wynette to Colin Irwin, "Stand by Your Record Producer," *Melody Maker,* Sep. 16, 1978

159 "Sometimes I think . . . too busy workin'," Wynette to Stuart Goldman, "Penthouse Interview: Tammy Wynette," *Penthouse,* Sep. 1980

159 "Personally, I'm not . . . enjoy bein' a woman," Wynette to Colin Irwin, "Stand by Your Record Producer," *Melody Maker,* Sep. 16, 1978

159–60 "After being barraged . . . without reservations," Sherrill to Dorothy Horstman, *Sing Your Heart Out, Country Boy*

160 "Women are very . . . They sell," Sherrill to Michael Thomas, "Tammy Wynette: A Little Tear in Every Word," *Rolling Stone,* number 108, May 11, 1972

160 "Epic Records did a poll . . . what to record," Wynette to anonymous, "Tammy Wynette Tops Country Music Field, but Don't Call Her Hillbilly," *Journal* [?], Tupelo, Mississippi, Mar. 29, 1973

160 "so skillfully . . . *Cosmopolitan* magazine," Jack Hurst, "Nashville's Good Ol' Hit Man," *Chicago Tribune Magazine,* Oct. 24, 1976

160 "We were in the middle of a lackluster recording session," Sherrill liner notes to *Stand by Your Man* (Epic CD EK 66018)

160 "like the back of my hand," Wynette to Peter Guralnick, "Tammy: The Only Time I'm Really Me," *Country Music* 7:5, Mar. 1979

160 "I was very intimidated by him," Wynette to Ralph Emery, "Tammy Wynette Tribute Night," *Nashville Now,* 1992

161 "If Tammy walked up . . . two words: 'What key?'" Randall Reise, *Nashville Babylon*

162 "He said, 'Do you . . . like that idea,'" Wynette to Peter Guralnick, "Tammy: The Only Time I'm Really Me," *Country Music* 7:5, Mar. 1979

162 "We wrote it so fast," Wynette, ibid.

163 "I have to feel a song to do it best," Wynette to Jack Hurst, "Tammy Wynette's Songs Echo Her Own Hard Times," *Chicago Tribune,* Dec. 24, 1975

163 "'Stand by Your Man' is a lot harder . . . Better song, too," Harris, *Today's Country with Crook & Chase,* TNN, Apr. 9, 1998

163 "a pig squealin'," Wynette to Burt Reynolds, *A Conversation with Burt Reynolds,* 1997 TV show

163 "I sounded like . . . blues singer," Wynette to Peter Guralnick, "Tammy: The Only Time I'm Really Me," *Country Music* 7:5, Mar. 1979

163 "He'd put it on and I'd slide the needle all the way across," Wynette to Emery, *The Ralph Emery Show,* week three of radio show, George and Tammy week, 1973

163 "I begged him . . . Pleaded," Wynette to Burt Reynolds, *A Conversation with Burt Reynolds,* 1997 TV show

164 "It became the . . . a genius," Wynette to John Gabree, "Tammy Wynette: Songs of Heartbreak, but a Happy Home," *Country Music* 1:8, Apr. 1973

164 "Brilliant recorded . . . their original intent," Simon Napier-Bell, *Black Vinyl, White Powder,* Ebury Press (UK), 2001

164 "soul-piercing," Mary Bufwack and Robert K. Oermann, *Finding Her Voice: The Saga of Women in Country Music*

164 "like it came . . . Pentecostal fervor," Bufwack and Oermann, ibid.

164 "the song's moral center is elusive," Daniel Cooper, "Still Standing," *Village Voice,* Oct. 27, 1998

165 "I didn't intend for it to be puttin' down men or anything," Wynette to Stuart Goldman, "Penthouse Interview: Tammy Wynette," *Penthouse,* Sep. 1980

169 "desperately wanted . . . the movies," Stu Phillips, *"Stu Who?": Forty Years of Navigating the Minefields of the Music Business*

169 "Billy hit me with a brick," Phillips, ibid.

169 "He wanted to have . . . wanted it all," Phillips, ibid.

170 "I earned a nice piece of change from that song . . . Thank you, Billy," Phillips, ibid.

170 "Jones got so embarrassed . . . and leave," Wynette to Ralph Emery, "Tammy Wynette Tribute Night," *Nashville Now,* 1992

171 "We tried every way in the world to record a song together," Wynette on *The Tammy Wynette Story,* 1990.

171 "I'd sing background . . . be on there," Wynette on *Country Profile,* Westwood One radio show, date unknown

171 "When we were onstage we were in our own little heaven," Jones to Nicholas Dawidoff, *In the Country of Country: People and Places in American Music*

171 "was not a great talker and he wasn't one to apologize, ever," Wynette to Ralph Emery, *The Ralph Emery Show,* radio show, Nov. 2, 1984

172 "called my mother . . . hang it up,'" Wynette on *Biography,* A&E, 1998

172 "One day when . . . what he says!'" Wynette to Joan Dew, "George and Tammy and Hank and Jeannie," *Country Music* 3:5, Feb. 1975

172 "Jones thought that was the greatest thing," Wynette on *Country Profile,* Westwood One radio show, date unknown

173 "acted real angry," Wynette, ibid.

173 "was stutterin' and stammerin'," Wynette, ibid.

173 "He's always makin' fun of my name," Wynette to anonymous, "Tammy Wynette Tops Country Music Field, but Don't Call Her Hillbilly," *Journal* [?], Tupelo, Mississippi, Mar. 29, 1973

173 "I never have met a woman with such a temper!" Jones, source unknown at press time

173 "He nipped and I nagged," Wynette, countless interviews, such as "Tammy Wynette: I Thought I Was on My Way to Heaven," Roger Hitts, *Star,* date unknown

178 "speeded onstage," Philip Elwood, "Fans Saw Little of the Joneses," *San Francisco Examiner,* Aug. 17, 1971

178 "left the distinct . . . back to Nashville," ibid.

179 "her full name, even in her presence," Joan Dew, "The George Jones Explosion," *Country Music,* Aug. 1977

179 "Nobody in the world sounds like she does," ibid.

179 "A little boy in men's clothes," Wynette to Ralph Emery, *On the Record with Tammy Wynette,* TNN, date unknown, circa Wynette's 1994 album, *Without Walls*

179 "The only man I ever knew who wore coordinated tennis outfits to mow the lawn," Wynette to Dew, *SBYM*

180 "It's very hard . . . he loves you," Wynette on *Country Profile,* Westwood One radio show, date unknown

180 "It's my prized possession," Wynette on George and Tammy week on *The Ralph Emery Show* radio, 1973

180 "George is the greatest," Wynette to Emery, *The Ralph Emery Show,* day three of radio show, Oct. 1971

ADDITIONAL NOTES: Author Ellis Nassour disputes Tammy Wynette being the first recipient of a gold record in country, saying Loretta Lynn already had one for her *Don't Come Home A-Drinkin'* album. "I was manager of artist relations for MCA/Decca and, while searching the books, found that Loretta was long overdue for a gold record. We presented it to her in Nashville at Fan Fair (I think) in October/November 1970. Then suddenly CBS/Columbia was claiming that Tammy received a gold record first, but that's totally untrue." Wynette's fan club newsletter stated that Lynn's album got the award a week after Tammy's. Press reports at the time said Wynette's *Greatest Hits* sold a million copies. An album needs to sell five hundred thousand copies to be an RIAA-certified gold album. Double that earns you platinum status, but the RIAA didn't begin certifying the awards until 1976. Perhaps Loretta got the first gold album and Tammy was the first to sell a million.

In regard to Wynette's initial recordings with George Jones for the Musicor label, the German 2009 Bear Family George Jones boxed set *A Good Year For the Roses: The The Complete Musicor Recordings 1965–1971 (Part 2)* collects together the handful of songs Wynette (obviously uncredited at the time) appears on: "Each Season Changes You," "Never Grow Cold," "How Much Rain," "The Hardest Part of All," "I'll Share My World with You," and a rerecording of "The Race Is On." (Outside of the first two numbers, she's nearly undetectable in the chorus, and I hear nothing of her on the last two. Tammy's not credited on another Musicor number she's definitely present on, "Love Me.")

Happy Never After

Author interviews: George Jones, Billy Sherrill, Earl "Peanutt" Montgomery, Charlene Montgomery, Lou Bradley, Ron "Snake" Reynolds, Dolores Edgin, Ray Walker, Jeannie Russell, Laura Cantrell, Maxine Hyder, Joan Dew, Scott Faragher, Tanya Tucker, Raeanne Rubenstein, Harvey Krantz, Bill Barnes, Al Clayton, Glenn Sutton, Jack Hurst, Eve Zibart, Huell Howser, Robert K. Oermann, Charlie Louvin, Patsy Sledd, Ed Grizzard, Jan Smith, Marshall Fallwell, Bobby Braddock, Norro Wilson, David Sloas, Nan Crafton, Merle Haggard

181 "How can anybody . . . of my life?" Wynette to Lorraine Chase, *Celebrities Offstage* TV show, 1989
181 "a musical dialogue . . . men and women," Joyce Maynard, "the lure of same-sex harmony in country," *New York Times*, Apr. 4, 1999
182 "They were fantastic . . . you beat 'em?" Loretta Lynn on *Biography*, A&E, 1998
187 "I like a man . . . has been exaggerated," Wynette to anonymous, *Journal* [?], Tupelo, Mississippi, Mar. 29, 1973
187 "Wallace's Woodstock," "Country Singers Join Wallace's Son at Rally," *uncredited, New York Times*, Jun. 12, 1972
188 "I sat slack-jawed . . . lotus blossom," Rosanne Cash in *The Nashville Portraits: Legends of Country Music,* Richard Carlin, Jim McGuire, William R. Ferris, Globe Pequot Press, 2007
191 "I learned . . . a plain human being," Wynette to Robert K. Oermann, "The Heartbreak's Over: Tammy's Finally Happy," *The Tennessean*, Aug. 13, 1982
193 "It's not exactly 'Moon River,'" Sherrill to Tom Roland, *The Billboard Book of Number One Country Hits*, Billboard Books, 1991
194 *"he* liked it," Larry Henley to Tom Roland, ibid.
194 "I'm cutting . . . and a chorus," Sherrill via Sutton to Don Cusic, "Notes on the Music," *Country & Western Classics: Tammy Wynette,* Time-Life Books, 1983
195 "I don't care . . . like it," Sherrill via Sutton to Tom Roland, ibid.
195 "I have a complex . . . really disturbs me," Wynette to Susan Toepfer, "What Women Really Want the Next Time Around: Straight Talk from Divorced Women, *Gallery,* Feb. 1976
195 "undergone nearly a dozen hospital stays," Bob Allen, *George Jones: The Life and Times of a Honky-Tonk Legend*
195 "like a woman going through her monthly cycle," Wynette to Dew, *SBYM*
196 "I never shot a gun at Tammy Wynette," Jones to Dotson Rader, "I've Learned What Love Means," *Parade,* Jul. 3, 2005

198 "If ever a home was broken up by outsiders, it was ours," Wynette to "S.T." [Susan Toepfer, I'm assuming], "Outsiders Broke Up Our Marriage," *Photoplay* 88:1, Jul. 1975

199 "There's no way . . . here to stay," Wynette to Emery, *The Ralph Emery Show,* day two of radio show, George and Tammy week, 1973

199 "George picked . . . that line," Wynette on *Country Profile,* Westwood One radio show, date unknown

203 "in good taste," Jones to Tom Roland, *The Billboard Book of Number One Country Hits*

204 "'Woman to Woman' was . . . a country hit," Wynette to Peggy Russell, "Tammy Wynette: Woman to Woman," *Country Song Roundup,* Oct. 1975

205 "Couldn't get no keys . . . away from y'all," Jones via my interview with Charlene Montgomery

206 "I always felt bad . . . Guy Lombardi [sic]," Jones, *George Jones Golden Hits* videotape (White Star 1683), 1994

206 "Tammy kept me awake all night, bawling about her career," Jones to Dotson Rader, "I've Learned What Love Means," *Parade,* Jul. 3, 2005

206 "It's just not . . . work out," Jones quoted in *SBYM*

206 "getaway bag," Wynette, ibid.

207 "A country music legend . . . as a team," Wynette to Joan Dew, "Tammy Wynette," *Country & Western Classics: Tammy Wynette,* Time-Life Books, 1983

207 "I couldn't convince her. Finally I said, 'I'll tell George you asked about him,'" Wynette to Yale Alexander, *Genre,* issue 13, Aug./Sep 1993

207 "George is one . . . destroy me with it," Wynette to Jane Smith, "Tammy Wynette Cries Out . . . 'I Love a Man Who Almost Destroyed Me,'" *Movie Life,* Jun. 1975

207 "broke up it just broke my heart, because I identified with them," ibid.

208 "I don't think she . . . quick way out," Jones, *Same Ole Me* videotape, Hallway Productions (PC 104), 1989

208 "There will never be anyone else for either of us," Randall Reise, *Nashville Babylon*

208 "It was almost like he was reading our minds," Wynette to Jack Hurst, "Tammy Wynette's Songs Echo Her Own Hard Times," *Chicago Tribune,* Dec. 24, 1975

209 "epic narrative . . . disillusioned breakup," Aaron A. Fox, *Real Country: Music and Language in Working-Class Culture*

209 "also signifies . . . loveless marriage," ibid.

210 "kept coming around just like he always did," Wynette to Dotson Rader, "Don't Tell Me I Can't Do Something, 'Cause I'll Show You I Can," *Parade,* Apr. 9, 1995

210 "There was no romantic . . . didn't want him," Lentz to Dolly Carlisle, *Ragged but Right: The Life and Times of George Jones*

210 "It was finally ended. It was over and done," Wynette to Rader, "Don't Tell Me I Can't Do Something"

210 "I remember it . . . about Jones," Wynette to anonymous, "57 Artists on the Records That Changed Their Life," *Musician,* Oct. 1994

211 "After Jones, I thought . . . my life together," Wynette to Lorraine Chase, *Celebrities Offstage* TV show, 1989

ADDITIONAL NOTES: There is a fantastic clip of Tammy doing "I Don't Think About Him No More" on a Kitty Wells tribute TV show floating around YouTube. The song was also recorded by Don Williams and Bobby Bare under the title "Poison Red Berries."

Tammy on the Run

Author interviews: Holly Ford, Linda Cayson, Jan Smith, Nan Crafton, Patsy Sledd, Van Abbott, Bobby Napier, Charley Abdon, Rusty Pence, Tim Watson, Joan Dew, Cliff Dew, Cathye Leshay, Georgette Jones, Jackie Daly, Martha Dettwiller, Steve Hoker, Karyn Sloas, Lou Bradley, Bobby Braddock, Lorrie Morgan, Linda Cayson, Jan Howard, Merle Haggard, Steve

Chapman, Sue Richards, Barbara Hutchison, Charlie Louvin, Sam Lovullo, Kelso Herston, Dianne Sherrill, Jan Smith, Nan Crafton, Jerry Hall, Charlene Montgomery, Jerry Taylor, George Jones

212 "Favorite colors . . . writings of Rod McKuen," undated Wynette bio
213 "I didn't find . . . on my own," Wynette to anonymous, "Tammy Wynette's Advice: Need the Valleys to Reach the Peaks," *Fayetteville Observer (North Carolina)*, Apr. 28, 1988
218 "I've taken her horse . . . a switch," Wynette to Jack Hurst, "The Queen of Broken Hearts," *Chicago Tribune*, Jan. 30, 1977
218 "I suppose I just know it's always going to be me and the girls," ibid.
218 "I have to support them. I always will," Wynette to Valerie Ridenour, "No Sad Songs for Tammy Wynette," *Country Song Roundup*, Jan. 1978
219 "was singing . . . a little bit,'" Sherrill to Michael Kosser, *How Nashville Became Music City, USA: 50 Years of Music Row*
219 "I can't bear . . . upbringing, somehow," Wynette to Joan Dew, *Cosmopolitan*, Apr. 1978
221 "Thank God . . . start writing," Wynette to Joan Dew, "Tammy's Story," *Country Music*, Jun. 1975
221 "Well, half of it's mine," Jones to Jack Hurst, "The Queen of Broken Hearts," *Chicago Tribune*, Jan. 30, 1977
223 "I tried to call . . . also been cut," Wynette to Lee D. Server, "The Heartbreak Queen of C&W," *Oui*, Jul. 1984
223 "a little time bomb of some sort," Wynette to unknown author, "Stand by Your Home!" *Star*, Jan. 21, 1992
223 "They insisted . . . on the inside," Wynette to Joan Dew, *Singers & Sweethearts: The Women of Country Music*
223 "We all took lie-detector tests," Wynette, ibid.
223 "They put him through hell," Wynette, ibid.
223 "He made me feel like a kid again," Wynette, ibid.
223 "The relationship . . . never the same," Wynette, ibid.
223 "The Gatlins ended up going to work for Larry," Wynette, ibid.
223 "We still . . . ever caught," Wynette to Lee D. Server, "The Heartbreak Queen of C&W," *Oui*, Jul. 1984
224 "At least I know . . . after my money," Wynette to Joan Dew, *Singers & Sweethearts: The Women of Country Music*
225 "Finally I got . . . water out," Wynette to Lee D. Server, "The Heartbreak Queen Of C&W," *Oui*, Jul. 1984
225 "dying laughing," Wynette to Valerie Ridenour, "No Sad Songs for Tammy Wynette," *Country Song Roundup*, Jan. 1978
225 "He looked . . . Burt Reynolds, don't it?'" ibid.
225–226 "She came to . . . said, "Wynette, I got to . . . ,'" Wynette to Mike Douglas, "Tammy Wynette Reveals Untold Secrets from Her 'Soap Opera' Life," *Star*, Dec. 13, 1984
226 "I just slid down in my seat," Wynette, ibid.
226 "I never checked up . . . no promises," Wynette, ibid.
226 "If you and I . . . blowing her a kiss," Wynette, ibid.
226 "I don't want to be known as Mr. Tammy Wynette," Tomlin to Joan Dew, "Tammy's Husband—Michael Tomlin," *Country Music* 5:1, Oct. 1978
226 "Nothing is sadder than a jaded lady," Wynette to Joan Dew, *Singers & Sweethearts: The Women of Country Music*
226 "When I married Michael . . . my Prince Charming," Wynette to LaWayne Satterfield, "At Last! Tammy Wynette Speaks Out on the Divorce That Turned Nashville Upside Down," *TV Mirror*, Jan. 1977
228 "I think she wanted to see Burt as much as she wanted to see a doctor," Daly to Tom Carter, *Tammy Wynette: A Daughter Recalls Her Mother's Tragic Life and Death* (hereafter *TW:ADR*)

228 "I guess you know it should've been you and me," Wynette to Jack Hurst, "Tammy Wynette puts her life to music—and now a book," *Chicago Tribune,* Jul. 13, 1977

228 "Michael was strictly . . . money from me," Wynette to Steve Tinney "Tammy Wynette—Wed 5 Times, Talks about . . . the Men in My Life," *National Enquirer,* 1978, exact date unknown

228–229 "The worst thing . . . some kind of record?'" Wynette to Joan Dew, *Singers & Sweethearts: The Women Of Country Music*

231 "I'm by no means a swinging single," Wynette to Susan Toepfer, "What Women Really Want the Next Time Around: Straight Talk from Divorced Women," *Gallery,* Feb. 1976

231 "Mom's compulsive . . . man in her life," Daly to Carter, *TW:ADR*

231 "It really used to get . . . real pain set in," Wynette to John Latta, "Heartbreak Star Tammy Wynette Finds Happiness—And Husband Number Five," *Star,* Jul. 11, 1978

232 "This is it for me . . . Richey does," Wynette to Joan Dew, *Singers & Sweethearts: The Women of Country Music*

232 "I look on the time . . . as Richey has," Wynette to Martha Hume, "I Found a Man to Stand by *Me,*" *Redbook,* volume 163, Oct. 1984

232 "He's very easy . . . found him," Wynette to Neil Pond, "Tammy Wynette," *Music City News,* Mar. 1989

232 "He means everything . . . got it right," Wynette to Gerry Wood, "Thirty Years of Hits for Tammy Wynette," *Music City News* 4:12, Mar. 25, 1997

233 "My favorite gospel singers were James Blackwood, Jake Hess, and Denver Crumpler," Richey post on Wynette Web site

234 "He's produced . . . name them all," Wynette to Suzie Guymon, "I'd Do It All Again: An Intimate Interview with the First Lady of Country Music," *This Is Las Vegas,* Jan. 11, 1980

234 "When I was quite young . . . great singing talent," Richey post on Wynette Web site

234 "It occurred to me . . . rest of my life," ibid.

235 "He's written I guess half the things I've done in my career," Wynette to Suzie Guymon, "I'd Do It All Again: An Intimate Interview with the First Lady of Country Music," *This Is Las Vegas,* Jan. 11, 1980

236 "cruel and inhuman treatment," Randall Reise, *Nashville Babylon*

236 "dreadfully afraid," Reise, ibid.

236 "Well, I'm history now . . . she divorces him," Richey to Lorraine Chase, *Celebrities Offstage* TV show, 1989

236 "secret love for Tammy," Richey in *Stand by Your Dream,* 1987 BBC documentary

236 "drinking heavily with two women," Richey to Ralph Emery with Tom Carter, *More Memories*

236 "just pulled . . . I wanted," ibid.

237 "We slipped out . . . nobody else knows,'" Wynette to Richard Morlock, "Tammy Wynette Reveals Heartbreak and Happiness of the Two Men in Her Life," *Star,* Jan. 27, 1981

238 "took an overdose . . . killed herself," anonymous to Joe Mullins, "Tragic Death of Girl Who Lost Hubby to Tammy Wynette," unknown tabloid and date

239 "I always said . . . needed each other," Wynette to Carl Arrington, *Us,* Oct. 3, 1978

239 "Your boobs are bigger . . . boobs were bigger," Sherrill via Wynette to Peter Guralnick, "Tammy: The Only Time I'm Really Me," *Country Music* 7:5, Mar. 1979

240 "There will be no more sad songs written," Sherrill via Wynette to Mary Campbell, "Wynette: Country Queen of Hurt and Lonely," *Connecticut Post (Bridgeport),* Jun. 20, 1989

240 "creates no problem for me," Richey, source unknown at press time

240 "often referred to as Mr. Wynette," Richey, ibid.

240 "I felt she was . . . happen any longer," Richey to Catharine S. Rambeau, "Tammy and George Richey—Still the Best of Friends," *Country Weekly,* date unknown (1990s)

240 "weeded out the bloodsuckers, leeches, and joyriders," Richey to Dolly Carlisle, "George & Tammy Will Duet Again, but Maritally She's Standing by Her Man No. 5, George Richey," *People,* Feb. 25, 1980

Mr. Tammy Wynette

Author interviews: Junette Young, Bobby Young, Jerry Eubanks, Michelle Broussard Honick, Diane Jordan, Alanna Nash, Jackie Daly, Tom Carter, Jan Smith, Carolyn Neal, Cathye Leshay, Yvonne Abdon, Bobby Napier, Karyn Sloas, Loretta Lynn, Jerry Taylor, Holly Ford, Agnes Wilson, Charley Abdon, Stanley Harman, Bud McComb, Jane Williams, Steve Hoker, Tony Kincaid, Tim Watson, Steve Chapman, Barbara Hutchison, Susan Nadler, David Sloas, Rusty Pence, Van Abbott, Robert Papazian, Joan Dew, Cliff Dew, Charlene Montgomery, Glen Sutton, Bob Moore, Bill Hullett, Jerry Kennedy, Ron "Snake" Reynolds, Earl "Peanutt" Montgomery, Linda Welborn, Nancy Jones, Lou Bradley, Billy Sherrill, Maxine Hyder, Larry Fullam, Dave Lindsey, Lorrie Morgan, Toni Wine, Linda Cayson, Stan Moress, Mike Martinovich, Jef Billings, Harry Langdon, Kevin Carlisle, Steve Buckingham

243 "I'll take care of you better than you'd ever imagine," Sam "Ace" Rothstein (Robert DeNiro) in *Casino,* directed by Martin Scorsese, Universal, 1995. The author's favorite film.

243 "I don't know . . . he provides," Victoria (Mrs. John) Gotti, as quoted by Gene Mustain and Jerry Capeci, *Mob Star: The Story of John Gotti,* Alpha, 2002

243 "I wanted to say . . . about her ex-husband," Junette Young, "A Battered Tammy Wynette Relives the Abduction that Nearly Killed Her," McCurran and Carlisle, *People,* Oct. 23, 1978

244 "I saw an arm with a pistol . . . he had a stocking on his face," Wynette to Lee D. Server, "The Heartbreak Queen of C&W," *Oui,* Jul. 1984

244 "drove around in circles," ibid.

244 "dragged me out . . . I'm gonna die," Wynette to Martha Hume, "I Found a Man to Stand by *Me,*" *Redbook,* Oct. 1984

245 "cuts and bruises," anonymous source, "Wynette Abducted, Released," *Chicago Tribune,* Oct. 5, 1978

245 "paused long enough . . . the gesture," Alan Carmichael and Laura Eipper, "Tammy Seized at Green Hills; Freed in Giles," *The Tennessean,* Oct. 5, 1978

245 "It was something we . . . dismiss the subject," Jackie Daley to Tom Carter, *TW:ADR*

246 "Where is Georgette?" anonymous, quoted by Laura Eipper, "Tammy Feels Long Series of Harassments Related," *The Tennessean,* Oct. 6, 1978

246 "Someone else is going to pick up your kid today," anonymous, ibid.

246 "We have no motive . . . take those," Nickens, ibid.

246 "She wasn't exactly treated like she would if she got a standing ovation," Nickens, ibid.

246 "He could possibly be here, I just don't know," Wynette onstage quoted by Katherine Freed, "Tammy on Stage: He May Be Here," *The Tennessean,* Oct. 7, 1978

246 "I'm still around, I'll get you"; "We missed . . . the next time," in "People" column, *Chicago Tribune,* Oct. 29, 1978

246–47 "Maybe whoever . . . no sense to me," Jones to Bob Allen, "The Decline and Fall of George Jones," *Country Music,* Jan.–Feb., 1979

247 "The whole affair was bullshit," Jones to Tom Carter, *ILTTIA*

247 "A hoax . . . a kidnapper," ibid.

247 "as saying . . . her continuing troubles," anonymous, quoted in "Miss Wynette's Troubles," *The Tennessean,* Oct. 6, 1978

247–248 "I think the press . . . I was a suspect," Wynette to Alanna Nash, *Behind Closed Doors: Talking With the Legends of Country Music*

248 "I lost a lot of respect for the Nashville Police Department," Wynette, ibid.

248 "were the only two . . . we didn't write," Wynette to Alanna Nash, "Tammy Wynette Stands by Her Man," *Saga* 59:2, Apr. 1981

248 "contain apparent distortions . . . these specimens," FBI report (FBI 95-HO-226559), Nov. 11, 1978

248 "We found out later . . . the phone," Wynette to Lee D. Server, "The Heartbreak Queen of C&W," *Oui*, Jul. 1984

248 "all preplanned . . . be kidnapped," Wynette to Stuart Goldman, "Penthouse Interview: Tammy Wynette," *Penthouse*, Sep. 1980

248 "He knew inside . . . made public," Wynette to Joe Edwards, "Letter Says Yes: Wynette Abductor in Jail," *Nashville Banner*, May 22, 1984

248 "made my blood run cold," ibid.

248 "It didn't happen . . . it was all made up," Wynette via Jackie Daly to Tom Carter, *TW:ADR*

249 "Richey had knocked her around," Daly, ibid.

249 "Based on what my mother told me about the kidnapping, I can't help wondering if Richey was responsible for our year of terror," Daly, ibid.

249 "hideous allegations," Richey to Bob Paxman, "George Richey Responds," *Country Weekly* 7:24, Jun. 13, 2000. (Note: material from this article has also been attributed to Gerry Wood, *Tales from Country Music*)

249 "sickened," Richey, ibid.

249 "for a number of hours," Richey, ibid.

249 "If the allegations . . . could refute her," Richey, ibid.

251 "You couldn't get . . . end of the night," Wynette to Patsi Bale Cox, "Tammy Wynette—A Very Personal Interview," *Country Song Roundup*, Oct. 1984

261–62 "At one point . . . in her grave!" Wynette to Jack Hurst, "The Tammy Wynette Story: Therein Lies a Troubled Tale," *Chicago Tribune*, Dec. 14, 1980

262 "It was kind of sad they didn't get it right," Wynette to Jim Asker, "Tammy Wynette: Heroine . . ." [missing rest of title] , *Free-Lance Star (Fredericksburg, Virginia)*, Jan. 14, 1989

263 "We were getting stale . . . people to record," Wynette, *Biggest Hits* liner notes, Epic (FE 38312), Oct. 1982

263 "I walked into his office . . . The tears started," Wynette to Stan Leventhal, "The Tammy Wynette Interview," *Country Rhythms*, Feb. 1982

264 "what was wrong with Nashville," Jimmy Bowen and Jim Jerome, *Rough Mix: An Unapologetic Look at the Music Business and How It Got That Way: A Life in the World of Rock, Pop, and Country, as Told by One of the Industry's Most Powerful Players*

264 "The great Billy Sherrill . . . work that way," ibid.

264 "gruff Yankee," ibid.

264 "had never developed a taste for," ibid.

264 "was determined to shake things up," ibid.

264 "all repeated their licks," ibid.

264 "try something different," ibid.

265 "What you're doin' is old," ibid.

265 "awful and antiquated," ibid.

265 "Nashville was stuck . . . New York and L.A.," ibid.

265 "make use of all the gadgetry," ibid.

265 "You dumb-ass hillbilly . . . I was crazy," ibid.

265 "There's no reason . . . a sledgehammer," Sherrill to Dan Daley, "Producer Billy Sherrill," MixOnline.com, Jul. 1, 2002

265 "Anything under five hundred thousand . . . made more money," Bowen and Jerome, *Rough Mix*

266 "We were always thinking . . . broader audience," Owen Bradley to Dan Daley, *Nashville's Unwritten Rules: Inside the Business of the Country Music Machine*

266 "You hear a lot about country artists getting divorced . . . do something about it," Jones, 1977, source unknown

267 "ruined a lot of voices," Sherrill to James Hunter, "The Ballad of No-Show Jones," *New York Times Magazine*, Mar. 15, 1992

267 "high, wispy cocaine sound," Sherrill, ibid.

269 "You saw things . . . costumes," Jones to Nicholas Dawidoff, *In the Country of Country: People and Places in American Music*

269 "I was very messed up in my mind . . . boiling over . . . ," Jones to Bob Allen, "The Decline and Fall of George Jones," *Country Music,* Jan.–Feb. 1979

269 "Peanutt just picked the wrong night to call me," Jones to Richard Felge, "Sing a Sad Song: George Jones," *Country Song Roundup,* 31:238, May 1979

270 *"Supposed* hole," Jones to Carter, *ILTTIA.* Italics mine.

271 "For months I . . . back together," Jones, ibid.

272 "The more anguish . . . career flourished," Jones, ibid.

273 "He said, 'Yeah . . . he hates me," Jones to Bob Allen, "The Decline and Fall of George Jones," *Country Music,* Jan.-Feb. 1979

274 "You like my fingernails . . . silly," Wynette/Jones exchange, undated press release, Wheeling, West Virginia, "Jamboree, USA"

274 "An interrogation of . . . Two Story House," Aaron A. Fox, *Real Country: Music and Language in Working-Class Culture*

274 "The title had . . . I wrote it," Wynette to Alanna Nash, "Tammy Wynette Stands by Her Man," *Saga* 59:2, Apr. 1981

274 "I knew exactly what I wanted," Wynette, source unknown at press time

274 "We climbed to the top, but we couldn't make it, because success really destroyed us," ibid.

276 "They lied again and stuck the money in their pockets," Jones to Mark Shwed, "The Possum Lying Low after Squabble," *Nashville Banner,* Jul. 22, 1981

276 "scared to death . . . beat up on me," Jones quoted by Mark Rose, "George Jones: Last Exit Off a Dark Highway," *Village Voice* 26:39, Sep. 23–29, 1981

277 "I didn't like the idea . . . could remember," Jones to Carter, *ILTTIA*

277 "She spent a lot of her slot bitching about me," Jones, ibid.

277 "I think Chips . . . a little bit," Wynette to Stan Leventhal, "The Tammy Wynette Interview," *Country Rhythms,* Feb. 1982

278 "I've made up my mind . . . Billy Sherrill's place," Richey via Wynette to Jack Hurst, "Tammy's Home after Her Little Fling with Pop," *Chicago Tribune,* Feb. 14, 1982

278 "my buddy" refers to Nelson Reilly, *Tammy Wynette Silver Jubilee Tourbook,* 1991

278 "a wonderful friend" refers to Jim Nabors, *Tammy Wynette: The First Lady of Country Music Souvenir Book,* 1978

279 "do like Barbara Mandrell . . . those casualties," Wynette to Jill Warren, "New Look, Show for Tammy," *Indianapolis Star,* Aug. 19, 1984

281–82 Moress suit based on Jul. 1988 newspaper clipping, unknown publication

"Don't Ever Get Married"

Author interviews: James "Bud" McComb, Maria McComb, Karyn Sloas, Steve Hoker, Barbara Hutchison, Charley Abdon, Jan Smith, Lisa Wallace, Jackie Daly, Martha Dettwiller, Kelli Haggard-Patterson, Michelle Broussard Honick, Rosemary Bowen-Jones, Billy Sherrill, David Sloas, Steve Chapman, Yvonne Abdon, "Super" Judy Vleck, Evelyn Resch, Beverly Clark, Dolly Parton, Steve Buckingham, Linda Cayson, Jane Williams, Evelyn Shriver, Scotty Kennedy, Susan Nadler, Charlie Louvin, Georgette Jones, Mike Martinovich, Tony Conway, Rusty Pence, Stanley Harman, Laura Cantrell, Wally Bishop, David Sloas, Lorrie Morgan, Ruben Garces, Loretta Lynn, Carolyn Neal

284 "Fragile? Good Lord! Fragile I am not!" Wynette to Robert K. Oermann, "The Heartbreak's Over: Tammy's Finally Happy," *The Tennessean,* 8/13/82

287 "I've tried marijuana . . . try it again," Wynette to Stan Leventhal, "The Tammy Wynette Interview," *Country Rhythms,* Feb. 1983

290 "I'm scared," Wynette in Daly to Carter, *TW:ADR*

290 "I hate you!" Daly, ibid.

290 "Mom stood . . . of the house," Daly, ibid.

290 "This was to form . . . she would crater," Daly, ibid.

290 "We all felt that she had set us up, and then betrayed us," Daley, ibid.

290 "I've lived my own soap opera for forty-three years," Wynette, Solters/Roskin/Friedman press release, Apr. 3, 1986

292 "I just fell . . . left the stage," Wynette to Larry King, *Larry King Live*, circa 1981

292 "They keep you . . . drug abuse," Wynette, ibid.

293 "put back on the very drugs she sought to escape," source unknown at press time

297 "There is no one . . . love her today," Richey post on Tammy Wynette forum, Jul. 19, 2007

297 "the pure panic . . . of cruelty," Terrence Rafferty, "Master of Doomed Love and Dark Surprises," *New York Times*, Nov. 25, 2007

297 "There have been so very many . . . my experiences on tape," Richey post on Wynette Web site, Oct. 24, 2006

298 Details on 1997 party with Tammy: *First Lady News 1:1*, spring 1997

299 "I find myself . . . baby on a schedule!" Wynette to Patsi Cox, "Tammy Wynette—A Very Personal Interview," *Country Song Roundup*, Oct. 1984

299 "We wanted it . . . plain country," Wynette to Robert K. Oermann, "Tammy Wynette Steps Up onto 'Higher Ground' for Fresh Start," *The Tennessean Showcase*, Nov. 8, 1987

300 "added those little turns like a steel guitar," Wynette, *Higher Ground* promotional material

300 "came up with . . . believe it," Buckingham, ibid.

300 "mostly live . . . as possible," Buckingham, ibid.

300 "Everybody was awestruck by her," Buckingham, ibid.

300 "But I still see her foot moving," O'Kanes via Buckingham, ibid.

300–301 "When you miss . . . used to be!" Wynette to Patsi Bale Cox, "Tammy Wynette—A Very Personal Interview," *Country Song Roundup*, Oct. 1984

301 "Not always together . . . sometimes one, two, sometimes all three," Wynette to Patrick Carr, "Tammy Wynette: It Feels Good to Feel Good," *Country Music*, Mar.-Apr. 1988

301 "when I wasn't hurting bad enough to have to," Wynette, ibid.

301 "I would demand a shot—and I usually got it," Wynette, ibid.

302 "Tammy Wynette, the teary-voiced . . . Franklin Road home," Kathleen Gallagher, "U.S. Marshals Freeze Tammy's Possessions," *Nashville Banner*, Sep. 21, 1988; Wynette's debt: "Country Music Star Describes $250,000 Debt," Jan Read, *Nashville Banner*, Oct. 20, 1988

302 "confided in me that Richey had asked her to borrow money from Burt," Daly to Tom Carter, *TW:ADR*

302 "Now it was public record," ibid.

307 "I was so dadgum nervous backstage I wished for a Valium the size of a half-dollar," "Random Notes," *Rolling Stone*, May 17, 1990

307 "grandma on the tour," Wynette to Ralph Emery, *Nashville Now*, circa 1990

307–08 "get mad and pitch . . . and go back," Wynette, ibid.

308 "Randy is responsible . . . traditional country," Wynette, ibid.

308 "Driving a powder blue Jag," Bill Drummond, 45

308 "snakeskin boots, fresh-pressed jeans, a wet-look perm," Drummond, ibid.

308 "I liked him," Drummond, ibid.

308 "Her fingers . . . pages of *Vogue*," Drummond, ibid.

308–09 "Bill, you're from . . . look into it," Drummond, ibid.

309 "an evil . . . in pitch," Drummond, ibid.

309 "She could not . . . sounds like shit?" Drummond, ibid.

309 "stretch them, squeeze them, get them all in time," Drummond, ibid.

310 "skintight mermaid outfit . . . meaning of that was," Wynette to David Zimmerman, "Wynette Treks to Alien Video Country," *USA Today*, Jan. 24, 1992

310 "voodoo video," Jones, Jones–Wynette press conference, 1996

310 "These guys are crazy," Wynette to David Zimmerman, "Wynette Treks to Alien Video Country," *USA Today*, Jan. 24, 1992

312 "The fallout was . . . came across," Hillary Clinton, *Living History*, Simon & Schuster, 2003

312 "How dare that bitch say that about me!" Wynette as quoted by Marisa Fox, "An American in Mu Mu Land," *Entertainment Weekly*, Feb. 7,1992

312 "mad as hell . . . time," Richey to anonymous, "An Upset Tammy Wynette Stands by Her Song," *Newark Star-Ledger*, Jan. 29, 1992

312 "With all that is in me . . . bright as yourself," Wynette statement, ibid.

312 "I didn't mean to hurt . . . sorry about that," Clinton statement, ibid.

312 "She's had to eat . . . count the ways?" Loretta Lynn to Calvin Gilbert, "Political Controversies Found Wynette and McGraw," CMT.com, Apr. 18, 2003

312 "Hey, she used . . . use her now," Wynette on *Remembering Tammy Wynette*, TNN, date unknown

314–15 "Her bedroom . . . eat on the carpet," Morgan to Beverly Keel, "Country Palace: Tammy Wynette's House Goes for $1.2 million," publication and date unknown (1990s)

316 "I just kind of cracked the whip," Parton to David Zimmerman, "'Honky Tonk Sisterhood Grit and Glory," *USA Today*, Oct. 29, 1993

317 "more at home with campy recitations than hip, new songs," Alanna Nash, amazon.com review (undated)

317 "There's a lot of jealousy . . . rock 'n' roll business," Parton to David Zimmerman, "Honky Tonk Sisterhood Grit and Glory," *USA Today*, Oct. 29, 1993

In Her Room

Author interviews: Evelyn Shriver, Karyn Sloas, Martha Dettwiller, Laura Cantrell, Rusty Pence, Mike Maiocco, Nancy Jones, George Jones, Harold Bradley, Norro Wilson, Charley Abdon, Raeanne Rubenstein, David Sloas, Yvonne Abdon, Alanna Nash, Jerry Taylor, Nanette Crafton, Tony Conway, Ruben Garces, Kelli Haggard-Patterson, Mike Martinovitch, Rusty Pence, Barbara Hutchison, Jan Howard, Lorrie Morgan, Loretta Lynn, Harry Benson, Linda Cayson, Susan Nadler

322 "The sad part . . . write about," Wynette to Pamela Lansden, "Never One to Stand By Idly, Singer Tammy Wynette Turns Actress and Makes a Capitol Investment," *People*, Sep. 26, 1986

322 "I had no reason to think it was life-threatening," Richey to Steve Dougherty and Michael Haederle, "Then Death Blinked," *People*, Jan. 31, 1994

322 "excruciating pain," Wynette to Ralph Emery, *On the Record with Tammy Wynette*, TNN, date unknown, circa Wynette's 1994 album, *Without Walls*

322 "she would have been brain-damaged," Richey to Steve Dougherty and Michael Haederle, "Then Death Blinked," *People*, Jan. 31, 1994

322 "I told Richey, 'I'm really getting frightened,'" Wynette to Ralph Emery, *On the Record with Tammy Wynette*, TNN, date unknown, circa Wynette's 1994 album, *Without Walls*

322 "I looked at . . . was no answer," Wynette, "Alive Again," *A Current Affair* TV show, date unknown (1990s)

322 "They told my family I wasn't gonna make it," Wynette to Ralph Emery, *On the Record with Tammy Wynette*, TNN, date unknown, circa Wynette's 1994 album, *Without Walls*

322 "I felt no pain, no fear, no anything," Wynette, ibid.

322 "I think it's God's way of telling me death ain't no big deal," Wynette, ibid.

322 "too late," Richey to Steve Dougherty and Michael Haederle, "Then Death Blinked," *People*, Jan. 31, 1994

323 "I'm not going . . . I'm very sorry," Wynette onstage as quoted by Lo-Mae Lai, "Tammy Wynette Collapses On Stage," *Star,* 1995, exact date unknown

323 "Yes, she's dying. She'll be dead at two fifteen this afternoon, why don't you print *that?*" Richey, *The Star,* unknown author/exact date, 1995

323 "Tammy received . . . with Tammy Wynette," *Rolling Stone* as quoted by anonymous in "God, Am I Going to Remember This Year," *Country Music Round-Up* 19:6 (UK), May 1995

324 "To the Queen . . . of England," John, quoted from photo of the framed and signed sheet music

324 "I never went in for the crossover song," "Tammy Wynette's Advice: Need the Valleys to Reach the Peaks," *Fayetteville Observer (North Carolina),* Apr. 28, 1988

326 "Are we both drag queens?" Brandi Wine to Tammy Wynette, YouTube clip

326 "My large following . . . white or whatever," Wynette to Yale Alexander, *Genre,* issue 13, Aug./Sep. 1993

327 "I've already been . . . to go again!" Wynette to Loretta Lynn, *Legends* TV show, 1990s

327 "I don't believe Nancy wants us to," Wynette to Neil Pond, "Tammy Wynette," *Music City News,* Mar. 1989

328 "It was real snowy that day," Wynette to Richard McVey II, "George Jones and Tammy Wynette: Two Good to Be True," *Country Song Roundup,* 1996, month unknown

328 "not that high anymore," Wynette, ibid.

328 "I was real tacky . . . go ahead,'" Wynette, ibid.

329 "I don't understand . . . happened to us," Wynette to Mark Cooper, "Wait 'Til You Get Home," *Mojo,* Oct. 1985

329 "They got dollar signs . . . rock stuff for kids," Jones to Patrick Carr, "George Jones Survives the Country Wars," *Country Music,* Jul./Aug. 1995

329 "There's only a handful . . . get rid of me," Wynette to Mark Cooper, "Wait 'Til You Get Home," *Mojo,* Oct. 1985

335 "as if they were . . . way they were," Wilson, *Tammy Wynette Remembered* liner notes, Asylum (62277-2)

337 "They called an ambulance to come take her away," Morgan, *Tammy Wynette: An American Tragedy,* 2001 documentary

338 "I can't spell!" Lynn, *Today's Country,* TNN, 1997

339 "I talked to her . . . wait on me," Lynn to Tracy Pitcox, *Legendary Conversations with a Texas Disc Jockey*

Death Ain't No Big Deal

Author interviews: Jackie Daly, Evelyn Shriver, Barbara Hutchison, Georgette Jones, George Jones, Nancy Jones, Karyn Sloas, Martha Dettwiller, Robert K. Oermann, Charley Abdon, Jan Smith, Raeanne Rubenstein, Susan Nadler, Carolyn Neal, Tony Conway, Jerry Taylor, Kelli Haggard-Patterson, Jane Williams, Norro Wilson, Lorrie Morgan, Jan Howard

343 "[Hank] was in too much . . . than death," Horton in *Hank Williams: Honky Tonk Blues,* directed by Morgan Neville, PBS American Masters series, 2004

343 "I think Tammy . . . she got in death," Shriver, countless interviews, such as "New Questions about Tammy Wynette's Death," *The Examiner,* Aug. 30, 2004

343 "was just sitting . . . his head," Daly, *Tammy Wynette: An American Tragedy,* 2001 documentary

343 "His eyes opened only halfway," Daly to Carter, *TW:ADR*

343 "I had been up for . . . up with me,'" Richey to Gerry Wood, *Tales from Country Music*

344 "I then noticed . . . in the kitchen," Richey, ibid.

344 "When I came out . . . in Pittsburgh," Richey, ibid.

344 "She is gone, Wallis, she is gone," Richey, ibid.

344 "We thought that 911 was for the living, not the dead," Sylvia Richardson to Roger Hitts, "Tammy Wynette was Beaten and Given Drugs," *Star,* May 4, 1999

345 "It seemed everyone knew before her own children," Gwen Nicholas, "What Killed Tammy Wynette?" *W* (Australia), Aug. 1999

345 "Obviously a lot . . . official word," Don Aaron to Kirk Loggins, "Police Weren't the First to Know," *The Tennessean,* Feb. 9, 1999

345 "in and out, drinking coffee and smoking," Daly, "Wynette's Family Seeks Answers," Feb. 6, 1999

345 "some kind of centerpiece for a ghoulish gathering," Daly to Carter, *TW:ADR*

345 "All I could think . . . in that shape," Daly, *Tammy Wynette: An American Tragedy,* 2001 documentary

345 "Every drop of pain medication was removed without my knowledge," Richey, *20/20,* 2000

346 "I could hear him screaming from the den," Fuqua statement Police report (complaint 98-164594)

346 "sick for a long time from a degenerative disease," Jones via Fuqua, ibid.

346 "I saw no signs of foul play," Fuqua, ibid.

346 "indwelling vena cava catheter," Marsh, Richardson death certificate, Apr. 7, 1998

346 "small bowel dismotility," Marsh, ibid.

346 "I had never heard . . . performed an autopsy," Wecht with Greg Saitz and Mark Curriden, *Mortal Evidence: The Forensics Behind Nine Shocking Cases*

346 "There is no way . . . not possible," Wecht, *20/20,* Feb. 19, 1999

346 "First she did not . . . autopsy on her body," Richey press conference, quoted by Brian Mansfield, "Reluctant Widower Allows Wynette Autopsy," *USA Today,* Apr. 15, 1999

346 "The world has lost . . . mourn Tammy Wynette," Dolly Parton, quoted by Anon, "Tammy Wynette 1942–1998," *Atlanta Journal and Constitution,* Apr. 8, 1998

347 "This woman walked through so much crap . . . nobody like Tammy, period," Wynonna, quote source unknown

347 "Tammy Wynette was an . . . miss her," Bill and Hillary Clinton, Anon, "Tammy Wynette 1942–1998," *Atlanta Journal and Constitution,* Apr. 8, 1998

347 "Her voice had a husky . . . strength and affection," Jon Pareles, "Tammy Wynette, Country Singer Known for 'Stand by Your Man,' Is Dead at 55," *New York Times,* Apr. 7, 1998

347 "We once made . . . been said," Sherrill to Brian Mansfield, "Love and Remembrances for 'One of a Kind' Wynette," *USA Today,* Apr. 8, 1998

347 "She was the epitome of a country star," Morgan in *Tammy Wynette: An American Tragedy,* 2001 documentary

347 "It was kind of like the death of country music," Morgan, ibid.

348 "I am just very glad . . . be sadder," Jones press release

350 "I may prepare . . . presumed none exists," Virginia W. Richardson, Jun. 1996 will

350 "It disappeared . . . know where it is," Tina Jones, quoted in "Wynette Fought Physical Ills for Years," *USA Today,* Apr. 12, 1999

350 "the estate of the insured," policy quoted by Daly/Carter, *TW:ADR*

353 "would wear my mother's jewelry and her clothes," Jones to Roger Hitts, "Tammy Wynette's Daughter Rips New Stepmom," *Star,* Feb. 13, 2001

353 "just completely, utterly disrespectful," Jones, ibid.

353 "May you sleep peacefully until I see you again," Richey, Country Music Hall of Fame induction as broadcast on TV

353 "Tammy's Kids Demand New Probe of Her Death," Roger Hitts, *Star,* date unknown

353 "It was always one of my favorite . . . make her proud," Jones to Wendy Newcomer, "Top Stars Remember Their Hero, Tammy Wynette," *Country Weekly,* Sep. 8. 1998

353 "You're a hypocrite . . . you pretend you're heartbroken, but you're sleeping with Sheila," Tina Jones, reported by Joe Mullins, "Tammy Wynette's Daughter Brands Her Dad a Cheater," *The Globe,* Dec. 1, 1998

353 "Richey and Sheila just stood there, looking like they wanted to be beamed up and out of the room," Daly to Carter, *TW:ADR*

354–55 "expressed regret . . . been provided," Levy, "Report of Investigation by Country Medical Examiner Narrative Summary," May 21, 1999

355 "This caused me . . . authorities that evening," Levy, ibid.

355 "extremely concerned," Levy, ibid.

355 "and urged that she be admitted to the hospital," Levy, ibid.

355 "he was not surprised . . . couple of days," Levy, ibid.

355 "Yes," Marsh via Daly to Carter, *TW:ADR*

355 "had we known about the medications," Levy, quoted by Kirk Loggins, "Autopsy for Wynette May Hinge on Narcotic Use," *The Tennessean,* Feb. 8, 1999

355 "that may have raised . . . held or not," Levy, ibid.

355 "In my medical opinion . . . in her lungs," Marsh statement, as quoted in "Doctor Affirms Blood Clots Killed Singer," *The Tennessean,* Feb. 9, 1999

355 "a thorough review," Levy, "Doctor Refuses to Exhume Wynette," *The Tennessean,* Feb. 11, 1999

355 "terminally ill . . . natural causes," Levy, ibid.

355 "Enough Versed . . . to kill a bull," George Jones to Don Imus, Jun. 2, 2000 fax

356 "in a hospital . . . cardiac function," PSYweb.com

356 "The Defendant, George B. Richardson . . . event of her death," lawsuit filed Apr. 5, 1999

356 "We contend that . . . what killed her," Ed Yarbrough, *Today Show,* as quoted in uncredited AP story, "Wynette's Doctor Disputes Contentions of $50 Million Suit," date unknown

356 "no basis in fact," Marsh statement, quoted in uncredited AP story, "Wynette's Doctor Disputes Contentions of $50 Million Suit," date unknown

356 "when the facts become known," Marsh, ibid.

356 "provided extraordinary medical care to a person who suffered extraordinary medical problems," Marsh statement, quoted by Jim Patterson, "Wynette's Body Exhumed, Autopsy Performed," *Northeast Mississippi Daily Journal,* Apr. 15, 1999

357 "so we can all move on," Richey, April 14 press conference, quoted by Pat Harris, "Wynette Controversy Continues . . ." in "Stargazing" column, *Music City News,* Jun. 1999

357 "I'm saddened that . . . part of this fiasco," Richey press conference, quoted by Jim Patterson, "Wynette's Body Exhumed, Autopsy Performed," *Northeast Mississippi Daily Journal,* Apr. 15, 1999

357 "I know exactly what's happening to Tammy today and I despise it," Richey press conference, quoted by Brian Mansfield, "Reluctant Widower Allows Wynette Autopsy," *USA Today,* Apr. 15, 1999

357 "What you have . . . in control," Sheila Richey at George Richey press conference, quoted by Jim Patterson, "Wynette's Body Exhumed, Autopsy Performed," *Northeast Mississippi Daily Journal,* Apr. 15, 1999

357 "heart failure with cardiac arrhythmia," Levy report, May 16, 1999

357 "chronic pulmonary emboli with pulmonary hypertension," Levy, ibid.

357 "That's what *everyone* dies of," Nancy Jones to Chet Flippo, "A Song of Survival: George Jones Considers His Recent Brush with Death 'A Final Warning,'" *TV Guide, Jul. 10, 1999.* Italics mine.

358 "intestinal dysmotility on pain management," Levy report, May 16, 1999

358 "It was an interesting . . . rarely seen," Wecht, ibid.

358 "one of the substances . . . in her death," Wecht, ibid.

358 "the medical examiner . . . her death," Wecht with Greg Saitz and Mark Curriden. *Mortal Evidence: The Forensics Behind Nine Shocking Cases*

358 "Dr. Levy . . . such a statement," Wecht, ibid.

358 "Why has not Richey . . . without a license?" Jones to Don Imus, Jun. 2, 2000 fax

358 "The answer is unequivocally, absolutely without question—no," Richey, *20/20,* 1999

358 "personally showed me how to," Richey, ibid.

358 "No, I was not told that," Richey, ibid.

358–9 "I knew her better . . . love of my life," Richey, ibid.

359 "In no way . . . not happen," Slaughter, ibid.

359 "I will stand by him no matter what," Slaughter, ibid.

359 "We will never . . . really happened," Richey, ibid.

359 "Much time and effort . . . an immediate autopsy," Wecht with Greg Saitz and Mark Curriden, *Mortal Evidence: The Forensics Behind Nine Shocking Cases*

360 "Wallis Marsh, UPMC Presbyterian, and University Health Center of Pittsburgh, settled out of court in April 2002." Copy of confidential settlement dated Apr. 16, 2002, obtained by the author.

360 "The First Lady of Country Music and she's buried in a damn wall," Nancy Jones to Julia Reed, *Queen of the Turtle Derby and Other Southern Phenomena*

360 "She doesn't even *know* anybody over there where she is," George Jones, ibid.

360 "My life will be lived . . . as long as I live," Richey, "My Wonderful Life with Tammy Wynette," *Country Weekly,* Jun. 2, 1998

361 June 2007 VIP fan meeting: anonymous source

361 "Absolutely not," Richey, *20/20* TV show, 2000

361 "Tammy was one . . . marriage from heaven," Sheila Richey to David Wright, "Secret Wedding for Tragic Tammy's Hubby and the Cheerleader," *National Enquirer,* date unknown

362 "I had just made . . . she passed away," Jones to Bob Cannon, "George Jones: Making the Right Choices," *Country Weekly* 6:30, Jul. 27, 1999

362 "It put the fear . . . miracle I'm alive," Jones, ibid.

364 "Now everybody's famous . . . nobody's interesting," Tina Brown to Michael Kimmelman, "The Former Queen of Buzz Conjures a Golden Heyday," *New York Times,* Jun. 11, 2007 "It's really a more narrow . . . limitations," Tony Brown 1993 BMI interview quoted in *Nashville's Unwritten Rules: Inside the Business of Country Music* by Dan Daley

ADDITIONAL NOTES: One last George Jones update. On December 7, 2008, Jones went to Washington, D.C., to receive his Kennedy Center honors. Originally George "passed on it," said Evelyn Shriver, who explained that Jones was instead determined to attend "a casino date in Nowhere, Oklahoma." The promise of a Learjet lured Jones to the nation's capital. Sitting up in the balcony with the other honorees, silent behind the omnipresent shades, George looked like his usual impenetrable and moody self—his hearing aid had died earlier that day. But he did appear to be enjoying a chuckle or two with then-president Bush as Garth Brooks warbled a tribute from the stage below. God knows what DeDoodle the Duck and the Old Man would have made of it all.

Index